Détente in Europe

Détente in Europe

The Soviet Union and
the West since 1953

J O H N   V A N   O U D E N A R E N

Duke University Press   Durham and London   1991

Library of Congress Cataloging-in-Publication Data

Van Oudenaren, John.
    Detente in Europe : the Soviet Union and the West since 1953 /
John Van Oudenaren.
      p. cm.
    Includes bibliographical references (p.   ) and index.
    ISBN 0-8223-1133-X—ISBN 0-8223-1141-0 (pbk.)
    1. Europe—Foreign relations—Soviet Union. 2. Soviet Union—
Foreign relations—Europe. 3. Detente. 4. World politics—1945–
I. Title.
D1065.S65V35 1991
327.4704—dc20
                                        90-25033
                                          CIP

Contents

Preface

This study was begun at the Kennan Institute for Advanced Russian Studies, Washington, D.C., in October 1987. My original intention was to write a book about détente in Europe, focusing on the network of political contacts, arms control forums, economic ties, and cultural exchanges that flourished in the 1970s and that more or less survived the deterioration in East-West relations of the early 1980s. At the time it was clear that Mikhail Gorbachev wanted to preserve and expand this network, which he saw as the basis for a future "common European home." In his early speeches he not only endorsed what had been achieved in the 1970s, but called for efforts to move "beyond détente." Just how far beyond and in what direction he eventually would go was unknown at the time—to outsiders and no doubt to Gorbachev himself.

As the research progressed it became clear that little of what we associated with the détente of the 1970s was really new. Efforts to trace regular summits, political consultations, bilateral economic institutions, and contacts between Soviet and West European nongovernmental organizations to their origins invariably led not to the 1970s or even the 1960s, but to the first two or three years after Stalin's death. Thus 1953 became a logical starting point for the study.

Subsequently, 1989 emerged as a logical endpoint. While it was generally recognized that the cold war ended in that year, in a sense détente, at least as we had known it, ended as well. Détente had always been a means of managing and mitigating the cold war in the absence of a solution to its fundamental causes; it was the relaxation of tensions rather than their elimination. As conflict in Europe faded, the continent indeed began to move beyond détente and into a new era. In this era a new order is being built, chiefly on the basis of institutions and patterns of cooperation established after 1953. Détente thus remains important for Europe's future, as well as a fascinating aspect of its past.

I wish to thank the Kennan Institute and the Rand Corporation for their generous support during the writing of this book, as well as for the stimulating environments they provided. Peter Reddaway, the secretary of the Kennan Institute during my stay there, and the entire staff were always helpful. I wish to thank especially my research assistants, Paul Midford and Jon Slusher, for their many trips to the Library of Congress and for their help in organizing a mass of data. At Rand, I would like to thank Jim Thomson, Jonathan Pollack, Karen Lee, Yogi Ianiero, Jim Small, Josephine Bonan, Maureen Jackson, Barbara Neff, Kathy Foyt, Melvin Fujikawa, Marjorie Behrens, Lilita Dzirkals, Steven Berry, and my secretaries, Linda Tanner, Valerie Bernstein, and Carol Richards, for their help on various aspects of the book. Professors William E. Griffith and James McAdams read early drafts and made numerous helpful suggestions. My sister, Claire Van Oudenaren, helped with the notes and bibliography. I would also like to thank Richard C. Rowson, director of Duke University Press, for seeing the book through to completion, and Enid Hickingbotham for her care and patience in editing the manuscript. I alone am responsible for the content of the book.

Finally, I would like to express my special thanks to my wife Carol and to my children, John, Daniel, and Laura, who were patient and supportive throughout.

I dedicate this book to the memory of my father.

Abbreviations

ACDA   Arms Control and Disarmament Agency
AFL-CIO   American Federation of Labor and Congress of Industrial
   Organizations
ASEAN   Association of Southeast Asian Nations
AUCCTU   All-Union Central Council of Trade Unions
CBM   confidence-building measure
CDE   Conference on Disarmament in Europe
CDU   Christian Democratic Union
CEC   Conference of European Churches
CFE   Conventional Armed Forces in Europe
CFM   Council of Foreign Ministers
CMEA   Council for Mutual Economic Assistance
CND   Campaign for Nuclear Disarmament
COCOM   Coordinating Committee
COMISCO   Committee of International Socialist Conferences
CPC   Christian Peace Conference
CPSU   Communist Party of the Soviet Union
CSBM   confidence- and security-building measure
CSCE   Conference on Security and Cooperation in Europe
CSU   Christian Social Union
DC (UN)   Disarmament Commission
DFU   German Peace Union
DGB   Deutsche Gewerkschaftsbund (Trade Union Organization)
DKP   German Communist Party
EC   European Community
ECE (UN)   Economic Commission for Europe
ECOSOC   Economic and Social Council
EDC   European Defense Community
EEC   European Economic Community
EFTA   European Free Trade Association
EKD   Protestant Church in Germany
ENDC   Eighteen-Nation Disarmament Committee
ENI   Ente Nazionali Idrocarburi

ESRO   European Space Research Organization
ETUC   European Trade Union Confederation
FAO (UN)   Food and Agricultural Organization
FBS   forward based systems
FCMA   Friendship, Corporation, and Mutual Assistance
FDP   Free Democratic Party (West Germany)
FMVJ   Fédération Mondiale des Villes Jumelées Cités Unies
FRG   Federal Republic of Germany (West Germany, 1949–90)
FSU   Friends of the Soviet Union
GDR   German Democratic Republic (East Germany, 1949–90)
GLCM   ground-launched cruise missile
GPO   U.S. Government Printing Office
HMSO   Her(His) Majesty's Stationery Office
IAEA   International Atomic Energy Agency
ICBM   intercontinental ballistic missile
ICFTU   International Confederation of Free Trade Unions
IFTU   International Federation of Trade Unions
IG   Metall (German) Metalworkers' Union
ILO   International Labor Organization
IMEMO   Institute of World Economy and International Relations
INF   intermediate-range nuclear forces
IPPNW   International Physicians for the Prevention of Nuclear
    War
IPU   Inter-Parliamentary Union
LRINF   longer-range intermediate-range nuclear forces
LTB   Limited Test Ban
MBFR   Mutual and Balanced Force Reduction Talks
MFA   Ministry of Foreign Affairs
MFN   most favored nation
MLF   multilateral nuclear force
NNA   neutral and nonaligned
NPT   (Nuclear) Nonproliferation Treaty
NST   Nuclear and Space Talks
ÖTV   Public Services and Transport Workers' Union (Germany)
PCC   Political Consultative Committee
PCF   French Communist Party
PCI   Italian Communist Party
PNG   persona non grata
PS   French Socialist Party
PSI   Italian Socialist Party
PSOE   Spanish Socialist Workers' Party

RFE   Radio Free Europe
RIIA   Royal Institute of International Affairs
SAK   Central Organization of Finnish Trade Unions
SALT   Strategic Arms Limitation Talks
SED   Socialist Unity Party
SFIO   Section Française de l'Internationale Ouvrière
SIDAC   Socialist International Disarmament Advisory Council
SMOT   Free Interprofessional Workers Association (Russian)
SNF   short-range nuclear forces
SPD   Social Democratic Party of Germany
SRINF   shorter-range intermediate-range nuclear forces
SSBN   strategic missile submarine
SSOD (UN)   Special Session on Disarmament
START   Strategic Arms (Limitation and) Reduction Talks
TUC   Trades Union Congress
UNESCO UN   Educational, Scientific, and Cultural Organization
UNGA UN   General Assembly
VOKS   All-Union Society for Cultural Relations with Foreign
   Countries
WCC   World Council of Churches
WEU   Western European Union
WFSW   World Federation of Scientific Workers
WFTU   World Federation of Trade Unions
WHO   World Health Organization
WPC   World Peace Council
WTO   Warsaw Treaty Organization

1 Introduction

Soviet and Western scholars generally agree that the most intense phase of the cold war began in the late 1940s and lasted until Stalin's death in early 1953. This period was followed by a change in East-West relations that has been described as a thaw, relaxation of tensions, or détente.[1] It did not eliminate the fundamental causes of hostility between East and West, and was in any case partly reversed by the Hungarian and Suez crises in the fall of 1956. Nonetheless, it set in motion a process leading to increased political, security, economic, and cultural contacts between the two parts of divided Europe. This book is about that process.

The dramatic developments of recent years—the collapse of communism in Eastern Europe, the reunification of Germany, and the accelerating pace of change in the USSR itself—were both a culmination and a negation of the process that began in the mid-1950s. The contacts that developed between East and West after 1953 no doubt helped to generate the pressures for change that led to the revolutions of 1989. Indeed, Soviet leader Mikhail Gorbachev's most reform-minded adviser, former Presidential Council and Politburo member Aleksandr Iakovlev, was himself a participant in one of the earliest Soviet exchange programs with the West.

At the same time, however, the upheavals of 1989 marked a sharp break with the pattern of East-West relations after 1953 and the beginning, as was generally recognized, of a new era in European history. Before 1989 few Western leaders expected the collapse of communism or the rapid reunification of Germany. Western countries pursued policies of détente precisely because they assumed that cataclysmic change was either unlikely or undesirable, and that the only realistic alternative was to seek gradual improvements in East-West relations and in conditions in the East, chiefly through dialogue and negotiation with the Communist authorities. Groups such as the West German Social Democratic Party (SPD) were in fact embarrassed when, after they had spent years developing cordial contacts with the Communists on the assumption that they alone could change the system, power passed overnight to a group of virtually unknown dissidents.

Whatever miscalculations there were on the Western side (and clearly there were many, on both the right and the left of the political spectrum), they pale beside those in the USSR, where the political elite utterly misjudged the course of relations with the rest of Europe. In the 1970s Leonid Brezhnev declared that socialism was "irreversible" and that the German question was irrevocably "closed." He also suggested that détente would strengthen communism in the East, even as it encouraged "progressive" changes in the West. Gorbachev had a more realistic view of Soviet prospects in Europe, but he too underestimated the pressures for change and the vulnerability of Communist regimes. As recently as June 1989 he was telling West German audiences that "history" would decide the ultimate fate of the German nation, but that for the present the main practical task was to join with the Soviet Union in building the "common European home."

From the perspective of the 1990s there are two reasons why the study of détente after 1953 is important. The first is to contribute to what promises to be an ongoing discussion about the relationship between it and the revolutionary developments of 1989 and beyond. Some aspects of détente no doubt helped to "subvert" the Communist system (or, to put it differently, to convince a new Soviet leadership that what previous leaders had defined as "subversion" was precisely what the system needed). But other aspects may have helped to maintain the status quo for longer than might otherwise have been the case. This, at any rate, was the accusation leveled by critics against the SPD and others.[2] The 1953–89 period thus is certain to merit ongoing study, as scholars attempt to understand which factors hastened and which might have delayed change in the East.

A second reason to study this period relates to the future. Although the old order was destroyed in 1989, a new order is being built out of institutions and patterns of cooperation that originated in the 1950s and 1960s and flourished in the 1970s and early 1980s. The role of the Conference on Security and Cooperation (CSCE) has been upgraded. The Nuclear Nonproliferation Treaty (NPT) of 1969 has taken on a new significance with Germany's reunification, as have the military confidence-building agreements of 1975 and 1986, the agreements between the European Community (EC) and the USSR, and many other bilateral and multilateral agreements and institutions that grew out of very different political circumstances but that now are being adapted to the post-postwar situation.

Despite its importance, détente in Europe has not been extensively studied. There are no up-to-date surveys of Soviet-West European relations and few monographs on specific issues, countries, or historical episodes.[3] In any case, much of the existing literature is not about policy but about "views," "images," or "perceptions," particularly on the Soviet side.[4] The book thus attempts to fill a gap in the literature. It concentrates on the policies of the Soviet and to some extent Western governments, as well as deals with political parties, churches, trade unions, and other nongovernmental organizations active in international affairs. It stresses the interactive character of East-West relations, showing how relations gradually developed after 1953, how ideological, political, and other barriers set limits to their development, and how such factors as the Berlin crisis, the Warsaw Pact invasion of Czechoslovakia, and the missile controversy of the early 1980s affected the development of relations. It draws upon a variety of Soviet and Western sources, but especially the texts of agreements and accounts of how they were negotiated. It uses but does not rely heavily on the writings of Soviet institute researchers and political commentators.

The book deals primarily with Soviet-West European relations, with the U.S. role discussed where it is especially relevant, as in the chapters on four-power negotiations and arms control. Eastern Europe is discussed in contexts where it played a unique or pioneering role, but in general it is assumed that the foreign policies of the East European countries paralleled those of the USSR (internally, of course, developments in Eastern Europe were distinctive, but that is an altogether different subject).[5]

Although the book is not intended to be an original contribution to international relations theory, it argues that détente after 1953 should be thought of not as a "code of conduct" or "rules of the game" (as is often done in the U.S. social science literature) but should be seen as an ongoing process governed by negotiated mandates and giving rise to permanent institutions. The role of process, mandates, and institutions is discussed in general terms in chapter two and demonstrated by example in subsequent chapters.

The organization of the book is as follows. Chapter two examines the legacy of the late Stalin period and the transition to détente after Stalin's death. It focuses on the two most important East-West institutions of the period, the Council of Foreign Ministers (CFM) and the United Nations Organization (UN) and their complete or partial breakdown in the late 1940s and early 1950s.

Chapter three focuses on the partial revival, at the Berlin Conference of 1954 and the Geneva summit of 1955, of the four-power process that was mandated in the Potsdam agreement. It shows how this revival failed to result in progress toward German reunification (although it did produce the Austrian State Treaty), but helped to launch, in accordance with the "spirit of Geneva," improved bilateral relations and expanded political, economic, and cultural contact. This chapter also discusses the residual role of four-power rights and responsibilities after 1955 and the unexpected revival (in the form of the "two plus four" talks) of four-power negotiations in early 1990 following the collapse of the East German state.

Chapters four to nine document the post-1953 development of Soviet-West European relations in different spheres. Chapter four deals with three levels of diplomacy: summits and other high-level meetings, political consultations between foreign ministries, and regular contact through embassies and diplomatic channels. Chapter five examines parliamentary visits and exchanges, cooperation between political parties, and trade union ties. Chapter six discusses three areas of arms control: nuclear, conventional, and confidence-building. Chapter seven outlines the development of bilateral and multilateral economic institutions. Chapter eight deals with cultural exchange, contacts between churches, and contacts between the Soviet and West European peace movements. Chapter nine examines CSCE and the "all European process" from its origins in the 1950s to its new role in the post-1989 order.

The final chapter deals specifically with the changes in Europe since 1989. It begins with a discussion of the Gorbachev leadership's approach to Europe in 1985–89, describes its efforts to shape change in 1989–90, and concludes with an assessment of the long-term outlook for Russia as a European power.

2   From Stalin to Khrushchev

The Cold War

The history of the cold war in Europe is certain to be rewritten as the newly democratic countries of Eastern Europe open their archives and as conceptual frameworks are adjusted in light of new data and the collapse of communism in 1989. Nonetheless, it is possible, using the best scholarship of the 1970s and 1980s, to draw a reasonably accurate picture of Soviet policy and objectives in the late 1940s to the early 1950s and by implication of the changes that took place after Stalin's death.[1]

In his *Russia's Road to the Cold War*, Vojtech Mastny showed that Joseph Stalin's wartime objectives were flexible and changed over time. In July 1941, one month after Hitler's attack on Russia, the Soviet government indicated to its British ally that its minimum aims were the retention of those territories gained in collusion with Germany after September 1939. By late 1943 Stalin had raised his expectations to accord with the approaching victory. He seemed to favor the formation of a continental security system in which there would be no sharp division between Communist and non-Communist spheres. Instead, Europe would be a differentiated collection of weak and pliable states stretching from Poland to the Atlantic, all of which would be subject to some degree of Soviet influence.[2]

The attempt to create such a system involved a mix of unilateral actions and bilateral and multilateral diplomacy. The Red Army and the Comintern (dissolved in 1943 but in fact continuing to function through the Soviet Communist Party) worked to establish Communist control or influence in various countries, while the Soviet government concluded treaties with Britain, France, Czechoslovakia, Poland, and Yugoslavia that laid the groundwork for a postwar security system in which the Soviet Union would have a significant voice.[3] Stalin sought to gain immediate international recognition of a series of faits accomplis along the USSR's periphery, but to postpone the resolution of most other questions. In this way he could cement his hold on territories of vital interest or where the risks of confrontation were low, while holding open the possibility of future gains in more distant and riskier regions. Thus in 1944 he tried to

obtain Charles de Gaulle's recognition of the proto-Communist Lub-
lin Committee and of the future western border of Poland, but refused to come to any understanding on postwar arrangements
between France and Germany, which "could be studied only in four-
way negotiation."[4]

This flexible approach to European affairs was maintained for as
much as two years after the war, as was shown by Charles Gati in
his *Hungary and the Soviet Bloc*. Gati argued the importance of a
German and Polish trade-off in Soviet policy of the 1940s. Stalin's
minimum and most vital war aims were the tight control of Poland
(probably through the imposition of a Soviet-type system) and the
extension of control over all or at least a part of Germany. He probably also assumed that Bulgaria and Romania could be transformed
into Communist satellites with a minimum of friction between the
wartime allies.

Elsewhere, however, Stalin took a more circumspect approach. He
saw Yugoslavia, Hungary, Czechoslovakia, Austria, and Finland as
an intermediate region in which, for both internal and geopolitical
reasons, Communist parties would exercise substantial power, but
would refrain from immediate takeovers so as not to "scare the An-
glo-Saxons."[5] In the rest of Europe Communists would participate
in but not dominate ruling coalitions. Eventual Communist seizures
of power were not ruled out in such countries as France, Italy, or
Greece, but for the moment they were not regarded as desirable. Stalin's objectives thus were both more and less ambitious than was
often assumed in traditional and revisionist histories. He was in less
of a hurry than was sometimes suggested to Sovietize all of what
would become known as Eastern Europe, but at the same time he
did not preclude Communist expansion in countries that later were
unambiguously thought of as part of the West.

The Council of Foreign Ministers and the United Nations

Stalin's flexible approach to the postwar order was reflected in Soviet
behavior in the two main East-West institutions to emerge from the
war, the Council of Foreign Ministers (CFM) and the UN. The former
was proposed by President Truman at Potsdam and was accepted by
Stalin and Churchill with relatively little debate, while the latter
was the brainchild of President Roosevelt and figured heavily in the
talks at Teheran, Yalta, and other wartime meetings.

As envisioned by Truman and Secretary of State James F. Byrnes,
the CFM was to be "the continuous meeting ground of the five prin-

cipal governments, on which to reach common understanding regarding the peace settlement."[6] It was to formalize the procedures that evolved at the Paris Peace Conference of 1919, at which the Council of Five had assumed responsibility for drafting the Treaty of Versailles on behalf of all potential signatories. Whereas in Paris the Council of Five met concurrently with the larger peace conference, the CFM was to finish its work before the convening of a conference, and thus avoid the complications arising from the presence of dozens of mostly small countries that had played some role in the war.[7]

The only controversies regarding the CFM concerned its membership and its relationship to a provision in the Yalta agreement stipulating that the British, U.S., and Soviet foreign ministers would meet periodically for consultations. Truman favored making France and China full members of the CFM. Stalin had reservations about the great power status of both countries but went along, as did Churchill, who was skeptical about the role of China. In the end the equality of France and China was purely nominal, however, since the Potsdam agreement stipulated which countries would participate in the drafting of which treaties. There also was some question about whether the CFM would duplicate or supersede the consultation provision in the Yalta agreement. It was decided that the CFM would deal primarily with the conclusion of the peace treaties "and should not be burdened with current problems."[8] In practice, however, the CFM superseded the Yalta arrangement, as only one consultative meeting of the foreign ministers was ever to occur.

The establishment of the other main postwar institution, the UN, was more controversial and required prolonged debate over organization, membership, and rules of procedure.[9] Stalin was determined to secure guarantees that the new organization would not be used against the USSR as the League of Nations had been after the Soviet attack on Finland in 1939. He insisted, therefore, upon a unanimity rule in the Security Council and a limited role for the General Assembly.[10] He also wanted a clear separation between the CFM and the UN. The latter was not to play a role in the peace settlement and its charter was not to qualify the rights of the victors in any way. In addition, the USSR favored a narrowly based organization that would concentrate on security issues and avoid involvement in economic and cultural affairs. Such questions were inseparable from ideology and in the prevailing Soviet view could not be made the basis for cooperation between antagonistic social systems. Therefore, the USSR chose not to participate in the World Bank or the International Monetary Fund, and opposed the establishment of the Economic and Social Council (ECOSOC). It did not, however, go all out to block the

U.S. effort to broaden the UN's range of activities, and by 1946 was itself participating in seven of the twenty-two specialized agencies that were then part of the UN system.

The CFM met for the first time in London in September 1945. The political atmosphere had deteriorated markedly since the Potsdam Conference because of differences over Poland and Western concerns about Soviet policy in occupied countries, but there was still a general expectation that the meeting would begin the process leading to a comprehensive peace settlement.[11] The main item on the agenda was the conclusion of peace treaties with Germany's former allies. At Potsdam President Truman had proposed that the victors draft treaties with Hitler's five former allies—Bulgaria, Romania, Hungary, Finland, and Italy—before making peace with Germany. This was to avoid a repeat of what had happened after World War I, when the allies concluded treaties with Turkey and Hungary years after the Treaty of Versailles. Western governments later concluded, however, that Truman had made a tactical mistake, as the USSR was able to insist upon Western recognition of Soviet-dominated countries in Eastern Europe before agreeing to address the issues of greatest concern to the West, Germany and Austria. The only real leverage the Western powers could exert in the negotiations concerning the five allies derived from the strong Western position in Italy, from which the USSR wanted to secure reparations and where it hoped to gain influence.

Foreign Minister Viacheslav Molotov's main objective in London was the normalization of Western relations with the nominally pluralist but Communist-dominated governments of Bulgaria and Romania, and he tried to force a favorable outcome on this issue by engaging in a series of complicated maneuvers involving the status of France and China. He eventually overplayed his hand, however, and caused the breakdown of the conference. A permanent secretariat was established in London in accordance with the Potsdam agreement, but the ministers left open the time and place of their next meeting.

It is possible, although unlikely, that the CFM could have broken down already in the fall of 1945 had it not been for the intervention of Byrnes. He was anxious to resume negotiations, and in November proposed that the ministers of the big three meet in Moscow under the consultation provisions of the Yalta agreement. British foreign secretary Ernest Bevin, the main victim of Molotov's behavior in London, was reluctant to attend such a meeting and confident that Molotov himself would eventually ask to reconvene the CFM, but he had little choice but to go along with Byrnes's suggestion.[12]

The December 1945 conference of foreign ministers was not a formal session of the CFM, but it resulted in two procedural breakthroughs. First, it resolved the disputes that had led to the break-down of the London session and thus made possible the scheduling of a second session of the CFM in Paris in April. Second, it resulted in a U.S.-U.K.-USSR agreement to sponsor a joint UN resolution mandating the establishment of an international commission for the control of atomic energy.[13] Neither the Soviet nor Western representatives at Yalta or Dumbarton Oaks had envisioned that disarmament, which had been somewhat discredited by the pacifism of the 1930s, would be a major area of UN activity. But in September 1945 Truman had gone before the U.S. Congress and proposed that the United States and Britain take measures to ensure that atomic power would be turned "into the channels of service to mankind."[14] This led to a November meeting with prime ministers Clement Attlee of Britain and Mackenzie King of Canada, at which the three governments adopted a proposal for the establishment of a UN disarmament mechanism.[15] In Moscow Bevin and Byrnes presented the proposal to Molotov, who downplayed the importance of controlling nuclear weapons but did not object to the plan and agreed to cosponsor the UN resolution.

In a strictly formal sense cooperation between the great powers reached its early postwar high point in the summer of 1946, when they succeeded, as called for in the Potsdam agreement, in convening a twenty-one-country peace conference to conclude work on the treaties with the five former German satellites.[16] The second session of the CFM took place in Paris in two sessions, April 25–May 15, and June 15–July 12. It made considerable progress on the five peace treaties but reached a deadlock on a number of issues. In late June Byrnes suggested that the CFM had gone as far as it could and that it should turn the completion of the treaties over to a full peace conference. Molotov strongly objected, however, arguing that such a conference could not be convened until the CFM had reached agreement on the final text of all treaties. He eventually yielded, however, in return for Western concessions on reparations from Italy and after the main outlines of the solutions to the remaining issues were agreed.

At the twenty-one-country conference the USSR controlled the votes of Poland, Yugoslavia, and to some extent Czechoslovakia (and of Byelorussia and the Ukraine, which were represented separately), but the majority of the participants were close to the West. Molotov thus displayed an extreme reluctance to allow the smaller countries a voice in the peace settlements or to resolve issues by majority votes. He argued that it was essential not to sow discord between the large and small countries and appealed for unity among the members of the CFM.[17] He did, however, adapt to the circumstances by forming temporary coalitions with smaller countries that happened to agree with the USSR on particular clauses or points in dispute. The Paris

Peace Conference thus completed its work in October 1946, and returned the treaties to the CFM for final approval at its third session in New York in November–December 1946.

Meanwhile, the first session of the UN got under way in London in January 1946. Much of the optimism about the world organization had already faded, but the USSR at least went through the motions of constructively participating in its work. The most dramatic confrontation of the session concerned the failure of the USSR to withdraw its troops from northern Iran, but this was resolved peacefully by the end of May. The USSR also established a pattern that was to last throughout the Stalin period, by vetoing the admission of new members, including Portugal and Ireland.

The UN arms control process also began in January, after the General Assembly passed the big-three sponsored resolution mandating the establishment of a UN Atomic Energy Commission.[18] According to its terms of reference, the commission was to make proposals for the elimination of atomic weapons and "for effective safeguards by way of inspection and other means to protect complying States against the hazards of violations and evasions."[19] It was ostensibly to fulfill this mandate that the United States put forward, in June 1946, the Baruch plan for the establishment of an international authority to control atomic energy. The USSR proposed an alternative resolution calling for a ban on the use, production, and possession of nuclear weapons and the destruction within three months of all stocks of weapons. The deliberations in the commission soon were deadlocked, as the USSR attacked the Baruch plan as a scheme for preserving the U.S. atomic monopoly under the fig leaf of international control, while the West accused the USSR of ignoring the commission's terms of reference by proposing a plan that made no provision for inspection or safeguards.[20]

In this as in other UN forums, Soviet representatives complained bitterly about the "mechanical majority" that allowed the United States to craft the terms of reference in such a way that U.S. proposals were consistent with these terms, while Soviet proposals were rejected on procedural grounds before their substance was even discussed.[21] Nonetheless, the USSR continued to work within the UN and even put forward organizational initiatives of its own. In October 1946 it proposed that the UN take up the question of a general reduction of armaments. Although it was later to focus almost exclusively on nuclear weapons, at the time the USSR sought to broaden the disarmament debate as a way of defusing support for the Baruch plan and drawing attention to U.S. overseas military bases. The General Assembly voted unanimously in December 1946 that a general reduction and regulation of armaments was necessary, and asked the Security Council to take measures toward that end.[22] This led to the establishment in February 1947 of the UN Commission for Conventional Armaments that was to discuss "all armaments and armed forces, except atomic weapons and weapons of mass destruction."

The Soviet attitude toward cooperation in the UN was expressed in high-level statements as well. In March 1946 Stalin told a U.S. interviewer that he attached "great importance" to the UN as a "serious instrument for the preservation of peace and international security." Molotov appeared before the fall session of the General Assembly and endorsed the work of the UN but, consistent with his statements and behavior at the Paris Peace Conference, stressed that it was "above all necessary to guarantee concerted action on the part of the great powers."[23]

The Turn to the Left

The Soviet turn to the left took place in two stages: in the late summer and early fall of 1947 following the announcement of the Marshall Plan, and in the summer and fall of 1949, after the formation of the Federal Republic of Germany (FRG) and the end of the first Berlin crisis. As a consequence of these events, Stalin abandoned the flexible, long-term, trade-off strategy, broke off most forms of contact with the West, and embarked on an unambiguous course that resulted in the clear division of Europe into two hostile camps.

Already in early 1946 there was growing disillusionment in the West with Soviet policy. George Kennan's "long telegram" arrived in Washington in February, and Churchill gave his "iron curtain" speech the following month.[24] Nonetheless, there was still enough ambiguity in Soviet policy to make Western governments reluctant to conclude that further postwar cooperation with the USSR was impossible. Stalin outraged the West by his actions in Eastern Europe and intransigence on atomic energy, but a semblance of dialogue continued in the CFM and the UN and its various commissions, committees, and specialized agencies.

While in retrospect it is clear that Stalin did not intend to launch a military attack against the West and may even have tried to restrain the Communist parties in Hungary, Yugoslavia, and Greece, he was prepared to let developments in Europe drift—to delay the onset of economic recovery and the conclusion of a peace settlement for Germany and thus perpetuate conditions favorable for the expansion of Soviet influence.

The United States and Britain already had begun to complain about Soviet economic policies in Germany in the spring of 1946. At the Paris CFM Byrnes protested that Germany was "split into four water-tight zones" and proposed that the ministers appoint special full-time deputies who could work on economic and related questions and report back to the ministers at the next session. But Molotov rejected this suggestion, arguing that the Allied Control Council in Berlin was adequate to deal with the problem.

In September 1946 Byrnes gave his famous Stuttgart speech in which he called for the economic unification of Germany and proposed the conclusion of a forty-year disarmament and demilitarization treaty for Germany, but the USSR and Poland seized upon the question of the Polish border to deflect the discussion of either proposal. In December 1946 the U.S. and U.K. authorities took the first step toward the establishment of a separate West German state by announcing the economic merger of their respective occupation zones. They were motivated by concern about the Communist threat, but even more by the pressures the unsettled situation in Europe exerted on their own economies and finances. They also were under pressure from a new German elite that was unwilling to accept prolonged occupation and inferiority of status for Germany.[25]

The creation of "bizonia" drew sharp protests from the USSR and set the stage for the fourth session of the CFM, scheduled for Moscow in March 1947. The atmosphere was further soured by Truman's speech to a joint session of Congress, delivered on the third day of the conference, requesting $400 million in aid for Greece and Turkey. The Truman Doctrine was not explicitly directed against the USSR, but it suggested a new readiness on the part of the United States to use its economic resources to halt the deterioration of conditions in friendly countries. At the Moscow CFM the Western powers again put forward a plan for the economic unification of all of Germany. Molotov countered by posing as the only champion of political unity. He also accused the Western powers—and especially the British—of failing to carry out the Potsdam decisions on demilitarization and reparations. The parties thus were unable to agree on calling a peace conference, and talks were suspended in mid-April.

Although the conference itself was the scene of harsh recriminations, Stalin showed no sign of wanting to break off the four-power dialogue or to disband the CFM. Shortly before Marshall returned to Washington he was granted a lengthy session with the Soviet leader, who attempted to smooth over the differences among the powers. "We may agree the next time, or if not then, the time after that."[26]

But the seeming moderation of Stalin's remarks had the opposite effect of what he probably intended, and helped to precipitate U.S. and British reactions that led to the worsening of relations and the first Soviet turn toward militancy. Marshall and Bevin both were taken aback by his indifference to the deteriorating economic conditions in Europe, and increasingly convinced that the Soviet objective was to drag out the discussions in the CFM while political and economic conditions worsened. As Bevin's biographer later wrote, Bevin's greatest fear "was that, by reviving hopes of a four-power settlement on Germany without any real intention of making concessions, the Russians might draw the Western powers back from working out a three-power alternative and in effect secure an extension of the deadlock which worked to their advantage."[27]

The failure of the Moscow conference thus contributed to the U.S. decision to launch the Marshall Plan, which Marshall proposed in rough form in a speech in June 1947, and to which Bevin took the lead in organizing a European response. In early July he and Foreign Minister Bidault of France met in Paris to organize a larger conference of interested participants. Although there was great uncertainty in the West about possible Soviet participation, they invited Molotov to attend the Paris meeting. He accepted, but left abruptly after learning that Britain and France planned to establish an all-European organization to implement the aid program. The USSR refused to participate in such an organization, and would not attend the organizing session of the Committee of European Economic Cooperation. It also blocked Hungary, Poland, Czechoslovakia, and Finland from participating.[28]

As Mastny later concluded, the Marshall Plan "spelled the bankruptcy of Stalin's preferred international order."[29] Stalin initially tried to continue an ambiguous course between cooperation and confrontation, as was seen in the decision to send Molotov to Paris. But the insertion of U.S. money and organizational impetus into Europe undercut the basis for such a policy. By shutting off the possibility of further gains in Western Europe and even threatening a rollback of Communist influence in Eastern Europe, the plan forced the USSR to abandon the policy of delay that it had pursued for more than two years after the German surrender.

The turn toward militancy manifested itself in September 1947 with the founding, at a secret meeting in Poland, of the Communist Information Bureau (Cominform), a grouping of the Soviet, East European, French, and Italian Communist parties.[30] In his opening speech to the organization's first session Andrei Zhdanov proclaimed the doctrine of the "two camps" and condemned the former policy, pursued by the West European parties, of joining coalitions dominated by non-Communists. In October 1947 the West European Communist parties and their affiliated trade unions launched a campaign of strikes and political violence directed against the Marshall Plan.

In this atmosphere little was to be expected from the fifth session of the CFM, which took place in London in November–December 1947. The Western powers again pressed for economic unification and the conclusion of an Austrian treaty, while the USSR posed as the champion of political unity and called for a German peace treaty. In the end the CFM made no progress in what Marshall called "a dreary repetition of what had been said and resaid at the Moscow conference."[31]

The breakdown of the London conference was followed by further moves toward consolidation in the West and growing militancy on the part of the USSR and the international Communist movement. In February 1948 the Communists mounted their coup in Czechoslovakia. This was followed a month later by an unsuccessful but possibly serious coup attempt in Finland and the very tense negotiations leading to the conclusion of the Finnish-Soviet mutual assistance treaty.[32] Communist parties throughout Eastern Europe began forcibly absorbing their socialist and social democratic allies in new socialist unity parties.

The growing militancy of Soviet policy was further reflected in the Berlin crisis.[33] In February 1948 the British, French, and Americans met to consider new steps toward creation of a unified Western zone. The Soviet government protested by withdrawing in March 1948 from the Allied Control Council and accusing the Western powers of "tearing up the agreement on control machinery."[34] In June the Soviets began the blockade of Berlin, ostensibly to protest a currency reform announced for the Western zones.

While the crisis reflected Stalin's turn to the left and the deepening of the cold war, it also showed that he had a lingering expectation that the instruments of postwar cooperation—the UN and the CFM—could still be used to advance Soviet interests. As Soviet forces began blocking access to Berlin the foreign and defense ministers of the eight European Communist countries met in Warsaw and issued a joint communiqué deploring developments in Western Germany and demanding a four-power conference to discuss demilitarization, the establishment of four-power control over the Ruhr, the establishment of a peace-loving and democratic government for the whole of Germany, and the conclusion of a peace treaty and payment of reparations. The Western powers refused to negotiate under duress and began the airlift to supply the city. As long as the prospects for the airlift remained uncertain, however, Soviet diplomatic probes continued. In September 1948 the USSR again called for a meeting of the CFM to discuss the question of Germany, "in accordance with the Potsdam agreement."[35] It was only in early 1949—after the city had been sustained through the worst part of the winter—that Stalin sought a face-saving way to end the crisis.

Through a series of informal probes Soviet representatives offered to suspend the blockade in exchange for Western agreement to attend a meeting of the CFM and to halt all steps toward establishment of the FRG. The Western powers again refused to alter their course, but the USSR was able, with Western encouragement, to seize upon the technicality that a West German state did not yet formally exist and thus agreed to lift its blockade in return for Western agreement to attend a conference at which German issues would be discussed. The CFM thus convened for the sixth and last time in Paris in late May 1949. It met for almost a month but led to no narrowing of the differences between the sides. The Soviets called for a "return to Potsdam," but recognized that a reestablishment of four-power control in Germany was unrealistic. The ministers adjourned by issuing a communiqué in which they agreed to meet again at a time and a place to be determined by mutual agreement, but no such meeting was ever to occur.

Soviet behavior in the UN largely paralleled the handling of the Berlin crisis. Soviet speeches became more vituperative (especially after Molotov's replacement by Andrei Vyshinskii in 1949) and proposals became even more propagandistic and non-negotiable.[36] Nonetheless, there was still a reluctance to walk out of forums that were seen as potentially useful. In 1947–48 the USSR actually increased its participation in the UN Economic Commission for Europe (ECE) as a counter to the growing U.S. involvement in the economic affairs of the continent. In May 1947 it sent a large delegation to the first session of the ECE, and as late as April 1948 it expanded its role in the organization by reversing an earlier decision not to participate in its technical committees.[37] Soviet representatives continued to participate in the work of the Atomic Energy Commission, even after it adopted, over Soviet objections, a report informing the Security Council that because of Soviet intransigence the commission was unable to fulfill its mandate and wished to suspend its work.[38] Soviet representatives also took part in the work of the Commission on Human Rights, and as late as December 1948 the USSR abstained rather than voted against the General Assembly resolution approving the Universal Declaration of Human Rights.[39]

The Soviet policy of grudging participation in both the UN and the CFM largely ended in mid-1949, after the creation of the FRG and the conclusion of the sixth and final session of the CFM. In October 1949 the USSR announced the establishment of the German Democratic Republic (GDR), which henceforth would figure in all Soviet initiatives on Germany and complicate immeasurably the simple calls for a "return to Potsdam." Elsewhere Soviet policy became more aggressive. In the spring of 1950 Stalin almost certainly approved North Korea's impending attack on the south. In December the USSR reportedly sent orders to the East Europeans to prepare for war.[40]

Thus by the summer of 1950 the radicalization of Soviet policy was virtually complete. Between October of that year and Stalin's death in early 1953 the USSR fought a rearguard action against West

German rearmament and integration into a Western defense organization by issuing notes of protests and calling for a reconvening of the CFM, but it showed little flexibility in actually bringing about a change in Western policy. In early 1951 the four powers met at the deputy foreign minister level at the Palais Rose in Paris, but after three months were unable to reach agreement on an agenda.[41] Even after the Western powers made major concessions the USSR raised new preconditions that suggested little real interest in a meeting.

The same turn toward militancy was seen in the UN. The three Soviet republics withdrew from the World Health Organization (WHO) in February 1949, and were followed by the East European member states in 1950. Czechoslovakia, the only bloc member of the Food and Agricultural Organization (FAO), left that body in 1950, the same year in which Poland and Czechoslovakia left the International Monetary Fund (IMF). The most drastic Soviet action was of course the decision in January 1950 to boycott sessions of the Security Council until the representative of Nationalist China was removed—a step that had adverse consequences for Soviet interests and was reversed on August 1 of the same year.[42] In April 1950 Soviet delegations walked out of both UN arms control commissions, ostensibly over the issue of Chinese representation. At the same time the USSR and the world Communist movement shifted their attention away from negotiations to the Communist-sponsored Stockholm appeal launched the previous month.[43] Between early 1950 and the middle of 1953 the USSR ceased to participate in the ECE's technical committees, and for the first time compelled the East European states to minimize their participation in these bodies.[44]

By 1951 Western observers were speculating that the USSR was preparing to withdraw from the UN and set up a rival organization of Communist states and representatives of the "peoples" of states remaining in the UN.[45] If Stalin ever considered this course he drew back from it. Nonetheless, Soviet and Eastern bloc participation in the UN system reached its nadir in 1952, the last full year of Stalin's rule. No change in policy toward the UN was seen until July 1953, when the USSR announced that it would take part in the UN Technical Assistance Program.[46]

A few Soviet actions of this period at first glance might suggest that there was a moderation in policy in the last part of Stalin's life. The most significant was the March 1952 note to the Western powers proposing the immediate convening of the CFM (with the participation of an all-German government) to discuss a united, neutral Germany with its own national defense forces.[47] But most scholars have concluded that Stalin was not really interested in promoting a united Germany (the offer begged the question of how an all-German government would be formed),[48] and that his main purpose was to stir up the domestic resistance to rearmament and NATO membership.[49] A second possible sign of moderation was the Soviet decision in the first half of 1952 to participate in the newly formed UN Disarmament Commission (DC). But like the August 1950 return to the Security Council, this was more to prevent the West from using the body against the USSR than a sign of renewed interest in negotiations, as was made clear in March 1952, when the DC became the focal point of the Soviet campaign against the alleged use of bacteriological weapons by U.S. forces in Korea.

Marshall Shulman Reappraised

In *Stalin's Foreign Policy Reappraised*, Marshall Shulman developed the thesis that the thaw in Soviet relations with the West that most observers contended began after Stalin's death in fact could be traced to 1949 and the end of the Berlin blockade. According to Shulman, in the last years of Stalin's life the USSR adopted a "quasi-right" strategy that was intended to provide a respite following the "aggressive militancy" of the first postwar period of Soviet policy, when a "left" line was pursued. The general features of the rightist line were restraint in overt acts of provocation and the encouragement of the development of "neutralism, nationalism, the Peace Movement, and anticolonial agitation," all of which represented a part of "a process of adaptation of the Communist movement to the great transformations in the character of international politics since the Second World War."[50]

While Shulman was undoubtedly correct in perceiving that Soviet *doctrine* was beginning to adjust to changing realities, it is not easy to square his thesis with the actions of the Soviet *government*. As has been seen, in the first four years after the war the USSR participated in six lengthy meetings of the CFM, as well as a twenty-one-nation peace conference. In these meetings it used flexible tactics to divide the West, first by currying favor with the United States while attacking Britain, and later by playing to French fears of an Anglo-U.S. sponsored revival of German power. In the same period the USSR participated in the UN and some of its specialized agencies, despite the fact that it was badly outnumbered and its substantive and procedural proposals routinely rejected by large majorities.

In 1949 the picture changed decisively. After the sixth meeting of the CFM the USSR agitated for a "return to Potsdam" but showed little flexibility in arranging a new meeting, even when it was offered the opportunity to do so on its own terms at the Palais Rose meetings of 1951. The hardened Soviet diplomatic position was accompanied by riskier behavior in the military sphere, including the sanctioning of the war in Korea and the undertaking of preparations for war in Europe. The same turn toward the left was seen in the UN, where the USSR virtually ceased to participate in the work of most agencies and commissions.

If, to use Shulman's definitions, a right phase of Soviet policy is "associated with 'peaceful coexistence,' flexibility of tactics, divisive exploitation of 'contradictions' abroad, and collaboration with other groups, classes or nations," while a left phase is marked by "an over-hanging consciousness of the inevitability of conflict, an emphasis upon those ideological aspects which deal with the class struggle and the necessity for revolutionary advance, a definite militancy of method, and a detachment of the Communist movement abroad from association with other elements of the national or international community,"[51] then it can be argued that Stalin pursued a rightist course in the immediate postwar period, and that he turned left only later.

As has been seen, the turn to the left took place in two stages, of which the second was more drastic: first, in September 1947 with the founding of the Cominform; and second, in mid-1949, following the failure of the sixth session of the CFM. In the first phase of leftist militancy he unleashed the Communist parties but did not burn his bridges to those institutions which still offered some hope of influencing Western policy. In the second phase he went further, and virtually ceased to participate in the UN or the four-power institutions.

To suggest that Shulman overstated the militancy of Soviet policy before 1949 while understating it for the subsequent period is not to endorse the revisionist thesis that the West *caused* the cold war and that Stalin's behavior was chiefly in response to external provocations. It is to suggest that Stalin emerged from World War II expecting to pursue a policy based on a double standard and that he turned left only when forced by Western policy to choose between incompatible courses of action. Initially he sought to consolidate Communist control in Eastern Europe while working to keep his options open in Western Europe, especially with regard to Germany. But, by launching the Marshall Plan and unifying the Western sectors of Germany, the United States and Britain undercut the assumptions upon which this policy was based. This in turn encouraged him to crush the surviving elements of pluralism in what soon came to be called Eastern Europe. Even in late 1947 and 1948, however, the USSR continued to hold back from irrevocably smashing the institutions of postwar cooperation. The Berlin blockade was not the first phase of a warlike policy that culminated in Korea, but rather a final effort to use a combination of force and four-power diplomacy to retain influence over events in West Germany. Only after this effort failed did Stalin respond by turning sharply left, virtually cutting off diplomatic and other forms of cooperation with the West and adopting a militant, "front from below" strategy.

Shulman's argument that Stalin in fact turned right during this period depends heavily on his view that the launching of the peace movement was an act of relative moderation. This view is seriously flawed. If after 1949 the international Communist movement began propagating the slogan of peace and attempting to use it against Western governments, this was in large part because the Soviet government was relinquishing many of its positions as a state actor in the international system, thus coming to rely more heavily on the Communist parties. In effect the Soviet leadership demanded that foreign Communist parties broaden their base through rightist slogans precisely because the Soviet state was embarking on a leftist course by eschewing such instruments of policy as participation in the UN, negotiations with the great powers, and contact with non-Communist, nonfellow-traveler groups in the West.

In any case, the suggestion that the Communist parties exercised restraint in the late Stalin period is itself questionable, as can be seen most graphically in a comparison between the two putsch attempts of the Austrian Communist Party. In May 1947, just after the conclusion of the Moscow CFM, the Austrian party, apparently with some backing from the Soviet occupation authorities, staged a riot that appeared aimed at precipitating the fall of the government and a Communist takeover. Nonetheless, when the Austrian authorities appealed to the Allied Council for help a Russian officer appeared at the main demonstration and successfully urged the crowd to disband. In contrast, in the much more serious coup attempt launched in September 1950 the USSR played no such restraining role and in fact rendered considerable help to the insurgents.[52]

In addition to taking the actions of foreign Communist parties as literal indicators of the orientation of the Soviet state, Shulman misinterpreted the meaning of some of the USSR's own attempts to reach out to Western public opinion and selected interest groups. He mentions, for example, the April 1952 International Economic Conference in Moscow as a sign of reviving Soviet interest in economic ties with the West and as such a sign of the moderate turn in policy.[53] But it is one thing to convene, under the nominal auspices of the World Peace Council, an economic conference that attracted a few renegade Western businessmen and that resulted in the formation of an international committee to promote East-West trade, and quite another to participate, especially on unequal terms, in established international institutions such as the UN ECE.[54] Similarly, it is necessary to distinguish between ventures such as the Moscow Conference in Defence of Peace of All Churches and Religious Associations in the USSR, which also took place in 1952 and attracted exactly four fellow-traveling clergymen from Western Europe, and the kinds of exchanges with legitimate Western religious organizations such as the World Council of Churches (still a strongly anti-Communist body in the 1950s) that took place immediately after World War II and that were resumed in the mid-1950s.[55] As will be seen in subsequent chapters, the innovative element in the Malenkov and Khrushchev policies was not that the USSR sought to mobilize Communists and fellow travelers in support of Soviet policy objectives, but that they reached out to organizations and institutions that they did not control and that were often overtly hostile to the USSR in a long-term effort to promote the "relaxation of tensions." Stalin did not adopt this approach, especially after 1949.

In sum, it seems justifiable to conclude that Soviet policy in Stalin's last years was more militant than that of the early postwar period, and that the policies of Georgii Malenkov and Nikita Khrushchev did indeed represent a sharp break with the immediate past as well as a resumption, in some ways, of the line pursued earlier in the 1940s.

Process, Mandates, Institutions

The behavior of the allies at Yalta and Potsdam was consistent with a broader historical pattern going back to the 1919 Paris Peace Conference and even the Congress of Vienna a century earlier. As international issues became more complex, as public and parliamentary opinion exerted greater influence on diplomacy, and as nationalism and ideology narrowed the scope for compromise and accommodation, governments found it increasingly difficult to negotiate solutions to international disputes. Instead, they often resorted to the expedient of agreeing to reach agreement *in the future* and establishing procedures for doing so. This pattern was seen at the wartime conferences, where the allies failed to reach agreement on a peace settlement but did set in motion a peace process. Yalta and Potsdam in effect issued mandates for postwar cooperation, as well as established institutions, such as the UN and the CFM, that were to implement those mandates. As has been seen, after the war the Yalta and Potsdam mandates either were violated outright or interpreted so divergently as to become sources of contention rather than blueprints for cooperation. For a time both sides fulfilled their commitments to participate in the processes established in 1945, but each accused the other of acting unilaterally in violation of these commitments. The CFM thus broke down without fulfilling the most important task assigned to it, completion of a treaty of peace with Germany, while the UN became increasingly ineffective.

The turn toward détente after Stalin's death brought a partial revival of the early postwar patterns of cooperation. The four powers met at the ministerial level in Berlin in January 1954 for the first time since 1949 to take up the questions of German reunification and an Austrian state treaty. New signs of life also appeared in the UN and its specialized agencies, as the USSR resumed and soon surpassed the levels of participation that had been seen in 1946–48.

However, this was largely a transitional phase. By the 1950s both the East and the West, in different ways and for different reasons, had concluded that formal negotiations in the old forums were likely to lead back to the same old deadlocks. The mandates of 1945 thus became increasingly irrelevant. Indeed, by the end of the 1950s Khrushchev was declaring that the Potsdam agreement was no longer valid, and waging a campaign against the UN and its secretary-general.

Nonetheless, the practice of issuing mandates—of agreeing to work toward future agreements and setting in motion processes toward that end—continued and became a distinguishing feature of the détente era. The first such agreement was the Geneva directive, which was issued at the end of the July 1955 four-power summit and which established procedures that would lead, the signatories claimed, to a settlement in Europe, disarmament agreements, and expanded economic and cultural contacts. As will be seen in the next chapter, the provisions of the Geneva directive were not fulfilled and it became, like the Yalta and Potsdam agreements, more a source of acrimony than a blueprint for cooperation. However, more modest but in the long run more enduring understandings came out of the initial round of Soviet-West European bilateral summitry in 1955 and 1956, and helped to launch détente as a mandated process. For example, in the Soviet-Norwegian communiqué issued at the conclusion of Prime Minister Gerhardsen's November 1955 trip to the USSR, both countries pledged to "cooperate towards a general relaxation of world tensions" as well as to expand their cooperation in economic, cultural, and other bilateral affairs.[56] Similar expressions of joint intent were concluded with Sweden, Denmark, Britain, and France.

As in the 1940s, agreements to engage in processes usually led to the establishment of institutions. The Geneva directive called upon the foreign ministers of the four countries to meet to discuss its implementation. President Dwight D. Eisenhower preferred the creation of more elaborate machinery, but this was blocked by the Soviets. Nonetheless, as will be seen in the next chapter, the Geneva directive did provide the basis on which the sides attempted to arrange high-level talks on the German question for the next five years. Many of the bilateral agreements also resulted in the creation of permanent institutions, such as ministerial and subministerial bodies charged with promoting trade or drawing up cultural exchange programs.

The willingness of the USSR and the Western powers to conclude agreements and to establish new institutions reflected a growing commitment on both sides to détente as a long-term process. After an initial period in the 1950s in which the Western powers (led by Konrad Adenauer and John Foster Dulles) stressed the need to build positions of strength, both to guard against Communist inroads in the West and to lay the basis for future negotiations, Western governments increasingly downplayed the importance of a negotiated settlement in Europe and instead linked change to an extended process. This shift culminated in the Harmel report of December 1967, in which the NATO countries committed themselves to seeking "a détente in East-West relations" which they described as "part of a long-term process to promote better relations and to foster a European settlement."[57]

West Germany at first lagged behind the other Western states in embracing this approach, but in time it too for all practical purposes abandoned the quest for German reunification through a negotiated settlement and looked instead to a process of overcoming the national division in the broader context of a global and continental détente. As a West German ambassador to the USSR later described the policy, "the goal we are working towards is to end the division of Germany as a result of a process which simultaneously defuses, and ultimately overcomes, the division of Europe together with the East-West confrontation."[58] Once it abandoned the quest for a negotiated solution within the old four-power mechanisms, West Germany became the most enthusiastic proponent of détente as a force for encouraging political change.

Soviet leaders initially were more reluctant than their Western counterparts to embrace détente as a process leading to political change. They began making favorable references to détente in the 1950s, but "relaxation" (the literal meaning of razriadka, the Soviet term for détente) was seen in essentially negative terms, and always coupled with an allusion to existing tensions (razriadka napriazhennosti).[59] The most important step toward removing these tensions, Soviet officials argued, was for the West to accept realities, including the division of Germany and the permanence of the socialist order in Eastern Europe. Détente thus was associated with the confirmation of the territorial and political (although not the social) status quo rather than with dynamic processes of change.

Notwithstanding the rhetoric, Khrushchev fully realized that in the absence of a negotiated settlement to the German problem a relaxation in East-West relations would tend to freeze the status quo and thereby contribute to a de facto settlement, even if the Western powers were not yet ready to grant one de jure. As will be seen in subsequent chapters, Khrushchev was in fact a strong supporter of "relaxation" and "normalization" in East-West relations, despite the fact that his frustrations over the situation in Berlin and East Germany led him to provoke a series of dangerous crises with the West. Later under Leonid Brezhnev, after West Germany and its allies had conceded what the USSR regarded as a de jure settlement, the Soviet view of détente became more dynamic. It was portrayed as a positive process that could be made irreversible and lead to an overcoming of the division of Europe on terms favorable to the USSR. This trend continued under Mikhail Gorbachev, who proclaimed himself an enthusiastic proponent of an "all-European process" that he claimed would lead to the creation of a "common European home."

The chapters that follow discuss the development of détente after 1953 as a mandated and increasingly institutionalized process. It discusses how both the USSR and the Western powers, building upon the mandates and institutions that grew out of the initial post-Stalin thaw, sought to use this long-term process to advance particular objectives and overall visions of a desirable European order. It focuses more on Soviet than on Western policy, but at various points it notes how Western conceptions of détente as a change-promoting process either coincided or clashed with Soviet conceptions. For the most part these conceptions clashed, thus ensuring that until quite recently détente was on balance a competitive process.

3   Geneva and the Four-Power Process

As was seen in chapter two, the breakdown of postwar cooperation and the deepening of the cold war were associated with the collapse of the CFM and the failure in the early 1950s to revive ministerial-level, four-power talks, while the turn toward détente after 1953 entailed a partial revival of four-power negotiations, culminating in the Austrian State Treaty and the July 1955 Geneva summit. Four-power dialogue subsequently died out, as the USSR refused to discuss reunification and as the Western powers grew increasingly indifferent to the German issue. By the early 1970s four-power rights played only a residual role in European affairs, chiefly in regard to Berlin. This chapter examines the four-power talks of the 1950s, their role in fostering a general East-West détente, and their subsequent breakdown. It also discusses residual four-power rights and responsibilities in the 1970s and 1980s, and the basis they provided for the dramatic and almost entirely unexpected revival of four-power talks in early 1990 following the collapse of the East German state.

The Resumption of Dialogue

The origins of the July 1955 Geneva summit usually are traced to Churchill's May 1953 speech to the House of Commons, in which he suggested that "a conference on the highest level should take place between the leading Powers without long delay."[1] Churchill had been calling for such a meeting for more than three years, both as a way of improving his own political fortunes and because he genuinely believed that a revival of the wartime dialogue would serve the cause of peace. In a campaign speech of February 1950 he spoke of the need for "a supreme effort to bridge the gulf between the two worlds."[2] Following his return to power in 1951, he privately raised the idea of an East-West conference with Truman, who did not believe that the Soviets really wanted a conference and stressed that while he would be willing to meet with Stalin in Washington, he would not go to the USSR.[3]

Truman's appraisal was probably correct, as Stalin did little to encourage hopes for an early meeting. In response to a query by a visiting journalist in 1952, he suggested that he would be willing to meet with President Truman in the USSR or, "if the offer should meet with objections," in Poland or Czechoslovakia. This offer was acidly dismissed by Secretary of State Dean Acheson, who questioned why a U.S. president "should travel for the fourth time halfway round the world" for a discussion that promised no sure success.[4] Nor was the USSR interested in a meeting at the foreign ministers' level, as was shown by the outcome of the 1951 Palais Rose Conference.

Although Stalin's death brought to power men with fundamentally different attitudes toward summitry and international travel, Malenkov and Khrushchev were careful not to rush into an East-West meeting. Their caution partly resulted from internal factors. Molotov had resumed the post of foreign minister that he had relinquished in 1949, and was a formidable proponent of maintaining a Stalinist line in policy toward the outside world.

But there also were procedural obstacles to a summit, as the sides could not agree on the prerequisites for and composition of a meeting that was likely to set a tone for years to come and to raise expectations throughout the world. Between March 1953 and the scheduling of a summit a little more than two years later governments and political leaders put forward at least six different formulas for a meeting. They included a big-three meeting of Britain, the United States, and the USSR, an informal big-two meeting between Britain and the USSR, a four-power meeting, a five-power meeting that included Communist China, a six-power conference involving both Communist and Nationalist China, and a conference of all European states.[5]

Each of these alternatives had tactical implications for the powers concerned, and each suggested continuity with or a resumption of patterns of cooperation that had developed in the mid-1940s and had been suspended in the cold war. The two- and three-power formulas recalled the wartime summits and the consultation process mandated at Yalta. The four-power formula suggested a reactivation of the Council of Ministers (CFM) and a "return to Potsdam." The five-power formula derived from the composition of the UN Security Council, which in turn was based on an earlier U.S. insistence on the importance of China as a great power. The "all European" formula was put forward by the Soviets as a European counterpart to the inter-American system established by the Rio Treaty of 1947, which was itself based on the right to "regional arrangements" and "collective self defense" enshrined in Article 51 of the UN Charter.

Within days of Stalin's death, Churchill wrote to Eisenhower to ask about separate or collective approaches to the new leadership.[6] The United States, France, and most of Churchill's own advisers were skeptical.[7] Eisenhower was wary of *any* meeting, which he associated with the sterile exchanges of the late 1940s and feared "would give our opponent the same kind of opportunity he has so often had to use such a meeting simultaneously to balk every reasonable effort of ourselves and to make the whole occurrence another propaganda mill for the Soviet."[8] But he also believed that if there *was* to be a meeting, France should be included. In his reply to Churchill he suggested that the United States, the United Kingdom, and "probably the French" should agree "upon some general purpose and program under which each would have a specific part to play."

By insisting upon the exclusion of China and the inclusion of France, the Western governments de facto committed themselves to a four-power formula. But this was more by default than the product of any positive attachment to the four-power arrangements of the 1940s. The immediate backdrop to these discussions was the 1950–52 exchange of notes in which the USSR had called for a CFM meeting to deal with the militarization of Germany, and there was considerable concern in the West that the USSR would use a four-power meeting at any level to try to derail West Germany's integration into the Western alliance.[9]

Following intense speculation in the Western press about an impending summit, Eisenhower invited Churchill and French prime minister René Mayer to a three-power meeting in Bermuda in June. The announced purpose was to advance "the cause of world peace," which was widely taken in the West to mean the finalization of plans for an East-West summit.[10] The USSR responded with a full-page *Pravda* editorial that began by praising Churchill who, "unlike other statesmen of the West, did not tie up his proposal for convening a conference with any preliminary obligations for one or the other side," but criticized the meeting as an attempt by the three Western powers to reach prior understandings "at the expense of the USSR."[11] It concluded that in going to Bermuda, Churchill was "in fact renouncing, if not the letter then at any rate the spirit of his proposal for the calling of a 'conference at the highest level,' because such a conference, in so far as it concerns the participation of the USSR, might take place only in the case when both sides approach the conference without any preliminary fixed demands." The *Pravda* editorial was widely seen in the West as an attempt to appeal to Churchill to exert pressures within the Western camp to convene an early summit.[12]

In retrospect it is doubtful that the Soviet leaders were bidding for such a meeting. In his memoirs Khrushchev credited Churchill with proposing a summit, but opined that the British leader "believed that the West could take advantage of the fact that the new Soviet government wasn't yet fully formed and therefore would be more vulnerable to pressure."[13] He also made the curious point that "the one reason we were able to agree to the Geneva meeting at all was that Malenkov had by then been released from his duties as Chairman." These remarks suggest that the internal Soviet situation may have been too unsettled to allow for an early summit. The riots that erupted in East Berlin in June 1953 no doubt instilled extra caution in the Soviet leaders as they contemplated the prospect of negotiations on Germany.[14] Thus the Soviet five-power and all-European conference proposals may have been intended to buy time and to ward off international pressures for an early meeting.

In July 1953 the three Western powers formally proposed a four-power foreign minister meeting with a two-part agenda: (1), the organization of free elections in Germany; and (2), "conditions for the establishment of a free all-German Government, with freedom of action in internal and external affairs."[15] The Soviet foreign ministry replied the following month and accused the Western powers of violating "existing agreements on Conferences of Ministers of Foreign Affairs" by coming to a preliminary agreement without Soviet participation.[16] The Soviet note acknowledged that a conference could be useful for discussing "measures which promote a general lessening of tension in international relations," but added that the "possibility should not be excluded of considering the question of in just what composition these or other problems of international relations should be considered." The note went on to call for a five-power conference with a slightly different agenda: (1), "measures for lessening of tension in international relations"; and (2), German reunification.

After a series of "harsh, argumentative or sometimes offensive Russian communications,"[17] in late November the Soviet government finally dropped its insistence on a conference involving China and accepted the idea of a four-power meeting of the foreign ministers, suggesting Berlin as a site.

The most noteworthy features of the Soviet reply were the choice of Berlin and the way the question of agenda was handled. The Soviet preference for Berlin was puzzling to Western observers, but in retrospect made perfect sense.[18] Whereas all sessions of the CFM had taken place on the territory of one of the four powers (London, Moscow, Paris, or New York), the January 1954 meeting was to be held in the former capital of Germany.[19] The shift reflected a declining Soviet interest in the four-power process and a corresponding increase in fostering a direct intra-German dialogue, if possible by associating the East and West German governments with the deliberations of the four powers.

On the question of agenda, the conference participants never did reach a preliminary understanding. In its note to the Western powers, the USSR stated that it was reluctantly agreeing to come to a meeting that did not include China, but that it was not accepting the proposed two-part Western agenda. In a conversation with U.S. high commissioner James Conant, Adenauer astutely noted the problems that could be posed by the absence of an agreed agenda, and pointed out that "there was an implied agenda [in the Soviet note] which placed European security before solution of [the] German problem."[20] He stressed that the West should insist on reversing the order in which these two points were discussed. In practice, however, there was no way either side could impose an order of procedure on the other. Thus began the practice of convening postwar conferences without an agenda and of leaving it to the participants to argue over the relative priority of a settlement of the German problem versus European security and the "relaxation of tensions."

The Berlin Conference convened in January 1954, in an atmosphere reminiscent of the meetings of 1945–49. The meeting did not constitute a formal revival of the CFM, but the participation of Molotov, Anthony Eden, and Dulles (a Republican adviser at earlier CFM meetings) suggested continuity with the late 1940s. In contrast to the four-power meetings that later were to take place in Geneva, there was little attempt by either side to influence public opinion by cultivating the media. Moreover, as in the late 1940s, Germany—East and West—still was treated as a defeated and occupied country, whose fate was subject to the deliberations of the victors.[21]

Nonetheless, the Berlin meeting was clearly a transitional event. Like the sessions of the CFM in the 1940s, it was conducted as a preliminary step toward the convening of a formal peace conference. The USSR continued to stress the importance of German unification, and may not have fully ruled out some form of unification combined with neutralization. It also continued to link the Austrian and German questions. This enhanced Soviet leverage over the German question, but also blocked the conclusion of the Austrian State Treaty that had been under discussion since 1947. At the same time, however, the conference saw the first Soviet proposals for "all European" political cooperation built around a Germany that would remain divided for an indefinite future. This was the basic formula that informed Soviet policy in the entire period from the Geneva summit to the reopening of the German question in late 1989.

The Berlin Conference

In his opening statement, Molotov took up where the exchange of notes had left off in December. He claimed that the USSR wanted to act in accordance with the Potsdam and other wartime agreements, but then constructed a chain of logic that placed Germany at the bottom of the list of topics to be tackled: German unification could be discussed only in the broader context of European security; European security was "closely linked to the fundamental problem of our day—the problem of decreasing international tension"; responsibility for decreasing tension had been assigned in the UN Charter to the five great powers—hence the need to consider a five-power conference as the first order of business.[22] In his reply, Dulles rejected the implication that the five powers had "a special mandate to run the affairs of the world," and urged Molotov to return to the main issue: "We four have met here in Berlin to discuss two concrete problems, Germany and Austria. For this discussion we have a special and unique responsibility as Occupying Powers. These two problems are capable of solution."[23]

Molotov later supported a request from the GDR to take part in the conference deliberations, and refused to be drawn into a discussion of the British-sponsored "Eden plan" for German unification based on free elections. He also introduced a draft of "basic points" for a German peace treaty providing for a united, neutral, and democratic Germany. To prepare the final treaty, he called for the convening of a conference of states concerned, including East and West Germany. Molotov also displayed little change in the Soviet position on Austria. He rejected a Western offer to sign the draft agreed to by the Soviet government in 1949, and introduced a new series of amendments that he argued were necessary to prevent a second Anschluss by militaristic circles in West Germany. These amendments, and especially a provision allowing for the stationing of Soviet troops in Austria after the conclusion of a treaty, were rejected by the three Western powers and the Austrians.[24]

While sidestepping the question of treaties for Austria and Germany, Molotov put forward the first of what was to be many versions of a general European treaty on collective security in Europe. The draft treaty stipulated that it would not affect the competence of the four powers "to deal with the German problem which shall be settled in accordance with decisions previously taken by the Four Powers." Pending such a settlement, however, the FRG and the GDR would "be parties to the treaty enjoying equal rights with other parties thereto."[25]

The results of the Berlin Conference were meager. It led to the convening of the 1954 Geneva Conference on Asia, but offered little hope for movement on European issues. The final communiqué of February 18 stated that the four ministers "have had a full exchange of views on the German question, on the problems of European security and on the Austrian question but they were unable to reach agreement upon these matters."[26] The breakdown of the conference was followed by a stepped-up Soviet campaign for the establishment of an all-European collective security system, but little movement toward a summit.

On March 31 the USSR proposed in a formal diplomatic note that it be permitted to join NATO and that the United States might become a member of the Soviet-proposed European security system.[27] The West rejected this offer, and on July 24 the USSR proposed an all-European meeting to discuss collective security. It followed up this offer on August 4 with another note calling for a four-power meeting to prepare the all-European conference. The three Western powers countered by stating that they would attend a four-power meeting, but only if the USSR signed the Austrian State Treaty and agreed to elections in Germany. The USSR rejected these preconditions, and in a note of November 13 that was addressed to all European countries, the United States, and Canada proposed the convening in Moscow of an all-European conference.[28] The Western powers declined the invitation, but the USSR and its allies went ahead with the meeting on November 29, thereby laying the groundwork for the conclusion the following spring of the Warsaw Treaty.[29]

Despite renewed entreaties from Churchill, throughout this period the Soviet leadership displayed little interest in a summit. After a further round of correspondence with a skeptical Eisenhower, in July 1954 Churchill dispatched a telegram to Molotov suggesting a personal meeting between himself and Malenkov.[30] Although many in the West and indeed inside the British cabinet had been fearful of just such a move by Churchill, the Soviets did not jump at the invitation. Molotov sent a reply in which he did not rule out a two-power meeting and which Churchill characterized as "encouraging," but soon thereafter the USSR relaunched the campaign for an all-European conference, thereby putting on hold all talk of a small, informal summit.[31]

While East-West diplomacy ground to a halt, there were important events on the Western side that, along with the leadership changes in the Kremlin, were to force a decisive break with the USSR's existing approach to European affairs. After a heated debate that pitted the Gaullists and Communists against the government, on August 30, 1954, the French National Assembly failed to approve ratification of the May 1952 treaty constituting the European Defense Community (EDC). This not only blocked further progress toward creation of a Western defense organization, but negated the May 1952 Convention on Relations Between the Three Powers and the Federal Republic of Germany that would have restored West German sovereignty, but whose coming into force had been made contingent upon ratification of the EDC treaty.

Alarmed by these developments, the Western powers moved quickly to establish an alternative means for integrating the Federal

Republic into a Western defense system. At the suggestion of British foreign minister Eden, a nine-power conference convened in London in late September, and hammered out the package of agreements that was to restore West German sovereignty, create the Western European Union (WEU), and secure the admission of West Germany as a member of NATO. In the final act of the nine-power conference the West Germans pledged to conduct policy in accordance with the UN Charter and to "undertake never to have recourse to force to achieve the reunification of Germany or the modification of the present boundaries of the German Federal Republic."[32] For their part, the Western powers declared that they recognized the Bonn government "as the only German Government freely and legitimately constituted and therefore entitled to speak for Germany as the representative of the German people in international affairs." They further affirmed that "a peace settlement for the whole of Germany, freely negotiated between Germany and her former enemies, which should lay the foundation of a lasting peace, remains an essential aim of their policy. The final determination of the boundaries of Germany must await such a settlement."[33] The three Western powers and the FRG also concluded a separate Protocol on the Termination of the Occupation Regime, in which the Western powers relinquished their rights as victors to station forces in West Germany. In a separate convention on the presence of foreign forces in the FRG the mission of allied troops was defined as "defense of the free world, of which Berlin and the Federal Republic form a part."[34]

The complex of agreements negotiated by the nine powers became known as the Paris agreements and were ratified in the spring of 1955. On May 5 the Allied High Commission proclaimed the repeal of the Occupation Statute, and on May 9 West Germany became the fifteenth member of NATO.

The Austrian State Treaty

The ratification of the Paris agreements and West Germany's accession to NATO were linked to the Soviet decision to conclude, after a delay of almost ten years, a state treaty ending the occupation of Austria.[35] The treaty in turn removed the last obstacles to the Geneva summit and paved the way for an across-the-board improvement in East-West relations. It also marked—although this was hardly recognized at the time—the USSR's final abandonment of efforts to achieve an all-German solution and the beginning of its pursuit of an increasingly explicit two-Germany policy.

As many in the West suspected at the time, Soviet policymakers probably believed—especially in late 1954 and early 1955—that negotiations with Austria might be used to slow or block ratification of the Paris agreements by encouraging the West German Social Democrats and others to continue campaigning for a neutral, re-unified Germany. But this motivation diminished over time, and became distinctly secondary after Malenkov's resignation in February 1955 and the resulting diminution of Molotov's influence. The Soviet leaders continued to press for an Austrian treaty, if anything with greater urgency, but for different reasons. Resigned to West Germany's becoming a part of NATO, they saw the treaty as a guarantee against a new Anschluss, as well as the price that needed to be paid to achieve a broad East-West relaxation of tensions in the absence of a German settlement. The shift in Soviet thinking occurred over a period of months, however, and was recognized by Western policy-makers slowly and unevenly.

On February 8 Molotov gave a long foreign policy speech to the Supreme Soviet that sent conflicting signals regarding Austria. He stated that "there is no justification for any further delay in concluding a state treaty with Austria" and that "a solution must be found which would rule out the possibility of a new annexation of Austria by Germany, and this requires the adoption of appropriate agreed measures by the four Powers in connection with the German question."[36] But he also stated that "it is necessary to convene without delay a conference of the four Powers for the examination both of the German question and the question of the state treaty with Austria."

In the West, the Soviet call for a treaty was seen almost exclusively as the start of a new campaign to derail the ratification of the Paris agreements and West Germany's accession to NATO. The U.S. Department of State acknowledged a few new elements in the Molotov speech, but concluded that the Soviets appeared to be demanding German neutrality, nonratification of the Paris agreements, and an early four-power conference as preconditions for an Austrian treaty.[37] Similar suspicions were voiced in London, Paris and Vienna.

In the ensuing weeks, however, some Soviet officials privately stressed that they were not trying to use the Austrian treaty to influence the intra-NATO debate regarding West Germany, but simply wanted an arrangement for Austria that would provide guarantees against an Anschluss with the FRG.[38] In late February Molotov himself began to clarify his intentions. He invited Austria's ambassador in Moscow, Norbert Bischoff, to the foreign ministry to discuss the Soviet proposals, and suggested that Austria and the USSR undertake high-level, bilateral talks aimed at reaching agreement on a treaty. But Molotov continued to stress the need for a four-power conference, thereby keeping alive suspicions that his real interest was Germany.

The Austrians feared the domestic political effects and long-term consequences of not seizing the opportunity for an agreement, but they were on the horns of a dilemma: if they proceeded too far in negotiating bilaterally with the USSR, they risked angering Britain, France, and the United States, who considered Austria still under occupation and regarded the restoration of its sovereignty as the sole responsibility of the four powers.[39] But the Austrians knew that if they pressed for an early four-power conference, they could be seen as accessories to a Soviet effort to derail ratification of the Paris agreements.

On March 14 the Austrian government officially replied to the Soviet offer by endorsing a conference of Austria and the four powers, but suggested prior clarification of two issues raised by the Soviets: guarantees against Anschluss and the form in which Austrian neutrality could be declared.[40] By this time an increasing number of Western officials were concluding that the Soviets genuinely were interested in a treaty. On March 5 Ambassador Charles Bohlen cabled from Moscow that "it does not appear that Soviet demarche is primarily a method of additional pressure to defeat ratification [of the] Paris agreements," which the Soviet government "must recognize as imminent."[41]

Ten days after receiving the reply from Vienna, the Soviets invited Austria to send a delegation to Moscow. They reaffirmed their stance that the treaty should be discussed at a four-power meeting, but dropped their insistence on scheduling such a meeting before beginning talks with the Austrians. This was a key concession that strongly suggested that the link between Germany and Austria had been severed. Nonetheless, uncertainty persisted about Soviet motives. From Austria, High Commissioner Llewellyn Thompson continued to argue that Germany was the real target of Soviet policy, while Bohlen claimed that the Soviets recognized the inevitability of West German rearmament and were only interested in preventing incorporation of Austria's Western sectors into NATO.[42]

Dulles tended to side with Thompson, and continued to approach a four-power conference with great caution. He and Eden both warned the Austrians against making concessions in Moscow, which Dulles called "a dangerous place to go alone."[43] Dulles also told the Austrian ambassador that the Western powers would not agree to participate in a conference at the ministerial level, since this would give Molotov an opportunity to raise questions, notably Germany and China, that the West was not prepared to discuss. He was, however, amenable to a conference of the ambassadors whose competence would be limited strictly to the Austrian question.[44]

The Soviets and Austrians hammered out the essence of a settlement during four days of meetings that began on April 12, 1955.[45]

The most important elements of the settlement were understandings on an Austrian declaration of neutrality and the withdrawal of
occupation forces, and on economic issues relating to the Danube
Shipping Company and the deliveries of Austrian crude oil in exchange for the return of properties seized by the Soviets.[46] Following
completion of the bilateral talks, the Soviet government addressed a
note to the Western powers, proposing that the foreign ministers of
the five countries meet to sign the document.[47] The Western powers
demurred, however, and instead called for a conference of ambassadors to go over the final treaty. The Soviets assented, although not
without strong propaganda attacks on the West for causing a delay.

The ambassadors convened in Vienna in mid-May 1955 for almost
two weeks of intense negotiations. The most contentious issue in
the talks concerned the relationship between the Austrian State
Treaty and the bilateral understandings reached in Moscow. The Soviet ambassador resisted any reference in the five-power treaty to the
bilateral agreement, which he claimed was a matter between Austria
and the USSR alone that was beyond the competence of the ambassadors.[48] But the three allied ministers were worried that the Austrians might be concluding a "broken treaty" with which the Soviets
could refuse to comply by charging Austrian nonfulfillment of the
bilateral economic agreement.[49] The USSR ultimately compromised,
but only after Dulles threatened to absent himself from the ceremonies in Vienna.[50] As will be seen, the ambassadorial conference
coincided with the final diplomatic exchanges leading to the Geneva
summit, and neither side was interested in a breakdown that would
have put the summit on hold.

The formal signing took place on May 15, 1955.[51] At a meeting of
the five foreign ministers the previous day Molotov unexpectedly
put forward the draft text of a four-power declaration guaranteeing
the permanent neutrality of Austria.[52] The Western powers requested time to study the draft, but generally were not amenable to
a guarantee. The United States had constitutional difficulties with
such a procedure, while the French and British had bad memories of
the guarantees of the 1930s.[53] At the same time, however, the Western powers did not want to respond negatively to the Soviet offer,
since they feared that this could precipitate a unilateral Soviet guarantee of Austria's neutrality that might imply a Soviet protectorate
over the country.[54] The Western powers finally decided, at the end
of 1955, to reject any kind of multilateral arrangement and instead
to recognize Austria's unilateral assumption of permanent neutrality
in bilateral exchanges of notes.[55]

The negotiations leading to the Austrian treaty demonstrated
both continuity and change in Soviet attitudes toward the rights and
responsibilities deriving from Potsdam and the other wartime con-

ferences. Molotov's calls for a four-power conference and a four-power guarantee were consistent with Soviet attempts from 1945 to 1954 to use the Potsdam arrangements as an instrument against real or alleged German "militarism." While the USSR tried to obtain a special status among the four powers by concluding a set of bilateral agreements with the Austrians, it was careful not to damage and in fact tried to strengthen its four-power rights. On the matter of Germany, however, Soviet behavior marked the virtual end of interest in trying to deal with the German problem through the four-power process. As was to be seen two months later in Geneva and even more clearly at the foreign ministers conference in the fall, the USSR was well on its way toward openly acknowledging a two-Germany policy premised on the preservation of the "achievements of socialism in the GDR."

Although the Soviet leaders were not particularly secretive about the fundamental change that had occurred in their approach to the problems of Germany and European security, the Western leaders had difficulty in coming to grips with the new reality. After remaining unduly skeptical about the prospects for concluding an Austrian treaty, they swung to the opposite extreme, and began to see the upcoming summit as the beginning of a process in which the pattern of the Austrian settlement might be applied—for better or worse—in Germany. Eden, for example, was convinced that the Western stance at Berlin in 1954 had paved the way to an Austrian settlement, and believed that the same kind of steadfastness on Germany would pay off.[56] Dulles had similar and if anything stronger views. In reality, however, the Soviet leaders had decided to conclude an Austrian treaty precisely because they had concluded that there would not be a German settlement, at least in the terms it had been understood since 1945.

The Geneva Summit

Preparations

The Western powers were divided as they approached the prospect of a summit. Before his resignation on February 5, 1955, French prime minister Pierre Mendes-France was the strongest Western supporter of a meeting, which he argued would facilitate rather than undercut ratification of the Paris agreements.[57] After Mendes-France was replaced by the more skeptical Edgar Faure, the British became the main backers of a summit, which they believed would help Eden in the upcoming elections.[58] The U.S. and West German governments were more negative. Eisenhower and Dulles feared that a summit would give the Soviet leaders a propaganda windfall, while

Adenauer preferred to strengthen his position at home before coming to grips with East-West issues. He believed that the Soviet view on Germany had "sharpened and hardened," and that it would be "very difficult to set up any plan to negotiate with the Soviets."[59] West German and U.S. suspicions regarding Soviet dealings with Austria also tended to argue against an early meeting.

Notwithstanding his own skepticism, on March 23, 1955, Eisenhower declared that he would be in favor of "exploratory talks," presumably at the foreign minister level, which could lead to a summit. He added three preconditions: that the talks follow the ratification of the Paris accords, that they result in something more substantive than just propaganda, and that they exclude China and "Germany."[60] Eisenhower's insistence on the exclusion of Germany was consistent with a pattern going back to the Palais Rose meetings, at which the Western powers sought to broaden the agenda to deflect Soviet calls for a return to Potsdam. Later, after the Paris agreements were ratified and West Germany was safely in NATO, the positions of the sides were to reverse: the Western powers would press for a narrow focus on German reunification (diluted over time by a growing interest in arms control), while the Soviets would all but refuse to discuss Germany and called for measures to promote a "relaxation of tensions." In mid-April the United States agreed in principle to attend a summit, but Eisenhower continued to insist that the meeting was to be "exploratory only" and that "no substantive problems or decisions should be considered." Its purpose would be to "locate areas of tension and disagreement, and assign them to working groups or to [an] organization such as the UN."[61]

Following ratification of the Paris agreements on May 5, on May 10 the three Western powers formally invited the USSR to a "two-stage" conference of heads of government and foreign ministers. The Western note suggested a brief meeting of the foreign ministers "to assist the Heads of Government in their task" that would be held a day or so before the summit itself. The summit in turn would be followed by another meeting of the foreign ministers, which would lead, it was hoped, to a sustained process of four-power negotiation. "This procedure would facilitate the essential preparation and orderly negotiation most likely to bring about agreements by progressive stages. The important thing is to begin the process promptly and to pursue it with patience and determination."[62]

On May 26 the USSR in essence accepted the Western invitation, although not without a long list of complaints about the "positions of strength policy" of the Western powers. The Soviet note stressed that the main task of the conference should be to "relax tensions," but appeared to welcome the Western plan for a series of meetings at different levels and the issuing of "instructions" by the heads of government to the foreign ministers.[63] After a further exchange of notes regarding time and place, the meeting was scheduled for July in Geneva.

As had been the case before the Berlin Conference of 1954, the agenda for the proposed summit was a subject of considerable debate, both within the West and between East and West. Initially Eisenhower did not regard German reunification as the central issue on the agenda. This position was shared by Adenauer, who was inclined to downplay the German issue and to believe that "a German settlement might follow only in the wake of a global U.S.-Soviet détente."[64] Ironically, it was the British and French who strongly insisted that the meeting deal with substantive issues, and that the West make German reunification the centerpiece of its strategy. Eden was especially forceful in arguing that "German unification [was] by far the most important of the questions to be discussed at the conference" and that progress on the German issue was the touchstone by which the conference would be judged.[65] The French also shared this general view—not out of any enthusiasm for reunification as such, but because they believed that reunification might come about in any case and that it was essential for the West to take the lead and to head off any dangerous Soviet neutralization offers.[66]

For their part, the Soviets made clear in diplomatic notes and premeeting commentary that they regarded the "relaxation of international tension" and the USSR's disarmament proposal of May 10 as the most important topics for discussion.[67] However, they were not interested in nailing down a precise agenda before the heads of government assembled in Geneva. In their note of May 10 the Western powers did not propose a specific agenda, but expressed the hope that the foreign ministers could make some progress on drawing up an agreed list of topics, if possible at the forthcoming meetings with Molotov on the occasion of the signing of the Austrian treaty. But Molotov refused to discuss the agenda either in Vienna or at the UN anniversary celebrations the following month in San Francisco.[68] The Soviet note of May 25 suggested that the heads of government could themselves determine the questions to be considered.[69]

The key event that crystallized Western thinking around the reunification issue was the USSR's note of June 7 (passed from the Soviet to the West German embassy in Paris), inviting Adenauer to come to Moscow to discuss the establishment of diplomatic relations.[70] Adenauer and the other Western leaders immediately suspected that the Soviets would try to push unification into the background at Geneva but make a bilateral offer in Moscow that the West German government would come under domestic pressure to accept. Therefore, he decided to hold off on the trip to Moscow until after the four powers had met, but believed that it was essential for the Western powers to show that they were making progress on the unification issue.[71]

A three-power working group that met in Paris to plan Western tactics and objectives recommended in its final report that "the Western powers should press for immediate reference of specified European questions to the Four Foreign Ministers. This should be done carefully and in precisely defined terms."[72] In addition, the three participating governments and the West Germans undertook detailed studies of various arrangements, including an arms control zone in Eastern Germany that if necessary could be tabled at the conference to advance the discussion on reunification.[73] Thus in a period of a few months the Western powers had come full circle on the German question—from fearing any discussion of it with the Soviet leaders to insisting that it be the main topic at the upcoming summit.

The Conference

The conference opened on July 18, 1955. In the first plenary session Eisenhower and Faure introduced a Western agenda that included German reunification, disarmament, European security, and certain other topics. Eisenhower reiterated his view that expectations for the single meeting should be modest, and that it was necessary to create conditions for the ongoing work of the foreign ministers. Faure went into detail on the German question, stressing the need for unification, ruling out neutrality, and proposing a general security organization that would provide guarantees against a revival of German aggression. He also outlined a plan to devote resources saved through disarmament to world economic development.

In his opening speech Eden focused exclusively on the German question. He reintroduced the plan for free elections that he had put forward at Berlin and, in an attempt to address the objections raised by Molotov at the previous conference, proposed a security pact and a demilitarized area between East and West that would provide the USSR with safeguards against German aggression.

Speaking last, Soviet premier Nikolai Bulganin put forward a two-stage plan for a "process of establishing a collective security system in Europe."[74] In the first stage, all states in Europe including, for the time being, the two Germanies would sign a nonaggression treaty and undertake certain disarmament measures, including a ban on atomic weapons in Europe and the withdrawal of all foreign troops from the continent. In the second stage NATO and the Warsaw Treaty Organization (WTO) would be dissolved and replaced by a system of collective security. Bulganin argued that "the Soviet government has been and remains a supporter of Germany's unification in accordance with the national interests of the German people and the interests of European security," but that the "remilitarization of Western Germany" had created a barrier to the realization of this goal. The main task, therefore, was to create a security system that would "facilitate the solution of the German problem and would create the necessary premises for uniting Germany on peaceful and democratic foundations."[75]

The foreign ministers met on the second day of the conference to draw up a formal agenda. Harold Macmillan, who was in the chair, suggested that four subjects had appeared in all of the speeches by the heads of government and should constitute the conference agenda: German reunification, European security, disarmament, and the development of East-West contacts.[76] Molotov agreed that disarmament, European security, the "German problem," and the development of economic and cultural contacts were subjects touched upon by all the heads of government, but wished to add three others: "the termination of the cold war, the encouragement of neutrality among the states of Europe and the problems of the Far East."[77] When Antoine Pinay noted that Molotov had listed the subjects in a different order from Macmillan, Molotov made what appeared to be an uncharacteristic tactical error and said that he had no objections to the order proposed by Macmillan. He refused to drop the three additional items, which it was agreed would be referred to the heads of government, but concurred in a suggestion that the press be informed of the decision regarding the four agreed agenda items. The Western ministers thus came away from the meeting surprised but pleased that they had secured preliminary agreement on their preferred agenda as well as managed to nail down the agreement in an announcement to the press.[78]

Western optimism began to wane at the plenary session that followed the morning meeting of the ministers. Bulganin again pressed for taking up three additional topics—ending the cold war, neutrality, and the Far East—and then turned to "the German question," which he called a more correct phraseology than the "question of the unification of Germany."[79] While repeating that the USSR had always favored German unity, he argued that unification could not be considered apart from the "remilitarization" of West Germany. Introducing a new theme, he noted that there were now two German states, and that it was necessary to consider the views of both. He claimed that the USSR was being realistic in not demanding nullification of the Paris agreements, but called for an equal measure of realism on the part of the West. Dismissing the political and arms control measures that Eden and Faure had introduced, Bulganin stated that "the USSR cannot place itself in a position where its security depends on guarantees by other states." The Western leaders countered with familiar arguments, and pressed for agreement on a procedure for tackling the German and other questions over time. Eisenhower proposed that the leaders "should ask the Foreign Ministers to suggest [a] kind of machinery which should be set up on when they would like to undertake [a] more detailed conference on [the] subjects of unification of Germany and European security."[80]

The second day of the conference thus concluded on a pessimistic note. Dulles came away from a private talk with Molotov believing "that the Soviets were not disposed to remit the problem of German unification within a framework of European security to a future meeting of the Foreign Ministers."[81] Although Bulganin had insisted that the USSR was willing to proceed from a recognition of the fact of the Paris agreements, Dulles remained haunted by the specter of a Soviet offer to the West Germans: "My present guess is that [the Soviets] want the conference to be a 'success' from the social standpoint but a total failure as regards German unification, so that Adenauer will go to Moscow knowing that his only hope is such hope as the Soviets may give him and that the Western powers cannot help him."[82] Eden also gained the impression that the Soviets were negative on the question of reunification, but detected certain differences between Molotov, who was adamantly opposed to any mention of Germany in a final conference document, and Bulganin and Khrushchev, who appeared more flexible.[83] Macmillan also believed that it should be possible to "extract" something from the Soviets on the German issue.[84]

The Western delegations accordingly agreed that they would begin to press Molotov "for a remitment of this subject to the Foreign Ministers to continue to work on the matter."[85] At the next session of the ministers Dulles, Macmillan, and Pinay stressed the urgency they attached to German reunification, and sought to secure agreement on procedures for future discussion of the topic. Molotov would not be moved, however. He again stressed the changed circumstances wrought by the Paris agreements, claimed that Bulganin had already given a full exposition on the German question, and that the topic was "exhausted." It was time to move to a consideration of the Soviet security proposals.[86] Molotov was receptive to the suggestion that another meeting of the ministers be held in October, but had reservations about the topics on the agenda. He thought it would be appropriate to continue to study the questions of European security and disarmament, but not German unification, which he said it would be "premature to study at this time."[87]

At the fourth plenary session that afternoon Bulganin spoke first and tabled the Soviet Union's draft "General European Treaty on Collective Security in Europe," to which he had alluded in his opening speech.[88] When Eisenhower, supported by Eden and Faure, continued to press for the establishment of machinery that would tackle both European security and Germany, Bulganin countered by stating that he did not want to reopen the discussion of the previous day's topic, about which there was nothing more to say. With the Soviets insisting that the German issue was exhausted and the West unwilling to discuss a European security scheme premised on the division of Germany, the conference appeared headed for a breakdown.

The outlines of a compromise began to emerge toward the end of the session when Eden suggested that Germany and European security were closely linked and that it might be worth studying a simultaneous approach to conclusion of a European security pact and unification. Bulganin responded favorably to this first hint that the West might be receptive to the Soviet security proposals. He agreed to a suggestion that the foreign ministers begin framing the text of a directive to the ministers, although not without adding that the directive should be clarified by a provision stipulating that the problem of establishing a system of collective security in Europe should not be made dependent upon the problem of German reunification. In the same session Eisenhower again called for the ministers to suggest a "kind of machinery which should be set up" and a more detailed conference on the subjects of unification and European security.

The following morning Molotov arrived at a scheduled meeting of the ministers with the text of a draft directive. It instructed the foreign ministers to "continue consideration of the problem of establishing a system of collective security in Europe," which would "facilitate settlement of the problem of German unification."[89] The West also prepared a draft. It stated that "Germany should be reunified through free elections in conformity with [the] national interest [of the] German people and security of Europe, thus discharging [the] common responsibility [of the] Four Powers."[90] While assigning precedence to the German issue, the Western draft added that "security for Europe should be sought by effective means which will respect and further the legitimate interests of all, including the inherent right of individual and collective self-defense."

For much of the remainder of the conference the delegations were preoccupied with the text of the directive. Eisenhower made headlines that afternoon with his Open Skies proposal, and there were parallel considerations of East-West contacts and disarmament. But it was clear that the outcome of the conference depended largely on the flexibility of each side in finding language that would indicate that progress had been made on the key issues of Germany and European security.

The following day, July 22, Molotov moved closer to the Western position, tabling a more detailed draft directive that contained four numbered points: European security, disarmament, Germany, and instructions for a further meeting. Under point three the draft instructed the ministers to consider the problem of German unification, which should be carried out "by means of free elections." However, it also stipulated that the ministers would address the German issue with the participation of representatives of the GDR and the FRG.[91] East German participation was clearly a nonstarter, having been ruled out before the conference by Adenauer.

Discussion of the draft directives continued throughout the day at the plenary session and in meetings of the ministers. The Soviets continued to hold out on two points: that European security had to be given priority over German unification; and that the directive had to provide for participation by representatives of the two German states. The dispute over order was, as Eden later wrote, "no mere point of procedure, but one of substance. . . . At the Potsdam Conference an agenda had been drawn up which had as its first two items the Italian Peace Treaty and the Austrian Peace Treaty. For two years thereafter the Russians had refused to discuss Austria until the Italian treaty had been concluded. If we met Russian wishes now, we must expect that they would insist on postponing the German problem until after agreement had been reached on both security and disarmament."[92]

As the ministers grappled with this question, Molotov's tactical error of three days earlier came back to haunt him, as Dulles, Macmillan, and Pinay pressed him on why the USSR refused to issue a formal directive whose wording paralleled that used in the preliminary agenda and released to the press. But Molotov refused to yield, and the ministers eventually concluded that they had no alternative but to conclude failure and to refer their work back to the heads of government, who it was agreed would meet in restricted session at 11 A.M. the following day.

The outcome of the conference thus was very much in doubt as its final day began.[93] In what was clearly a Soviet attempt to break the impasse by circumventing Eden and Dulles, shortly after breakfast Marshal Georgii Zhukov privately came to see Eisenhower and urged him to break the deadlock.[94] Zhukov argued that the German question was "very important, and a question of principle," but that it was "still a special problem not comparable in his view with the great issues of war and peace." But Eisenhower, who had been well briefed by Dulles, held firm, and criticized Molotov for insisting upon a directive that did not list the subjects in the order in which the heads of government and the ministers themselves had considered them.

The deadlock finally was broken when all parties agreed to a British suggestion that both subjects somehow be tackled in parallel. Bulganin "was willing to merge the two subjects in a single paragraph of the directive, so long as security was mentioned first."[95] Although not entirely satisfied with this arrangement, the Western powers "could not contemplate the breakdown of the Conference on a point which world opinion would consider to be procedural, even though in fact it was not. This directive was the best we could get and it was good enough, if the will to work was there."[96]

The Directive

The outcome of the Geneva summit thus was a compromise three-point directive to the ministers, who it was agreed would meet again in October. The section entitled "European Security and Germany" consisted of two paragraphs, the first of which instructed the ministers to "consider various proposals," including the Soviet project for a security pact, and the second of which contained clear and rather forceful language on Germany, including agreement that "settlement of the German question and the reunification of Germany by means of free elections shall be carried out in conformity with the national interests of the German people and the interests of German security."[97] These paragraphs, along with two others entitled "Disarmament" and "Development of Contacts between East and West," constituted what might be called the Geneva mandate, which both sides sought to use for the next five years to gain negotiating leverage and to rally alliance and domestic support.

The directive ran from the heads of government to the ministers as a collective body, although not without certain procedural complications. In the restricted session on the last day of the conference, Bulganin finally replied definitively to Eisenhower's proposal for the creation of post-conference "machinery," and rejected the suggestion that the heads of government set up groups or subcommittees to deal with the German question, since "these were procedural matters to be determined by the foreign ministers."[98] The nonexistence of a preestablished structure of committees weakened the Western position on reunification, and made it much easier for Molotov to claim that the German issue had to be addressed after rather than in parallel with the discussion of European security. The directive also stipulated that the ministers "will make whatever arrangements they may consider desirable for the participation of, or for consultation with, other interested parties." Although the West had managed to avoid any reference to the GDR, the Soviets later were able to claim that this passage provided for participation in future four-power talks by representatives of the two German states. In the section on disarmament, it was somewhat unclear whether the directive called for the ministers to work in parallel with the UN sub-committee, or merely contribute to its efforts in an unspecified way.

The directive was not a compromise in the sense in which that term is used in such nonpolitical areas of negotiation as trade and the purely technical aspects of arms control. The compromise occurred strictly on the level of language, with virtually no convergence of views on matters of substance. This point was well understood by Khrushchev, who later wrote that the directive "was formulated in such a way as to leave each delegation with the possibility of interpreting it in its own way. The wording was the result of various compromises which allowed all of us to sign. We didn't want to disperse without having anything to show for the meeting. On the other hand none of us wanted any point in the statement to be interpreted as a concession in principle or policy to the other side."[99] In this sense the directive was similar to the CSCE Final Act of almost exactly twenty years later which, in its most controversial provisions, was also a purely linguistic rather than a substantive compromise.

The way the Geneva directive was adopted illustrates an aspect of the mandating process with general relevance for East-West relations. As Khrushchev's remarks suggest, an event—in this case the summit—created a shared interest in a document even though the substantive differences between the two sides were too large to justify one. Both sides then used the pressure of the event to try to get the best possible agreement. As was to happen in the drafting of the Final Act, the Western powers enjoyed a certain leverage over the USSR owing to the latter's relatively greater commitment to a favorable outcome. As Eisenhower recalled, "it had become evident to us that the Soviet delegation wanted in the final communiqué some kind of 'paper' agreement that would be acceptable to world opinion."[100] The U.S. delegation "seriously discussed" whether to leave the meeting to protest Soviet positions on Germany and Eastern Europe and indicated that it would not sign any written document that did not contain "an unequivocal pledge to authorize free elections in Germany."[101] But the USSR was able to exert a degree of counter-leverage on the West, which did not want to see the process break down or at least do so in a way that could not be blamed on the other side. As Eden's remarks suggest, there were limits to how far the Western leaders could push, and in the end the USSR won an important victory in listing Germany after—and by implication making it subordinate to—the broader issue of European security.

In addition to its substantive provisions, the directive mandated an ongoing process that the West hoped would be progressively institutionalized. This mandate was weaker than what the West originally hoped to secure, but stronger than what the pessimists on the

Western delegations feared was obtainable. It did not instruct the ministers to establish, as Eisenhower had proposed, a machinery for furthering German unification, but it did require the ministers themselves to meet and to address a detailed agenda.

The Western powers thus came away from Geneva fairly optimistic about the future, and confident that they had fulfilled their basic objective of initiating a process that would lead to a resolution of the division of Europe on favorable terms. Adenauer wrote to Eisenhower praising the results of the meeting, noting that "it is especially valuable that agreement with the Soviets was successfully reached upon a common agenda, which provides a useful basis, in the Western interests, for future negotiations."[102] Reporting to the National Security Council shortly after his return from the summit, Dulles said that "the West must keep pressing the German unification issue. He predicted, but did not wish to be held to his prediction, that we might get unification in the next two years."[103] Eden was less effusive, but even he called the directive "good enough," and expected progress when the foreign ministers convened in October.

The Foreign Ministers Meeting

Having been forced by Western bargaining strategy to endorse unification by means of free elections, the Soviet leaders after Geneva tried to enforce their interpretation of the ambiguous directive, but without damaging the "spirit of Geneva" and the prospect of a further relaxation of tensions. On their way back to Moscow Bulganin and Khrushchev stopped in Berlin for meetings with the East German leaders, at the conclusion of which they issued a communiqué stating that "both parties proceed from the premise that the German problem cannot be settled without the participation of the Germans themselves, without a rapprochement between the German Democratic Republic and the German Federal Republic."[104] Bulganin further developed this theme in his report on the conference to the Supreme Soviet on August 4, 1955. While adopting a positive tone and acknowledging that "all the participants in the conference . . . showed a desire for a positive result," he took a hard line on Germany, arguing that the existence of the Paris agreements meant that the settlement of the German question had to be sought "in another way, by easing international tension in Europe, by eliminating military groupings in Europe and by creating an effective European collective security system."[105]

The USSR also took steps (following the conclusion of the Moscow meetings with Adenauer, which are discussed in chapter four) to shore up the political and legal status of the GDR. On September 20 the two countries concluded a broad political treaty, Article 1 of which stated that the GDR "is free in solving questions of its home and foreign policies, including relations with the German Federal Republic."[106] As part of its new relationship with the GDR, the USSR declared that it was transferring certain control functions relating to East Germany as a former occupation zone to the GDR authorities. This step presaged Khrushchev's actions later in the decade, but stopped short of precipitating a full-fledged Berlin crisis by explicitly stipulating that the movement of military personnel and freight between West Germany and West Berlin would be permitted "on the basis of the existing four-power agreements."[107] To visiting Westerners such as Canadian foreign minister Lester Pearson, Khrushchev argued that the policy of the Western powers was "to impose solutions" on the USSR that it would not tolerate, and that there could be no solution to the German problem as long as the FRG remained in NATO.[108]

For their part, the Western powers, despite growing signs that the optimism of the summer had been misplaced, started to draft a series of proposals and plan a negotiating strategy that they hoped would lead to progress in the upcoming talks.[109] In September a tripartite group (with occasional West German participation) met in Washington to study an overall Western approach.[110] It was supplemented by three other groups: one that met in Bonn to discuss various aspects of the Eden plan and all-German disarmament; another that met in Washington to discuss disarmament; and a Paris group concerned with East-West contacts.

Although the Western delegations recognized the need to comply with what they regarded as the letter of the Geneva directive, they not surprisingly tended to shade their interpretation of it in the direction of their original summit proposals and to downplay the concessions they had made.[111] For their part, the Soviets did not even attempt to disguise their intention to ignore the delicate compromise contained in the directive. According to the instructions that Molotov carried to Geneva, "the cardinal issue is that of assuring security in Europe, while the German question is specific and should be subordinate to the settlement of the main question, that of European security."[112] At the same time, however, Molotov was instructed to do nothing to damage the spirit of Geneva: "It must be borne in mind that the representatives of the three Western powers may attempt to exacerbate the discussion of one issue or another, particularly the German question. While adhering to the USSR's principled stand, the delegation shall avoid aggravating the discussion and try to give the discussion of the questions on the conference agenda a constructive and calm character."

The conference began on October 27. In his opening statement Molotov repeated familiar arguments regarding the need for a relaxation of tensions, but was blunt on the German question, arguing that the two German states had different social systems and that a "mechanical" merger was unacceptable.[113] Molotov also argued that disarmament was the most important problem facing the conference, and expressed interest in discussing East-West contacts. At the end of the first session Pinay tabled the official Western proposal responding to item one of the directive, which precipitated a long and fruitless wrangle with Molotov over conference procedures.[114]

The next day Macmillan again introduced the Western proposal, to which Molotov replied with the first of many arguments and counterarguments concerning compliance with the July directive. Alluding to the dispute at the summit over order, he maintained that the Western draft did not correspond to the directive, "which placed European security before German reunification."[115] Dulles responded with a similar charge, asking when the Soviet representatives would "give us their views about the first part of the question which had been remitted to us by the Heads of Government."[116] Macmillan returned to the same theme the following day. "The Soviet Government have not done their duty, because they have expressed no views on German reunification. The Western governments have presented a complete picture. Will not the USSR do the same? For I must repeat that the new security proposals of the Soviet government are still based on the partition of Germany. That is not in conformity with the directive."[117]

On October 31 Molotov finally put forward the USSR's ideas on the German question. He proposed that representatives of the two German states first be invited to address the conference. On November 2 he went somewhat further, and tabled a proposal for an all German council, without making provision for free elections.[118] The Western delegations rejected the council proposal as incompatible with the directive. They also tried to teach Molotov a lesson by proposing that the West German government—the only one recognized by all four conference participants—be invited to address the conference.[119]

While these fruitless exchanges on Germany took place, Molotov remained, at least initially, faithful to his instructions not to "aggravate the discussion" and to work in a calm and constructive manner. In his speech of October 31 he referred favorably to Eden's proposal for an arms limitation zone in central Europe and put forward a counterproposal that envisioned, among other things, ceilings on the number of troops each of the four powers could station within the zone. He also modified the Soviet European security treaty proposal, and hinted at progress in East-West contacts.[120] But by the end of the first week of the conference the Western ministers were forced to acknowledge a hardening of Soviet policy on Germany. Although Dulles continued to profess that a step-by-step approach eventually would produce movement on the Soviet side, even he concluded that the Soviet position on Germany was a "retrogression" from Molotov's position in Berlin two years earlier.[121]

In areas other than Germany, however, the Soviets were showing elements of flexibility. This created a dilemma for the Western governments and brought to the surface differences that had been submerged by the need to forge a common strategy. Already by the third evening of the conference the unofficial West German observer inquired whether the United States would be disposed to break up the conference—as Adenauer might have preferred—if the Soviets proved unwilling to engage on the reunification issue.[122] The British and French, in contrast, had domestic political reasons to avoid a breakdown.[123] As they became increasingly convinced that a dangerous Soviet offer to West Germany was not in the cards—that, as the Norwegian foreign minister had argued to Macmillan, the Soviets would not surrender the GDR even in exchange for neutrality—they had less cause to allow their own policies toward the USSR to be driven by Adenauer's needs on the German issue.[124]

In what was perhaps the most perceptive comment on the conference, on November 7 Bohlen sent a memorandum to Dulles in which he noted that "in essence our position suffers from the inherent disadvantage of putting forth specific proposals on the basis of a hypothetical situation, in this case the unification of Germany. Molotov, I would say, is clearly aware of this factor and is seeking to concentrate discussion on security without, however, having the slightest intention of meeting the basic condition on which our proposal rests."[125]

Any lingering hopes for progress on the German issue were dashed during the second week of November, when Molotov returned from a brief visit to Moscow apparently with new instructions to take a harder line on Germany. This he had little difficulty doing, delivering a "retrograde" speech in which he attacked the monopolists and Junkers.[126] The meetings ground on for another week, and were concerned chiefly with disarmament and East-West contacts, where new disputes arose as well.

On the penultimate day of the conference the ministers met in restricted session to decide their future course. Molotov expressed interest in scheduling another meeting, but in a reply that foreshadowed the procedural disputes that were to arise in the CSCE process more than two decades later, Pinay gave the Western view that the mandate for the conference had come from the heads of government, and that they would have to decide on its continuation.[127] Thus the ministers agreed to adjourn, producing only a two-paragraph communiqué stating that they had discussed the issues remitted to them, would report the results back to their respective heads of government, and had agreed "to recommend that the future course of the discussions of the Foreign Ministers should be settled through diplomatic channels."[128]

In the aftermath of the conference Dulles continued to profess long-term optimism about the prospects for reunification, but concluded that for the immediate future it was best to shift emphasis toward promoting West European integration. Adenauer drew similar conclusions, probably with even less reluctance than Dulles, as did the French.[129] For their part, the Soviets continued to exude optimism and to give the impression that time was on their side. Molotov had failed to secure agreement to another meeting of the foreign ministers, but until the fall of 1956 the momentum generated by the Geneva summit continued to help Khrushchev and Bulganin as they worked to normalize relations with Western countries on a bilateral basis.

While the immediate outlook for Soviet diplomacy in Europe thus was bright, the remainder of the 1950s was to prove more frustrating for Khrushchev than the optimism of late 1955 seemed to justify at the time. The Soviets were themselves in part responsible for this turn of events, as they destroyed the spirit of Geneva with their behavior in the Suez and Hungarian crises a little less than a year later. But they also suffered from the residual influence that the reunification issue exerted on Western policy and from the compromises they had been forced to make in the summer of 1955.

As the outcome of the foreign ministers meeting suggested, the mere reiteration of an agreed document could not force the USSR to abandon what it regarded as its vital interests, namely control of the GDR. But the Geneva mandate was used by the Western powers in other ways. As one astute observer later wrote, the "premises of 1955" provided the "main functioning guideline for Western policy until 1960."[130] They helped to maintain Western unity at the governmental level and served to insulate public opinion in Western countries from Soviet propaganda appeals by providing Western governments with effective and easily understood responses. They also undoubtedly helped to maintain discipline in the bureaucracy. By calling attention to the importance of orderly procedure, the completion of stages and the evaluation of results, the Geneva directive virtually ruled out the kind of frenzied ad hoc activism that later came to characterize East-West and especially Soviet-U.S. relations. For these reasons, the directive was a source of endless frustration to the Soviet leaders, as well as an irritation to Western activists who wanted to experiment with new approaches to the East.[131] This frustration was reflected in the procedural disputes that raged for the remainder of the decade and that eventually culminated in the second Berlin crisis.

Procedural Disputes, 1957–59

The Soviet leadership could not rewrite the Geneva directive, but it was able to undercut the process that the Western powers hoped to establish at Geneva. Although Molotov had shown a mild interest in securing Western agreement to another meeting of the four foreign ministers, in the course of the next year the USSR adopted a policy of scrupulously avoiding any meetings that followed the four-power format, and especially any meeting or series of meetings that followed the West's preferred pattern of preparatory meetings alternating with summit-level contacts. In doing so, of course, it had to be careful that it did not engineer its own isolation, make itself too obviously responsible for the division of Germany, or unilaterally renounce its own four-power rights. The Soviet decision to avoid four-power meetings was helped along by the Suez and Hungarian crises, which both convinced Khrushchev that it was no longer necessary to regard Britain and France as first-rate powers and led to a temporary Western diplomatic boycott of the USSR that forced Khrushchev to look for dramatic and surprising ways of reengaging the West in negotiations.

Khrushchev was not able to make any real progress toward overcoming his post-Hungary isolation until the second half of 1957, after he had turned back the internal challenge of the "anti-party group" and scored a notable international success with the launching of the first Sputnik. In December 1957 Bulganin (by then largely a figurehead who had barely survived the power struggle earlier in the year) began a letter writing campaign calling for a multilateral summit. In separate notes to the governments of the NATO countries he proposed a new heads of government conference at which the resumption of the arms talks "in an appropriate forum" could be discussed.[132] A few days later the Supreme Soviet passed a resolution endorsing, among other things, "a personal meeting of the leading statesmen of the Powers."

The background to the campaign for a summit was the Soviet decision in the fall of 1957 to withdraw from the UN Disarmament Commission. This decision (which is discussed in more detail in chapter six) was linked to Khrushchev's growing self-confidence about the economic and strategic competition with the West. The Sputnik success was followed by a massive propaganda campaign, chiefly orchestrated by Khrushchev, which stressed the economic and military aspects of the breakthrough. By December, however, the Soviet leadership had concluded that this campaign had "gone too far," and that it was time for new diplomatic initiatives.[133] The NATO decision to deploy medium-range missiles in several countries of Western Europe (taken in December 1957) offered a further incentive to improve the political atmosphere and resume the arms control talks.

Although directed at a large number of Western and neutral countries, Bulganin's letters were in part a smokescreen behind which the Soviet leaders angled for a bilateral meeting with the U.S. leaders.[134] At the 1957 New Year's Eve party in the Kremlin, Khrushchev praised the wartime coalition and generally gave the impression of a desire to settle world issues with the United States alone. He ended his speech with a toast to President Eisenhower and praised a recent letter from Indian prime minister Jawaharlal Nehru that had called for a bilateral U.S.-Soviet summit.[135]

Meeting in Paris a week after Bulganin's round of notes was sent, the NATO heads of government rejected his call for a summit, but offered to meet at the foreign minister level.[136] In reply to this offer, in January 1958 Bulganin sent a new round of letters in which he ruled out a conference of foreign ministers, stating "the Soviet Government attaches primary importance to having the proposed negotiations take place at the very highest level, with the participation of the heads of government."[137] Bulganin's letter was addressed to the heads of government of nineteen countries, including the NATO countries and the more important neutrals, all of whom he invited to meet "within two or three months" to discuss a nine-point agenda. Seven of the points dealt with disarmament or security, one with trade, and one with the Middle East. Bulganin did not propose to put Germany on the agenda, but argued that the passing of the cold war and the development of international cooperation would "facilitate the settlement of the German question on the basis of drawing the GDR and the FRG closer together."

In addition to ruling out a foreign ministers conference, Bulganin sought to counter charges that the USSR had reneged on the Geneva directive. As he wrote to Eisenhower,

[S]ome in the West are trying to ascribe to the Soviet Government the non-fulfillment of some decisions of that [the Geneva] Meeting concerning the German question. You will undoubtedly recall that neither in the statements of N. S. Khrushchev nor in my statements at the Meeting was there even a hint that the Soviet Union would agree to the platform on the German question as proposed by the Western powers. . . . At the Geneva Meeting and thereafter, we stated quite definitely that the reunification of Germany could not take place without a rapprochement and agreement between the two sovereign German states.[138]

Most prominent among the "some in the West" was of course Dulles, who had stressed Soviet noncompliance with the Geneva directive ever since the breakup of the 1955 ministerial meeting, and who repeated the same charges at a news conference two days later. Dulles suggested that the USSR could make the greatest contribution to a new meeting by carrying out previous obligations, "and most particularly . . . the agreement which was arrived at at the last summit meeting."[139] Eisenhower's formal reply to Bulganin was more moderate in tone, but in essence the same. He informed the Soviet leader that the three Western powers would be prepared to come to a summit, but that "prior to such a meeting these complex matters should be worked on in advance through diplomatic channels and by our Foreign Ministers."[140] Macmillan also replied by suggesting that "as a matter of convenience" it would be best to convene a meeting consisting of the foreign ministers of the same countries that had met at Geneva in 1955, adding that this would "not prejudice the ultimate composition of a subsequent meeting of Heads of Government."[141]

On February 1 Bulganin again rejected the idea of a foreign ministers meeting,[142] but at the end of the month the Soviets partially relented and proposed the holding of a preliminary conference of foreign ministers in April 1958, provided the discussion was "strictly limited to questions relating to the organizational side of preparation for a meeting at the Summit."[143] The Western powers countered by proposing that the impasse be resolved through exchanges in Moscow between Andrei Gromyko and the Western ambassadors.[144] The USSR accepted this offer, but reiterated its position that any presummit talks could not deal with substantive matters. In an aide-mémoire of April 11 it stated that "the Soviet Government deems it expedient to restrict the exchange of views through diplomatic channels to a minimum of questions relating directly to the organization of a meeting of ministers of foreign affairs, that is, questions of the date and place for the ministers meeting and the composition of the participants."[145]

Although not completely satisfied with this arrangement, the three powers decided to go ahead with consultations.[146] They were surprised, however, when Gromyko refused to receive the three ambassadors together, claiming that to do so "would be tantamount to a four-power conference in which three states of the North Atlantic alliance and only one state of the Warsaw treaty organization would be taking part." Gromyko went on to suggest that the consultations be expanded to include the ambassadors of Czechoslovakia and Poland. The Western powers rejected the inclusion of any East European countries but, unable to secure a four-power ambassadorial meeting, eventually agreed to hold parallel bilateral consultations.[147]

As will be seen in chapter six, the newly expressed Soviet concern for NATO-Warsaw Pact "equality" and the resulting effort to elevate the diplomatic status of Czechoslovakia and Poland also was reflected in the arms control discussions under way at the time.

In their parallel bilateral meetings with Gromyko, the Western ambassadors presented a draft agenda of questions to be considered at a summit. It included disarmament, "reunification of Germany in accordance with the terms of the 1955 Directive of the Four Heads of Government to the Ministers of Foreign Affairs," and several other subjects.[148] The Soviet response was predictably negative and led, for all practical purposes, to the suspension of the consultations. On June 16 the government of Hungary announced that former premier Imre Nagy had been executed after a secret trial, thereby setting off violent demonstrations in Western capitals and organized counter-demonstrations at Western embassies in Moscow. Many in the West believed that the Hungarian announcement, which undoubtedly was cleared in Moscow, was designed to scuttle the Moscow talks.[149] Rising tensions in the Middle East also helped to push talk of a summit off the political agenda.

Thus by the summer of 1958 Khrushchev had reached an impasse in his policy toward the West. He had failed to restructure the UN arms control process or to resume summitry on Soviet terms. These procedural failures underscored a more serious substantive failure: the Soviet inability to secure the legitimation of the GDR and, by implication, of the postwar division of Europe. The situation was not helped by the issuing of a lengthy draft treaty of friendship and collaboration on July 15, 1958, that incorporated many earlier Soviet proposals but that the Western powers refused to accept even as the basis for discussion.[150]

In retrospect it is likely that the foreign policy impasse that confronted Khrushchev in the fall of 1958 played a role in his decision to launch the second Berlin crisis. After a good harvest that appeared to bolster his confidence and a seemingly successful visit to China, on November 10 he announced his intention to terminate four-power rights in Berlin and to sign a peace treaty with East Germany. On November 27 the USSR announced that as a result of violations on the Western side it considered the Potsdam agreements no longer valid.[151]

The USSR further underlined its rejection of the four-power arrangements by making an extraordinary bid to settle the German and Berlin problems through direct talks with West Germany. Using the Austrian ambassador as an intermediary, Gromyko informed the West German government that the USSR was interested in concluding a peace treaty that would be signed by both German states, and that could be followed by a step-by-step rapprochement between East and West Germany. As a precondition, the USSR insisted that West Germany renounce atomic armament. Gromyko asserted that this was the last occasion on which the USSR would be willing to discuss the German question with the FRG.[152] After some apparent hesitation in Bonn, the West Germans rejected the Soviet offer.

The three wartime allies thus retained the lead in responding to Soviet proposals on Germany, with West Germany deliberately assigning itself a background role. In January 1959 the Soviet government followed up its December notes with a proposal for a conference of all states that had fought against Germany, to be held within two months either in Warsaw or Prague. The conference would consider a peace treaty, a draft of which was appended to the note.[153]

The United States, acting on behalf of the Western powers, replied with a proposal for a four-power foreign ministers conference.[154] The U.S. reply did not comment on the substance of the draft treaty, but suggested that the conference "deal with the problem of Germany in all its aspects and implications." For the first time the United States proposed to include advisers from the two German states as "consultants" to the conference. Shortly thereafter Macmillan went to the USSR for "exploratory" talks that helped to ease the crisis but that also suggested a degree of disunity on the Western side.[155] In a note of March 2 the Soviet government relented on the question of a ministerial conference, stating that while it preferred a heads of government meeting, it would be willing to attend a meeting of the foreign ministers of the four powers, Poland, Czechoslovakia, and the two German states. On March 26 the United States replied by suggesting it would be best to begin with a meeting of only the four powers responsible for Germany. Khrushchev accepted this proposal, and on May 11, 1959, the first four-power conference since 1955 convened in Geneva.[156]

Khrushchev's motives for finally agreeing to a four-power meeting remain obscure, but they probably had to do with his desire to find a way out of the Berlin crisis. He also had won a partial victory by compelling the four powers to sit down with the East Germans, if only as "consultants," and probably assumed that the discussion would gravitate toward the narrow problem of West Berlin rather than the broader issue of reunification. Dulles had resigned and thus would not be able to assume the role he had played at Geneva, while in France de Gaulle's return to power gave reason to believe that France would be less willing to press the reunification issue than it had been in 1955.

When the conference opened the Western powers immediately tabled a new peace plan that contained a number of concessions, including a provision for the establishment of a Mixed German Committee consisting of twenty-five members from the FRG and ten from the GDR, the offer of a "common declaration" that had points in common with the Soviet proposed nonaggression treaty, and suggestions for deep force reductions in Europe.[157] The Soviets responded by reintroducing their treaty of January 10, but the conference soon bogged down. The Western powers wanted the four powers to establish a process leading to free, all German elections and eventual reunification, while the Soviets called for the conclusion of peace treaties with the two German states, who would then decide whether and if so how they wanted to unite.

While failing to produce any movement on the German issue or Berlin, the conference did result in getting the arms control talks back on track, largely on Soviet terms. After discussing "the method by which further negotiations on the question of disarmament could be most effectively advanced," the four powers announced that they had agreed to set up "a committee to consider disarmament matters" that would be comprised equally of representatives from the East and the West: on the Western side, the four traditional participants plus Italy; on the Eastern, the USSR, Bulgaria, Czechoslovakia, Poland, and Romania.[158]

The conclusion of the ministerial meeting was followed by Khrushchev's September 1959 visit to the United States, which Eisenhower hoped would be a prelude to a four-power meeting yielding real progress on European issues, but which in fact appeared to prejudge the outcome of future four-power meetings. In their final session at the president's farm in Gettysburg the leaders agreed, as recorded in their final communiqué, "that the question of general disarmament is the most important one facing the world today."[159] This was not only factually incorrect (the crisis in Berlin was clearly the "number one" problem), but ran counter to the Geneva directive, which had specified an agreed East-West agenda that lent equal weight to European security-Germany, disarmament, and East-West contacts. The agreement reversed the order that the West had fought for at Geneva, and undercut the parallelism that had structured the recent Western proposals at the foreign ministers conference. At a subsequent press conference Eisenhower revealed that he had made two further concessions: he agreed to intervene with de Gaulle and Macmillan to arrange an early summit, and he recognized the "abnormal" character of the Berlin situation and acknowledged the need to seek a solution "which would safeguard the legitimate interests" of all parties concerned, including the East Germans.[160] Khrushchev came away from the summit pleased with the outcome, and confident that he had reached important understandings with Eisenhower over the heads of the leaders of France and West Germany.[161]

The End of the Four-Power Process

The post-Geneva four-power process came to an abrupt end with the abortive Paris summit of May 1960. This meeting technically ended before it began, as Khrushchev demanded that de Gaulle yield him the floor and then launched into a forty-five-minute harangue in which he proposed that the leaders "postpone this conference for about six to eight months." When Macmillan later sought assurances that Khrushchev was not forcing a breakdown of the conference, the Soviet leader was blunt: "This is not the beginning of the Conference. That has not started yet. We regard this meeting as preliminary."[162]

In the Western literature it sometimes is suggested that Khrushchev had badly wanted an East-West summit and that the U-2 shoot-down was a tragic incident that deprived East and West of an opportunity for serious talks.[163] While it is true that Khrushchev campaigned for a summit, he also had always resisted another four-power meeting, seeking to associate India, Poland, Czechoslovakia, and other countries with the process and to broaden the agenda beyond those subjects discussed in 1955. From this perspective, the U-2 incident could have been welcome to Khrushchev in providing an excuse not to come to Paris.

That Khrushchev did come to Paris suggests that he may have wanted to have it both ways: to humiliate Eisenhower in a personal encounter and then break off the meeting. As de Gaulle later suggested, the Soviets might have wanted "to extricate themselves from a conference which they no longer desired after having clamored so loudly for it."[164] An alternative explanation is that Khrushchev overplayed his hand, underestimating de Gaulle's toughness while overestimating the effect that Macmillan would have on Eisenhower.[165] After receiving some kind of apology from Eisenhower, he might have wanted the conference to continue. He would have had two possible motives for desiring such a scenario. He may have wanted Eisenhower to visit the USSR and knew that this depended upon a successful outcome in Paris; or he may have genuinely wanted to engage on the Berlin and German questions, despite the fact that he had won only partial victories on the key questions of participation and agenda.

Whatever the causes, Paris clearly spelled the end of the four-power process. The Western powers had used up an enormous amount of leverage in getting Khrushchev to accept a conference that basically followed the Geneva format, in that it excluded the Soviet allies, included only the four powers, and had been prepared by a conference of foreign ministers.

In the course of the 1960s Western diplomats made a number of efforts to revive the four-power talks in some form, but the process was clearly dead. During a December 1965 visit to Moscow British foreign secretary Michael Stewart renewed the proposal for a four-power body to consider European security questions that was first made at the 1959 foreign ministers conference. According to British accounts of the meeting, Gromyko "rejected any attempts to force Russia to discuss reunification of Germany," which he claimed was beyond the competence of the four powers and could only be done by the two Germanies and only after the FRG had abandoned its "aggressive policy" in favor of disarmament.[166] Henceforth the Soviet position was clear: reunification was a matter to be settled between the two German states, which in turn required full recognition of the GDR.

After the start in 1966 of the campaign for a European security conference the USSR went further, and virtually ruled out reunification even by agreement between the German states. In the late 1960s and early 1970s the preeminent goal of Soviet European policy was, in fact, to secure formal international acknowledgment that the German issue was closed and that the existing territorial and political order was immutable. The USSR pursued this goal by promoting the European security conference and in its responses to the *Ostpolitik* of successive West German governments.

In 1966 the West Germans proposed to the USSR a bilateral non-aggression treaty, which they believed would help to counter the effects in Eastern Europe of Soviet attacks on German "revanchism," supersede the "enemy states clauses" in the UN Charter, and in time lead to improved relations with the USSR. The West Germans believed that such a treaty would open the way to a more comprehensive détente in Europe, without compromising their long-term, constitutionally enshrined commitment to reunification. The Soviets, in contrast, saw the negotiation of such a treaty as a way, along with the security conference, to close the German question.

After a long and stormy set of negotiations that was complicated by the Prague Spring, the Soviet invasion of Czechoslovakia, and the Nuclear Nonproliferation Treaty, in August 1970 the Social Democratic-Free Democratic government of Willy Brandt signed a bilateral treaty with Moscow.[167] Although the text was brief and straightforward, the Soviet and West German governments had fundamental if submerged differences regarding its meaning, which in turn reflected differences over the ultimate resolution of the German question. The West Germans stressed that the treaty, while it outlawed armed aggression, did not preclude peaceful and negotiated change, including reunification. West German foreign minister Walter Scheel made these points in a letter to Gromyko that accompanied the treaty.[168] The USSR, in contrast, interpreted "inviolability" to mean unchangeability even by peaceful means, and over the next two decades took numerous steps to reinforce their point. It was not until early 1990 that the USSR reversed its position on this issue and agreed that the German people could exercise their fundamental right to self-determination by choosing to reunify, provided the four powers approved the "external aspects" of reunification in an appropriate international agreement.

Remnants and Revival

The breakup of the Paris conference had left unresolved the simmering crisis in Berlin. For the remainder of Eisenhower's term the Soviets and East Germans tried to whittle away at the status quo in the city but refrained from launching a major new crisis.[169] Following John F. Kennedy's inauguration, Khrushchev resumed the political offensive, calling for the conclusion "without delay" of a German peace treaty. Soviet pressures initially were directed at West Germany, but soon were felt in the United States, where the new administration was inclined to approach European issues from a new perspective.

In March 1961 the administration informed the Soviet government that "all discussions on Berlin must begin from the start." According to Arthur Schlesinger, "this was a move to disengage Kennedy from the concessions the Eisenhower administration had made in 1959 and even more from the ones we had been informed Eisenhower was ready to make at the summit meeting in Paris."[170] Notwithstanding these brave words, the new administration was at best able to achieve a stalemate. At Vienna in May 1961 Khrushchev presented Kennedy with a formal aide-mémoire in which he threatened to sign, by December, a peace treaty with East Germany that would abrogate Western rights in Berlin.[171] Kennedy defended the Western position but may have conveyed to Khrushchev an impression of weakness, not least by announcing that the U.S. force in Berlin was "token in nature" and by seeming to accept at face value Khrushchev's threat to make war.[172]

The building of the Berlin wall in August 1961 and the tense U.S.-Soviet confrontations in the fall of that year lent new urgency to the U.S. desire for a negotiated solution.[173] The French refused to negotiate with the Soviets, but in September Secretary of State Dean Rusk, British foreign secretary Alec Douglas-Home, and Gromyko held a series of exploratory meetings on Berlin.[174] Berlin was also the

main subject of an extraordinary correspondence between Khrushchev and Kennedy that began in the same month. Khrushchev used
his letters to angle for an early bilateral summit, to which the U.S.
president was "cautiously receptive."[175] The trilateral meetings and
the Kennedy-Khrushchev correspondence did not result in a formal
solution to the Berlin problem, but they encouraged Khrushchev to
moderate his demands. On October 17 he withdrew his threat to sign
a separate peace treaty, thereby ending the most acute phase of the
second Berlin crisis.

However, in February 1962 the Soviets resumed their harassment
of air traffic and the following month Rusk and Gromyko had ex-
tensive discussions regarding Berlin on the periphery of the Eighteen
Nation Disarmament Committee sessions in Geneva. Gromyko proposed the continuation of bilateral talks on a formal basis between
Rusk and Soviet ambassador Anatolii Dobrynin in Washington.[176]
The State Department was skeptical of bilateral talks, and preferred
"to keep things within the four-power process."[177] But under White
House pressure Rusk met with Dobrynin from mid-April to late
May. The United States put forward a variety of possible solutions,
all of which were unacceptable to the NATO allies and seemingly at
variance with the maintenance of four-power rights in West Berlin,
not to speak of greater Berlin or Germany as a whole. (They included
adjudication by the World Court, an all-Berlin free city, parallel
Western and Communist peace conferences, the use of Berlin as a
UN headquarters, and an international access authority.)[178]

Rusk believed that the best approach was to "talk the question to
death," and in the long run may have been correct.[179] But from the
perspective of the 1960s Khrushchev was extremely pleased with the
outcome of the second Berlin crisis. Looking back on these events
from retirement, he noted that Stalin had tried to take advantage of
the Berlin situation but had "suffered a defeat." In contrast, he had
"forced Kennedy and the Western allies to swallow a bitter pill."[180]
Khrushchev's account was self-serving, but it contained a large element of truth. He had used Berlin to pressure the Western powers to
scale down their expectations of what was possible in negotiations
on Germany, to divide the French and West Germans from the British and the Americans, and to foster the further development of a
special U.S.-Soviet relationship that was resented in Europe. Having
secured these objectives, and with the wall in place and East Germany enjoying a new measure of stability, Khrushchev allowed the
crisis to gradually wind down.

The Soviets continued their harassment of U.S. military convoys
until as late as September 1963, and in June 1964 the USSR and the
GDR sought to buttress their legal position regarding Berlin by signing the Treaty of Friendship, Mutual Assistance, and Cooperation

that designated West Berlin an "independent political entity."[181] But the Soviets and East Germans never seriously threatened another full-fledged crisis, even though for the remainder of the 1960s they harassed traffic on the autobahns to the city whenever a "demonstrative West German federal presence" was exercised.[182] For their part, the Western powers remained interested in a stabilizing settlement that would minimize the risk of future crises as well as strengthen the legal and political ties between West Berlin and the FRG, but saw little opportunity to pursue such a settlement, as Soviet-West German relations remained frozen and East-West disputes flared over nuclear issues, Eastern Europe, and Vietnam. However, in early 1969, following a particularly severe incident precipitated by the East Germans but amid renewed signs of a broader East-West détente, the Western powers signaled a renewed interest in a Berlin agreement.

The Western offer elicited a fairly positive response from the Soviets, who were beginning to distance themselves from the East Germans on this issue.[183] In a July speech to the Supreme Soviet Gromyko suggested that the USSR would be "ready to exchange opinions on the subject of how to prevent complications concerning West Berlin" with "the other powers, our allies in the war, who bear a share of the responsibility for the situation in West Berlin."[184] At the same time he reiterated the "unique status in international law" of West Berlin and stressed that there could be no encroachments on the sovereign rights of the GDR, one of which he claimed was sole control over the access rights to West Berlin.

In August 1969 the Western powers formally proposed talks on a Berlin agreement, and after wrangling about the agenda and other modalities, negotiations began in late March 1970. While the USSR was not enthusiastic about such an agreement, it was forced to respond to the linkage strategies of the Nixon and Brandt governments. The United States made conclusion of a Berlin agreement a precondition for U.S. participation in Brezhnev's pet project for a European security conference, while the West Germans linked ratification of the 1970 Treaty of Moscow to a successful outcome in the Berlin talks. Soviet ambassador Valentin Falin argued to Egon Bahr, Brandt's chief foreign policy adviser, that by tying ratification of the bilateral treaty to a Berlin agreement West Germany was giving the Western powers an unacceptable veto over its own policy, but failed to break the linkage. The West Germans, in fact, were major players in the Berlin negotiations, even though the four Potsdam powers ostensibly took the leading roles.[185]

The ambassadors of the four powers signed the Quadripartite Agreement on September 3, 1971, and it went into force on June 3 of the following year.[186] It incorporated both Western and Soviet compromises, along with a considerable degree of ambiguity. The USSR abandoned its claim that the GDR was solely responsible for access to West Berlin. This point appears to have been contested in East Berlin, and East German party leader Walter Ulbricht's fall in the spring of 1971 probably was related to his intransigence on this issue.[187] The USSR also acknowledged that "the ties between the Western Sectors of Berlin and the Federal Republic of Germany will be maintained and developed." The West Germans regarded this "dynamization" of the Berlin situation as a great success.[188] It was offset, however, by a disagreement over the meaning of "ties" (sviazi, liens), which the Soviets insisted meant transport and communications links, and the West argued included ties of a political nature.

In exchange for these points the Western powers acknowledged the validity of the Soviet claim that West Berlin was not a "constituent part" of the FRG, but without obtaining explicit recognition of the Western position that East Berlin was not a part of the GDR.[189] The Western powers agreed on the inadmissibility of "constitutional or official acts" in West Berlin by officials of the West German government, the Parliament, and the parliamentary party groups. The agreement did not explicitly acknowledge four-power rights, but it was concluded by the four acting, in the words of the preamble, "on the basis of their quadripartite rights and responsibilities, and of the corresponding wartime and postwar agreements and decisions of the Four Powers, which are not affected." France was particularly insistent on maintaining its four-power rights, even going so far as refusing to agree to the issuing of an official German text.[190]

Taken as an isolated document, the agreement represented a partial victory for the West, and was characterized as a major achievement by individuals as varied in political outlook as Bahr and Henry Kissinger.[191] Following its conclusion there were few incidents of East German or Soviet interference with Western access to the city. Nevertheless, the Western powers expended an enormous amount of negotiating capital to secure the agreement. It was the one concession that West Germany demanded in exchange for ratification of the Soviet–West German treaty of August 1970 and that the Western powers collectively sought for their participation in a European security conference. It was thus in essence an agreement that ambiguously reaffirmed rights that already belonged to the Western powers, unambiguously denied West Germany certain other rights, and did so in exchange for substantial concessions on unrelated issues.

The other remnant of the four-power process that retained a residual role in Soviet–West European relations was the Potsdam agreement. As has been seen, in 1958 the USSR repudiated the agreement, claiming that the Western powers had failed to implement its provisions and that the USSR was under no further obligations to work for the restoration of German unity. But in the 1970s the USSR in effect took back some of the rights and responsibilities it had surrendered. It chose not to reject the letter of West German foreign minister Scheel that was sent to Gromyko after the signature of the 1970 Soviet-West German treaty, it joined with the three Western powers in publishing, in November 1972, a document on four-power rights following the decision of the two German states to apply for membership in the United Nations, and it negotiated a "Berlin clause" in the CSCE Final Act.[192] In retaining its four-power rights, the USSR kept a useful instrument for influencing East Germany as well as sustained the legal basis upon which German unification might be negotiated in the future.

Throughout the 1970s and 1980s Western experts sometimes speculated about whether or under what circumstances the USSR might reopen the German question. Although officially the Soviet government never waivered in its commitment to the territorial status quo, many in the West saw potential for change in this stance, and believed that the USSR might at some point reopen the German question as part of a neutralization ploy intended to lure West Germany away from NATO. It thus came as a great surprise when the German question was reopened and the four-power talks revived, not as a result of Soviet machinations but through Soviet weakness and the virtual collapse of the East German state. After having tried for decades to negate or at least downplay four-power rights and responsibilities, for a brief period in late 1989 and early 1990 the USSR became their greatest proponent, as it sought to use its World War II victor status to head off the reunification of Germany. These developments are discussed in chapter ten.

Conclusions

One of Khrushchev's main foreign policy achievements was to reshape the character of Soviet interaction with the West. In chapter two it was seen that in 1949 Stalin retreated into self-isolation, in part because he was unable to use the most important postwar institutions, the CFM and the UN, to advance Soviet objectives. The challenge for Stalin's successors was to overcome this isolation, but to do so without reviving the "unequal" institutions of the 1940s and without accepting the major points on the Western agenda: German reunification by free elections, verified disarmament, and measures to open up Soviet society.

At the 1955 Geneva summit Khrushchev and Bulganin were forced to accept more of this agenda than they would have preferred.

To conclude the summit on a favorable note and secure a promise of further meetings they had to accept the Geneva directive, which mandated a process toward German reunification. While the USSR soon made clear that it had no intention of living up to the promises contained in the directive, it managed to hang on to many of the gains that were reaped from the spirit of Geneva. Even after the Suez and Hungarian crises Soviet isolation was far less than what it had been in 1953. As will be seen in chapter six, the Soviet leaders faced similar challenges and made similar gains in the disarmament area. To lend credence to peaceful coexistence and to gain influence over Western policies, Khrushchev wanted to conduct a more active arms control and disarmament policy. But he was frustrated at being forced to participate in institutions that were dominated by the West. In 1957 the USSR disengaged from and ultimately destroyed the UN arms control process. Khrushchev then used the Berlin crisis and an orchestrated campaign of nuclear threats to establish new, more equitable arms control institutions and to replace the UN-mandated arms control agenda with his own project for complete and general disarmament.

But Khrushchev's achievements with respect to European security and disarmament were essentially negative. Although he demonstrated that the Western powers could not pressure or entice him into a structured process for solving political and disarmament issues on terms favored by the West, he did not succeed in pressuring the West to accord de jure recognition to the GDR or to accept his security and disarmament proposals. With the notable exception of the Limited Test Ban Treaty of 1963 there were no arms control breakthroughs until the Brezhnev period. Similarly, a breakthrough on the German question came only later under Brezhnev and even then only after the USSR had scaled down some of its demands.

In any case, Brezhnev's breakthroughs of the early 1970s, which at the time were ascribed an epoch-making significance in Soviet commentary, in a longer-term perspective proved to be ephemeral. Within two decades it was shown that the USSR lacked the internal political and economic strength to permanently enforce the division of Germany. Contrary to anything that Khrushchev and Brezhnev would have predicted, for a brief period in 1989 and 1990 residual four-power rights again became central, as the USSR became the strongest advocate of a four-power meeting to negotiate the terms of reunification, and even tried unsuccessfully to use its victor's rights to secure a permanent military and political presence in Germany.[193]

4   Diplomacy

Summitry

The 1950s

Although the Geneva meeting failed to resolve the issues of greatest importance for the West, it changed the political atmosphere and made possible the first high-level political contacts between the USSR and Western Europe.[1] After a decade in which there had been no meetings with heads of Western governments, in 1955 and the first ten months of 1956 Nikolai Bulganin and Nikita Khrushchev received or were received by the leaders of Finland, West Germany, Sweden, Norway, Denmark, Belgium, Britain, and France. This was in addition to the Geneva meeting itself, the meetings with the Austrian leaders in the spring of 1955, the rapprochement with Marshal Tito in Belgrade, and the November 1955 trip to India, Burma, and Afghanistan.

The USSR took the initiative in arranging virtually all of these trips, but pursued different objectives with different Western leaders. As was noted in chapter three, the Austrian leaders were literally summoned to Moscow for discussions of the state treaty and the separate Soviet-Austrian bilateral understandings. The Soviets respected the four-power role in the Austrian negotiations, but they tried to make their bilateral understandings with the Austrians the "essence" of the settlement.[2]

Like the meeting with the Austrians, Finnish president Juho Paasikivi's September 1955 visit to Moscow was part of the overall Soviet adjustment to the new situation in Europe caused by West Germany's accession to NATO. In the summer of 1955 the Soviet government informed Paasikivi that it was prepared to return to Finland the Porkkala base that was occupied after World War II, provided the Finns agreed to renew the 1948 Treaty of Friendship, Cooperation, and Mutual Assistance (FCMA) (due to expire in 1958) for another twenty years. Paasikivi gladly accepted the offer and went to Moscow to sign the relevant agreements. The deal reflected the broad post-Stalin assessment of policy toward Europe and the emerging view of neutrality as a positive force in international affairs. Instead of seeking to hold open the option of Finnish membership in the WTO, the USSR sought to make neutrality more attractive to members of NATO. This was a shift from 1954, when it was feared that Finland would be pressured to accept the Soviet invitation to attend a European security conference as a prelude to its incorporation into an Eastern collective security system.[3] Soviet forces left Porkkala in January 1956, and in his speech to the party congress the following month Khrushchev made the first official acknowledgment of Finland's status as a neutral country.

Although in many respects very different from the Austrian and Finnish summits, the Soviet-West German meeting of September 1955 also reflected Soviet adjustment to the new European order. The USSR took the lead in inviting a reluctant Adenauer to Moscow. The chancellor and his advisers had grave misgivings about initiating a bilateral dialogue, which they feared would prejudice Bonn's legal contention that there was only one German state. But with 10,000 Germans still held in Soviet prisons and labor camps, Adenauer had little choice but to accept the invitation.[4]

In planning sessions before the trip, the West Germans discussed possible ways to finesse the recognition issue while making progress on reunification and the release of the prisoners. They decided to propose the establishment of bilateral commissions for economic matters, cultural matters, prisoners of war and detainees, and general political matters (diplomatic relations, unification, and European security) that would conduct negotiations with the Soviet government before the establishment of full diplomatic relations (West Germany and the USSR would exchange "diplomatic agents").[5] The purpose of deferring the establishment of full diplomatic relations was to make clear that there could not be "normal" relations with the USSR as long as Germany was divided. Adenauer also wanted to stress that the ultimate resolution of the German question was a matter for the four powers to decide and that there were limits to what the USSR and West Germany could negotiate bilaterally. As he told a U.S. official, he intended to "speak strictly as John the Baptist in the wilderness, making it plain to the Russians that they would receive the true gospel in Geneva."[6] To underscore this point the West Germans planned to omit any explicit reference to unification in the terms of reference for the envisaged political commission, which they feared could be interpreted as inconsistent with the Geneva directive and four-power responsibilities.[7]

Much of this planning proved irrelevant when the visit got under way. Led by Bulganin, the Soviet negotiators called for the immediate establishment of diplomatic relations. They rejected the West German proposals for the establishment of bilateral commissions and the exchange of diplomatic agents, and insisted that all questions, including the repatriation of prisoners of war (who the Soviets insisted were war criminals), could be discussed only after diplomatic normalization. Khrushchev argued that it would be unrealistic for the USSR to demand that the FRG leave NATO; all he wanted was mutual recognition "proceeding from the existing situation."[8] While the Soviets insisted that the sole agreed purpose of the discussions was to establish relations, Adenauer appealed to the meeting's terms of reference (embodied in the June exchange of diplomatic notes) and argued that "we are come here to restore *normal* and *good* relations between two peoples; and not just to restore normal *diplomatic* relations, which were only a small part of a larger task."[9]

As the talks moved toward breakdown, Bulganin informally put forward a simple but brutal proposal: release of German nationals detained in the USSR in exchange for the establishment of relations. After some agonizing in the German delegation, Adenauer agreed.[10] To salvage their position on the broader issues, the West Germans asked the Soviets to accept two unilateral letters setting forth their reservations on the questions of frontiers and relations with the GDR. The Soviets initially refused and said they would send unilateral letters spelling out the Soviet position. But they later softened their stance, thus enabling Adenauer to cover his retreat.[11]

The "complete collapse of the West German position" was so at variance with the previsit posture of the Bonn government that some in the West, notably Bohlen, found it "difficult to conceive" that there were not additional, secret understandings between the Soviets and West Germans.[12] But in fact there were no such understandings. The West German collapse was simply that, and was brought about by a mix of summit-level pressures, Soviet bargaining tactics, and unresolved problems from the Second World War.

Adenauer was unable to delay mutual recognition until after the resolution of the German question, but for the remainder of the 1950s and even into the 1960s the West Germans lagged behind the French, British, and Italians in developing extensive bilateral relations with the USSR. The government and society in general remained cool to most Soviet overtures and wary of agreements or forms of cooperation that might further prejudice future negotiations on Germany. The Soviet leaders, in contrast, saw advantages in improved relations with West Germany and, until the souring of relations in the Berlin crisis, pressed for the expansion of economic and cultural cooperation.

Although in the 1970s a view took hold in Western academic circles that the USSR feared West German economic and potential military power (and thus desired a U.S. military presence in Europe as a check on Bonn), the diplomatic record of the mid-1950s suggests that the Soviet leaders in fact saw certain advantages in West Germany's relative rise and were alert to possibilities for a special Soviet-West German relationship. At the four-power ministerial meeting in November 1955 Molotov told Pinay that he was confident that the Soviet social system would hold up in front of the new West Germany, whereas the British and French would not.[13] The following spring Khrushchev made similar arguments to the leaders of the British Labour Party, and went so far as to defend the Ribbentrop-Molotov pact and to threaten a new Rapallo.[14] When Christian Pineau and Guy Mollet came to Moscow in May 1956 Khrushchev stressed the complementarity of the Soviet and West German economies and the prospects for a new Rapallo.[15] While Khrushchev retained a certain residual fear of German power, he sometimes suggested—with how much sincerity it is difficult to judge—that Germany no longer was to be regarded as a serious military threat. He told Canadian foreign minister Pearson that "the allies might as well face up to the fact that the Germans will not fight having had enough of war."[16]

In sum, once it was clear that reunification was not a realistic possibility, the Soviet leaders had little to fear and much to gain from a West Germany that was clearly "number two" in Europe—too small to challenge the USSR but large enough to cause concern in France and Britain. On the other hand, Adenauer was undoubtedly correct when he concluded on the basis of his conversations in Moscow that the thing the Soviet leaders most feared was an association between the United States and West Germany.[17]

The Khrushchev-Bulganin meetings with the leaders of Norway, Denmark, and Sweden were less directly connected with the USSR's 1955 shift to an explicit two-Germany policy but were generally consonant with the effort to promote an East-West détente "proceeding from the existing situation." Prime Minister Einar Gerhardsen went to Moscow in December 1955 for what the Norwegians hoped would be talks with primarily an economic and cultural focus. Gerhardsen had gone before Parliament and stated that "between Moscow and Oslo there were no problems of a political nature" and that questions such as Norway's role in NATO would not be discussed. But Khrushchev used the talks to argue that neutrality would be a better option for Norway, and Gerhardsen agreed to a concluding communiqué that recorded his assurances that Norway would not pursue a policy that could further "aggressive" designs against the USSR or make its territory available for foreign bases in time of peace.[18] Although the assurances in the communiqué did not go beyond those already given to the USSR through diplomatic channels, Gerhardsen was criticized in Norway and elsewhere for failing to keep politics out of the discussions as he had promised he would.[19]

Danish prime minister H. C. Hansen was more forceful in fending off Soviet pressures to offer assurances about Denmark's basing policy during his March 1956 visit to Moscow. The concluding communiqué focused exclusively on economic and cultural contacts, and Hansen's success in avoiding political-military subjects was greeted as a positive result by other NATO governments.[20] Khrushchev revealed something of his thinking about the Stalin era when he told Hansen that the USSR was determined to bring about the dissolution of NATO, which had come into being only because of the "war psychosis" caused by Soviet policies.[21] The Hansen visit also was instrumental in leading to a bilateral trade agreement concluded later in 1956.

Prime Minister Tage Erlander of Sweden went to Moscow in March 1956, and won explicit Soviet endorsement of Sweden's neutrality, which previously had been criticized in the Soviet press and official statements. But the hosts also set a pattern for the future by suggesting that Sweden's neutrality should be "active" and contribute to the solution of international problems. This was an indirect way of saying that Sweden should work to draw Denmark and Norway away from NATO—a prospect that the USSR had rejected in the late 1940s and early 1950s by condemning with equal force both NATO and the proposed Scandinavian Defense Community.[22] One of the most contentious issues at the summit was the Wallenberg case. The Swedes proposed the formation of a binational commission to investigate the case, but the Soviets refused and reproached Erlander for bringing up the subject. But the Soviets eventually did agree to accept information handed over by the Swedes and to mention the case in the concluding communiqué.[23]

By early 1956 the increasingly bilateral focus of Soviet policy toward the West was reflected not only in summits but in a new round of treaty proposals. In January 1956 Bulganin proposed a U.S.-USSR treaty of friendship and cooperation.[24] In his report to the Twentieth Party Congress the following month, Khrushchev praised "nonaggression treaties" and "treaties of friendship," which he declared the USSR was ready to conclude with "appropriate states."[25] In March 1956 Italian Communist leader Togliatti returned from the USSR proposing a bilateral nonaggression pact and offering to play a role in arranging contacts between the Italian and Soviet governments.[26] But Western governments invariably rejected these offers, which were seen as too political for bilateral meetings and implying agreement on fundamental issues that were expected to be resolved in the four-power negotiations.[27] Instead they preferred to keep the focus of bilateral meetings on culture and economics and, in the special case of Britain and France, on tensions in the Middle East.

The British-Soviet and Franco-Soviet summits in the spring of 1956 were outgrowths of the four-power meeting the previous summer. Eden recalled that at a Soviet dinner in his honor in Geneva "Marshal Bulganin drew me out onto the terrace" and "began to speak of a visit by me to Moscow." Eden replied that it was the turn of the Soviet leaders to come to Britain, and issued an invitation on the spot, which Bulganin informally accepted.[28] Faure and Pinay also discussed a bilateral summit, and were scheduled to go to Moscow in the fall of 1955 before the convening of the October conference of foreign ministers.[29] But after an unfavorable Soviet vote on Algeria in the UN General Assembly the French cabinet voted to defer the visit. The first postwar summit between the USSR and France thus did not occur until May 1956, several months after Guy Mollet had replaced Faure as prime minister.

At Geneva both the British and the French had envisioned a process of four-power meetings at the summit and foreign ministers' level, which they expected would lead to the gradual resolution of the German and other contentious issues. A bilateral meeting between the British and Soviet leaders could serve to move along the multilateral process, much the way the wartime visits of Eden and Churchill to Moscow had prepared the way for later meetings of the big three. But the failure of the November foreign ministers conference dashed these expectations and inevitably gave the London meetings a heavily bilateral focus.

Eden proposed a two-part agenda that the Soviets accepted: Anglo-Soviet relations and a review of world affairs. The global review was divided into four parts: Europe, the Middle East, the Far East, and disarmament.[30] But Germany and European security were not extensively discussed and not even mentioned by Bulganin in his report to the press on the conference.[31] The final communiqué issued by the two leaders affirmed "a joint desire to work for the easing of international tension," but noted bluntly that the sides had "failed to reach agreement on the means of settling European problems."[32]

In contrast, non-European questions played a major role in the talks. Soviet attacks on British colonialism had grown so violent during Khrushchev's recent tour of Asia that Eden seriously considered calling off the summit in protest.[33] But the British cabinet chose not to do so, and Eden remained hopeful that he could use the meeting to secure promises of Soviet restraint in the Middle East. The final communiqué expressed the "firm intention" of both countries "to do everything in their power to facilitate the maintenance of peace and security in the Near and Middle East." But in the ensuing months the USSR did little (from the British point of view) to carry out this pledge.[34] In addition to the lengthy communiqué, the leaders issued a separate document on cultural relations and a list of items that the USSR planned to purchase from Britain in the 1956–59 period. The chief result of the summit thus was to promote bilateral economic, cultural, and technological exchange and thus to normalize relations in the absence of a broader European settlement.

The failure of the November four-power talks and the delay caused by the dispute over Algeria also changed the character of the Franco-Soviet summit. In the parliamentary debate the previous summer over whether the government should accept the Soviet invitation, French officials explained that they saw the trip as a "continuation of the international loosening of tensions rather than the opening of precise negotiations."[35] This was consistent with the overall Western line that the real business of settling the disputes left over from World War II would take place in a properly prepared great-power conference. However, in a magazine interview that appeared shortly before his trip to Moscow, Mollet declared that the Western powers had made a mistake at the July 1955 summit by putting European security and disarmament ahead of disarmament on their agenda.[36] Mollet's remarks were both a reflection of and a further contribution to the marginalization of the German issue that took place after November 1955. Khrushchev and Bulganin praised Mollet for the interview, while the West German foreign minister was sharply critical.

Like the British, the French hoped that direct talks with the Soviet leaders would strengthen their position in the Middle East. Mollet tried to obtain the benevolent neutrality of the USSR in the worsening conflict in Algeria and seems to have believed that Khrushchev actually favored a continued French presence in North Africa to prevent the United States from replacing France in the region (but could not afford to reveal this position because of Chinese and Third World anticolonial sentiment).[37] Armed with this illusion, Mollet proceeded to negotiate ambiguous and rather disappointing language on the issue.[38] The two governments also signed a lengthy joint communiqué and a separate cultural declaration which gave impetus to the development of ties in various fields.

The post-Geneva round of Soviet-West European summitry came to an abrupt end with the Suez and Hungarian crises in the fall of 1956. In October Belgian prime minister Achille van Acker went to Moscow for what was the last visit by a NATO head of government for the next two and one-half years. Soviet behavior with regard to Suez shattered whatever remaining illusions the British and French had about Soviet restraint in the Middle East; while the crushing of the Hungarian uprising dampened enthusiasm for the expansion of cultural and other bilateral ties. The Belgians promptly denounced the cultural agreement signed earlier in the month. A return visit to Moscow that Eden had scheduled for May 1957 was put on hold by Macmillan, while Soviet visits to France and Scandinavia were postponed indefinitely.[39]

Khrushchev was by no means happy with this enforced isolation. As the Yugoslav ambassador in Moscow concluded in May 1957, the Soviet leaders "start from the assumption that the consequences of the war in the Middle East and of the Soviet armed intervention in Hungary must be removed and that the atmosphere in international relations which prevailed in 1955 and the first half of 1956 must be restored."[40] But apart from two meetings with Finnish leaders in 1957 and a meeting with Austrian chancellor Julius Raab in 1958 there were no Soviet-West European summits until early 1959.

The revival of high-level diplomacy in 1959 ironically was spurred by the Berlin crisis and the resulting deterioration in East-West relations. In February British prime minister Macmillan took it upon himself to visit Moscow to explore a solution to the crisis (and to enhance his own prospects for election). Macmillan's visit was followed by Khrushchev's trips to the United States later in 1959 and to France in the spring of 1960. The USSR also made breakthroughs with Italy, whose leaders had been very cautious about meetings with the Soviets, which they feared could legitimate the Communist Party at home. In February 1960 President Giovanni Gronchi became the first Italian head of state to visit the USSR, and was followed by Prime Minister Amíntore Fanfani in August 1961.

The one casualty of the resumption of summitry was high-level Soviet interest in the smaller West European countries. In July 1959 Khrushchev unexpectedly cancelled a trip to Sweden, Finland, Norway, and Denmark scheduled for the following month. The Soviet foreign ministry blamed the cancellation on press coverage and the activities of organizations "hostile to the USSR" in the Scandinavian countries (although not in Finland), but it was widely believed that Khrushchev had decided to forgo these meetings in order to meet with Eisenhower and to concentrate on his campaigns for a Berlin settlement and complete and general disarmament.[41]

What is striking in retrospect about the renewed bilateral diplomacy of 1959 and 1960 is the different way the USSR and the Western powers regarded these meetings. Despite the disappointments of 1955, Western leaders still tended to characterize their bilateral talks with the USSR as informal or "exploratory," and to insist that the *real* negotiations would take place at a future date and in the proper forum. In writing to Adenauer to explain the reasons for his 1959 trip, for example, Macmillan stated that his primary purpose was "to try to discover something of what is in the minds of the Soviet leaders. I shall make it clear that I am not coming to negotiate . . . it will still be some time before the Western allies will be able to decide on the lines which they are to take with the Russians at any conference."[42] Similarly, in explaining his instructions to Robert Murphy, the State Department official who was to arrange for Khrushchev to visit the United States, Eisenhower wrote that he was to "specify that we were thinking not of negotiation but of mere discussion and especially to express my hope that the foreign ministers, resuming their meeting, would make such progress as would justify a meeting of the four heads of government."[43] Eisenhower wanted to extend a "qualified invitation," and Murphy was to convey that Khrushchev would be welcome in the United States only if progress was made in the 1959 conference of foreign ministers.[44]

Khrushchev was more realistic about the probable course of East-

West diplomacy. As was argued in chapter three, he had concluded that four-power talks on Germany were not in the interest of the USSR, and recognized that even in the absence of such talks Western governments probably would go forward with developing cultural and economic ties and in conducting arms control negotiations. Khrushchev was basically correct. The bilateral summits of 1959 and 1960, which the Western leaders stressed were to have an informal, preparatory character, in fact became the model for East-West meetings in the 1960s and 1970s; while the four-power meetings, whose importance was stressed by Western governments, soon died out completely. The 1959 Khrushchev tour of the United States, which Eisenhower regarded as an addition to a preparatory meeting, was to become the model for White House and State Department planners, as both the Nixon and Reagan administrations yearned for a repeat of this coast-to-coast extravaganza.[45] Much the same happened in France, where de Gaulle remained in power long enough to implement a reversal of his own policy. Of the three Western leaders, de Gaulle was the least enthusiastic about any kind of meeting with Khrushchev but decided, once a four-power summit became inevitable, to host his own bilateral summit with the USSR (the United States and Britain already having done so).[46] But long after the May 1960 summit had marked the end of four-power summitry, Khrushchev's bilateral visit of April 1960 continued to serve as a model for the Franco-Soviet summits of the 1960s with their emphasis on trade, culture, and political tourism.

Although Khrushchev had a keen appreciation of the role of high-level meetings with the Western powers and used these meetings to promote his agenda of disarmament and the relaxation of tensions, he was too erratic and too preoccupied with the Berlin and German issues to make high-level meetings the centerpiece of his policy or to pursue regular summitry for its own sake. Following the abortive Kennedy-Khrushchev summit of June 1961 and the building of the Berlin wall later in the summer, the domestic and international climate deteriorated to the point that even sporadic high-level meetings with Western leaders were no longer possible. In fact, 1962 and 1963 were the only years since 1955 in which no such meetings occurred.

In what may have been a bid to revive his flagging domestic and international fortunes, at the end of his term in office Khrushchev became more active in promoting bilateral summits. His moves in this direction were facilitated by the U.S.-Soviet détente that followed the Limited Test Ban Treaty of 1963. In the summer of 1964 he made his postponed trip to Denmark, Sweden, and Norway and dispatched his son-in-law Aleksei Adzhubei on a private visit to Bonn to explore a trip to West Germany.[47] In September it was announced that Khrushchev had accepted a long-standing invitation to visit the FRG, but his ouster a few months later intervened and it was almost another decade before a Soviet leader set foot on West German soil.[48]

Notwithstanding the policy setbacks he suffered and the controversies they evoked at home, Khrushchev scored a major achievement in establishing bilateral summitry, which did not exist in the interwar period or in the first decade after the war, as a major institution of East-West relations.

The 1960s

The second major period of Soviet summit diplomacy was in the mid-1960s. The Kosygin-Brezhnev regime, having recovered from the setbacks of the early 1960s and having found its bearings at home, began to use high-level meetings with France, Italy, the Nordics, and others to expand political and economic ties, pressure the United States and West Germany to change their policies, and promote the convening of a European security conference.[49]

The new regime moved quickly to exploit tensions between the United States and Turkey over the conflict in Cyprus. In January 1965 Nikolai Podgornyi led a parliamentary delegation to Turkey—the first such Soviet group to visit the country since 1933.[50] In April it was announced that Gromyko would visit Turkey the following month, thus becoming the first Soviet foreign minister to do so.[51] Aleksei Kosygin used the occasion of his first interview with a foreign correspondent to call for a Soviet-Turkish nonaggression pact.[52] In August Suat Urguplu became the first Turkish prime minister to visit the USSR in thirty-three years.[53] In December 1966 Kosygin paid a return visit, the first ever by a Soviet (or Russian) premier.

In April 1966 Gromyko made the first postwar visit to Italy by a Soviet foreign minister. This meeting paved the way for a trip to Italy by Soviet president Podgornyi in January 1967.[54] Podgornyi's visit, which technically was in return for the Gronchi visit of 1960, was the first to Italy by a Russian head of state since that of Czar Nicholas II in 1909. Podgornyi also became the first Soviet president to visit the Holy See and be received by a pope. Relatively frequent meetings also took place with Austria, Sweden, and Finland.

Soviet diplomacy in this period combined elements of both Khrushchev's impetuous drive for an immediate legal settlement to the German and Berlin problems and Brezhnev's subsequent mechanical, depoliticized approach that ignored underlying political differences in favor of ritual pronouncements of support for détente. France by this time was prepared to set aside the most contentious political issues and to pursue a détente that de Gaulle hoped would "dismantle the Iron Curtain piece by piece" through "economic, cultural, technical and touristic" agreements.[55] But Kosygin refused to accept an exclusive focus on "low politics." "We talk détente, they talk security,"[56] was how French foreign minister Couve de Murville summed up several days of dialogue during de Gaulle's 1966 visit to the USSR. "Security" meant recognition of the political status quo, preferably by an all-European conference at which both German states were represented. Other Western countries heard similar messages. As U.S. and British negotiators pursued the nuclear nonproliferation treaty they were repeatedly confronted with Soviet efforts to link arms control to progress on the German question.

At the same time, however, Kosygin and Brezhnev did not follow Khrushchev's example and break off dialogue by precipitating crises in Berlin or elsewhere. Nor did they altogether spurn the French, Italians, and others eager for more extensive economic and cultural cooperation, or the Americans and British when they sought to institutionalize an East-West arms control dialogue. The exception that proved the rule was West Germany: it remained isolated and the object of Soviet vilification until it agreed to the Eastern treaties that once and for all were to solve—so Brezhnev thought—the German question on Soviet terms.

De Gaulle's July 1966 trip and Kosygin's return visit in December were probably the most important meetings of the decade.[57] They laid the groundwork for the special relationship between France and the USSR that was to flourish in the 1970s and that became the USSR's preferred model for relations with all the NATO countries. The Soviet leaders also broached the idea of a Franco-Soviet political treaty with de Gaulle, and received a noncommittal, although not entirely negative, reply.[58]

While less noteworthy than the meetings with de Gaulle, Soviet-British summitry also reached a pre-Thatcher high point. In 1966 Prime Minister Harold Wilson made two trips to Moscow, one in February and another in July, and Kosygin reciprocated with a February 1967 trip to London. During this London visit Kosygin proposed to a joint session of Parliament that Britain and the USSR conclude a "treaty of friendship, peaceful cooperation and nonaggression" and even managed to enlist a certain amount of British support for this project.[59] In these meetings, Wilson sought Soviet help in ending the Vietnam War, both because of Britain's traditional closeness to the United States and because Britain had been, along with the USSR, cochair of the Geneva Conference of 1954 and thus had certain special responsibilities for Southeast Asia. In retrospect it is clear, however, that Wilson failed to secure any Soviet help in ending the Vietnam War, while placing himself in a *demandeur* position on other issues.[60] (During Wilson's second trip to Moscow his hosts went so far as to delay by two hours a dinner they had scheduled in his honor so that they could attend a Vietnam solidarity rally.)[61]

From the Soviet perspective the summits of the 1960s had two important results. First, they gave a dramatic impetus to the further institutionalization of bilateral relations. As will be seen in subsequent chapters, many of the permanent institutions of economic cooperation, such as the joint economic commissions, date from this period. The first Kosygin-de Gaulle summit resulted in an agreement to conduct regular political consultations and in the issuing, in addition to the usual communiqué, of a freestanding, political declaration expressing agreement on various international issues.

Second, the meetings helped to move the Western countries toward Soviet positions on the key issues of Germany and the convening of a European security conference. While it is doubtful that the meetings in themselves led West European governments to change their minds or adopt new positions on these issues, they provided occasions for sharpening points of divergence within the West and pointing out areas of convergence between Soviet and West European views. By inducing Western governments to put their thoughts on European security questions on paper, Kosygin scored considerable success in locking in advantageous positions and in codifying differences between the FRG and its most important European partners.

This pattern was apparent already in the 1965 meetings between Gromyko and Couve de Murville. At the conclusion of their April meeting in Paris the two men issued a communiqué reporting that "it was emphasized that the USSR and France, as European powers, have a vital interest in . . . an agreed solution to these problems [i.e., Germany]."[62] In the press conference that followed Gromyko claimed that French and Soviet positions on the German issue coincided at a number of points, and that "France starts from the fact that two German states exist." This caused the Quai d'Orsay to issue a brief statement reiterating that France had not changed its policy and did not recognize the GDR. Nonetheless, damage had been done in West Germany, and Foreign Minister Gerhard Schröder went before Parliament to warn against the "Europeanization of the German question."[63]

Kosygin also used meetings with Western leaders to place the European security conference on the East-West agenda and to edge Western governments toward support. At the end of their February 1966 talks in Moscow Kosygin and Wilson issued a communiqué in which both sides pledged "the encouragement of efforts leading to the establishment of comprehensive cooperation between all the countries of Eastern and Western Europe."[64] Although not in itself counter to British or Western policy, the formulation "all the countries of Eastern Europe" implied recognition of East Germany, while the "establishment of comprehensive cooperation" was an opening wedge toward endorsement of a European security conference.

In the joint communiqué issued at the conclusion of Kosygin's June 1966 visit to Finland both governments declared that they believed it would be useful to hold a conference on European security. The de Gaulle-Kosygin communiqué of December 1966 noted that there had been "a discussion on the question of convening in the future a general European conference to examine problems of security in Europe and the establishment of general European cooperation."[65] This did not imply French endorsement of the idea, but the very mention of "discussion" in such a document helped to establish the conference as an agenda item.

At the conclusion of the February 1967 talks between Kosygin and Wilson in Britain it was stated that the sides "considered the question of convening a conference to discuss the problem of safeguarding security and developing cooperation in Europe" and "agreed that such a conference could be valuable, subject to the necessary preparation."[66] They further agreed that "all countries of Europe" should be among the participants at such a conference, and decided to continue an exchange of views on the subject. "Countries" allowed the British to sidestep the issue of East Germany's unrecognized statehood, but the wording was welcomed by the Soviets as implying British support for East German participation, without a counterbalancing reference to U.S. and Canadian participation. This formulation was repeated in subsequent USSR-U.K. communiqués in 1967 and 1968.[67]

In the communiqué issued at the end of Podgornyi's visit to Italy in January 1967 the sides noted the potential utility of a conference and "agreed to undertake further study of the question."[68] "Study" was not quite support, but it represented an advance from passive interest toward parallel action on the part of both governments. At the end of Kosygin's visit to Stockholm of July 1968, Sweden and the USSR agreed to "conduct consultations with interested states on questions connected with the convening of a conference."[69]

Thus by 1968 Kosygin, building upon Khrushchev's breakthroughs but for the most part avoiding his mistakes, had developed summitry into perhaps the most effective institution of Soviet-West European relations. With France he began what Brezhnev later called the "tradition" of Franco-Soviet summit talks.[70] He made progress toward the long-standing Soviet goal of "normalizing" the European territorial and political situation by conducting multiple bilateral discussions on issues that formerly were seen as the province of the four powers. In addition, Kosygin used summits to promote the further development of bilateral relations. These meetings and the documents they produced led to the founding of numerous bilateral institutions with top-level mandates to expand cooperation in political, economic, cultural, and other areas. Notwithstanding these successes, the Kosygin era in Soviet summit diplomacy came to an abrupt end with the Warsaw Pact invasion of Czechoslovakia, as meetings were put on hold and as Kosygin himself soon yielded his foreign policy portfolio to Brezhnev.[71]

The Brezhnev Era

The third major phase of Soviet summit diplomacy began in August 1970 with Willy Brandt's trip to Moscow. A number of features characterized this new phase. First, Brezhnev replaced Kosygin as the most important figure in Soviet foreign policy and the most sought-after interlocutor for foreign leaders. Second, the summit process was extended to new countries such as Portugal, Cyprus, Spain, and Greece, and state visits were held with countries that had formerly exchanged only official or working visits. Third, summits were institutionalized with the two most important countries of Western Europe—West Germany and France. Between the 1970 meeting and the last summit in 1983 before the initial Western deployments of intermediate-range nuclear forces (INF), Soviet and West German leaders met on average once every eighteen to twenty months. Franco-Soviet summits occurred at similar intervals. Moreover, after the erratic start of the 1950s and 1960s, U.S.-Soviet summitry was firmly established under presidents Richard Nixon and Gerald Ford. While U.S.-Soviet meetings focused on strategic arms control and conflict in the Third World, they played a major role in settling issues relating to talks on force reductions in central Europe, CSCE, and the Berlin agreement.

In October 1970 Brezhnev broke with protocol and became the first Soviet party leader to welcome a non-Communist leader to the USSR by meeting President Georges Pompidou at Vnukovo Airport.[72] Brezhnev made his first trip to a Western country in October 1971, when he went to France and was received with the honors normally accorded a head of state. Brezhnev's assumption of the foreign policy portfolio caused a few protocol problems for governments squeamish about conducting business with a man who had no governmental status, but was on balance favorable to Soviet interests. It meant that three members of the Politburo—Brezhnev, Kosygin, and Podgornyi—played some role in meetings with foreign leaders. Brezhnev chiefly concentrated on the intensification of the summit process with the key countries, while Kosygin and Podgornyi had meetings with the leaders of countries that had not previously had high-level contact with the USSR.[73]

Brandt's original plans for *Ostpolitik* certainly did not envision a process of institutionalized summitry. The 1970 trip, the first by a West German leader since that of Adenauer in 1955, was arranged on the spur of the moment, largely at Soviet initiative. According to Brandt's account, Foreign Minister Scheel was in Moscow to complete and sign the nonaggression treaty when, "prompted by talks with the Russians, . . . [he] telephoned me to suggest that I should also come to Moscow for the signing."[74] Brandt agreed, was hosted by Kosygin, but also met privately for four hours with Brezhnev. The treaty was signed, as originally planned, at the ministerial level, but Brandt and Kosygin attended the Kremlin signing ceremonies and "Brezhnev turned up unannounced" as well.[75]

The second Brandt summit came about by similarly unorthodox means. In early September 1971, just after the conclusion of the Quadripartite Agreement, Brandt was asked by the Soviet ambassador if he "would visit Brezhnev in the Crimea for a few days in the middle of the month—unofficially, without protocol or obligations."[76] Despite heavy criticisms at home, Brandt accepted and, accompanied by his foreign policy adviser Egon Bahr and one foreign ministry expert, held several days of talks with Brezhnev on CSCE, central European force reduction talks, and bilateral relations. It was only after these two unusual meetings that Brezhnev became, in May 1973, the first Soviet leader to visit the FRG.

The development of regular Soviet-West German summitry deprived France of its status as a privileged interlocutor, as the Soviet leadership encouraged France and West Germany "to compete for the honor of having the best relationship with the USSR."[77] Despite his own basically suspicious attitude toward the USSR, Pompidou had five meetings with his Soviet counterpart that produced an array of economic, technological, and political agreements. The most important Franco-Soviet understanding of the period was probably the sweeping thirteen-point October 1971 Principles of Cooperation Between the USSR and France, which mapped out joint efforts in numerous fields and which in the course of the next few years was referred to repeatedly by officials from both sides.[78]

Throughout this period Britain, which to some extent had taken the lead in bilateral summitry in the late 1950s and had had four summits in the 1966–68 period, was the odd country out. The Conservative government of Edward Heath did not have a single top-level meeting with the Soviet leadership, and talks at the foreign minister level were infrequent. After returning to power in 1974 Wilson made one trip to Moscow in 1975, and foreign ministers David Owen and Gromyko exchanged visits in 1976 and 1977, but meetings were not regularized. Not until the beginning of the Gorbachev era did the tempo of USSR-U.K. diplomacy accelerate.

In contrast to Khrushchev, who was indifferent to institutionalized summitry, Brezhnev spoke warmly of the value of continuous personal contact between leaders and sought to regularize meetings with most of the major countries. Largely at Soviet insistence, the joint communiqués concluded at Brezhnev's summits contained ponderous formulations that endorsed future high-level meetings, without going as far as to stipulate an ironclad commitment to follow-on summits within a set period of time. At the conclusion of the second Brandt visit to the USSR, for example, it was stated that the sides were determined "to work consistently for the improvement and development of relations. . . . In this context, meetings and exchanges of views between political leaders will play a special role. It was agreed that such meetings will be held also in the future."[79]

Like Kosygin in the 1960s, Brezhnev used meetings with Western leaders to accelerate the convening of the European conference and to shape its outcome. At the conclusion of their Oreanda talks in September 1971, Brandt and Brezhnev issued a joint communiqué in which both sides promised to have early consultations with each other and with their allies "in order to accelerate the holding of the conference."[80] In exchange for this pledge Brandt secured wording on conventional force reduction talks that, while committing the Soviet side to nothing precise, was more favorable to the West than anything previously offered. Two months later Pompidou and Brezhnev came out in favor of a "properly prepared all-European conference" and agreed "to begin an active and all-round preparative work both by way of bilateral contacts and—as soon as possible—in the framework of multilateral contacts." In the final communiqué issued at the May 1972 Moscow summit, the United States agreed that as soon as the Berlin agreement was concluded the CSCE should be convened "at a time to be agreed by the countries concerned, but without undue delay."[81] The phrase "without undue delay" proved to be the key endorsement that led to the convening of the preliminary stage of the conference in late 1972.[82] Once the actual conference got under way, Brezhnev used virtually every meeting with U.S. and West European leaders to press for its rapid conclusion.

Brezhnev was the only Soviet leader (before Gorbachev) to realize any of the many Soviet proposals for an all-European summit. Throughout the 1973–75 negotiation of the CSCE Final Act the USSR persistently pressed for a top-level conclusion to the conference. The irony of Brezhnev's approach, however, was that his near-obsession with a summit-level conclusion to the CSCE gave Western negotiators leverage over the content of the Final Act, thereby undermining the value to the USSR of the conference it so badly desired. As a U.S. participant noted, "the dynamics of the Conference depended almost entirely on the Soviet desire to bring the CSCE to a successful summit conclusion. This was the engine that powered the whole undertaking, and all Western strategy could do was to channel the Soviet effort by indicating what the Soviets would have to do"—chiefly in the areas of human rights and confidence-building measures—"to get what they wanted."[83]

The Soviet leadership on occasion sought to counter this leverage by signaling that it was losing interest in the project and a concluding summit. For the most part, however, Brezhnev sought to cure the drawbacks of summitry with more summitry. He tried in bilateral meetings with Western leaders to commit governments to a CSCE summit, and thus to deprive negotiators at the working level of the leverage they derived by dragging out the pace of the conference. He "hoped to obtain early commitments from Western leaders to a date for Stage III of the Conference, and thus to generate internal pressures from Western governments on their own negotiators to finish the work in time to meet the agreed schedule."[84] By late 1974 the Soviet leadership apparently was convinced "that a Stage III summit in the late spring or early summer of 1975 was virtually in the bag." Thus to some extent it was able to reverse "the time pressure the West had previously sought to use against Moscow, and apply it as leverage against those countries that theoretically had less interest than the Kremlin in an early conclusion [to the CSCE]."[85] In seeking to commit Western leaders to the summit Brezhnev also was not above trying to play one country against another. Kissinger recalled a 1974 meeting between Brezhnev and Nixon that "was largely a recital by Brezhnev of which Western European leaders had already agreed to the Soviet proposal to conclude the conference at the summit level"; adding that "much of this was news to us."[86] When Belgian prime minister Leo Tindemans refused to commit to a specific date for a Helsinki summit during his June 1975 visit to Moscow, he was told by Gromyko that Valéry Giscard d'Estaing and Wilson had already aligned their positions with that of the USSR, and asked whether it was reasonable for Belgium to fight such a useless rearguard action.[87]

The Brezhnev-era summits also were the occasion for the conclusion of numerous "basic principle" agreements between the USSR and West European countries that were patterned on but often went beyond the 1966 Franco-Soviet political declaration. Brezhnev badly wanted to conclude a friendship treaty with France on the occasion of his first major trip abroad in 1971, but this was rejected as "premature" by President Pompidou.[88] Instead, France and the USSR signed a political agreement on principles of cooperation. The 1971 agreement was supplemented by the 1975 Declaration on the Development of Friendship and Cooperation, and the 1977 Joint Declaration. Other bilateral declarations that followed the Franco-Soviet model were the 1978 Joint Declaration with West Germany, the 1972 Declaration on Principles of Good Neighborly Relations and the 1978 Declaration on Principles of Good Neighborly Relations and Friendly Cooperation with Turkey, the October 1979 Greek-Soviet Declaration on the Principles and Further Extension of Good Neighborly Relations, and numerous other bilateral agreements. These agreements were not treaties spelling out precise and concrete obligations, but political commitments regarding joint efforts and common goals that presumably had some effect on other governments, national bureaucracies, and public opinion.

While Brezhnev concentrated on relations with a few major countries, Kosygin and, until his eclipse in 1977, Podgornyi also were active in meeting Western leaders. Kosygin continued to have frequent meetings with the Austrians, Swedes, and Finns, the focus of which was often trade and economic matters. He also played the key role in meetings with the leaders of Spain and Greece, two of the last European countries to hold high-level meetings with the USSR. In September 1978 George Rallis became the first Greek foreign minister to make an official visit to Moscow. In response to an invitation issued during the Rallis visit, in October 1979 Konstantinos Karamanlis made the first trip to the USSR by a Greek prime minister.

Podgornyi took the lead in one of the more curious episodes in the history of Soviet summit diplomacy, the flurry of royal visitors to Moscow during a five-week period in 1975. In May Queen Margarethe of Denmark traveled to Leningrad and Moscow, thus becoming the first European sovereign to visit Russia since the October Revolution. She was followed, in early June, by Grand Duke Jean of Luxembourg, and later in the month by King Baudouin of Belgium. These trips effectively broke an informal boycott of the USSR that had been maintained by all the European monarchs as a result of the Bolsheviks' murder of the czar and his family.

From the Soviet point of view these visits, which were hosted by Podgornyi and did not involve Brezhnev, were substantive and successful. The Danish foreign minister accompanied the queen for talks with Podgornyi and Gromyko, and the sides made progress toward a ten-year Soviet-Danish agreement on economic and industrial cooperation that was signed a few months later. The Luxembourgian and Belgian sovereigns brought their premiers and foreign ministers. Luxembourg concluded agreements on air transport and scientific, technical, and cultural cooperation. During the Belgian visit foreign ministers Gromyko and Renaat van Elslande concluded a joint political declaration in which the sides pledged "to contribute to the development of the process of the international relaxation of tension" and to seek to make this process "irreversible." The two sides also agreed to hold regular consultations on matters of mutual interest.[89]

At the conclusion of each of these visits it was announced that President Podgornyi had accepted invitations to pay a return visit. None of these visits took place, however, before Brezhnev assumed the presidency from Podgornyi in June 1977. Brezhnev either was too busy (especially in light of his declining health) or seen in Moscow as too important to travel to these small countries. Thus in combining the posts of president and general secretary the Soviet leadership deprived itself of certain options in dealing with the second-tier European states. Meanwhile, unreciprocated royal visits to the USSR continued. King Carl Gustav of Sweden visited in 1978, where he was hosted by President Brezhnev, and King Juan Carlos of Spain traveled there in 1984.

Brezhnev's passion for summitry was in many ways the key to his entire foreign policy. While it is easy in retrospect to dismiss his approach as little more than a manifestation of his personal vanity, there was in reality a convergence, at least for a time, between Brezhnev's personal preferences and the advancement of Soviet foreign policy objectives. Building upon the work of Khrushchev and Kosygin, between 1970 and 1975 Brezhnev used high-level meetings to promote the institutionalization of Soviet-West European cooperation in many areas, both bilaterally and by seeing the security conference to a successful conclusion. Like his predecessors, he had a strong sense of the value of high-level meetings as mandating events. In his speech to the Helsinki Conference he argued that the CSCE summit should "become the main link [kliuchevim zvenom] in the process of détente."[90] At summits held after August 1975 the USSR "strived to include a statement on commitment to the Helsinki accords in [all] final documents, agreements and joint communiqués" as part of its effort to "consolidate the political results of the European Conference."[91]

In the late 1970s Brezhnev's policy in Europe lost momentum as his health declined and he was less able to travel or to impress foreign visitors with his vigor and determination. When he did meet with leaders, such as Giscard d'Estaing and Schmidt, the results were often hollow or ephemeral. The Franco-Soviet and Soviet-West German declarations of 1977 and 1978 were not comparable to the breakthroughs of the 1966–75 period. For a time the hollowness of Brezhnev's policy was not apparent to himself, to many in the West, and, despite much retrospective criticism in the Gorbachev period, to the top foreign policy professionals in the USSR. Brezhnev had developed a conception of détente that was mechanical and depoliticized, and that did not require the kind of dramatic proposals and breakthroughs that later came to be associated with Gorbachev. His basic message to Western Europe was that the continent had been transformed by the agreements of the early 1970s and that what remained to be accomplished was the steady, businesslike implementation of those agreements, the supplementing of political with military détente, and the establishment of détente as an irreversible process. Summits resulted in new trade and cultural agreements, joint statements of principle, and discussions of, if not actual progress toward, military détente, all of which seemed to confirm steady movement toward a desired endpoint.

These meetings took place at a time that the USSR and the Warsaw Pact were steadily building up conventional and nuclear force advantages in Europe. West European leaders such as Helmut Schmidt used summits to protest the military buildup, but Brezhnev seems to have concluded—perhaps because other aspects of bilateral relations continued to develop normally—that these protests were largely pro forma and that Western Europe had come to accept the legitimacy of Soviet theater superiority. The summits of the 1970s thus may well have contributed to the shock felt by Brezhnev, Iuri Andropov, and Konstantin Chernenko when NATO signaled its determination to redress the nuclear imbalance with its 1979 dual-track decision. Although it can never be proven, a case can be made that Western governments in the 1970s would have been more successful in communicating their real concerns to Moscow if they had had fewer meetings.

The value of Brezhnev's mechanical approach to détente appeared to be confirmed in 1980, as a deep U.S.-West European split developed over the Soviet military buildup and U.S.-Soviet tensions in various parts of the Third World. In contrast to what had happened after the invasions of Hungary and to a lesser extent Czechoslovakia, the Soviet invasion of Afghanistan did not result in an extended period of political isolation. Giscard d'Estaing met Brezhnev in Warsaw in May 1980 and Schmidt followed with a visit to Moscow several weeks later. According to a terse joint announcement, Brezhnev and Giscard d'Estaing discussed "initiatives directed at lessening the existing tension" and bilateral relations.[92] The Brezhnev-Schmidt talks were more substantive, and led to a Soviet agreement (discussed in chapter six) to begin arms control talks with the United States on nuclear weapons in Europe.

In retrospect, however, these meetings marked the end of the Brezhnev era in diplomacy. As was to become clear later in the decade, Brezhnev's détente had failed to counter two developments with implications for Soviet interests: instability along the Soviet periphery and NATO's plans to offset perceived Soviet military superiority. Conflict over the first led to the breakdown of institutionalized Franco-Soviet summitry; over the second to the suspension of the West German-Soviet dialogue.

In the electoral campaign of 1981 Socialist Party candidate François Mitterrand criticized his predecessor for his trip to Warsaw and vowed that he would not meet with a Soviet leader until Soviet troops left Afghanistan.[93] Mitterrand later modified this stance, but there was, nonetheless, a highly unusual four-year break in top-level Franco-Soviet meetings following Mitterrand's inauguration. While the French were chiefly responsible for the breakdown of Franco-Soviet summitry, the Soviet side forced the suspension of high-level dialogue with the West Germans. Brezhnev made a final trip to Bonn in November 1981 during which he tried to dissuade Schmidt from carrying out the deployment part of the dual track decision, and he also encouraged the

West German peace movement in its campaign against the deployments. Following the coalition change in late 1982, Chancellor Kohl and Foreign Minister Hans-Dietrich Genscher met with Andropov in Moscow in July 1983 for a chilly, unproductive meeting. But with the initial INF deployments in late 1983, the FRG "forfeited the role of preferred partner."[94] Kohl attended the funerals of Andropov and Chernenko, but was "accorded only formal treatment" by Gorbachev. Soviet-West German summitry did not resume its traditional pattern until 1989, when Gorbachev finally made a return visit to Bonn after the West Germans had made an extraordinary number of unreciprocated visits to Moscow.

Gorbachev as Summiteer

In his first four years as general secretary Gorbachev assigned a relatively low priority to meetings with West European leaders. In October 1985 he went to France in an attempt to revive the special Franco-Soviet relationship. In his speech to the National Assembly and on other occasions in France he pointed to many of the innovations that later were to occur in Soviet policy toward Western Europe. He unveiled a series of new arms control proposals and stressed the concept of the "common European home."[95] But Gorbachev appears to have come away from Paris somewhat disappointed with the results, and did not respond to other West European governments eager to host the new Soviet leader. Unofficial Soviet spokesmen fed speculation about trips to Italy, Greece, and other countries, but nothing came of these rumors.[96] Gorbachev welcomed many European leaders in Moscow, but in his own international travels began to concentrate on the United States, India, and Eastern Europe.

Apart from the intrinsic importance that the USSR attached to relations with these countries, Gorbachev appeared to believe that he could better promote his new thinking in meetings with their leaders than by resuming the long-established pattern of Soviet-West European summitry. The Soviet media portrayed the Delhi Declaration that Gorbachev and Rajiv Gandhi signed in October 1986 as a kind of mandate to Gorbachev from the nonaligned world to persist in his proclaimed efforts to create a new international order.[97] Although the Soviet relationship with the United States was very different from that with India, Gorbachev attributed the same global (and in the case of Reykjavik, epochal) significance to his meetings with the head of the other superpower. After the November 1985 Geneva summit *Izvestiia* editorialized on the theme of "Living and Acting According to the Geneva Mandate," claiming that "Geneva issued a mandate for [the great science of living together] to be learned. Now we have only to start living and acting according to the Geneva mandate."[98] Soviet commentary after Reykjavik was even more effusive.

Like Khrushchev, who on numerous occasions called for high-level, multilateral meetings to deal with "burning issues," Gorbachev saw summits as a way of accelerating the pace of East-West relations. In July 1988 he called for a "European Reykjavik" to impart momentum to the conventional arms control mandate talks in Vienna (see chapter six). While in the West this proposal was seen as a ploy to drive a wedge between the United States (which was not explicitly mentioned as a participant) and its European allies, its intent was probably not to exclude the United States (which Gorbachev must have known was unrealistic) but to take arms control away from the cautious and slow-moving Vienna negotiations and to place it in a more political forum where decisions could be made more quickly and where pressures would be brought to bear on Western leaders.[99] Western governments rejected this and subsequent calls for an all-European arms control summit. (As in 1973, they held out the promise for a high-level meeting at the *conclusion* of the arms control process rather than at its outset, and thus perhaps gained a bit of leverage over the USSR.)

In this period Western Europe was to some extent an object of Soviet-U.S. summitry. The initial breakthrough to the "zero option" was made at Reykjavik, and one of Gorbachev's most concrete European conventional arms control proposals was presented to the U.S. president at the 1988 Moscow summit. To the extent that any Soviet-West European meetings took place, Britain and France were the preferred partners, while West Germany was kept at arm's length. Mitterrand made a return trip to the USSR in July 1986, but the visit was low key and planned around the launching of a second French astronaut on a Soviet space vehicle. Prime Minister Thatcher (who had welcomed Gorbachev to Britain in December 1984 when he was heir apparent and leader of a parliamentary delegation) made a more extensive visit to the USSR in May 1987, and also was favored by a Gorbachev stopover on the way to Washington. During the May visit Thatcher and Gorbachev reportedly argued at length about the validity of nuclear deterrence, and the sides concluded agreements on space, culture, and education.[100] Glasnost was very much apparent during the trip, as Thatcher was granted a long television interview with three rather inexperienced journalists which she used to defend her views, especially on nuclear deterrence.[101]

Despite almost desperate pleas from Bonn, Gorbachev refused to come to West Germany. Although it was the USSR that had broken off regular summits and thus might have been expected to be the *demandeur* in the matter of their resumption, the West German government was placed in a weak position by domestic politics, by the resumption of Franco-Soviet summitry, and by the aggressive courting of Gorbachev by President Reagan and Prime Minister Thatcher. In mid-1987 the Soviet government stepped-up contacts with virtually every political leader in West Germany but Kohl. In July President Richard von Weizsäcker went to Moscow for a state visit. Other prominent West German visitors included Bavarian prime minister Franz-Josef Strauss in December 1987 and Lothar Späth, the prime minister of Baden-Württemberg, in February 1988. Foreign Minister Genscher made five unreciprocated visits to Moscow (prompting criticism in Germany) before Eduard Shevardnadze made a return visit in January 1988.[102] A Kohl visit to Moscow finally took place in October 1988, four months after the ratification of the INF treaty and the final removal of the main irritant in Soviet-West German relations in the 1980s. The Soviet welcome was restrained (as *The Economist* remarked, "on the whole it was the steely, not the cuddly, Mr. Gorbachev whom Mr. Kohl met"[103]), even though the West Germans brought a large contingent of businessmen and concluded a number of deals, including a DM 3 billion line of credit, up to that time the largest ever offered by a Western country.

The real upsurge in Gorbachev's summit diplomacy toward Western Europe did not occur until 1989, following Reagan's retirement and the successful conclusion of the Vienna CSCE review conference. In April Gorbachev went to Britain on an official visit that was originally scheduled for December 1988 but that had been postponed because of the earthquake in Armenia. Setting a tone for his trips later in the year, Gorbachev pressed his vision of a nuclear-free Europe and met with British business leaders to urge them to invest in the USSR. The two countries signed an investment protection agreement and several other minor understandings, and Gorbachev invited Queen Elizabeth to the USSR.[104]

But as in the 1970s, improving Soviet relations with West Germany meant that Britain and France were relegated to secondary if still important roles as the FRG became the USSR's preferred partner. The high point of Gorbachev's 1989 diplomacy thus was his visit to West Germany in June 1989. From the Soviet perspective the centerpiece of the trip was a joint declaration that went beyond the Schmidt-Brezhnev statement of 1978 and endorsed "new political thinking" and the vision of a united Europe.[105] Like many Brezhnev-era summits the visit also resulted in bilateral agreements in various fields, including a treaty on the protection of investments and the establishment of a Bonn-Moscow hotline. The other hallmark of the Gorbachev visit was the nearly euphoric reaction of the West German public, which Soviet commentators found gratifying but which caused concern in other Western capitals.[106]

The trip to West Germany was followed by a brief visit to France shortly before the 200th anniversary of the French Revolution, which Gorbachev linked to the October Revolution.[107] Not to be outdone by the West Germans, the French concluded twenty-one cooperation agreements, although not a grandiose political declaration. The cooperation agreements were mostly minor, but included an investment protection agreement and agreements in training, agriculture, high definition television, and space. Gorbachev completed his visit to France with a speech to the Parliamentary Assembly of the Council of Europe in Strasbourg in which he pressed for further nuclear reductions in Europe and proposed several projects, including a transcontinental train and a European television satellite—intended to give economic substance to the common European home.[108]

With the conclusion of his 1989 visits to Britain, West Germany, and France, Gorbachev reestablished the centrality of summitry in Soviet-West European relations. Overlooking somewhat the experience of the early 1970s, Vitalii Zhurkin, the director of the Academy of Sciences Institute of Europe, concluded that "for the first time since the war summit meetings are becoming a kind of permanent institution, built into the European system of international relations."[109] The established pattern continued into the fall of 1989, with Gorbachev's successful trips to Finland, Italy, and the Vatican. The trips to Helsinki and Rome both produced sweeping bilateral declarations, similar to the one concluded in Bonn but tailored to Finnish and Italian circumstances.[110] The trip to Italy also was noteworthy for the large number of economic agreements concluded, including one setting up a working group of experts to study the conversion of defense industries to civilian production.[111]

While Gorbachev more or less continued Brezhnev's practice of concentrating on the United States and the three main West European countries (his talks in Ireland in 1988 and his 1989 visits to Italy and Finland represented a partial break in this pattern), the chairman of the Soviet Council of Ministers, Nikolai Ryzhkov, followed the pattern established by Kosygin in concentrating on such countries as Sweden and Austria. It is noteworthy that in the period in which Gromyko served as president, he did not go to Western Europe on symbolic visits, although he did perform important protocol functions at home, such as during the visit of President von Weizsäcker in 1988. The relatively low-key roles played by the prime minister and president (before October 1988) were more than counterbalanced, however, by the increased weight of Shevardnadze and the importance of his meetings with such Western counterparts as George Shultz, Genscher, and Roland Dumas. A leading reformer and close political associate of Gorbachev, Shevardnadze quickly mastered his brief and conducted much of the negotiation that led to such agreements as the INF treaty, the concluding document of the Vienna CSCE meeting, and the 1990 understandings with West Germany regarding German reunification.

Summitry, 1953–90

A Soviet head of government did not go abroad on official business until 1940, when Molotov, who was then both foreign minister and chairman of the Council of People's Commissars, traveled to Berlin for negotiations with Ribbentrop and a personal meeting with Hitler. Stalin, who assumed Molotov's governmental post in May 1941, went to Teheran, Potsdam, and Yalta, but showed little interest in a continuation of summitry after 1945. Not until 1955 did Stalin's successors venture outside Soviet-controlled territory.

In contrast, from 1955 onward the USSR had summits with West European governments in every year except 1962 and 1963. As has been seen, these meetings clustered in four groups: the mid-1950s; the mid-1960s; the early to mid-1970s; and the late 1980s. In the first period the USSR participated in four-power meetings and bilateral summits with Britain, France, and West Germany, as well as initiated contacts with Finland, Sweden, Norway, and Denmark. In the second period it shunned the FRG but reactivated summitry with France and Britain and intensified contacts with the Nordics, Turkey, Italy, and the Vatican. In the third period the USSR made strenuous efforts to institutionalize summitry with France and West Germany, had high-level meetings with traditional partners in Italy and Nordic Europe, and had its first high-level meetings, including royal visits, with the Benelux, Cyprus, Spain, Greece, and Portugal. The high point of this period was the all-European summit in Helsinki, which Brezhnev regarded as a great personal triumph. In the most recent period Gorbachev concentrated on the United States and the four largest countries of Western Europe, but also traveled to Finland, Ireland, and Spain, and seemed prepared to go to Greece. Like Brezhnev, he also campaigned for an all-European summit, and managed to secure Western agreement to attend a "Helsinki II" as early as late 1990.

Throughout this period Soviet leaders displayed certain general preferences regarding the conduct of summits. They were tough bargainers on venue. Differences with the West on this issue went back to the wartime summits, all of which took place on Soviet-controlled territory, and continued into the early postwar period.[112] The first post-Stalin, East-West summit (excluding the visit of the Austrian leaders to Moscow in early 1955) took place on neutral territory in Geneva, and Britain and the United States insisted on hosting their first postwar bilateral summits with the USSR.[113] In *all* other cases except the Vatican it was the Western country whose leader made the initial trip to Moscow before a return visit was made by a Soviet leader.

The Soviet leadership was most flexible on venue when it badly needed a summit to overcome temporary isolation. Kosygin met with Prime Minister Mauno Koivisto of Finland on an icebreaker in the

Gulf of Finland (it was announced that the two men were fishing) some six weeks after the Warsaw Pact invasion of Czechoslovakia. In 1980 Brezhnev took the unprecedented step of meeting French president Giscard d'Estaing in Warsaw, when doing so proved useful in enabling the USSR to escape the temporary diplomatic isolation following the invasion of Afghanistan.

The USSR was most inflexible on venue when it wanted to show displeasure or when it had its interlocutor in a *demandeur* position. The most memorable example was in 1961, when President Urho Kekkonen of Finland took the train to Moscow and then flew to Novosibirsk for talks with Khrushchev aimed at defusing the crisis in Finnish-Soviet relations. That the Soviet leader refused to interrupt his tour of Siberia to engage in talks with a head of state was a gesture of calculated contempt. Kosygin's refusal in 1967 to come to Washington rather than Glassboro and Gorbachev's Reykjavik gambit both were directed at politically weak U.S. presidents badly in need of a summit for domestic political reasons.

Soviet leaders also were tenacious on the question of summit timing. They did not allow themselves to be rushed into meetings for which they felt they were not prepared or which, more importantly, would take place during times in which the USSR's international position was "objectively" disadvantageous. Khrushchev's remarks on Soviet caution after Stalin's death already have been noted. The USSR also tended to schedule summits in pairs or packages in what probably were efforts to dilute the leverage any one Western leader, and in particular a U.S. president, could exert on his Soviet counterpart.

This pattern was already apparent in the mid-1950s, when Khrushchev and Bulganin lessened somewhat the significance of their trips to Geneva and London by scheduling a series of high-level meetings in Moscow. In the 1970s and 1980s Soviet leaders made rather transparent attempts to put Washington in its place by scheduling U.S.-Soviet summits in tandem with meetings with the French leadership. In 1967 Kosygin stopped in Paris to meet with de Gaulle before going on to the United Nations in New York and his Glassboro meeting with President Johnson. In 1974 Brezhnev stopped in Paris to meet with Pompidou on the way back from Washington. In July 1985 the French and Soviet governments simultaneously made the surprise announcement that Gorbachev would travel to Paris in October, thus upstaging the U.S.-Soviet meeting planned for Geneva.

When engaged in high-level discussions with the Western powers that touched upon the interests of the East European states, Soviet leaders made a point to stop in East European capitals to display solidarity and to issue bilateral or unilateral statements that affirmed the Soviet interpretation of what had been or shortly was to be agreed in talks with the West. Khrushchev and Bulganin stopped in East Berlin on their way back from Geneva in 1955.[114] Brezhnev cushioned the effect of his first trip to Bonn with visits the preceding week to Poland and East Germany. At the conclusion of both visits joint communiqués were issued affirming Eastern interpretations of the Quadripartite Agreement and the agreements signed with the FRG. The Soviet leadership continued although slightly downgraded this practice in 1989 when it sent Shevardnadze to East Berlin on the eve of Gorbachev's trip to Bonn.[115]

While very tough and precise on questions of timing and venue, the Soviet leadership generally was deliberately nonchalant about agenda. In the preparations for the 1955 Geneva summit Molotov argued against the adoption of a formal agenda.[116] Brezhnev's last minute invitations to Brandt in 1970 and 1971 virtually precluded careful negotiation through diplomatic channels of a summit agenda. In his account of his 1975 meeting with Brezhnev, Harold Wilson recalled that he arrived in Moscow without having established an agenda beforehand and only discussed this matter with Kosygin in the car on the way from the airport to the city. Kosygin stated that "the Soviet Government had no strict protocol or agenda to suggest, but he hoped we would feel that the discussions should be entirely free."[117] Gorbachev took the pattern one step further when he all but deceived President Reagan about what he hoped to discuss at the summit he proposed to hold in Reykjavik.

While the USSR preferred little or no preparation going *into* summits, it usually favored as many formal documents as it was able to secure to come *out* of these meetings. As bilateral summitry took hold in 1955 and 1956 the Soviet side pressed for the adoption of very long and detailed joint communiqués. In the 1960s communiqués tended to be shorter, but were supplemented by joint statements and declarations regarded as politically more significant and legally more binding.[118]

By the mid-1950s documents resulting from high-level meetings had for all practical purposes supplanted the political treaty as the main instrument of Soviet diplomacy toward the West.[119] The USSR still regularly proposed nonaggression and friendship treaties to Western governments, but was almost always rebuffed. Indeed, between the conclusion of the Austrian State Treaty in 1955 and the upheavals in Eastern Europe in late 1989, the 1970 Moscow agreement with the FRG was the only political treaty concluded by the USSR with a West European country. Political treaties did not come back into fashion until the second half of 1990, when the USSR and Germany signed the Treaty on Good-Neighborliness, Partnership, and Cooperation, and when Britain, France, and Italy followed the German pattern and decided to conclude similar agreements with Moscow.

With the political treaty all but obsolete, in the détente period there emerged what might be called a diplomacy of process in which communiqués and joint statements performed some of the functions that previously were served by treaties. Unlike in traditional diplomacy, where the main objective was the negotiation of treaties, the focal point of diplomacy after 1953 often became the high-level meeting itself. To the extent that meetings produced results, they were embodied not in treaties but in communiqués and other documents that described a process: the fact that the leaders had met, the atmosphere surrounding their talks, and often the time and the place suggested for the next meeting. Process in effect became the substance of diplomacy.

These documents did not so much codify the status quo as lay out guidelines for the future. As a standard Soviet text on diplomacy noted,

communiqués, joint statements and declarations adopted by two countries (*particularly if there are no treaty relations of a political nature between them*) define the trends of the further development of relations between those countries and map out the fields of common interests and cooperation. . . . The provisions contained in them provide guidelines and stimuli for the work of the departments and organizations. . . . The sides make references to the relevant clauses . . . in discussing whatever concrete question may appear.[120]

In drafting these documents the Soviet side not surprisingly paid close attention to language. A consistent if low-key Soviet objective was to secure the inclusion of Soviet-defined terminology in bilateral agreements. In the communiqués concluded in London and Moscow in 1956 Britain and France both affirmed the principle of peaceful coexistence. France subsequently banned the phrase from bilateral documents, while British practice varied, depending upon whether Conservative or Labour governments were in power. Harold Wilson overruled foreign office objections to the phrase,[121] but most governments tended to reject its inclusion in bilateral documents, and some professional diplomats were surprised when it appeared in the 1972 U.S.-Soviet basic principles agreement.[122] Soviet negotiators also tried to write the phrase into the CSCE Final Act, but were rebuffed by the delegations from the European Community. "Friendship" was another loaded term that was the object of dispute. At their Moscow meeting in June 1977 Gromyko expressed to Genscher his hope for "the development of relations to the point of friendship." During Brezhnev's 1978 visit to Bonn the Soviet side unsuccessfully tried to introduce the word "friendship" into a Soviet-West German document.[123]

In the mid-1980s the Soviet government was deeply disturbed as a number of Western countries insisted upon dispensing altogether with a concluding document. Sweden, which always had been somewhat leery of concluding written agreements with Moscow, suspended the practice in the mid-1970s.[124] In 1986 the USSR issued a detailed "unilateral communiqué" at the conclusion of Prime Minister Ingvar Carlsson's Moscow talks, but failed to induce the Swedes to sign a joint document.[125] In October 1985 Mitterrand broke with the practice that was begun by Guy Mollet in 1956 and institutionalized by presidents de Gaulle, Pompidou, and Giscard d'Estaing and decided not to issue a joint statement at the conclusion of Gorbachev's first Western summit. In premeeting talks Soviet diplomats pressed for a joint document and Gorbachev himself raised the matter in his talks with Mitterrand. But the French remained adamant and the Soviet side eventually agreed to a compromise solution proposed by the French: the two leaders held a joint press conference at which each man issued a unilateral statement summarizing his view of the talks.[126] (The joint press conference subsequently became a very popular aspect of bilateral summitry, and was used again by Mitterrand as well as by Chancellor Kohl, President George Bush, and other Western leaders.) A year after the dispute with France the Soviet government attempted to pressure Dutch prime minister Ruud Lubbers to agree to a communiqué at the end of his forthcoming visit to the USSR. The Dutch traditionally did not sign such documents, and rebuffed a Soviet request that the two sides "record" an alleged convergence of views on such issues as the importance of continued adherence to the 1972 U.S.-USSR Treaty on the Limitation of Anti-Ballistic Missile Systems and nuclear testing. Ambassador Anatolii Blatov used an interview with a press organ of the Dutch Inter-Church Peace Council to call for strengthening areas of agreement by issuing a document, but this tactic failed and no communiqué was issued.[127]

At the end of the 1980s joint statements and communiqués came to be regarded with less suspicion as relations improved. The Soviet-West German joint statement of June 1989 was as grandiose a document as any ever concluded between the USSR and a West European country. Soviet officials stressed that while the statement reflected the particular importance of West Germany, it could serve as a model for agreements with other countries as well.[128] Gorbachev's trips to Finland and Italy and Canadian prime minister Brian Mulroney's visit to Moscow also resulted in unprecedentedly broad statements of agreement on political and philosophical questions. In these agreements the USSR sought achieve bilateral and multilateral endorsement of such new slogans as "new political thinking" and "common European home," but also made important concessions to its partners; for example, by endorsing Finnish neutrality and the German idea of a European peace order.

CSCE and All-European Meetings

As was seen in chapter three, as far back as 1954 the USSR began proposing high-level, all-European meetings. With the sole exception of the 1975 Helsinki summit, which occurred at the high point of Soviet global influence and was in any case used by the West to gain leverage in the drafting of the CSCE Final Act, Western countries rejected these calls for multilateral summits. This pattern persisted into the Gorbachev period, as was seen in the Western reaction to Soviet calls for a "European Reykjavik." It began to change in early 1990, however, as Western governments came to regard institutionalized, all-European summits and ministerial meetings as a useful way of responding to the sweeping political changes in the East.

After the January 1989 Vienna CSCE follow-up conference the USSR suggested that the next such meeting, scheduled for Helsinki in 1992, take place at the summit level. In his May article in *Pravda*, Zhurkin proposed that in the "common European home" the institution of summitry "could be multilateral as well as bilateral." In July the Warsaw Pact Political Consultative Committee (PCC) endorsed an all-European summit that would "define tasks for the future" and strengthen European security to a "qualitatively new level."[129] At his September 1989 meeting with the foreign ministers of the twelve EC countries Shevardnadze pressed for an all-European summit (to be preceded by a working meeting of the foreign ministers).[130]

Western governments at first were reluctant to commit in advance to what Soviet commentators were calling "Helsinki II," even though Soviet calls for such a meeting became increasingly urgent. In a speech in Rome on November 30 Gorbachev suggested that the recent changes in Europe made it desirable to hold a thirty-five-nation summit as early as 1990.[131] In his speech to the Political Commission of the European Parliament the following month, Shevardnadze further suggested that the participants in the summit could sign the European conventional arms control agreement expected to be ready by the fall of 1990 as well as "examine and elaborate an agreed approach to the present state of affairs on the continent."[132] Shevardnadze also proposed that the heads of government "found a tradition of yearly meetings of the heads of state on a systematic basis."

Western governments remained somewhat cautious about these proposals, and suggested initially that the leaders of the thirty-five should meet only to sign the arms control agreement. There was some concern in the West that the Soviet interest in an early, all-European summit was linked to developments in Germany and the Soviet desire to stop or at least slow the progress toward reunification. Such a meeting would have resulted in a multilateral reaffirmation of the political and territorial status quo, and would have produced the signature of an East German leader on an authoritative, all-European document.

Notwithstanding these concerns, in January 1990 the leaders of the EC countries endorsed the holding of an all-European summit by the end of the year. French president Mitterrand saw such a meeting as a way to help Gorbachev politically, while the West Germans had concluded that the prospect of an all-European meeting late in 1990 would help rather than hinder the solution of the German question on favorable terms. The United States remained skeptical but gradually came to accept the prevailing European view that such a meeting might be useful in inducing Gorbachev to drop his opposition to German reunification in NATO.[133]

The convergence of Soviet and Western views on the question of an all-European meeting led to the Paris summit of November 1990, at which representatives of the thirty-four countries (East Germany having ceased to exist) signed a conventional arms control agreement and an important political declaration. As in 1975, the West had been able to use the Soviet desire for a high-level meeting to exert pressure on the USSR in the negotiation of agreements—in this case the Conventional Armed Forces in Europe (CFE) treaty and the final settlement of the German question. For their part, the Soviet leaders saw the institutionalization of all-European meetings at various levels as a guarantee that they would remain a power in Europe, despite the reunification of Germany and the effective demise of the WTO and CMEA.

In addition to calling for annual summits, the USSR after 1985 put forward many proposals to upgrade the role of the foreign ministers, thereby reversing a long-standing trend. After the breakup of the CFM in the late 1940s and the abortive revival of four-power talks in the 1950s, the importance of ministerial meetings in Soviet-West European relations had steadily declined. By the 1960s foreign ministers were increasingly cast in the role of "sherpas" whose main function was to prepare for higher-level meetings. Gromyko helped to achieve breakthroughs in relations with France, Turkey, and Italy, although even in this secondary role he often was upstaged by parliamentary delegations that included members of the Politburo. With some countries summits became more frequent than ministerial meetings, or took place even before separate ministerial meetings were held. There were some exceptions to this general rule—notably in relations with some smaller countries or in periods such as the early 1980s when political tensions and the health of Soviet leaders made summits impossible— but on balance the role of the foreign minister in Soviet-West European diplomacy declined, notwithstanding Gromyko's growing power *within* the Soviet leadership.

This situation changed after 1985, as Shevardnadze began to play an increasingly prominent role in Soviet foreign relations. The shift from the Brezhnev-era emphasis on ritualized meetings to concrete agreements on the central issues—recognition of the European Community, arms control, and perforce the reunification of Germany—entailed a new role for negotiation, not all of which could be conducted at the summit level. Recognizing this factor, the Soviets made increasingly elaborate proposals for formalizing the role of the ministers in ways that had not been seen since the four-power meetings of the 1950s. At Reykjavik Gorbachev tabled a draft "Directives to the USSR Minister of Foreign Affairs and to the U.S.A. Secretary of State," containing an outline of the Soviet proposals discussed at the meeting.[134] Other Soviet officials elaborated new approaches to arms control based on a larger and more formal role for both ministers and national leaders. Georgii Arbatov, for example, suggested an approach in which

a fundamental accord at the highest level or at a very high level (that is, at the foreign minister's level) would be reached on a particular question or group of questions after a more or less long period of consultations at the level of experts or key officials of foreign ministries and other departments. . . . At this high level appropriate concrete directives could be given to those who will have to translate this accord into the language of juridically well-drafted documents, and in a very brief time.[135]

Shevardnadze's bilateral meetings with foreign counterparts also became more complex and results oriented, as plenary sessions were supplemented with subministerial working groups tasked with finding solutions in specific problem areas. Following a pattern established in U.S.-Soviet talks, during his January 1988 visit to Bonn he and West German foreign minister Genscher agreed to expedite their work by setting up working groups concerned with bilateral affairs, questions of security and disarmament, and humanitarian problems.[136] A similar procedure was followed during Shevardnadze's October 1988 visit to Paris. He and Foreign Minister Dumas agreed to set up four working groups to discuss disarmament, regional problems, various aspects of humanitarian and cultural cooperation, and bilateral relations.[137] These temporary groups later evolved into permanent ministry-to-ministry working groups under the auspices of the bilateral consultation agreements (discussed below).

The Soviet proposals of late 1989 calling for regular summits under CSCE auspices also envisioned new and highly formalized roles for the foreign ministers. In his December speech in Brussels, Shevardnadze suggested the establishment of an all-European committee of foreign ministers that would receive directives from and present proposals to meetings of national leaders. In an article published in *Izvestiia* in May 1990, he proposed the establishment under CSCE auspices of a council of greater Europe—a summit-level body that would meet at least once every two years—and called for setting up a committee or council of foreign ministers that would meet more frequently to prepare the meetings of the leaders and monitor the fulfillment of their decisions. In addition, *troiky*—consisting of the former, current, and future chairmen of these councils—would be "endowed with mandates of some kind for holding urgent consultations."[138] These ideas were discussed in bilateral sessions between Shevardnadze, Genscher, and other Western ministers, and were endorsed by the NATO countries at their July 1990 London summit. As will be seen in chapter ten, most of these ideas were put into practice at the Paris summit in the fall of 1990, following the settlement of the German issue and the successful negotiation of the European conventional arms control treaty.[139]

Consultations

In addition to high-level meetings and contact through diplomatic channels, Soviet-West European diplomacy after 1953 came to be based on a network of bilateral consultation agreements and institutionalized consultations between foreign ministries. The USSR generally took the initiative in proposing these consultation arrangements, but often was rebuffed by Western governments wary of agreements or practices that might grant the USSR a *droit de regard*.[140]

The consultation clause in the 1948 Treaty of Friendship, Cooperation, and Mutual Assistance between the USSR and Finland was the most sensitive point in the negotiations. In the final version of the treaty Article 2 stipulated that "the high contracting parties will consult each other in the event of the existence of a threat of military attack provided for under Article 1."[141] This article referred to an attack by Germany on Finnish territory or on Soviet territory via Finland. With the Finnish example partly in mind, other West European governments either rejected consultation agreements outright or insisted that such agreements could be invoked only by mutual agreement, rather than unilaterally as in the Soviet-Finnish and in many Soviet-Third World agreements.

The Soviet collective security proposals of 1954 and 1955 included provisions stipulating both crisis and regular peacetime consultations. The general European treaty that Molotov put forward in Berlin in 1954 stipulated that "whenever, in the view of any party to the treaty, there is a danger of an armed attack in Europe against one or more of the parties to the Treaty, the latter shall consult one another in order to take effective steps to remove the danger and to maintain security in Europe."[142] Bulganin presented essentially the same draft treaty to the July 1955 four-power summit.[143] Bulganin's other major proposal at Geneva, a NATO-Warsaw Pact treaty of nonaggression, also stipulated that the parties to the treaty would "undertake to consult one another in the event of differences and disputes which might constitute a threat to the maintenance of peace in Europe."[144] Molotov's 1954 draft treaty also proposed the creation of permanent institutions "to implement the provisions of the treaty concerning consultation among its parties." The 1955 Warsaw Treaty, which was put forward as a multilateral collective security treaty providing for accession by other states, included a similar clause stipulating that the contracting parties "shall consult with one another on all important international issues affecting their common interests, guided by the desire to strengthen international peace and security."[145]

In the late 1960s and early 1970s sweeping all-European proposals gave way to concrete if modest bilateral agreements providing for regular and in some cases emergency consultations. During President de Gaulle's June 1966 talks in Moscow, France came under strong Soviet pressure to conclude a separate consultation protocol.[146] The French resisted, but de Gaulle and President Podgornyi signed a separate political declaration in which France and the USSR agreed to "consult regularly on European and international issues of mutual interest" as well as on bilateral issues. The agreement did not spell out any set period between consultations, nor did it mention crisis situations.[147]

In October 1970 presidents Pompidou and Podgornyi signed a joint protocol spelling out more concrete obligations. Three of the four operative provisions in the agreement dealt with consultation. The first provision obliged the sides to "immediately contact each other with the object of concerting their positions" in the event of situations arising "which, in the opinion of both sides, would create a threat to peace, a violation of peace, or would cause international tension."[148] In the second provision the two countries agreed to "extend and deepen political consultations on major problems of mutual interest." Four specific areas were spelled out: détente in Europe; "the situation in all regions of the world where international security is threatened"; topics of mutual interest under discussion at "multilateral international talks," including at the UN; and "any other questions concerning which the sides may find it useful to have an exchange of views." The fourth point of the protocol stipulated that the consultations "should be held regularly." In specific terms, "the ministers of foreign affairs or representatives especially appointed for these purposes will meet whenever necessary, and, in principle, twice annually." In his report to the Twenty-Fourth Party Congress in 1971 Brezhnev singled out this protocol as an important step that "expanded the possibilities" for Soviet-French cooperation.[149]

The 1970 Franco-Soviet protocol was unusual and precedent setting in that it was aimed at bringing the foreign ministers of the two countries into regular contact for purposes of planning, policy concertation, and exchange of information. In previous collective security, non-aggression, and other political agreements going back to the Congress of Vienna the emphasis was on the obligation of states (or "sovereigns" in older agreements) to consult in certain circumstances. In practice, this usually meant consultation through ambassadors, supplemented on occasion by meetings at the political level. In contrast, in the 1970 agreement it was stipulated that the foreign ministers or "representa-

tives especially appointed for these purposes" (that is, *not* ambassadors in the normal performance of their duties) would meet. In practice
this opened the door to regular meetings between subministerial officials from the Soviet and French foreign ministries. The shift from ambassadorial to ministry-to-ministry consultations was of particular
interest to the centralized Soviet bureaucracy, but it also reflected the
general trend in contemporary diplomacy away from reliance on ambassadors and toward increasingly direct exchanges between capitals.

Although the French appeared to believe that the 1970 agreement
was an expression of the privileged political dialogue between Paris
and Moscow, shortly after its conclusion the USSR undertook efforts to
sign similar agreements with other European (as well as Third World)
states, often by pointing to the agreement with France as a precedent.
The first such agreement was concluded in May 1971 with Canada and
was signed in Moscow by prime ministers Kosygin and Pierre Trudeau.
According to the Canadian ambassador in Moscow, Gromyko presented the draft of the protocol to him two weeks before the summit.
The Canadians also were under the impression that they were to play a
special role in Soviet foreign policy, as they were told by Soviet officials
that the USSR saw Canada playing a role in North America analogous
to that of de Gaulle's France in Europe.[150]

The agreement with Canada was somewhat less detailed about
agenda topics than the Franco-Soviet protocol and stipulated that consultations would be held in principle once each year, as well as in situations that, in the opinion of both sides, would endanger peace. The
Canadians were somewhat more reserved than the French about the
object of these emergency consultations and agreed only to "exchange
views on what might be done to improve the situation," rather than to
work, as the French had agreed, at "concerting positions."[151] A Soviet-
Italian protocol, signed in Moscow in October 1972, also at the prime
minister level, was closer to the Canadian than to the French agreement. It specified only that talks would be held "regularly" at times
"established by mutual consent."[152]

A protocol with Britain was concluded by Prime Minister Wilson
during his March 1975 visit to Moscow and was the first such agreement to be signed by General Secretary Brezhnev rather than Kosygin.
The text followed the basic formula of the other protocols in providing
for both emergency and regular consultations, but a few new elements
were introduced, the most notable of which was the explicit emphasis
on reciprocity. "The consultations will be carried out on the basis of
reciprocity at all appropriate levels and will have a regular character.
Either side is free to recommend the holding of such consultations, including the time and the level at which they should be held. The Ministers of Foreign Affairs or their representatives will meet whenever
the need arises and in principle at least once a year."[153]

A 1976 Danish-Soviet protocol more or less followed the British and Italian models in providing for annual consultations on a range of subjects and emergency consultation by mutual agreement. This protocol was not signed in Moscow at the summit level, but by Gromyko on a visit to Copenhagen. It was the first post-Helsinki protocol, and provided for consultations on implementing the CSCE Final Act.[154] Greece signed a similar agreement in February 1985 during Andreas Papandreou's visit to Moscow.[155]

In the 1970s West Germany and Belgium did not sign separate consultation protocols but merely agreed to the incorporation of language on consultations in other documents. In the joint declaration issued at the conclusion of Chancellor Schmidt's 1974 visit to Moscow the sides agreed to "conduct regular consultations on important questions concerning bilateral relations as well as on international problems of mutual interest."[156] The timing and level of the consultations would be determined by mutual agreement through diplomatic channels. The foreign ministers or their representatives would meet "whenever the sides considered it necessary" and in principle not less than once each year. There was no allusion to consultation in emergency situations. The declaration that was signed at the time of President Brezhnev's 1978 visit to Bonn strengthened this commitment. In it the sides pledged "to consistently continue [an] exchange of views, including in the form of regular consultations, and at all suitable levels, with the aim of expanding the basis for agreement."[157] An agreement with Belgium also was contained in a political declaration rather than a separate protocol. In the declaration signed by Prime Minister Leo Tindemans during the 1975 royal visit to Moscow, both sides agreed to "broaden the practice of regular consultations at various levels on all problems of mutual interest" and pledged that the object of these consultations was to further the goals of the CSCE. There was no emergency clause in the Soviet-Belgian declaration.[158]

The USSR continued to urge other countries in Western Europe to sign consultation agreements, but many were reluctant to do so. The foreign ministries of such countries as Norway, Sweden, and the Netherlands traditionally were wary of political agreements with the USSR, which they feared could open the door to a partial Soviet *droit de regard* over their policies.[159] But even those states that were reluctant to conclude a formal consultation *agreement* did not oppose the *practice* of holding subministerial consultations with the USSR. Norway and the USSR had fairly regular consultations on UN and CSCE issues. Spain began a pattern of consultations in 1985, even though no formal agreement was concluded. Austria and Finland did not have political consultation agreements with the USSR but the foreign ministries of both countries maintained regular contact with their Soviet counterpart.

West Germany and the USSR finally signed a freestanding consultation protocol in January 1988 during Foreign Minister Shevardnadze's first visit to Bonn. Soviet-West German consultations were already fairly well institutionalized, but there was considerable reluctance on the German side to sign a formal agreement out of concern about a possible *droit de regard*.[160] The 1988 agreement stipulated that the foreign ministers or their representatives would meet at least once each year to discuss significant international and bilateral questions. Topics singled out for discussion included disarmament, regional conflicts, global problems, and cooperation in the fields of economics, science, environmental protection, culture, and humanitarian relations. The protocol also contained an emergency clause, stipulating immediate contact in the case of a crisis situation.[161]

The motives underlying the Soviet interest in concluding consultation agreements are not entirely clear and appear to have evolved over time. One of the few explicit Soviet treatments of this subject appeared in the 1986 Dictionary of International Law, which defined international consultation as "an institution of international law which has developed over recent decades" and distinguished between two types of consultations: those "held to coordinate positions," and those "intended to resolve international controversies."[162] The "resolution of international controversies" is a vague term that could apply to situations in which the USSR was on the defensive and seeking to avert sanctions or pressures exerted upon it by the outside world, or to situations in which it was involved in a dispute with a smaller neighbor and wanted to "consult" as a means of exerting pressure.

There was, in fact, precedent in both Russian and Soviet history for using consultation provisions to bring pressure on weaker neighbors. In 1948 Tito's chief ideologist, Edward Kardelj, was summoned to a midnight meeting in Molotov's office, handed two sheets of paper, and ordered to sign. The agreement imposed upon the Yugoslavs, which allegedly was in response to their unauthorized conversations with Bulgaria regarding the formation of a Balkan federation, obliged them to undertake mutual consultations on foreign policy questions. According to Yugoslav sources, the Soviets denounced the agreement several months after it was signed.[163]

During the October–November 1961 note crisis with Finland the Soviet government requested joint military consultations under the 1948 treaty, "in view of the threat from Western Germany." The background to this request was the formation in Finland of an anti-Kekkonen coalition, which announced plans to contest the presidency in the elections scheduled for January 1962. Although tensions in Europe were running high at the time over the Berlin crisis, the USSR appears to have used the broader international situation as a pretext to interfere in a purely domestic matter. The crisis continued for a period of weeks and was not resolved until the Finnish president made his unusual trip to Novosibirsk for personal talks with Khrushchev. After the meeting it was announced in a joint communiqué that "the Soviet Government found it possible to postpone for the time being the consultations it had suggested."[164] The Finns thus emerged from this crisis with their domestic autonomy intact, but at the cost of adjusting their foreign policy in an actively pro-Soviet direction. This interpretation is supported by the wording of the communiqué, which dealt not only with Finnish-Soviet relations and the alleged problem of Germany but with developments in the Nordic area as a whole and Finland's future relationship to them. It recorded Khrushchev's assent to postpone the consultations, but concluded: "Mr. Khrushchev emphasized that the Soviet Government hoped that the Finnish Government would closely follow developments in Northern Europe and the Baltic area and, if necessary, would bring its considerations on taking appropriate measures to the notice of the Soviet Government."[165] Although the communiqué did not explicitly state that Kekkonen acceded to Khrushchev's request ("hope"), the implication of the document was that the USSR had agreed to ease its direct pressures on Finland in exchange for Finland's undertaking certain foreign policy actions directed at its neighbors.

Although the Yugoslav and Finnish incidents give grounds to suspect that the Soviet foreign policy establishment may have regarded obligatory consultation as a potential instrument of pressure on smaller states, other evidence suggests change in the reasons behind the Soviet interest in consultation agreements. By the 1970s and 1980s consultation probably was seen less as a way of pressuring other governments in crises than of obtaining information and ensuring that a Soviet voice was heard on issues of interest to the USSR.

Regular consultations also were useful in promoting Soviet arms control and foreign policy initiatives. They did so, not so much by providing channels through which Soviet officials could promote these initiatives on their merits (if this occurred, so much the better), as by enabling the USSR to call for multilateral consultations as the "next stage" following extensive and virtually automatic bilateral discussion of any Soviet proposal. For example, in January 1983 the Warsaw Pact PCC put forward its Prague Political Declaration, calling for the conclusion of a NATO-Warsaw Pact treaty on the mutual nonuse of military force. In May 1984 the PCC sent a follow-up message to NATO member states in which it noted that the Pact proposal "held an important place in the consultations that were held on a bilateral basis" in the previous year and that the time had come to take "a new step in examining the treaty proposal to commence consultations on a multilateral basis."[166] The USSR later adopted a similar approach in trying to launch negotiations on short-range nuclear forces in Europe.[167]

Arms control consultations with France and Britain also proceeded somewhat in the direction of the bilateral negotiations on arms control that the USSR repeatedly proposed but that these countries rejected. In April 1986 the British received a bit of a surprise when they learned that Viktor Karpov, at the time the USSR's chief negotiator at the U.S.-USSR nuclear weapons talks in Geneva, would head the Soviet team coming to London to conduct consultations on arms control. Karpov had never played this role before with Britain or any other country, and his selection was seen as an attempt to foster the impression of a bilateral U.K.-USSR nuclear weapons negotiation, as Gorbachev had proposed in October 1985 but Britain had rejected.[168]

Soviet-West European foreign ministry consultations covered all regions and functional topics. With France there was a stress on extra-European as well as European issues, along with disarmament.[169] Britain and the USSR tended to discuss arms control and many extra-European issues. With Italy there was some concentration on the Middle East. West Germany and the USSR used consultations to help resolve some of the human rights, legal, and consular problems growing out of the presence of German minorities in the USSR. With many countries the USSR was eager to have a round of consultations devoted to the UN General Assembly (either in July or in late August to early September, before the opening of the fall session), and before new stages in the CSCE process, such as the opening of a review conference.

West European foreign ministries initially preferred to conduct these consultations at the political director level, but as the number of consultations and the specificity of their agendas increased talks between political directors were supplemented by talks involving lower-ranking officials with particular regional and functional areas of responsibility. Annual meetings between the planning staff of the Soviet foreign ministry and its counterparts in the major Western countries also took place under the aegis of these agreements. On the Soviet side these consultations usually were conducted by one or more members of the collegium of the Ministry of Foreign Affairs (MFA) (usually a first deputy or deputy foreign minister). The ambassador accredited to the consulting country also often participated.

Until the Gorbachev period the Soviet government seemed more interested in concluding consultation agreements as visible symbols of détente than in the actual conduct of the consultations themselves, which often were sterile and perfunctory. Even those countries that signed consultation agreements tended to fulfill their provisions only minimally, holding meetings the required one or two times each year. But as the pace of change in Soviet policy quickened the consultation process was invigorated. In 1987–89 there was an explosion of mid-level consultations with European governments as foreign ministries reacted to the improved East-West atmosphere and the increased Soviet activism in arms control and regional, global, and European issues. One official claimed that in 1988 Britain and the USSR had eighteen rounds of political consultations.[170]

In his 1989 meetings with the leaders of West Germany, France, Italy, Canada, and Finland, Gorbachev expressed strong interest in stepping up political ties at all levels. He and West German chancellor Kohl pledged support for "intensive dialogue embracing both traditional and new subjects of bilateral relations."[171] In the Soviet-Italian declaration Gorbachev and Giulio Andreotti "agreed in particular to invigorate—on the basis of the 1972 protocol on consultations, which has fully proved its worth as a foundation for bilateral dialogue—political contacts at all levels."[172] Canada and the USSR agreed to "develop a political dialogue at various levels, including the practice of regular consultations between foreign ministries, the subject matter of which will be extended."[173]

There was also movement toward a further institutionalization of consultations through the establishment of permanent working groups or what some Soviet writers refer to as consultation commissions.[174] France and the USSR established eight working groups dealing with such matters as disarmament, European affairs, North-South relations, the rule-of-law state, the Near East, Latin America, and other regions. West Germany and the USSR set up five permanent working groups: for bilateral issues, arms control, humanitarian affairs, regional issues, and economics.[175] These groups apparently grew out of the temporary groups that were used during Foreign Minister Shevardnadze's meetings with his French and West German counterparts. During Soviet deputy foreign minister Vladimir F. Petrovskii's November 1989 visit to Paris, France and the USSR further agreed to an unspecified arrangement intended to "impart a systematic character to a dialogue between the foreign policy agencies of the two countries, specifically in the settlement of regional conflicts."[176]

The ambitious consultation agreements of the 1980s also laid the basis for what promised to be an even more extensive, treaty-based consultation regime in the post-cold war era. Article 6 of the September 1990 USSR-FRG Treaty on Good-Neighborliness, Partnership, and Cooperation contains a legal commitment to regular consultations, including annual meetings at the summit level, meetings between foreign ministers at least twice a year, regular meetings between defense ministers, and the intensification of work by existing joint commissions. In addition, Article 7 of the treaty contains an unprecedented commitment to emergency consultations which are to be used by the sides to "harmonize their positions and achieve understanding on the measures appropriate to improve or overcome the situation." In contrast to all previous emergency consultation clauses in Soviet-West

European agreements, this clause can be invoked unilaterally by either side. The treaties with France and Italy that were concluded in October and November 1990 also contained extensive consultation provisions.

Diplomatic Relations

The Role of Embassies

Summits, frequent meetings between foreign ministers, foreign ministry consultations, and more recent innovations such as direct conversation by telephone (favored by Chancellor Kohl and presidents Gorbachev, Mitterrand, and Bush) inevitably have diminished the relative importance of embassies and communication through diplomatic channels. Nonetheless, the exchange of diplomatic representatives has remained the most basic of international political institutions, and has continued to play a role in Soviet-West European relations. Diplomatic representation has been especially important to the USSR, which waged a long struggle to secure recognition from many countries and which, given the nature of the Soviet system, long relied on embassies and trade missions to maintain the kinds of contacts that in other countries were left to businesses and other nongovernmental organizations.[177]

In the early 1920s there were sharp debates in Europe about whether it was proper to establish diplomatic relations with the Bolshevik regime.[178] By 1924 most of the major West European countries granted de jure recognition, but Spain waited until 1933, Belgium and Luxembourg until 1935, the Netherlands and Canada until 1942. Switzerland and the USSR did not establish relations until 1946, after a long delay caused by the murder on Swiss soil of a Soviet diplomat. The last West European states to establish relations with the USSR were Ireland in 1973, Portugal in 1974, and Spain in 1977 (the USSR had broken ties in March 1939 after the republican defeat in the civil war).[179] (The USSR and the Vatican exchanged missions and appeared to be moving toward the establishment of full diplomatic relations in 1990, although the Vatican remained wary of Soviet policy toward predominantly Catholic Lithuania, and thus did not fully normalize relations.)

After Stalin's death diplomatic relations evolved into what might be called an absolute institution, as it became increasingly difficult to imagine a diplomatic break between the USSR and a major Western country. During the second Berlin crisis the Western powers discussed a possible break if Khrushchev carried out his threat to interdict Western convoys, but in view of their decision not to take such a step during the first Berlin crisis it is doubtful they would have chosen this option.[180] In March 1961 President de Gaulle recalled the French ambassador from Moscow to protest the USSR's recognition of the provisional government in Algeria, but stopped well short of a break.[181] In response to the Treholt case of 1983 the government of Norway recalled its ambassador for a period. Italy recalled its ambassador to Bulgaria to protest that country's involvement with the attempt to assassinate Pope John Paul II on Italian soil, but most West European governments were reluctant to consider a diplomatic break even in the event a "smoking gun" was found linking the Soviet KGB to the assassination. For its part, after 1945 the USSR never broke relations with a West European country and recalled ambassadors only rarely. The most noteworthy instance occurred in October 1961 when it recalled its ambassador from the Netherlands (and expelled the Dutch ambassador) after he was involved in a fist fight with Dutch police over the custody of a Soviet defector's wife.[182]

The USSR had a pervasive influence on the norms and customs governing the behavior of diplomatic personnel, mainly in the interwar period but to some extent after World War II as well. Under Lenin and Stalin Soviet diplomatic and trade missions were major sources of tension with host governments.[183] After Stalin's death the activities of Soviet diplomatic missions became less of an issue in Soviet-West European relations, as host governments ceased to question what was shipped in diplomatic pouches or with whom Soviet representatives conspired. There was also genuine improvement in Soviet behavior, as little evidence surfaced of direct contacts between Soviet missions and groups engaged in violent revolutionary activities.

While Soviet embassies in Europe shed their insurrectionary associations, they remained heavily involved in espionage and "unacceptable" interference in domestic affairs, both of which at times resulted in strained relations with various countries.[184] In the 1970s and 1980s Soviet officials were expelled from every country in Western Europe, including Finland.[185] Most of these expulsions were low-key incidents involving a small number of individuals, but a few led to major blow-ups with long-term effects on bilateral relations. In the most memorable case, in September 1971 Britain expelled ninety Soviet officials and announced that another fifteen who were temporarily out of the country would not be allowed to return.

Expulsions of Soviet diplomats from Europe increased in the early 1980s as Western governments toughened enforcement and as the USSR appeared to step up its military and industrial espionage activities. In April 1983 France expelled forty-seven Soviet officials after French intelligence turned up evidence of an extensive industrial espionage ring.[186] In April and September 1983 Britain and the USSR engaged in a series of three tit-for-tat exchanges that resulted in the expulsion of thirty-six Soviet citizens from the United Kingdom and thirty-four British citizens from the USSR.[187] In addition, the USSR cancelled at least one scheduled U.K.-USSR exchange to protest the expulsions. (In the early Gorbachev period there may even have been a certain hardening of Soviet policy regarding expulsions, as was seen in the very tough line that was taken in the Zakharov-Daniloff affair with the United States the following year.)

Defining "unacceptable" interference in domestic affairs is a matter of judgment and has varied over time and from country to country.[188] A legitimate function of embassies is to maintain contact with diverse sectors of society, and it is inherently difficult to judge precisely when such contacts assume an unacceptable character. In 1981 a Soviet diplomat was expelled from Denmark for offering to pay for the placement of advertisements in Danish newspapers in which prominent Danes backed the establishment of a Nordic nuclear-free zone. In the same year Swiss authorities closed down the Novosti office in Berne for similar involvement in "active measures" and expelled a first secretary attached to the Soviet embassy.[189] As the INF crisis came to a head in late 1983, Soviet ambassador to West Germany Vladimir Semenov warned the chairmen of the political parties, members of Parliament, journalists, and others in positions of influence about the dangers of taking a "step hostile to peace."[190] Eventually these activities became so objectionable that the West German minister of economic affairs complained to Prime Minister Nikolai Tikhonov about them, characterizing Semenov's behavior as "an unfriendly act of pressure."

Some of this activity continued after Shevardnadze became foreign minister in 1985, but the USSR also took steps to improve the image and effectiveness of its embassies in foreign capitals. New ambassadors were appointed to virtually all major countries, and Shevardnadze displayed an interest improving the day-to-day work of Soviet representatives that was largely absent in Gromyko.[191] Soviet embassies began holding frequent formal press conferences for the first time in 1986, following the Twenty-Seventh Party Congress.[192] Soviet diplomatic personnel stepped-up informal contacts with Western journalists, and even Soviet military attachés began to meet with the foreign media, usually to promote Soviet arms control initiatives but also on the occasion of the release of *Whence the Threat to Peace*, the Soviet riposte to the Pentagon's *Soviet Military Power*.[193] The Soviet embassy in Copenhagen even took out two-page advertisements in Denmark's two largest morning newspapers to inform readers about the Twenty-Seventh Party Congress.[194]

While Soviet missions in Western Europe generally were highly active, foreign missions in Moscow were rather constrained. They often had only limited access to the Soviet leadership and little or no access to the media. Khrushchev tended to take ambassadors very seriously, but he also used diplomatic receptions for political theater. He would arrive at an embassy with a large entourage and make one or another ambassador the target of his latest threats and blandishments.[195]

Brezhnev and Kosygin went to the opposite extreme and had virtually no contact with foreign diplomats. They generally did not attend embassy receptions or receive ambassadors, and thus gave rise to complaints from Western governments about the absence of reciprocity.

Reversing the trend of the Brezhnev period, Gorbachev and Shevardnadze worked to enhance the status of Western (and other foreign) ambassadors in Moscow. In December 1985 Gorbachev met with the Moscow diplomatic corps and declared that "trust between states begins with ambassadors."[196] Shevardnadze made himself more accessible to foreign ambassadors than Gromyko had been and used meetings with groups of ambassadors for certain symbolic purposes. In February 1989, for example, he met with the representatives of the EC countries to underscore the new political dialogue between the USSR and the European Community.[197]

The Diplomatic Channel

While embassies play important symbolic and public relations roles, after World War II their involvement in negotiations was largely supplanted by direct high- and working-level talks between governments. There was one exception to this general pattern. Given the importance of agenda, representation, and other procedural matters, ambassadors continued to play an important role in preparatory and exploratory talks before formal meetings and conferences. As was seen in chapter three, the Western ambassadors in Moscow were heavily involved in the procedural disputes that preceded the convening of the 1959 four-power conference of foreign ministers and the 1960 Paris summit. Embassies later played an essential role in establishing multilateral forums such as CSCE, MBFR, and the conventional stability talks. In 1972 governments unwilling to commit themselves to a preparatory or even an exploratory phase of CSCE agreed to hold "consultations" at which the terms of reference for the actual conference were worked out.[198] The larger countries flew in teams of experts to conduct these consultations, but the cover of an ambassadorial conference enabled the participants to settle such questions as agenda and rules of procedure in advance. The formula of embassy consultations was used again in 1986–89 to work out the mandate and modalities for the conventional stability talks.

There also has been a residual role for written communications between embassies and foreign ministries, or what traditionally has been called the diplomatic channel. This channel serves as an irreducible fallback which governments use to reestablish contact when talks in more visible forums break down. As was seen in chapter three, the foreign ministers of the four powers concluded their failed November 1955 meeting by consigning the arrangement of future meetings to the diplomatic channel. When Warsaw Pact negotiators walked out of the arms control talks in late 1983, the East German representative to the MBFR talks informed the last plenary session that the four Eastern participants "proposed to agree on the date of resuming the negotiations later through diplomatic channels."[199] Diplomatic channels also have been assigned roles in implementing the provisions of arms control and other cooperative agreements, and are essential for registering protests, formally conveying the texts of proposals, and conducting many kinds of routine business.[200] In the Soviet case embassies also have been responsible for delivering appeals from the Supreme Soviet to the presiding officers of foreign parliaments and messages and appeals from the Communist Party of the Soviet Union (CPSU) to foreign socialist and other political parties.

For much of the postwar period the style of Soviet diplomatic communications was more formal than that of Western governments. The Soviet government was inclined to use the traditional diplomatic note, whereas Western governments were more likely to instruct their ambassadors to deliver their remarks orally and to leave behind an unofficial "nonpaper" that did not require a formal reply. Beneath the facade of formality, however, Soviet diplomats were highly conscious of the potential propaganda value of official communications. A standard Soviet text on diplomacy noted that "it has become the rule" for diplomatic correspondence "to be drafted with an eye toward [its] publicity effect—whether immediate or eventual" and that all "Soviet diplomatic documents have two addresses: they are addressed at one and the same time both to the governments and to the peoples."[201]

The USSR claimed credit for inventing what it called the government statement. According to a standard Soviet diplomatic handbook, "previously, correspondence by notes was conducted, as a rule, between ministries of foreign affairs and embassies . . . and not directly between governments." But after the Second World War "the practice of correspondence by notes directly between governments was established by the USSR." This rise in the level of the correspondence was attributed to the increased "importance of the international aspects of the policy of governments in the nuclear age and the [increased] responsibility of governments to the peoples in all matters relating to the resolution of the question of war and peace."[202]

Soviet diplomacy also made extensive use of letters from the Soviet general secretary or prime minister to foreign leaders. Technically such letters are diplomatic notes, delivered by ambassadors to foreign ministries. The USSR did not invent the practice of summit-level correspondence, but Soviet leaders put such letters to particular use in diplomatic and propaganda campaigns. Soviet enthusiasm for summit-level letters reached its peak in the mid-1950s when Bulganin used them to draw attention to the "burning issues" of the day and to promote the Soviet agenda. The U.S.-Soviet correspondence launched by Bulganin after the Geneva summit (and conducted by both countries with an eye toward European opinion) continued for five years and involved the exchange of seventy-two letters, thirty-one of which were by Eisenhower and forty-one by Bulganin, Khrushchev, or Kliment Voroshilov, the chairman of the Presidium of the Supreme Soviet, or titular head of state.[203] Bulganin initiated similar but less extensive correspondences with other world leaders, prompting Macmillan to complain that the Soviets were "making dangerous use of this new game of sending simultaneous letters to the various allied governments and then exploiting any difference which resulted from microscopic examination of the answers."[204]

After a lull in the 1960s caused by the failure of the Paris summit and the less flamboyant style of Kosygin the summit-level letter returned in force in the 1970s and 1980s. Brezhnev's letters often conveyed implicit or explicit threats. In January 1978 he sent a series of "bullying letters" to West European leaders, warning them that deployment of the "neutron bomb" would endanger détente,[205] and in December of the same year he sent letters to the leaders of Britain, France, Italy, and West Germany warning of unspecified consequences if these countries sold weapons to China.[206] Brezhnev and Andropov also sent numerous letters in the course of the 1979–83 campaign against the NATO INF deployments.

Unlike in the 1950s, when the Soviet government often published the texts of letters (compelling Western governments to do likewise), in the 1970s and 1980s an aura of pseudo-confidentiality often surrounded summit-level correspondence. Summaries or texts of letters were leaked to the press, leading both the Soviet and Western governments to accuse each other of attempting to manipulate correspondence for propaganda advantages. After the initial INF deployments took place in late 1983 Andropov sent harsh letters to the leaders of the basing countries. *Pravda* subsequently accused West German chancellor Kohl of "shameless deception" when he failed to characterize the letter to him in sufficiently gloomy terms. In another noteworthy case, in November 1985 the West German newspaper *Bild* published the text of a nine-page letter from Gorbachev to Chancellor Kohl, in which the Soviet leader warned West Germany against participating in the U.S. Strategic Defense Initiative (SDI). The West German chancellery publicly accused the Soviet embassy of responsibility for the leak, while the Soviet embassy denied the charge.[207] In a practice going back to Lenin, Soviet leaders also frequently sent letters to private individuals and heads of nongovernmental organizations. Such letters usually were in response to inquiries and appeals and were given wide publicity in the Soviet media. Along with scientists engaged in arms control activities, schoolchildren concerned about nuclear war were among the most frequent recipients of such letters in the 1970s and 1980s.[208] During the campaign against the INF deployments Andropov also wrote directly to members of the West German Bundestag to encourage them to oppose the Bonn government.[209]

Official Protests

Protests are a special category of diplomatic correspondence that deserve additional comment. There is no prescribed way to issue a protest, which can take the form of a note, government statement, or letter. Western governments generally summon embassy representatives of the recipient country to the foreign ministry. The Soviet foreign ministry also calls in foreign ambassadors or their representatives, but in the 1950s and 1960s it often delivered politically visible protests in the form of diplomatic notes conveyed by ambassadors to host governments.[210]

Deciding when to issue formal protests is a matter of judgment, and practice has varied according to circumstances. In offering guidelines to policymakers Soviet writers have stressed legal factors. According to K. Anatoliev, "a protest is lodged against such actions by another state or group of states that are unlawful from the standpoint of international law, violate the generally accepted standards of international intercourse, and are of a provocative nature or else are fraught with a threat to security and peace." The author went on to state that when lodging a protest "it is particularly important to prove the existence of a delict (an offense against the law), which in fact is what gives grounds for the protest," and noted that it was best to make direct reference to a document such as the UN Charter or other appropriate treaty or agreement in order to make the protest as convincing as possible.[211]

Soviet writers never listed protests by subject, but eight broad categories of protests relevant to Soviet-West European relations in the 1953–89 period can be identified: (1) protests to third countries about West Germany; (2) protests addressed directly to West Germany; (3) protests relating to Berlin; (4) protests about NATO and other Western military activities; (5) protests in espionage and persona non grata (PNG) cases; (6) protests about press coverage; (7) protests about protests; and (8) protests addressed to individuals and nongovernmental organizations.

After the breakdown of the CFM in 1949, diplomatic notes were the Soviet government's main channel of communication on German issues. As the Western powers took the various steps leading to the creation of a West German state and its incorporation into the Western alliance, the Soviet foreign ministry issued a stream of notes charging violations of the Potsdam agreements and, in the case of Britain and

France, of their bilateral treaties with the USSR.[212] In 1954 it protested to the Western powers the Paris agreements and West Germany's pending accession to NATO.[213] In February and May 1963 it delivered notes to France concerning the signing and ratification of the Franco-German Treaty of January 1963, which it characterized as a "war treaty" that would lead to West German access to nuclear weapons.[214] As recently as July 1984 the USSR protested the decision by the Western European Union (WEU) to lift remaining restrictions on the kinds of arms that West Germany could produce, which it argued (in memoranda to all members of the WEU and the signers of the Potsdam agreement) violated the Potsdam agreement, the Moscow Treaty of 1970, and the CSCE Final Act.[215]

While treating the FRG as the object of understandings between the USSR and third countries and protesting alleged violations of these understandings, the Soviet foreign ministry also complained directly to the authorities in Bonn. In 1957 and 1958 Bulganin addressed a number of harsh letters to Adenauer about the deployment of U.S. nuclear weapons on German soil. In January 1967 the Soviet ambassador in Bonn delivered to the West German government a harshly worded document entitled "Declaration of the Soviet Government on the State of Affairs in the Federal Republic of Germany" that referred to the "enemy states" provisions of the UN Charter.[216] In March 1981 the USSR lodged an official protest with Bonn after the education ministers of the West German states decided to produce textbooks containing maps of Germany within its 1937 borders. The Soviet protest regarding the WEU's decision to lift restrictions on West German arms production was sent, with some changes in wording, to Bonn as well as other capitals.[217] The West German government issued a sharp reply to the Soviet document, which it characterized as unacceptable interference based on charges without substance.[218]

The USSR also repeatedly protested to the Western powers and to the FRG about any extension of political contacts between the latter and West Berlin. Examples of activities protested include talks between the U.S. secretary of state and the mayor of Berlin, conferences of West German state officials in the city, and visits by NATO or West German defense officials.[219] As recently as November 1988 the USSR protested when the government of France sanctioned the formation of Euroberlin, a joint venture between Air France and Lufthansa, which it claimed was a violation of the Quadripartite Agreement.[220] The USSR also protested the establishment of links between West Berlin and the European Community. In early 1975, for example, it protested a decision by the EC to establish a European Center for Vocational Training in West Berlin,[221] and in 1979 and 1984 it protested the city's participation in direct elections to the European Parliament.[222]

Protests about military activities directed against the USSR have concerned both NATO as an organization and particular military programs undertaken by the alliance or its member states. The first kind of protest was common in the late 1940s and early 1950s, as the USSR sought to block formation of the alliance and the accession of new members, while the second predominated after 1955. In 1949 the USSR issued notes of protest at every step in the formation of the alliance: as countries debated whether to sign the treaty, after they had done so, and as parliaments debated ratification. It later protested when new members sought admission to the alliance, including Greece and Turkey in 1951, and Spain in 1981. In September 1981 the Soviet chargé d'affaires in Madrid handed a note to Spanish foreign minister José Pedro Pérez-Llorca warning of "negative consequences" for Spain if it carried through with plans to join NATO.[223] Pérez-Llorca rejected the note, which he characterized as unacceptable interference in Spain's affairs.

Protests concerning particular military activities are too numerous to recount in detail. Protests about nuclear weapons have been especially common, and were one of the main themes in the Bulganin letters of 1957–58. In late 1983 Andropov sent protest notes to the five West European countries scheduled to receive U.S. INF missiles. According to a British source the tone was "resentful to the point of anger, and even threatening."[224] Later in the decade the USSR protested to Britain about its reported supply of missiles to resistance forces in Afghanistan.[225]

Norway has been the recipient of a unique class of protests concerning alleged military activities on the Svalbard (Spitzbergen) archipelago. Under the terms of the Svalbard Treaty of 1920 (to which the USSR acceded in 1935), Norway has sovereignty over this territory, but the islands are to be kept free of naval bases and fortifications. Norway is responsible for ensuring adherence to this provision.[226] The USSR frequently protested alleged violations of the demilitarization provisions of the 1920 treaty. In 1951 it protested what it called Norway's responsibility for placing Svalbard and Bear Island under the "competence" of the NATO integrated command, and accused the Oslo government of allowing the islands to be used as NATO naval bases. In 1959 and 1960 the USSR protested Norway's plans to build new airfields on the islands.[227] In the mid-1960s it protested Norway's decision to allow the European Space Research Organization (ESRO) to construct a telemetry station on Svalbard. The USSR also complained to Denmark about military activities in Greenland. In February 1987 the MFA called in the Danish chargé d'affaires in Moscow to receive an official protest regarding the construction by the United States of a new phased array radar at Thule, which the USSR claimed was a violation of Article 6 of the 1972 ABM treaty. The day after the protest was delivered in Moscow the Soviet embassy in Copenhagen supplied the text to a reporter from a left-wing publication waging a campaign against the radar.[228]

These repeated protests about military matters sometimes created a dilemma for recipient governments. To reply to such protests was to dignify their content and to take the first step down a slope leading to the formalization of a commitment to the USSR. Norway's experience illustrates the point. In 1949 and 1951 most prospective NATO members replied to Soviet notes of protest by stressing their own defensive intentions but being careful not to say anything that could be construed as a commitment to the USSR. Norway defended its right to enter a regional collective security pact under the UN Charter, but also assured the Soviet government that "the Norwegian Government will not join in any agreement with other States involving obligations to open bases for the military forces of foreign powers on Norwegian territory as long as Norway is not attacked or exposed to threats of attack." The USSR promptly responded by offering to conclude a bilateral nonaggression pact that would obviate the need for any other collective security arrangement. The second note tried to elicit more definite pledges on the basing question by claiming that the Norwegian government had "not given a clear answer to the Soviet Government's question as to whether or not Norway's entry into the Atlantic Alliance will lead to her undertaking obligations in regard to the establishment of air or naval bases on Norwegian territory." In its reply the Oslo government reiterated its earlier points about bases and rejected the call for a nonaggression pact, pointing out that both countries had already eschewed aggression by adhering to the UN Charter.[229] Although Norway claimed that it alone had the right to determine its basing policy and could change this policy at any time, the USSR treated the exchange of notes as an international commitment rather than an exchange of information about a unilateral policy decision.

While quick to protest Western military activities, the Soviet foreign ministry often responded with harsh counterprotests to Western complaints about its own military forces. In April 1983 the government of Sweden delivered to the USSR a protest note based on the findings of the commission investigating incursions by Soviet submarines into Swedish territorial waters. The note demanded, among other things, that the Soviet navy be given "such instructions that the violations of Swedish territory cease."[230] In a subsequent meeting with Prime Minister Olof Palme, Ambassador Boris Pankin stated that the Soviet government regarded the Swedish note as "unfriendly" and demanded that the Swedish government "call to account" those responsible for the findings of the submarine commission.[231] The Soviet government responded in a similar manner to another Swedish protest the following year that concerned the incursion of a Soviet interceptor into Swedish airspace.[232]

Before glasnost protests about Western media coverage of the USSR were a common source of diplomatic acrimony. On many occasions Soviet embassies protested to host governments, in effect requesting that they take action against the local media. In October 1984, for example, the Soviet ambassador in Stockholm lodged an official protest with the Swedish foreign ministry about publication of a book purporting to reveal Soviet espionage activities in Sweden.[233] In March 1984 the Soviet embassy in Paris demanded that the French government block publication of confidential documents outlining Soviet industrial espionage activities in the West.[234] In early 1985 the Soviet ambassador in Paris lodged a protest about an article in *L'Express* that had identified the KGB resident in France and detailed his activities.[235] In April 1985 the Soviet embassy in Paris issued a statement protesting the failure of the French government to censor a program produced by actor Yves Montand that portrayed a hypothetical Soviet attack on Western Europe.[236] The Soviet government also protested direct statements by Western leaders that were regarded as provocative. In January 1981 Italy's ambassador was summoned to the foreign ministry and handed a protest regarding a recent interview with French television by President Sandro Pertini in which he suggested that there might be links between the USSR and the Italian terrorist Red Brigades organization.[237]

Soviet embassies supplemented government-to-government protests by complaining directly to the editors and journalists of the offending media. In December 1982 the Soviet embassy in Paris sent letters to the directors-general of French radio and television and to the editors of French newspapers protesting speculation in the French media about an alleged Bulgarian role in the attempt to assassinate Pope John Paul II and asking the recipients to publish the full text of a TASS statement on the subject.

Consistent with its general policy of denying that its representatives abroad engaged in espionage, the USSR usually protested expulsions of its diplomatic personnel. One day after Britain announced action against the 105 Soviet officials in 1971, the British ambassador in Moscow was summoned to the foreign ministry and presented with a note rejecting all charges and associating Britain's action with an alleged "general British policy line" of "creating obstacles in the path of a détente, particularly in European affairs" and requesting that Britain rescind the expulsions. When the British government turned down this request, the USSR retaliated with the expulsion order.

Among the most unusual Soviet protests were those registered with political parties or other nongovernmental organizations. Complaints to editors and media representatives already have been mentioned. Other protests were addressed to political parties and members of parliament. In one of his diaries François Mitterrand recalled an incident in 1974 when he received at his home Soviet ambassador Stefan Chervonenko, who had come to deliver an official protest from the CPSU to the French Socialist Party regarding the situation in Portugal. According to Mitterrand, the ambassador alluded to the activities of the Socialist International in that country and declared: "The Central Committee of the Communist Party of the USSR wishes you to know that our leaders will not tolerate any foreign interference in the affairs of Portugal."[238]

A test of Soviet policy in the future will be whether such protests continue. In the past some Soviet complaints to Western governments reflected genuine concern about matters in which the USSR had a legitimate interest, but many were a form of pressure and harassment. The number of such protests to West European governments appears to have declined in recent years (although there is no central registry of protests, some of which may not even be publicized). On the other hand, in 1989 the Soviet foreign ministry began issuing protests on various matters to the newly democratic countries of Eastern Europe. The USSR has also agreed, in the September 1990 Treaty on the Final Settlement on Germany, that there is no longer any legal basis deriving from Potsdam and the other World War II agreements upon which it can protest to the Federal Republic of Germany or third countries about various activities on German soil. It remains to be seen, however, whether the USSR will formulate new protests to the united Germany on the basis of the Final Settlement Treaty itself or the sweeping USSR-FRG bilateral agreements that were also concluded in the fall of 1990.

5 Parliaments, Political Parties, and Trade Unions

Parliaments

International contacts among parliamentarians first were institutionalized in 1889, with the founding in Paris of the Inter-Parliamentary Conference for International Arbitration. In 1899 the organization changed its name to the Inter-Parliamentary Union (IPU) to reflect its broadening interests, but arbitration remained a prime concern. Members of the Russian Duma attended IPU conferences between 1906 and the outbreak of World War I in 1914.[1] After the revolution the Bolsheviks made no attempt to reaffiliate with the IPU. They opposed arbitration, identified the IPU with "bourgeois pacifism" and an incorrect line on international issues, and drew a sharp distinction between parliamentary democracy and their system of proletarian democracy based on workers' soviets.[2]

The Soviet attitude toward parliamentary contacts changed somewhat in the 1930s. A delegation from the Supreme Soviet went to Turkey in 1933 to participate in celebrations of the tenth anniversary of Atatürk's revolution, and the influence of bourgeois parliaments was tacitly recognized in the popular front strategy of 1935. The 1936 Stalin constitution also reorganized the Soviet legislature, establishing a pseudo-parliamentary system based on universal direct suffrage and territorial constituencies rather than the election of deputies from production units.[3]

The trend toward superficial accommodation with Western parliamentarism continued during World War II and immediately thereafter. During the war the USSR exchanged parliamentary delegations with Britain and expressed interest in joining the IPU. In 1946 a Bulgarian group attended a preparatory meeting of the IPU and discreetly inquired about membership for the Supreme Soviet. The USSR subsequently was invited to send a delegation to the first postwar IPU Conference, scheduled to take place in Cairo in 1947, but for reasons that are not clear the Supreme Soviet ultimately chose not to participate. Groups from Bulgaria, Czechoslovakia, Hungary, Romania, and Yugoslavia—all prewar members of the IPU—did attend, but in 1949 the East European parliaments suspended their participation in IPU activities, and there were no further overtures to the IPU from them or the Supreme Soviet until after Stalin's death.

Bilateral Relations

The USSR resumed bilateral parliamentary exchanges in 1954. Building upon the wartime contact with Britain, in August of that year the Supreme Soviet invited the Houses of Commons and Lords to send an all-party delegation to the USSR the following month.[4] There was one other official exchange in 1954: a visit to the USSR by a Finnish delegation.

The revival of bilateral exchanges was paralleled by new initiatives toward the IPU, first by the East European parliaments and later by the Supreme Soviet. In 1954 inter-parliamentary groups from Bulgaria, Hungary, Romania, and Czechoslovakia were reconstituted. By the end of the year these groups were participating in the IPU and calling on it to "broaden its membership."[5] In February 1955 the Supreme Soviet issued an appeal to the parliaments of the world calling for "the establishment of direct relations between Parliaments, the exchange of parliamentary delegations, [and] the hearing of delegations from one country by the Parliament of another country." Contact of this kind, the appeal explained, would "answer the desire of the peoples of the world for friendly relations and for cooperation."[6] On June 29 the deputies to the Supreme Soviet formed a national parliamentary group, which applied for and was granted membership at the IPU's annual conference in Helsinki later in the year.[7]

IPU membership was followed by an upsurge in bilateral exchanges. In June 1955 a delegation of the Swedish Riksdag came to the USSR at the invitation of the Supreme Soviet.[8] In September a visiting delegation of French Deputies and Senators traveled to the USSR and was received by Khrushchev.[9] Later in the same year the Supreme Soviet hosted official delegations from Austria, Belgium, and Luxembourg.

Within two years of resuming bilateral exchanges the Supreme Soviet was exploring ways to institutionalize its contacts with Western parliaments. In October 1956 a group of Soviet delegates announced the formation of a standing Soviet-Franco Parliamentary group, and it was expected that a counterpart Franco-Soviet group soon would be formed. But establishment of the first formal link between the Supreme Soviet and a Western parliament was delayed by the Suez and Hungarian crises. A Soviet delegation was scheduled to visit France in November, but asked to postpone the trip indefinitely.[10] A standing Franco-Soviet parliamentary group eventually was formed in late 1957, after a delegation of French parliamentarians made a post-Suez visit to Moscow. Over one hundred deputies representing all parties joined the group, whose purpose was to develop regular contacts with its Soviet counterpart.[11] In 1958 Italian-Soviet and Soviet-Italian as well as British-Soviet and Soviet-British groups also were formed.

The idea for these standing bilateral groups may have come from the Western side, and specifically from West European Socialists and Social Democrats looking for a politically safe way to establish contact with the CPSU. In his meetings with Khrushchev and Bulganin in Britain in 1956 British Labour Party leader Hugh Gaitskell complained about Soviet attempts to deal with Labour through the British Communist Party and its associated fronts, and suggested the formation of an Anglo-Soviet Parliamentary Committee that would be comprised of representatives from all parties and that would provide an untainted forum through which Labour and the CPSU could maintain contact.[12]

The group formed in 1958 served this purpose. In early 1959 Mikhail Suslov traveled to Britain as a Soviet parliamentarian, and in September of that year a Labour Party delegation headed by Gaitskell went to the USSR as guests of the Soviet parliamentary group. Labour later ceased to have such Gaitskellian qualms about unmediated contacts with the CPSU, but the parliamentary cover continued to play a role in Soviet and East European dealings with the West German Social Democratic Party (SPD) into the 1980s.

The Supreme Soviet also tried to enlist Western parliaments in joint foreign policy actions, but generally was unsuccessful in this regard. It issued appeals on various international issues to Western and Third World parliaments, some of which called for closer forms of inter-parliamentary cooperation in the foreign policy sphere. In May 1957, for example, the Supreme Soviet passed a resolution calling for the establishment of a USSR-U.K.-U.S. inter-parliamentary committee that would exchange opinions on possible steps leading to a ban on nuclear testing.[13] This offer was conveyed to the British Parliament through the Soviet embassy in London, but mainly elicited a sharp protest from the foreign office, where it was seen as a ploy to intensify opposition pressures on the government.

There was, in fact, a rather close correlation between improvements in relations between governments and the level of inter-parliamentary contacts, as the latter were used by governments to open doors and symbolize improving ties. In 1956 the French authorities decided that a parliamentary delegation had to go to Moscow before the prime minister could accept Bulganin's invitation to visit. The visit of Jacques Chaban-Delmas, president of the French National Assembly, to the USSR in early 1960 paved the way for Khrushchev's visit to France some months later. Similarly, Podgornyi's visit to France in February 1964, while technically a parliamentary mission, had almost the character of an intergovernmental summit.

After the initial breakthroughs of the 1950s, the development of additional formal parliamentary relationships proceeded slowly. By

1967 the Supreme Soviet had managed to conclude group-to-group agreements with only three additional parliaments, one of which—the Belgian—was West European. (The others were the Japanese Diet and the Mexican Parliament.) Further breakthroughs did not occur until the general warming of Soviet-West European relations in the early 1970s. In February 1971 an all-party, West-German-Soviet group was constituted within the Bundestag, and a counterpart group was formed within the Supreme Soviet in May of that year. In June 1972 the first Soviet parliamentary delegation was welcomed in the FRG, and a West German group made a return visit in the fall of the following year.[14] The Austrian Parliament also established a bilateral group in the early 1970s.[15]

In addition to failing to institutionalize its relations with many Western parliaments, the Supreme Soviet had difficulty in sustaining even a modest level of ad hoc exchanges. After the promising start of 1955 and the first part of 1956, the Suez, Hungarian, and Berlin crises dampened the pace of contact. The number of exchanges increased in the 1960s, but cancellations and indefinite postponements occurred in response to the 1968 Warsaw Pact invasion of Czechoslovakia and again in 1979–81, as tensions heightened over Poland, Afghanistan, and INF. Delegations from the Supreme Soviet came to Britain as guests of the Parliament in November 1966, March 1973, and December 1984.[16] British groups made return visits in May 1968, April 1977, and May 1986.[17] The five-year break after 1968 and the seven-year break after 1977 were in large part attributable to the Soviet invasions of Czechoslovakia and Afghanistan.[18] But even these fairly infrequent exchanges could play an important role in bilateral relations, as was seen most vividly in December 1984 when Gorbachev, a Politburo member who was widely believed to be Chernenko's probable successor, assumed his parliamentary role to lead the Supreme Soviet delegation to Britain.[19]

After an initial visit to the USSR in 1973, an all-party delegation of the Bundestag did not travel to the USSR until November 1985. A second such delegation went to the USSR in August 1986, and a Supreme Soviet delegation made a return visit to West Germany in October 1986.[20] But after Chancellor Kohl made his remarks comparing Gorbachev to the Nazi propaganda chief Joseph Goebbels the Supreme Soviet postponed another West German delegation scheduled to visit the USSR in the fall of 1986.

Franco-Soviet parliamentary contacts were less subject to disruption. France underlined its desire for continuity in relations with the USSR when the president of the National Assembly, Chaban-Delmas, went to Moscow in January 1980—less than a month after the Soviet invasion of Afghanistan—and met with Brezhnev as well as Soviet parliamentarians. (Ironically, Chaban-Delmas broke off his visit after two days to protest the arrest and exile of Andrei Sakharov, which was announced an hour after the meeting with Brezhnev.)[21] Other leading French parliamentarians stressed the importance of contacts with the Supreme Soviet, "regardless of fluctuations in the external political situation."[22]

In the 1980s the relative importance of all-party parliamentary exchanges declined somewhat, as meetings between the Foreign Affairs Commission of the Supreme Soviet and counterpart committees in Western parliaments became more common. These more issue-specific exchanges focused less on the promotion of general international understanding than on the main policy issues of the day. On the Soviet side, they enabled a relatively small number of parliamentarians with full-time jobs in the foreign policy establishment to increase their access to influential Western parliamentarians as well as, during trips to Western capitals, to government officials and the media.

In November 1982 the Supreme Soviet announced the formation of a special section of the USSR parliamentary group on the problems of peace and disarmament, one of whose purposes was to activate "contacts with analogous foreign sections and organizations."[23] In March 1985 the Supreme Soviet invited Attilio Ruffini, the Christian Democratic chairman of the Defense Commission in the Italian Chamber of Deputies, to Moscow for an exchange of views. This was the first Soviet exchange with the defense committee of a NATO country.[24] At the same time, the Soviet side remained interested in further extensions of the formula pioneered by the French National Assembly in 1957, and used these more targeted meetings to promote the formation of all-party groups. During a March 1987 exchange of foreign affairs commissions with the Spanish Cortes, for example, Aleksandr Iakovlev suggested that "we ought to think of setting up Soviet-Spanish parliamentary groups within the framework of [our] exchanges."[25] Such groups, nonetheless, remained an exception in Soviet-West European parliamentary relations.

Multilateral Relations

As noted, a Soviet parliamentary group entered the IPU in 1955, whereupon it became a leading advocate of the "politicization" of organization. Along with Third World and other Communist delegations, the Soviet group was responsible for shifting the IPU's agenda from such traditional areas of concern as dispute resolution and the study of parliaments to day-to-day political issues of interest to governments.

While Soviet participants helped to promote the politicization of the IPU, they were not always pleased with the outcome of IPU deliberations on controversial issues. The Supreme Soviet long was unable to secure admission of the East German and North Korean parliaments, even though their West German and South Korean counterparts were represented. Soviet prestige suffered a blow in 1967 when the IPU Secretariat cancelled a meeting scheduled to take place in Moscow after the Soviet group refused to guarantee the admission of parliamentarians from South Korea.[26] The IPU also could become a forum for international criticism of Soviet foreign policy. Parliamentarians from Europe and the Third World condemned the invasions of Hungary and to a lesser extent Czechoslovakia. The IPU condemned the Soviet invasion of Afghanistan and "deeply deplored" the shooting down of KAL 007.[27]

On the other hand, the IPU generally was responsive to appeals for peace and disarmament, the main items on the Soviet agenda. The Soviet parliamentary group was able to secure passage of resolutions obliquely supportive of Soviet foreign policy initiatives and to enlist IPU involvement in propaganda undertakings staged by the Soviet government.[28] An assistant secretary from the IPU's resident staff attended the October 1973 World Congress of Peace Forces in Moscow, and the chairman of the USSR Inter-Parliamentary Group published a glowing report of the Congress in the *Inter-Parliamentary Bulletin*.[29]

From the Soviet perspective, the IPU also was important in providing a mechanism for the establishment of an all-European parliamentary assembly. The idea of a regional meeting of European parliaments went back to the 1966 Canberra session of the Inter-Parliamentary Council, at which the Yugoslav delegate introduced a resolution proposing a regional conference.[30] The Soviet attitude at first was skeptical. The IPU Council authorized parliamentarians from Yugoslavia and Belgium to explore the organization of a conference. Soviet and East European parliamentary groups objected when East Germany was not included on the list of participants and when the Belgians circulated an agenda that included free flow of persons and other items that the USSR preferred not to discuss. But these obstacles to a regional meeting eventually gave way as the East Germans were admitted to the IPU in 1972 and as the USSR and the West moved toward agreement at the governmental level on the agenda of the impending European security conference. Henceforth, the USSR became among the most enthusiastic proponents of a regional parliamentary forum.

With the Finns serving as hosts, the first European Inter-Parliamentary Conference convened in early 1973, in the same city and at approximately the same time as intergovernmental preparatory consultations for the CSCE. The Soviet delegation was led by Aleksei Shitikov, a leading parliamentarian and head of the Soviet Committee for European Security. The USSR had three apparent objectives for the meeting: to generate parliamentary pressure on Western governments for an early convening of the CSCE; to adopt a "final act" that would serve as a model for the governmental agreement expected to come out of the CSCE; and to institutionalize parliamentary contacts at the all-European level.[31]

Each of these objectives was at least partially achieved. The conference's final act expressed support for "the convening of a Conference on Security and Cooperation in Europe (CSCE) on a governmental level as soon as possible after the positive conclusion of the multilateral preparatory consultations in Helsinki."[32] More important than the endorsement itself was the fact that the assembly drew media and parliamentary attention to the low-key and preparatory intergovernmental consultations, and thus helped to generate interest in a project that was as yet more important to the Soviet than to Western governments. In terms of content, the final act was also relatively favorable from the Soviet perspective. The Western parliamentarians were not pushovers, but they could not negotiate in six days what the professional diplomats took over two years to achieve in Geneva. The final act thus contained a number of formulations that Western delegations later fought to keep out of the CSCE Final Act. To what extent precedents established in the parliamentary document influenced the intergovernmental negotiations is impossible to tell, but presumably they had some effect.[33]

On the matter of institutionalization, the USSR and its allies won only a partial victory. The Finns proposed the establishment, under IPU auspices, of a "Euroforum" for the consideration of European questions. The Finnish proposal was supported by the Soviet and East European representatives, but opposed by many Western parliamentarians, some of whom were concerned about "rushing into hasty institutionalization of this kind of meeting," and others of whom suggested that the same purpose could be achieved by "adding an extra session of a few hours" devoted to European issues at regular IPU conferences.[34] The conference adopted a compromise proposal by asking the Inter-Parliamentary Council "to authorize the organization, within the framework of the IPU's activities, of meetings at suitable intervals." Following discussion and approval by the IPU, such meetings were held in Belgrade in 1975, Vienna in 1978, Brussels in 1980, Budapest in 1983, Bonn in 1986, and Bucharest in 1989.

Each of these conferences adopted resolutions mandating increasingly extensive parliamentary links, with growing emphasis on the détente process. The 1975 Final Act endorsed the intensification of bilateral and multilateral parliamentary contacts.[35] The 1978 Resolutions contained a similar appeal, but also called on "parliamentarians to strengthen the bilateral sections in existence within the

National Groups" and "to promote the creation of new sections to form a network of interparliamentary contacts aimed at promoting détente."[36] This formulation, which was repeated in more urgent terms in the 1980 Concluding Resolutions, constituted a multilateral endorsement of the USSR's preferred formula for the establishment of parallel sections modeled after the USSR-France/France-USSR arrangement of 1957.[37] The 1983 Resolution repeated all of the earlier recommendations, but for the first time called for the encouragement of contacts between parliamentary committees dealing with foreign affairs and with military and defense questions.[38] Soviet support for this language reflected the growing Soviet interest in working through the Foreign Affairs Commission of the Supreme Soviet and the formation of a section for disarmament the previous year. The 1986 Resolutions reaffirmed all previous recommendations, but called on the national groups "to organize fora, symposia, round tables and other meetings at the regional and subregional levels, with a view to taking up issues regarding the strengthening of security and co-operation in Europe."[39]

The USSR traditionally enjoyed certain advantages in such multilateral parliamentary gatherings. First, it benefited from the fact that its delegations were tightly coordinated and expressed a uniform viewpoint, whereas the Western groups were divided within and across national lines. The USSR also could expect virtually automatic support from East European delegations on votes and resolutions, as well as from most of the Communist members of Western delegations.[40] Second, the USSR had the advantage of greater continuity in selecting its delegations. The two most prominent Soviet delegation heads of the 1970s and 1980s, Shitikov and Lev Tolkunov, were *apparatchiks* who, unlike most Western and many Third World parliamentarians, did not have to fear losing their seats in elections. (Many West European parliamentarians elevated from backbench to cabinet status also were lost to international parliamentary activities.) Third, and related to the previous point, Soviet delegates did not face conflicting demands from their constituents or from other European or Atlantic parliamentary bodies, and thus had a certain incentive to encourage the proliferation of international meetings. In the discussions of the early 1970s regarding the creation of a parliamentary Euroforum, a Danish representative complained about the increasingly loaded schedule of international parliamentary meetings and of the growing conflict between these meetings and the requirements of their constituencies. Other Western parliamentarians voiced similar concerns.[41]

In addition to having smaller overall demands on their time, Soviet parliamentarians did not have to fear the unexpected schedule conflicts that arise in many countries when governments fall and national elections are called. They thus had an interest in adhering to a rigid schedule of international meetings. As hosts of the first European Parliamentary Conference, the Finns originally scheduled the meeting for November so that it would coincide precisely, in accordance with Soviet wishes, with the opening of the CSCE inter-governmental preparatory consultations. When the Bundestag was dissolved unexpectedly in September and elections scheduled for November 19, the West German delegation informed the IPU that it would not be able to send a delegation to Helsinki in the middle of November, and asked the council for a brief postponement. This request was strongly, if in the end unsuccessfully, opposed by the Soviets and their allies.[42]

While the USSR became an increasingly active participant in the IPU and in all-European, inter-parliamentary conferences, it remained hostile or indifferent to cooperation with West European and North Atlantic parliamentary bodies that excluded the USSR and its allies: the European Parliament, the Assembly of the WEU, the North Atlantic Assembly, the Council of Europe, and the Nordic Council. The Soviet attitude was consistent with an overall opposition to supranational integration in Western Europe, as well as reflected the security and human rights orientations of these bodies. Soviet opposition manifested itself not only in negative commentary in the press, but also in the fact that the Warsaw Pact and the Council for Mutual Economic Assistance (CMEA) made no attempt to establish multilateral parliamentary assemblies that could serve as possible partners for these bodies.

The Soviet attitude toward cooperation with subregional parliamentary bodies began to change in 1985 after Gorbachev's accession to power. In May of that year he met with Gianni Cervetti, an official of the Italian Communist Party (PCI) and head of the Communist group in the European Parliament. In December 1985 a delegation from the Socialist group in the European Parliament went to the USSR as guests of the Soviet parliamentary group and the Soviet Committee for European Security. TASS described the visit as "a step toward establishing ties between the USSR Supreme Soviet and the European Parliament."[43] A delegation from the European People's Party (Christian Democratic) group in the European Parliament made a similar visit in March 1987.[44]

In February 1987 the Supreme Soviet invited the WEU Assembly to send a delegation to Moscow for talks. This overture was consistent not only with a new approach to East-West parliamentary links, but with the Soviet call for an East-West dialogue on security issues that was launched in the January 1983 Prague Political Declaration and given a new impetus in the June 1986 Budapest appeal. The Soviet invitation was greeted with caution in the WEU, but accepted after an 11–2 vote in the assembly, with the British delegates formally opposed.[45] A delegation of Soviet parliamentarians made a return visit to the WEU Assembly in July 1989, and an agreement was reached to hold meetings at least once each year, alternating between Paris and Moscow. The subject of these meetings would be limited to the "military-political aspects of European security."[46]

Exchanges of parliamentary delegations of the Parliamentary Assembly of the Council of Europe began in mid-1987, and in June 1989 the USSR, along with Poland, Hungary, and Yugoslavia, was accorded a special "guest status" in the Council of Europe.[47] The Supreme Soviet was allotted eighteen nonvoting seats in the Parliamentary Assembly, and members of the Soviet parliament were permitted to address plenary sessions and attend sessions of working commissions to which they were invited. The Soviet government also announced its readiness to adhere to certain Council conventions in the fields of environment, culture, education, and television.[48] Later in the same month a delegation from the Council of Europe went to Moscow for talks with the Supreme Soviet and the foreign ministry.[49] In July Gorbachev led a Soviet delegation to the Council, and delivered an important speech to a plenary session in Strasbourg in which he noted that "interparliamentary ties are of undoubtedly major significance for adding dynamism to the common European process."[50] At the conclusion of Gorbachev's visit it was agreed to establish a joint Soviet-Council of Europe working group that would develop proposals for contact and cooperation. Iuri Deriabin, the head of the MFA's European Security and Cooperation Department, was named the chief of the Soviet side of the working group, which met for the first time in Strasbourg in September 1989.[51] These developments would not have been possible without the changes in the Soviet human rights situation that had taken place in the previous four years, and probably not without the relative democratization of the Soviet parliament in the spring of 1989.

On the same day that Gorbachev was speaking in Strasbourg a delegation from the North Atlantic Assembly was in the USSR for the first time at the invitation of the Supreme Soviet, and held talks with Defense Minister Iazov, officials from the CMEA, and Deputy Foreign Minister Petrovskii.[52] Another innovation was the joint visit by Rita Süssmuth, president of the Bundestag, and her French counterpart, Laurent Fabius, to Moscow in November 1989. Gorbachev received the two parliamentarians and welcomed a proposal by them for regular trilateral working contacts among the committees of the three parliaments in the areas of law, environment, and international relations.[53]

As the USSR revised its policies regarding cooperation with West European parliamentary organizations it was to be expected that it would try to create an East European counterpart to these organizations. Representatives of the Warsaw Pact member-state parliaments met in Sofia in November 1983 and issued an appeal to the parliaments of the CSCE participating states urging them to block the impending INF deployments, but the meeting did not result in any steps toward a permanent Warsaw Pact parliamentary committee.[54] However, in the summer of 1987 the chairmen of the Pact member-state parliaments agreed to hold annual meetings on a rotating basis to examine ways to "add dynamism to the general European process" through inter-parliamentary cooperation. At a September 1988 meeting of bloc parliamentary leaders the Soviet representative, Iuri Khristoradnov, declared that the USSR was in favor of creating a multilateral commission of the socialist country parliaments, which he said would "help improve coordination of foreign policy actions on a parliamentary level, strengthen the position of the socialist community in the United Nations, and open an additional channel in the IPU for cooperation with interparliamentary organizations of the capitalist countries."[55] Closer coordination of parliamentary ties among Warsaw Pact member states was linked to a new effort to create an all-European parliamentary assembly. In July 1987 the Polish Sejm proposed the convening of a meeting of the chairmen of the parliaments of states participating in the CSCE. The chairmen of the East bloc parliaments immediately endorsed the offer in an "Appeal to the Parliaments and Parliamentarians of CSCE Countries," and the proposed meeting took place in Warsaw in December 1988.[56]

By early 1989 it appeared that the Warsaw Pact was moving toward the formal establishment of a parliamentary body that would give substance to the claim that the Pact was becoming a more "political" organization.[57] But it soon became clear that the USSR had waited too long to take this step, and that at the very moment that a Pact parliamentary body would have been most useful for foreign policy purposes it had become impossible to convene because of domestic upheavals within the Communist world. The newly pluralist parliaments of Eastern Europe had little interest in bolstering Eastern institutions, and hastened to step up their own links with West European parliaments and parliamentary bodies. Nor could the Soviet leadership be confident that independence-minded Soviet deputies from the Baltics and other republics would not use such a forum to promote their own agendas.

The New Supreme Soviet

The restructuring of the Soviet parliament in 1989 was mainly connected with Gorbachev's internal reforms, but it also had implications for the USSR's parliamentary diplomacy and indeed for Soviet

foreign policy in general. Following the first competitive multican-
didate elections since the October Revolution, in May 1989 a new
Congress of People's Deputies convened in Moscow. The Congress
in turn elected a smaller Supreme Soviet to replace the existing body
and chose Gorbachev as its chairman.[58] The new body was still less
powerful than its Western counterparts, but it was endowed with
real authority on both domestic and international matters and soon
showed that it was prepared to challenge the government, the CPSU,
and even Gorbachev.

Although partial and incomplete, the democratization of the Soviet parliament transformed the nature of Soviet-West European parliamentary ties. As a leading Soviet parliamentary official himself
acknowledged, past parliamentary meetings often were "nothing
more than formal protocol." Unlike its predecessor, the new Supreme Soviet was "directly involved in making political decisions,
including decisions on international matters,"[59] and this inevitably
affected its relations with other parliaments. Supreme Soviet delegations were warmly received throughout Western Europe, doors
were opened in traditionally critical forums such as the Council of
Europe, and proposals put forward for even more extensive parliamentary links.[60]

Gorbachev also took advantage of his new status as the USSR's
leading parliamentarian in his conduct of foreign policy. On his first
foreign trip after his election as chairman of the Supreme Soviet he
visited the West German Bundestag and met with President Süssmuth and some of her colleagues to discuss both substantive issues
and the further development of parliamentary ties.[61] On subsequent
trips to France, Finland, and Italy, he also went out of his way to
stress his parliamentary status.[62]

The new parliament was better configured than its predecessor to
interact with Western parliamentary committees. It established an
International Affairs Committee and a Committee for Defense and
State Security Questions, each of which had three permanent subcommittees. The committees broke new ground by holding substantive hearings and even inviting foreign officials and experts to testify.
The Defense and State Security Committee developed new links
with Western defense committees, as well as worked with the group
for the Public Monitoring of the Reduction of Soviet Armed Forces
and Armaments, a public organization set up in 1989 in part "to
maintain contacts with representatives of the public abroad" and to
"invite foreign public figures and parliamentarians" to Soviet self-
monitoring activities.[63]

Members of the new Soviet parliament also showed that their interests in international contact went beyond the traditional drum-
ming up of support for Soviet foreign policy initiatives. Stressing

their desire to obtain information that they regarded as necessary to fulfill their new roles, committees were eager to study Western parliamentary practices and to learn about Western conditions and policies. Moreover, exchanges quickly extended beyond their traditional focus on foreign policy and arms control to include labor, environmental, and other domestically oriented commissions and committees.

It remained to be seen, however, how much real authority the new parliament would exercise over Soviet foreign and defense policy and whether it would use foreign contacts to promote policies and international agreements not necessarily endorsed by the president or the ministries. The international affairs and defense committees included such establishment stalwarts as Valentin Falin, Georgii Arbatov, and Marshal Akhromeev, and radical deputies charged that the apparatus of the parliament, which was tightly controlled by Gorbachev and Lukianov, retained a firm grip on inter-parliamentary exchanges.[64] But whatever its shortcomings, the new parliament was more representative and more powerful than any previous Soviet legislative body and as a consequence enjoyed far more credibility in the West.

Ties between the Soviet and other European parliaments entered a new stage in mid-1990, after the West proposed the creation of a parliamentary wing of the CSCE process. The November 1990 Paris summit endorsed the establishment of an Assembly of Europe that was expected to include parliamentarians from all of the CSCE participating states.

Party-to-Party Relations

Socialist Parties

Relations between the CPSU and the Socialist and Social Democratic parties of Western Europe long were overshadowed by the bitter ideological and political rivalry between the Second and Third Internationals. The Communist and socialist movements both claimed to be the heirs of Marx, and each blamed the other for the breakup of working class unity after World War I. Communists accused the socialists of "opportunism" and of selling out the true interests of the working class, while socialists condemned the antidemocratic methods and subservience to a foreign power that characterized the Communist movement.

The Bolsheviks founded the Communist International—or what became known as the Comintern—in March 1919. In the summer of 1920 the new international promulgated its famous "Twenty-One Conditions," which included a demand that parties in other countries adopt Leninist methods of internal organization. Most Western socialist parties split, with a part becoming "bolshevized" and joining the Soviet-sponsored international and a part retaining its traditions and adhering to the old Second International. Between 1920 and 1922 there was talk of contact and cooperation between the rival internationals, and in 1922 a unity conference was held in Berlin. But the meeting "began and ended in violent mutual recriminations," and was in fact the last official meeting between representatives of the Socialist International and the Soviet Communist Party until 1979.[65]

In the interwar period the Comintern primarily followed a "front from below" strategy. Communists sought to penetrate the socialist-oriented trade unions but spurned cooperation with the Socialist parties. Soviet embassies maintained some contact with party leaders, but the Soviet government rebuffed Western efforts to send prominent socialists to Moscow as ambassadors.[66] Unofficial delegations of Western socialists made visits to the USSR and were given carefully controlled glimpses of Soviet reality, but the Bolsheviks tried to avoid working through the party leaderships. The hosts controlled the composition of delegations and determined their itinerary.[67]

The only partial exception to this general pattern was in the 1930s, when the USSR urged foreign Communists to form popular fronts against the rising Nazi and fascist dangers. The main emphasis in the popular front era was on horizontal cooperation between Socialist and Communist parties, but the USSR also stepped up its direct ties with Western Socialist parties. Prominent socialists, such as Attlee, were invited to the USSR for talks with an array of Soviet officials.[68] But the popular fronts collapsed in 1939 with the announcement of the Hitler-Stalin Pact, and whatever margin of trust the USSR had gained in socialist circles was destroyed.[69]

During World War II many in the British Labour Party—the only surviving Socialist party in Europe besides those of Sweden and Switzerland—hoped that the Anglo-Soviet alliance would establish a basis for cooperation between the parties. In the spring of 1942 Labour's National Executive Committee announced that it was prepared to send a delegation to Moscow to seek an understanding with the CPSU on restoring unity in the postwar era.[70] Labour reaffirmed this decision at the 1943, 1944, and 1945 conferences, and at one point requested the Soviet ambassador in London to arrange a delegation visit to Moscow. But Stalin rebuffed these overtures. He was displeased by Labour's failure to back the second front, and was in any case wedded to the traditional Soviet stance in favor of horizontal links between Labour and the British Communist Party.[71] In late 1942 the Communists made the first of several wartime requests for affiliation with Labour. Some constituencies favored a merger, but all resolutions to that effect that were introduced at Labour's annual conferences were defeated.[72] Stalin finally received an official Labour Party delegation in July 1946, but he would not be drawn into a discussion of the socialist-Communist split and of ways to heal it.

Relations between the socialists and Communists deteriorated after the war, although they did not reach a low point until after the founding of the Cominform in September 1947. With its return to power in the summer of 1945 Labour's interest in a party-to-party channel to the Kremlin declined, while the Soviets held Labour responsible for Britain's stances on such issues as Poland and reparations from Germany.[73] Relations were especially damaged by developments in Eastern Europe, where Socialist and Social Democratic parties continued to exist but were coming under increasing Soviet and Communist pressure. The leaders of these parties (presumably with backing from the USSR but also with an eye to their own survival) called for the creation of a World Federation of Trade Unions-type (WFTU) international comprised of both Socialist and Communist parties. The Western socialists rejected this idea, but deferred the establishment of a new international that the Eastern parties would have been prevented from joining. Instead they formed a loose organization known as the Committee of International Socialist Conferences (COMISCO). The Eastern European Socialist parties attended some of the conferences convened under COMISCO's auspices, and for a time a split was averted.[74]

The Communist coup in Czechoslovakia in February 1948 and the forcible absorption of the East European parties by the Communists in the course of that year dashed all hope for an understanding between the socialist and Communist movements. COMISCO became more overtly anti-Communist, and in May 1949 expelled the Italian Socialist Party (PSI) for refusing to dissolve its pact with the Communists.[75] After a series of preliminary meetings in June 1951 the Western parties gathered in Frankfurt to establish a new Socialist International. Characterized by the official journal of the Cominform as a gathering of "hardened Wall Street agents," the Frankfurt meeting adopted a declaration that rejected capitalism but affirmed that socialism could be achieved only on the basis of political and social freedom guaranteed by democratic political systems. In place of the liquidated parties of Eastern Europe, the International welcomed into its ranks Socialist parties in exile. It strongly discouraged cooperation by member parties with the Communists, and held up the fate of the East European socialists as a warning of the dangers of cooperation with domestic or foreign Communists.[76]

The Soviets had in any case long since abandoned the coalition strategies they favored in the immediate postwar period. At its founding the Cominform condemned the alliance strategies previously pursued by the French and Italian parties. There was no change in this stance until after Stalin's death. In his report to the Nineteenth Party Congress in October 1952 Malenkov attacked the British, French, and West German parties, which he claimed were "directly responsible" for the hostile policies of the Western "ruling circles." He also accused the parties in Sweden, Denmark, Norway, Finland, and Austria of following the larger parties and "fighting the peaceloving and democratic forces of the peoples."[77]

A change in Soviet attitudes toward the non-Communist left began shortly after Stalin's death and first was reflected in informal contacts. Harold Wilson, who as president of the Board of Trade under Attlee had had extensive dealings with the Soviet government, made a private visit to Moscow in June 1953 and saw both Molotov and Anastas Mikoian.[78] In August 1954 a Labour delegation on its way to China made what was expected to be a brief stopover in Moscow. But "local municipal authorities" suggested a longer stay and the delegation, which was led by Attlee and Aneurin Bevan, was accorded an unprecedented welcome, as virtually the entire Politburo turned up at a dinner in honor of the delegation hosted by the British ambassador.[79]

The Soviet leadership was aware of the differences between party leader Hugh Gaitskell, who favored a tough line toward the USSR and who supported a strong, rearmed West Germany, and those like Bevan and Hugh Dalton who took a different line. Molotov and Khrushchev both dwelt upon the theme of German rearmament and its alleged dangers. Khrushchev "made a very blunt speech" in which he spoke of the "differences in the Labour Party and even in the delegation," and asked how some of Bevan's published views on Germany were compatible with the Labour Party's official support for the European Defense Community (EDC).[80] It also was arranged for Bevan to make an early return visit to the USSR.[81]

Efforts to build ties with the socialists continued in 1955 and were bolstered by the bilateral summits discussed in chapter four. The CPSU put out feelers to the Austrian, British, Danish, and Finnish Socialist parties for different forms of contact and cooperation. One such overture was made on the occasion of Norwegian prime minister Gerhardsen's December 1955 visit to Moscow, when Khrushchev, acting in his capacity as first secretary of the CPSU, handed Gerhardsen (who was also leader of the Norwegian Labor Party) a seven-point memorandum outlining specific forms of permanent cooperation, including party, trade union, and youth exchanges.[82] The Norwegians rejected most of Khrushchev's proposals but did agree to exchange journalists from party newspapers.[83]

In his report to the Twentieth Party Congress in February 1956 Khrushchev claimed that the Communist parties were the "most active and consistent fighters against the war danger," but acknowledged that "many other social circles are also opposing war." He regretted that "in many countries the working class has been split for many years," and called for "unity of the working class, of its trade unions, unity of action of its political parties, the Communists, the socialists and other workers' parties."[84] This was a sharp reversal of the Malenkov line of 1952. At the end of March Ponomarev published a major article in *Pravda* appealing for working-class unity. This and other Soviet gestures prompted the Moscow correspondent of the *New York Times* to conclude that the "drive to win the sympathy and cooperation of Socialist parties is rapidly emerging as the dominant theme of Soviet policy in Europe."[85] In another move that most observers believed was intended to facilitate a rapprochement with the socialists (and with the Yugoslavs), on April 17 Mikoian announced the dissolution of the Cominform.[86]

The Socialist International dismissed these gestures as cosmetic. Its council met in Zurich shortly after the conclusion of the CPSU Congress and issued a resolution that acknowledged a change of Soviet tactics but stated that this was "not adequate proof of a genuine change in the principles and policies of Communist dictatorship."[87] It reaffirmed its rejection of "any united front or any other form of political co-operation with the parties of dictatorship" and stated that the International considered a "minimum precondition, even for the possibility of talks on an international basis," to be the reestablishment of free labor movements in those countries where they had been suppressed.

Despite the strong stance of the council, individual Socialist parties found it difficult to rule out all forms of contact with the CPSU. As Haakon Lie of the Norwegian party argued, "we have to accept the idea of delegations on an official basis as an inevitable consequence of relations between our governments."[88] He went on to outline certain guidelines that were to be followed in the sending and receiving of delegations, including that their members be selected by official organs or democratic methods (rather than by the Soviet hosts, as had been common in the 1930s), that the socialists provide their own delegation secretaries and interpreters, and that members be briefed beforehand by experts on the USSR. Another leading social democratic theoretician drew a distinction between "multiplication of contacts which penetrate the Communist monopoly of propaganda" and "formal delegations based on the pretence of the alleged common aims of Communists and Socialists."[89]

The deep mutual suspicions between the Soviets and the Western socialists were highlighted during the Khrushchev-Bulganin visit to Britain in the spring of 1956. In mid-March a second secretary at the Soviet embassy in London urgently contacted Labour backbencher Richard Crossman to inquire about Labour's plans for the upcoming visit. The embassy staffer made clear that the Soviet side was interested in talks—that it "would seriously like to discuss politics with [Labour] as much as with the Government."[90] Labour had been planning to meet with the Soviets as a matter of courtesy, but there was some question in the leadership about the advisability of substantive talks on political issues. Crossman and others were receptive, but Gaitskell was adamant that "there can be no question of formal talks with the Russians."[91] Instead, he worked out an arrangement with Prime Minister Eden whereby he and the deputy leader of the party would be invited to a government-sponsored luncheon at Chequers where they could have an informal talk with Khrushchev and his delegation. Before the luncheon Gaitskell reaffirmed his position that "it was obviously impossible for us to talk about the major subjects which they [the Soviet delegation] were discussing with the Government, such as the Middle East, disarmament, etc.," but he did agree to raise two issues of special concern and about which he believed a direct dialogue with the USSR was justified: the nature of Soviet-Labour Party relations and the plight of the socialists and social democrats in Eastern Europe.[92]

It was in the discussion of the first topic that Gaitskell complained to Khrushchev about persistent Soviet attempts to deal with Labour through Communist-controlled organizations, and he suggested that the USSR approach the non-Communist Anglo-Soviet Committee of the British Council or consider forming an Anglo-Russian Parliamentary group. According to Gaitskell's account, Khrushchev and Bulganin "showed some guarded approval of the idea of an Anglo-Soviet Parliamentary Committee," but defended the role of the Communist-controlled organizations. In any case Khrushchev was less interested in the mechanics of contact with Labour than in the substance of its policies, and launched into a strong attack on the party for its attitude toward the USSR.

The second topic on Labour's agenda came up the following evening at a Labour-hosted dinner that achieved considerable notoriety at the time. The British participants asked about the fate of imprisoned social democrats in Eastern Europe and the status of Jews in the USSR. Khrushchev replied with a paranoiac speech in which he dismissed the prospects for disarmament, defended the Hitler-Stalin pact, and suggested that the British, in Crossman's paraphrase, "should join with the Russians because, if not, they would swat us off the earth like a dirty old black beetle."[93] Khrushchev left the meeting in a rage and, although things were smoothed over a bit on the following day, remained resentful and would not invite Gaitskell to Moscow until 1958.[94]

Relations between the CPSU and the Section Française de l'Internationale Ouvrière (SFIO) developed somewhat more smoothly. In

April and May members of the executive committee of the party made an official visit to the USSR.[95] But the Soviet leaders got on rather poorly with Guy Mollet, the SFIO prime minister who went to Moscow later in the month and whom the Soviet leaders deliberately attempted to shock with their coarse humor.[96] Mollet reportedly made a bad overall impression by limiting his stay to only three days and by beginning and ending his speeches with affirmations of French loyalty to the Western alliance.[97]

The Hungarian and Suez crises brought an end to the modest post-Stalin thaw in CPSU-Socialist Party relations. Khrushchev later made sporadic attempts to win over the Western socialists and to use them as pressure groups against conservative governments, but serious Soviet interest in the non-Communist left in Europe did not revive until the late 1960s. Khrushchev continued to cultivate Bevan, who traveled to the USSR in the summer of 1957 for "a few days of intimate discussion" with Khrushchev at his summer home in the Crimea. This time the main topic of concern to Khrushchev was not Germany, but the Middle East and Britain's own atomic program. According to Michael Foot, Bevan's biographer and himself a prominent member of the Labour Party's left wing, Bevan came away from the talks convinced "that an arms embargo leading to a Middle East settlement *was* possible, if only the West would undertake an intelligent initiative" and that a cessation of nuclear tests "could start the world on the road to disarmament."[98]

In October 1957 Khrushchev sent letters to several Western Socialist parties in which he asked them to meet with Soviet representatives to discuss ways to avert a Middle East war.[99] Gaitskell and Bevan agreed that it would be unconstitutional for an opposition party to negotiate with a foreign government, and reported the approach to Prime Minister Macmillan.[100] The Norwegian Labor Party also declared that it did not wish to carry on its own foreign policy, and forwarded the letter to the government.[101]

Soviet policy in Eastern Europe continued to have a dampening effect on CPSU-Socialist Party relations. Gaitskell was scheduled to go to the USSR in the summer of 1958, but cancelled his plans when it was announced by the Hungarian authorities that Imre Nagy and three associates had been tried and executed for their involvement in the uprising of 1956.[102] The Socialist International condemned the executions, and individual parties ruled out further contacts with the USSR.[103]

Just as the Berlin crisis led to stepped-up contacts at the state level, CPSU-socialist relations began to thaw somewhat in early 1959 as officials in Labour and the SPD became involved in the search for a way out of the crisis. In March 1959 a Soviet delegation led by Suslov traveled to Britain as guests of the Labour Party group in the Anglo-

Soviet Parliamentary Committee, and in September Bevan and Gaitskell led a return delegation to the USSR.[104] By this time Khrushchev (who was about to leave for his trip to the United States) appears to have lost interest in Labour, which was approaching an election that most experts believed it could not win.[105] But the visit was significant in that it resulted in a joint communiqué that expressed agreement on a number of international issues, including the need for a three-power agreement on the cessation of nuclear tests, support for a zone of controlled disarmament in Europe, and the desirability of an early summit conference. The specific points of agreement were only slightly at odds with British governmental policy and in themselves not all that controversial, but for an opposition party to record them in a joint document was a break with past practices.

The Berlin crisis also led to a flurry of Soviet contacts with the SPD. In March 1959 SPD chairman Erich Ollenhauer crossed into East Berlin for a meeting with Khrushchev to discuss the SPD's Deutschland Plan for German reunification. It was reported that West Berlin Mayor Willy Brandt also had been asked to meet with Khrushchev, but had declined.[106] Later that month Carlo Schmid of the SPD parliamentary group and Fritz Erler, party vice chairman, went to Moscow for longer and more formal discussions, at the end of which Khrushchev embarrassed his guests by unequivocally rejecting their plan and bluntly informing them that "no one wants reunification."[107]

The SPD was sharply criticized at home for its dealings with the USSR. Ollenhauer was especially singled out by those who thought that his trip to East Berlin implied acceptance of the Soviet claim that the city was part of the GDR, while Brandt was praised for rejecting the invitation. But it later was revealed that Brandt had taken the initiative in trying to arrange a meeting in East Berlin with the Soviets (working through his friend and fellow social democrat Bruno Kreisky, at that time state secretary in the Austrian foreign ministry) and that the Berlin Senate had blocked his trip. The Soviets were so interested in a meeting with Brandt—which would have promoted their concept of a "three-state" Germany—that they held up approval of the Erler-Schmid visit.[108] Khrushchev's behavior throughout this episode—his desire to receive Ollenhauer and Brandt in East Berlin, his hesitation about having Schmid and Erler come to Moscow, and his blunt rejection of their Germany plan— suggests that he had little interest in courting the West German socialists *qua* socialists and was mainly seeking to improve his position in the Berlin crisis. Brandt was of interest as the mayor of Berlin and not as a socialist.

The essentially negative Soviet attitude toward the Social Democratic parties was confirmed in the 1961 CPSU program, which contained a sharp attack on the "contemporary right-wing social-democrats," whom it characterized as "the most important ideological and political prop of the bourgeoisie within the working-class movement."[109] While some in the Soviet foreign policy establishment no doubt realized that better relations with the West European socialists could serve Soviet foreign policy objectives and for that reason might have preferred to downplay ideological differences, those officials directly responsible for contacts with the non-Communist left continued to view these parties through the Leninist prism. Western socialists gave vivid accounts of how persistently Suslov, Ponomarev, and other CPSU officials sought to promote the obsolete notion of working-class unity under Communist hegemony. Christian Pineau, a former French foreign minister who went to the USSR in 1963 as part of an SFIO delegation, recalled that Otto Kuusinen, Ponomarev, and other interlocutors "insisted on discussing, despite our opposition, the problems of rapprochement between the PCF [French Communist Party] and the SFIO."[110]

CPSU attitudes toward the non-Communist left began to change somewhat in the mid-1960s, as anti-Communist sentiment in Europe weakened and as prospects for socialist-Communist cooperation improved in several countries. The CPSU made a number of direct appeals, both public and private, for contact and cooperation with Socialist and Social Democratic parties. A delegation of the SFIO visited Moscow in the fall of 1963, and the two parties issued a communiqué that acknowledged a "large measure of agreement regarding the need to consolidate international détente."[111] In a private meeting with Brandt in late 1966 Ambassador Abrasimov broached the possibility of talks between the SPD (of which Brandt was chairman) and the CPSU, but this was rejected by Brandt.[112] Soviet commentators also expressed guarded interest in the West European "new left." Although they deplored its spontaneous tendencies and its flirtation with Trotskyism and Maoism, they saw improved prospects for united action on certain issues.

One of the difficulties that the ruling Communist parties faced in reaching out to the non-Communist left was the sectarianism of the West European Communist parties. Brezhnev reportedly complained to Polish leader Władysław Gomułka and Walter Ulbricht about the Swiss and Dutch Communist parties, which he claimed adopted a hard rhetorical line but had never managed to do anything for the working classes of their own countries. Even Ulbricht acknowledged that East Germany had tried to win over the radical students of West Berlin, but that "the comrades"—the Communists of the SED-controlled West Berlin Socialist Unity Party—"were much too clumsy."[113]

Nonetheless, after a relatively short break caused by the Prague

Spring (which occasioned sharp attacks on social democracy in the Soviet press and temporarily strengthened the hands of the sectarians in the international Communist movement) and the ensuing invasion, the CPSU continued its evolution to a less hostile stance toward the socialists. In March 1969 Suslov gave a major speech at a Moscow conference marking the fiftieth anniversary of the Comintern in which he rejected as "sectarian" the thesis of the Comintern's Sixth Congress according to which social democracy was to be regarded as the "main danger."[114] These remarks were partly directed at Ulbricht, who was resisting any rapprochement with the rival SPD. There was also a resumption of contacts with Western socialists, although often under a parliamentary cover that satisfied Western insistence on avoiding anything that appeared to suggest the establishment of formal party-to-party links. For example, in August 1969 Helmut Schmidt, the leader of the SPD group in the West German Bundestag, went to Moscow for a four-day official visit—the first by an SPD leader since the unsuccessful Erler-Schmid visit a decade earlier.[115]

The growing Soviet interest in the non-Communist left was in part a response to changes in the policies of these parties. In 1966 the Finnish Social Democrats formed a coalition with the Communists, and there were pressures on the Socialist International to rethink its policy against cooperation with Communists in domestic and international settings. In 1968 the Bureau of the International appointed a study group to look into the question. It recommended no change in the existing policy, and the International's 1969 Eastbourne Congress adopted a resolution warning that "Communist parties, in seeking united action with Social Democratic parties, generally have as their ultimate goal Communist party hegemony and one-party rule."[116]

But it was increasingly clear that the International could not control the electoral and coalition strategies of its member parties. In 1972 the French Socialist Party (PS) of François Mitterrand concluded a common program with the PCF.[117] At the April 1972 meeting of the Socialist International Bureau it was decided that member parties should be free to determine their own bilateral relations with other parties, including the Communists.[118] This change was more a recognition of the existing state of affairs than a dramatic shift, but it had symbolic importance and was welcomed in the East.[119] The Soviet government, which was suspicious of the Finnish Social Democrats, suspected the PS of Atlanticist tendencies, and saw numerous advantages in "businesslike" dealings with "bourgeois" governments, was not necessarily interested in seeing Communist-Socialist Party coalitions succeed, but it welcomed the lessening of socialist hostility toward the Communists.

In the early 1970s the focus of Soviet interest in the Western socialists shifted from domestic radicalism to foreign policy concerns—from socialism to peace. The June 1969 International Conference of Communist Parties issued a call for socialist-Communist cooperation "to establish an advanced democratic regime today and to build a socialist society in the future."[120] In contrast, at the Twenty-Fourth Party Congress Brezhnev declared that "the CPSU is prepared to develop cooperation with the Social Democrats both in the struggle for peace and in the struggle for socialism, without, of course, making any concessions in ideology and revolutionary principles."[121] In his May 14 speech in Tbilisi Brezhnev reiterated his readiness to work with the social democrats "in the international arena."[122] He also noted that the leaders of the Socialist International would be meeting in Helsinki later in the month and appealed for their support on behalf of détente. Three months later *Pravda* published a major article on the International that attracted widespread attention in socialist circles.[123]

1972 marked the beginning of a period in which CPSU-socialist ties in Western Europe were progressively institutionalized. In November a delegation led by the two copresidents of the Belgian Socialist Party traveled to the USSR to discuss bilateral and international issues and the development of party-to-party relations. At the conclusion of the trip, which included meetings with Ponomarev and Vadim Zagladin, the CPSU and the Belgian Socialist Party issued a joint communiqué in which they stated that "the delegations believe that the actions to attain joint efforts of Communist and Socialist parties and other progressive and democratic forces should be treated favorably."[124] They further agreed that "realistic possibilities exist for . . . further cooperation in the interests of the cause of peace. . . . In this connection both delegations support the continuation of contacts." A CPSU delegation paid a return visit to Belgium in June 1973, and a further trip by the Belgians took place in 1974.[125]

In June 1973 the first official delegation of the British Labour Party's National Executive Committee since the Bevan-Gaitskell trip of 1959 visited the USSR. Labour officials blamed the fourteen-year gap on East-West tensions and the invasion of Czechoslovakia. Labour's renewed interest in direct contact had been kindled largely by the impending start of the CSCE and in particular by Labour's strong interest in the Mutual and Balanced Force Reduction (MBFR) talks in Vienna. According to a semi-official account, "the National Executive believed that, on the eve of the European Security talks in Helsinki, it was time for a Labour Party initiative to improve Anglo-Soviet relations."[126] At Labour's request the invitation was extended not by the CPSU but by the Institute of World Economy and International Relations (IMEMO), the leading Soviet foreign policy institute attached to the Academy of Sciences. The involvement of IMEMO was intended to highlight the informational focus of the visit and to downplay the ideological connection, but had little practical effect on the visit, which appears to have been managed by Ponomarev. Three years later the National Executive Committee issued a return invitation to IMEMO and was surprised to learn that the Soviet side had picked Ponomarev to head the delegation. Coming on the heels of an unpopular visit by trade union leader Aleksandr Shelepin a year earlier, the presence of the "Stalinist" Ponomarev provoked demonstrations and protests in Parliament. Nevertheless, Ponomarev met with Prime Minister Callaghan and called for the further development of CPSU-Labour ties.[127]

François Mitterrand led a delegation of French socialists to the USSR in the spring of 1975 and was received by Suslov and Ponomarev. The communiqué issued at the conclusion of the visit expressed agreement on a range of international issues. The French delegation "expressed its appreciation of the constructive contribution of the USSR to the process of international détente," and both parties "resolved to do all in their power to make international détente historically irreversible."[128] The two parties "agreed to develop their contacts further under the most appropriate forms and procedures."[129] It was decided to convene two meetings "in order to discuss the economic crisis and the problems of Europe." The first such meeting took place in Paris in late 1977 and dealt on an expert level with such issues as disarmament, EC-CMEA relations, and implementation of the CSCE Final Act.[130] Another breakthrough with a West European Socialist party occurred in 1977, when a delegation of the Spanish Socialist Workers' Party (PSOE), led by Felipe González, traveled to Moscow for meetings with Suslov and Ponomarev. González reaffirmed his party's intention to stay out of NATO, and he and Suslov signed the now familiar communiqué affirming a mutual commitment to party-to-party cooperation.[131]

In addition to cultivating bilateral contacts, the CPSU began to reassess its attitude toward the Socialist International, particularly after the election of Willy Brandt as president in 1976. Press treatment of the organization slowly improved during the 1970s,[132] but the first contact between the CPSU and the International did not occur until April 1978, when the USSR and the United States were invited to send representatives to a conference in Helsinki sponsored by the International's Study Group on Disarmament and the Finnish Social Democratic Party. The United States sent a governmental arms control representative to discuss the Strategic Arms Limitation Talks (SALT), while the USSR sent Ponomarev at the head of a large delegation.

In his speech to the conference Ponomarev called for the establishment of "stable, consistent" socialist-Communist cooperation and outlined several proposals toward that end, including meetings between representatives of the Soviet party press and the social democratic media, a joint conference of disarmament experts to be held in Moscow, and the establishment of joint study and research groups on disarmament problems.[133] The Soviet media echoed Ponomarev's line, calling for the creation of "machinery for permanent joint actions by Communist and Social Democratic parties on disarmament questions."[134]

The International did not agree to institutionalize its relationship with the CPSU, but in the fall of 1979 it sent a delegation from its Study Group on Disarmament to Moscow for what was the first official meeting between representatives of the Socialist International and the CPSU, and the first CPSU contact with a non-Communist international since the Berlin Conference of 1922.[135] The delegation was accorded high-level attention, including a meeting with Brezhnev. Socialist International disarmament specialists subsequently made periodic visits to Moscow. In October 1985 a second Socialist International conference on disarmament was held in Vienna, and again the USSR sent a large delegation headed by Ponomarev.[136]

Brezhnev's personal involvement in contacts with the Western Socialist and Social Democratic parties was reflected in his reports to the Twenty-Fifth CPSU Congress in early 1976 and the Twenty-Sixth Party Congress in 1981. His 1976 report was the first in which a general secretary singled out individual Socialist parties for praise. It noted that "contacts with the Socialist and Social Democratic parties of a number of countries, including Finland, Belgium, Japan, Great Britain and France, have expanded noticeably. We appreciate what has been achieved here, and we shall continue to work along these lines."[137] In his 1981 report Brezhnev commented favorably for the first time on the development of contacts with the Socialist International and specifically with the Socialist International Disarmament Advisory Council (SIDAC), a permanent body that had grown out of the ad hoc Study Group on Disarmament of the late 1970s.[138] He again singled out five individual parties for praise, citing, as in 1976, the parties in Belgium, Finland, and Japan, but substituting the Spanish PSOE and the Swedish Social Democratic Party for British Labour and the French PS.

Brezhnev's caution in associating himself with Labour and the PS may have been linked to the INF controversy that was raging at the time. The December 1979 NATO dual-track decision that the USSR bitterly opposed was largely the work of social democratic leaders in Britain and West Germany, and was supported by the socialists in France and Italy and the Labor parties of the Netherlands and Norway. Nonetheless, as the INF debate unfolded and as the left lost power in Britain and later Germany, the missile issue provided a basis for expanding contacts with the CPSU and the Soviet government.

In September 1980 the CPSU Central Committee wrote to the Labour Party's National Executive Committee asking for cooperation in reducing INF in Europe.[139] Labour did not take up this offer, but in the course of the next several years it abandoned all previous inhibitions about the constitutionality of negotiations with the USSR. In May 1983 the party's National Executive Committee sent a letter to the Central Committee of the CPSU asking whether the USSR would cut its medium-range missiles and warheads "by an equivalent amount in return for the phasing out of the British Polaris missiles."[140] At first the Soviets offered only vague and noncommittal replies. With French and British nuclear systems playing such a large role in the Soviet anti-INF campaign, the Soviet leadership was probably wary of directing attention to Labour opposition to British systems lest it weaken the case against the deployment of additional U.S. missiles.[141] But once the campaign had failed the Soviets gave a more favorable reply. In talks with party leader Neil Kinnock in late 1984 Chernenko announced that "the USSR would be prepared to reduce and physically liquidate a part of its medium-range missiles in the European part of the USSR that would be equal to the number of nuclear missiles liquidated by the British side."[142] In the same meeting Chernenko indicated for the first time that the USSR was prepared to resume negotiations (in a broader framework that included strategic and space-based weapons) with the United States on INF.[143]

The INF issue also had major effects on relations between the CPSU and the SPD. Throughout the 1970s the West German Social Democratic Party did not develop the kind of relationship with the CPSU that took shape with other Western parties.[144] There was some contact through the Socialist International and statements by Soviet authors began appearing in the SPD press for the first time in the late 1970s,[145] but the SPD did not send and receive delegations representing the party executive or sign joint communiqués with the CPSU.

By the last year of the Schmidt government this began to change. In June 1981 Brandt led an SPD delegation to Moscow for talks with Brezhnev and other Soviet leaders.[146] As the INF controversy intensified contacts between the SPD parliamentary group and the Soviet leadership increased dramatically. At the height of the controversy Andropov sent a letter to the SPD delegates in the Bundestag warning against deployment.[147] Individual SPD parliamentarians made frequent trips to Moscow, and often were given hints of potential Soviet moves in the Geneva negotiations.

Formal institutionalization of SPD-CPSU links began in March

1984 when SPD leader Hans-Jochen Vogel went to Moscow to meet with General Secretary Chernenko.[148] The SPD had been casting about for ways to build bridges to the Soviet regime following the first INF deployments, and decided to propose the formation of a joint SPD-CPSU working group to study ways of lowering arms expenditure to divert funds to the developing world.[149] The topic chosen was one that was thought likely to be of interest to the CPSU but not overburdened by the INF dispute. Chernenko accepted Vogel's offer and the first SPD-CPSU working group was formed shortly thereafter. Drafting delegations were exchanged and a joint paper was to have been produced by the fall of 1985.

In the summer of 1984 the SPD announced that it was intensifying its efforts at dialogue with the Eastern parties with the object of serving as a "bridge" while the arms control process was interrupted by the U.S. elections.[150] Joint working groups were established with the East German Socialist Unity Party (SED) to discuss a chemical weapons-free zone in central Europe, with the Polish United Workers' Party (PUWP) to consider "means of building mutual trust," with the Hungarian Workers' Party to discuss economic cooperation, and with the Czechoslovak Communist Party to consider environmental issues. These groups met on a regular basis and produced a number of joint proposals and initiatives, the most noteworthy of which were the June 1985 SPD-SED agreement on a proposal for a chemical weapons free zone in central Europe and a 1986 agreement for the creation of a nuclear-free zone in the same region.[151] The Czechoslovak Communist Party associated itself with both proposals, which were presented to the governments of East Germany, West Germany, and Czechoslovakia. The Basic Values Commission of the SPD and the East German Academy of Sciences (attached to the SED) also concluded, in August 1987, a joint document on "The Battle of Ideologies and Joint Security."[152] The SPD and the PUWP concluded two agreements, a February 1988 joint declaration on confidence- and security-building structures in Europe and a June 1989 working paper on confidence- and security-building measures and arms limitation in the Baltic.[153] In October 1987 the CPSU-SPD working group, tasked with producing a joint paper on disarmament and development, finally delivered the product, some two years behind schedule. (The slippage in the deadline was caused, SPD officials believed, by the replacement of Ponomarev by Anatolii Dobrynin, who was less familiar with European issues.) A second working group on questions of building a "common European home" was founded in September 1988.[154]

By the mid-1980s SPD interactions with the Eastern Communist parties had taken on a quasi-governmental form. Party leaders met, usually at "summits" in Eastern capitals, to draw up mandates authorizing the creation of joint working groups and establishing their terms of reference. The working groups then met periodically to carry out their assigned tasks. In presenting their results to the party leaders, the groups mimicked the language used in such intergovernmental forums as the CSCE. The February 1988 SPD-PUWP Joint Declaration on Criteria and Measures for Establishing Confidence-Building Security Structures in Europe, for example, contained preambular language stating that "the Group is continuing its work on the basis of the mandate contained in the communiqué on the talks held in Warsaw on October 1, 1987, between Mr. Wojciech Jaruzelski, First Secretary of the PUWP Central Committee, and Mr. Hans-Jochen Vogel, SPD chairman, and on the foundation of the joint declaration of November 25, 1985."[155]

While ties between the CPSU and the SPD improved, relations between the Soviet party and the PS and the PSI deteriorated somewhat. Already in early 1979 the PS sponsored colloquia on Stalinism and other aspects of Soviet life that reflected the sea change in French intellectual attitudes toward the USSR. Articles in the Soviet press criticized the PS for these activities and suggested that it was abandoning understandings that had been reached with the CPSU in 1975 and that were codified in the Brezhnev-Mitterrand communiqué.[156] The PS also suspended party-to-party contacts with the CPSU following the imposition of martial law in Poland. The Soviet press also attacked the "rabid anticommunist Craxi," who was described as "being looked on with increasing favor across the Atlantic."[157]

But the deterioration was partially reversed beginning in late 1982. In October 1982 the French Socialist leaders Pierre Joxe and Claude Estier went to the USSR as members of an all-party exchange of foreign affairs commissions where they met with Ponomarev and Zagladin to arrange a resumption of ties, beginning with the acceptance of an invitation to the December 21 celebration of the sixtieth anniversary of the founding of the USSR.[158] The following year President Mitterrand reversed his earlier stance against top-level governmental contacts between France and the USSR, which also had a positive effect on PS-CPSU relations.

Lingering tensions in relations with the Socialist parties were further dampened after Gorbachev's accession to power in March 1985. The new leader took a strong interest in CPSU ties with the West European left and began to develop personal relationships with many of its leading figures. His first foreign visitors included Brandt, Palme, Craxi, and a delegation from SIDAC.[159] Palme was credited by some Soviet officials with impressing upon Gorbachev the importance of the nuclear testing issue, which was reflected in his August 1985 declaration of a unilateral test moratorium.

The new edition of the CPSU program, the draft of which was published in October 1985, dropped the attacks on the right-wing leaders of the Social Democratic parties contained in the 1961 version and stressed the part that CPSU cooperation with Socialist, Social Democratic, and Labor parties could play "above all in preventing nuclear war."[160] It called for "the fruitful and systematic exchange of opinions" and "parallel or joint actions" against the danger of war. Another symbolic change was the decision of the CPSU to invite these parties to send delegations to the Twenty-Seventh Party Congress. Twenty-one parties, including most of the major ones in Western Europe, accepted the offer and generally sent low-ranking but nonetheless official representatives. The French PS represented the Socialist International at the latter's request.[161] Socialist parties also were represented at the November 1987 celebrations marking the seventieth anniversary of the Bolshevik Revolution.

Observers from the CPSU attended their first congress of the Socialist International in Stockholm in June 1989. The congress was especially noteworthy in that it approved a new declaration of principles to replace the Frankfurt document of 1951. More than a decade in preparation, the declaration affirmed the socialist commitment to freedom but dropped the anti-Communist strictures of the earlier document. According to Karen Brutents of the International Department, the new document differed "advantageously from the Frankfurt declaration of 1951, because it does not carry the imprint of the 'cold war'."[162] In a post-congress assessment *Pravda* asserted that thanks to the dialogue under way since 1979 "the positions of the CPSU and the Socialist International on disarmament issues today virtually coincide."[163]

Neither the East European Communists nor the West European Socialist parties proposed the establishment of formal, multilateral Communist-socialist links, but movement in this direction began in 1985 when Socialist parties in the Netherlands, Belgium, and Denmark and Communist parties in Bulgaria, Hungary, and the GDR agreed to hold annual meetings to discuss disarmament, trade, and other issues.[164] In contrast to previous periods, however, the CPSU was more wary than the socialists and social democrats of institutionalizing multilateral contacts. CPSU officials rhetorically supported overcoming the historic rift in the working-class movement, but warned against "according priority to the organizational factor."[165] With the disarray in the world Communist movement and the absence of a unified center, the CPSU might have concluded that it would be at a disadvantage in a multilateral forum and that the Western parties might use such a forum both to further weaken the West European Communists and to woo the East European Socialist parties.

In any case, the smooth development of socialist-Communist

links soon was rudely shaken by developments in Eastern Europe. After the overwhelming defeat of the Polish Communist Party in the free elections of June 1989 the West European socialists (and especially the SPD) became increasingly vulnerable to charges that they had sided with the forces of oppression against the peoples of Eastern Europe. Stung by these criticisms, in September the SPD announced that it would expand its dialogue with the churches and opposition in the GDR. This provoked a harsh reaction from the SED and the cancellation of a planned exchange of delegations.[166] By October the SPD was establishing contacts with a newly founded East German Social Democratic Party and with the Hungarian Socialist Party. The previous month party leaders received Lech Walesa in Bonn and announced that they wanted to expand ties with Solidarity.[167]

Although at the time the Soviet leadership was still insisting that Article 6 of the Soviet constitution would be retained and that the USSR would remain a one-party state, Gorbachev was widely credited with promoting pluralism in Eastern Europe, and CPSU relations with West European Socialist parties did not suffer from the up heavals in Eastern Europe. Indeed, in late 1989 the CPSU leadership began promoting the idea of a forum of left-wing forces in Europe and managed to drum up some support for this idea during Gorbachev's October visit to Finland.[168] Over the longer term, however, officials in the West European parties faced questions about the extent to which they should continue to rely on links with the CPSU or whether they should reach out to the informal groups and nascent political parties then forming throughout the USSR. The newly formed Socialist and Social Democratic parties of Eastern Europe were granted observer status at a February 1990 Berlin meeting of the Confederation of European Community Socialist Parties (a grouping of sixteen parties from EC countries), but neither the CPSU nor any Soviet socialist party was represented at the gathering.[169] A Russian Social Democratic party held its constituent congress in May 1990, following the adoption in the USSR Congress of People's Deputies of constitutional amendments legalizing the formation of new political parties, and a second congress in October 1990 after the USSR Supreme Soviet passed a more detailed law on public associations (including political parties). The Russian Social Democratic party immediately began developing ties with the Socialist parties in Italy, Austria, France, Sweden, and Germany. It also applied for membership in the Socialist International, and expected its request to be considered at the International's next congress in 1992. However, the Soviet law on political parties banned the acceptance of contributions from foreign sources, thereby limiting the assistance that the Russian Social Democratic party could derive from its European contacts. For its part, the CPSU was increasingly demoralized and too preoccupied with its internal problems to devote much effort to building links with foreign Socialist parties or even to maintaining long-standing ties with other Communists. This was seen most dramatically in July 1990, when the CPSU decided not to invite any foreign parties—Communist or Socialist—to attend its stormy Twenty-Eighth Party Congress.

Nonsocialist Parties

Soviet contacts with "bourgeois" political parties began to occur with some frequency in the 1960s, mainly under the auspices of the Supreme Soviet. In July 1969, for example, a delegation from the West German Free Democratic Party (FDP, the sole opposition party to the country's ruling grand coalition) was invited to Moscow and met with Prime Minister Kosygin. Delegations from the Center Party of Finland also exchanged visits with the USSR. In the 1970s many nonsocialist parties established de facto bilateral relations with the CPSU through the Soviet Committee for European Security. A public organization that was founded in 1971 as an offshoot of the Soviet Peace Committee and that at one point maintained ties chiefly with Communists and fellow-travelers, the committee gained in stature as it became a major point of contact for Western "bourgeois" political parties.[170]

The first formal relationship between the Soviet Communist Party and a "bourgeois" party in Europe was not established until December 1986, when the CPSU and the Center Party issued a joint communiqué in which they "confirmed their readiness to continue to develop mutual contacts and cooperation for the benefit of our countries and peoples and in the interests of peace and international security."[171] The CPSU also began forging links with the West German Greens, whose social base and position in the class struggle was somewhat indeterminate. During the April 1986 visit of a Greens delegation to the USSR the two parties discussed the establishment of joint working groups and reached an informal agreement to exchange delegations and articles for publication in the party press.[172] In January 1989 Aleksandr Iakovlev (in West Germany for the congress of the German Communist Party [DKP] met with Otto Lambsdorff to discuss prospects for developing ties between the CPSU and the FDP.[173]

In July 1988 Karen Brutents of the CPSU's International Department told a foreign ministry conference that "favorable conditions are shaping up for us to establish and promote contacts with the widest spectrum of working class, revolutionary democratic, left-wing, democratic and other parties, movements and organizations," including "non-working class parties affiliated to the Liberal International, the Christian Democratic World Union or the International Democratic Union."[174] In May 1989 Valentin Falin, the head of the International Department, went to Vienna for the first high-level contacts between the CPSU and the European Democratic Union, the organization of West European conservative parties that includes the British Conservatives and the Christian Democratic Union/Christian Social Union (CDU/CSU).[175] Iakovlev accompanied Gorbachev on most of his trips to Western Europe, and devoted much of his time to meetings with nonsocialist as well as Socialist parties. In Finland in October 1989, for example, he met with Finnish parties from across the political spectrum.

The peoples democracies of Eastern Europe, which technically remained multiparty states even after the Communist takeovers of the 1940s, also played a role in developing contact with nonsocialist parties of Western Europe. The West German FDP established links with Poland's Democratic Party and the Liberal-Democratic Party of East Germany.[176] The Bulgarian Agrarian Party hosted delegations from the Center Party of Norway, the Flemish wing of the Belgian Christian Social Party, and other conservative, agrarian based parties of Western Europe.[177] The West German CDU/CSU traditionally shunned contact with parties that were seen as regime puppets, but in 1987 even it joined in the general trend. In April 1987 a four-member delegation from the CDU parliamentary group made a six-day visit to Hungary at the invitation of the National Council of the Hungarian Patriotic People's Front.[178]

The USSR welcomed these contacts, but was itself a one-party state and thus had no easy way to establish its own links with the bloc parties in Eastern Europe or to monitor and coordinate their contacts with West European parties.[179] But in 1987 the USSR's Union of Consumers' Cooperatives (Tsentrosoiuz) signed an agreement with the Polish Democratic Party in which both organizations pledged to "collaborate in international forums on questions of the struggle for peace and mutual understanding among the peoples and on cooperation in environmental protection."[180] On other occasions the Soviet Committee for European Security provided the mechanism by which the USSR was able to participate in multilateral activities involving the minor East European parties. In November 1986, for example, Tolkunov led a committee delegation to a mini-conference on security that was held in Finland and that brought together West and East European center, agrarian, and liberal parties.[181] Similar party-level "mini-CSCEs," as they were called by the leadership of the Finnish Center Party, subsequently took place on an annual basis.[182]

But any hopes that the Soviet authorities may have had of using the non-Communist parties of Eastern Europe as instruments for dealing with Western Europe were dashed by the events in Poland in August 1989, when two of the hitherto docile parties in the national front, the Democratic and United Peasant parties, broke with the Communists and made possible the election of Solidarity's Tadeusz Mazowiecki as prime minister.[183] In subsequent months the bloc parties in Czechoslovakia and East Germany also jettisoned their Communist allies in an effort to gain credibility, while in East Germany the head of the Liberal Party, Manfred Gerlach, briefly served as caretaker president. But most of these parties were discredited by long years of subservience to the Communists, and were either unable to survive in open political competition or unwilling to serve as instruments of Soviet policy at home or in contacts with the West.

By late 1989 the CPSU's monopoly on political power in the USSR was in any case beginning to crumble, raising the prospect not only of new ties between the CPSU and the Western European "bourgeois" political parties, but of relationships between newly founded Christian Democratic, Liberal, and other parties in the USSR and various union republics and their Western counterparts. In early 1990 the Soviet Congress of People's Deputies repealed Article 6 of the Soviet constitution, thereby opening the way to the establishment of a multiparty system. The CPSU remained the dominant force in the country, however, and most West European political parties moved cautiously in forging relationships with the new political parties opposing Gorbachev.

Trade Union Ties

As was seen in the previous section, in the interwar period the Comintern preferred dealing with the non-Communist trade unions to cooperation with the Socialist parties. Soviet and West European trade unions established contact already during the civil war, when British, German, Swedish, and other labor organizations supported the Bolsheviks with demonstrations, solidarity campaigns, and in some cases strikes to hamper the allied intervention. The British trade unions also lobbied for diplomatic recognition and the restoration of trade, which they saw as essential to combating unemployment at home.[184] In 1920 a combined Labour Party-Trades Union Congress (TUC) delegation traveled throughout the USSR and produced a detailed and for the most part objective report on conditions in the country.[185] By 1927 one hundred labor delegations—most of them from Europe—had traveled to Russia as guests of the Soviet trade unions.[186]

In addition to seeking contact with individual European trade unions, the Bolsheviks organized, in July 1921, the Red International of Labor Unions, or Profintern, as a rival to the International Federation of Trade Unions (IFTU) formed in Amsterdam two years earlier.[187] The All-Russian Central Council of Trade Unions had denounced the Amsterdam venture as an "international union of conciliators" and called for a workers' boycott.[188] The bulk of the Profintern's membership was made up by the Russian trade unions, and no attempt was made to maximize the number of individual members from other countries. Communists and Communist sympathizers who were members of IFTU affiliates were told to stay in their unions and to win them over to the Profintern rather than to force splits as had been done in the socialist parties. The Profintern also made direct overtures to the IFTU and called for the convocation of an international unity conference. But the IFTU rejected cooperation and in 1923 decided to have no further contact with the Profintern.

Establishing a pattern that persisted in the West European trade union movement after World War II, the IFTU drew a distinction between a Communist trade union international and the Soviet trade unions. As one writer described the attitude of the British trade union leaders, they were "disdainfully contemptuous of native Communists, uncritically respectful of Russian ones, and loth to acknowledge any connections between them."[189] Thus in 1922 the IFTU suggested that if the Russian trade unions left the Profintern, they would be welcome in the IFTU.

The USSR thus came to rely, by necessity rather than choice, on the All-Union Central Council of Trade Unions (AUCCTU) rather than the Profintern as its chief instrument for dealing with the Western trade unions. M. P. Tomskii, the head of the AUCCTU, spent two months in England in the spring of 1924 (where he was formally attached to the Soviet trade delegation) and established close contact with the left wing of the TUC. Tomskii seems to have favored joining the IFTU, but this was resisted by Aleksandr Lozovskii, the head of the Profintern, and ultimately blocked by Zinoviev and the Comintern.[190] Tomskii also tried to institutionalize the relationship between the AUCCTU and the TUC. In 1924 he proposed that the two trade union movements "establish permanent regular connections." The TUC reacted warily to this offer, but it did agree to an extended but purely educational trip to the USSR in the fall of 1924.[191]

At the June 1924 Fifth Congress of the Comintern, Lozovskii suggested that international trade union unity could be advanced by the formation of bilateral committees uniting, for example, French and Italian miners or German and Czech transport workers, or even Russo-Polish or Anglo-Russian committees linking workers in all industries.[192] Lozovskii's ideas later were reflected in a concrete proposal by Tomskii for an AUCCTU-TUC committee that would be empowered to "act jointly." After discussions with a somewhat hesitant TUC leadership, in 1925 the two federations agreed to form an Anglo-Russian Trade Union Unity Committee, "the first important organizational manifestation of [working-class] reunion" to result from the strategy of the united front.[193]

It soon became clear, however, that the two sides had different conceptions of the role the committee would play. The British believed that they had secured ironclad commitments against interference in each other's internal affairs, and grew increasingly irritated as the Soviets violated these understandings, most notably in the general strike of 1926. The Soviet trade unions also engaged in what the British saw as extraneous politicization.[194] More fundamentally, the TUC saw the committee as a unique and temporary mechanism by which it could mediate between the Soviet trade unions and the IFTU, while the Soviets saw it as a first step toward international trade union unity, based not on the dissolution of the Profintern and AUCCTU adherence to the IFTU but on equality between the Communist and non-Communist trade union movements at both the national and international levels. These divergences were compounded by the severe deterioration in Anglo-Soviet relations at the state level, and the TUC withdrew from the committee in September 1927.

Informal U.K.-USSR trade union contacts continued intermittently, but the committee marked the high point of relations in the interwar period. In 1935 TUC general secretary and IFTU president Walter Citrine made a private visit to the USSR and was received by ranking officials, including Molotov.[195] The Soviets urged him to put aside the experiences of the 1920s and work for unity in the face of the fascist danger, but they were not successful, as Citrine went as far as to walk out of a meeting of Russian trade union officials when he learned that Lozovskii, at the time still secretary of the Profintern, was in the room.[196]

It was not until World War II that formal AUCCTU-TUC contacts were resumed. At its September 1941 Edinburgh Congress the TUC authorized its General Council to begin talks with the Soviet AUCCTU concerning the establishment of a single trade union international. The Soviet side responded positively, and agreed to participate in the preliminary meetings that eventually led to the founding in 1945 of a World Federation of Trade Unions. The TUC also sent a message to the AUCCTU pledging British support for the war effort and proposing the formation of an Anglo-Soviet Trade Union Committee.[197] The Soviets immediately accepted and an exchange of delegations began in October 1941 and continued throughout the war.[198] The British intended the committee as a gesture of solidarity and patterned it on an existing wartime Anglo-French

Trades Union Council rather than on the Anglo-Soviet committee of the 1920s.[199] For their part, the Soviet leaders hoped to use the committee as a lever against the Churchill government on wartime policy and as "a first step in the struggle for international trade union unity."[200] Nonetheless, as the war drew to a close, the activities of the Anglo-Soviet committee wound down and by 1945 the organization had all but ceased to function. The committee was never formally disbanded, however—a point that was later stressed by Soviet writers and trade union officials in appealing for a strengthening of AUCCTU-TUC ties.[201]

Although more firmly based than the party-to-party contacts established in the 1940s, East-West trade union unity broke down following Stalin's turn to the left in the fall of 1947. In what appears to have been an attempt to enlist the WFTU in the Soviet campaign against the Marshall Plan, in November 1947 Communist militants made a bid for total power within the organization, and by 1948 the WFTU had become deadlocked on all key issues. Led by the British, Dutch, and U.S. trade union centers, in January 1949 the major non-Communist affiliates seceded from the WFTU with the aim of setting up a rival organization. This resulted in the establishment, in December of that year, of the International Confederation of Free Trade Unions (ICFTU).

The Soviet trade unions sought to renew contact with the free trade unions only after Stalin's death. In November 1953 the USSR informed the International Labor Organization's (ILO) director general that it had decided to accept the obligations of membership, but also requested certain changes in the structure of the ILO, including increased representation for workers in the tripartite structure of the organization. The ILO refused to alter its structure to ensure Soviet participation, but in April 1954 the USSR, the Ukraine, and Byelorussia accepted the obligations of the ILO constitution without reservation. The ICFTU challenged the credentials of the Soviet workers' organizations, but narrowly lost a bitter fight to deny them participation.[202]

Soviet delegates soon were involved in efforts to politicize the organization. In 1956 the Soviet delegate to the ILO Conference introduced the first of many resolutions calling for disarmament and the relaxation of tensions, and in 1957 the Soviet delegate read a special message from Bulganin urging it to support the Soviet proposals introduced in the UN Subcommittee on Disarmament.[203]

The AUCCTU also began putting out feelers to the TUC and other Western trade union federations for bilateral exchanges and other forms of contact. On the eve of the TUC's annual congress in September 1954, Nikolai Shvernik, the head of the AUCCTU, sent a message of greeting in which he called for a "resumption of the activities of the Anglo-Soviet Trade Union Committee" and invited the congress to send a delegation to the USSR for discussions on "problems of common interest to the trade unions of the two countries."[204] Shvernik's intervention may have been intended to influence a congress vote on a resolution introduced by the Communist-leaning engineering union calling for a discussion between the ICFTU and the WFTU. After a heated debate in which Arthur Deakin of the TUC attacked the Shvernik telegram as unwarrantable interference, the resolution lost by a large margin.[205]

In September 1955 the WFTU also appealed directly to the ICFTU for a restoration of trade union unity, but the offer was swiftly rejected.[206] Foreshadowing the course that the Socialist International was to take in March 1956, the ICFTU issued guidelines that in effect banned member union and trade union center contact with the Soviet and East European trade unions. Despite "persistent overtures from the W.F.T.U. and its various affiliates to establish fraternal relations and exchange delegations,"[207] this policy was generally followed until the mid-1960s, albeit with some exceptions and compromises. Because of its integral relationship with the Labour Party the TUC found it almost impossible to shun all contact with the AUCCTU. As early as 1959 the Soviets included a vice-chairman of the AUCCTU on a parliamentary delegation to the USSR. The official met with Labour's trade union group and urged British trade union delegations to come to the USSR.[208] Moreover, some member unions, such as the woodworkers and the coalminers, were under strong Communist influence and maintained ties in defiance of TUC and ICFTU policy.

The one country where the USSR decisively breached the Western boycott was Finland. During their June 1957 visit, Khrushchev and Bulganin surprised their hosts by asking the Finnish foreign ministry to arrange for them to address the fiftieth anniversary celebrations of the Central Trade Union Organization (SAK) that were then taking place in Helsinki. The ministry deferred to the SAK, which declined to issue the invitation. Nevertheless, the two leaders turned up anyway to watch the festivities.[209] The Khrushchev-Bulganin gambit was followed by the formation later in 1957 of the Soviet-Finnish Permanent Trade Union Commission, the only such body in Soviet-West European relations and still the most advanced form of institutionalization in bilateral trade union relationships. The commission was comprised on the Soviet side of representatives of the AUCCTU and on the Finnish side of representatives of the four Finnish trade union centers. It met annually to draw up a protocol of exchanges as well as to formulate joint positions on peace and disarmament.[210]

The AUCCTU's road to formal cooperation with the British, West German, and other important trade union centers was much more arduous, as patterns established during the cold war began to break down only in the late 1960s. The first official AUCCTU-TUC exchange since the 1940s took place in September 1966, when a TUC delegation undertook a ten-day, fact-finding tour of the USSR. The stated purpose of the visit was to "examine the role of Soviet trade unions and to study Soviet industry" while avoiding all "political" subjects.[211] The TUC visit was closely watched by other European members of the ICFTU, who were "particularly interested to see whether the Russians [would] cooperate with the western trade unions on technical, bread and butter issues . . . without injecting politics."[212]

The development of regular ties between the AUCCTU and the West German trade union federation, the *Deutsche Gewerkschaftsbund* (DGB) paralleled the British pattern, with some differences. Unlike in the British case, there were no Communist-dominated DGB affiliates that had maintained ties with the AUCCTU and no indirect links to Soviet trade unionists through the SPD (which unlike Labour had no "organic" relationship with the trade unions). Thus in attempting to court the West German trade unions the Soviets were starting from a base of zero. In addition, there were several barriers to cooperation that were unique to the German situation. The Soviets were not happy that DGB affiliates had branches in West Berlin, while the West Germans were more sensitive than other West European trade unionists to the repressive aspects of Communist trade unionism. They had watched in the 1940s as a major part of the German trade union movement was subordinated to the East German Communist Party and renamed the "Free" DGB (*Freie Deutsche Gewerkschaftsbund*). There was also the curious matter of Shelepin, who was even more controversial in Germany than in Britain. It was under his leadership that the KGB had killed, in Munich in 1959, the Ukrainian nationalist Stefan Bandera, and a West German judge had ruled Shelepin responsible for the murder.[213]

The initial breakthrough with the German unions came via Czechoslovakia in September 1965, when the leadership of the Transport and Public Employees Union (*Öffentliche Dienste, Transport und Verkehr*, ÖTV) accepted, with the approval of the DGB executive, an invitation to attend a World Congress of the International Society for the Study of Living Conditions and Health in Karlovy Vary.[214] At the congress ÖTV leader Heinz Kluncker held discussions with Soviet and other East European trade union representatives and proposed several "information exchanges." In March 1966 Kluncker led a small delegation to the USSR. The focus of the trip was health and related issues, but the Soviet trade unionists devoted considerable time to foreign policy themes and specifically to the alleged dangers of West German aggression, which they said were of great concern to Soviet workers.

As much to gain control of the process as out of genuine interest, in December 1966 the DGB sent its own delegation on an initial twelve-day visit to the USSR, thus establishing the first direct contact between the Soviet and West German trade union centers.[215] After considerable debate within the trade union movement, in January 1967 the DGB executive adopted its Guidelines for Travel in Eastern Bloc Countries, which on the one hand set an official stamp of approval on trade union exchanges but on the other stressed the need for—and difficulty of—breaking through the Communist bureaucracy and establishing effective contact with the Soviet workers.[216]

Over the next eighteen months about thirty trade union exchanges took place between the DGB and counterparts in the USSR, Hungary, Romania, and Czechoslovakia, although disputes over territorial and status questions still blocked contact with Poland and the GDR.[217] The DGB shared the TUC's approach of stressing nonpolitical themes and of exchanging information in areas "in which there were no fundamental differences of outlook between trade union organizations." Thus in June 1968 DGB chairman Ludwig Rosenberg went to Moscow to work out an intensified program of expert exchanges in the areas of social security, industrial safety, wage settlements, labor rationalization, and worker training.[218]

The invasion of Czechoslovakia brought a quick end to the trend toward the institutionalization of trade union ties. The DGB severed all exchanges in response to the invasion.[219] The TUC's General Council withdrew an invitation to the AUCCTU to send a representative to its centenary congress in September, and issued a resolution strongly condemning the invasion. "In light of this invasion," the resolution stated,

the General Council have come to the conclusion that it would no longer be useful to pursue current contacts with the trade union Movement of the USSR or with those of the countries associated in the attack. These contacts were resumed in recent years in the expectation, now shown to be completely unjustified, that the Soviet Government was moving towards an attitude of greater independence for the satellite countries, greater freedom for its own citizens, and in particular greater freedom for the trade unions of these countries to reflect the experience and the working-class interests of their members.[220]

The resolution urged all TUC affiliates to "reconsider their attitude" toward exchanges of delegations with any of the invading countries, and many individual unions in fact cancelled visits to the USSR and Eastern Europe.[221]

Despite agitation within some individual trade unions for a resumption of exchanges, the DGB ban on contact was maintained throughout 1968 and most of 1969.[222] Informal DGB-AUCCTU contacts resumed in December 1969, when Heinz Oskar Vetter, the newly elected head of the DGB, made a brief stopover in Moscow on his way back from a trade union meeting in Japan. At Vetter's request, the German ambassador arranged for him and his delegation to meet informally with Shelepin to discuss the further development of trade union ties.[223] The two leaders agreed to step up contacts, beginning with an AUCCTU visit to the FRG in the spring of 1970.[224]

The AUCCTU put forward a written proposal for an agreement on contact and cooperation that the DGB representatives agreed to take back to Bonn and to discuss at a future meeting of the executive committee, which subsequently declared its willingness to conclude such an agreement. Negotiations quickly bogged down, however, over the Berlin question. The AUCCTU insisted that under no circumstances could any trade union representative from West Berlin come to the USSR under West German auspices, while the DGB insisted that it had to maintain the "integrity of its organization" and would not discriminate against its West Berlin locals.[225] Exchanges continued on an ad hoc basis, however. An AUCCTU delegation traveled to the Federal Republic in May 1970. At the conclusion of the visit the sides issued a joint communiqué covering trade union and economic issues, but not recording any convergence (or divergence) or views on broader political or foreign policy themes.[226] The DGB also initiated exchanges with the central trade union federations of Poland and Bulgaria in 1970 and East Germany in 1972.[227]

The Soviet side demonstrated the importance it attached to the development of trade union contacts in early 1972 by tacitly retreating on the Berlin issue. The Soviets badly wanted the DGB to send a delegation to the Fifteenth Congress of the AUCCTU, scheduled for March, and informally assured the West Germans that if they were to include a West Berliner in their delegation he would receive a visa. The AUCCTU delivered on this promise, and a DGB group went to Moscow, where it met with Shelepin to work out a further program of exchanges.[228] It is also noteworthy that Brezhnev used his speech to the congress to make an important gesture toward the European Community by for the first time recognizing its existence.[229] He further underlined the significance attached to trade union ties by meeting with Vetter and a delegation from the DGB during his first trip to the FRG in May of the same year. Throughout 1973 additional regional and industrial groups were exchanged, and in May of that year the first delegation of DGB trade union journalists visited the USSR under AUCCTU auspices.[230]

TUC-AUCCTU ties were not formally restored until July 1973, when a delegation led by General Secretary Vic Feather traveled to Moscow and concluded an agreement committing both sides to bilateral exchanges across a broad front.[231] The meeting's final communiqué dealt not only with trade union matters, but with broader foreign policy issues as well. It stated, for example, that the "trade unions of the USSR and Great Britain [had] identical goals and common positions on many questions, including the struggle for peace."[232] The sides welcomed the first stage of the CSCE, the Paris accords on Vietnam, and other recent developments.

In March 1975 it was announced that a delegation of the AUCCTU, led by Shelepin, would pay a return visit to Britain the following month. This announcement provoked a storm of criticism, largely because of Shelepin's past role as head of the KGB. The TUC and the Soviets went ahead with the visit, however, which was accompanied by major demonstrations and was cut short by a day.[233] Despite the controversy surrounding his visit, Shelepin pushed ahead with an ambitious and well-prepared agenda. He proposed a broad program of cooperation that included further exchanges of delegations, exchanges of trade union journalists, and exchanges between corresponding industrial unions, all of which were agreed to in a joint communiqué.[234] The two federations also agreed to look into the question of whether to revive the wartime Anglo-Soviet Trade Union Committee. According to Shelepin, "there are now conditions for such a committee to be restored."[235] Sentiment for such a step was considerably weaker on the British side, however, and the matter was simply referred to the General Council for further discussion.[236] In addition to reviewing the state of trade union relations, the final communiqué addressed broad political themes and even made certain concrete policy recommendations. It called, for example, for disarmament, for an early summit-level conclusion to the CSCE, and for settlements in the Middle East and Cyprus.

While institutionalizing its bilateral links with the West European trade unions, in the early 1970s the AUCCTU also stepped-up efforts to promote global and European trade union unity. The USSR's maximum goal remained some form of reunification of the WFTU and the ICFTU. This objective was endorsed by the TUC in the communiqué concluded at the end of Shelepin's visit to Britain, and by the TUC Conference of 1975, but it did not enjoy broad support throughout Europe. Short of overcoming the split of 1949, the USSR was interested in the more modest goal of creating a pan-European forum that would bring together free and Communist, Western and Eastern trade unions, preferably to discuss and formulate actions on political and security issues. The Soviet campaign for the creation of such a forum began in 1969, when the AUCCTU proposed that the WFTU and ICFTU cosponsor an all-European trade union conference on European security issues. This idea was rejected by the ICFTU, which continued to eschew contact with the WFTU on the grounds that it was an instrument of Soviet foreign policy.[237]

After repeated overtures in bilateral settings the AUCCTU finally managed to make a breakthrough in the ILO context.[238] In July 1973 the TUC, the DGB, and the Swedish trade union federation met in Vienna with Soviet, East German, and Hungarian trade unions to discuss a pan-European meeting within the framework of the ILO. An informal consultative meeting took place in January 1974 in Geneva and led to the convening, a year later, of an official pan-European trade union conference on Humanization of the Work Environment—an appropriately nonpolitical theme insisted upon by the West European participants. Such meetings were subsequently institutionalized within the ILO framework, and all-European trade union conferences were held on such topics as the use of toxic substances in industry (1975), problems relating to the working environment (1977), and the working environment, vocational training, and youth employment (1980).

Another avenue toward pan-European cooperation that the AUCCTU explored was Soviet and East European affiliation with the European Trade Union Confederation (ETUC), a loose gathering of West European trade union centers that had been established in the early 1970s to deal with the new problems posed by West European economic integration and the growth of the multinational corporation, which were seen as challenges to the trade unions that cut across national borders. Shelepin discussed gaining observer status in the organization with the TUC and also made an approach to Vetter, but his bid for association was rejected largely because of opposition from the DGB and some other trade union centers.[239]

Thus by the mid-1970s the USSR had scored certain successes in its trade union diplomacy, although it was unable to secure its maximal objectives. Bilateral exchanges had recovered from the 1968 setback and were increasingly institutionalized. In 1974 over four hundred Soviet and West German trade union leaders traveled to each other's countries, up from fifty in 1970. In Britain the level of exchange was roughly the same, with about thirty delegations on each side traveling back and forth.[240] On the multilateral level the AUCCTU was pursuing several paths toward the creation of a pan-European organization. Meanwhile, the American Federation of Labor and Congress of Industrial Organizations (AFL-CIO) had withdrawn in 1969 from the ICFTU, precisely over the issue of contacts with Communist trade unions, and U.S. influence over the West European trade union movement was at a low point.[241] Soviet writers especially praised the overtly political content of Soviet trade union exchanges with the West, which they saw as a sign of the growing "realism" on the part of European trade union leaders.[242]

During the second half of the 1970s the rapid development of Soviet-West European trade union ties was not sustained. There was no backward movement, but exchanges were increasingly routinized and the AUCCTU made little progress toward a pan-European trade union forum with a political agenda. Nonetheless, from the Soviet perspective the long investment in developing trade union ties soon was to pay off, as AUCCTU contacts with the West proved largely immune to the political shocks that increasingly damaged government-to-government (and many nongovernmental) contacts between 1978 and 1983.

In January 1978 a group of Soviet workers announced that they had formed an independent trade union, SMOT (*Svobodnoe mezhprofessionalnoe obedinenie trudiashchikhsia*, or Free Interprofessional Workers Association), and intended to apply to the ILO for recognition. They also sent, via Amnesty International, an appeal to trade union organizations in the West asking for support and recognition. In response to these developments the AUCCTU used its channels to the West to neutralize support for SMOT and to limit international criticism of its suppression. In response to TUC inquiries, the AUCCTU sent a letter to the General Council that outlined the Soviet system for dealing with labor disputes, listed new state-sponsored trade unions that had been founded in recent years, and "expressed the view that the concept of a trade union implied an association of people of the same occupation or employed in the same enterprise" and that "a group composed of complainants claiming to be a trade union could not pretend to pursue trade union objectives, and that the Soviet trade unions therefore saw no reason to support such a group."[243] The TUC claimed that it was satisfied with the AUCCTU reply, and stated that the mere fact that the AUCCTU had chosen to reply "appeared to confirm that by consistently pursuing a policy . . . of dealing with selected sensitive issues away from publicity, the General Council had been able to open and sustain a channel for exchanges . . . that could not otherwise take place." The TUC's rather tortured language was the result of an internal compromise, and the meaning not entirely clear. What the TUC seemed to be saying, however, was that by not publicly criticizing the USSR it had been able to maintain contact with the AUCCTU through which it was able to learn that there was in fact nothing to criticize.

The ICFTU took a stronger stance and announced in June that it had decided to submit a formal complaint to the ILO alleging contravention of the ILO convention on freedom of association. Although the ILO rebuffed SMOT's application for membership (explaining that its charter made no provision for the recognition of individual unions),[244] it did launch an inquiry into the treatment of those workers who were seeking to form a new union. Soviet representatives claimed that SMOT leader Vladimir Borisov was mentally ill and that other members had been jailed for criminal activities unrelated to trade union affairs, but after a two-year inquiry the ILO's Committee on Freedom of Association issued a report highly critical of Soviet practices.[245] In a separate matter, the ILO earlier had sent messages to the USSR, the Ukraine, and Byelorussia charging that Soviet legislation making work a moral obligation violated an international convention prohibiting forced labor.[246]

Another shock weathered by the AUCCTU's international policy was the Soviet invasion of Afghanistan, which, unlike the occupation of Czechoslovakia eleven years earlier, did not result in strong West European trade union responses. The TUC General Council adopted a statement expressing "grave concern at the new threats to peace arising from the Soviet military intervention." But it had relatively little to say about the intervention as such, and instead dwelt at length on the fact that the "action could only harm progress towards détente and strengthen those who sought to justify increasing defense expenditure." Using established channels of communication with the Western trade unions, the AUCCTU defended the invasion. In a letter to the General Council it charged that NATO governments were using the situation in Afghanistan as a pretext to undermine détente and pointed to the INF decision as proof of this contention.[247] Whether the AUCCTU letter had any effect is difficult to say, but the TUC did not curtail contact with the AUCCTU as it had done in 1968.

The DGB also condemned the invasion of Afghanistan, but called for the maintenance and intensification of dialogue with the East. In its resolution concerning Afghanistan, the DGB's executive committee declared that the federation would "continue its contact with trade union organizations in the East European countries and will use these contacts to develop its own positions regarding the preservation of peace and détente, and will emphatically point out that these goals are endangered by the Soviet military intervention."[248] There was thus no break in Soviet-West German trade union contacts. Already in February 1980 a delegation from *Industriegewerkschaft Metall* (IG Metall, the Metalworkers' Union), led by its chairman and his two deputies, made a scheduled trip to Moscow for annual consultations with the Soviet metalworkers' union. The union went through with the visit, it explained, "in order to demonstrate that it would proceed fundamentally with making its contribution to the policy of détente."[249]

Another East-West shock to affect trade union ties was the 1980–

81 crisis in Poland and the imposition of martial law in December 1981. The crisis initially had only a minor effect on TUC-AUCCTU ties. The TUC was asked by the Polish government to call off a planned visit to Poland, and this incident influenced at least one union to cancel a visit to the USSR.[250] Effects on DGB-AUCCTU relations were even more limited, as the DGB was less heavily involved in attempts to find facts and mediate in the early stages of the conflict and seemingly less sympathetic to the Poles in general.

While bilateral contacts proved largely immune to the developments in Poland, there were sharp repercussions in the ILO, where several Western trade unions pressed for the creation of a commission of inquiry to determine whether Poland was in compliance with the ILO charter. The Polish and other East European governments initially succeeded in heading off an inquiry,[251] but a commission of experts was formed in June 1983. Poland refused to cooperate with the commission and boycotted ILO sessions. After the commission delivered a 144-page report that was highly critical of the Polish government, the Poles gave notice, through a Ukrainian delegate, that they would be withdrawing from the organization within two years.[252] The Soviet and other Eastern trade unions also threatened to withdraw, charging the ILO with having violated its own convention, which prescribed that trade union activities be guided by the constitutional statutes within a given country. The Soviet press accused "political intriguers" (politikany) within the ILO of politicizing the organization.[253] It was clear, however, that the Soviet trade unions had no wish to withdraw from an organization which they themselves hoped to politicize using the peace issue. Indeed, Poland eventually reversed its own decision to withdraw after it managed to secure ILO registration of its new state-sponsored trade unions in May 1987.

Having successfully institutionalized its relations with the West European trade union movements and weathered the political crises of the late 1970s and early 1980s, the AUCCTU concentrated on attempting to mobilize international trade union support for Soviet foreign policy. As Stepan Shalaev wrote in 1984, "the questions of international solidarity of the working people in the struggle against the threat of war and for strengthening peace and curbing the arms race occupy the most important place in all contacts of the Soviet trade unions with foreign trade unions."[254] At the same time, however, Soviet trade union officials showed that they were still capable of a highly sectarian approach to the Western trade unions that undercut prospects for joint action on foreign policy matters. The most noteworthy example of this was in 1984 when the Soviet coal miners' union reportedly gave financial support to striking British miners—an action that irritated the British government, embarrassed the mainstream of the TUC and the Labour Party, and probably was seen as foolish by many Soviet foreign policy specialists.[255]

Soviet proposals in the ILO generally failed to win broad support. As a Soviet delegate lamented at the 1983 general conference, "deplorably . . . the ILO, whose aim is to defend the interests and rights of the working people, has so far failed to determine its place in the struggle for preserving peace and preventing the threat of war."[256] The Soviet trade unions, therefore, became involved in a long list of secondary efforts that had peace as their focal point. These efforts, none of which were very successful, included the annual proclamation (beginning in 1982) of September 1 as the International Day of Trade Union Peace Actions, support for a grouping of Balkan trade union federations campaigning for the creation of a Balkan chemical-free zone, the formation in May 1982 of an International Trade Union Committee for Peace and Disarmament, and the creation in March 1983 of the European Commission of the WFTU.[257]

These efforts, many of which were launched under Brezhnev and given a new impetus in the anti-INF campaign of the early 1980s, continued under Gorbachev, whose positive image and active diplomacy facilitated the further development of trade union contacts. In January 1987 the General Council of the TUC voted, after considerable debate, to send a delegation to the congress of the AUCCTU— the first since the TUC's withdrawal from the WFTU in the late 1940s. Although supported most forcefully by the "hard left" unions (for example, TASS, the white-collar section of the engineering union led by Communist Ken Gill), the motion received broad support.[258] In all about thirty delegations from trade unions affiliated with the ICFTU attended the Eighteenth Congress of the AUCCTU in early 1987.[259]

The presence of Western delegations did not prevent the AUCCTU from adopting a fairly militant final resolution that called for "unity of action in the international trade union movement," and stressed the need, in developing cooperation with trade unions of capitalist countries, "to promote in every possible way the mobilization of the trade union movement to participate widely in antiwar measures, the assertion of new political thinking, and the shaping of public opinion opposed to the policy of confrontation being pursued by the U.S. administration and its closest allies." The resolution also declared that "Soviet trade unions will continue and step up work on strengthening all-European trade union cooperation, in whose development certain positive trends have become apparent."[260]

Another breakthrough occurred in October 1987 when Gorbachev received a delegation from the ICFTU, the first ever to visit the USSR.[261] The meeting came about at ICFTU rather than Soviet initiative, and was an outgrowth of the West European trade unions' growing involvement in security issues. At its November 1981 meeting the organization's executive board adopted an appeal on disarmament, and the June 1983 Oslo World Congress adopted a more extensive Statement on Peace, Security, and Disarmament.[262] These documents were fairly balanced and criticized Soviet as well as U.S. armament programs, but they reflected a new mobilization on security issues and an unprecedented willingness to make specific recommendations on policy matters. The USSR welcomed the ICFTU's growing politicization, although this was partially offset by ICFTU support for Solidarity in Poland and SMOT in the USSR.[263]

In 1987 the ICFTU set up a study group on security issues, and shortly thereafter it informed the Soviet authorities that it wanted to go to Moscow as "part of a program of discussions with top world leaders" (which included stops at the UN, NATO, and Washington for a meeting with President Reagan). It also stressed that it was not interested in contacts with the AUCCTU.[264] The Soviet side respected these initial ground rules, although it clearly hoped to use the peace issue to promote an ICFTU-AUCCTU or even ICFTU-WFTU dialogue. In his session with the delegation Gorbachev stressed that there was much in the 1983 Oslo statement with which he agreed, but he firmly turned aside questions regarding human rights.[265] Gorbachev reportedly concluded the two-and-one-quarter-hour meeting by saying that "the ice had been broken" and that he looked forward to continued exchange.[266]

As Gorbachev's reforms encouraged the reemergence of a Soviet civil society, Western trade unions were increasingly faced with the dilemma of balancing their existing ties with the AUCCTU with their interest in encouraging the development of new trade unions free of political control.[267] The West European trade unions did not take up the cause of the new unions in a major way, but by the summer of 1989 (marked by miners' strikes in various parts of the USSR) it was clear that the days of the AUCCTU monopoly were numbered and that in the future Western trade unions would face a more complex situation as they sought contact and cooperation with their counterparts in the USSR.

For its part, the official AUCCTU became so preoccupied with the deepening domestic crisis in the USSR that it shifted its main concern from promoting peace to securing aid for the Soviet economy. In 1990 the ILO agreed, with AUCCTU encouragement, to launch a program of assistance for the Soviet trade unions. Gorbachev signaled his approval of this step by announcing that he would attend the ILO Conference in June 1991. Individual members remained highly dissatisfied with the performance of the AUCCTU, however. At the Nineteenth Congress of Soviet Trade Unions in October 1990 the AUCCTU leadership acknowledged that the organization was out of touch with the country's workers and unable to cope with the economic crisis. The Congress voted to disband the AUCCTU and to replace it with a new organization, provisionally called the All-Union Confederation of Trade Unions of the USSR. The new organization was expected to continue the AUCCTU's international activities, albeit on a more decentralized basis.

6　Arms Control

The Institutional Setting

As was seen in chapter two, in the late 1940s and early 1950s the USSR and the West maintained a rudimentary arms control dialogue. Whereas the Council of Foreign Ministers broke up in 1949 and never reconvened, UN arms control institutions functioned continuously from June 1946 until April 1950. After a break of less than two years during the Korean War, a new UN Disarmament Commission (DC) was established in January 1952 and remained in session until the Soviet walkout of November 1957.

The DC grew out of an October 1950 proposal by President Truman to the General Assembly in which he called for the creation of a consolidated disarmament commission that would consider "all kinds of weapons."[1] Truman's interest in general disarmament reflected the growing perception in Washington that the almost exclusive pursuit of total nuclear disarmament that had characterized Western policy in the last five years was no longer appropriate, given the USSR's emergence as a nuclear power and the new importance of the conventional balance in Europe. Recognizing the same basic factors, the USSR also reversed its stance by downplaying conventional reductions and focusing almost exclusively on the demonization of the atomic bomb and other weapons of mass extermination.

While the USSR opposed the merger of atomic and conventional arms control talks, it participated in the various ad hoc committees and subcommittees that drafted the resolution from the General Assembly mandating the creation of a new commission. The resolution was approved in January 1952, and provided for the establishment of a body with the same permanent membership as the former Atomic Energy Commission and Commission for Conventional Armaments, both of which were dissolved. According to its terms of reference, the commission was to discuss four subjects: (1) regulation, limitation, and balanced reduction of armed forces and armaments; (2) elimination of all weapons of mass destruction; (3) effective international control of atomic energy; and (4) establishment of an adequate system of safeguards.[2] The USSR proposed an alternative mandate to the commission that followed the main themes of the

Stockholm appeal and that was rejected in the General Assembly by a large majority.[3]

The commission met in New York in June 1952 and soon was deadlocked over rival plans of work proposed by France and the USSR. The French plan was adopted by majority vote, but the USSR refused to accept it as a basis for talks.[4] The commission thus made no progress toward agreement and by the end of 1952 its only accomplishment was to forward a report of its activities to the General Assembly.

The deadlock in the commission resulted in a situation similar to that of 1948, when members of the international community not participating in the talks pressured the great powers to continue their deliberations. In November 1953 several smaller powers introduced a General Assembly resolution instructing the DC to "study the desirability of establishing a subcommittee consisting of representatives of the Powers principally involved, which should seek in private an acceptable solution" to questions of disarmament.[5] This led to the founding of the London Subcommittee, which became the forum for all disarmament negotiations until the end of 1957.

The USSR and its allies abstained in the General Assembly vote mandating the establishment of the subcommittee. This marked a return to the practice, which the USSR had abandoned in 1948, of not opposing resolutions mandating the creation of new UN institutions. The Soviet bloc also participated in the selection of the "powers principally involved." The West proposed a committee of five with the usual list of members—the USSR, the United States, the United Kingdom, France, and Canada—while the USSR suggested the addition of Czechoslovakia, India, and the People's Republic of China (PRC). The West prevailed and a Subcommittee of Five was constituted.

The post-Stalin leadership's turn to détente initially manifested itself in a certain enthusiasm for disarmament, later replaced by disillusionment and determination to end the talks. On May 10, 1955, the USSR put forward a sweeping proposal which, as was seen in chapter three, was the centerpiece of its diplomacy at the Geneva summit. It contained three elements—a ban on the use and production of nuclear weapons, conventional reductions, and the establishment of a control organ—to be carried out in two stages by the end of 1957.[6] The proposal was a step away from the propagandistic approach of the Stalin period, in that it addressed the problem of control and envisioned step-by-step implementation.

Although the USSR followed the accepted practice of introducing the proposal to the subcommittee in the form of a draft General Assembly resolution, there were already indications that it wanted to move disarmament out of the UN. At the July 1955 Geneva summit

Molotov argued "that the Heads of Government mandate should run not to UN representatives but to the Foreign Ministers." According to Dulles, the apparent purpose of Molotov's position was to assure that the ministers were occupied with disarmament and thus had less time to consider German unification, "and also to hamper our dealing with our UN disarmament representatives except through proven machinery."[7] The Soviet leaders ultimately yielded on this issue, and the heads of government reaffirmed the work of the subcommittee and instructed their representatives on it, "in the discharge of their mandate from the United Nations," to "take account in their work of the views and proposals advanced by the Heads of Government."[8]

At the October 1955 conference of foreign ministers Molotov made several probes that again seemed aimed at downgrading the role of the UN subcommittee and promoting direct government-to-government talks. Soviet draft documents made no mention of the UN subcommittee, and in one negotiating session Molotov asked "whether the whole question should be narrowed down to the Subcommittee alone" or whether "the Ministers also were instructed to work on this question."[9] But these were mere probes, and the Soviet government gave no indication that it was disturbed with the subcommittee. In his speech to the Twentieth Party Congress Khrushchev appeared to endorse the UN arms control dialogue by urging acceptance of the Soviet proposals on the table in London.

By the spring of 1956, however, it was clear that Khrushchev was wary of becoming enmeshed in a Western-dominated arms control process located in the UN. He objected to the verification schemes put forward by the West and showed increasing irritation at the composition of the subcommittee. During his trip to Britain in April 1956 he asked several Western interlocutors whether there was need "to reach formal agreement and sign documents. Supposing we take a unilateral decision and disarm a million men, would there be no response from your side from such a gesture? We want to do it but we are not ready to have controllers in our bedrooms."[10] On May 14 the USSR issued a statement on disarmament in which it castigated the "futility" of the entire work of the UN subcommittee and announced that the USSR was unilaterally reducing its armed forces by 1,200,000 men.[11] In his letter to Eisenhower of June 6 Bulganin characterized the subcommittee as a factor "retarding progress" and called upon the United States to follow the USSR in making unilateral reductions.

The Suez and Hungarian crises further lowered Khrushchev's view of France and Britain as powers, as well as convinced him that NATO as a whole was susceptible to Soviet nuclear threats.[12] In the spring of 1957 Harold Stassen, Eisenhower's chief arms control negotiator, exceeded his instructions and held a bilateral meeting with his Soviet counterpart that provoked a crisis with the allies and earned him a severe reprimand from Dulles. Stassen had gained the impression "that the Soviets now believed that progress would be furthered through informal Soviet-American negotiations rather than within the United Nations."[13]

In the summer of 1957 the USSR launched a determined assault on the subcommittee. On August 27 it rejected a package of partial disarmament measures, and three days later the subcommittee sessions were for all practical purposes suspended.[14] In his speech to the UN General Assembly on September 20, Gromyko attacked the "narrow and unrepresentative composition" of the Disarmament Subcommittee and asked: "How can one expect the Subcommittee to achieve positive results when four of its five members are countries of NATO" and when "whole continents like Asia and Africa are not represented."[15] The following month the USSR proposed that the Disarmament Commission be enlarged to include the entire membership of the United Nations.[16]

The Soviet representative on the First Committee of the UN General Assembly (where the proposal was taken up) attacked both the inequality of representation on the UN disarmament bodies and the ability of the Western powers to use the General Assembly to shape their terms of reference:

How can it be viewed as anything but an ultimatum when the U.S.A., Britain and France try to impose a disarmament solution on the General Assembly which is based completely on the Western powers' position and which presupposes that the Disarmament Commission and Subcommittee continue to negotiate on disarmament, stipulating in advance that the participants in the negotiations be guided by the proposals of the Western powers? It is completely clear that such an approach dooms the disarmament talks before they begin.[17]

The timing of the Soviet decision to break up the subcommittee can be explained both by tactical considerations and Khrushchev's assessment of broad historical trends. The immediate cause may have been the German elections of September 1957. With the SPD waging a "campaign against atomic death" in opposition to the deployment of tactical nuclear weapons in West Germany, Khrushchev might have calculated that he could best influence the elections by engineering a deterioration of East-West relations. But Khrushchev also sensed a disproportion between the USSR's growing military strength and the disadvantageous international forums in which it was forced to discuss disarmament. On August 26 the USSR tested its first intercontinental ballistic missile (ICBM) and on October 2 it launched the first Sputnik.

On November 11 the USSR announced that it no longer would participate in any negotiations in the Disarmament Commission or its subcommittee. Although there was little support in the world community for Gromyko's proposal to expand the Disarmament Commission to include all UN members, a number of countries were sympathetic to Soviet complaints about the "unrepresentative" character of the UN disarmament bodies. On November 19 the General Assembly rejected, by a vote of 46–9–24, the Soviet proposal of October 28, but adopted a resolution put forward by Sweden, India, Japan, Canada, Paraguay, and Yugoslavia which raised the membership of the DC to twenty-five (making Czechoslovakia, Poland, and twelve other countries members). However, the USSR refused to reconsider its position and continued to boycott sessions of the DC.

In a December speech to the Supreme Soviet Gromyko hinted at a new formula for the resumption of talks within the UN context. After criticizing the "utterly abnormal situation" in the subcommittee, where "the USSR was opposed by four members of the North Atlantic bloc," Gromyko repeated that the USSR would accept as a forum a Disarmament Commission enlarged to include all UN members, or "the establishment of a somewhat narrower Disarmament Commission in which the Socialist countries and the countries pursuing a neutral policy would account for at least half the members."[18]

After the Soviet walkout from the subcommittee the only noteworthy arms control developments of 1958 were the holding at Western initiative of two "technical" conferences concerned with monitoring nuclear tests and the prevention of surprise attacks. Because these were expert talks, the West accepted the principle of equal representation. The first set of talks got under way on July 1 and involved the participation of experts from four NATO and four Warsaw Pact states. The second conference opened on November 10 and brought together experts from five Eastern and five Western countries. "Thus a pattern was being established in arms control negotiations of Soviet representatives equal in number to Western representatives."[19]

The 1959 four-power foreign ministers meeting got the arms negotiations back on track by agreeing to establish a Ten-Nation Disarmament Committee composed of five Eastern and five Western powers. The committee, which was to convene in Geneva in early 1960, differed from all previous disarmament forums in that at Soviet insistence it was not formally linked to the United Nations.[20] This also meant that for the first time since 1946 disarmament talks were not structured by an explicit General Assembly mandate.

In the absence of such a mandate, East and West scrambled to define the goals and objectives of the talks. In his speech to the General Assembly on September 18, Khrushchev launched his campaign for general and complete disarmament, which he suggested could be carried out by all states over a period of four years.[21] Khrushchev's proposal marked a departure from the increased emphasis on partial measures in Soviet proposals since May 1955, and was inconsistent with the 1952 mandate of the Disarmament Commission, which called for the elimination of weapons of mass destruction but only the "regulation, limitation and balanced reduction" of all other weapons and forces. Publicly the West went along with Khrushchev's superficially attractive goal of complete disarmament, but in practice it remained wedded to partial measures.[22]

Notwithstanding this enormous buildup, the talks in the committee lasted for a little more than three months. East and West both put forward plans for general and complete disarmament, although the Western plan was in reality a package of modest partial measures coupled with a call for studies of how to proceed toward comprehensive disarmament. In June the USSR and its allies withdrew from the committee.[23]

Thus, despite having won an important victory in reshaping the arms control process, Khrushchev did not seriously try to work in the equal Ten-Nation Disarmament Committee. Soviet writers blamed the Eastern walkout on Western intransigence, but came close to acknowledging that concern about propaganda lay behind the action. The ten-power meetings "had convincingly shown that the Western Powers did not want real disarmament" and that "under such circumstances, the prolongation of discussions would have done nothing but harm. The fact that talks were continuing would have given the peoples a false sense of security. . . . Such illusions are extremely harmful as they weaken the efforts of the masses in the struggle for peace and disarmament."[24] Khrushchev was determined not to get bogged down in detailed negotiations and instead chose to wage a high-profile campaign for general and complete disarmament. This campaign culminated in his appearance at the October 1960 session of the General Assembly, which he tried to convert "into a summit conference of sorts . . . on the argument that disarmament negotiations, which had failed in other forums, should be carried on by heads of government."[25]

The election of a new U.S. administration later in the fall had no immediate effect on Khrushchev's course, but was to have substantial long-term implications. Just as it abandoned the search for a Berlin (and broader German) solution within the four-power context, the Kennedy administration largely completed the bilateralization of the arms control process. In March 1961 Adlai Stevenson, the U.S. ambassador to the UN, announced in the First Committee that the United States and the USSR had decided to jointly propose that the General Assembly take up "the problem of disarmament and all pending proposals relating to it."[26] Pursuant to this agreement, in June, July, and September of that year Valerian Zorin and John McCloy held discussions regarding both the substantive provisions of and an acceptable forum in which to negotiate a comprehensive disarmament agreement.[27] No agreement was reached on a forum or "the question of the composition of the negotiating body,"[28] which the USSR was unwilling to discuss until the two powers had concluded agreement on the "basic provisions" of a disarmament plan that would be put to the body. But after some resistance the United States yielded and on September 20, 1961 the two powers jointly submitted to the General Assembly their recommendations regarding the principles to serve as the basis for "future multilateral negotiations on disarmament."[29] The question of forum was resolved in late 1961 with the announcement of the formation of an Eighteen-Nation Disarmament Committee (ENDC), with the United States and the USSR designated as "permanent cochairmen." The membership was comprised of the members of the Ten-Nation Committee, and eight new members, all of which were neutral or nonaligned, and seven of which were from the developing world (Sweden was the one developed country added).[30]

The Zorin-McCloy agreement was not followed by progress toward disarmament, either partial or "complete and general." Indeed, it seemed to have the rather paradoxical effect of dampening Soviet enthusiasm for what had been the main theme of Soviet propaganda and diplomacy for more than two years.[31] The main result of the Zorin-McCloy exercise thus was procedural: it established a precedent for direct U.S.-Soviet arms negotiations and in effect made UN bodies the implementing agents for agreements reached between the United States and the USSR outside the UN framework. This was a reversal of what had been envisioned in 1945, when it was thought that the United Nations would be the mandating agency whose resolutions would be implemented by the member states.[32]

Nuclear Arms Control

Testing and Nonproliferation

The bilateralization of the international arms control process after 1961 paved the way to the conclusion of two agreements, the Limited Test Ban Treaty of 1963 and the Nuclear Nonproliferation Treaty of 1968, both of which had implications for Soviet-West European relations.

A ban on nuclear testing was first proposed by the USSR as part of its comprehensive disarmament plan of May 10, 1955. Later that year the Soviet Union offered to conclude a separate ban on testing, but the Western powers argued that until progress was achieved in other areas of arms control they could not accept a separate ban. This position was at first widely understood by Western public opinion, but became increasingly unpopular over time.

In early 1958 Khrushchev declared a unilateral moratorium on testing, placing the Western powers under intense pressure to discuss a ban in isolation from other arms control issues. It was partly to defuse these pressures that the United States called for the 1958 meeting of experts on nuclear testing. The meeting produced a measure of agreement on key issues, and encouraged President Eisenhower to suggest, in the summer of 1958, a meeting of the three states with nuclear weapons—Britain, the United States, and the USSR—to negotiate an agreement on the suspension of tests.

France's disenchantment with arms control dates from these talks. As latecomers to the nuclear race who had not yet developed their arsenal, the French were bound to resist any arrangements that would make doing so more difficult. In the debate concerning the establishment of separate talks on testing the veteran French negotiator Jules Moch delivered a passionate warning against the separation of the testing issue from other aspects of arms control, arguing that this would institutionalize the inequality of the nuclear haves and have-nots.

I am ... speaking most especially to the representatives of the non-atomic Powers and I say to them with all the persuasive force of which I am capable: "Watch out. By accepting, out of weariness, a solution which stills your immediate anxiety, you are seriously and in fact dangerously mortgaging the future of your States, for the benefit of a confirmed monopoly of nuclear weapons. ... [Y]ou will have sacrificed—for a long time, nay definitively— the essential to the incidental."[33]

This appeal went unheeded, however, and the tripartite talks got under way on the last day of October 1958.

In January 1959 Britain and the United States delinked their support for a test ban from other arms control issues, thereby theoretically clearing the way to agreement. But differences regarding control and verification as well as recurring Soviet attempts to link a ban on testing to other arms control and political issues continued to block an agreement. The trilateral talks adjourned in 1960, and the testing issue was transferred to the newly established ENDC, which soon became the scene of inconclusive debates in which the neutral countries attempted to mediate between East and West.

In April 1963 the United States and Britain decided to go back to the three-power negotiating formula. Kennedy and Macmillan addressed a joint letter to Khrushchev, expressing their readiness to send "very senior representatives" to Moscow to discuss a ban. Without indicating any great enthusiasm for the idea, Khrushchev agreed to receive the envoys.

Picking up a proposal that Britain and the United States had floated several years earlier, in a speech given shortly before the start of the talks Khrushchev suggested that the USSR was ready to conclude an agreement banning tests only in the atmosphere, in outer space, and under water. He appeared to erect a new obstacle to an agreement, however, by linking the test ban to his pet proposal for a NATO-Warsaw Pact nonaggression pact. The chief U.S. negotiator, Averell Harriman, and his British counterpart, Quintin Hogg (Lord Hailsham), thus arrived in Moscow not knowing whether Khrushchev was interested in a complete ban, a partial ban, or no agreement at all.

The Western negotiators made a perfunctory defense of the comprehensive proposal that was still formally on the table at the ENDC, but in accordance with their instructions quickly began to explore the prospects for a partial ban that would sidestep the verification issue. Khrushchev raised the nonaggression pact, but soon revealed his willingness to conclude a partial ban even in the absence of such an agreement. Thus the way was cleared to a rapid conclusion of the treaty, which was initialed on July 25 and formally signed on August 5.[34]

As far as Western Europe was concerned, the *least* noteworthy aspect of the treaty was the agreement to end testing in the three environments. Most countries were neither interested in nor capable of conducting nuclear tests at the time. In this sense the treaty was, as de Gaulle remarked, "rather like asking people to promise not to swim the Channel."[35] The three countries that were conducting atmospheric tests and that signed the treaty were under international and, in the case of Britain and the United States, domestic pressure to suspend such tests, which could have been done by unilateral action. The real significance of the treaty for Western Europe lay in the determined effort mounted by the sponsors to get other countries to accede to what had been signed in Moscow. The West Germans acquiesced rather sullenly, and the French, who had long since parted company with their allies on arms control issues, refused outright. The treaty was "resented in at least some quarters" and even "sometimes described as an agreement between opponents against friends."[36]

The other effect of the limited test ban (LTB) was to dramatically improve the prospects for a nuclear nonproliferation treaty. Prior to the mid-1960s nonproliferation was not a major preoccupation of either East or West, but by the mid-1960s it had become the single most important issue in U.S. policy toward the USSR. In August 1957 the Western powers submitted to the UN subcommittee, as part of a package of measures, a proposal that each party to the treaty undertake not to transfer out of its control any nuclear weapons or to accept transfer to it of such weapons "except where, under arrangements between transferror and transferee, their use will be in conformity with paragraph III."[37] The referenced paragraph stipulated the right of states to use nuclear weapons for individual or collective self-defense against armed attack. The USSR thus in effect was being asked to legitimate both the use of nuclear weapons as a means of self-defense and to sanction intra-alliance nuclear sharing. Its reaction was predictably negative. In response, it put forward a plan that would have banned both the transfer of nuclear weapons and the stationing of such weapons in foreign countries.

As was evident already in this exchange of proposals, the West and especially the United States tended to regard intra-alliance nuclear sharing and the stationing of U.S. weapons on foreign soil as compatible with, and indeed supportive of, the goal of limiting nuclear proliferation. Countries able to rely on a credible U.S. "extended" deterrent would have no need to seek to acquire nuclear weapons of their own. In contrast, the USSR regarded these two things as antithetical to each other. Countries that did not have nuclear weapons had no need to "import" surrogate U.S. power, but were to seek their security in the kinds of political measures traditionally favored by the USSR, such as nonaggression pacts and no-use guarantees.

One of the ways the United States sought to bridge this gap was to focus on the control of nuclear weapons rather than their deployment and possession. In January 1964 President Johnson sent a message to the ENDC, proposing an agreement barring the transfer of nuclear weapons "into the national control of states which do not now control them."[38] Unlike previous Western nondissemination proposals, the Johnson offer was not part of a package of other arms control measures. At the time NATO was finalizing plans for a multilateral nuclear force (MLF) in which the United States would provide nuclear warheads for sea-based delivery systems manned by non-U.S. crews. The United States would retain control over the warheads, but the nonnuclear allies, and especially West Germany, would have a greater role in NATO nuclear operations. The USSR, which strongly opposed the whole MLF concept, submitted a memorandum to the ENDC calling for a ban not only on the transfer of nuclear weapons to other governments, but also "provisions to guarantee that such a transfer of nuclear weapons or access to them shall not take place indirectly, through military blocs, for example, through the so-called multilateral nuclear force of NATO."[39] The Soviet memorandum identified the MLF as the chief nonproliferation danger confronting the world, and Soviet representatives argued that no agreement could be reached as long as the plan remained under consideration.

Despite the negative Soviet response, in 1965 the United States submitted a draft treaty to the ENDC that focused on the issue of national control. In an amplification of the Johnson statement, the draft not only banned the transfer of weapons into the national control of any nonnuclear state, but also ruled out "any other action which would cause an increase in the total number of States and other organizations having independent power to use nuclear weapons."[40] This language did not satisfy the USSR, which escalated its attacks on the MLF and presented a draft treaty with sweeping prohibitions on intra-NATO nuclear sharing arrangements.

The Soviet draft prohibited the transfer of nuclear weapons "directly or indirectly, through third states or groups of states not possessing nuclear weapons." It also barred nuclear powers from transferring "nuclear weapons, or control over them or their emplacement or use" to military units of nonnuclear allies, even if the weapons were placed under joint command. Nuclear states party to the treaty were to agree not only not to transfer nuclear weapons in any form, but were to undertake not to accord to nonnuclear states "the right to participate in the ownership, control or use of nuclear weapons."[41] The Soviet draft was so sweeping that Johnson was led to conclude that it would have raised doubts that "we could have carried out even the kind of intensive consultations on nuclear matters within NATO that we planned to develop."[42]

After additional months of deliberations in which the United States was unable to convince the USSR to negotiate on the basis of national control, in the fall of 1966 the United States proposed private bilateral talks with the USSR. These talks resulted in a tentative draft agreement that both powers agreed to "sell" to the world community. Following arduous consultations between the United States and its allies and further bilateral talks with the Soviets, in August 1967 the United States and the USSR submitted separate but identical texts of the draft to the ENDC.[43]

Although the USSR had made major modifications in its original draft, notably by dropping the provisions explicitly barring various forms of participation in alliance arrangements by nonnuclear states, the key articles on the obligations of nuclear and nonnuclear states were closer to Soviet than to U.S. preferences. Whereas the first U.S. draft barred the transfer of weapons "into the national control" of nonnuclear states, the version submitted to the ENDC with the USSR barred the transfer of "nuclear weapons . . . or control over such weapons." The elimination of the alliance option, as one West German expert termed it, was a major Soviet victory.[44]

On June 12, 1968, the General Assembly approved a resolution endorsing the text of the treaty and requesting the depository governments to open it for signature.[45] Formal signing ceremonies took place in Washington, London, and Moscow on July 1. However, establishment of the international nonproliferation regime was delayed somewhat by the August 1968 Warsaw Pact invasion of Czechoslovakia and by lingering differences over controls. Italy announced that it would delay consideration of the treaty, but signed it in January 1969. West Germany did not sign until November 1969. Moreover, most of the West European countries delayed ratification until 1975, after the European Atomic Energy Community (Euratom) had concluded an agreement on safeguards with the International Atomic Energy Agency (IAEA). France refused to sign. In contrast, the East Europeans all signed on July 1, 1968, and with one exception ratified it by the middle of the following year. Romania ratified the treaty in early 1970.

Thus by the end of the 1960s the Limited Test Ban Treaty and the Nuclear Nonproliferation Treaty (NPT) had become an essential part of the structure of East-West relations in Europe. Particularly with the latter treaty, the USSR had gained a legal and political safeguard against attempts even in the distant future by West Germany, a combination of European powers, or neutrals such as Sweden, to develop an independent deterrent. The LTB and NPT did not give the USSR direct leverage over the French and British nuclear forces, but they simplified one of its potential security dilemmas by placing a limit on one dimension of the West European nuclear threat.

The continuing relevance of the NPT was underscored in the summer of 1987 when the USSR invoked its provisions to exert pressure on West Germany to abandon, as part of the "double zero" INF agreement, its Pershing IA missiles, the warheads for which were owned and controlled by the United States.[46] Two years later the prospect of German reunification made the NPT even more topical, as the USSR sought assurances that the new Germany would be permanently barred from access to nuclear weapons.

The NPT also had limited utility against the United States. Article 6 of the treaty, which obliged the nuclear powers "to pursue negotiations in good faith on effective measures relating to the cessation of the nuclear arms race at an early date," was in effect a mandate from the international community to the United States and the USSR. It is noteworthy that in January 1984, following the Soviet walkout from the INF talks, the USSR for the first time explicitly charged the United States with failing to honor this obligation.[47]

U.S. and Soviet Forces

With the conclusion of the multilateral treaties of the 1960s, the focus of nuclear disarmament in Europe shifted to U.S. and Soviet weapons located in or presumably targeted on Western Europe. In

the 1950s the Soviet media coined the phrase "forward based systems" (FBS) to refer to all U.S. nuclear or nuclear-capable systems
that had less than continental range but which, because they were
deployed in or near Europe, could reach the USSR.[48] While complaining about these systems, the USSR did not advance proposals designed specifically to eliminate them. Soviet-proposed agreements
to ban foreign military bases or denuclearize particular regions
would have had the effect of eliminating most FBS, but this was not
their primary rationale. One exception to this general pattern occurred in the unique circumstances of the Cuban missile crisis, when
Khrushchev offered to remove the Soviet missiles from Cuba in exchange for the removal of U.S. missiles from Turkey.[49]

The earliest Soviet efforts to negotiate specific limits on U.S. FBS
were made in SALT. At the first round of the talks the U.S. delegation
received a "nasty shock" when the Soviet representatives unexpectedly raised this issue.[50] In tabling the USSR's "Basic Provisions for
Limiting Strategic Armaments," chief Soviet negotiator Vladimir Semenov declared that a mutually acceptable agreement would have
to "provide for a radical solution of the question of bases beyond the
limits of national territories."[51] The United States countered by arguing that FBS were not strategic and thus outside the scope of the
talks. Although the USSR failed to achieve the desired "radical solution," it did not drop the FBS demand. As Smith observed, "failure
to settle this question finally blocked a comprehensive SALT I treaty
limiting offensive arms."[52] The result was an interim offensive
freeze which sidestepped the FBS issue.[53]

The SALT II treaty of 1979 also worked around the FBS problem,
albeit in a way that seemed to strengthen the U.S. position. It placed
explicit numerical limits on Soviet and U.S. offensive forces of intercontinental range without taking into account FBS. It thus established a precedent for arms control agreements based on the U.S.
definition of a strategic weapon. The basis for the agreement was an
impromptu decision that Brezhnev took at the November 1974 Vladivostok summit over the resistance of his closest advisers.[54] But in
subsequent commentary the Soviet government stressed that it did
not regard the Vladivostok compromise as a precedent for future
agreements. At the 1979 Vienna summit at which SALT II was
signed, Brezhnev told President Carter "that it would be impossible
to agree to new reductions until the sides had also dealt with U.S.
nuclear systems based in Europe and with the nuclear weapons of
[the U.S.'s] British and French allies."[55]

While the Soviets objected to the exclusion of FBS from SALT, the
West Europeans were also dissatisfied with the negotiations, albeit
for reasons precisely the opposite of those advanced in Moscow. The
West Germans in particular were unhappy about negotiations that

failed to consider weapons that were of less than intercontinental range but that were capable of striking European territory.[56] This threat had long been a matter of concern in Western Europe, but it was heightened by the Soviet attainment of strategic parity with the United States and the Soviet deployment of the SS-20 missile and the Backfire bomber. After unsuccessfully urging President Carter to modify the U.S. approach and to raise the SS-20s in SALT, West German chancellor Schmidt went public, and warned in a 1977 speech in London about the dangers of the growing East-West nuclear disparity in Europe.[57]

The U.S. preference for keeping "grey area systems" out of SALT thus was a middle-of-the-road solution that satisfied neither the USSR nor its allies. While the Soviets complained about a U.S.-Soviet asymmetry that they claimed was inconsistent with the principle of "equality and equal security," the West Europeans worried about a Soviet-West European imbalance that implied a lesser degree of security for them than for the two main powers. To address the West European concern the United States would have had to negotiate a SALT III agreement that from the Soviet perspective would have widened the perceived U.S.-Soviet "inequality." To address the Soviet complaint it would have had to accept a treaty that would have subordinated West European security even further to the dictates of U.S.-Soviet equality.

There was probably no way to reconcile the Soviet demand for equality vis-à-vis the United States with the West European insistence on security vis-à-vis the USSR, although the issue might have been finessed as it had been in SALT I and II. What brought the matter to a head were NATO's plans to upgrade its own theater nuclear systems that began to take shape in 1977 and culminated in the "dual track" decision of December 1979. In his meetings with Brezhnev in Bonn in 1978 Schmidt raised the SS-20s and the possibility of Western countermeasures. But in this as in other meetings Brezhnev professed to be the injured rather than the injuring party, and complained about U.S. planes and aircraft stationed in West Germany capable of hitting the USSR.[58] NATO thus went forward with its own deliberations, and ultimately settled on a plan to deploy, beginning in late 1983, 108 Pershing II ballistic and 464 Tomahawk ground-launched cruise missiles in five NATO countries, provided no arms control agreement rendering the deployments superfluous was concluded.

The USSR launched an all-out but ultimately unsuccessful campaign to block implementation of the decision. In an obvious gesture to the West Germans, in October 1979 Brezhnev announced from East Berlin that the USSR was withdrawing 20,000 troops and 1,000 tanks from East Germany.[59] Dozens of Soviet officials descended upon West Germany to lobby the Bundestag and to rally opposition

to the formal approval of the NATO plan. But these efforts failed, forcing the USSR to make good on its earlier warnings that it would not
negotiate under the threat of the impending deployments. It did not
respond to U.S. offers to begin the talks that were called for in the
two-track decision.[60]

The USSR did not relent on the question of negotiations until the
summer of 1980, following a stormy six months marked by bitter
East-West recriminations over the Soviet invasion of Afghanistan,
growing West European disillusionment with U.S. policy under President Carter, and the beginnings of the massive West European anti-
INF movement. At the conclusion of his June 30–July 1 visit to Moscow, Schmidt announced that Brezhnev had informed him that the
USSR was ready to enter talks with the United States on the limitation of theater nuclear weapons, without setting as a precondition
cancellation of the deployment part of the two-track decision.[61] This
stance was confirmed in a joint party-government statement published on July 5, which stressed, however, that the question of
medium-range nuclear missiles in Europe had to be addressed "simultaneously and in organic connection with the question of American forward-based nuclear means."[62]

This announcement led to a September 25 meeting in Washington
between Gromyko and Secretary of State Edmund Muskie at which
the modalities of the INF talks were discussed. The two governments
issued a brief communiqué announcing that after an exchange of
views "regarding the beginning of discussions on questions of limiting arms which were raised in previous contacts between the parties," representatives of the sides had agreed to meet in Geneva in
October.[63] The vagueness of the joint statement, which was in effect
the terms of reference for the impending talks, reflected the gap between the sides concerning the question of what actually was to be
negotiated. The United States was interested mainly in Soviet SS-4,
SS-5, and SS-20 missiles, while the USSR reserved the right to discuss all categories of weapons not covered in SALT.

At the "Carter Round" of the INF talks the United States advanced
a general set of propositions, including that there should be equal
limits on both sides' long-range missiles and that these limits should
be worldwide in scope. The Soviet side put forward a "freeze" proposal that would have kept the Soviet INF force intact while blocking
any Western deployments. After this preliminary exchange, there
was a long delay caused by the elections in the United States and the
inauguration of a new administration. Negotiations did not resume
until late November 1981. In the intervening year the USSR intensified its propaganda against the dual track decision and tried to encourage the rapidly growing West European peace movement.[64]

The history of the INF negotiations has been told elsewhere and need not be recounted here.[65] But it is necessary to address two questions about the INF episode that, depending upon how they are answered, lead to different conclusions about Soviet policy and intentions toward Western Europe in the 1980s: (1) whether a nonzero arms control solution to the dispute was possible, and (2) why Gorbachev ultimately opted for an arms control solution to the INF dispute rather than sticking with the posture of unilateral defiance that he inherited from his predecessors.

The answer to the first question is almost certainly no. In their formal offers the Soviet negotiators never suggested they would accept a compromise that allowed the deployment of a single new U.S. missile in Europe. Soviet negotiators stressed that they would not "bless" any deployments, and in one plenary session Iuli Kvitsinskii, the chief Soviet negotiator, remarked that the real nuclear balance between the superpowers in Europe was 10,000–0 in favor of the United States, thus implying that the United States did not have the right to keep missiles in Europe for which the USSR had no counterpart.[66] In March 1982 the USSR declared a moratorium on its own SS-20 deployments and in December 1982 it offered to reduce the level of SS-20s to that of the French and British deterrent forces, but at no point did the USSR formally suggest a U.S.-Soviet balance at levels above zero.

While Soviet stubbornness in the negotiations sometimes was attributed to resistance by the military, political considerations probably played at least as important a role in Kremlin decisionmaking. The political leadership had reasons to oppose any agreement that ran counter to prevailing Soviet conceptions of European political realities. As a British journalist covering the talks concluded, "the Soviets have consistently stressed that the issue is political and strategic. . . . Arms control treaties codify the strategic relationship between the signatories. . . . What is at issue in Geneva is the strategic relationship between Western Europe and the USSR. Moscow wants to have a nuclear monopoly on the continent. Its aim is to remove from Europe all U.S. nuclear weapons capable of striking the USSR."[67] The political leadership also knew that any sign of wavering in the "principled" Soviet opposition to any U.S. deployments would undercut the West European peace movement, the leaders of which were arguing that the initial appearance of Pershings on European soil would constitute an immediate threat to peace.

The one piece of evidence that might undercut this interpretation is the "walk in the woods" episode of 1982, which seemed to suggest that at one point the Brezhnev regime contemplated accepting some number of U.S. systems in Western Europe. Soviet motives in this episode remain obscure, but can be inferred from accounts by the chief U.S. negotiator, Paul Nitze, of his dealings with Kvitsinskii.[68]

Alarmed at the prospect that public pressure in Western Europe could derail the entire INF deployment, in July 1982 Nitze sought out his Soviet counterpart and asked for his help in fashioning "a joint exploratory package for consideration of both governments." Under the terms of the formula eventually worked out, each side was to be allowed seventy-five INF launchers in Europe, while the United States would abandon the Pershing II part of its planned deployment and the USSR would freeze its SS-20 force in Asia. According to Nitze, the content of the package was 20 percent Kvitsinskii's and 80 percent his own. Kvitsinskii did reveal that he was negotiating on authority from Foreign Minister Gromyko, although it is unclear whether this authority entailed anything more than permission to listen to Nitze.

For the United States, the advantages of the walk in the woods formula were largely political; the disadvantages mainly military. For the USSR, the reverse was true. The United States would have forgone the strongest element of the deployment package, but in so doing might have defused public pressures in Europe while ensuring the coupling of Western Europe and the United States through a re-duced but by no means trivial deployment. The USSR would have dramatically diminished the threat posed to it by the INF deploy-ments, but would have sanctioned the general principle that U.S. missiles could be deployed in Europe, as well as established that the USSR could be forced to trade away existing forces in exchange for Western agreement to scale down plans to deploy. Faced with this complex mix of advantages and disadvantages, neither government saw fit to go through with the deal. After more than two months of intra-agency debate Nitze was instructed to inform Kvitsinskii that the United States had rejected the proposal. Upon receiving this news, Kvitsinskii reaffirmed the USSR's formal position calling for cancellation of the entire NATO deployment, and broke off further "back channel" contacts with Nitze.

Soviet motives in this episode remain obscure. The weight of ev-idence seems to suggest, however, that Kvitsinskii was involved in a fishing expedition, possibly hoping to start the unraveling of the NATO position by securing an informal agreement to cancel the Pershing part of the decision. Nitze himself later came to believe that the formula would have been repudiated in Moscow, no matter how the United States had responded. Once Kvitsinskii learned that Washington had rejected the offer, he was quick to reiterate the USSR's formal stance, lest *its* standing in Western Europe, particu-larly with the peace movement, begin to unravel.

It is also noteworthy that when, in March 1983, the United States formally tabled something close to the walk in the woods formula, the offer was swiftly rejected by Kvitsinskii, who stressed that the

USSR would not bless any U.S. deployments. On the other hand, on November 12, ten days before the West German Bundestag was to vote on accepting the Pershings, Kvitsinskii contacted Nitze to initiate an informal discussion of a compromise based on the walk in the woods formula. Nothing came of this episode, which appeared to be an eleventh hour maneuver aimed at derailing the Pershing deployments without publicly committing the USSR to accepting subsequent U.S. deployments. In December 1983 the Soviets made good on previous threats and walked out of the INF talks to protest the first deployments in Britain and West Germany.

The second question—why Gorbachev opted for an agreement rather than maintaining a position of defiance—is more difficult to answer. To address this question it first is necessary to qualify the assertion often made that Gorbachev accepted the zero option proposed by NATO in 1981.[69] The 1987 INF agreement differed from the 1981 proposal in important respects and was in any case concluded in an entirely different political context. It contained not one but "two plus" zeroes: in addition to missiles with ranges between 1,000 and 5,500 kilometers, it banned those in the 500–1,000 kilometer range category as well as eliminated, through a side understanding, the West German Pershing IA missiles. Nevertheless, Gorbachev's willingness to come to closure on INF represented a change in previous Soviet arms control policy, in that it tacitly accepted the equating of U.S. missiles stationed *in* with Soviet missiles targeted *on* Western Europe and permitted a mutual trade-off on that basis.

Gorbachev's actions in 1985 did not suggest that he came into power prepared to adopt the radical solution to INF contained in the Washington treaty. He was fortunate in that the Chernenko regime, in talks between Gromyko and Secretary Shultz in September 1984 and January 1985, had managed to resume INF negotiations as part of the three-forum Nuclear and Space Talks (NST) dealing with strategic offensive weapons, strategic defenses, and INF. These talks began in March 1985, just as Gorbachev took office. On the negative side, after a period of hesitation and backsliding the government of Belgium announced, in mid-March, that it would go through with the ground-launched cruise missile (GLCM) deployments, thereby turning aside Soviet calls for a defection from the INF decision.[70]

Gorbachev's own first step was to announce a moratorium on further deployments of SS-20s and to invite the United States to take a reciprocal action.[71] This offer was partly directed at the Netherlands, which had announced that it would make a final decision regarding the deployment of GLCMs on Dutch territory in November 1985 and that the decision would depend upon the number of Soviet missiles deployed.[72] In talks with European leaders Gorbachev revived the Andropov proposal of late 1982—the reduction of Soviet SS-20s to the level of French and British forces—and appeared to angle for a freeze in the U.S. deployments.[73]

On October 1 the Soviet delegation in Geneva tabled a comprehensive arms control proposal that accepted in principle the U.S. call for 50 percent cuts in strategic warheads, but in so doing again defined as strategic all weapons capable of striking the other side's territory. In the same proposal the USSR offered to reduce its INF in Europe to the level of British and French systems. In a speech to the French National Assembly two days later Gorbachev revealed details of the Soviet offer. He endorsed a separate INF treaty providing for the "speediest mutual reduction" of medium-range nuclear weapons in Europe, as well as called for direct talks between the USSR and Britain and France regarding their nuclear systems.[74]

Although this approach was later dropped, the reraising of the perennial FBS issue in the Strategic Arms (Limitation and) Reduction Talks (START) context was a long step backward and suggested no movement away from the stance that had led to the INF deadlock in the first place. Nonetheless, many on the Western side hoped that there was enough ambiguity in the package to allow for progress. Secretary of State Shultz claimed that "implicit in their new position may be a grudging acceptance of the presence of some U.S. INF missiles in Europe defending our allies."[75] At the first Reagan-Gorbachev summit the following month the sides endorsed an interim INF agreement, which many in the West assumed would provide for equal U.S. and Soviet ceilings at some level above zero.

Signs of a less ambiguous Soviet approach to INF appeared some six weeks after the Geneva summit, when Gorbachev unveiled his three-stage plan for the elimination of nuclear weapons by the year 2000.[76] The first stage of the plan, which was to last five to eight years, called for the "liquidation" of all U.S. and Soviet INF "in the European zone" and a freeze on French and British nuclear arsenals. These provisions strongly suggested that in negotiating the interim agreement endorsed in the Geneva statement the USSR would be unlikely to accept reduced but equal levels of Soviet and U.S. INF, or even a phased approach in which both sides would be allowed to keep equal but reduced levels of launchers in Europe while working toward their eventual elimination.[77]

After the January 15 plan fell flat with world opinion the Soviet negotiators in Geneva shifted their attention to less radical arms control outcomes. In May and June 1986 the USSR introduced a new START proposal that dropped INF and FBS from consideration. This step, along with the Reagan-Gorbachev correspondence carried out over the summer, again led U.S. negotiators to conclude that the USSR was moving toward acceptance of a nonzero outcome—that it had distanced itself from the utopian elements of the January 15 plan and was ready to conclude a treaty providing for one hundred INF on each side. At this point Gorbachev wrote to Reagan proposing that the two leaders meet in Reykjavik, "on the pretext of putting the finishing touches on a separate INF deal."[78]

Exactly what happened at Reykjavik is likely to remain unclear, even after the relevant documents are declassified; but the upshot of the meeting was an irreversible U.S.-Soviet commitment to the total elimination of INF.[79] According to Gorbachev, the USSR came to Reykjavik with a proposal for the complete elimination of "medium-range missiles" (the Soviet term for longer-range intermediate-range nuclear forces [LRINF]) in Europe. He also offered to freeze shorter-range intermediate-range nuclear forces (SRINF) at existing levels and to begin negotiations on their eventual elimination, as well as agreed to restrictions on Soviet missiles in Asia, to be counterbalanced by equal limitations on U.S. missiles deployed on U.S. territory.[80] After some wrangling over details, Reagan apparently accepted the Soviet offer.

In the West, particularly in government circles in Western Europe, there was dismay that Reagan apparently had agreed to eliminate all U.S. INF and there was hope that the United States would "walk back" its position to the 100/100 formula that was much discussed before Reykjavik.[81] But Reagan resisted this notion and Gorbachev himself scoffed at the idea that the USSR would ever recognize the right of the United States to deploy new missiles in Western Europe. Gorbachev and Shevardnadze also criticized those Western leaders who had voiced doubts about the understandings reached in Reykjavik.[82]

For the remainder of 1986 and the first two months of 1987 the USSR insisted that its Reykjavik proposals were a package and that it would not "delink" INF from START and SDI. But most Western observers believed that it was only a matter of time before Gorbachev would agree to a separate INF treaty based on the "zero option." As expected, Gorbachev made an announcement to this effect on February 28, 1987, and linked it to his comprehensive program for the creation of a nuclear-free world.[83] Shultz immediately declared his intention to go to Moscow to work out the remaining obstacles to a treaty.

The most important remaining issues were verification and collateral constraints on missiles with ranges of 500–1000 kilometers (SRINF). The SRINF issue was of particular concern to the European allies, who feared that large numbers of Soviet missiles in this category would continue to threaten Western Europe after the U.S. Pershing II and cruise missiles were removed. In talks in Moscow in mid-April Shultz conveyed these concerns to Gorbachev, making clear that the West was interested in at least a theoretical right to match Soviet SRINF deployment levels, whether or not this right was exercised in practice. Gorbachev responded by accusing the West of planning another "counterarmament." According to Gorbachev's account, Shultz "tried to convince us that the U.S. must have the right to build up its arsenal by having a number of missiles of this class deployed until the USSR completely eliminates its missiles."[84] Rejecting this "reversed logic," Gorbachev proposed the complete elimination of SRINF by both sides. Soviet officials subsequently made clear that such a double-zero agreement also would have to include the U.S. warheads for seventy-two West German Pershing IA missiles, which NATO regarded as third-country systems outside the scope of the U.S.-Soviet talks.

Gorbachev's offer of a second zero placed the Western alliance in a difficult position. To reject the offer would have made governments vulnerable to charges, already being voiced in the Soviet media, that they were planning a new counterarmament in the 500–1000 kilometer range while forgoing a chance to achieve highly asymmetrical cuts in the Soviet force of SS-12s and SS-23s. To accept the offer, on the other hand, risked starting a "cascade of zeroes" whose logical endpoint was the complete denuclearization of Europe. A number of West European politicians favored holding open the option of a third alternative, namely a legal right-to-match in the SRINF category that the West probably would not exercise, at least not right away.[85] But Shultz in effect sided with Gorbachev in pressing the double zero on the alliance by insisting that NATO either agree to deploy new SRINF in Europe—a political impossibility at the time—or permanently forgo the option in the treaty. Meanwhile, the USSR did nothing to reassure nervous West Europeans, as the Soviet media stressed that a nuclear-free Europe was in fact the Soviet objective and attacked those Western politicians who did not share the same goal.

Despite considerable behind-the-scenes grumbling, few European politicians were willing to accept the domestic political costs of battling against the Shultz-Gorbachev SRINF arrangement. NATO thus endorsed the second zero at the June session of the North Atlantic Council in Reykjavik, leaving the West German Pershing IAs, verification, and INF deployed outside Europe the main points of dispute between the sides. Gorbachev provided further impetus to an agreement in his July interview with the Indonesian newspaper *Merdeka*, in which he offered to eliminate all Soviet missiles stationed east of the Urals, provided the United States give up its right to retain one hundred INF on U.S. territory.[86] U.S. officials hailed the Soviet move as a major concession that would ease concerns in East Asia and simplify verification. But the move also had advantages for the USSR. Relinquishing the Asian missiles allowed Gorbachev to proclaim that an "entire class of weapons was being eliminated" (which was duly echoed on the U.S. side), thus lending credibility to his denuclearization rhetoric. It also was a political gesture to China, Japan, and the countries of the Association of Southeast Asian Nations (ASEAN), and obviated the need for the USSR to have its territory divided, in an international agreement, into zones where missiles could and could not be deployed while U.S. territory was not similarly affected.[87]

Throughout the summer of 1987 the Soviets mounted a major propaganda campaign against the *Bundeswehr's* Pershing IAs, charging that by trying to exempt them from U.S.-Soviet negotiations the FRG was defining itself as a nuclear power in violation of its obligations under the NPT.[88] Yielding to this campaign, in August Chancellor Kohl announced that West Germany would forgo modernization of the Pershing IA missiles. The USSR welcomed this decision, but sought to decisively breach the NATO principle that third-country systems were not subject to bilateral negotiations by asking for and to some extent obtaining guarantees from the United States that the Pershing IA warheads were being eliminated in accordance with the agreement.[89] The remaining verification issues were resolved in the fall, and the treaty was signed at the December 1987 Washington summit.

In rejecting an interim solution that would have provided for some U.S. LRINF as well as in offering a second zero to deal with the problem of circumvention at the SRINF level, Gorbachev followed the absolutist line of his predecessors and refused to acknowledge the right of the United States to keep "even one missile" in Western Europe. But unlike his predecessors, Gorbachev was ready to eliminate comparable Soviet missiles in order to achieve an agreement. This was not a cost-free step. By trading away "legitimate" Soviet for "illegitimate" U.S. missiles, it could be argued that the USSR was implicitly recognizing the "legitimacy" of the latter. An INF agreement also had the further disadvantage of undercutting the West European peace movement and the Social Democratic parties, which at the height of the INF campaign had accepted the reasonableness of the Brezhnev-Andropov stance on INF.[90] In addition, the agreement entailed the destruction of far larger numbers of Soviet than U.S. missiles, and thus was resented by some in the Soviet military concerned about one-sided concessions.

One of the ways that Gorbachev finessed the problems raised by the treaty was to portray it as a landmark step on the way to a nuclear-free world. In effect he managed to sidestep the whole question of "equality" that had so obsessed Brezhnev by embedding the INF problem in the broader context of a program for European and eventually global denuclearization (equality at zero). Since *all* nuclear weapons were going to disappear fairly soon *anyway*, it did not matter which side was making the greater numerical sacrifice or giving up weapons to which it was in principle entitled in exchange for other weapons that in principle had no right to exist.

After the signing and ratification of the treaty Gorbachev and especially Foreign Minister Shevardnadze stressed that while it required the USSR to give up a larger number of weapons than the West, its strategic implications were asymmetrically beneficial to the USSR. In a speech to a foreign ministry conference in July 1988 Shevardnadze argued that the INF treaty took "into account that these [INF] missiles are of different value from the standpoint of Soviet and American security" and that "thanks to it the American nuclear presence has been moved away from our borders."[91] To what extent such claims were made to defend the treaty against possible domestic critics is impossible to say, but it appeared that Shevardnadze himself strongly believed in trying to move all U.S. weapons of mass destruction as far as possible from the state borders of the USSR.

With the conclusion and initial steps toward implementation of the INF treaty, European nuclear disarmament had gone through three stages. In the first stage, which lasted from the initial U.S. deployments in the 1950s until the beginning of SALT, the USSR attempted to block or limit U.S. deployments through propaganda and political appeals to European governments and leaders, but was unable to use arms control to gain leverage over U.S. forces in Europe. For their part, Western governments were not unduly concerned about Soviet nuclear weapons presumed to be targeted on Western Europe, which they assumed were designed to counterbalance U.S. strategic superiority by holding Western Europe hostage.

In the second stage, which spanned the decade from 1969 to 1979, the USSR continued to campaign against U.S. weapons in Europe in the traditional manner (and even enjoyed a degree of success in the 1977–78 neutron bomb episode), but also tried to use SALT to promote at least the beginnings of an arms control solution to the problem of U.S. nuclear weapons in Europe. It was unable to impose curbs on these weapons, as the United States successfully defended its position that they were outside the SALT terms of reference. But as has been seen, some in Western Europe were increasingly unhappy with the exclusion of Soviet INF from SALT, which led them to press for extending the arms control talks to Soviet and U.S. substrategic systems.

The third stage began in 1979, when the USSR secured agreement from the United States that it would discuss its European-based nuclear weapons in a special subforum of SALT. This period was characterized by intense and initially fruitless negotiations (interrupted for about fourteen months in 1983–85) concerning U.S. and Soviet weapons in Europe, and culminated in the INF treaty of December 1987 that banned the deployment of any U.S. ballistic and cruise missile with ranges between 500 and 5,500 kilometers.

The INF treaty opened a fourth stage in the East-West controversy over nuclear weapons in Europe. The USSR called for rapid progress toward a denuclearized continent and tried different tactics to advance this goal. Throughout 1987 and 1988 it held out for the inclusion of battlefield nuclear weapons in the envisioned Conventional Armed Forces in Europe (CFE) talks. In the face of adamant Western and especially French opposition to their inclusion the East abandoned this position in mid-1988, and instead began to press for a separate negotiating forum to deal with reducing and eventually eliminating short-range nuclear forces (SNF) in Europe. There were also bilateral initiatives. In December 1987 Erich Honecker wrote to Chancellor Kohl proposing talks on the elimination of battlefield nuclear weapons along the intra-German border.[92]

As will be seen below, however, by the end of the decade the nuclear issue was increasingly difficult to separate from broader political questions concerning change in Eastern Europe, German reunification, the role of the alliances, and the future of the U.S. and Soviet presence in Europe. While governments debated the procedures for negotiating SNF, in both the East and the West public opinion increasingly determined policy. In the first half of 1989 the United States was forced to postpone, in the face of strong public and parliamentary opposition, plans to modernize its Lance missiles stationed in West Germany. One year later the USSR began pulling all of its SNF out of Eastern Europe following the unexpected collapse of the Communist regimes in those countries and the virtual disintegration of the Warsaw Pact.

Strategic Confidence-Building and No-First Use

In addition to negotiating quantitative and qualitative limitations on their forces, in the 1970s and 1980s the United States and the USSR concluded agreements on measures to improve strategic deterrence and crisis stability through operational constraints.[93] These measures included the nuclear hotline, the 1972 Agreement on Prevention of Incidents On and Over the High Seas, the 1973 Prevention of Nuclear War Agreement, agreements requiring advanced notifications of test ICBM launchings, and the nuclear risk reduction center agreement of 1987. Unlike the confidence-building measures that were negotiated in the CSCE process and that are discussed below, these U.S.-Soviet measures did not impose direct obligations on the West European states. They had implications for NATO, however, in that they could influence the peacetime deployment of U.S. forces earmarked for the defense of Europe or affect the way the United States responded to Soviet actions in a crisis. These agreements also served as models and precedents for Soviet-West European arrangements. Several West European countries established hotlines linking their capitals to Moscow and concluded incidents at sea agreements with the USSR, and in 1990 the thirty-four states participating in the CSCE process agreed to the establishment of a modest all-European conflict prevention center.

The United States proposed most of the U.S.-USSR measures adopted. In formulating these proposals the United States generally took a technical approach. It favored measures that would minimize the likelihood of accidents, miscalculations, and unauthorized acts by the forces of either side, but that would not impose constraints on the political and strategic options available to the United States and its allies in a crisis.

The Soviet approach was different. In periods of high tension the USSR opposed agreements that would have improved the political atmosphere and lessened public and alliance pressure on the United States to actually reduce nuclear forces. When the USSR was more receptive to discussing confidence-building measures it adopted a more political approach, and usually called for agreements that would impinge in some way on defense cooperation between the United States and its allies. In the START talks, for example, it proposed a ban on close approaches by strategic forces to either side's territory or territorial waters, a ban on close approaches by bombers to either side's airspace, and the creation of sanctuaries where nuclear submarines could not be exposed to antisubmarine warfare.[94] On the eve of the Reagan-Gorbachev Moscow summit the USSR temporarily blocked conclusion of a technical agreement providing for the notification of ballistic missile launchers by attempting to broaden its scope to include aircraft and ships, and suggesting provisions that would have prevented each side from carrying out specified aircraft operations and naval maneuvers in zones near the other's territory.[95]

The USSR also proposed various declaratory measures that the United States either rejected outright or sought to "depoliticize" in some fashion. Early in the SALT talks, for example, the Soviets approached the head of the U.S. delegation with an informal offer to discuss a U.S.-Soviet agreement banning the first use of nuclear weapons.[96] Kissinger recalled that in April 1972, as he and Brezhnev made final preparations for the Moscow summit, the Soviet leader proposed that both sides come to an understanding that they would not be the first to use nuclear weapons against each other.[97] Brezhnev floated the same idea with Nixon several weeks later. Although these initiatives were rejected, the USSR scored a partial success with the 1973 Agreement on the Prevention of Nuclear War, which caused unease in Europe and which Kissinger himself later came to regard as a mistake.[98]

In June 1982 Brezhnev announced (through Foreign Minister Gromyko) to the second UN Special Session on Disarmament (SSOD) that the USSR was unilaterally adopting a no-first-use policy.[99] The announcement was followed by a campaign to bilateralize this pledge by pressuring the Western powers to follow suit. In December 1982 a combined session of the CPSU Central Committee, the Supreme Soviet, and the Supreme Soviet of the RSFSR issued an appeal, "To the Parliaments, Governments, Political Parties, and Peoples of the World," calling on all powers "to assume a similar obligation."[100] In the Prague Political Declaration of the following month the members of the Warsaw Pact claimed that they expected "that after the USSR unilaterally adopted the commitment not to be the first to use nuclear weapons, all the nuclear powers which have not yet done so will do the same."[101] Soviet commentators were encouraged by a flurry of interest in no-first use in the West (and especially among retired U.S. officials), but adoption of such a policy and even more so its formalization in an international agreement ran counter to NATO strategy and was not considered seriously by most member-state governments.[102]

The USSR was more successful in securing U.S. agreement to a somewhat vaguer declaratory measure at the 1985 Reagan-Gorbachev summit. The joint statement issued by the two leaders affirmed "that a nuclear war cannot be won and must never be fought." This wording had implications for SDI (with its essentially war-fighting rationale) and was seen by some Western observers as qualifying U.S. nuclear guarantees to allies.[103] Moreover, there were differences of nuance between the English and Russian versions of the statement that lent credibility to these concerns.[104]

Nuclear-free Zones

For much of the postwar period the United States and its allies generally supported the creation of nuclear-free zones in the Third World but opposed their extension to Europe, where they relied on nuclear weapons to counter Soviet conventional military preponderance. The USSR generally favored nuclear-free zones in all parts of the world. It put forward its own proposals for nuclear-free zones in Europe as well as endorsed those of other countries, notably Poland, Romania, Bulgaria, Finland, Sweden, and Yugoslavia.

The first Eastern proposal for the creation of a nuclear-free zone in Europe was put forward in October 1957 by Polish foreign minister Adam Rapacki in a speech to the UN General Assembly. As elabo-

rated in diplomatic notes of December 1957 and a government memorandum of February 1958, the zone was to include the territory of
the FRG, the GDR, Poland, and Czechoslovakia, and would require
the assumption of certain obligations by the four powers. The USSR
endorsed the plan in October 1957 and again in Bulganin's January
1958 letters to foreign leaders.

Soviet sources usually trace the idea of a Nordic nuclear-free zone
to a speech in 1963 by Finnish president Kekkonen. In fact the USSR
first proposed the zone in January 1958. During the previous fall
there had been considerable discussion in NATO regarding the possible deployment of nuclear weapons in Denmark and Norway. Both
governments subsequently made clear that they did not wish to
change their nonnuclear, no foreign base policies and within NATO
the topic was dropped. But the USSR seized upon the controversy
and tried to transform unilateral statements of policy into bilateral
commitments. In a letter to Prime Minister Hansen of Denmark Bulganin noted that "your country's and Norway's refusal of nuclear
weapons, taken together with the fact that there are no nuclear weapons in Sweden and Finland, means that a good basis arises to turn all
northern Europe into a zone free of atomic and hydrogen weapons."[105] He also supported the zone in a letter to Prime Minister Gerhardsen of Norway.[106] The following year Khrushchev offered to
guarantee a nuclear-free zone in the region.[107]

Soviet support for a nuclear-free zone in the Balkans also dates
from the late 1950s. In September 1957 Romanian prime minister
Chivu Stoica sent messages to the five other Balkan states proposing
that they take part in a conference aimed at creating a regional
"peace zone" free of all foreign military bases.[108] The USSR endorsed
the offer, but it was rejected by Greece and Turkey. In a January 1958
meeting with a delegation of Italian Communist peace partisans Foreign Minister Gromyko volunteered that the USSR would welcome
Italy's becoming part of a Balkan nuclear-free zone, and hinted that
in return for Italian participation the USSR would refrain from stationing nuclear weapons in Albania.[109] These proposals elicited little
support in the NATO countries, and in 1959 Greece and Turkey
agreed to host U.S. nuclear weapons. This prompted Romania to revive, in June 1959, its 1957 proposals and to call for a top-level conference to discuss the creation of a nuclear- and missile-free zone in
the region. The USSR endorsed the Romanian proposal, and again
suggested extending the zone to Italy and the Adriatic. It also proposed that the zone be guaranteed by the governments of the four
powers.[110] Greece and Turkey again rejected the offer. (Three years
later the U.S. missiles in Turkey were caught up in the drama of the
Cuban missile crisis.)

Thus by the end of 1959 the USSR had endorsed proposals which, if implemented, would have created a nuclear-free *cordon sanitaire* along its entire Western periphery.[111] In doing so it was reacting to the real danger posed by the deployment of U.S. theater nuclear weapons, but also trying to turn its military concerns to political advantage by linking the proposed zones to the erosion of existing political and military alliances. According to an authoritative 1959 article in *Izvestiia*, formation of a northern nuclear-free zone could "mark the first stage of a shift by all Northern countries to positions of neutrality."[112]

Soviet efforts to advance the various zone proposals were frustrated both by a general suspicion of Soviet motives and by political problems unique to each of the zones. The Rapacki plan would have entailed Western recognition of the GDR and thus was a nonstarter in the political context of the late 1950s. In the Balkans the Albanians opposed the nuclear-free zone and actually wanted the stationing of Soviet rockets on their territory.[113] In northern Europe, the one area that was already de facto nuclear free, Soviet military installations on the Kola Peninsula and naval deployments in the Baltic undercut the appeal of all zone proposals. The USSR rejected suggestions that it include parts of its own territory in the proposed zone, arguing that its forces on the Kola were not directed against countries in the region but against the United States and Britain.[114]

Despite these obstacles, the USSR and its allies intermittently put forward nuclear-free zone proposals throughout the 1960s and early 1970s.[115] In the spring of 1963 President Kekkonen of Finland made a concrete proposal for a Nordic nuclear-free zone which the USSR quickly endorsed.[116] In May 1963 the USSR addressed an appeal to sixteen states asking them to declare the Mediterranean region a nuclear-free zone and offering to guarantee not to target the region with its own weapons.[117] In late 1964 Rapacki renewed his call for a central European nuclear-free zone as part of the Eastern effort to block the MLF. In 1968 the USSR endorsed a joint proposal by Bulgaria and Yugoslavia for a nuclear-free zone in the Balkans and the Mediterranean. In the first Brezhnev peace program of 1971 the USSR pledged "to promote the creation of nonnuclear zones in various regions of the world."[118] In 1974 the USSR proposed that the United States and the USSR remove all nuclear-armed ships from the Mediterranean.[119]

Beginning with the Belgrade follow-up conference of 1977–78 CSCE became the principal forum in which the USSR and its allies promoted nuclear-free zones. In his report to the Twenty-Sixth Party Congress in 1981 Brezhnev declared that "the decisions of the European conference are in fact aimed at making all of Europe such a zone."[120] This rather loose interpretation of the CSCE Final Act (in which the words "nuclear" and "zone" did not even appear) presaged the Soviet position at the 1984–86 Stockholm Conference on Disarmament in Europe (CDE), where the Eastern bloc proposed that the conference work toward the creation of nuclear-free zones in various parts of Europe.

Northern Europe was of greatest interest and offered the best prospect for a breakthrough. The Soviet navy introduced nuclear missile-carrying submarines into the Baltic for the first time in the fall of 1976, which had the initial effect of increasing skepticism about the zone even in Sweden. But the neutron bomb and INF debates later in the decade and the nuclear rhetoric of the Reagan administration early in the 1980s heightened public aversion to nuclear weapons and increased interest in measures deemed useful in keeping the region out of conflict. Soviet authorities claimed that all five of the Nordic countries had declared that they were "in principle" in favor of the zone and that it was being discussed at the regular meetings of the Nordic foreign ministers. (Technically it was not.) Soviet writers also were gratified by the "substantial advances in Sweden's position" following the return to power of the Palme government in 1982.[121]

But even here the obstacles to realization of the zone remained formidable. The running aground of a Soviet submarine in Swedish territorial waters in October 1981 and the Treholt affair of 1984 damaged Soviet credibility in the region.[122] Soviet military installations on the Kola Peninsula and in the Baltic region also remained problems for Soviet diplomats seeking to promote the zone.

Brezhnev displayed a new readiness to address the latter problem in June 1981 when he told an interviewer from the Finnish Social Democratic newspaper that while "the guarantees of non-use of nuclear weapons against countries included in the zone is the chief obligation and undoubtedly the obligation of utmost importance for those countries that the USSR is prepared to assume," he did "not preclude the possibility of considering the question of some other measures applying to our own territory in the region adjoining the nuclear-free zone in the north of Europe," and that the USSR would be "prepared to discuss this question with the countries concerned."[123] A month later, however, Novosti put out a statement reiterating the traditional Soviet stance. It claimed that the military potential of the Kola Peninsula was "part of the global strategic balance between the United States and the USSR and . . . not aimed at the Nordic countries."[124] The quid pro quo for reductions on Kola would have to be limitations on activities in "the international waters of the North Atlantic, where rocket-carrying American submarines and carriers are constantly in operation."

Under Andropov the USSR issued less ambiguous pledges regarding possible concessions involving Soviet territory. In a written reply to a group of Finnish peace organizations in 1983 Andropov essentially reiterated the Brezhnev pledge of two years earlier. He also pledged for the first time, at a dinner for visiting Finnish president Mauno Koivisto, that the USSR was prepared to discuss extending the zone to the Baltic.[125] The Baltic pledge was directed especially at Sweden, which had suggested that the withdrawal of the six submarines deployed in 1976 should be the main Soviet concession in exchange for unequivocal Swedish support for the zone.[126]

It is difficult to say what effect Andropov's offers had on public and elite sentiment, but the Nordic nuclear-free zone idea inched forward in the mid-1980s.[127] Nordic political parties favoring the zone hosted a conference of parliamentarians in Copenhagen in late 1985. To the irritation of some in the Norwegian government, prime ministers Palme of Sweden and Sorsa of Finland attended the meeting, thus lending it higher political visibility than it otherwise would have had.[128] The parliamentarians subsequently formed a five-country parliamentary commission that went to Moscow in October 1988, where it reportedly was told that the USSR was prepared to withdraw its SNF from the Kola Peninsula if a zone was established.[129] On the governmental level the ministers of the five Nordic countries agreed in May 1986 that the political directors of the five foreign ministries would meet periodically to consider the question. The conservative government of Kåre Willoch had opposed formation of such a group, but Norway reversed its policy after the Labor Party returned to power in 1985.[130]

The Gorbachev leadership reiterated Soviet interest in the zone and began to pursue the idea more energetically as part of its overall denuclearization campaign. It removed any remaining ambiguity about whether the USSR was prepared to take more than declaratory measures to further its realization. During his November 1986 visit to Finland hosted by the Finnish Social Democratic Party Egor Ligachev announced that the USSR was prepared to make four unilateral steps which he claimed would promote the creation of a Nordic zone. He stated that the USSR already had dismantled its medium-range missile launchers on the Kola as well as most of such launchers in the Leningrad and Baltic military districts, that it had offered to withdraw Soviet strategic missile submarines (SSBNs) from the Baltic, endorsed additional confidence-building measures for the North and its adjacent seas, and called for the enhancement of confidence-building measures in the naval field, which he suggested could be done by "drawing on the positive experience" of the 1972 U.S.-Soviet incidents at sea agreement and the similar agreement concluded with Britain in 1986.[131] In his October 1987 speech in Murmansk, Gorbachev endorsed the steps announced by Ligachev, affirmed Soviet readiness to discuss "possible measures applicable to Soviet territory," and called for making the zone a component of a broader

Arctic "zone of peace." He also reiterated the Soviet willingness to guarantee the zone and mentioned the various ways a guarantee could be extended.[132] In March 1989 Soviet officials also announced that of the 500,000 troops to be eliminated from the Soviet armed forces, 20,000 would be from regions facing northern Europe.[133] The USSR also announced that it was withdrawing two of its six Golf-class submarines stationed in the Baltic. During his visit to Finland in October Gorbachev announced that the Soviet navy would withdraw the remaining four submarines by the end of 1990, and repeated the Soviet pledge to guarantee, along with other nuclear powers, the nuclear-free status of the Baltic.[134] He further claimed that the USSR no longer had any medium or short-range missiles "on operational status in areas adjacent to the north of Europe."

After largely dropping off the East-West agenda in the mid-1960s, the central European zone resurfaced during the INF controversy of the early 1980s and was given a new impetus by the Independent Commission on Disarmament and Security (the Palme Commission). The commission, which constituted itself in September 1980 and issued a final report in April 1982, recommended the establishment of a battlefield-nuclear-weapon-free zone, starting with central Europe and ultimately extending to the northern and southern flanks of the two alliances. It did not pronounce definitively on the geographic boundaries of the proposed zone, but suggested, for "illustrative purposes," 150 kilometers on both sides of the intra-alliance border.[135]

Although the Soviet government cooperated with the commission, it displayed little enthusiasm for its variant of the zone concept. In a footnote appended to the report, Georgii Arbatov, the Soviet member of the commission, "expressed doubts about the arms control value of this proposal," which he argued would be "of small military significance, would be difficult to negotiate and could create an unfounded impression of enhanced security." Instead, Arbatov called for a "genuine zero-option for Europe," including "radical reductions up to a complete ban of all medium-range and tactical nuclear weapons."[136] TASS reported that the USSR had formally accepted an offer from Palme to take part in multilateral talks on setting up the zone, but called the 150-kilometer proposal inadequate, given the range of existing weapons.[137] Soviet commentators later amplified these remarks, claiming that the Palme proposals proceeded "in the same direction as the efforts being made by the socialist countries," but did not go far enough.[138]

From the Eastern perspective, in addition to diverting energies from the campaign against U.S. INF deployments, a battlefield zone failed to singularize countries in ways that would undercut the strategic unity of the Western alliance. The Palme proposal was based on technical military criteria (however dubious) rather than on a political relationship between the USSR and the Western participants. The Palme report was welcome, however, for the role it later played in stimulating the SPD to begin discussions with the East Germans regarding a nuclear-free corridor in central Europe. At the conclusion of their meeting in East Berlin in September 1985, SPD chairman Brandt and East German leader Honecker announced the creation of a joint working group to discuss the establishment of such a corridor. The group met six times over the course of the next year, and in October 1986 the parties announced agreement on the "Principles for Creating a Nuclear-Free Corridor in Central Europe." The USSR promptly endorsed the proposal.[139]

In one important respect the SED-SPD proposal was more congenial to Soviet interests than the Palme proposal. It stipulated that three years after the realization of the corridor the governments concerned would start negotiating to expand the zone, "for example, [to] an area as defined in the Vienna talks between NATO and Warsaw Treaty Organization countries."[140] Qualifying language was inserted stating that expansion would depend on other factors such as the conventional balance and "the overall development of East-West relations," but the door was opened to discussion of a Rapacki-type zone.

Soviet support for the Balkan nuclear-free zone cooled in the 1960s and 1970s as it became primarily a device by which Romania sought to expand its autonomy within the Warsaw Pact, but revived in the 1980s as the overall importance of nuclear-free zones in Soviet diplomacy increased.[141] In January 1985 Prime Minister Papandreou threatened to order the removal of all U.S. nuclear weapons from Greek territory if there was no progress toward the creation of a Balkan nuclear-free zone. These remarks were widely seen as posturing by Papandreou, but nonetheless were welcomed in Moscow.[142] Reflecting changing Soviet attitudes, Bulgaria warmed to the zone idea, and at the Vienna CSCE review conference joined with Romania to introduce a proposal for "zones of peace and good neighborly relations free from nuclear and chemical weapons."[143] At the February 1988 Belgrade conference of the foreign ministers of the Balkan countries (the first such meeting since the early 1930s) Bulgaria and Romania both canvassed support for a Balkan zone. During his visit to Yugoslavia the following month, Gorbachev told his hosts that the USSR was ready to "give all necessary guarantees should it be decided to establish a zone free of nuclear and chemical weapons in the Balkans."[144] The USSR continued to support a Mediterranean zone, either linked to or separate from a wider Balkan initiative. The Warsaw Pact Political Consultative Committee (PCC) declaration of January 1983 called for transforming the Mediterranean into a "zone of peace."[145] In March 1986 Gorbachev called for negotiations on the simultaneous withdrawal of the Soviet and U.S. fleets from the Mediterranean.[146]

The USSR also endorsed movements by local authorities to declare cities and other administrative units nuclear-free zones. The municipal nuclear-free zone movement began in November 1980, when Manchester, England, declared itself such a zone, and by the spring of 1984 170 municipal councils in Britain had made similar declarations. In Italy there were approximately 250 nuclear-free municipalities.[147] In a letter to Kenneth Livingstone of the Greater London Council Gorbachev declared that "in this we perceive the peoples' realization of their responsibility for the world's fate and their intention to act in forms available to them. The edifice of peace is made of separate bricks. Détente is made up of tiny grains."[148] According to one Soviet specialist, by mid-1987 there were already 3,200 nuclear-free cities throughout the world (none of which were in the USSR or Eastern Europe).[149]

No-Use Guarantees

Soviet offers to guarantee, on a bilateral basis, nonnuclear states against nuclear attack were a more limited variant of the nuclear-free zone concept. In the 1950s and early 1960s the USSR frequently threatened nonnuclear states with nuclear attack. Philip Mosely observed in 1962 that the USSR had "addressed blackmail notes to more than 30 governments, in which it [had] threatened their peoples specifically with nuclear destruction unless they abandon[ed] certain policies and postures of which Moscow disapproves."[150] Most of Bulganin's January 1958 letters contained explicit and regionally nuanced atomic threats. Writing to the prime minister of Greece, for example, Bulganin predicted that NATO plans "would bring great calamities on the Greek people." To Portugal's António Salazar he wrote that "the presence of foreign-controlled war bases . . . offers no escape from the disastrous consequences of modern war, especially in view of the development of military techniques." To those countries such as Norway and Denmark that did not have nuclear weapons on their soil, Bulganin expressed "great satisfaction" with their nonnuclear policies, but also warned against the danger of establishing U.S. bases.[151] Khrushchev added a strong personal flavor to Soviet nuclear threats, not only in speeches and letters but in personal encounters with foreign leaders and ambassadors. Khrushchev's private warnings reached a crescendo in the summer of 1961, shortly before the building of the Berlin wall (which suggests that he might have seen such threats as a way to forestall Western reactions). He told the British ambassador that he could destroy Britain with eight nuclear bombs.[152] Shortly thereafter he complained to Italian prime minister Fanfani about U.S. missiles stationed in southern Italy and boasted that "he could blast them out of the orange groves."[153] Gromyko and other Soviet officials apparently were under instructions to take part in this campaign as well.[154]

Although as recently as the early 1980s some Soviet officials reverted to the pattern of the Khrushchev era and hinted at the nuclear destruction of other countries,[155] under Brezhnev the USSR largely abandoned this practice as counterproductive. Instead, it offered to guarantee not to target countries that did not have nuclear weapons on their territory. Although superficially reassuring, such guarantee proposals in fact contained an implicit threat by promising a lower level of security to those countries not opting to become nuclear-free.

The question of guarantees by nuclear powers to nonnuclear states first arose in the nonproliferation negotiations of the 1960s. Critics of the NPT argued that it would create two classes of states and would consign the nonnuclear powers to a lower level of security. In response, the sponsoring powers discussed various formulas that would guarantee nonnuclear states against attack or intimidation by states possessing nuclear weapons. The USSR put forward the "Kosygin formula" that would have guaranteed nonuse only against nonnuclear states that did not have nuclear weapons on their territories.[156] This was rejected by the United States and Britain as an attempt to use the NPT to promote the emergence of nuclear-free zones. The United States eventually agreed to what were called "positive security assurances." In separate, identical statements to the Security Council, the United States, Britain, and the USSR agreed that aggression with nuclear weapons or the threat of such aggression by a nonnuclear state against a nonnuclear party to the treaty "would create a qualitatively new situation" that would require Security Council action.

At the 1978 UN Special Session on Disarmament each of the nuclear powers bowed to Third World pressures and offered separate and somewhat different assurances that they would not use or threaten the use of weapons against nonnuclear states. While the United States basically reaffirmed its Security Council statement of 1968, the USSR submitted a document in which it declared that it "will never use nuclear weapons against those States which renounce the production and acquisition of nuclear weapons and have no nuclear weapons on their territories." It further offered "to conclude special agreements to that effect with any such non-nuclear State" and called upon the other nuclear powers to follow the Soviet lead.[157] It subsequently launched a campaign in the UN and in the Conference on Disarmament for the conclusion of an international convention embodying the proposed guarantees.[158] In his report to the 1981 Twenty-Sixth Party Congress Brezhnev recalled this pledge. Two months later he used a reply to questions submitted by an Athens newspaper to suggest a bilateral guarantee agreement with Greece.[159] Similar offers later were made to the Netherlands, Spain, and other countries.[160] Moreover, in December 1982 the UN General Assembly adopted a resolution (by a vote of 108–17 with the Western states opposed) calling for the negotiation of an international convention "to assure non-nuclear-weapon States against the use or threat of use of nuclear weapons."[161] But no Western government responded positively to these Soviet offers, although some interest was displayed in opposition political parties.

British and French Nuclear Weapons

It often has been difficult to tell to what extent Soviet military and civilian policymakers were genuinely concerned about these forces and to what extent they were interested in using them to defend their own policies or to gain compensation from the United States in U.S.-Soviet negotiations.[162] In the 1940s and early 1950s the USSR did not make a concerted effort to block British acquisition of nuclear weapons. Britain was still treated by the USSR as a great power, nonproliferation in itself was not a Soviet (or Western) policy goal, and the British Communist Party was not a major political force that could be mobilized in an antinuclear campaign.

Even more striking is how little the USSR did in the late 1950s and early 1960s to derail the British nuclear program, which by then was under attack by the Campaign for Nuclear Disarmament (CND) and threatened by economic and financial constraints. On several occasions leaders of the Labour Party asked Khrushchev whether the USSR would exercise restraint in its own weapons programs if Britain were to forgo certain options, thereby practically inviting him to meddle in the British domestic debate. But each time Khrushchev was bluntly negative. In 1957 he told Bevan that British renunciation of the hydrogen bomb would not make the slightest difference to the USSR.[163] When Gaitskell asked him in 1959 whether unilateral disarmament by Britain would elicit a Soviet response, he replied, "we do not want our grandchildren to call us fools."[164] Nor did Bulganin and Khrushchev complain unduly about British nuclear weapons in their meetings and correspondence with Eden and Macmillan.

The Soviet attitude toward the French nuclear program was somewhat harsher, although for reasons that seem to have had little to do with the program as such. When France exploded its first nuclear device in February 1960, TASS issued a statement condemning the action, but more for the fact that it was taken while the USSR was observing a unilateral moratorium on tests and because the test took place in the Sahara in defiance of African and Asian opinion.[165] The statement said nothing about the dangers of France acquiring nuclear weapons.

Soviet officials stressed that because the tests were conducted by a member of NATO, they placed the USSR in "an unequal position."[166] Khrushchev charged that France was "perfect[ing] nuclear weapons in the interests of its Western allies."[167] In view of the known U.S. hostility to the French program, this line of argument suggests that the USSR may have been more interested in justifying its own decision to resume testing than in blocking France's acquisition of nuclear weapons. On one of the few occasions that Khrushchev linked the French tests to the dangers of proliferation, it is noteworthy that he did not question the reasonableness of de Gaulle's desire "to conduct an independent policy," but instead raised questions about "other countries" (presumably Germany) that might adopt the same logic.

What the USSR probably found most disturbing about French behavior was de Gaulle's defection from the arms control process in the early 1960s. Whereas membership in the nuclear club spurred Britain to arms control efforts that were welcomed in Moscow, the belated development of France's program and the political vision that drove it dictated an "empty chair" policy that clashed with the USSR's growing political stake in arms control talks. Pineau recalled a meeting with Khrushchev in which the Soviet leader referred more than ten times to France's refusal to sign the LTB and in which he accused France of trying to sabotage détente.[168] On balance, however, the USSR did not allow differences over nuclear issues to block improvement of relations with de Gaulle, and did not encourage the French Communist Party to wage an all-out campaign against the *force de frappe.*

In the 1960s the USSR acknowledged the conuclear status of Britain and France in special political and confidence-building agreements. During de Gaulle's first meeting with Kosygin in 1966 France and the USSR established a direct teletype link patterned after the U.S.-Soviet hotline. Britain followed suit during Kosygin's February 1967 visit to Britain. These understandings were followed by accidental measures agreements patterned on the 1971 U.S.-Soviet Agreement on Measures to Reduce the Risk of Outbreak of Nuclear War.[169] France and the USSR concluded such an agreement in July 1976; Britain and the USSR in October 1977. Britain's status as a sponsor of the NPT also served as the basis for a modest special relationship. Nonproliferation was a major subject in U.K.-USSR bilateral exchanges in the 1960s, and during the 1975 visit to Moscow of Prime Minister Wilson the two countries signed a joint Declaration on Nonproliferation of Nuclear Weapons.[170] The USSR and France concluded a similar declaration during Brezhnev's June 1977 visit to Paris, even though France reaffirmed its intention not to sign the NPT.

In the 1970s the USSR made sporadic efforts to involve France and Britain (and China) in arms control negotiations. In his report to the Twenty-Fourth Party Congress Brezhnev called for the convocation of a disarmament conference of the five nuclear powers, but provided no details about the relationship of this conference to SALT.[171] This proposal elicited no support from the other four nuclear powers and was quietly dropped from the next edition of the Brezhnev "peace program." The USSR also made private but unsuccessful diplomatic approaches to Britain and probably France proposing that they accede to the U.S.-Soviet agreement on the prevention of nuclear war.[172]

In 1978 the USSR responded favorably to France's decision to join the Conference on Disarmament, and agreed to meet the French condition that the USSR and the United States relinquish their cochairmanship. But in its own presentation to the special session the USSR called for new talks on the complete elimination of nuclear weapons and suggested that "an appropriate preparatory committee" could be used to prepare a new forum in which all the nuclear powers and a certain number of nonnuclear states would participate.[173] France and the other nuclear powers rejected this offer.

During the INF controversy of 1979–83 Soviet proposals emphasized the threat to the USSR of British and French nuclear weapons, but not the creation of new forums in which to discuss these weapons. When Gromyko was asked point blank by President Carter whether the USSR "was sincere about involving the other three countries—France, Great Britain, and China in the future SALT III talks," he gave an "equivocal" answer rather than a clear yes.[174] In June 1983 the USSR formally proposed a quantitative and qualitative freeze on all nuclear weapons to be agreed by all the nuclear powers, but it appeared to suggest that the freeze might initially apply only to U.S. and Soviet forces.[175]

With the defusing of the INF crisis in 1984 and Gorbachev's accession to power the following year, Soviet officials displayed a somewhat greater interest in direct negotiations with third countries. As noted in chapter five, in November 1984 the CPSU replied positively to the British Labour Party's offer for a bilateral agreement involving the elimination of British nuclear forces. Gorbachev repeated this offer in the January 1986 letter to Kenneth Livingstone, head of the Greater London Council.[176]

In his October 1985 speech to a joint session of the French parliament Gorbachev called for a "direct dialogue" with France and Britain on their nuclear forces. The speech was followed by formal proposals to both countries for direct talks on nuclear weapons.[177] Gorbachev's January 1986 plan for the complete elimination of nuclear weapons by the year 2000 called for Britain and France to freeze their arsenals in the first stage of the plan, to eliminate their tactical nuclear weapons and cease all tests in the second stage, and to abolish their forces in the final stage of the plan. It did not, however, suggest how British and French participation in the plan would be negotiated.[178]

At Reykjavik Gorbachev again separated British and French systems from U.S. INF, thereby paving the way toward the conclusion of the zero-option treaty. But Soviet officials made clear that any efforts by the British or French to slow the momentum toward a zero or double-zero U.S.-USSR INF treaty would result in Soviet demands that third country forces be brought back into the negotiations.[179] Whether these threats had any effect on dampening official opposition in London and Paris to the INF treaty beyond the influence already exerted by domestic and intra-alliance politics it is impossible to know.[180]

Soviet experts also claimed that the ministry of foreign affairs drew upon detailed analyses to determine whether the USSR could afford to conclude an INF treaty that did not take account of British and French systems. According to one of the experts familiar with a computer model that was used, analysts concluded that "the military strategic nuclear parity which exists between the USSR and the U.S.A. is characterized by a substantial dynamic margin, the so-called 'margin of safety' for both sides."[181] Models then were used to calculate "the existing dynamic margin of the USSR-U.S.A. military parity," which in turn enabled the USSR to accept the zero option. According to the same expert, British and French systems were considered in this analysis.[182]

After the signature of the INF treaty, Soviet officials began giving more thought to ways of bringing French and British nuclear weapons into the arms control talks. At the July 1988 foreign ministry conference a working group of experts concluded that "a major cut in Soviet and U.S. strategic armaments and the introduction of rigid controls on their modernization could result in European nuclear powers revising their attitude to participation in nuclear disarmament."[183] There also was a lively debate on this issue among foreign ministry officials, some of whom were sharply critical of the 1987 analyses for underestimating the importance of West European nuclear forces.[184] But neither France nor Britain softened its stance on nonparticipation in nuclear arms control talks, even though U.S.-Soviet progress toward a START agreement was expected to intensify domestic and international pressures for a change in this position. These expectations were confirmed in 1990, when Gorbachev strongly pressed the United States to give formal assurances that U.S.-U.K. nuclear cooperation would end after the completion of the planned Trident D-5 program.[185]

Briefings

While West European governments never engaged in direct negotiations with the USSR, they did receive Soviet briefings on arms control and disarmament issues. Before 1985 Soviet ambassadors often called on host governments to provide written or oral versions of developments in the U.S.-Soviet arms control process. The Soviet embassy in Bonn, for example, delivered memoranda to the chancellor's office after each round of the NST talks in Geneva.[186] Arms control also was a frequent topic in the bilateral consultations discussed in chapter four. In addition, the USSR occasionally sent special envoys to European capitals, usually after party congresses and other major events.

The United States also consulted regularly with its West European allies on arms control issues and generally enjoyed certain advantages over the USSR in the consultation process.[187] U.S. credibility was higher, and U.S. ambassadors usually were better informed on arms control issues than their Soviet counterparts. Soviet special envoys were more qualified than resident ambassadors, but could do more harm than good by raising expectations that were not fulfilled. In 1971, for example, the British awaited a visit from Deputy Foreign Minister Semën K. Tsarapkin, expecting information that could lead to a breakthrough on conventional arms control talks in central Europe, but were disappointed when Tsarapkin merely informed them about the Twenty-Fourth Party Congress peace program and sought to elicit British reactions to the call for a five-nation nuclear disarmament conference. Above all, the United States had an enormous advantage over the USSR in that it was able to use the NATO machinery in Brussels for purposes of consultation.

These traditional Western advantages were diminished somewhat after the 1985 Reagan-Gorbachev Geneva summit, as the United States and the USSR both began sending special envoys to national capitals on the occasion of all ostensibly important arms control developments. The USSR dispatched teams in early 1986 after Gorbachev's announcement of a plan for the complete elimination of nuclear weapons by the year 2000; in the fall of 1986 following the Reykjavik summit; in December 1986 to mark the start of the first post-Reykjavik round of the NST talks; and in March–May 1987 after Gorbachev made his "double zero" INF proposal. On some occasions Soviet briefers were designated personal envoys of Gorbachev, charged with delivering "oral messages." In July 1986, for example, a team of envoys was dispatched "to emphasize the importance of solving the problems of disarmament at an earliest date while a war-starting decision is still taken by the leaders of states, and not by computers."[188] The reasons for Gorbachev's personal involvement in delivering an essentially routine piece of propaganda were unclear, but it ensured that the envoys were received at high levels and that the message attracted media attention.

East European and neutral and nonaligned (NNA) governments seemed to genuinely appreciate being informed by envoys from Washington and Moscow, but in NATO capitals roving teams of U.S. and Soviet envoys were regarded as a mixed blessing. They competed in selling their respective proposals, presented different versions of what transpired in important meetings, and in general heightened the circus atmosphere already surrounding summits and other high-level U.S.-Soviet meetings.[189] The presence of a Soviet briefer helped to lend credibility to the most one-sided or utopian Soviet proposals, as Western governments inevitably received the briefer at an appropriate level, announced that it was "studying" the proposals, welcomed the fact that they were made, and so on. Soviet briefers also had numerous opportunities for media appearances (in which they could offer "inside" information disparaging U.S. proposals), and on occasion meddled in domestic politics. On trips to West Germany, for example, Soviet briefers made it a point to accord the government and the SPD equal treatment. After Reykjavik Viktor Karpov saw both Egon Bahr and Chancellor Kohl, even though in Britain he met only with Prime Minister Thatcher and not with the Labour Party leaders.

Conventional Arms Control

Background

Before 1955 Soviet conventional arms control policy largely consisted of ritual attacks on foreign military bases and repetition of the Soviet proposal for one-third reductions in the forces of the great powers. The USSR adhered to the percentage reduction approach even after the Western powers put forward, in May and August 1952, proposals based on manpower ceilings on the forces of the five powers: 1–1.5 million each for the United States, the USSR, and China, and 700,000–800,000 each for France and Britain. The USSR rejected these offers as well as a modified version of March 1955 that would have lowered French and British levels to 650,000 men each.[190]

The Soviet commitment to the percentage approach began to weaken with the prospect of German rearmament. The May 1955 proposal that figured prominently at the July 1955 Geneva summit essentially accepted the Western-proposed force levels for the five powers, but also called for an international treaty obliging all states to freeze conventional forces and expenditures at the levels of December 31, 1954.[191] Such a freeze would have aborted West German rearmament, which got under way in earnest only in 1955. The May 1955 proposal also contained the familiar provision for the "liquidation of all foreign military, naval and air bases."

At the Geneva summit Bulganin reiterated the proposal of May 10 and claimed that the Soviet government had "accepted the proposal made by the three powers in regard to conventional armaments" and that "now we are entitled to expect that these powers would take a step which would ensure agreement on the prohibition of atomic weapons."[192] Bulganin's assertion was only partially correct, as in fact the Western powers had not proposed a freeze on the force levels of other powers. Bulganin later modified the Soviet stance to call for limits of 150,000–200,000 on the forces of other states, and the USSR formally tabled a proposal that included a provision limiting the armed forces of "all other States" to this level and suggesting that exact numbers could be determined "at an appropriate international conference."[193]

Throughout this period neither the proposals introduced by any of the powers nor the fora in which these proposals were to be negotiated were specifically European. The approach was global and concentrated on the great powers, all of which had substantial forces stationed outside Europe. Even after the USSR began trying to use arms control to stop the development of the West German army it did not do so by proposing limits on European forces, but by the indirect route of a global freeze or numerical ceilings on the forces of "all other states."

The first steps toward a Europeanization of conventional arms control came not from the USSR but from the West. As was seen in chapter three, at the January 1954 Berlin foreign ministers conference Molotov rejected the Eden plan for free all-German elections on the grounds that it did not provide the USSR with adequate safeguards against the danger of a unified, remilitarized German state. Eighteen months later the Western powers went to Geneva with proposals designed either to allay Soviet concerns or to show that these concerns were spurious and were being used as a pretext to thwart unification.[194]

In his opening speech to the first plenary session Eden introduced two proposals, a security pact and an agreement "as to the total of forces and armaments on each side in Germany and the countries neighboring Germany," both of which he linked to the question of German unification.[195] His intent was not to Europeanize arms control, but to introduce an arms control component into the discussion of the European political order and German reunification. Later in the conference, the British offered another proposal—a plan for a system of joint inspection that would operate "in unspecified areas of agreed extent on either side of the line dividing Eastern and Western Europe."[196]

While the proposals made "in connection with European security" were intended to facilitate movement on the German issue by alleviating Soviet concerns, the inspection scheme appeared to go in the other direction by making the inner-German border a structural element of a permanent and potentially expanding arms control enterprise. For this reason, the proposal caused intense irritation in Bonn, where it was seen as "premised on the acceptance of the ongoing division of Germany."[197]

At the foreign ministers meeting in the fall of 1955 the USSR and the Western powers both elaborated upon their earlier proposals. The Western powers spelled out more concretely what they were prepared to do to assure the USSR that a reunified Germany would not pose a threat to its security. In addition to renouncing the use of force and withholding support for aggressors, they offered to negotiate, "in a zone comprising areas of comparable size and depth and importance on both sides of the line of demarcation between a reunified Germany and the East European countries, levels for armed forces [that] would be specified so as to establish a military balance."[198] This proposal, which was formally submitted on behalf of the three Western powers by Foreign Minister Pinay of France, was not billed as a disarmament measure but as part of a proposed "treaty of assurance" intended to make German reunification more palatable to the USSR. It was submitted and discussed under Item 1 (European security and Germany) in the conference agenda and described as part of the Western response to that part of the Geneva directive calling for the reunification of Germany by means of free elections. Molotov's contribution to the discussion of Item 1 was to introduce yet another version of the General European Treaty on Collective Security in Europe.[199] When two weeks later the conference turned to its second agenda item—disarmament—Molotov reintroduced the Soviet draft proposal on force reductions that Bulganin had made at Geneva. The Western powers repeated their confidence-building proposals of July.[200] Pinay, who again spoke on behalf of the West, made only a perfunctory reference to the British proposal "to undertake practical experiments on problems of inspection and control."[201]

Thus the basic approaches of the sides were clear. Under Item 1 (European security and Germany) the West was in favor of a regional arms control plan to facilitate German reunification. Under Item 2 (disarmament) it was offering a grab bag of confidence-building measures. The USSR, in contrast, was not interested in reunification and stuck with its global approach. In addition, Molotov showed some interest in Eden's zone proposal of July, to some extent confirming German fears that it would help to reinforce the division of Germany.[202]

The USSR's partial measures proposal of March 1956 basically followed the global approach of the May 10 proposal, but contained a new element under the heading "Creation in Europe of a zone of limitation and inspection of armaments." The proposal called for ceilings on the forces of the four powers in the zone, total denuclearization of the zone, and joint inspection measures.[203] The Soviet Union put forward a modified version of this proposal in March 1957, and in April Bulganin wrote to Macmillan to suggest, among other things, that "the Soviet Government would be willing to resume discussion of the proposals, made some time ago in a general form by Sir Anthony Eden, on the creation of demilitarized zones in Europe and of areas of restricted armaments," provided the corresponding proposals by the USSR, such as that for an aerial inspection zone in Europe, could also be discussed.[204] The Soviet intent was to associate the USSR's new zonal proposals with those put forward by Eden and thus to delink the British proposals from the political context in which they had been made. In his reply, however, Macmillan reiterated the political assumptions underlying the Western disarmament offensive of 1955, reminding Bulganin that "these proposals were put forward as part of a comprehensive settlement which, in accordance with the directive approved by the Heads of Government at the summit conference, was intended to provide concurrently for a reunification of Germany in freedom and for the establishment of a security system to meet the legitimate defense requirements of the USSR and other European States."[205]

The Rapacki proposals of 1957 and 1958 essentially built upon the Soviet partial measures proposal of March 1956. They focused on denuclearization and conventional reductions within a central European zone and separated disengagement from the broader political question of reunification. Rapacki's first proposal dealt almost exclusively with nuclear weapons, but had a tenuous link to conventional reductions. The Polish government declared that it had "reasons to state" that acceptance of its proposal would "facilitate the reaching of an agreement relating to the adequate reduction of conventional armaments and of foreign armed forces stationed on the territory of the states included in the zone."[206] In November 1958 Rapacki circulated a second version of the plan that was intended, by placing greater emphasis on conventional forces, to meet objections raised by Western governments. The revised plan would be implemented in two stages. In the first stage denuclearization of central Europe would begin and control measures would be introduced. This would be followed by talks on the reduction of conventional forces in the zone leading to an "appropriate reduction." In the second stage denuclearization would be completed.[207]

In 1959 Soviet interest in zonal arms control began to fade. At the conclusion of Macmillan's February–March visit to the USSR, Britain and the USSR agreed that "further study could usefully be made of the possibilities of increasing security by some method of limitation of forces and weapons, both conventional and nuclear, in an agreed area of Europe, coupled with an appropriate system of inspection.[208] But later in the year Khrushchev launched his campaign for complete and general disarmament, thereby shifting the focus back to global ceilings without region-specific subcomponents. Equally important, as Khrushchev made clear that he was not interested in German reunification in any form, he deprived governments and nongovernmental actors in the West of any further motivation to look to zonal arms reduction as a potential means to encourage political change.[209]

The USSR's first proposal for complete and general disarmament, issued in September 1959, did lay out a plan for the complete elimination of conventional forces in stages. The first stage called for setting British and French force strength at 650,000 men each (as in the proposals of 1955), and limiting the United States, China, and the USSR to 1.7 million men each. Levels for other states were not spelled out, but were to be negotiated at a "special session of the UN General Assembly or at a world conference on general and complete disarmament." The second stage of the plan called for the complete elimination of foreign military bases, and represented a step back from the Soviet proposal of March 1956, which tacitly accepted such bases by calling for negotiated ceilings on U.S., French, and British forces in the central European region.[210]

The declining Soviet interest in negotiated conventional arms control coincided with the decision by Khrushchev, which he announced to the Supreme Soviet on January 15, 1960, to unilaterally reduce the size of the Soviet armed forces by one-third over the course of the next two years.[211] As in the spring of 1956, Khrushchev's impatience with the arms control process, his dislike of verification measures, and his conviction that nuclear weapons alone were truly important—both for military planning and arms control—encouraged him to act unilaterally.

In June 1960 the USSR submitted to the UN a draft "Basic Provisions of a Treaty on General and Complete Disarmament" that indicated even less interest in negotiated conventional disarmament. The first stage of the new proposal dealt exclusively with banning nuclear weapons (except for a provision for the withdrawal of troops from foreign bases), while conventional reductions were deferred to the post-nuclear future. In 1962 the USSR submitted a draft treaty to the UN that closely followed the June 1960 proposal.[212]

Throughout the period of the complete and general disarmament campaign the USSR introduced only one plan for partial measures that was somewhat negotiable. This was an eight-point memorandum submitted to the General Assembly in September 1961 entitled, "Measures to Ease International Tension, Strengthen Confidence among States, and Contribute to General and Complete Disarmament." This document called for the freezing of military budgets, renunciation of the use of nuclear weapons, renunciation of war propaganda, and conclusion of a nonaggression pact between NATO and the Warsaw Pact.[213] The fifth item of the memorandum dealt with the withdrawal of troops from foreign territory, and proposed a first-step "agreement to reduce the number of all foreign troops stationed in Germany by one-third or by some other accepted proportion over a given period of time and to institute the necessary control over the execution of this measure." This positive gesture relating to Germany may have been intended to deflect attention from the erection of the Berlin wall, which had taken place the previous month.

For the remainder of the decade, however, conventional arms control was relegated to a very minor status in East-West relations. The United States and Britain concentrated on the test ban and nonproliferation treaties, while the USSR went from indifference to seeming hostility. In December 1964 the new Kosygin-Brezhnev leadership submitted to the UN an eleven-point "Memorandum of the Soviet Government on Measures for the Further Reduction of International Tensions and Restriction of the Arms Race" that included, in addition to provisions on testing and proliferation, a call for measures to prevent surprise attack and a proposed reduction of the total strength of armed forces.[214] But in his message to the Geneva Conference of January 1966 Kosygin dropped all mention of troop reductions and measures to prevent surprise attacks. The change reflected the growing Soviet stress on the nuclear proliferation issue (and in particular the interest in heading off an expanded nuclear role for West Germany), the USSR's own post-1965 conventional buildup in central Europe, as well as reaction to the Vietnam War and a sensitivity to Chinese charges that the USSR was facilitating the transfer of U.S. troops from Europe to Asia.[215] Late in the decade the Western powers became increasingly concerned about the U.S. involvement in Vietnam, the possibility of large unilateral U.S. force cuts, and the Soviet proposal for a European security conference, all of which encouraged them to press for European force reduction talks. As will be seen, however, until well into the 1970s the Soviet response was largely negative.

MBFR: Background

Western interest in the talks on Mutual Reduction of Forces and Armaments and Associated Measures in Europe, or what in the West generally came to be called the Mutual and Balanced Force Reduction (MBFR) talks, first surfaced in the 1967 Harmel report on the future tasks of the alliance. The report concluded that NATO had two primary functions: "to maintain adequate military strength and political solidarity to deter aggression" and "to pursue the search for progress towards a more stable relationship in which the underlying political issues can be solved."[216] The commitment to solving the "underlying political issues," and specifically the German problem, was consistent with Western declarations of the 1950s and early 1960s, but the report did not link movement on these issues to progress in arms control. It went on to note that the allies were "studying disarmament and practical arms control measures, including the possibility of balanced force reductions."

At their Reykjavik meeting in June 1968 the NATO ministers issued a declaration on force reduction talks that set forth the principles they believed would have to govern a successful negotiation. The most important were that the reductions "should be reciprocal and balanced in scope and timing" and consistent with "the vital security interests of all parties."[217] The ministers also endorsed a direct approach to the USSR by a representative of the alliance.[218]

The Soviet response to the NATO appeal was negative. At the time the Warsaw Pact was pressing its campaign for a European security conference. Western governments did not expressly stipulate that participation in the conference was conditional upon Soviet acceptance of MBFR but, in fact, the West had decided to make force reduction talks a counter-issue to the conference. This led to considerable frustration on the Soviet side, which was unwilling to get bogged down in a lengthy arms control process to which the West could hold the security conference hostage. The USSR claimed that it was disposed in principle to force reduction talks, but suggested that such talks could succeed only if they took place after the political conference had been convened. The Pact countries also suggested some form of organizational link between MBFR and the political conference, thereby establishing a counterlinkage making Eastern participation in MBFR conditional upon the convening of the conference.

The August 1968 Warsaw Pact invasion of Czechoslovakia and the resulting deterioration in political relations temporarily blocked movement toward either a European conference or force reduction talks. But by the spring of 1970 progress toward both had resumed.

At the Rome meeting in May 1970 the North Atlantic Council adopted a declaration inviting "interested states" to hold "multilateral exploratory talks on mutual and balanced force reductions in Europe, with special reference to the central region."[219] To give effect to the declaration, the ministers asked the Italian foreign minister to transmit the declaration through diplomatic channels to "all other interested parties" and to solicit their reactions.

TASS characterized the NATO invitation as "full of reservations intended to confuse the clear-cut problem and to drown in endless procedural questions the urgent proposal [that is, the European security conference] that meets the most vital interests of the peoples of Europe."[220] Despite this largely negative reaction, the following month the Pact took an important but conditional step toward the Western position. In its June 1970 Budapest Memorandum it expressed readiness to discuss the "reduction of foreign forces," either "in the body whose creation at the all-European conference is proposed, or in another forum acceptable to the interested states."[221] But the bulk of the memorandum dealt with the proposed security conference which, it was hinted, was a Soviet precondition for talks on arms control.

In 1971 Brezhnev made two sets of remarks which further raised Western expectations. In his February report to the Twenty-Fourth Party Congress he declared that the USSR was "for the dismantling of foreign military bases" and "for the reduction of armed forces and armaments in areas where military confrontation is especially dangerous, above all in central Europe."[222] Although a step toward the Western position, Brezhnev's reference to talks concerning central Europe was only one element in his comprehensive peace program, and was ranked far below references to political initiatives such as the convening of an all-European conference. Two months later he made his famous Tbilisi speech, inviting the West to "taste the wine" of arms control in Europe.

Because such large conclusions later were drawn from this speech,[223] it is worthwhile to examine its relevant passages in detail. As noted in chapter five, the passage on force reductions was preceded by an appeal to an upcoming meeting of the Socialist International, at which Brezhnev's pet project of a European security conference was on the agenda. The Soviet leader noted that among the social democrats about to gather in Helsinki were "a good many representatives of ruling parties." Although he did not make the point explicitly, he clearly had in mind the West German SPD. Brezhnev then declared:

The interests of the workers' movement and the interests of peace the world over demand that those who will be making decisions in Helsinki not forget about the monstrous crimes the imperialist aggressors are committing in

Vietnam, Cambodia and Laos and on the seized territories of the Arab countries. The interests of European security demand that they not forget the will of their own peoples, who want the complete elimination of the legacy of the "cold war" and the speediest possible creation in Europe of an atmosphere of cooperation and good-neighbor relations. Otherwise, the session's participants will only confirm that their "international" continues to prefer to heed not the voice of the masses but those who determine NATO policy.[224]

The anti-U.S. tone, the appeal to the socialists to distance themselves from NATO policy, and the call for the "complete elimination of the legacy of the 'cold war'" (a Soviet codeword for recognition of the territorial and political status quo) strongly suggest that these remarks were not meant as a preface to a Soviet call for the United States to maintain its military forces in Europe. This was made even clearer in the subsequent passage:

In connection with the West's reaction to the proposals advanced at the [Twenty Fourth Party] Congress . . . , some NATO countries are displaying an appreciable interest, and in part some nervousness as well, on the question of the reduction of armed forces and armaments in central Europe. Their representatives ask: Whose armed forces—foreign or national—and what armaments—nuclear or conventional—are to be reduced? . . . In this connection, we too have a question to ask: Do not such curious people resemble a person who tries to judge the taste of a wine by its appearance alone, without touching it? If there is any vagueness, this can certainly be eliminated. All that is necessary is to muster the resolve to "taste" the proposals that interest you, which, translated into diplomatic language, means to enter into negotiations.[225]

Although these remarks may have had an *effect* on the U.S. Senate, their tone, context, and content suggest that this was not their intended audience. The "negotiations" endorsed by Brezhnev did not refer to MBFR as envisioned by NATO but to his own proposals at the party congress.

Subsequent events tend to support this interpretation. Although pressures for the adoption of a Mansfield-type amendment continued until the middle of 1973, the USSR strenuously resisted progress toward the convening of a conventional force reduction forum. As one of the closest Western observers of Soviet policy noted at the time, the Tbilisi speech could "hardly be described as a source of Soviet movement toward force reduction talks."[226] In June 1971 the NATO foreign ministers sought to probe the meaning behind Brezhnev's remarks by announcing their readiness to appoint, "at the appropriate time," a representative responsible to the (NATO) Council who would conduct "exploratory talks" with the USSR and other interested governments to work out the time, place, arrangements, and agenda for the negotiations.[227] Initial Soviet commentary on the NATO offer was negative. According to TASS, the NATO communiqué "contains lengthy statements on the desirability of mutual and balanced force reductions, but it gives no concrete answer to the recent initiative of the USSR, which offered to hold talks on the reduction of armed forces and armaments in central Europe."[228] A few days later, Soviet deputy foreign minister Tsarapkin flew to London for talks with British officials in which he reiterated the Soviet willingness to discuss troop reductions, but only within the framework of a general European security conference.[229]

Further evidence that Brezhnev viewed MBFR mainly as a way of advancing the European security conference was provided by the Brandt-Brezhnev summit in Oreanda (the Crimea) in September 1971. According to Brandt, "Brezhnev drew no real distinction between the terms of reference that were subsequently assigned to the conferences in Helsinki and Vienna."[230] Similarly, during his December 1971 visit to Denmark and Norway Kosygin suggested that the proposed force reduction talks could take place within a subcommittee of the security conference.[231]

In an effort to stimulate Soviet interest in talks, a little more than a month after the Oreanda summit the NATO Council appointed Manlio Brosio, the former secretary-general of NATO, to explore procedural matters with the Soviet and other governments. France, which withdrew from the NATO integrated command in 1966 and opposed a bloc-to-bloc approach to arms control, chose not to associate itself with the Brosio mission. The USSR subsequently declined to receive Brosio on the grounds that it too was opposed to bloc-to-bloc discussions and thus would not deal with an individual who represented no government but had only a mandate from NATO. This position was reiterated in the declaration issued at the conclusion of the January 1972 Prague summit, which argued that "the examination and determination of ways toward solving this question should not be the prerogative of the existing military alliances in Europe. Appropriate agreement could be reached on the way of conducting talks on this question."[232]

The USSR did not formally abandon the position that European force reduction talks should take place within the context of the European security conference until the May 1972 Nixon-Brezhnev summit, at which it agreed in principle to the establishment of a special forum for the reciprocal reduction of armed forces in central Europe. In exchange, Nixon agreed to begin preliminary talks on CSCE later in the year.[233] Even after this understanding was reached, however, the USSR showed little enthusiasm for the talks, and only fulfilled the letter of its commitment to Nixon by agreeing to begin the preparatory phase of the talks on the last day of January 1973.[234]

Soviet foot dragging at this time no longer reflected opposition to MBFR as such, but a changed attitude toward its relationship with CSCE. Having been forced by the West to convene MBFR in parallel with the CSCE, the USSR reversed its earlier position on linkage. Whereas previously it had suggested that MBFR be subordinated to CSCE, it now opposed any connection between the two forums. In January 1973 Brezhnev told journalists that "the actual implementation of a concrete reduction of forces will be examined after the European security conference."[235] Shortly thereafter he had intensive discussions with French president Pompidou in which he managed to turn French hostility to MBFR to his advantage by establishing a united position against any linkage between it and CSCE. According to the final communiqué, the sides agreed that an all-European conference was a major initiative in European and world politics and should not be made dependent on any other negotiations.[236] At the Helsinki CSCE consultations Soviet delegates were instrumental in blocking Norwegian and Swedish suggestions that a link be established between CSCE and MBFR.[237]

While the USSR had effected a tactical reversal by resisting any link between the two forums, the underlying logic of the Soviet position was the same. The USSR had always claimed that security in Europe was primarily a political matter and that arms control could only take place after and in relation to the overarching goal of political normalization. This could have been accomplished by relegating arms control to an "organ" that would be subordinate to the CSCE. But when the Western powers did not accept this solution, the USSR moved to block any arrangement that would link CSCE and MBFR on a parallel rather than a hierarchical basis and give the West opportunities to hold an agreement in the former hostage to progress in the latter.

In sum, the background to the MBFR talks offers little evidence for the view that the USSR wanted these negotiations as a way of keeping the United States militarily engaged in Western Europe. As has been seen, Brezhnev reluctantly was brought to accept the talks in exchange for Western participation in the European security conference. The one piece of evidence usually cited to support the contrary view, Brezhnev's Tbilisi speech, can be explained away when the context and audience of the speech are understood. The Nixon administration may have deserved credit for its skilled use of Brezhnev's words to influence the Senate, but the speech itself was a weak reed upon which to base theories about Soviet-West European relations.[238]

MBFR: The Preparatory Phase

The main Soviet goals in the preparatory phase of MBFR were to en-sure that the talks would not be used by the West to undo the rela-tively favorable political and military situation that was evolving on the continent. The Western side had itself eschewed the practice, which it had pioneered with the Eden plan of 1955, of trying to use zonal arms control to promote a negotiated political settlement (the Harmel report maintained a tenuous link between arms control and a settlement by suggesting that force reductions could build trust that would facilitate a resolution of the "underlying political is-sues"); but the USSR remained wary of the potential use of arms control to challenge the European political order. For this reason it had always insisted that ratification of postwar borders and recog-nition of the GDR precede negotiations on force reductions.

The USSR thus refused to acknowledge the existence of the asym-metries that the West hoped would be the very subject of the nego-tiations. At the preparatory consultations it objected to inclusion of the word "balanced" in the title of the negotiations or indeed any-where in the negotiating mandate,[239] and insisted that the talks pro-ceed from the assumption that a balance already existed and that the purpose of the talks was to preserve that balance at lower levels. The East ultimately prevailed on this issue, in part because the West was the overall *demandeur*, but also because a precedent had been set in bilateral negotiations. At the Oreanda summit Brandt had aban-doned the Western stipulation, which had appeared in NATO com-muniqués since 1968, that reductions be "reciprocal and balanced in scope and timing." In its place he accepted Soviet-proposed language that the reductions be "without detriment to the participating states (*bez ushcherba dlia uchastvuiushchikh gosudarstv*)." At Soviet in-sistence this language was incorporated in the MBFR terms of refer-ence.

The Soviet refusal to acknowledge geographic or force-level asym-metries reflected an understandable desire to protect perceived Pact military advantages in the upcoming talks. But it also had a political dimension. The USSR could not have acknowledged the validity of Western concerns about geographic asymmetries without compro-mising long-standing positions on the role of U.S. forces along the Soviet periphery. Having campaigned for so long against foreign mil-itary forces and bases, it was not about to concede that the U.S. in-terloper should be *compensated* for Soviet proximity to central Europe.

Political considerations also applied to the Soviet handling of force-level disparities. As one writer noted shortly after the talks be-gan, the Soviet preference was for a "political" arms control process that would "help to secure Russia's political goals via symbolic reductions in NATO-WPO forces."[240] The USSR was concerned not only that an admission of force imbalances could weaken its hand in the negotiations, but that the mere discussion of the balance would undercut a relaxation of political tensions. This point was suggested by Brezhnev in his speech to the October 1973 World Congress of Peace Forces in which he set the tone for the Eastern approach to MBFR. He stressed that it was important not to damage the security of any of the parties or to "violate the existing balance of forces in central Europe and on the European continent in general," but also warned that Western attempts to "disturb the existing balance of power" would "become a bone of contention and an object of unending disputes."[241]

The East also insisted on the inclusion of "armaments" in the title (which would ease discussion of stockpiles of prepositioned NATO equipment), and purported to be mystified by the Western concept of associated measures. In the end these differences provided the basis for a compromise, as the East agreed to discuss associated measures and the West dropped its objection to the inclusion of armaments.[242]

Other points of dispute concerned the status of the various participants and the geographic applicability of both reductions and associated measures. The West originally favored two zones, with the associated measures to be applied more widely than the reductions. This would have facilitated verification and given states on the flanks a larger stake in the talks. Foreshadowing disputes that later were to erupt in CSCE over confidence-building measures, the USSR insisted that the associated measures be confined to the reduction zone and ruled out any extension to Soviet territory lying immediately east of the zone.[243]

Another dispute concerned the definition of the guidelines area. The East insisted that Hungary be a special rather than a direct participant, and argued that forces stationed in Hungary did not pose a threat on the central front. Although this issue had military implications, the main reason for Eastern insistence on this point was probably political. With Hungary in the guidelines area, all Soviet forces stationed in Eastern Europe would have been subject to negotiation, whereas many U.S. forces in Western Europe would not have been. Excluding Hungary thus was essential to securing equality of treatment with the United States.[244] Unwilling to concede this point of principle to the East but fearful of blocking progress toward the talks, the West reserved its position on the future status of Hungary, but for all practical purposes the Soviets had won their point.

Although the main issues were largely resolved by early June, the USSR continued to show its reserve toward MBFR by refusing to commit to a date for the start of formal negotiations. It finally did so during the June 1973 Nixon-Brezhnev summit, where it was agreed that talks would begin in Vienna on October 30.[245] On June 28 the Vienna participants issued a final communiqué that for the next fifteen years was to serve as the MBFR terms of reference. As one writer summed up the document, "the box score on concessions . . . favored the Soviets."[246] The parties declared that they were "agreed that specific arrangements will have to be carefully worked out in scope and timing in such a way that they will in all respects and at every point conform to the principle of undiminished security for each party" and agreed that "any topic relevant to the subject matter may be introduced for negotiation" by any state.[247] The words "balanced" and "conventional" did not appear in the document. This was to be a considerable hindrance to the Western side as it attempted to pursue the goals it had had in mind when it first proposed the talks.

MBFR: The Negotiations

The East put forward its first draft MBFR agreement on November 8, 1973, one week after the start of the formal negotiations. The proposal called for all direct participants to reduce their forces in the guidelines area on an equal basis, beginning with collective Eastern and Western reductions of 20,000 men and their associated armaments by the end of 1975, followed by additional reductions by each party of 5 percent in 1976 and 10 percent in 1977. The forces of non-indigenous countries would be withdrawn to national boundaries, while those of countries in the guidelines areas would be disbanded.[248] The proposal also called for reductions of approximately similar types of forces on both sides, including armored, infantry, combat aviation, and air defense units, "as well as units and subunits equipped with nuclear weapons." The inclusion of nuclear forces had been foreshadowed several weeks earlier by Brezhnev in his speech to the World Congress of Peace Forces, in which he stressed that "units equipped with nuclear weapons should be subject to reduction too."[249] The proposal did not spell out verification or associated measures, but reverted to the old Soviet formula of obligatory consultation, suggesting that each party "could have an established right to ask about the implementation of bilateral or multilateral consultation between the interested sides and if need be demand consultation between all states party to the agreement."[250]

On the surface the Eastern proposal was not a flagrantly one-sided document, but it did appear aimed at enhancing the Eastern strategic position to the detriment of NATO as well as reflected, in the ostensibly technical language of arms control, certain Soviet preferences regarding the European political order. The proposal made no allowance for Western concerns about geographical asymmetries. When the Western delegations complained about this fact, arguing that the proposal took no account of the large numbers of forces that would remain in the Western military districts of the USSR, Eastern negotiators correctly replied that these forces were outside the negotiations area, and hence not subject to discussion at Vienna.[251] The proposal also took no account of force-level asymmetries. By calling for absolute and percentage reductions of existing forces, it sidestepped the question of the force imbalance even within the MBFR zone itself. By calling for percentage cuts in the forces of each direct participant the proposal further suggested a Soviet interest in obtaining a *droit de regard* over the forces of each of the Western participants located within the guidelines area. This was of particular concern to West Germany, the only major military power whose military forces were entirely based within the MBFR guidelines area. Finally, the Eastern proposal was virtually silent on verification and associated measures. The one measure suggested was at best an attempt to sidestep more stringent measures and at worst a Soviet attempt to introduce through arms control the kind of political consultation scheme it had been recommending for Europe since 1954.

The West, which had been taken by surprise by the Soviet draft, put forward its own proposal on November 22. Before doing so, however, it tabled data on the forces of the two sides on which its proposal was based. The Western offer called for the establishment of common ceilings of 700,000 ground force manpower, to be achieved in two successive phases. In the first phase, the United States and the USSR would make 15 percent reductions in their forces in the guidelines area. This would require the United States to withdraw 29,000 (15 percent of 193,000) and the USSR 68,000 (15 percent of 460,000) soldiers. The Soviet forces were to comprise one tank army of five divisions and 1,700 main battle tanks. Foreshadowing the data dispute that was to dominate the MBFR talks for most of their existence, the East rejected the Western data while refusing to provide numbers of its own.

The East made the first modification of its initial proposal in October 1974, when it called for an "initial step" agreement of 20,000 men by each side by the end of 1975, with 10,000 men each to be withdrawn by the United States and the USSR, 5,000 men each by Poland and West Germany, and the remainder by the other participants. The United States and the USSR would take their reductions in the first half of the year, the other countries in the second half. The initial reductions would be tied to an obligation to continue negotiations toward further reductions. The singling out of U.S. and Soviet forces represented a very modest step toward the Western position that a first-phase reduction should deal exclusively with these forces. In December of the same year the East introduced a "no increase" proposal that called on the direct participants to ascribe to a joint declaration pledging that they would not increase their forces for the duration of the talks. This was the first of several Eastern freeze proposals, and was made shortly after West Germany announced a restructuring program that was to add three brigades to the *Bundeswehr*.

The completion of the CSCE led to somewhat greater Soviet enthusiasm for MBFR. Brezhnev no longer had a motive to delay progress in MBFR to prevent it from overshadowing the political conference. On the contrary, the Helsinki summit was followed by a stepped-up Soviet campaign for "military détente" and a corresponding increase in the high-level attention accorded to MBFR and other arms control forums. Soviet interest in MBFR was further stimulated by the West's Option 3 proposal of December 1975, in which it offered to trade U.S. nuclear for Eastern conventional forces. The West proposed the withdrawal of 1,000 U.S. nuclear warheads, 54 U.S. nuclear-capable F-4 aircraft, and 36 Pershing IA missiles in exchange for the withdrawal of the same 5-division tank army singled out in the proposal of November 1973. The goal of the reductions was to reach combined collective ceilings of 900,000 men, of which 700,000 would be ground forces.[252]

The nuclear element in Option 3 clearly was of interest to the East, which responded in February 1976 with a sweeping counterproposal that was timed to precede by a few days the opening of the Twenty-Fifth Party Congress and the issuing of another Brezhnev peace program. It called for equal percentage reductions of U.S. and Soviet forces, reductions on each side of 300 tanks, 54 nuclear-capable aircraft, and unspecified but equal numbers of tactical missile launchers and warheads and certain other forces. All other participants would freeze their forces at existing levels, but would agree to undertake percentage reductions in a second stage. A new element in the Eastern proposal was the willingness to reduce Soviet and U.S. forces in the first stage of a two-stage plan. The significance of this step toward the West was undercut, however, by the East's insistence that the agreement contain an ironclad commitment to reductions in the second stage by the West Europeans.[253]

Following the exchange of proposals in late 1975 and early 1976, the focus of the talks shifted to the problem of data, where it largely remained for the next ten years. On June 1, 1976, the East tabled data showing that it had (as of January 1) 987,000 men in the guidelines area, of which 805,000 were ground force personnel. These data showed a Warsaw Pact superiority of only 14,000 for ground forces, compared with the West's estimate of 157,000. Although the West questioned the validity of the Eastern data, the mere fact that they were provided represented a step forward that was welcomed by the West. Nonetheless, the talks remained deadlocked.

In what may have been an attempt to try to circumvent the deadlock, Brezhnev used his famous January 1977 speech at Tula (in which the USSR formally eschewed the pursuit of military superiority) to defend the Soviet approach to MBFR and to float the idea of a series of bilateral dialogues to supplement the Vienna negotiations. "At the talks on the reduction of troops and armaments in Central Europe we are told, in effect: You reduce more and we'll reduce less. Such a position, of course, cannot move the talks forward." He went on to state that "we have no objections to discussing questions related to this topic at any level and at any site: Vienna, Bonn, Washington, Moscow, wherever it is convenient."[254]

In April 1978 the West introduced a modified proposal based on common collective ceilings that attempted to meet Eastern concerns about non-U.S. reductions by agreeing to the principle that the overall size of the manpower reductions to be taken in stage two would be specified at the time a stage one agreement was concluded.[255] The April offer represented only a modest step toward the Soviet position, but it set the stage for the extensive discussions of MBFR by Brezhnev and Schmidt during the Bonn summit the following month. Brezhnev argued strenuously for conclusion of a joint statement claiming that an approximate balance of forces existed in Europe. Schmidt resisted Brezhnev's entreaties, and German and Soviet negotiators finally agreed on a compromise formulation: "The two sides deem it important that no one strive for military superiority. They proceed from the premise that approximate equality and parity are sufficient to ensure defense."[256] The USSR later pointed to this formulation as proof that Schmidt had acknowledged the existence of a balance, whereas the West Germans treated balance as a mutually acknowledged goal rather than a description of the existing state of affairs. The 1978 formulation thus became a standard element in Soviet statements attacking Western intransigence on the data issue.

A few weeks after the Brezhnev-Schmidt meetings the East put forward a counterproposal that narrowed many of the conceptual differences between the sides without, however, offering anything new on the data issue. The East for the first time agreed to common collective ceilings of 900,000 men, of which 700,000 would be ground forces. Instead of focusing on the reduction or freezing of existing levels, the East "accepted the concept of an outcome of parity."[257] In addition, it implicitly accepted the concept of collectivity of manpower limitations. The West cautiously welcomed movement on these matters of principle, but raised questions about the effect they would have on the actual shape of an agreement. As the Dutch representative noted, "because the data discrepancy remains unresolved, the potentially useful Eastern acceptance of the principle of parity is not yet of practical value."[258] Eastern acceptance of the collectivity principle also was highly qualified. The East dropped its insistence on national ceilings, but it proposed that reductions be made proportionate to the numerical strengths of the different countries. To ensure proportionality, it introduced a formula that would have prevented countries from increasing their forces to make up for unilateral reductions by other members of the same alliance.

In November 1978 the East put forward another variant of its freeze proposal, suggesting that the sides undertake unilateral commitments not to increase their overall manpower strength during the course of the negotiations. This proposal was probably a response to growing concern in the Warsaw Pact about NATO conventional improvements under the Long-Term Defense Plan adopted the previous year, as well as to growing pressures in Eastern Europe for limitations on the growth of military spending. A month later the West modified its position to accommodate Soviet pressure for de facto national subceilings by pledging that it would give assurances that all non-U.S. direct participants would take a significant share of the overall ground force reductions necessary to reach the common collective ceilings at the end of phase two. The East took six months to respond to this proposal before offering, in June 1979, an arrangement under which participants on both sides would make reductions "approximately proportionate" to their share of forces in the reduction area. Prior to signature of the agreement, all states would notify each other of the size of their forces in the area.

By the end of 1979 MBFR was increasingly overshadowed by the INF dispute. In what was clearly an attempt to influence West German deliberations on the impending two-track decision, in October 1979 Brezhnev announced from East Berlin the unilateral withdrawal of 20,000 Soviet troops from the GDR. He claimed that these withdrawals had nothing to do with MBFR, and would not be charged against Soviet reductions in a future agreement.[259] For its part, in December 1979 the West offered a new proposal for an interim phase one agreement, the key element of which was reductions by the United States of 13,000 and the USSR of 30,000 men. The most noteworthy feature of the Western proposal was its heavy emphasis on associated measures. Seven items were suggested, including prior notification of out-of-garrison activities, exchange of observers at notified activities, prior notification of ground force movements, annual inspections to monitor compliance, declared exit and entry points for the movement of troops into the guidelines area (with foreign observers to be stationed at these points), exchanges of information, and agreement to noninterference with national technical means of verification. The Western associated measures package broke the pattern of the last six years in that it called for applying the provisions on prior notifications and exchanges of observers to significant portions of the Western USSR. Whatever the arms control rationale for this approach, it was inconsistent with the MBFR mandate and elicited a sharp response from the Soviet foreign ministry, which sent notes of protest to the participating states.

The East countered in July 1980 with its own first-phase U.S.-Soviet reduction proposal and a package of associated measures. The latter were to be applied only in the reductions area, and included the periodic convening of a mixed commission to monitor compliance, limitations on the size of military exercises, advance notification of large troop movements, prior notification of exercises, and the establishment of temporary control points at which foreign observers could monitor the withdrawal of forces being reduced under the agreement. The Eastern reduction numbers were identical to those tabled by the West—13,000 and 20,000—but were conditioned upon agreement that no country could exceed 50 percent of the overall collective levels of 900,000 men in the guidelines area. The latter provision was a result of the discussions in June between Brezhnev and Schmidt, who is reported to have suggested the 50 percent rule as a way of meeting Soviet concerns about a possible unlimited West German buildup without incorporating into the MBFR agreement an explicit and politically unacceptable cap on the size of the Bundeswehr.[260] In November 1980 the East put forward yet another freeze proposal, this time calling for a "gentleman's agreement" that the non-U.S. and non-Soviet participants not change the mix of forces in their respective alliances.

Additional exchanges on the data dispute took place throughout 1981. In another attempt to circumvent the dispute, in December the East suggested that the sides establish a working group to begin drafting early in the new year. Transition to the drafting stage, according to a Soviet source, would give the talks a "really businesslike character."[261] At the beginning of the next round of talks in February 1982 the East tabled a draft treaty that could provide a basis for the drafting exercise. But the West refused to begin drafting in the absence of even a rudimentary convergence of views on data and associated measures.

In July 1982 the West countered with its own draft treaty. It provided for combined collective ceilings of 900,000 total and 700,000 ground forces, to be achieved by staged reductions over a seven-year period. In the first stage the United States and the USSR would take reductions of 13,000 and 30,000 respectively. The proposal also contained the same package of associated measures offered in 1979. However, the Western proposal reversed a long-standing NATO position by dropping the phased approach in favor of a single agreement which would spell out the obligations of all participants.[262] The elimination of the linkage issue shifted the focus of the negotiations almost exclusively to the two remaining problem areas: data and associated measures.

In the first half of 1983 the East put forward two proposals that contained a few minor substantive concessions probably intended to promote an image of Eastern flexibility as the campaign against INF neared its peak. In February it proposed an initial symbolic withdrawal, within one year and on the basis of mutual example, of 13,000 U.S. and 20,000 Soviet troops and their associated armaments. These withdrawals would be outside the framework of an MBFR agreement. They would not be subject to verification, and would not be dependent upon explicit or implicit agreement on the numbers of U.S. and Soviet troops remaining in the guidelines area.[263] The reasons for this somewhat odd approach to an initial stage of U.S. and Soviet withdrawals were unclear, but the proposal was consistent with other Soviet proposals for arms control by mutual example made during this period (for example, the no-first use declaration of 1982 and the various INF moratoria declared by Brezhnev and Andropov). At the same time all direct participants in the talks would undertake a collective freeze by "mutual political commitment."

In June the East tabled a draft agreement providing for manpower and armaments reductions to agreed common ceilings of 900,000 men (700,000 ground and 200,000 air force) on each side. There would be no prior agreement on data, but each side would itself determine the size of the reductions it would have to take to reach the agreed ceilings. National subceilings would not be stipulated in the agreement, but it would be understood that "those participants in the agreement who maintain large units in central Europe should assume an essential share of the total volume of the armed forces reduction in their alliance."[264]

The Eastern package offered little that was new. It virtually ignored the Western package of associated measures, and did not provide for obligatory verification of the U.S. and Soviet withdrawals or of the freeze. It did provide for "invitation, on a voluntary basis, of observers from both sides for the withdrawal and reduction" of forces and for the establishment, after the conclusion of the reductions, of three or four permanent control posts on either side for the observation of the rotation of troops to and from the central region.

In any case, few in the West believed that the USSR would conclude even a modest MBFR agreement with the INF deployments pending. In December 1983 the Eastern delegations refused to set a date for the resumption of the MBFR talks, prompting concern that the East would not return to the talks and instead would concentrate on the CDE (scheduled to convene in January 1984). These concerns proved misplaced, however, as the Eastern delegations returned to MBFR on March 16, 1984, after a suspension of a little more than two months.

Western governments came back to the talks eager to show public opinion that they could do business with the USSR, even after the INF deployments. Thus in April the West introduced a modified proposal that demonstrated unprecedented flexibility on the data dispute.[265] It called for agreement on only a portion of the forces to be reduced and suggested dialogue and exchange of information aimed at resolving the dispute or, at a minimum, pinpointing its source. But the East rejected the Western offers and continued to criticize NATO for its alleged intransigence on the data issue.

In February 1985 the East put forward a set of basic draft provisions containing the earlier 13,000/20,000/one-year formula for symbolic U.S. and Soviet reductions and a no-increase pledge for all other direct participants. In response to Western criticisms of the "political commitment" suggested in the previous Eastern proposal, the new draft envisioned a formal freeze agreement. In what appeared to be an attempt to respond to Western concerns about verification, the proposal provided for the establishment of three or four observation posts on each side that would be used to verify the initial Soviet and U.S. withdrawals and that would then be dismantled. The East also accepted the Western position that most of the proposed U.S. and Soviet reductions be in identifiable combat units, which not only would facilitate verification of the withdrawals but enhance their military significance.[266]

While characterizing the new Eastern offer as disappointing, the British and West German governments favored dropping the data requirement, which they hoped would pave the way toward a rapid agreement.[267] Although there were considerable misgivings at the working level in most NATO countries, by December 1985 the alliance had decided to take this step, in effect making the most substantial concession ever offered by the West in MBFR.[268] In a counteroffer based largely on the East's draft, NATO for the first time offered to set aside its requirement for prior agreement on data, calling instead for carefully verified and modest, first-phase reductions from existing (and disputed) levels of forces. The NATO counteroffer scaled down the proposed reductions to 5,000 U.S. and 11,500 Soviet soldiers, and reverted to its pre-1982 two-negotiation concept by deferring all non-U.S. and Soviet reductions to a subsequent phase of negotiation.[269]

Western governments expected that this concession would result in rapid progress and a possible agreement, but soon were disappointed. In February 1986 the East tabled a draft agreement that the West characterized as a completely inadequate response to its recent concessions. The new proposal called for reductions of 6,500 U.S. and 11,500 Soviet men and associated armaments within a year of signature. But the draft merely elaborated in treaty form the basic provisions of February 1985 and "contained nothing new and in effect ignored the most recent Western initiative."[270] In regard to verification, the Eastern position actually moved backward. Although Gorbachev had made an explicit reference to entry-exit points in his January 15 statement on the elimination of nuclear weapons by the year 2000, the February draft stipulated that military personnel involved in routine rotation would not pass through the points—a reversal of the East's position of 1983.

Gorbachev's 1986 Decision

Although it is unlikely that Gorbachev had decided by February 1986 to kill off MBFR, the East's February draft presaged this action. Instead of moving, as the West had hoped, toward a symbolic first-stage agreement, Gorbachev dramatically upped the ante by proposing, in an April 18, 1986, speech in East Berlin, an agreement on "substantial reductions in all the components of the land forces and tactical air forces of the European states and the relevant forces of the U.S.A. and Canada deployed in Europe."[271] Gorbachev further suggested that the proposed reductions "cover the entire European territory from the Atlantic to the Urals." While he did not specify where he hoped to negotiate these reductions, it was clear that the proposals would require the establishment of a new forum or, at a minimum, the renegotiation of the MBFR terms of reference.

The East Berlin speech was followed by the June 11 Budapest appeal, which called for an initial one-time reduction of 100,000 to 150,000 troops each by NATO and the Warsaw Pact within one or two years of the conclusion of an agreement, and for larger cuts that would result by the early 1990s in an approximately 25 percent reduction in NATO and Warsaw Pact land and tactical aviation forces. The appeal also called for agreement on measures to "lessen the danger of sudden attack" and endorsed on-site inspection through the establishment of an "international consultative commission" comprised of representatives from NATO, the Warsaw Pact, and neutral and nonaligned states.[272]

The appeal mentioned three possible forums in which these measures could be negotiated: a "second stage" of the CDE, a "special" forum that would include all of the European states, the United States, and Canada, and an expanded MBFR that would bring in additional European states under a new mandate. Press commentary and informal remarks by Eastern officials suggested that the USSR preferred the first alternative, and that the other two suggestions were fallbacks that could be adopted if the first stage of the CDE failed to produce an agreement or if the Western countries refused to abandon MBFR.

As will be seen, the Gorbachev proposals spelled the death knell for MBFR. The negotiators continued to meet in Vienna, with the Western delegates half-heartedly reproaching the East for attempting to "escape forward" from an agreement, while their Eastern counterparts called for a quick agreement on symbolic troop cuts that would wrap up MBFR and set the stage for negotiations in a new forum.[273] Both sides were essentially marking time, however, waiting for new talks to begin. (MBFR formally ended on February 2, 1989, after the mandate for the new CFE talks was adopted.) But this depended upon the outcome of the Stockholm CDE—itself the culmination of an East-West dialogue on confidence-building that went back to 1955.

Confidence-Building Measures

Background

The first postwar confidence-building measure (CBM) proposals were put forward by the West at the Geneva summit, and included Eden's central European plan and Eisenhower's Open Skies proposal. The latter was for a strictly bilateral venture and did not envision the inclusion of West European or other third country territory. It called for the United States and the USSR "to give each other a complete blueprint of our military establishments . . . from one end of our countries to the other," and for each country "to provide within our countries facilities for aerial photography to the other country."

Accounts of the Geneva meeting often stress Khrushchev's strong and spontaneous rejection of Open Skies as a system of espionage.[274] But the Soviet leaders later moderated their response. Although they probably never considered accepting Open Skies, they saw it as a useful basis for discussion with the West. It provided a pretext for Bulganin's first personal letter to Eisenhower, which was written in extremely conciliatory terms and succeeded in its basic objective of launching an extended correspondence whose main topic was arms control.

Apart from this important procedural consideration, Bulganin was able to score substantive points in the public discussion of aerial inspection. Open Skies was basically a publicity stunt, and it was not difficult for the Soviet side to point out its flaws.[275] In his letter to Eisenhower Bulganin observed that "both our countries are not acting singly" and suggested that any aerial inspection regime would have to consider military installations on third countries.[276] The USSR later incorporated a vague and heavily qualified commitment to aerial inspection in its March 1956 conventional arms reduction proposal, which stipulated that at some point "the countries concerned shall consider the possibility of using aerial photography as one of the methods of control."[277]

The early sparring over aerial inspection illustrated a point that was to apply generally to confidence-building measures in the next few decades. Proposals for such measures almost always had a hidden political agenda. In proposing Open Skies Eisenhower was hoping to repeat his Atoms for Peace triumph of 1953 and to demonstrate that Soviet society was closed and secretive. With his vague counterproposal Bulganin sought to rebut these charges and to deflect attention to U.S. overseas bases. At least as important as these submerged polemics over secrecy and foreign bases was the political symbolism of the way in which proposed zones were geographically defined. The Soviets liked the Eden proposal of 1955 because it appeared to sanction the division of Germany. Accordingly, in November 1956 the USSR put forward a plan that combined elements of the Eden proposal and Open Skies by providing for an 800-kilometer-wide aerial inspection zone on each side of the East-West demarcation in Europe.

In April 1957 the West countered with a complicated offer, for "illustrative purposes," of two wedge-shaped zones, one in Europe, the other in Alaska and Siberia.[278] From the Western perspective these zones had the virtue of including large parts of Soviet territory, some (but not all) of Western and Eastern Europe, and part of the United States (most of Alaska, but none of the continental United States). The use of wedges defined by longitudinal lines running south from the North Pole obviated any reference to the demarcation line in Germany.

A few weeks later the USSR responded with its own proposal to create two zones. The first would encompass most of Eastern and Western Europe, but very little of European Russia. The second zone would include that part of Siberia east of 108° East longitude and all U.S. territory west of 90° West longitude (the western two-thirds of the continental United States and all of Alaska). The proposal would have created zones roughly equal in size, but was heavily weighted in favor of the USSR. Most of the Soviet territory that would have been covered was wasteland, while the U.S. zone contained a considerable proportion of the U.S. population, industry, and military infrastructure. Nonetheless, it was the first Soviet proposal that was not designed around the German border, and as such was greeted positively by the West. The United States came back in August 1957 with two still more complicated proposals, one of which would cover all Soviet, U.S., and Canadian territory, while the other would cover only these countries' territory north of the Arctic Circle, those parts of Greenland and Norway north of the Arctic Circle (Swedish and Finnish territory would be exempt), along with sub-Arctic parts of Siberia and all of Alaska.[279]

Underlying the discussion of these lines of demarcation were questions of political status as well as concerns about security. The USSR did not want to include substantial parts of European Russia if its geopolitical equivalent, the continental United States, was excluded. The West Europeans did not want a European zone that excluded nearly all of European Russia. The West Germans did not want the inner-German border used as a line of demarcation, nor were they enthusiastic about a zone that included all of Germany but excluded all or parts of the other major powers. The neutrals were wary of getting caught up in the whole scheme.

With the development of satellite photography and the seeming obsolescence of aerial inspection as a means of building confidence, complicated formulas based on geographic coordinates disappeared from the arms control agenda. But many of the issues that figured in these discussions were to resurface in the 1970s, when confidence-building measures were placed on the CSCE agenda by the NATO, neutral, and nonaligned countries. In addition, of course, Open Skies received a new lease on life when the idea was revived in a different form by President Bush in May 1989 and greeted more positively by the USSR than in 1955.

The Helsinki Precedent

The fact that some Western countries pressed for the inclusion of confidence-building measures (CBMs) in the CSCE Final Act was a reflection of a hidden agenda that went beyond the measures themselves. The NATO countries were less interested in CBMs per se than in ensuring that the CSCE dealt in some way with military questions and thus contradicted the Soviet claim that security was largely a political problem that could be solved by the recognition of existing borders and declarations of peaceful intent. The neutral and nonaligned shared this view, but also wanted to use CBMs as a bridge to the MBFR talks, in which they did not participate.[280] In contrast, the USSR had two reasons for wanting to exclude discussion of CBMs from the conference. First, it wanted a rapid outcome and therefore did not want the conference bogged down by highly technical military and arms control issues. Second, the Soviet foreign and defense establishment was suspicious of CBMs as such, which were openly proclaimed in the West as a means to dilute Soviet and Warsaw Pact secrecy.

At the 1972–73 preparatory consultations that formulated the CSCE's terms of reference the Western delegations managed to secure a vague commitment to the negotiation of concrete CBMs. Paragraph 23 of the Final Recommendations directed the relevant committees and subcommittees of the conference to submit "appropriate proposals on confidence-building measures such as the prior notification of major military maneuvers on a basis to be specified by the Conference, and the exchange of observers by invitation at military maneuvers under mutually acceptable conditions."

To comply with this mandate, the USSR's "General Declaration," which Gromyko presented on the opening day of the conference, contained a brief paragraph proposing that the participating states agree to notify each other of major maneuvers in "specified areas" and exchange observers by invitation "at such maneuvers."[281] In the subcommittee that dealt with CBMs, however, the USSR did not introduce a concrete proposal, but merely reintroduced the relevant passages of the "General Declaration."[282] Britain introduced the West's proposal, which called for the notification of all CSCE-participant states of any maneuver "in Europe" involving a division or more of troops. Notification was to take place sixty days in advance of the maneuvers and was to provide considerable detail.[283]

In responding to the Western draft the Soviet negotiators made clear their preference for a minimalist regime. The USSR was willing to notify, five days in advance, major land maneuvers (those involving forces equal in strength to an army corps) within fifty kilometers of an international border, but only to those states adjoining the border. Exchanges of observers would be limited to maneuvers subject to notification.[284] This regime would have exempted most of the USSR's territory, and would have required it to give notice of maneuvers on that part of its territory that was covered only to Norway (the one NATO state with which it shares a border in Europe), Finland, and several of its own allies.

In June 1974 the Soviets offered to widen the frontier zones they were advocating to 100 kilometers and to lower the proposed period of notification to ten days. In September 1974 they hinted that they might accept "all of Europe" as a notification zone, provided exceptions were made for the USSR. In January 1975 NATO declared that it would be willing to exempt all but a 700-kilometer strip of Soviet territory along this border, but the Soviets rejected this offer. Behind the Soviet stance was not only a desire to minimize outside intrusion into Soviet military affairs, but also a political objection to any agreement that would cover extensive areas of Soviet territory while exempting the United States.[285] In private talks with West European leaders Brezhnev explicitly linked Soviet intransigence on the geographic issue to the presence of U.S. forces in Europe. In the summer of 1975, for example, he told British prime minister Wilson and foreign secretary Callaghan that "if the United States would remove all their nuclear weapons from West Germany, he would undertake to notify us of the movement of every Soviet military unit—even a single regiment—right up to the Urals."[286]

The negotiators eventually reached a compromise that exempted all but 250 kilometers of Soviet territory in Europe.[287] All participating states were to be notified, twenty-one or more days in advance, of maneuvers involving more than 25,000 troops. At Soviet insistence it was agreed that notification would be on a voluntary basis. The signatories further agreed to invite other participating states, "voluntarily and on a bilateral basis," to send observers to such maneuvers.

After 1975 the USSR and its allies compiled a rather mixed record in implementing these provisions of the Final Act. From 1975 to 1983 NATO and the NNA announced thirty-four major maneuvers and invited observers to twenty-nine, whereas the Warsaw Pact announced eighteen major maneuvers and invited observers to six. In 1980 the USSR ceased inviting observers to Warsaw Pact exercises and turned down all invitations to attend NATO exercises, presumably to avoid incurring a moral obligation to reciprocate.[288] In addition, the USSR committed one flagrant violation when, at the height of the crisis in Poland, it failed to provide information regarding the *Zapad-81* exercise that involved 100,000 men and was widely seen as intended to intimidate the Poles.[289]

CDE: Background

The USSR's preference for a minimal confidence-building regime and its relatively poor record of compliance suggested little receptivity in Moscow to new Western proposals in this area. Many in the West, therefore, were surprised when the USSR seemingly reversed its earlier position and negotiated, in the Stockholm CDE, a set of binding CBMs applicable to the entire region from the Atlantic to the Urals.

The CDE was a Western initiative. In 1977 the government of France decided to undertake a reconsideration of its "empty chair" arms control policy, which it believed was coming under increased domestic and international scrutiny. In May 1978 President Giscard d'Estaing went before the first UN Special Session on Disarmament and put forward a series of proposals, one of which was for a conference on disarmament in Europe that would deal with conventional force asymmetries.[290] Shortly thereafter France circulated a memorandum to all states participating in the CSCE (and Albania) in which it proposed a two-stage conference. Stage one would consider binding

CBMs in the region from the Atlantic to the Urals, and stage two would deal with negotiated limits on conventional air and ground forces. The French hoped that this proposal would demonstrate interest in European arms control, while blunting the mounting Soviet campaign for a "military détente" based on no-first-use and related nuclear issues.

Like previous confidence-building proposals, the French offer had a latent political agenda. In proposing to extend CBMs to the Urals, the French sought to highlight the deficiencies of the MBFR guidelines area and to point up the discrepancy between the USSR's efforts to pose as the champion of European security and its refusal to participate on an equal footing in a European security regime.[291] But the French offer had certain elements in common with several Eastern proposals, without which it is doubtful that the CDE ever would have been launched.

In November 1976 the PCC had proposed that all thirty-five CSCE participants conclude a treaty pledging not to be the first to use nuclear weapons against each other.[292] At the first CSCE review conference (convened in Belgrade in October 1977) the USSR tabled a draft program of measures to consolidate military détente, one of which was the conclusion of a nuclear no-first-use agreement among the CSCE participants. The USSR remained unenthusiastic about CBMs, but proposed that maneuvers involving more than 50,000–60,000 men be banned in Europe. It also called for special multilateral consultations among the thirty-five to discuss all aspects of military détente and especially the Eastern proposals.[293] NATO governments rejected the Soviet offer on procedural as well as substantive grounds, arguing that special consultations would be tantamount to a conference that would detach the military aspects of security from the CSCE and downgrade the relative importance of issues such as human rights. However, there was growing interest among some Western governments (although not in the United States) in strengthening the security component of the CSCE as a way of compensating for the obvious deficiencies of MBFR.

Drawing up the Mandate

Initially neither the French proposal of 1978 nor the various all-European offers by the Warsaw Pact envisioned a formal link to the CSCE process. The Pact characterized its 1976 no-first-use proposal as a step toward fulfillment of the "indicated aims" of the Final Act, but did not suggest that the multilateral consultations proposed at Belgrade become an integral part of the CSCE process. In May 1979 the Warsaw Pact called for a political-level conference on military détente and disarmament in Europe and proposed that interested states immediately undertake consultations aimed at defining the modalities for such a conference.[294] The Pact suggested that all participants in the conference sign an agreement pledging not to be the first to use either nuclear or conventional arms. Such an agreement "would in fact be equivalent to concluding a nonaggression pact between all the participants of the Helsinki conference."[295] The Pact also pressed for a political-level opening of the Madrid follow-up meeting scheduled for the following year, and stated that "a constructive approach to and productive work of the proposed all-European conference on problems of military détente would be of great significance for the success of the Madrid meeting."[296] However, it did not suggest a direct link between the Madrid meeting and the proposed conference, which could convene in 1979, well before the start of the Madrid meeting.

By the summer of 1979 the French and their allies had concluded that creating an autonomous negotiating forum not linked to CSCE would play into Soviet hands by elevating military détente above other aspects of East-West relations. Therefore, they decided to introduce their proposal at Madrid in a way that would make the CDE an integral part of the CSCE process.

The Madrid meeting opened in November 1980, and France, Poland, Sweden, Romania, and Yugoslavia put forward draft proposals for a European conference on disarmament. The French draft dealt exclusively with exchange of information, technical measures to diminish the potential for surprise attack, and measures of verification. It expanded the zone of applicability to the Urals, linked the proposed negotiating forum to the CSCE, and excluded nuclear weapons.

The Polish draft contained mainly declaratory measures and had a pronounced nuclear emphasis. It did not envisage an ongoing link between the conference and the CSCE. Its list of possible concrete measures followed the proposals put forward by the Warsaw Pact in December 1979, and included a reduction of the threshold for announced maneuvers from 25,000 to 20,000 men, extension of the advance notification period from twenty-one to thirty days, and a restriction on the size of maneuvers to 40,000–50,000 men. The Polish draft left open the question of the zone of applicability, which was to be decided at the conference itself. In remarks to the conference, however, Pact-country delegates discouraged speculation about any extension of the zone of application beyond the 250-kilometer strip of Soviet territory agreed at Helsinki.

Despite the differences between the two approaches, in February 1981 the Warsaw Pact countries (and the NNA) accepted the French draft as a basis of discussion. Several days later Brezhnev made a major shift in the Soviet position regarding geographic applicability when he declared in his report to the Twenty-Sixth Party Congress that the USSR was prepared to extend the zone of applicability to the Urals, "on the condition that the Western states make a corresponding extension of the area of measures of trust."[297] Soviet delegates in Madrid would not specify precisely what would constitute a "corresponding extension," which could have meant anything from the whole of the United States and Canada, to an area of the North Atlantic as wide as the zone from the western border of the USSR to the Urals, to relatively small areas adjacent to Europe.[298] During the February–July 1981 session of the conference the East made further concessions by agreeing to accept some form of linkage with the CSCE and agreeing that the proposed conference should aim to establish obligatory and verifiable confidence- and security-building measures (CSBMs).[299] The Soviet delegates stressed, however, that negotiation of these measures should not prejudice the further discussion of declaratory measures.[300]

Western governments (and especially the United States) were determined to resist a sweeping extension of the zone of applicability, but were prepared to show some flexibility. In July 1981 the Americans informed the Soviet delegation that they would be willing to include military activities in the air and sea space adjacent to European territories, provided they were an integral part of land operations. Although this offer was rejected at the time by the USSR, it later became the basis for the "functional approach" used in Stockholm and made the tacit basis for the CDE agreement.

The conclusion of the Madrid meeting was delayed by the crisis in Poland and the resulting deterioration in East-West relations, but in September 1983 the sides finally reached agreement on a concluding document that contained a mandate for the CDE. For reasons having to do with the dynamics of the CSCE process (discussed in chapter nine) and the leverage the West was able to exert within it, the Madrid mandate was closer to NATO than to Warsaw Pact preferences. It stipulated that the first stage of the conference "will be devoted to the negotiation and adoption of a set of mutually complementary confidence- and security-building measures. . . . They will be of military significance and politically binding and will be provided with adequate forms of verification which correspond to their content."

The question of geographic applicability was solved more in accordance with Western than Soviet preferences, although there was a degree of ambiguity in the mandate. It was agreed that the CSBMS

will cover the whole of Europe as well as the adjoining sea area and airspace.[*] [In this context, the notion of adjoining sea area is understood to refer also to ocean areas adjoining Europe. (Footnote inserted in the original).]

As far as the adjoining sea area[*] [the same footnote is referenced] and airspace is concerned, the measures will be applicable to the military activities of all the participating states taking place there whenever these activities affect security in Europe as well as constitute a part of activities taking place within the whole of Europe.

The West also prevailed on the issue of linking the CDE to the broader CSCE process. The CDE was to "begin a process of which the first stage will be devoted to the negotiation and adoption of a set of mutually complementary confidence- and security-building measures." This process was described as an "integral part of the multilateral process initiated by the CSCE." This meant that at the next CSCE review conference, which was scheduled to take place in Vienna beginning in late 1986, the participating states would have the opportunity to review the results of the Stockholm conference, as well as other aspects of the CSCE process and on that basis decide whether to renew or alter the CDE mandate.

On the other hand, the mandate did not stipulate that the CDE would be limited to conventional weapons, thereby leaving the USSR an opening to promote its no-first-use and nuclear-free zone proposals. The definition of Europe in the mandate was fairly narrow and did not constitute the "corresponding extension" demanded by Brezhnev, but it was vague enough to allow the USSR and its allies to raise naval and air activities deemed by the West to have little relevance to the conventional balance in Europe.

The Stockholm Conference

The CDE convened in Stockholm in January 1984 under the shadow of the initial INF deployments and the suspension of other arms control forums.[301] Gromyko outlined the basic Soviet goals for the conference in his opening speech. After a bitter attack on U.S. foreign policy and the INF deployments, he called for the conclusion of a nuclear no-first-use agreement and an agreement banning the use of either nuclear or conventional forces.[302] In addition to these "two major confidence-building measures," he alluded to other possible declaratory measures, including the establishment of nuclear-free zones. He also suggested that the conference consider an expansion of the concrete provisions contained in the Final Act, but did not offer specific ideas for doing so.[303]

A few days later the West tabled the first proposal of the conference. It called for the adoption of six binding measures: exchange of military information, exchange of forecasts of notifiable activities, notification of military activities, observation of certain military activities, compliance and verification measures, and the development of better means of communication for use in urgent situations. The

USSR did not formally table its counterproposal until early May, although Gromyko and the chief Soviet delegate, Oleg Grinevskii, made known its general outlines in speeches to the conference.[304] The Soviet draft also contained six elements: a nuclear no-first-use pledge, a treaty on the nonuse of force, nuclear-free zones, a freeze and reduction of military budgets, a ban on chemical weapons in Europe, and improvement in the CBMs of the Helsinki Final Act.

There was thus a wide disparity between the East's heavy emphasis on declaratory measures and the West's outright rejection of such measures and its exclusive focus on concrete military-technical CSBMs. The Soviets essentially "refused to concentrate on concrete CSBMs for the first year of the conference."[305] For their part, the Western delegations argued that declaratory measures were outside the terms of reference of the conference and would not be discussed. As the chief U.S. delegate stated, "the stringent criteria of the mandate automatically excludes vague political declarations of benign intent, such as pledges of nonaggression or repetitions of other commitments undertaken in the United Nations Charter or the Helsinki Final Act."[306] NATO delegations claimed that a nonuse of force pledge would be inappropriate at a time when the USSR was conducting a war in Afghanistan, that it would intensify pressures for a nuclear no-first-use agreement, and that such an agreement was in any case superfluous, given the prohibition on the use of force in other international agreements.[307] There thus appeared to be little basis for a positive outcome.

Moreover, unlike MBFR, which could drag on indefinitely, the CDE took place against a deadline set by the Madrid mandate. Consistent with their position that the CDE had to remain subordinate to the Vienna review conference, the NATO delegations had made it clear that they would not allow the CDE and the CSCE to run concurrently. September 19, 1986, thus was an effective deadline for the CDE.

Prospects for the negotiations improved dramatically in June 1984, when President Reagan announced in a speech to the Irish Parliament that the United States was willing to enter "discussions on reaffirming the principle not to use force" if doing so would "bring the USSR to negotiate agreements which will give concrete, new meaning to that principle."[308] Soviet negotiators at Stockholm had suggested that if the United States signaled a receptiveness to the Soviet position on declaratory measures in Stockholm, the USSR would be willing to talk about resuming bilateral nuclear arms control talks. It is likely, therefore, that the Reagan statement was at least tacitly linked to Gromyko's visit to Washington later in the year and the start of a dialogue leading to the NST talks in early 1985. Almost a year went by, however, before the USSR, under new leadership, began to signal that it was interested in an agreement.

In the spring of 1985 the NATO countries put forward a comprehensive proposal that called for notification at least forty-five days in advance of troop movements involving at least 6,000 men, extensive exchanges of military data, and exclusion of most air and naval exercises. The USSR and its allies complained that the measures proposed by NATO were unfair in that they applied to much of the USSR while "not one inch of U.S. territory was involved."[309] To compensate for this alleged unfairness the East proposed measures dealing with air and naval activities, U.S. reinforcements for Europe and possible transits through Europe, and other measures clearly outside the scope of the Madrid mandate.[310] While Western negotiators charged their interlocutors with ignoring the conference mandate and attempting to win back points that had been lost at Madrid, the West regarded the new proposals as a step forward from the exclusive emphasis on declaratory measures. By the summer of 1985 the Pact was calling for notification, thirty days in advance, of maneuvers involving a minimum of 20,000 troops, 200 aircraft in the air simultaneously, or 30 ships plus 100 aircraft. It remained opposed to the exchange of military data and was vague on the question of verification, preferring to stress national technical means and obligatory consultations.[311]

Over the course of the next year the USSR made a number of concessions that ultimately paved the way to an agreement. NATO made concessions as well, but they were less dramatic. Having basically secured its preferred formula for an agreement in the Madrid mandate, the West had to give way on essentially quantitative parameters. The USSR, in contrast, had to yield on what it had proclaimed were matters of principle, agreeing, in effect, to operationalize the general approach contained in the Madrid document with which it did not agree and which it had tried to revise in the course of the negotiations.

Gorbachev personally took a hand in modifying Soviet positions, usually in settings calculated to maximize the political effect. In his January 1986 statement on the complete elimination of nuclear weapons he proposed "setting aside" naval activities to the "next stage of the conference."[312] The West could not agree in advance that naval issues would be on the agenda of a second-stage Stockholm conference. This was not only substantively unattractive, but ran counter to the NATO view that the CDE was a creation of the CSCE and had no competence to perpetuate itself or to establish its own agenda. But the Soviets did not insist on a firm commitment regarding the future agenda and one important obstacle to agreement thus was removed.

During his July 1986 meeting with French president Mitterrand, Gorbachev further announced that the USSR was prepared to defer agreement on the notification of air activities and hinted at forth-coming movement on verification. On August 19, the first day of the final round of the talks, Grinevskii announced that the USSR was ready to agree to one to two inspections per year on its territory, thus accepting the principle of on-site inspection and coming close to meeting the West's minimum demands in this area.

These changes set the stage for adoption of a final document in September 1986, just in time for the formal date of adjournment. The agreement stipulated that all military activities involving 13,000 troops or more (or 300 or more tanks) had to be notified. Notification was to include detailed information and be provided forty-two days in advance. In place of the voluntary provisions in the Final Act it was agreed that observers had to be invited to activities involving more than 17,000 troops for land forces or 5,000 amphibious or para-chute troops. In addition, the signatories agreed to provide annual calendars of military activities subject to notification. Activities in-volving more than 75,000 troops had to be communicated two cal-endar years in advance.[313]

All signatories agreed to accept up to three inspections per year on their territory to ensure compliance with the notification provi-sions. Requests for inspection could not be refused, and inspections were to begin not more than thirty-six hours from the time a request was made. Inspectors would be permitted on the ground and in air-planes provided by the inspected state. The inspections were to apply to all of Europe from the Atlantic to the Urals.[314]

In the first two years in which the agreement was in effect (1987 and 1988), Western governments were satisfied with, although not overly enthusiastic about, its implementation. The signatories ex-changed a total of forty-seven notifications: NATO seventeen, the Warsaw Treaty Organization (WTO) twenty-five, and the NNA five.[315] Under the provisions for on-site inspection, NATO and the WTO each carried out nine inspections, the NNA none. The United States and the USSR each were inspecting states on five occasions, Britain and the GDR twice, Bulgaria, Turkey, and West Germany each once. In terms of the territory inspected, West Germany was inspected five times, the USSR four, and East Germany three.[316] There also were dozens of maneuver observations.

U.S. officials praised the USSR for the way it received U.S. in-spectors, but some governments were less satisfied. West Germany carried out only one inspection—at a Soviet exercise in the GDR in August 1988—and complained about Soviet efforts to obscure the course of events. There were also complaints about the USSR's be-havior as an inspecting state. In the summer of 1988 West Germany lodged an official protest about the conduct of Soviet inspectors, who appeared more interested in nuclear sites adjacent to the maneuver than to the maneuver itself.[317] The behavior of Soviet inspectors reportedly improved at their next inspection—in Britain in October 1988.

The USSR also accused the NATO countries of CDE violations. In September 1988 it charged that Britain had committed a violation on West German territory by failing to notify a series of nine military activities that the USSR claimed was, in fact, a single exercise comprised of 69,000 men. In October of the same year the USSR accused West Germany of failing to announce two years in advance a U.S.-French-West German exercise using 170,000 troops. The Western countries rejected the charges, arguing that they had conducted four separate exercises, all of which they had given notification of one year in advance.[318] The common thread running through these Soviet complaints was an effort to draw attention to large-scale NATO exercises.

Western governments also complained about the East's minimal compliance with the observation provisions of the CDE agreement. According to one report, Eastern units "practiced with fictitious unit designations or covered identification numbers; peacetime bases were kept secret; helicopter flights over the exercise terrain were almost always denied; new major equipment was seldom shown; night observations not offered." Nonetheless, Western observers still considered "the events to be profitable."[319] More importantly, the inspection provisions of the CDE agreement, however minimally observed, were regarded as a major breakthrough that set a precedent for Soviet acceptance of on-site inspection provisions in the INF treaty of the following year.

Military Contacts and Exchanges

Exchanges of military delegations are listed as a confidence-building measure in the CSCE Final Act, which urges the participating states to promote such exchanges "with due regard to reciprocity and with a view to better mutual understanding." This was a Spanish rather than an Eastern proposal, but the USSR had long advocated military exchanges as an instrument of political détente.[320]

The earliest Soviet proposals for military contacts were made during the initial post-Stalin thaw. After receiving Eden's invitation to visit Britain at the 1955 Geneva summit Khrushchev is reported to have immediately "raised the question of other visits—military missions, naval visits, etc."[321] He also pressed the United States to consider an exchange of military visits.[322]

An exchange of naval squadrons between Leningrad and Portsmouth took place in October 1955, with the Soviets sending six ships (two cruisers and four destroyers) and the British a more powerful squadron composed of an aircraft carrier and five supporting vessels.[323] In April 1956 it was announced that the Danish and Soviet navies would exchange ship visits in Copenhagen and Leningrad during the summer, and other Western countries soon followed suit.[324] There were also mutual ship visits with the Swedish navy. In May 1956 Marshal V. D. Sokolovskii invited high-ranking Western air force officers to attend the Soviet Aviation Day show in Moscow the following month. Twenty countries, including the United States (where the invitation was highly controversial),[325] Britain, France, and Norway sent delegations to the display, at which the Soviet air force unveiled seven new or modified aircraft models.[326]

After the initial breakthroughs of 1956 there was little movement toward the establishment of regular or permanent military links. Naval visits became a rarity. No further exchanges took place with Britain until 1966, when a single British warship called upon a Soviet port. A Soviet destroyer was to make a return visit in June 1967, but abruptly turned back to the Baltic in what was interpreted in Britain as a protest against British naval links with Israel, which at the time was engaged in the Six-Day War with the Arab states.[327]

In the 1970s a number of European countries, including France, Britain, Sweden, Turkey, and Finland, began to develop fairly extensive ties with the Soviet military. In 1973 France and the USSR concluded a military exchange agreement similar to those already in use in the areas of trade and cultural cooperation. The chiefs of staff agreed to meet every two years to work out a program of exchanges. During Wilson's visit to Moscow in 1975 it was announced that the sides had "reached agreement on an exchange of visits between the armed forces." In accordance with this agreement, Britain and the USSR began exchanging delegations of officers from the Frunze Academy and the British Army Staff College, and ship visits were resumed in 1976.[328] West Germany was somewhat of an exception to the general pattern, as there were virtually no ties between the Red Army and the Bundeswehr. West Germany and the USSR did not even exchange military attachés until 1978.[329]

In the early 1980s many of these exchange programs broke down. To protest the Soviet invasion of Afghanistan, NATO military attachés ceased attending celebrations marking the anniversary of the October Revolution. In January 1980 Britain announced the cancellation of all military exchanges with the USSR. After a Soviet submarine ran aground in Swedish territorial waters in 1981, Sweden cancelled a scheduled visit to the USSR by the commander in chief of the Swedish armed forces and did not resume military contacts until almost six years later.[330] U.S. defense secretary Caspar Weinberger curtailed the rather minimal level of U.S. exchanges with the

Soviet military to protest the shooting of Major Arthur Nicholson in Berlin in 1984.

By the mid-1980s, however, the USSR had largely recovered from the setbacks sustained earlier in the decade and was forging new ties with Western military and defense establishments. Whereas in the early 1970s the focus of Soviet military exchanges had been on the neutrals and on countries such as France and Turkey that the USSR may have hoped to draw away from the NATO mainstream, in the 1980s the emphasis was on contacts with the most important NATO countries, above all the United States, and on contacts with NATO itself.

The Soviet decision to cultivate direct contacts with NATO was foreshadowed in the January 1983 Prague Political Declaration, in which the Pact for the first time made a direct appeal to the Western alliance. The declaration called for the member states of both alliances to conclude a treaty on the nonuse of military force, to undertake a "commitment to examine jointly practical measures to avert the threat of a surprise attack and also to contribute to the development of mutual exchanges of military delegations and visits of naval ships and air force units," and for the start of "direct talks" between the member states regarding a freeze and subsequent reductions in military budgets.[331] In June 1983 the leaders of the Pact countries outlined detailed plans for a NATO-WTO member state conference on a budgetary freeze, and similar proposals were made in March 1984 and October 1985. In an editorial of October 1985 *Pravda* stated that even though the USSR and its allies were in favor of "overcoming the division of Europe into opposing groupings in the more or less foreseeable future," they also sought a "modus vivendi that would blunt the acuteness of recent confrontation" and believed that "there [was] no lifetime taboo on the possibility of establishing contacts between the Warsaw Pact and NATO as organizations."[332]

In his April 1986 Berlin speech Gorbachev implied a role for NATO by proposing that the advisory commission responsible for verification be comprised of representatives from NATO, the Warsaw Pact, and neutral and nonaligned states. Thereafter the USSR made strenuous efforts to raise the level of exchanges with Western defense and military establishments. In late 1986 Marshal Viktor Kulikov, the supreme commander of the Warsaw Pact forces, Herbert Krolikowski, the general secretary of the PCC, and Ambassador Stefan Todorov, the chairman of a Warsaw Pact working group on conventional arms control, sent separate letters to their NATO counterparts suggesting the establishment of direct contacts for the purpose of discussing doctrinal and conventional arms control issues.[333]

At its May 1987 meeting in East Berlin the PCC adopted the "Document on the Military Doctrine of the Warsaw Pact States" in which it called for NATO-WTO consultations "with the aim of comparing the military doctrines of these alliances," in order to reduce suspicion and to ensure that "the military concepts and doctrines of the two military blocs and their members are based on principles of defense."[334] The proposed consultations would also deal with "imbalances and asymmetries" as a way of facilitating progress on arms control. The Pact also continued to promote a bloc-to-bloc budgetary freeze proposal, and issued a new document on that subject in April 1987.[335]

Soviet and Warsaw Pact activism toward NATO was accompanied by a burgeoning of contacts between the U.S. and Soviet defense establishments, which in turn foreshadowed new or revived Soviet-West European bilateral military contacts.[336] In April 1989—a little more than a month after the completion of the Soviet withdrawal from Afghanistan—French defense minister Jean-Pierre Chevenement went to Moscow, the first such visit since 1977.[337] At the Paris summit of July 1989 Soviet chief of staff Mikhail Moiseev and his French counterpart resumed the practice of concluding two-year exchange agreements by signing a protocol on mutual contacts for 1990–91.[338] In accordance with an agreement reached during the April 1989 Thatcher-Gorbachev summit, in July 1989 Dmitrii Iazov became the first Soviet defense minister to visit Britain, and in May 1990 Tom King became the first British defense minister to make a return visit.[339] In the same month a Swedish defense minister made the first such visit to the USSR in a decade.

Even more significant were the breakthroughs in Soviet-West German military relations. Defense Minister Scholz accompanied Chancellor Kohl to Moscow in October 1988, thus becoming the first high FRG civilian defense official to visit the USSR. In May 1989 Admiral Dieter Wellershoff became the first West German inspector general to visit the USSR. He and General Moiseev concluded a three-year program of exchanges for the period 1989–91 that included the exchange of delegations from military academies and units, the joint publication of articles in military newspapers and journals, visits of warships, and the exchange of delegations between the Voroshilov Academy and the Bundeswehr's Higher Military Command Academy.[340] The first naval visits took place in October 1989, when three West German ships called at Leningrad, and a Soviet squadron made a return visit in early 1990.[341] Marshal Sergei Akhromeev, retired from the armed forces but serving as Gorbachev's top military adviser, accompanied him to West Germany in 1989 and had meetings with Defense Minister Stoltenberg and Admiral Wellershoff.[342] West Germany and the USSR also concluded their first militarily relevant bilateral agreement: an incidents at sea accord similar to those already in place with the United States and Britain. The USSR and the Netherlands concluded a similar agreement in June 1990, but Sweden reportedly rejected a Soviet offer to conclude such an agreement during Defense Minister Roine Carlsson's September 1990 visit to Moscow.[343]

Vienna and the Passing of Soviet Superiority

The East Berlin and Budapest proposals of April and June 1986 caused some concern in the West that Gorbachev was turning his back on a modest agreement in order to pursue more grandiose and possibly unattainable objectives, but on balance the Western response was positive. On May 30, 1986, the North Atlantic Council announced the establishment of a high-level task force to discuss the new proposals and prepare a Western response.[344] Within this group the United States argued that the new conventional force reduction talks should be separate from the CSCE and include only the twenty-three bloc members (sixteen NATO, seven Warsaw Pact), while France favored an institutional link to CSCE and the inclusion of all thirty-five participating states. The USSR and its allies backed the French, accusing the United States of seeking to discriminate against the neutral and nonaligned and to blunt the uniquely "all European" character of the impending talks.

In December 1986 the North Atlantic Council approved the first report of the task force and set forth substantive criteria for the negotiation of improved conventional stability in Europe.[345] NATO proposed two distinct negotiations, one that would include the thirty-five and continue the work of the CDE, and another that would involve just the twenty-three and that would be concerned with reduction toward conventional stability. The declaration left somewhat vague the relationship of the twenty-three-country forum to the CSCE process, and reflected lingering French and U.S. differences over this question.[346]

Four days prior to NATO's December Brussels declaration Poland formally introduced to the Vienna conference an Eastern draft mandate for a post-CDE arms control forum.[347] It called for supplementing the Madrid mandate by bringing reductions within the purview of the CDE, which would continue to elaborate new CSBMs, but under a revised mandate that would explicitly include independent air and naval exercises. The Polish draft did not rule out discussion of nuclear weapons, the exclusion of which was stipulated in the Brussels declaration. NATO was not prepared to introduce a draft mandate until the summer of 1987, but the basic thrust of its approach had been spelled out in its December 1986 document.

In early 1987 the governments of the thirty-five agreed to a complicated two-part procedure for negotiating a mandate that it was hoped would bridge the gaps between the sides and allow formal talks to get under way. Beginning in February 1987 the twenty-three would hold consultations to draw up a mandate for force reduction talks. These consultations were to take place at the Vienna embassies of NATO and Pact countries, and thus not formally "within the context of the Vienna Conference."[348] At the same time representatives of all thirty-five would meet as the "S" or security working group of the Vienna conference to evaluate the CDE and decide whether to renew or supplement the Madrid mandate. NATO and Warsaw Pact participants would provide regular reports on the progress of the twenty-three to the working group of the thirty-five, thereby maintaining a loose link between the two sets of talks. In agreeing to this procedure the East tacitly abandoned its position in favor of a combined post-CDE forum under CSCE auspices.

The negotiations in these two bodies took almost two years and involved a complex set of linkages and counterlinkages, as both East and West tried to maintain a balance between the security and non-security components of the CSCE as well as to achieve their goals within each of these components. The whole process was further complicated by simmering differences between France and the United States over the nature of the link between the twenty-three and the CSCE process, and by differences between Romania and her Warsaw Pact allies.

Both mandates were formally adopted at the close of the CSCE review conference in January 1989.[349] Neither the East nor the West got all of what it wanted, but the West came out ahead, in part because the USSR had placed itself in the *demandeur* position in badly wanting a new all-European arms control forum. Very little of Poland's 1986 draft mandate proposal survived in the concluding document, while the outlines of the Brussels declaration were at least discernible. The document reaffirmed the Madrid mandate as the basis for a further stage of the CDE, thereby ruling independent air and naval activities outside the forum's terms of reference.

The mandate for the reduction talks took the form of a chairman's statement annexed to the Vienna document. The objective of the talks was "the establishment of a stable and secure balance of conventional armed forces . . . at lower levels," the elimination of disparities prejudicial to stability and security, and, as a matter of priority, elimination of the capability for launching a surprise attack and for initiating large-scale offensive action. While these objectives were largely of Western origin, they were counterbalanced somewhat by the old MBFR language ruling out damage at any stage to any participant's security. In another Western victory, the mandate for the conventional arms reduction talks stated that "nuclear weapons will not be a subject of this negotiation."[350] Naval forces and chemical weapons also were excluded.

While the delegations in Vienna labored over procedural issues, there was uncertainty and debate in both the East and the West about the substance of a future arms control agreement.[351] In his speech to the Twenty-Seventh Party Congress in February 1986 Gorbachev claimed that the USSR was interested "in restricting military potential within the limits of reasonable sufficiency," but went on to state that the character and levels of these limits were set by the actions of NATO and the United States.[352] It thus was difficult to tell how "sufficiency" differed from the traditional Soviet stress on parity. Throughout 1986 Soviet officials promoted the two-stage reduction scheme outlined in the Budapest appeal, raising concerns in the West that Gorbachev might be interested in preserving the same force imbalance at lower levels or in simply promoting his denuclearization campaign. Western governments were raising their sights from what they had tried to achieve in MBFR, and wanted to secure asymmetrically large reductions in Soviet and Warsaw Pact forces. It was unclear, however, whether the USSR would accept an "unequal" agreement, and uncertain whether Western public opinion would support such a negotiating posture.[353]

In early 1987 Gorbachev began to sound a new theme and to call for the elimination of NATO-Warsaw Pact imbalances in specific force categories. Soviet officials intimated that the Pact was ahead in tanks and certain other categories, but that NATO had advantages in ground attack aircraft, armed helicopters, and naval forces. They did not acknowledge an overall Pact superiority, but only a balance of imbalances that could be rectified by reducing to the level of the side with the smaller forces.[354] Nonetheless, the acknowledgment of asymmetries was an advance in the Soviet position and probably a response to NATO's December 1986 document setting forth the criteria for a stabilizing arms control agreement.

The government of Poland further complicated matters in May 1987 by putting forward a plan for a reduction of both conventional and nuclear forces in a zone that included Poland, Czechoslovakia, the two Germanies, the Low Countries, Hungary, and Denmark.[355] The USSR did not appear very enthusiastic about what became known as the Jaruzelski plan, but nonetheless endorsed it. In the same month the PCC adopted the "Document on the Military Doctrine of the Warsaw Pact States," which declared that henceforth the Pact would plan and deploy its forces strictly for defense, based on the principle of reasonable sufficiency. The Pact also suggested that the goal of the conventional talks should be a radical restructuring of forces on both sides in accordance with defensive principles.[356]

The new emphasis on eliminating asymmetries in particular force

categories gave rise to proposals (which Western officials found puzzling in light of Soviet behavior in MBFR) for an official, verifiable,
and very detailed exchange of data. In March 1988 the Foreign Ministers Committee of the Warsaw Pact issued an appeal to all NATO
and CSCE-participating states calling for the "holding as soon as possible [of] an exchange of data on the armed forces and conventional
arms of the Warsaw Pact countries and NATO in Europe."[357] Soviet
officials argued the importance of an *official* exchange of data rather
than the tacit agreement (or even agreement to disagree) that had
marked previous arms control negotiations.[358]

At the June 1988 Moscow summit Gorbachev outlined to President Reagan a three-stage conventional arms control proposal that
was to begin with an exchange of data to establish which side was
ahead in various force categories. Reagan rejected the proposal on
procedural grounds, claiming that the United States could not negotiate for its allies,[359] but the following month the Warsaw Pact PCC
issued a detailed public account of what had been offered in Moscow.[360] The first stage would entail the mutual elimination of imbalances and asymmetries in the conventional forces of both sides
following the proposed data exchange. At the end of the first stage
the sides would agree on the general principles to govern reductions,
which would occur in the second stage and would eliminate 500,000
men and associated arms on each side. The third stage would entail
a complete restructuring of each side's military forces to assure that
they were strictly defensive and incapable of carrying out a surprise
attack. As in the Soviet MBFR proposals of December 1974, November 1978, and November 1980, both sides would pledge not to increase their forces for the duration of the talks.

In the West there was still skepticism and debate about Soviet
motives and intentions. The Soviet stress on defense could be seen
as an element of the Soviet denuclearization policy, in that it put
further pressure on NATO to modify its (allegedly offensive) doctrine
of flexible response and possible nuclear first use. The Warsaw Pact
had always declared that its military doctrine was defensive, and it
was apparent that the Soviet military was dragging its feet on translating the new declaratory doctrine into new policies at the operational level. Western defense planners were also concerned about
operational minimums and other esoteric concepts, and feared that
because of geographic and military factors the USSR might be in a
position to offer asymmetrically large mutual reductions that would
be politically attractive but that in purely military terms would leave
NATO in a worse position than before an agreement.[361]

Soviet credibility received an enormous boost in December 1988
when Gorbachev announced to the UN General Assembly that in the
next two years the USSR was planning to reduce its forces by 500,000

men and to withdraw six tank divisions comprising 50,000 men and 5,000 tanks from East Germany, Czechoslovakia, and Hungary.[362] At a meeting with the Trilateral Commission the following month Gorbachev revealed that Soviet forces in Europe would be cut by 240,000 men, with the rest of the reductions to be taken in the eastern and southern parts of the USSR. The East European allies also announced unilateral reductions in their forces and military budgets.

These developments set a positive tone for the start of the CFE negotiations in early 1989. The actual negotiations were not scheduled to begin until March, but at the January 1989 CSCE follow-up meeting that adopted the CFE mandate the ministers outlined their goals for the talks. Shevardnadze stated that the "declared fundamental goal" of the USSR was "to end any foreign military presence and bases on the territories of other countries."[363] He also signaled that the USSR was dropping its quest for an exchange of data, and outlined a series of unilateral steps that the USSR would take to provide the West with more information, including the release, by the end of January, of Warsaw Pact "numerical data on troops and armaments of the sides in Europe."[364] At the formal opening of the CFE talks Shevardnadze proposed a three-stage agreement, the first stage of which would, as in previous Soviet offers, eliminate imbalances and asymmetries. He again downplayed the importance of agreement on data, remarking that it was necessary to avoid the sterile debate that had characterized MBFR.[365] NATO tabled a set of rules for stability, and called for setting limits for each alliance of 20,000 tanks, 16,500 artillery pieces, and 28,000 armored troop carriers.

The early stages of the CFE were partly overshadowed by a new controversy, stirred up by the INF treaty and continuing signs of political ferment in the East, concerning the future of nuclear weapons in Europe and especially U.S. short-range missiles based on West German soil. Western governments agreed in principle that NATO nuclear strategy required the maintenance of some residual U.S. nuclear capability in Europe, but were divided on what this meant in practice. The British opposed further theater nuclear negotiations until the conventional imbalance was redressed and called for a "firebreak" at the 500-kilometer level, while the West Germans pressed for immediate negotiations and the deferral of NATO nuclear modernization plans. The United States attempted to strike an intermediate position, but was clearly worried about the pressures for total denuclearization that were apparent in the FRG.

In what was clearly a gesture to the West Germans, in January 1989 Shevardnadze announced that Soviet forces withdrawing from East Germany, Hungary, and Czechoslovakia would take their short-range nuclear weapons with them. This was seen as militarily insignificant but potentially important in swaying German opinion.[366] In

April 1989 the Warsaw Pact formally proposed the beginning of separate negotiations on tactical nuclear weapons in Europe, including dual-capable systems. The West Germans were inclined to accept the offer; the Americans and British to defer negotiations until after a conventional arms control agreement was concluded and implemented—probably well into the 1990s.

On his trip to Bonn in June 1989 Gorbachev urged the West Germans not to accept deployment of new U.S. systems, and in his Strasbourg speech the following month he underlined the potential U.S.-European divergence of interests on the denuclearization issue: "The final goal here is the complete elimination of this weaponry. It threatens only Europeans, who are certainly not preparing to fight each other. So why is it needed and who needs it?"[367] He also offered to make further unilateral reductions, provided the NATO countries moved toward negotiations on short-range systems. Privately Soviet officials and institute researchers began to hint that the USSR might be prepared to conclude an agreement sanctioning the maintenance of some kind of "minimal deterrent" in Europe,[368] and Soviet researchers began elaborating a detailed, semi-official plan for nuclear reductions to a level of mutual minimum deterrence.[369] It was clear, however, that over the long run the USSR would continue to press for virtual denuclearization and that political support for NATO's nuclear deterrent was on the wane, especially in West Germany. The NATO countries, and in particular the United States, thus were under growing pressure to address the questions of both conventional and short-range nuclear forces in Europe.

On May 25 the Pact offered its first detailed CFE proposal with specific numerical limits. It called for three sets of ceilings on forces and equipment: country ceilings, foreign deployment ceilings, and alliance ceilings. No country could have more than 920,000 men in the Atlantic-to-the-Urals region or more than 350,000 troops deployed outside its territory, while each alliance would be limited to 1,350,000 troops in Europe. The proposal also called for alliance-wide limits of 20,000 tanks, 24,000 artillery pieces, and 28,000 troop carriers, and ceilings in a central European region of 8,700 tanks, 7,600 artillery pieces, and 14,500 armored troop carriers. The latter numbers were close to the 8,000, 4,500, and 11,000 ceilings proposed by the West in these categories, and appeared to signal a very serious Soviet interest in an agreement. The Pact also called for limits on strike aircraft and helicopters, which NATO wanted excluded.[370]

Given the huge quantitative disparities between NATO and Warsaw Pact forces and the relative weight of the Soviet military in Europe, virtually all of the single-country and alliance ceilings were well above NATO levels (and thus would not require cuts), but well below those of the USSR and the Pact. The Soviet leadership had in effect made a decision to make large and virtually unilateral reductions, albeit in the context of a negotiated agreement. The Western response was overwhelmingly positive, and the United States came under strong domestic and European pressure to counter with concessions on issues of special interest to the Soviets, notably reductions in aircraft and foreign troop presence.

NATO formulated its response to both the Eastern conventional and nuclear proposals at its May 29–30 summit. It approved a proposal by President Bush that was intended to meet Soviet demands on several points, notably the inclusion of combat aircraft, attack helicopters, and manpower. The proposal accepted the Pact offer to limit tanks, armored troop carriers, and artillery to 20,000, 28,000, and 16,500–24,000 respectively for each side. It called for reducing U.S. and Soviet ground and air forces in the central region to 275,000—a cut of about 30,000 for the United States and as much as 325,000 for the USSR. However, it did not include alliance-wide or central region troop ceilings, and thus did not constrain non-U.S. forces in Europe or British, French, and other allied deployments in West Germany.

The alliance also papered over the rift on the short-range nuclear issue by agreeing to accelerate the conventional arms control talks and pledging "to enter into negotiations to achieve a *partial* reduction of U.S. and Soviet land-based missile forces of shorter range to equal and verifiable levels," after conclusion of a conventional agreement.[371] To meet West German demands for early nuclear negotiations the alliance pledged that it would try to reach a conventional agreement within six to twelve months and complete the reductions by 1992 or 1993.

There were still some important differences between the sides. The East wanted ceilings to apply to stored equipment (including the 4,000 tanks the United States had in reserve in West Germany), while the West wanted to count only equipment deployed in units. The sides also differed on the counting of aircraft. NATO wanted to limit all types of aircraft, while the Pact wished to exclude air defense fighters and interceptors on the grounds that they were defensive. Shevardnadze also raised the issue of non-U.S. NATO forces, noting that together Britain and France had 100,000 troops in Germany.[372]

Nonetheless, by mid-1989 the prospects for the first all-European arms reduction agreement were seen as increasingly good. There were lingering concerns in various Western capitals about denuclearization, verification, and the effect of Soviet disarmament on NATO cohesion, but on balance Western officials were surprised and delighted that the USSR seemed prepared at last to give up the conventional superiority which had played such an overwhelming role in East-West and intra-Western affairs since the 1950s. Progress toward an agreement continued during the summer and fall, and at times was slowed as much by intra-Western differences over various issues as by East-West bargaining.[373]

The second all-European arms control forum, the thirty-five-country talks on CSBMs, also got under way in Vienna in March. Following the pattern established at Madrid, Stockholm, and again at the Vienna review conference, the USSR's primary objective in these talks appeared to be to secure the inclusion of, or at a minimum, draw attention to naval and air activities. Bulgaria, Czechoslovakia, and the GDR tabled a proposal that included provisions for the notification of naval exercises, limitation of major naval exercises to no more than fifty ships and ten to fourteen days, and other naval measures, thereby provoking the familiar procedural wrangles over the CDE mandate.[374] The East also called for additional ground force-related CSBMs, with emphasis on limiting the size, frequency, and duration of military maneuvers.[375]

The most striking feature of the Eastern approach was its emphasis on the creation of permanent, all-European security institutions. Eastern proposals in this area were patterned in part on the U.S.-Soviet risk reduction center agreement of May 1987, but also drew upon ideas developed by the West European left and its defense counter-experts. In May 1987 the joint working group of the PUWP and the parliamentary group of the SPD reached agreement on a proposal for the establishment of a European council for confidence building. This was followed, in July 1988, by an SED-SPD joint statement proposing the establishment of a "zone of confidence and security in central Europe," along with permanent "confidence centers" for the exchange of information to prevent crises, joint observation posts in strategic areas, a system of joint satellite monitoring, and the establishment of direct bilateral communications to prevent crises.[376] Gorbachev endorsed the proposal in his speech to the Polish Sejm several days later.[377]

The Warsaw Pact began translating these ideas into formal proposals in 1989. In his concluding speech to the Vienna follow-up conference Shevardnadze called for "greater persistence in the realization of the idea of a European war risk reduction center."[378] The East's March 1989 CSBM proposal contained provisions for regular consultations on various matters, the establishment of a risk reduction center, and the development of special crisis communications systems. Western governments retained much of their traditional skepticism about excessive institutionalization in the security sphere, but support for such measures was growing. One day after an unpiloted Soviet Mig-23 crashed into a farmhouse in Belgium in July

1989 West Germany, the Netherlands, and Belgium proposed a NATO-Warsaw Pact hotline.[379]

Alongside the main negotiations in Vienna two additional CSBM forums were agreed to in 1989 and convened in early 1990: the Open Skies talks and the seminar on military doctrine. President Bush revived the Open Skies idea in May 1989 as part of his effort to gain the arms control initiative from Gorbachev, possibly expecting him to follow Khrushchev's example and turn the offer down. But in September Foreign Minister Shevardnadze and Secretary of State Baker agreed to jointly call for an international conference on Open Skies. Canada and Hungary offered to host the conference, and meetings were scheduled for February 1990 in Ottawa and April in Budapest.

The seminar on doctrine was a Soviet idea whose origins went back to the January 1983 Prague Political Declaration and subsequent efforts to draw attention to NATO's first-use doctrine and the Warsaw Pact's own defensive restructuring. NATO agreed to the seminar in October, which took place in Vienna at the chiefs-of-staff level in January–February 1990.

While talks continued and forums proliferated, arms control was increasingly overshadowed by the political upheavals in Eastern Europe and the prospect of German reunification. In the main CFE talks the virtual breakdown of the Warsaw Pact called into question the rationale for the bloc-to-bloc format. Already in November 1989 the non-Communist government of Poland announced large unilateral cuts in its armed forces, while Hungary and Czechoslovakia pressed for and ultimately achieved agreements for the complete withdrawal of Soviet forces from their territory outside the framework of a CFE agreement. The impending reunification of Germany created an even more problematic situation. East German forces technically were counted in the Warsaw Pact totals, even though it was increasingly clear that the GDR soon would be absorbed by a NATO member. At the Vienna seminar on doctrine the Soviet military was virtually isolated, as representatives of the newly democratic states of Eastern Europe made no secret of their sympathies for the West.[380] The Ottawa Open Skies conference was thoroughly overshadowed by the German question, and failed to reach agreement on an aerial inspection regime. It appeared that the USSR was pulling back from an agreement, possibly in response to military resistance at home.[381]

By early 1990 Western governments found it increasingly difficult to synchronize their arms control proposals with the rapid political changes sweeping through Eastern Europe. The Bush administration was under strong domestic and international pressure to abandon the proposal to limit U.S. troops in the central region to 275,000—a number that seemed fairly bold when it was tabled in May but that by the end of the year was seen as unrealistically high. At the same time the administration was increasingly wary of a conventional "zero option"—a Soviet proposal or series of proposals calling for mutual withdrawals of U.S. and Soviet forces in Germany down to zero. The United States, therefore, sought to break the previous U.S.-Soviet symmetry by proposing unequal levels for the two countries.

The USSR had, of course, a long history of insisting on absolute equality vis-à-vis the United States, and there was considerable uncertainty about whether it would accept asymmetrical levels of forces. However, in a sudden reversal Shevardnadze agreed, in talks with Secretary Baker on the edges of the Ottawa meeting, to a plan that would allow both countries to have 195,000 troops in central Europe but would permit the United States to have an additional 30,000 outside the central zone. The agreement was controversial in both the USSR and the United States, albeit for different reasons.[382] Critics of Shevardnadze in the USSR objected to what was seen as yet another unilateral concession, while U.S. military planners worried that German domestic political factors might result in U.S. force levels in Germany falling to zero *in any case.* The United States then would be permitted to station no more than 30,000 air force and army personnel in the rest of Europe (mainly the U.K., Italy, and Spain)—a level that was seen as dangerously low.

As noted in chapter three, the bilateral meetings on the periphery of the Ottawa Conference also resulted in an agreement to convene the two plus four talks on the external aspects of German reunification. Soviet officials insisted that West German and foreign troop levels in Germany had to be addressed in the new forum, as well as at CFE. The maximum Soviet objective seemed to be to retain a permanent Soviet military presence in Germany based on four-power rights. Alternatively, the USSR seemed to want to have the option of trading the withdrawal of Soviet forces in East Germany for U.S. withdrawal from the West.[383]

The Western powers argued that limitations on German forces should not even be discussed in the two plus four talks, which could lead to the creation of a special security regime for Germany reminiscent of the one established in the Treaty of Versailles. Consistent with the 1954–55 understandings between West Germany and its allies, the Western powers argued that British, French, and U.S. forces were not in West Germany as occupiers, but at the request of a sovereign government with which they were collectively engaged in the "defense of the free world." The Western powers were not averse to placing limits on German military power, but argued that such limits had to be addressed in the Vienna CFE talks rather than as part of the final German settlement.

In the end the USSR did not have the bargaining power to force a solution along its preferred lines. At the same time, however, the Germans were forced to agree to what was in effect a special military regime for Germany. At the conclusion of the July 1990 Stavropol summit the German government announced that it was prepared to give a binding declaration at the CFE talks that within three to four years of the coming into effect of a European arms control agreement it would reduce the strength of a unified German army to 370,000.[384] It also reaffirmed its commitment not to acquire chemical, biological, or nuclear weapons. In exchange the USSR dropped its objections to German membership in NATO and agreed to withdraw its troops from the eastern part of Germany by the end of 1994.

Foreign Minister Genscher fulfilled the pledge of the West German government to make a binding declaration to the CFE talks on August 30, 1990. Genscher stated that German reductions would commence with the entry into force of the first CFE agreement, and that within three to four years the German military would reach a level of 370,000 personnel, of which 345,000 would belong to the ground and air forces. Subsequently, the West Germans yielded to pressures by the Soviets and moved away from their earlier insistence that Germany not be "singularized" as part of the reunification process. Article 3 of the Treaty on the Final Settlement with Respect to Germany incorporated the text of Genscher's statement to the CFE negotiations. While this article did not explicitly constitute an imposition by the four powers of a limit on the size of German forces, it clearly diluted the unilateral character of the German declaration and created a somewhat murky legal situation.[385] The West German retreat on this question was compounded by the fact that the final German settlement was embodied in a treaty rather than, as the Bonn government preferred, a less authoritative international document. While the form of the agreement was different from what the West Germans originally wanted, its substantive provisions were highly favorable. The limit of 370,000 was close to Kohl's opening position in the negotiations and far above the 200,000 level favored by the Soviets.

The settlement of the German question made conclusion of a CFE agreement both more attainable and, given the link between the German reductions and the entry into force of the agreement, more necessary for all parties concerned. The Soviets, who had been stalling at CFE throughout the spring, began to negotiate in earnest. Having lost their East German ally and agreed with the governments of Czechoslovakia and Hungary to withdraw all their forces from those countries by July 1, 1991, the Soviets were for all practical purposes committed to complete withdrawal from Eastern Europe, even in the absence of a CFE agreement. In early September Soviet ambassador Grinevskii suggested that in view of the changed political situation and the Soviet withdrawals the United States should be limited to 70,000–80,000 troops in Western Europe, rather than the 225,000 agreed to earlier in the year. Secretary of State Baker replied that all of the previous troop-level ceilings had been overtaken by events, and that the United States no longer considered itself bound by the 225,000 commitment made in Ottawa.[386] In the end the United States and the USSR both agreed, with the concurrence of their allies, to drop personnel ceilings from the CFE agreement.

Baker and Shevardnadze reached agreement in principle on all of the major issues holding up conclusion of the treaty at their meeting in New York in early October. They agreed that each alliance would be limited to 20,000 tanks, 30,000 armored combat vehicles, 20,000 artillery pieces, and 2,000 helicopters (with somewhat lower sub-ceilings for active units). Within these ceilings, any one country could have up to 13,300 tanks, 20,000 armored combat vehicles, 13,700 artillery pieces, and 1,500 helicopters. These single-country ceilings were relevant only to the USSR, which was the only country with forces in Europe at anything near these levels.[387] Baker and Shevardnadze failed to settle the question of combat aircraft totals for each alliance, but the more important number—5,150 maximum for any one country—was established.

The U.S.-USSR agreement was quickly endorsed by the NATO allies of United States, but became a source of contention between the USSR and its nominal East European allies, who began to squabble over the allocation of national totals within the Warsaw Pact ceilings. The USSR wanted to keep the highest possible level of tanks—13,300—leaving 6,700 for the other five members of the organization. The five asserted a right to a share of 7,200, and thus wanted to cut the Soviet total to 12,800.[388] In early November the USSR and its allies worked out a compromise under which it would be permitted to keep 13,150 tanks and 13,175 artillery pieces, or slightly less than the single-country ceilings allowed in CFE treaty, with the remainder of the alliance subceiling totals allotted to the other members of the Pact. This understanding paved the way for the signature of the treaty, which took place at the Paris summit on November 19.

In the final treaty combat aircraft limits were set at 6,800 for each alliance, of which the USSR would be permitted to keep 5,150, plus an additional 430 naval aircraft not covered by the treaty. Manpower was not limited by the treaty, but the signatories pledged to begin immediate negotiations toward a second agreement covering this category. In addition to the overall ceilings on forces in the region from the Atlantic to the Urals the treaty established four subzones in which tanks, armored combat vehicles, and artillery were limited to specified subceilings. (There were no subzonal ceilings on aircraft or helicopters.) In Subzone 4.4, composed on the Western side of Germany and the Low Countries and on the Eastern side of Czechoslovakia, Hungary, and Poland, each side was limited to 7,500 tanks, 11,500 armored combat vehicles, and 5,000 artillery pieces. Subzone 4.3 included, on the Western side, Denmark, France, Italy, and the U.K., and, on the Eastern side, the USSR's Baltic, Byelorussian, and Carpathian Military Districts as well as all of the territory comprising Subzone 4.4. Subzone 4.4 limits for tanks, armored combat vehicles, and artillery were set at 10,300 tanks, 19,260 armored combat vehicles, and 9,100 artillery pieces for each side. Subzone 4.2 included, on the Western side, Portugal and Spain, and, on the Eastern side, the Moscow, Volga-Ural, and Kiev Military Districts, as well as all of the territory comprising Subzones 4.3 and 4.4. Limits for Subzone 4.2 were set at 15,300, 24,100, and 14,000 for the three categories of weapons, with lower subceilings for active units.

The inclusion of Subzone 4.4 within Subzone 4.3 and of Subzone 4.3 within Subzone 4.4 was an ingenious device that allowed the USSR, which in the future would not have any forces in Subzone 4.4, to compensate by keeping higher levels of forces in the other subzones. In addition, the treaty established a flank subzone that did not encompass the other subzones and that included Greece, Iceland, Turkey, and Norway on the Western side and Bulgaria, Romania, and three Soviet military districts on the Eastern side. Force levels in the flank subzone were derived by subtracting the totals for Subzone 4.2 from the permissible totals in the entire Atlantic-to-Urals region. The establishment of the subzones divided Soviet territory into four juridically defined regions (the portions of the USSR located in Subzones 4.3 and 4.4, the flank subzone, and the region beyond the Urals) without affecting U.S. or even other European territory in a similar manner. The USSR thus accepted an agreement that, in addition to mandating highly asymmetrical numerical cuts, impinged upon Soviet territory in a way that previous Soviet leaderships had rejected as discriminatory and politically unequal.

The treaty also established an intrusive verification system that included on-site monitoring of the destruction of excess weaponry, exchanges of data, and large numbers of on-site inspections to verify compliance. In addition, the members of NATO and the Warsaw Pact signed a non-aggression declaration stating that they were "no longer adversaries and will establish new relations of partnership and mutual friendship." It added that the signatories had an "obligation and commitment to refrain from the threat or use of force" against each other. The Paris summit also produced a document on CSBMs that strengthened the provisions of the Stockholm agreement and assigned certain tasks to the new conflict prevention center.

The signing of the two agreements in Paris opened a new and

somewhat uncertain period of arms control in Europe. On the one hand, the signatories had made a political commitment to further talks. On the other hand, there was considerable skepticism in many military establishments about further large reductions. German military planners assumed that over the long run the USSR—or Russia or a future Russian confederation—would remain the preeminent land and nuclear power in Europe, and thus were reluctant to commit to forces smaller than 370,000, especially in light of the uncertainty surrounding the U.S. military presence in Europe. These uncertainties were compounded in late 1990 and early 1991, as the Soviet military made clear that it was opposed to the highly asymmetrical character of the Paris agreement and determined to resist its implementation. NATO governments charged the Soviet Union with violating the letter and spirit of the agreement, and in early 1991 were considering delaying its ratification.

7   Economics

The development of Soviet-West European economic relations after World War II was shaped by the experience of the interwar period, which saw both a substantial revival of Russia's trade with the West and ongoing conflict caused by divergent Soviet economic practices and Comintern support for world revolution. After veering toward autarky under war communism, in the 1920s the Soviet authorities began restoring business relations with traditional partners. In the spring of 1920 they began talks with Britain that led to the temporary trade agreement of 1921. This agreement provided for the exchange of official representatives with limited diplomatic privileges, allowed the Russian federation to establish a trade mission in Britain, and barred the British government from attaching Soviet property as compensation for old debts.[1] Two months later the Bolsheviks concluded a provisional economic treaty with Germany that accorded de jure recognition to the Soviet foreign trade monopoly and full diplomatic privileges to its representatives in Berlin. The provisional agreement was superseded by the Rapallo Treaty of 1922 which, for all its political notoriety, was essentially an economic agreement.[2] The USSR also granted concessions to foreign businesses seeking to invest on Soviet territory, obtained commercial credits (initially from Sweden but later from Germany and other countries), and established the first mixed companies chartered abroad but owned and controlled by the Soviet state.[3]

Although few of the economic agreements of the 1920s and 1930s remained in effect after World War II, the interwar period established important precedents for how the Soviet state related to the international economic system. First, the USSR succeeded in forcing foreign companies and governments to recognize the state monopoly on trade. In the end the Soviets probably hurt themselves by maintaining this monopoly, as many Western firms may have been dissuaded from trade with the USSR because of the added costs it imposed; but Western governments never mounted a political challenge to the monopoly. Second, the USSR managed to win diplomatic status for its foreign trade representatives and extra-territoriality for its trade missions. Third, it won de facto and de jure most favored nation (MFN) status from most countries, even though the

Soviet state trading monopoly and the internal pricing system rendered such status problematic and potentially damaging to the granting country. Fourth, it managed to normalize its trade relations without addressing the Bolshevik repudiation of czarist and Kerensky government debt. The debt issue created a psychological barrier for Western companies and governments, but did not stop the USSR from conducting business with the outside world.[4] As will be seen in this chapter, these precedents began to lose their validity only in the late 1980s, as the USSR moved toward a free-market system, decentralized its foreign trade apparatus, and even belatedly decided to clear up the problem of czarist debt.

Bilateral Relations

Trade and Credit Agreements

After lagging behind most other West European countries in the interwar period, after World War II France took the lead in developing trade ties with the USSR. In December 1945 the de Gaulle government concluded the Agreement on Trade Relations and on the Status of the USSR Trade Mission in France that included a MFN clause.[5] The 1945 agreement provided the legal basis for bilateral trade until 1951, when it was replaced by the Agreement on Reciprocal Trade Relations, the provisions of which were reaffirmed in subsequent agreements and remain in force today.[6] In December 1947 Britain and the USSR signed a trade and finance agreement under which the Soviet Union resumed the export of grain in exchange for locomotives and other industrial products.[7] The Temporary Commercial Agreement of 1934 remained in effect, as did most of the provisions of the 1941 agreement under which Britain had supplied wartime aid to the USSR.[8] Trade with Sweden revived, helped along by a 1 billion kronor ($280 million) credit—repayable over fifteen years at 3 percent interest—that the Swedish government provided in 1946.[9]

The USSR also restored trade relations with two former enemy states, Finland and Italy. Finland and the Soviet Union signed a commercial treaty in 1947 which was supplemented by provisions in the Friendship, Cooperation, and Mutual Assistance Treaty of 1948 that called for the strengthening of bilateral economic ties.[10] Largely because of political factors, in 1951 Finland and the USSR signed a five-year trade and payments agreement, the first "long-term" Soviet-West European economic understanding. Soviet-Italian economic relations got off to an inauspicious start after World War II, owing to the poor state of political relations and to Soviet demands, rejected by both Italy and the Western powers, that Italy pay huge reparations for its part in Germany's invasion of Russia. (Finland did pay extensive reparations.) But in 1948 the two countries concluded the Treaty on Commerce and Navigation, the provisions of which remain in force and were reaffirmed by an exchange of letters in 1975.[11]

Direct trade between the USSR and West Germany began in 1952, even though political disputes blocked the conclusion of a formal trade agreement for another six years. In the absence of diplomatic relations between the FRG and the countries of Eastern Europe, the Bonn government prodded leading West German industrialists into forming, in 1952, an Eastern Committee (Ostausschuss) that assumed responsibility for economic negotiations with the East. Beginning in 1953 Soviet representatives made approaches to the West Germans for the conclusion of a governmental trade agreement, but were rebuffed by the Adenauer government, which linked the expansion of economic relations to progress on political issues.[12]

Thus, even before Stalin's death, the USSR and most West European countries had established a legal and institutional framework for trade, in some cases by building upon interwar agreements. The existence of a framework did not in itself promote trade, however, and leaders on both sides sought to use the post-Stalin thaw to give a political impetus to trade. In April 1953 the ECE hosted a series of simultaneous, bilateral trade negotiations which, as one observer noted, "whetted the appetite" of West European governments for trade by increasing awareness of export opportunities.[13] They also provided the occasion for the first direct talks between representatives of the Soviet and West German governments. The consultations did not entail meetings between official delegations (which would have been politically controversial in the West), but were talks among trade specialists appointed as temporary consultants to the executive secretary of the organization. Following the consultations the USSR and its allies dramatically stepped up their participation in the ECE and its working bodies, thus returning to and eventually surpassing the level of involvement seen in the late 1940s. Nonetheless, Soviet-West European trade relations were far from normalized, as was seen in the decision by the United States in 1954 to block Denmark's export of oil tankers to the USSR.

The 1955 Geneva summit had little direct influence on East-West trade but substantial indirect effects. Bulganin and Khrushchev agreed to Western suggestions that the development of East-West contacts be placed on the agenda. It soon became clear, however, that East and West had radically different ideas regarding the kinds of contacts to be discussed. While the Western delegations criticized the closed and secretive nature of Soviet society and called for measures to liberalize the flow of people and information, the Soviet leaders concentrated on the elimination of Western-imposed barriers to trade. These differences were papered over in the Geneva directive, which instructed the foreign ministers to study, "by means of experts," measures to eliminate barriers to trade as well as to "bring about such freer contacts and exchanges as are to the mutual advantage of the countries and peoples concerned."

At the November meeting of the four foreign ministers the underlying divergences became more apparent. Acting on behalf of the Western powers, France put forward a seventeen-point plan that focused heavily on human and cultural contacts, while Molotov introduced a plan consisting of five points, four of which dealt with economic matters. Point one of the Molotov proposal called for "applying the principle of the most-favored nation treatment in the fields of trade and navigation." Point two concerned shipping and the removal of "existing restrictions on sea communications with certain states." Point three dealt with cooperation in the field of atomic energy; and point four called for "participation in international specialized agencies . . . of all states desiring to cooperate in the work of these agencies."[14] Working groups were set up to discuss the French and Soviet proposals, but no progress was made.

While the four powers made little progress on trade issues, the "spirit of Geneva" did help to facilitate trade. The governments of Norway, Sweden, and Denmark were eager to secure new export markets, and used their post-Geneva meetings with Khrushchev and Bulganin to pursue this objective.[15] Gerhardsen's trip to Moscow in late 1955 produced a three-year Norwegian-Soviet trade agreement, together with a protocol covering exchanges for 1956. During Prime Minister Erlander's visit to Moscow in March 1956 Sweden and the USSR managed to overcome a major obstacle to trade by settling claims arising from the annexation of the Baltic states, where Swedish companies had had major investments. Danish prime minister Hansen used his visit during the same month to smooth over some of the lingering tensions from the tanker incident of 1954. France and the USSR concluded their first long-term (1957–59) agreement on reciprocal commodity deliveries, and Britain and the USSR also agreed to expand trade during the Bulganin-Khrushchev visit to London.

The gradual breakdown of Western barriers to trade with the USSR made a profound impression on Khrushchev, who was personally bitter at his country's exclusion from the benefits of trade but also naively impressed by the "complementarity" of the Soviet and West European economies, which he expected would lead not only to vast increases in trade but to political leverage over West European governments. During the 1955 summit with Adenauer he and Bulganin painted a glowing picture of the prospects for Soviet-West German cooperation.[16] Although Adenauer tried to dampen talk of economic breakthroughs and stressed the primacy of the political issues, Khrushchev came away convinced that pressures from the German business community had severely undercut Adenauer's ability to bargain on political issues.[17]

While believing that he could exploit economic interests within West Germany to pressure Adenauer, Khrushchev also hoped to use the prospect of Soviet-West German economic ties to gain leverage over France and other West European countries. Pineau recalled that when he defended the West's policy of economically integrating West Germany to ensure its peaceful intentions, Khrushchev countered by raising the specter of a Soviet-West German economic rapprochement that would be disastrous for France: "You forget that [Germany's] economy is much less complementary with yours than with that of the USSR. When you begin to compete with German industry, it will turn toward the USSR where it will be able to find an appropriate area of expansion. That will be the time of a new Rapallo. Then you will be sorry that you didn't listen to us."[10] This misplaced confidence in the political importance of economic ties may have been behind the otherwise inexplicable position of the USSR on economic issues during the negotiation of the Austrian State Treaty. Conclusion of the treaty was delayed by Soviet insistence that certain Austrian assets (which the USSR claimed had belonged to Germany) remain in Soviet hands. Mastny noted that it is "not easy to understand Soviet intransigence on this point," and suggested that the issue was one of prestige rather than substance.[19] An alternative explanation is that the Soviet leaders thought that they could retain political leverage over Austria through partial control of its economy.

The Suez and Hungarian crises ended the initial post-Stalin relaxation in Soviet-West European relations, but had only modest effects on the development of bilateral economic ties. In 1957 Italy concluded a four-year agreement for the 1958–61 period, along with a new agreement on payments.[20] After arduous negotiations that concerned, among other things, unrepatriated German prisoners, in April 1958 West Germany and the USSR concluded the three-year Agreement on General Questions of Trade and Navigation that granted the USSR MFN status within the limits set by West German membership in the EEC.[21] In May 1959 Britain leapfrogged the other major West European countries by concluding a five-year trade agreement, the first between the two countries in almost twelve years.[22] In a separate agreement also concluded in 1959, Britain and the USSR agreed to exchange claims stemming from World War II. Not until 1967, however, was a final settlement achieved.[23]

In the following decade the 1957–59 trade agreements generally were renewed, in some cases with their terms lengthened and special protocols attached. Italy concluded four-year trade agreements for the 1962–65 and 1966–69 periods. Britain renewed its 1959 treaty in 1964, 1969, and in all subsequent five-year periods. France renewed its three-year trade agreement for 1960–62 and 1963–65, and concluded its first five-year trade agreement for 1965–69. Similar agreements were concluded for 1970–74, 1975–79, and all subsequent five-year periods.[24] West Germany was an exception to the general pattern. Its 1958 trade agreement was renewed in 1961, but allowed to expire at the end of 1963, largely as a result of the unresolved dispute over the status of Berlin.

In themselves, the bilateral agreements removed only some of the economic and political barriers to trade. They contained lists of products that the signatories were prepared to exchange, but did not establish binding commitments to particular levels of trade or specific transactions. Actual sales remained dependent upon the negotiation of terms between firms and state trading organizations. The gap between the provisions of these agreements and actual performance was a source of frustration to the Soviet leaders, who failed "to understand that a Western state guarantee of a right to export or import, given to a private enterprise, is not an obligation to trade."[25] In any case, the USSR was unable to pay for a large volume of imports. After the Swedish loan of 1946 it was another twelve years before the Soviet Union again was able to borrow in the West.[26] In addition, the Soviet ability to earn hard currency through exports was limited by internal factors and by Western restrictions on the import of many Soviet products, including petroleum. Britain banned the purchase of Soviet oil in 1941.[27] The U.S. and British-controlled oil majors blocked Soviet sales to third countries, thereby preventing the USSR from regaining even the share of the world market held by Russia before World War I and in most of the interwar period. Other Soviet exports were subjected to rigorous Western import quotas.

These barriers began to break down in the late 1950s. In 1958 Britain breached the credit embargo by extending a five-year loan for the purchase of textile machinery and equipment. The following year a German bank provided a five-year credit for the purchase of fishing boats. Western barriers to Soviet energy exports began to erode in 1957, when Ente Nazionali Idrocarburi (ENI), the Italian national oil company, demonstrated that it was possible to defy the oil majors by purchasing Soviet oil. ENI concluded its first major agreement with the USSR in 1960, and by the following year was obtaining 72 percent of its oil from Soviet sources, all of it at cut-rate prices. Attracted by the same prices, West Germany and several other European countries also became substantial importers.[28] Even the British ban on imports of Soviet petroleum was partially lifted in 1961.

By the early 1960s Western opponents of trade with the USSR no longer could hope to maintain absolute bans and boycotts. Instead they sought to regulate terms and limit levels of perceived dependence. NATO recommended that credits to the USSR be limited to repayment periods of five years or less.[29] The five-year limit lasted until 1964, when it was breached by the British, who provided a $278 million credit on fifteen-year terms for the purchase of complete plants; and by the French, who lent $322 million on ten-year terms. In 1965 the government of Italy provided a $110 million, ten-year credit for general purchases. The following year Italy extended a fourteen-year, $367 million credit for the purchase from Fiat of what was to become the Togliatti motor works.

In 1961 the Commission of the European Economic Community recommended that each member adopt measures to ensure that the share of Soviet oil in its total imports would not increase. Italy objected, however, and the recommendation did not become policy. Largely as a result of U.S. pressure, the Coordinating Committee (COCOM) that monitored technology exports to the East blacklisted shipping companies involved in the transport of Soviet oil and took other measures to slow the expansion of Soviet energy exports to the West. Again in response to U.S. pressure, in 1962 all NATO members and Japan embargoed further sales of large diameter pipe to the USSR, which planned to use the pipe to build the Druzhba pipeline to transport oil to the West. But like the EEC Commission recommendation of 1961, these measures were only partly effective. There was no shortage of ships to transport oil, and the pipe embargo lasted only until November 1966. It helped to delay the construction and limit the capacity of the pipeline, but it did not reverse the generally upward trend in Soviet exports of energy to Western Europe.[30]

The Soviet leaders thus had reason to be gratified by the partial normalization of trade ties and the breakdown of the credit and energy embargoes. There were, however, two other developments that threatened to negate the gains achieved in the 1950s. The first was West European economic integration, which Soviet analysts claimed was unsustainable in the long run but which in the short run had negative implications for Soviet-West European economic relations. Countries that joined the European Economic Community (EEC) or the European Free Trade Association (EFTA) in effect accorded more favorable trade treatment to fellow-members than to nonmember countries, including those such as the USSR to which they had earlier granted MFN status. This practice was legal under the General Agreement on Tariffs and Trade (GATT), but as a nonsignatory of the GATT the USSR protested that countries joining the EEC and EFTA were violating their MFN pledges. The USSR pressured Finland to renegotiate its bilateral trade treaty with the USSR in exchange for allowing it to become a de facto member of EFTA, but did not have the leverage to gain comparable concessions from other EEC or EFTA members.[31]

The second trend was Western Europe's financial recovery and its shift from a deficit to a surplus region. In the late 1940s and early to mid-1950s dollar-short West European countries were interested in bilateral commodity exchange agreements that enabled them to obtain Soviet grain and raw materials in exchange for industrial goods. The major West European currencies were not convertible, and Soviet-West European trade was based on a clearing system of bilateral settlements. After 1957 this system gradually was replaced by payment in convertible currencies.[32] Italy led the way in 1958 with a new agreement on payments that replaced the previous lira clearing settlements, and all other West European countries (except Finland) eventually followed suit.[33] In the early 1970s Austria became the last West European country to change over to the new system.[34]

The USSR would have preferred to maintain and strengthen the existing pattern of balanced commodity trade but failed to do so. In negotiating the 1958 trade agreement with West Germany it sought to establish a system of clearing account credits to be mutually granted at an agreed rate of interest.[35] The West Germans refused and the Soviets were forced to accept a system of payments based primarily on convertible marks. In 1960 the Franco-Soviet agreement on payments of 1953 was replaced by a system of settlements in francs or other convertible currencies.[36] During discussions with de Gaulle in 1960 Khrushchev tried to achieve a Franco-Soviet arrangement that would provide for fully balanced exchanges, with the USSR supplying France mainly with raw materials and France exporting industrial goods to the Soviet Union. The French rejected this proposal as impractical and disruptive of France's relations with other suppliers.[37]

These adverse developments in the areas of trade and finance were accompanied by growing signs of internal problems in the Soviet economy. Khrushchev remained optimistic about Soviet economic prospects, but his Sputnik-era euphoria was increasingly tempered by a recognition of the remaining economic and technological gaps between the USSR and the most advanced countries of the West. As Philip Hanson noted, Khrushchev first expressed concern about Soviet economic performance in the early 1960s.[38] These concerns eventually led to the Kosygin reforms of 1965, whose failure doomed substantial economic reform until the Gorbachev period.

Permanent Institutions

The failure of the Soviet economy to keep pace with changing conditions in Western Europe led to increased interest on both sides in the creation of permanent institutions that could provide a political and administrative stimulus to trade and offset some of the barriers created by the Soviet system. Soviet interest in such institutions represented a break with the pattern of the interwar period, in which the USSR showed little interest in creating bilateral economic institutions and was even reluctant to work with Western organizations that were specifically tasked with administering trade with the USSR.

In 1921–22 Soviet trade officials suggested to representatives of the German government that Germany establish a central agency to handle all matters concerning German-Soviet trade. But the Soviet authorities later concluded that the advantages of being able to play different German firms against each other outweighed the inconvenience caused by the absence of a single counterpart organization. By the end of the 1920s they were directing "sharp attacks against all and any attempts on [the German government's] part to coordinate German business dealings with the USSR through a central agency."[39] The only exceptions to the general Soviet aversion to institutionalization were the bilateral chambers of commerce. An all-union Western chamber of commerce was founded in Leningrad in November 1921, and was given responsibility for maintaining relations with chambers of commerce in the industrialized countries. A British-Russian chamber of commerce that had been founded in 1916 by a group of British and Russian firms was revived, and similar joint chambers were organized with the United States in 1925 and Germany in 1928.[40]

The U.K.-USSR trade agreement of 1947 took a modest step toward the creation of a permanent bilateral institution by providing for the appointment by each government of representatives who would meet to draw up, from the agreed lists of commodities available for exchange, a balanced program of shipments. These representatives were empowered to arrange for the appointment of other representatives, who would meet at least once each year, alternately in London and Moscow, to discuss the fulfillment of the agreement and to make recommendations to both governments "designed to improve, develop and widen the basis of trade between the two countries."[41] This permanent review mechanism was allowed to lapse during the cold war but was revived in the 1959 trade agreement.[42] In many ways it anticipated the joint commission agreements of the late 1960s and early 1970s.

The other step toward the institutionalization was the revival of chambers of commerce and bilateral business councils. Patterned after the British-Russian organization founded in 1916, the joint chambers were technically nongovernmental entities that brought together Western firms, Soviet foreign trade organizations, and representatives of the USSR all-union chamber of commerce. A Finnish-Soviet chamber of trade was formed in 1947. The British-Soviet chamber was reactivated after the war, all but ceased to function in 1951, but was reactivated in 1953. An Italian-Soviet chamber of commerce was established in 1964, and a Franco-Soviet chamber was established by intergovernmental agreement during de Gaulle's 1966 visit to the USSR. In West Germany, the East Committee of the German Economy came to function as the Western side of what was in effect a joint chamber of commerce. Most other West European countries established similar bodies.

The importance of the joint chambers eventually was overshadowed by the formation of permanent, mixed commissions comprised of government and industry officials. The commission concept went back to the mid-1950s, when the first such bodies were established to administer scientific and cultural exchanges. During his visit to Finland in 1954 Mikoyan proposed that the USSR and Finland conclude a far-reaching accord on scientific and technological exchange. The Finns regarded the Soviet proposals as incompatible with their own legislation on licenses and intellectual property, and made a counterproposal that included a plan for a mixed commission to facilitate exchange.[43] In August 1955 Finland and the USSR concluded the Agreement on Scientific and Technical Cooperation that established the bilateral Commission for Scientific and Technical Cooperation.[44] Soviet sources describe the commission as the first of its kind in the history of relations between states with different "social systems."[45] The commission was to meet annually and review implementation of the agreement. Its first session was in Moscow in March 1956, and resulted in a one-year program of exchanges of information and personnel.[46] Another precedent was the November 1955 agreement between Norway and the USSR to establish a committee of experts that would plan the joint development of hydroelectric resources on the frontier between the two countries.[47] The proposal for the commission came from Norway which, like Finland, may have been searching for ways to accommodate Soviet interests in a way compatible with its own economic and legal system.

In the late 1950s and early 1960s de facto joint trade commissions gradually evolved, as working-level officials met to draw up annual trade protocols specifying commodities and levels of trade.[48] The first formal agreement to establish a joint commission was concluded in June 1966, during de Gaulle's first postwar trip to the USSR. The de Gaulle-Kosygin declaration provided for the establishment of a mixed commission (*Grande Commission*) that was to meet at the ministerial level and was charged with responsibility for Franco-Soviet commercial, economic, scientific, and technological cooperation under all bilateral agreements.[49] In addition, a mixed commission for scientific, technical, and economic cooperation (*Petite Commission*) was set up to monitor implementation of the 1966 agreement of the same name.[50]

The de Gaulle-Kosygin arrangements established a pattern that was copied by virtually every other West European country. In April 1966 Italy and the USSR concluded the Agreement on Scientific and Technical Cooperation that established a joint commission on the Franco-Soviet model.[51] In 1967 Finland and the USSR concluded an agreement that provided for the establishment of a second permanent bilateral mechanism, a standing intergovernmental commission for economic cooperation. On the basis of an understanding between Brezhnev and Brandt at the 1971 Oreanda summit, West Germany and the USSR established a single mixed commission.[52] The Long-Term Agreement on Trade and Economic Cooperation concluded in July 1972 (replacing the 1961 agreement that had been allowed to expire in 1963) provided the commission with a written charter similar to that contained in other Soviet-West European bilateral agreements.[53]

The development of Soviet-British bilateral institutions followed a somewhat different course, although the end result was essentially the same. In 1967 the Confederation of British Industry and the Soviet State Committee for Science and Technology established eight working parties for the facilitation of technological cooperation. The following year the two governments concluded the Agreement for Cooperation in the Fields of Applied Science and Technology which coopted these nongovernmental groups. The agreement stipulated that fields of cooperation were to be "determined by joint Working Parties, the British and Soviet members of which shall be appointed by their respective governments."[54] The working parties were to examine possibilities in three areas—long-term technological research and development, industrial technology, and long-term industrial development—and make joint recommendations to the governments. The U.K. minister of technology and the USSR chairman of the State Committee for Science and Technology would meet once a year to review the agreement. In January 1971 the two countries established a permanent intergovernmental commission for scientific, technical, and economic cooperation that absorbed and rationalized the existing network of working groups.[55]

Whereas in the Soviet-British case working groups formed first and were then rationalized under a commission, with other countries establishment of the commissions was followed by the formation of permanent or ad hoc working groups. The number and types of groups varied from country to country, but their overall number tended to increase over time. By the 1970s the Soviet-Finnish Commission for Scientific and Technical Cooperation had twenty technical and scientific and twenty-one scientific working groups. The Finnish-Soviet Standing Intergovernmental Commission established another seven permanent working groups (machines and equipment, ferrous metals, chemicals, forest industry, energy, transport and communications, and border trade), one of which (machines and equipment) had an additional eight subgroups.[56] The Franco-Soviet Petite Commission set up twelve working groups devoted to particular industrial sectors, as well as special working groups for the exchange of economic information, the licensing of patents, and the development of technical standards. The Soviet-Italian commission started out with six sectoral working groups, which was later increased to nine.[57] At its first meeting in 1972, the Soviet-West German commission established a single working group to examine possibilities for intensifying cooperation in the fields of raw materials, energy, and industry.[58] This group met for the first time in September 1972 and set up six subgroups of experts in the fields of ferrous metallurgy, chemistry, diesel engineering, machine building, power engineering, and certain fields of mining.[59] Other expert groups later were established, including one for banking and financial questions.[60] With a few countries the USSR established joint commissions exclusively devoted to a dominant sector of industry, such as the Norwegian-Soviet fisheries commission and the Greek-Soviet shipping commission.

In the 1970s and 1980s this ramified structure of commissions and working groups came to play an important part in Soviet-West European economic and political relations. Under the economic agreements of the 1960s and early 1970s the commissions had an overall mandate to work to expand bilateral economic ties. The agreements stipulated that the commissions would meet on a regular basis to pursue certain tasks, such as the promotion of trade. In fulfillment of these mandates (which often were supplemented by new instructions issued at summits or other high-level meetings), the commissions submitted to the governments agreed proposals and recommendations, usually embodied in protocols signed and published after each commission session. To help in drawing up such proposals and recommendations the commissions in turn issued instructions to their working groups. The Soviet sections of the bilateral commissions usually were headed by a deputy prime minister, while Western sections usually were chaired by cabinet ministers. Commission sessions thus provided the occasion for fairly high-level exchanges of views.

The commissions generally proved resistant to political shocks. Western governments and businessmen were reluctant to disrupt their work in response to such Soviet actions as the invasions of Czechoslovakia and Afghanistan or the imposition of martial law in

Poland. On a few occasions the USSR did allow politics to disrupt the work of the commissions. Following the mass expulsion of Soviet diplomats from Britain in 1971 the Soviet side of the U.K.-USSR commission requested that the 1972 commission session not be held. The activity of the sectoral working groups also was suspended for a year. But the commission resumed its normal activities in April 1973. In late 1986 the Soviet side abruptly canceled a meeting of the Soviet-West German commission, apparently to protest remarks by Chancellor Kohl in which he compared Gorbachev to the Nazi propaganda minister Joseph Goebbels. The commission resumed its regular activity the following year.

The commission structure was generally supported by West European political and business leaders, but was regarded with skepticism by some in the West. The commissions placed "upon the Western government the burden of identifying the most suitable participants among its own national agencies and firms and of encouraging and organizing their participation."[61] Some Western critics argued that this governmental involvement was corrosive of the free-market system. But defenders of the commissions stressed their very modest effect on Western business practices and their potential for giving Western businesses greater insight into Soviet economic planning and requirements.[62]

While the commissions became the preeminent Soviet-West European bilateral economic institutions, the joint chambers continued to play a role in facilitating trade.[63] In each of the major West European countries several hundred firms generally became members of the national joint chamber. More than 650 U.K. firms were members of the British-Soviet chamber. The Italian-Soviet chamber included 280 Italian firms and 73 Soviet organizations.[64] More than 200 French firms were members of the Franco-Soviet chamber.[65]

The chambers organized exhibitions of products available for export and import and promoted contacts and the exchange of information. As an incentive to membership, the Soviet authorities provided special discounts and business services to members traveling in the USSR. In some countries the chambers made a special effort to involve small- and medium-sized businesses in trade. The French chamber even published a quarterly journal, *Commerce and Cooperation*, in French and Russian, and maintained a permanent office in Moscow.[66]

As will be seen, after 1987 the role of the chambers increased as they were called upon to facilitate interfirm contacts and to help in establishing joint ventures. This new role was reflected in the opening of new Moscow offices,[67] in a dramatic increase in the number of member firms, in new joint publications and databases, and in the fact that countries such as Turkey, Malta, and Greece for the first time formed joint chambers.[68]

Economic and Industrial Cooperation

As economic relations with Western Europe were progressively institutionalized in the 1960s, Soviet officials expressed growing impatience with traditional trade relationships and began to suggest ambitious schemes for increasing the structural interlinkages between the Soviet and West European economies. In a speech to the Confederation of British Industry in early 1967 Prime Minister Kosygin called for Britain and the USSR to undertake joint planning, initially for 1968–70 and then for the period up to 1975. According to Kosygin, planning would serve Soviet needs while insulating British industry from world market fluctuations. It would "mean that you will have a very clear perspective of the development of our trade in the next eight years and can plan development of your industries accordingly. We will accordingly develop production of various commodities in our country and supply you."[69]

Nothing came of the joint planning proposal, but the USSR did conclude comprehensive cooperation agreements with various countries that pointed toward a more comprehensive interlocking of economies, in part by combining elements that were dealt with separately in earlier trade and technological exchange agreements. The first such agreements were the 1966 Agreement on Scientific, Technical, and Economic Cooperation with France, the 1967 agreement with Finland establishing the Standing Intergovernmental Commission for Economic Cooperation, and the 1968 Agreement on Economic, Scientific, and Technical Cooperation with Austria.[70]

The shift from "trade" to "cooperation" in the titles of these agreements involved "more than a change in nomenclature." As a U.S. official wrote,

Whereas trade agreements were essentially prescriptive, with each of the parties undertaking specific obligations such as to accord most-favored-nation treatment to the exports of the other, the cooperation agreements are more hortatory. The signatories assume few concrete obligations, but rather undertake to exert their best endeavors toward fulfillment of the objectives of the agreement. Hence the prevalence of terminology such as "facilitate," "encourage" and "promote" in these agreements.[71]

A prime Soviet objective in the cooperation agreements was to secure Western governmental backing for major long-term East-West projects. The 1969 U.K.-USSR five-year trade agreement stipulated that both governments would "encourage and promote the conclusion of long-term agreements between Soviet foreign trade organizations and British firms for the purpose of cooperation in developing production facilities in both countries." According to one Soviet commentator, this provision was "fundamentally new" in that it pointed to the development of new forms of economic cooperation not encompassed by traditional trading arrangements.[72] The Franco-Soviet trade agreement for 1970–74 endorsed the construction of industrial complexes as well as stipulated that "part of the product turned out by these complexes is [to be] imported by interested organizations and firms in the other country to the full value of the supplied equipment and rendered services."

In the 1970s long-term economic and industrial cooperation became the dominant theme of Soviet economic diplomacy.[73] In April 1971 Finland and the USSR concluded the ten-year Treaty on the Development of Economic, Technical, and Industrial Cooperation. This was followed by the Franco-Soviet Intergovernmental Agreement on Economic, Technical, and Industrial Cooperation of October 1971, the Soviet-West German Agreement on the Development of Economic, Industrial, and Technological Cooperation of May 1973, the U.K.-USSR ten-year Agreement on the Development of Economic, Scientific, Technological, and Industrial Cooperation of May 1974, the Soviet-Italian Long-Term Economic Cooperation Agreement of July 1974, and similar agreements with most other European countries.[74]

These agreements established new patterns of interaction between governments, joint commissions, commission working groups, and industry. The agreements themselves generally were quite brief (one to two pages, comprising between six and ten articles), but were important in that they issued mandates to the commissions or other bilateral institutions. In Article 1 the parties generally agreed to "develop," "extend," or otherwise promote economic cooperation. The remaining articles then stipulated that the commissions would submit to both governments, by a given date, a ten-year program of specific projects and proposals. The ten-year programs generally were adopted by the governments within about eighteen months of the conclusion of the initial cooperation agreement.

In July 1973 France and the USSR concluded the ten-year Program for the Extension of Soviet-French Cooperation in Economics and Industry. Soviet-West German, Soviet-Italian, and other programs also were concluded in 1973 and 1974.[75] During Wilson's February 1975 visit to the USSR Britain and the Soviet Union concluded two long-term programs, one for cooperation in science and technology, the other for economic and industrial cooperation.[76] Most such agreements contained lists of specific cooperation projects.

Brezhnev, who at one time may have been more skeptical than Kosygin about the value of extensive East-West economic interdependence, was an enthusiastic backer of these agreements and the large-scale industrial cooperation they appeared to promise. In his talks with Brandt in 1970 and 1971 he called for "bold and sincere cooperation on a grand scale, with targets set for decades ahead," and declared that he "was in favor of 30-, 40- or 50-year trade agreements."[77] In talks with Helmut Schmidt in 1974 he spoke of a "transition from classical trade to larger projects," preferably of twenty to thirty years duration.[78]

In addition to their value in promoting Soviet-West European trade, the cooperation agreements had a political rationale. Under the Treaty of Rome competence for the conclusion of trade agreements between members of the European Economic Community and third countries was to have been transferred from individual governments to the EC Commission in 1969. (The March 1957 Treaty of Rome established the European Economic Community. A separate treaty, also concluded in Rome in March 1957, established the European Atomic Energy Community [Euratom]. The six signatories of the Rome treaties had also concluded a treaty in Paris in 1951 establishing the European Coal and Steel Community [ECSC]. In a treaty signed in Brussels in 1965 [effective from July 1, 1967], the six agreed to combine the EEC, Euratom, and the ECSC into a single institution known as the European Communities, or more commonly, the European Community [EC]. The EC is supervised by the EC Commission.) Because of the Soviet attitude toward the Community, the members agreed to allow member states to trade with the USSR under the provisions of bilateral trade agreements until the end of 1974, when all existing agreements were allowed to lapse.

Technically, the ten-year economic cooperation agreements were consistent with the transfer of authority in trade matters to the EC Commission, which did not extend to the promotion of exports and other activities that fell under the rubric of economic cooperation. But in negotiating these agreements and the protocols intended to implement them the USSR sought "to transfer provisions from trade agreements to the ten-year cooperation agreements, and thereby to provide a legal basis for the continuation of bilateral [trade] negotiations on a national basis."[79] Member-state governments reacted differently to these efforts. Some appeared to welcome the cooperation agreements as a way to retain substantial national control over trade with the USSR, while others objected to Soviet tactics. France accepted clauses dealing with trade in its July 1973 cooperation program, whereas West German negotiators reportedly rejected Soviet efforts to incorporate similar clauses in the 1973 cooperation program.[80]

In the late 1970s the terms of several of the Soviet-West European cooperation agreements were lengthened considerably, not for any apparent economic purpose but to symbolize the stable nature of the political relations and to satisfy Brezhnev's penchant for very long-term agreements. In 1977 Finland and the USSR concluded the Long-Term Agreement for Developing and Extending Trade, Economic, and Industrial Cooperation Up to 1990, the first intergovernmental economic agreement with a West European country that was to run for more than ten years. A year later the West Germans outdistanced the Finns, as Schmidt and Brezhnev signed the twenty-five-year Agreement on the Development and Deepening of Long-Term Cooperation in the Field of Economy and Industry. The agreement consisted of little more than a list of industries and technologies in which the sides agreed to cooperate, and was criticized in the FRG as a vacuous document whose main purpose was to satisfy Brezhnev's desire for politically symbolic but commercially meaningless long-term agreements.[81]

Economic and Political Implications

Thus by the end of the Brezhnev era the USSR had managed to institutionalize its economic and commercial relations with all of its major and most of its smaller partners in Western Europe. The pace and character of the institutionalization process differed from country to country and was shaped by economic and political circumstances, but each country went through the same basic stages, and all (with the partial exception of Finland) arrived at more or less the same point in their economic relations with the USSR.

For each country the first step was the conclusion of a commercial or trade and navigation treaty governing the general conditions for commerce. These agreements provided for nondiscriminatory tariff treatment and often contained provisions dealing with shipping, transport, customs, and other matters. Such agreements were concluded with most West European countries in the late 1940s or early 1950s. Throughout the 1950s these agreements were supplemented, usually on a one-year basis, with trade agreements or protocols specifying the level and composition of trade. Toward the end of the decade the terms of these agreements were in many cases lengthened to two, three, and in one case five years.

In the mid-1950s the USSR and most West European countries concluded scientific and technological exchange agreements. Although originally thought of on the Western side as cultural rather than economic in character (to use CSCE parlance, as belonging to Basket III rather than Basket II), these agreements laid the groundwork for the comprehensive cooperation agreements of the late 1960s and early 1970s. They did so by providing for greater governmental involvement in the promotion of exchange through periodic review meetings and the establishment of joint commissions. In this period working-level economic officials also established de facto economic commissions, as they met each year to implement annual trade agreements.

In the late 1960s permanent economic institutions, such as the joint commissions, were established and began to play the leading role in promoting trade with the USSR by identifying opportunities and clearing away obstacles. Joint chambers of commerce also continued to expand. By the early 1970s the focus of Soviet-West European economic relations shifted from classical trade to economic and industrial cooperation. Ten-year cooperation agreements were concluded, and the joint commissions were instructed to implement these agreements by drawing up detailed programs, most of which were valid also for ten years.

Views differed both within and between East and West on the significance of this institutional structure. Brezhnev clearly regarded its development as a major achievement that would constrain Western policy and contribute to making détente irreversible. In his speech to the 1976 Berlin Conference of Communist Parties, for example, he claimed that it was "extremely important to create ... the material fabric of peaceful cooperation in Europe, a fabric that would strengthen ties among European peoples and states and would give them an increasing stake in the preservation of peace for many years to come. I have in mind various forms of mutually advantageous cooperation—trade and production cooperation and scientific technical ties."[82]

Many in the West were more skeptical, and suspected that some of the new institutions reflected little more than the desire of governments to "produce some impressive new accord on the occasion of each major state visit."[83] The truth was probably somewhere between these two extremes. The institutionalization of Soviet-West European economic relations did constitute a political success for Soviet policy. It made the imposition of economic sanctions or a return to economic warfare increasingly improbable. Whereas in the 1940s and 1950s Western companies often were in an adversarial relationship with their governments as they attempted to push against politically imposed constraints on trade and credits, in the 1970s and 1980s government and company officials were associated in the common enterprise of actively trying to promote East-West trade.

At the same time, however, this institutional structure played only a limited role in stimulating trade that would not have occurred in its absence. As trade volumes increased dramatically in the course of the decade, it was natural for people such as Brezhnev to conclude that agreements and institutional arrangements helped to cause this growth. In reality, purely economic factors, such as increases in the price of energy and recession in the West, probably played a much larger role. In the 1980s the volume of Soviet-West European trade in fact plunged, as meetings of commissions and long-term cooperation programs were unable to offset the effects of falling energy prices and other purely economic factors.

Developments under Gorbachev

In *Perestroika: New Thinking for Our Country and the World*, Gorbachev remarked that "the building of the 'European home' requires a material foundation—constructive cooperation in many different areas."[84] But Gorbachev did not claim that Soviet economic dynamism was an irresistible magnet attracting European businesses. Gorbachev's predecessors all were deeply impressed by the crisis- and recession-prone character of Western economies and as a consequence seemed to assume that Western businesses and governments were strongly attracted to "stable, long-term" ties with a planned and constantly growing economy. Gorbachev was not completely immune to this kind of thinking, but he seemed to have a better understanding that Western companies were motivated more by the desire for profit than the fear of recession. He also knew that the Soviet and East European economies were themselves vulnerable to recession.

Gorbachev's more realistic attitude toward Soviet economic prospects led him to downplay the creation of added layers of intergovernmental bureaucracy and to look for ways to inject Western capital and technology at the enterprise level.[85] The most tangible result of this attention to enterprise-level contacts was the decision to permit joint ventures with foreign firms. The USSR law on joint ventures went into effect in January 1987.[86] Within a year Soviet enterprises and ministries had advanced 320 specific proposals for projects in such areas as agro-industry, chemical and wood processing, and machine building. By the middle of 1988 thirty-one joint ventures were under way, most with partners from Western Europe. Nine ventures were with firms from West Germany, four with firms from Finland, and four with firms from Italy.[87] By August 1989 the number of joint ventures had risen to 722, of which about 100 were with West German firms.[88] As part of the effort to attract foreign capital, the USSR also began concluding investment protection agreements with most West European countries,[89] and even agreed to compensate, on a country-by-country basis, foreigners who had lost property in Russia after the October Revolution.[90]

But Western businesses were unhappy with many of the restrictions placed on the ventures, and many of the announced projects were either small or consisted of letters of intent that did not result in an immediate flow of capital into the USSR. Soviet officials were also disappointed that many of the ventures were in the service sector and that Western firms seemed relatively uninterested in the production of goods. In late 1988 the Soviet government issued a revised set of guidelines to make participation more attractive, but the Western response was still rather tepid. By late 1989 Western firms were having increasing difficulty getting paid even for exports to the USSR, which further dampened enthusiasm for deeper involvement in the Soviet economy.[91]

West European countries—and especially the FRG—responded to the Soviet hard currency crisis by extending large loans and lines of credit that allowed their companies to be paid and trade to continue. For its part, the USSR took another major step to attract foreign investment when Gorbachev, in a presidential decree of October 1990, authorized foreign companies to establish wholly-owned subsidiaries in the USSR with the right to repatriate their earnings.

The new Soviet emphasis on enterprise- and firm-level cooperation did not diminish the importance in Soviet eyes of the existing structure of governmental and mixed institutions, whose work was adapted to the new conditions. Chambers of commerce, which traditionally played a role in establishing contacts between enterprises and in arbitrating disputes, began to concentrate on setting up joint ventures. Soviet officials also reaffirmed the importance of the joint commissions, but argued that under new conditions they had to "act more dynamically and flexibly" as well as "orient expert and working groups to new forms of cooperation."[92] Within the framework of most existing commissions new working groups on agriculture, light industry, and finance were established. The finance groups became involved in resolving problems, such as taxation and repatriation of profits, that were raised by the establishment of joint ventures.

During Gorbachev's July 1989 visit to Paris, France and the USSR signed a "protocol of intent" regarding the complete reorganization of the commission structure established in the 1960s. The two existing commissions were to be replaced by a "single joint intergovernmental organ" that would have mainly coordinating and consultative functions, while the sectoral working groups would be used to facilitate cooperation between firms and enterprises.[93] In early 1990 the USSR-FRG commission assumed an important new role in helping to coordinate the economic aspects of German unification and to fulfill West Germany's pledge to assume responsibility for East Germany's trade agreements with the USSR. In Article 6 of the September 1990 Treaty on Good-Neighborliness, Partnership, and Cooperation Between the USSR and the FRG, the signatories pledged that "the joint commissions already in existence will examine the possibilities for intensifying their work. New mixed commissions will be set up as required following bilateral agreement." The USSR thus remained highly committed to the commission formula, despite its intention to shift to an economy based in part on private ownership and a free market.[94]

The European Community

Soviet opposition to the formation and development of the European Community has already been noted. This attitude grew out of a recognition of the commercial disadvantages of West European integration, as well as a long-standing and almost instinctive opposition to the formation of European subgroupings that excluded the USSR. Already at the October 1943 Moscow Conference of Foreign Ministers the USSR sought to enlist British and U.S. support against the plans of several European governments in exile to form postwar federations.[95] After the war it pressured Finland not to join the Nordic Council, which was established in 1952 by representatives of Denmark, Norway, Sweden, and Iceland. The USSR withdrew its objections in 1955, but largely because it expected that Finnish membership might help to draw Denmark, Norway, and Iceland away from NATO.[96]

In opposing West European integration, the USSR traditionally followed a dual approach: on the one hand it criticized the Community for its inward and exclusive character, while on the other it proposed all-European or global alternatives to it. Until the early 1970s the all-European proposals were unrealistically premised on the dissolution of the EEC and its sister organizations, Euratom and the European Coal and Steel Community. Subsequently they allowed for its continued existence, but sought to subordinate its development to a larger multilateral design and to the maintenance of existing bilateral patterns of trade and economic cooperation.

The most obvious forum for the promotion of all-European initiatives was the ECE. In the spring of 1956 the USSR submitted to this organization its draft "All-European Agreement for Economic Cooperation," that provided for MFN treatment and prohibited all restrictions on trade that were not applied to all signatories.[97] In March 1957 the Soviet foreign ministry proposed a further series of all-European economic measures, including the establishment of a Europe-wide atomic energy research institute, all-European cooperation in the building of civilian atomic power stations, multilateral cooperation in the building of hydroelectric power stations, a trade agreement among all interested European countries, and mutual economic and financial aid to promote development.[98] Coming one week before the signing of the Treaty of Rome, these proposals clearly were directed at the EEC and Euratom. At the April 1957 session of the ECE the Soviet delegation formally introduced these ideas in slightly modified form.

In late 1956 IMEMO published seventeen "theses" on the Common Market and Euratom which contained a definitive Marxist-Leninist analysis of West European economic integration.[99] The analysis stressed the importance of the EEC as a vehicle for West German expansionism and revanchist designs. To some extent this reflected real concerns about Germany, but it was also calculated to appeal to anti-German sentiments in France and other countries. The French Communist Party was in fact the USSR's main ally in the fight against the Community.

The Soviet campaign against the EEC persisted into the early 1960s. At a major international conference on contemporary capitalism that took place in August 1962 IMEMO put forward a revised thirty-two theses on the Community that reflected little change of attitude.[100] Shortly thereafter Khrushchev published an article on the world socialist system in which he contrasted the CMEA, which he claimed fully respected the sovereignty and independence of its members, with the EEC, which he portrayed as an instrument of external domination.[101] Khrushchev also personally argued with European leaders against the Community, often invoking his favorite concept of complementarity. He told the visiting Italian trade minister, for example, that the EEC was a "marriage against nature. . . . [E]ven if it is regulated by law, nature will see to it that it will be broken because in this marriage, if I may say so, there are not two sexes, male and female, but only two males."[102]

In the mid-1960s the USSR began taking a somewhat more relaxed attitude toward the EEC. De Gaulle's veto of Britain's entry in January 1963, France's "empty chair" policy of 1965, and disagreements over agriculture seemed to vindicate the expectation that the Community's own internal "contradictions" would prove decisive. While the USSR continued to oppose the very existence of the EEC, some Soviet commentators unofficially expressed interest in the approach of the Italian Communist Party, which argued that the Communists should accept the reality of the Community but work to democratize it from within. Khrushchev's 1962 article in *Kommunist* had already hinted at a new approach by raising the possibility of cooperation "not only between separate states with different social systems, but also between their economic unions."[103] The USSR also did not try to stop its East European allies from concluding agreements with the Community to protect their access to traditional markets.[104] As a supplier mainly of fuel and raw materials, the USSR was less affected by the EEC's market quotas and external tariff, and thus could afford a more intransigent stance.

Nonetheless, by the early 1970s and the impending accession of Britain, Ireland, and Denmark, the USSR increasingly faced a choice between refusing to deal with the Community and thus depriving itself of influence over its development, and recognizing the EC but in so doing appearing to sanction a political process to which it was deeply opposed. Brezhnev tried to sidestep this choice by reverting to Khrushchev's old idea of cooperation between the opposing economic unions. In a March 1972 speech to the congress of the Soviet trade unions he stated that "the USSR is far from ignoring the present situation in Western Europe, including the existence of such an economic grouping as the 'Common Market'. Our relations with its members will depend, naturally, on the degree to which they, on their part, recognize the reality existing in socialist Europe."[105]

In May 1973 Finland became the only West European country to conclude an agreement with CMEA. The timing of the agreement (the USSR presumably could have asked the Finns for such an agreement at any time in the 1960s) suggested that it was intended to serve as a model for a future CMEA-EC agreement. It provided for the establishment of a Finnish-CMEA joint commission that met for the first time in 1973, and that established five working groups and numerous subgroups. Based on the work of the commission, in 1975 Finland and the CMEA concluded the first of many multilateral cooperation agreements. These agreements, which covered such areas as international truck traffic and paper production, built upon and further promoted intra-CMEA standardization by establishing a uniform set of obligations between Finland on the one hand and all or some of the members of CMEA on the other.[106]

In August 1973 Nikolai Fadeev, the general secretary of the CMEA, met with Ivar Norgaard, Denmark's minister of foreign economic affairs and at the time chairman of the EC Council of Ministers, and proposed that the organizations exchange official representatives. The EC and its member-states rejected this offer on the grounds that the two organizations were not comparable and out of concern that any strengthening of CMEA's role would limit the freedom of maneuver of the East European states.

While hinting at a symbolic accommodation with the Community, the USSR remained intransigent when it came to matters of substance. In late 1974 the EC submitted to the USSR proposals for the establishment of a legal trade regime to replace the existing network of bilateral trade agreements, which were due to expire at the end of the year. The USSR (and the other CMEA members) rejected this offer, leaving the Community little choice but to make special legal arrangements to accommodate the peculiar Soviet stance. To get around the legal problems associated with the expiration of the bilateral agreements the members of the EC exchanged letters with the USSR, affirming that the principles set forth in earlier agreements would continue to be applied. This arrangement sidestepped the question of whether the agreements themselves were still in force, as the USSR insisted but the Community denied.[107] The Soviet Union refused to negotiate with the Commission regarding fishing rights, which in 1977 led the Community to exclude all Soviet fishing fleets from its 200-mile economic zone.[108] It also tried to block EC participation in the CSCE. Soviet representatives refused to agree to the listing of Commission officials with national delegations and at one point challenged a representative of the Commission when he took the floor.[109] Nonetheless, the USSR ultimately acquiesced in an arrangement under which Prime Minister Andreotti was able to sign the Final Act both for Italy and the EC.

The USSR launched its first really serious effort at a CMEA-EC agreement in early 1976, following conclusion of the Helsinki conference the previous summer. In February CMEA put forward a draft accord that Western analysts characterized as "without question a masterpiece of drafting skill."[110] It conferred a form of recognition on the EC, but without conceding it jurisdiction over any substantive aspect of economic or trade policy. Article 1 declared that the agreement established "official relations" between CMEA and the EC. But the draft avoided any mention of Community bodies such as the Council of Ministers or the Commission. Article 6 called for the member countries of both organizations to grant each other MFN status "on the basis of existing agreements or corresponding agreements which will be concluded between given countries." To further establish the principle of bilateralism Article 11 stipulated that cooperation *between countries* would be regulated by bilateral and multilateral agreements *between these countries*. The second part of the article acknowledged some role for the "organs" of CMEA and the EC, which would conclude agreements with member countries and with each other. To implement the agreement Article 14 called for establishment of a mixed commission that would be composed of representatives of the member states of the two organizations and of the two organizations themselves. Formal talks on an agreement began in 1977, but there was little progress and they were broken off in 1980, in part because of the general deterioration of relations that followed the Soviet invasion of Afghanistan.

In the early 1980s the USSR displayed little interest in an accord with the EC. It was unhappy about the EC rapprochement with China and the conclusion of a separate agreement with Romania.[111] Soviet commentators were increasingly critical of the European Parliament, and looked askance at perceived West European efforts to compensate for lagging progress toward economic unity by heightening the political and potentially the security identity of the Community.[112]

Soviet and East European interest in an EC-CMEA agreement revived in 1984. In their declaration, "Maintenance of Peace and International Economic Cooperation," issued in June of that year, the leaders of the CMEA countries "reiterate[d] their readiness to conclude an appropriate agreement between the CMEA and the EEC with a view to facilitating the further expansion of trade and economic contacts existing between the member countries of these organizations."[113] Upon taking power the following year, Gorbachev signaled a strong personal interest in a CMEA-EC agreement. In May 1985 he met with Gianni Cervetti, a PCI official who was chairman of the Communist faction in the European Parliament.[114] A week later he met with Italian prime minister Bettino Craxi (Italy at the time was chair of the EC Council of Ministers) and suggested that it was "time to establish mutually beneficial economic relations in economic affairs" between the two organizations. He also stated that "insofar as the EEC countries act as a 'political entity,' we are prepared to seek a common language on concrete international problems with it."[115] This was the first positive Soviet assessment of the EC's political character, and signaled a major rethinking in Moscow that Gorbachev and Shevardnadze later publicly acknowledged.[116]

In June 1985 the Polish ambassador in Brussels delivered a letter to EC Commission president Jacques Delors from CMEA secretary Viacheslav Sychev proposing early talks between the two organizations. This was the first official CMEA approach to the EC since 1980.[117] Responding to these probes, in June 1985 the EC foreign ministers agreed to resume the talks with CMEA that had been broken off in 1980. In October 1985 CMEA sent the EC the draft of a joint declaration establishing official relations. The EC responded in January 1986 by setting forth several preconditions for the establishment of relations between the two groupings, the most important of which was that an agreement on relations had to be accompanied by the establishment of bilateral relations between the EC and the individual European members of the CMEA. Unlike in the 1970s, the USSR agreed to this stipulation, as was conveyed in an April 1986 letter from Sychev to the Commission and in subsequent communications from CMEA member states.[118]

CMEA-EC negotiations thus were to proceed in parallel with talks between the Community and the European members of CMEA. Hungary had already announced its intention to begin negotiations with the EC on a bilateral trade pact in 1984, and Romania had concluded an agreement with the EC in 1980, but the other countries held back.[119] Bulgaria, Poland, and Czechoslovakia communicated with the Commission in May 1986.[120] In July 1986 the EC declared that it was satisfied with the Eastern response, and in late September delegations of experts from the EC Commission and from the CMEA secretariat held exploratory talks in Geneva to discuss ways and means for establishing official relations between the two organizations. The talks, the first in six years between the organizations, concluded with an understanding that the sides would begin negotiating a joint declaration recording the establishment of relations between the two organizations.[121] In accepting this approach the USSR dramatically scaled down its ambitions for an initial EC-CMEA agreement. Mutual recognition was to be the first step, with trade and economic issues deferred to subsequent bilateral and multilateral negotiations.

The USSR, which along with East Germany traditionally had the strongest aversion to bilateral dealings with the EC, was the last CMEA country to convey its willingness to conclude a bilateral agreement with the Community.[122] But in November 1986 it sent a letter to the Commission expressing its readiness to begin a bilateral dialogue, and in January 1987 formal talks began between the Soviet government and the EC regarding mutual recognition.[123]

Unlike the East Europeans, who were almost exclusively interested in improving their access to EC markets, the USSR at first appears to have been interested as much in the political as the economic implications of ties with the EC. Gorbachev's 1985 meetings with Craxi and Cervetti highlighted the political aspects of Soviet-EC dialogue, as did suggestions that the establishment of CMEA-EC relations take place at a high-level meeting.[124] Gorbachev's first official communication with the EC was a February 1986 letter setting out his ideas on a possible Middle East peace conference.[125] Later in 1986 Oleg Bogomolov wrote that the CMEA's "moves to normalize relations with the EEC are prompted not so much by business motives as by the need to strengthen European security, build confidence, and gradually overcome the disunity of Europe."[126]

Political factors remained important in Soviet thinking, but were counterbalanced in 1987 and 1988 by an increasing awareness of the potential economic benefits of an accommodation with the EC (and of the likely costs of not reaching an accommodation). This awareness was the result both of the USSR's own deepening economic crisis and of the 1986 Single European Act mandating the creation of a single European market by the end of 1992. In his speech to a July 1988 conference at the foreign ministry Shevardnadze noted that "integrational processes are developing rapidly in Western Europe," and criticized the ministry for failing to conduct research on how this would affect Soviet interests.[127] The following spring IMEMO published a detailed study entitled *The Consequences of the For-*

mation of a Joint Market in the European Community, which concluded that it would be "considerably more difficult to realize the task of increasing exports of the USSR's industrial products to the EC's joint market."[128]

Formal EC-CMEA talks began in March 1987, but quickly bogged down over Berlin, an issue that had more to do with Soviet attitudes toward Germany than with the EC.[129] CMEA contended that the Community did not have the authority to negotiate on behalf of West Berlin, which was not a member, while the Community insisted that the city was covered in all EC international agreements. The CMEA delegation offered a draft declaration that in the view of EC negotiators contained too many phrases about "peace policy and the process of détente," which the EC preferred be eliminated to leave a more concise, matter-of-fact statement.[130] These issues were cleared away in a series of negotiating sessions in Geneva, and in June 1988 the sides initialed a joint statement declaring that the organizations had decided to establish official relations, and that the specific areas, forms, and methods of cooperation would be determined by mutual agreement in subsequent negotiations. The Berlin issue was finessed by a provision stating that the declaration would "apply to the territories in which the Treaty establishing the European Economic Community is applied."[131] Sychev characterized the agreement as "one more brick [in] the edifice of our common European home."[132]

Following formal signature by representatives of the EC Council and Commission and their CMEA counterparts, the two organizations began consultations to consider ways to implement the general goals expressed in the declaration.[133] It quickly became clear, however, that the negotiations toward a more substantive EC-CMEA agreement would progress very slowly, owing to the incompatibility of the two organizations, the growing fissures within the CMEA, and the preference of the EC for bilateral deals. Areas considered appropriate for an umbrella agreement included cooperation in environmental matters, standardization, energy infrastructure, and science and technology.[134]

Consistent with the understandings reached in 1986 before the CMEA-EC negotiations began, the bloc-to-bloc recognition agreement was followed by the announcement of recognition and trade agreements between the Community and individual members of the CMEA. Hungary led the way on June 30, 1988, by signing a ten-year trade and cooperation agreement with the EC.[135] The USSR, East Germany, Bulgaria, and Hungary established diplomatic relations with the Community in August, and were followed by Poland a month later. Czechoslovakia concluded a trade agreement with the EC in

December 1988, followed by Poland in September 1989. The USSR and the EC began formal negotiations on a trade and cooperation agreement in July 1989.

In 1989 the USSR and the Community also began a formal political dialogue. In January of that year Shevardnadze met with Spanish foreign minister Francisco Fernández-Ordóñez in his capacity as chairman of the EC Council. The following month he met with EC ambassadors in Moscow, and with the foreign ministers of the twelve at the UN General Assembly in September and in Brussels in December. The highlight of Shevardnadze's Brussels trip was his visit to NATO, but he gave his most important speech at a meeting of the Political Commission of the European Parliament. When French president Mitterrand made a quick trip to Kiev to meet with Gorbachev in December 1989, he was received not only as the president of France but as the head of the EC Council, and thus a spokesman for the Community regarding recent developments in Eastern Europe.[136] While the USSR accepted the political identity of the EC, it remained alert to potentially negative implications for Soviet interests, as was seen most vividly in August 1989, when the Soviet foreign ministry unexpectedly sent an aide-mémoire to the Austrian government raising questions about the compatibility of Austria's neutral status with its pending application to join the Community.[137]

After hard bargaining on economic and political issues, in late November 1989 the USSR and the EC finished work on the bilateral trade and cooperation agreement.[138] The USSR was unable to secure de jure MFN status or the removal of all quotas on its exports to the Community, and Soviet negotiators were unhappy with what they saw as the EC's failure to carry out the 1988 pledge to develop EC-CMEA and EC-individual country relations in parallel. As a *Pravda* commentator complained, the EC was "showing preference for the growth of bilateral ties with CMEA countries. This hardly corresponds to the letter and spirit of the joint declaration or the principle of parallelism provided for in it."[139] Nonetheless, the agreement was the most extensive of any yet concluded between the EC and an Eastern country, and included such areas as nuclear energy and safety, industrial standards, economic statistics, environmental protection, tourism, insurance, and banking. It established a joint USSR-EC commission that held its first session in March 1990. Meanwhile, the EC-CMEA agreement became increasingly irrelevant, as the newly democratic countries of Eastern Europe made clear their intention to leave the Eastern trading bloc and to seek membership in the Community.

8 Culture, Churches, and the Peace Movement

Cultural Exchanges

Under Lenin and Stalin the USSR drew little distinction between the promotion of Soviet culture and the recruitment of foreign Communists and fellow-travelers. Cultural contact was the responsibility of bilateral friendship societies, which functioned as Communist fronts. The first foreign friendship society was founded in Denmark in 1924, and similar organizations were established shortly thereafter in other countries.[1] In 1925 the All-Union Society for Cultural Relations with Foreign Countries (VOKS) was established to coordinate links with such groups. In 1927 VOKS, several other Soviet organizations, and the British Communist Party convened a Moscow world congress of friendship societies, at which the International Association of Friends of the Soviet Union (FSU) was formed. The purpose of the FSU was to subordinate the friendship societies to a central secretariat under Soviet control. Henceforth, the societies were national sections of the FSU.[2]

The national sections of the FSU were closely identified with the local Communist parties and had difficulty attracting support from other segments of the population. In the 1930s the FSU secretariat directed the sections to broaden their appeal, but it proved difficult to attract non-Communist members and to force organization leaders to downplay their Communist sympathies. Never a thriving organization, the FSU and its national sections all but ceased to function after the Hitler-Stalin pact and the subsequent German occupation of most of Europe.

June 1941 revived the fortunes of the organization in those parts of Europe not overrun by the Germans. In Britain a national section was reactivated and an array of subinstitutions, including a Society for Cultural Relations between the Peoples of the British Commonwealth and the Soviet Union, helped to attract thousands of non-Communists into the movement in support of Soviet friendship. As Europe was liberated bilateral friendship societies in Finland, France, Italy, and Eastern Europe were transformed into mass organizations.

After the war Stalin encouraged the work of the Communist-dominated friendship groups, but showed no interest in cultural contact that was not subject to Communist control. After unsuccessfully opposing the establishment of ECOSOC as a constituent part of the UN, the USSR declined to join the UN Educational, Scientific, and Cultural Organization (UNESCO).[3] It also showed little interest in cultural exchange with the United States or with those European countries, notably Britain and France, that made proposals to Moscow.[4]

By late 1947 Andrei Zhdanov's aggressive campaign against foreign influences in Soviet life virtually precluded international exchange.[5] In Eastern Europe the friendship societies remained mass organizations, but the post-liberation enthusiasm wore off as they became routine public organizations within the Communist bureaucratic structure. Elsewhere in Europe the friendship societies lost whatever mass support they had gained and operated as transparent Communist fronts. Soviet demands that national sections of the FSU defend Soviet policy and denounce their own governments accelerated the decline. By 1949 the British Labour and other Socialist parties were instructing their members to refrain from participation in FSU-related organizations.

The friendship groups managed to attract some non-Communist support, chiefly from prominent Protestant clergymen, but as Barghoorn concluded, between 1948 and 1953 "most of the contacts between Russia and the non-Communist world, especially Western Europe and America, were between Soviet delegations and foreign communist or fellow-traveler groups, or between visiting groups composed mainly or at least partly of such persons and Soviet communist party and government agencies."[6] Finland was a partial exception to the general pattern. With its large Communist Party and special relationship to the USSR, it continued to support a mass Finland-USSR society. President Juho Paasikivi became its first chairman, and was later succeeded by President Kekkonen.[7] In the 1948 Treaty of Friendship, Cooperation, and Mutual Assistance the Finns and Soviets also negotiated a clause that called for strengthening cultural ties between the two countries.

Soviet interest in cultural contact with non-Communist groups in the West began to pick up only in the early post-Stalin period. At the arms control talks in the spring of 1954 a senior Soviet official informally described to his U.S. and British counterparts "new and unannounced Soviet decisions to encourage close cultural and economic relationships with the West."[8] In December 1954 the president of the Soviet Academy of Sciences published an article in *Izvestiia* advocating Soviet participation in scientific and technological exchanges. In April 1955 the USSR joined UNESCO, and in the same year Soviet scientists, historians, and cultural figures participated in international conferences for the first time since the 1920s.

The expansion of East-West contacts was also on the agenda of the July 1955 Geneva summit. The Soviet leaders were placed somewhat on the defensive by Western demands that they open up Soviet society and eliminate barriers to the flow of people and information; but they agreed, in the Geneva directive, to instruct the ministers to study measures to "bring about such freer contacts and exchanges as are to the mutual advantage of the countries and peoples concerned."

At the foreign ministers meeting in the fall of 1955 Molotov introduced a five-point plan that dealt mainly with economic contacts but that contained one item concerning cultural exchanges, exchange of publications, and the expansion of sports and tourism.[9] Acting on behalf of the West, the French offered a more detailed seventeen-point plan that called for everything from the freer exchange of information to the initiation of direct air transport services.

The substantive differences between the sides soon were reflected in procedural wrangles. When the experts met to discuss the two proposals, the Western delegations called for setting up two working groups, one for economics and one for exchanges. They hoped that this would prevent the Soviets from linking human contacts to their demands on trade. The Soviet delegate preferred to begin with a broad discussion of exchange in general, but eventually yielded and agreed to the establishment of separate working groups.[10]

The working group for exchanges spent much of the conference arguing over an agenda. The Soviets proposed that the group examine only those elements common to both proposals. Although this approach had been used by the heads of government in Geneva and had been turned to advantage by the West, within the working group it meant exclusion of precisely those issues—termination of jamming, access to publications, ending of censorship—that the Soviets regarded as part of their internal affairs and refused to put on the agenda. The Western delegations thus operated from a position of weakness, and were often forced to defend their right to address "non-agenda items."[11]

As the end of the conference approached and the ministers took up the inconclusive results of the expert meetings, Molotov proposed that his opening draft be used as the basis for a concluding document, but the Western powers refused. They argued that even those parts of the Molotov draft that "could be considered to fall within the terms of the Directive" were only "generalised statements of good intention" that did little more than endorse existing group exchanges while doing nothing to break down barriers to the flow of information or movement by individuals. The West thus came away from Geneva claiming that the USSR had not complied with the July 1955 directive with respect to human contacts, just as it had not done so in regard to the weightier issues of German reunification and international disarmament. But Western officials also claimed that certain barriers to communication had been eliminated. According to Dulles, "the process now started is almost sure to go on. It may proceed unevenly, but the process now started is, we believe, not easily reversed."[12]

The summits that followed the Geneva meetings led to expanded bilateral agreements on cultural exchange. During the 1955 Gerhardsen visit to Moscow, Norway and the USSR agreed to widen exchanges in science, industry, culture, and sport.[13] During Tage Erlander's visit the following spring Sweden and the USSR agreed to continue developing cultural and scientific contacts and pledged in the final communiqué that "state organizations in both countries administering cultural contacts with foreign countries would be instructed to further the expansion of all such contacts in a suitable way."[14] At the conclusion of Khrushchev's 1956 visit to Britain, the U.K. and the USSR issued the Joint Declaration on the Further Development of Contacts between the U.K. and the USSR in which they agreed to take steps "directed toward ensuring a freer exchange of information by the spoken and the written word" as well as to promote group exchange.[15] The following month France and the USSR concluded a ten-point agreement, also issued as an appendix to the communiqué, in which they agreed to "study new kinds of institutions that would contribute to the further improvement of cultural relations" and to begin negotiations at the working level toward a cultural agreement.[16] By late 1956 the USSR had concluded cultural agreements with Norway, Denmark, and Belgium, and was engaged in discussions with several other countries.

The Soviet attitude toward these agreements was somewhat ambivalent. While the USSR was interested in exchanges as part of its campaign to overcome international isolation and to foster the "spirit of Geneva," it had less need than Western countries to conclude formal cultural agreements. It already had access to Western societies through the Communist parties and front organizations, and was especially reluctant to conclude a cultural agreement with France, where it was able to circumvent official and semiofficial cultural organizations by dealing with organizations with direct ties to the French Communist Party, many of whom could combine politics and profit by hosting popular groups such as the Moscow circus.[17] In contrast, individuals and organizations from the West faced formidable political, administrative, and financial obstacles in trying to gain access to Soviet society. One of the main British objectives in cultural exchange negotiations with the USSR was to obtain a more realistic sterling-ruble exchange rate so as to make British travel to the USSR more practical.[18]

The initial attempts on the Western side to create bilateral cultural institutions grew out of these practical concerns, as well as out of efforts to separate scientific and cultural exchange from the political and propaganda activities of the local Communist parties. In a move to undercut the Anglo-Soviet Friendship Society and the British Communist Party, in May 1955 the British foreign office announced that it had asked the quasi-official British Council to undertake the promotion of closer cultural relations with the USSR and that the council in turn had set up a five-member Soviet Relations Committee that had approached the Soviet embassy with proposals for cultural and scientific exchanges.[19] The friendship society offered its help to the new committee, but was rebuffed. In June the committee reached an agreement with the Soviet embassy on stepping up exchanges, mainly of professional delegations.[20] While the USSR was not willing to disavow the Communist friendship society, it agreed to deal with its non-Communist rival on the basis of at least apparent equality. Nonetheless, concerns about lack of reciprocity and the favored position of the Communist friendship societies remained irritants in U.K.-USSR cultural relations at least until the conclusion of the first major exchange agreement in 1959.[21] In countries with larger and more active Communist parties, notably France and Italy, the problem was even worse.

The Soviet invasion of Hungary brought the initial period of expanding cultural contacts to an abrupt if temporary end. The Norwegian and Danish parliaments refused to ratify the agreements signed earlier in the year. The Belgian parliament denounced the cultural agreement signed in October 1956. Exchanges with the USSR were dramatically cut back in all countries, and some Soviet delegations were asked by their hosts to interrupt their stays in the middle of the Hungarian events. Norway, Switzerland, the Netherlands, and Spain even withdrew from the Olympic Games in Melbourne to avoid contact with Soviet teams.

Exchanges resumed in the second half of 1957, in many cases after repeated demarches from Soviet embassies and representatives in Moscow. The general trend in this period was toward the conclusion of formal cultural cooperation agreements, in which Western governments, to some extent exploiting the USSR's eagerness to overcome its post-Hungary isolation, sought to obtain assurances that cultural events would not be channeled through Communist front organizations.

To meet Western concerns as well as to upgrade the effectiveness of its cultural exchange programs, in 1957 the Soviet government announced the formation of the State Committee for Cultural Relations with Foreign Countries, which provided a legitimate governmental counterpart to the governmental and nongovernmental bodies in the West charged with concluding and implementing bilateral cultural agreements. In February 1958 the Soviet press announced the formation of a new public organization, the Union of Soviet Societies for Friendship and Cultural Relations with Foreign Countries.[22] Henceforth, the negotiation of cultural agreements was the responsibility of the State Committee, while implementation was assigned to the Union of Soviet Societies. (This system was modified slightly in 1967, when the State Committee was dissolved and its functions transferred to the Cultural Relations with Foreign Countries Department of the MFA.)[23]

The Union of Soviet Societies was the successor organization to VOKS, and was designed to preserve a propagandistic and mobilizational element in Soviet cultural policy. Under its auspices were formed Soviet societies ostensibly dedicated to the promotion of cultural contacts and friendship with foreign countries. Societies dedicated to relations with Communist countries generally were called "friendship societies" while those associated with Western and Third World countries were simply called "societies." USSR-Finland and USSR-France societies were founded in January 1958, a USSR-Italy Society in February, and a USSR-Great Britain Society and a Soviet-Belgian Friendship Society in April of the same year. By the end of 1959 the USSR had established similar societies for Austria, Denmark, Greece, Iceland, the Netherlands, Norway, and Sweden. Societies for Switzerland, Ireland, Luxembourg, and Malta were established in the early 1960s, and for Portugal and Spain in the 1970s.[24] A USSR-FRG society was not formed until November 1972, when the Institute for the Development of Relations with the Federal Republic of Germany that had been established in 1970 was transformed into the Soviet section of a USSR-Federal Republic of Germany Society.[25] The members of the Soviet societies generally included Communist Party officials, delegates to the Supreme Soviet, trade union leaders, athletes, cosmonauts, artists, and scientists.

These bodies served as the Soviet counterpart to Western groups such as the British Council, but also maintained contact with the older, Communist-dominated organizations. The Soviet authorities, in fact, may have hoped to bolster the successor organizations to the old FSU-affiliates by promoting more even-handed seeming forms of contact. (It now could be argued that groups promoting friendship with Britain existed in the USSR, just as groups promoting friendship with the USSR existed in Britain—even though in reality both were controlled by Communist parties.) But these organizations were increasingly dominated by aging, working-class members who were poorly equipped to champion Soviet culture in the West.[26]

These organizational innovations were accompanied by a rapid increase in the number and complexity of bilateral cultural agreements. After prolonged negotiations between the State Committee and the cultural section of the French foreign ministry, in October 1957 France and the USSR concluded an agreement on cultural and scientific exchanges for the year 1958. The agreement provided for the establishment of a mixed commission that was to meet on a biannual basis to work out specific programs.[27]

In April 1958 West Germany and the USSR jointly announced that they would begin negotiations on exchanges, and in May 1959 they concluded their first cultural, scientific, and technical exchange agreement. The agreement was valid for 1959 and 1960, and assigned responsibility for implementation to the Central Exchange Office on the West German side and to the State Committee of the USSR.[28] At the conclusion of Macmillan's March 1959 trip to the USSR he and Khrushchev issued a joint document on cultural exchanges in which they agreed that representatives of the British Council would meet for talks with the State Committee to draw up a program of exchanges for the coming year, and possibly to establish a framework for longer-term exchanges.[29] In late March the two organizations signed a one-year program that doubled the volume of exchanges and gave the British Council increased status in bilateral contacts.[30] To administer the agreement, the council transformed its Soviet Relations Committee into an independent Great Britain-USSR Association, with a board of directors that included prominent personalities from the major parties and that remained free of association with the Communist Party.[31]

In December 1959 Britain and the USSR concluded their Agreement on Relations in the Scientific, Technological, Educational, and Cultural Fields. It was valid for 1960–61, and was the first comprehensive exchange agreement concluded between the two countries. It provided for cooperation in many fields, and named the British Council, the Royal Society (for the Improvement of Natural Knowledge), and other organizations as implementing agents on the British side. In addition, it was agreed that representatives of each government would meet each year "to review progress and to discuss further developments in the whole field of scientific, technical, educational and cultural relations between the two countries."[32] The 1959 U.K.-USSR agreement subsequently was renewed every two years, with frequent amendments and appended minutes and protocols.[33] In February 1960 Italy and the USSR concluded their first cultural and scientific exchange agreement, which also provided for the establishment of a mixed joint commission that would meet biannually to formulate two-year exchange programs.[34]

The development of Soviet-West German cultural relations largely paralleled trends in the economic sphere. Because of the general deterioration in bilateral relations and the specific problem of Berlin, the two-year agreement of 1959 was not renewed in 1961. The Soviet government argued that the federal government had no authority to negotiate cultural agreements on behalf of West Berlin, and throughout the 1960s Berlin complicated ad hoc cultural events.[35] Only after conclusion of the political agreements of the early 1970s did Soviet-West German cultural relations reach the level common elsewhere in Europe. Brezhnev's 1973 visit to West Germany resulted in a comprehensive cultural agreement in which the Berlin issue was handled by a reference to the Quadripartite Agreement. (During the same visit, however, the USSR refused to conclude an anticipated agreement on scientific and technological cooperation when the Bonn government insisted that it should apply expressly to research institutions located in Berlin.)[36] The agreement was to run for an initial period of five years, after which it was to remain in force indefinitely, unless denounced by either of the contracting parties.[37] It called for both governments to promote cooperation in the cultural field between governmental organizations, academies, schools, and research institutes, for increased tourism, and for the promotion of cooperation in film, television, radio, and sports. To implement these goals, the agreement provided for the establishment of a mixed commission that would meet to draw up two-year programs of cooperation as well as handle administrative and financial details. The West German side of the commission was to be made up of a working group of the FRG-USSR Society, the Soviet side by representatives of the USSR-FRG Society. Sessions of the commission would be presided over by a representative of the host contractual party, thus ensuring continued direct involvement of the two governments. In accordance with the agreement, two-year Soviet-West German programs were concluded without interruption after 1973.

The basic framework of Soviet-West European cultural exchanges thus was established by the early 1960s (later in the case of West Germany), and remained fairly stable. There were a few noteworthy attempts by Western governments to establish more ambitious institutional frameworks for cultural cooperation. During Kosygin's 1967 visit to Britain the two governments agreed in principle to establish an Anglo-Soviet consultative committee that would consist of "leading figures in culture, science, sport, and other fields, which would study the possibilities of expanding . . . contacts . . . and which would submit appropriate recommendations for consideration by the two sides."[38] But negotiations to formally establish the committee were suspended following the Soviet invasion of Czechoslovakia, and the committee did not meet until April 1971.[39] During Wilson's 1975 visit to the USSR he and Kosygin agreed to another pioneering venture, the establishment of a USSR-U.K. "round table" whose members "would be distinguished representatives of public life, science, culture, commerce, the press and other fields" and which would hold annual meetings alternating between London and Moscow. Responsibility for organizing these meetings was assigned on the British side to the Royal Institute of International Affairs and on the Soviet side to IMEMO.[40]

On a few occasions political disputes led to a temporary suspension of exchanges. The strong Western reaction to the 1956 invasion of Hungary already has been noted. Following the 1968 Warsaw Pact invasion of Czechoslovakia Soviet exchanges with many European countries were curtailed. This was done largely at the initiative of nongovernmental organizations, however, as governments maintained an air of normalcy. Even Britain, whose government strongly condemned the Warsaw Pact action, signed a new agreement on cultural exchanges with the USSR in December 1968.[41] Apart from the boycott of the Moscow Olympic Games by West Germany and Norway, the Soviet invasion of Afghanistan had a minimal effect on Soviet-West European exchanges. Following the imposition of martial law in Poland, Britain announced certain sanctions on the USSR, including a reduction in the scope of various technical cooperation agreements. West Germany also announced that it was suspending bilateral negotiations on the pending scientific exchange agreement. But in general the trend in Western Europe was to insulate exchanges from external political shocks, and even these marginal measures were taken largely with an eye toward defusing U.S. pressures.

The Soviet government took the high road on exchanges, and generally refrained from severing contacts for political motives. But a general wariness about the subversive implications of certain forms of contact nonetheless served as an overall brake on the development of contacts. As a prominent Soviet official observed,

the development of cultural exchanges demand[s] that attentive consideration be given to the specific features of various countries and regions, that foreign cultural productions which reach our country via the channels of cultural exchanges be carefully selected, and that major comprehensive measures in connection with events of this kind be well considered and prepared. Particular attention must continue to be paid to the ideological, political, and moral tempering of cadres traveling to foreign countries.[42]

While remaining wary of Western subversive influences, the Soviet cultural bureaucracy was encouraged by the leadership to politicize exchanges and to use them to generate support for Soviet foreign policy objectives. In her 1986 report to the session of the Union of Soviet Societies, Z. M. Kruglova, chairman of the union presidium, stressed that "the movement for friendship with the USSR has become an integral part of the peace-loving forces' movement to avert the threat of war," as is confirmed "by the practice of carrying out within the [Union of Soviet Societies] sphere antiwar actions and international meetings, seminars, conferences and round tables."[43] At the same time, however, Kruglova criticized certain shortcomings in the work of the Union of Soviet Societies, and stressed the need to "adopt a differentiated approach to developing relations with the public of each country and to take care about the ideological thrust and political content of measures."

The tendency toward politicization was most apparent in the zealous Soviet pursuit of sister-city relationships and town twinnings, which were ostensibly designed to promote cultural and human exchanges at a decentralized level but which had an increasing focus on peace. The earliest town twinnings dated from World War II, when the citizens of Coventry, England, and Dijon, France, independently expressed their solidarity with the citizens of Stalingrad.[44] In the 1950s town-twinning with the USSR largely was confined to Communist-controlled municipalities in France and Italy. In 1957 French Communists played a major role in setting up the United Towns Organisation (better known by its French title, the *Fédération Mondiale des Villes Jumelées-Cités Unies*, or FMVJ). In 1964 Soviet cities active in twinnings and exchanges founded the Association for Relations between Soviet and Foreign Cities. One of the stated objectives of the Association was "to involve in the [sister city] movement larger numbers of peace-supporters both in the Soviet Union and abroad."[45]

U.K.-USSR sister city pairings included (in addition to Coventry-Volgograd) London-Moscow, Manchester-Leningrad, Birmingham-Kiev, Nottingham-Minsk, Leeds-Ivanovo, Cheltenham-Sochi, and Margate-Yalta.[46] Franco-Soviet pairings included (in addition to Dijon-Volgograd) Le Havre-Leningrad, Calais-Riga, Marseilles-Odessa, Bordeaux-Leningrad, Nice-Yalta, Menton-Sochi, Saint-Ouen-Podolsk, and formerly Brest-Tallinn.[47] The first West German-Soviet sister city pairing was set up in 1975, and involved Saarbrücken and Tbilisi. It became a focal point of DKP activity, and for many years remained the only such relationship.[48] By 1985 the number of pairings had increased to "more than 24,"[49] and by 1989 to three dozen. Pairings included Dortmund-Rostov-on-the-Don, Hagen-Smolensk, Bielefeld-Novgorod, Münster-Ryazan, Kiel-Tallinn, Ludwigshafen am Rhein-Sumgait, Hamburg-Leningrad, Bremen-Riga, and Mainz-Baku.[50] In the Kohl-Gorbachev joint statement of June 1989 the Soviet and West German governments pledged to promote city partnerships as "building blocks of European peace and cooperation."[51] The number of pairings between Soviet and Finnish cities was predictably large. At the end of the 1960s there were forty-five, including Helsinki-Moscow, Turku-Leningrad, Tampere-Kiev, and Kemi-Volgograd. Other significant pairings with cities in neutral countries included Göteborg-Leningrad and Linz-Zaporozhye.

In November 1985 the Foreign Affairs Commission of the Supreme Soviet held a special meeting devoted to further efforts in this area. In his address to the meeting Ligachev called for the increased participation of Soviet cities in "different antiwar activities" and for further efforts in the United Towns Organization and a related grouping, the World Union of Hero-Cities and War Victim Cities. Ponomarev claimed that the multiplication of Soviet sister city relationships "demonstrate[d] the groundlessness of the stories told by our adversaries about socialism as an allegedly 'closed society'."[52] In addition to playing upon the hero/victim theme, the Soviet Association for Relations between Soviet and Foreign Cities pressed for the convening of annual meetings that would bring together all of the sister cities from a given West European country and their Soviet partners. The representatives of the twin towns of Finland and the USSR began to hold annual meetings in the late 1970s, and similar meetings took place with all the Swedish sister cities. These annual meetings were fairly political, and usually concluded with joint appeals to end the arms race or similar propaganda documents.

Because most West European countries are highly centralized and have no important layer of government between the local and national levels, there was little scope for ties between union republics and West European counterparts such as developed between Yugoslavia and individual Soviet republics, and those that began forming in the 1980s between republics and U.S. states and Canadian provinces.[53] Austria and West Germany, both of which are federal republics, were important exceptions to the general pattern. Formal relations between North Rhine Westphalia, the largest of the West German *Länder*, and the Russian republic were established in 1972.[54] The Saarbrücken-Tbilisi town-twinning relationship was supplemented with a region-twinning arrangement between Saarland and Georgia during Minister-President Lafontaine's trip to the USSR in May 1986.[55] These *Land*-republic links had both cultural and economic aspects. During RSFSR leader Vorotnikov's visit to Düsseldorf in September 1988 North Rhine Westphalia and the RSFSR concluded an agreement on setting up a joint working group to draw up programs of art and cultural exchanges for a three-year period, but the German authorities were also interested in promoting exports by local firms.[56] Lothar Späth visited the USSR in February 1988 and concluded an industrial cooperation agreement between Baden-Württemberg and the USSR, and in September 1989 Rhineland-Palatinate became the second West German state to conclude such an agreement.[57]

State and local governments also sponsored the special days, weeks, and months devoted to the study of Soviet cultural and economic achievements, and contributed to corresponding events in the USSR devoted to West European achievements. The Soviet Union inaugurated a month of Soviet-Icelandic friendship as early as October 1955.[58] Finland and the USSR established a friendship month lasting from November 7, the anniversary of the October Revolution, to December 6, the Finnish independence day.[59] West German-Soviet days became an annual event in the 1980s that brought together trade unions, industrialists, cultural groups, and local politicians. The Days of the Soviet Union in Mannheim in the fall of 1985, for example, lasted almost a month and included 120 cultural, scientific, and industrial activities and events.

The Gorbachev period witnessed a dramatic upsurge in Soviet-West European exchanges, as the USSR became more flexible and less wary of subversion and as Western governments sought to respond positively to the Soviet reform program. During Prime Minister Thatcher's 1987 visit to the Soviet Union Britain and the USSR concluded a "Memorandum on Mutual Understanding Regarding New Avenues of Cooperation in the Areas of Information, Culture, and Education," in which both sides pledged to promote new activities in these areas.[60] Under an agreement between the U.K.-USSR Association and the USSR-U.K. Society a USSR week was held in Birmingham in 1988 and a British week in Kiev in 1990. The 1987 memorandum "expressed the hope" that "such festivals will be held on a more regular basis in the future." Before the Gorbachev period, Britain and the USSR had had only two such festivals, a Soviet festival in Leeds in 1966 and a British festival in Novosibirsk in 1978. In October 1988 West Germany and the USSR concluded environmental and cultural agreements that showed a new degree of Soviet flexibility on the Berlin issue. In a compromise worked out over many months it was agreed that the lists used to administer Soviet-West German exchanges could include individuals and organizations from West Berlin, with the West Berliners marked with an asterisk. Previously the Soviets had insisted upon separate lists.[61] In November 1988 France and the USSR began regular consultations on the question of cooperation in the field of information.[62]

Other breakthroughs grew out of Gorbachev's visits to the major countries of Western Europe in the spring and summer of 1989. They included agreements on the opening of cultural centers in national capitals, youth exchanges, cooperation in the exchange of archives, and the holding of annual public forums.[63] (The latter began in 1989 with France and West Germany, and brought together specialists in various fields who were tasked with working out new ideas for contact and cooperation.) In November 1989 the USSR took part in an informal all-European meeting of culture ministers, hosted by French minister of culture Jacques Lang, that one Soviet commentator described as a meeting intended to explore "the outlines of a common European home of culture."[64]

Viewed from a foreign policy perspective, the Soviet approach to cultural contacts under Gorbachev was an evolutionary development of patterns established in the Khrushchev and Brezhnev periods. As in trade and economic relations, the structure of official and semiofficial contacts and agreements continued to expand, often spurred by summit agreements. From a domestic perspective, however, change under Gorbachev was much more radical. With the advent of glasnost, Soviet authorities made little attempt to control the flow of subversive information into the West through cultural exchange. Indeed, *Moscow News*, the official publication of the Union of Soviet Societies and long a vehicle for Soviet propaganda in the West, became one of the leading reform journals in the USSR and was seen by party conservatives as a force for subversion against socialism. Under *khozrashchet* performers and cultural organizations were given the freedom to negotiate their own agreements with Western sponsors, in part for economic reasons.[65] Increasingly the main barriers to cultural contact were set not by political and administrative factors but by financial constraints and the size of the market for various kinds of culture. Meanwhile, the traditional Communist-dominated friendship societies, which had long been in decline, faced an increasingly uncertain future as older members died off, as the Communist parties weakened, and as the USSR cut its direct and indirect subsidies to these organizations.[66]

These changes caused great difficulties within the Soviet cultural establishment, and made it all but impossible to coordinate the activities of the Soviet ministry of culture, the MFA, republican ministries, the Union of Soviet Societies, and the Soviet Committee for the Defense of Peace. By 1989 it was clear that many groups in the USSR were using contacts with the West to assert positions which clashed with those held by the authorities in Moscow. Kievans participating in a new city partnership with Munich, for example, used their first trip to West Germany less to promote Soviet foreign policy than Ukrainian nationalism.[67] Above all, there was a pronounced depoliticization of many cultural exchanges, not through Western pressure or Soviet governmental decree, but because many of the individual participants were no longer motivated to take part in state-sponsored peace propaganda. As a Soviet participant in Open Doors week in Finland noted in late 1989, the week was marked by the absence of "something that everyone was sick and tired of: the calls to fight for peace."[68] Even more profound changes occurred in 1990, as the union republics declared their sovereignty and as authority over culture gravitated to them and to other bodies such as the Moscow and Leningrad city soviets. Whereas in the past the authorities in Moscow encouraged town twinnings and relations between republics and foreign counterparts as a way of promoting Soviet foreign policy goals under the cover of an artificial pluralism, by 1990 the USSR was beginning to disintegrate, leaving control over contacts with the outside world increasingly in the hands of republican and local governments rather than the Kremlin.

The Churches

Persecution of religion in Russia after the revolution was severe, and by 1938 it is estimated that only 500 churches—less than 1 percent of the prerevolutionary total—remained open. Churches were cut off from contact with the outside world, and there was no attempt by the state to use religion for foreign policy purposes.[69] Contact between the Russian Orthodox Church and foreign churches resumed only during World War II, which Western experts generally agree saved the church from extinction.[70]

The Church proved useful to the state in fulfilling three wartime and early postwar tasks: consolidating Russian control over the Orthodox populations in the Baltic republics and Eastern Poland, improving the Soviet image in the Western democracies, and enlisting traditional Russian patriotism in the war effort. Church help was solicited on the basis of a new church-state bargain: "Essentially, the State granted certain minimal concessions to the Church, marginally sufficient to ensure its continued survival in the country, in return for the Church's unwavering support in political activities."[71] In September 1943 Stalin personally sanctioned this bargain by meeting with the three leading Church hierarchs.

Restoration at home was followed by limited contact with churches abroad. The first official reception of a foreign church delegation took place three days after Stalin's meeting with the hierarchs, when the archbishop of York attended the *Sobor* then taking place in Moscow. A delegation of the Russian Orthodox Church made a return visit to Britain in 1945.

When the war ended Stalin chose not to reimpose the prewar policy of trying to eradicate Russian Orthodoxy. This decision was based primarily on domestic factors, but foreign policy considerations played a role as well. The state sanctioned the further development of the Church's international ties, and in 1946 the Department of External Church Relations headed by Metropolitan Nikolai was established by the Moscow Patriarchate.

In policy regarding international contacts, Church and state authorities drew distinctions between the three main branches of Christianity. They were most supportive of contact with the Orthodox world. At the *Sobor* of 1945 the overwhelming majority of the churches in the Orthodox world acknowledged the Moscow Patriarchate as the legitimate representative of the Russian Orthodox Church. This paved the way toward extensive contact between the Moscow Patriarchate and the autocephalous and autonomous Orthodox churches, most of which were located in Eastern Europe and the Middle East. These contacts were "defensive" and system-consolidating, and fundamentally different from the contacts later cultivated with the Protestant churches of Western Europe. The "tasks assigned to the Moscow Patriarchate in the period from 1945 to 1948 evidently amounted to the consolidation of the eastern bloc of churches under the aegis of the Moscow Patriarchate and the Committee for the Affairs of the Russian Orthodox Church which stood behind it."[72]

At the other extreme, Church and state authorities were unremittingly hostile toward the Roman Catholic Church, which was seen as an instrument of foreign political penetration and a threat to Soviet control in the recently acquired western borderlands. This hostility was manifested in severe persecution of Catholics in Lithuania, and in the decision to forcibly sever the historic bonds between the Vatican and the Uniate Church of the Ukraine. In March 1946 the Uniate Church convened a synod of "terrorized priests that proclaimed the union with Rome made in Brest-Litovsk in 1596 null and void."[73] The Roman Catholic Church refused to acknowledge the Lvov Synod as valid, and continued to support an underground Uniate Church.

Soviet policy toward the Protestant churches tended to follow trends in political relations with the West. Until 1948 the political authorities tolerated and possibly even encouraged Russian Orthodox Church contacts with the Western Protestant establishment. On the occasion of his visit to Britain in 1945 Patriarch Nikolai met with W. A. Visser t'Hooft, the Dutch clergyman who was in the process of founding the World Council of Churches (WCC). This meeting led to a regular correspondence between the Patriarchate and the World Council in Process of Formation.

Russian interest in the WCC was partly motivated by the same defensive considerations that encouraged greater activism in the Orthodox world. In his letters to Western Protestants Nikolai sought to elicit information about the relations between other Orthodox churches and the WCC. Other communications from the Russian Church hinted at a desire to use association with the WCC against the émigré churches. Among Russian churchmen there also was concern, probably shared in Soviet political circles, that the WCC could become a "Protestant Vatican" that would constitute a united front of all non-Orthodox Christians against the USSR.

In July 1948 the Russian Church decided unequivocally against association with the WCC. At the Sobor of 1948 the Moscow Patriarchate condemned all participation in the organization.[74] The Sobor also issued "An Appeal to Christians of the Whole World" which, although ostensibly addressed to all churches, had an inward-looking character and contrasted the Catholic-Protestant West with the Orthodox East. This was the religious equivalent of the Zhdanovist turn against all things foreign. For the remainder of the Stalin period the only contacts between the Russian Church and the WCC were occasional letters accompanied by published materials from Church conferences. In 1950 the USSR urged the WCC to endorse the Stockholm appeal, but this was done by means of letters from Pierre Joliot-Curie, the French Communist who headed the World Peace Council (WPC), rather than through the Russian Orthodox Church.[75]

Having abandoned efforts to forge ties with the Protestant establishment, the Russian Orthodox and other churches in the USSR concentrated on attracting support for the Soviet peace campaign from religious fellow-travelers and Western clergymen willing to take part in Communist-sponsored enterprises. The Russian Orthodox Church became a charter member of the Soviet Peace Committee at its founding in 1949, and the patriarch issued "An Appeal to All Christians for the Defense of Peace," on the occasion of the first World Congress of Supporters of Peace.

In December 1951 the Patriarchate invited Martin Niemöller, the German nationalist pastor, to visit the USSR in an apparent attempt to enlist the churches in the campaign against West German rearmament. The trip caused a sensation in West Germany, where it was welcomed by many as an optimistic sign but denounced by Chancellor Adenauer as a "stab in the back." In 1952 the Patriarchate took the lead in organizing the Conference in Defence of Peace of all Churches and Religious Associations in the USSR. It attracted three Protestant pastors (from Austria, Denmark, and the Netherlands) and a member of the synod of the Old Catholic Church in Austria.[76] This was hardly an impressive showing, and demonstrated the difficulties associated with any effort to enlist individual Western clergymen in the Soviet peace campaign when relations with official religious bodies were nonexistent.

After Stalin's death the Church began expanding its contacts beyond Communists and fellow-travelers. In 1954 delegations from the Church of Scotland and the German Protestant Church (EKD) visited the USSR, and there was some talk of establishing contact between the Church of Scotland and the Russian Orthodox Church in "matters concerning the defense of peace." In June 1955 a delegation of the Dutch Ecumenical Church visited the USSR. In the same month, on the occasion of Prime Minister Nehru's visit to the USSR, the Church was represented for the first time at a Kremlin reception for foreign visitors. Informal contacts between the Russian Orthodox Church and the WCC resumed in 1954, and in March and July 1956 delegations of the WCC's two most influential affiliates, the U.S. National Council of Churches and the Church of England, visited the USSR, the latter to attend an Anglican-Orthodox theological conference.[77]

A major objective of the Russian Church in these exchanges was to broaden Western support for the Soviet peace campaign. Initially this was attempted by the rather naive expedient of urging churches in the West to adopt a positive attitude toward the WPC. In early 1955 Nikolai informed the WCC by letter that "we are convinced that the World Council must give up its one-sided and even biased estimate of the activity of the WPC. How it would befit the dignity of the World Council of Churches if its representatives would take part in the work of the WPC."[78] The Russian Church was aware of the WCC's interest in expanding its largely Protestant membership base, and sought to parlay the promise of association with the WCC into greater support for Soviet propaganda efforts. At the same time, the Russian Church showed that it was less interested than in the past in trying to use the WCC to undermine the émigré churches. The "defensive," system-consolidating phase in Church policy had shifted to one of outreach toward the West.

The first meeting between the Russian Church and the WCC was scheduled for January 1957, but was postponed (at the request of the Russians) because of the crisis in Hungary. It eventually took place in the Netherlands in August 1958, and resulted in an agreement under which the Russian Church would send observers to meetings of the WCC. Nikolai spoke at length about peace and attempted to have a declaration on the presence of British and U.S. forces in Lebanon included in the minutes of the meeting. In the joint communiqué issued at the close of the meeting it was stated that the delegations shared a "deep concern for world peace with justice and freedom," and that the WCC and the Moscow Patriarchate would continue to exchange views on the "great international problems of our time such as disarmament, atomic warfare and nuclear weapon testing" with the object of achieving "agreement about the different ways toward peace which each is following."[79]

In 1959 and 1960 Soviet representatives attended WCC meetings in the West, and in December 1959 Visser t'Hooft led a WCC delegation on an unofficial visit to the USSR.[80] In 1961 the Russian Orthodox Church applied for membership in the WCC and was accepted by a vote in the General Assembly. The Orthodox churches of Bulgaria, Romania, and Poland also were admitted, and a year later five other Soviet churches—the Lutheran churches of Latvia and Estonia, the Armenian Apostolic Church, the Georgian Orthodox Church, and the Union of Evangelical Christians/Baptists in the USSR—also became affiliates.

The decision of the Russian Church to join the wcc coincided with a wave of antireligious persecution in the USSR. Begun in 1959 at Khrushchev's behest and ended only after the leadership change in 1964, the campaign resulted in the closing of an estimated 8,500 of the Orthodox Church's 16,000 parishes. Added pressures were applied to individual believers, including expulsion from party organs and educational institutions, loss of jobs, forcible separation of children from believing parents, and in some cases imprisonment and death.[81] The connection between the Church's rising international profile and its worsening position at home is unclear.[82] One explanation for the upsurge of international activism by the Church is that the political authorities pressed the Church into greater activity in order to block or delay Western recognition of the internal persecution. An alternative possibility is that the Church was acting on its own initiative and sought membership in the wcc in order to "secure its own existence."[83] Whatever the reasons, the effect of membership was to mitigate international reaction to the antireligious campaign.

The first official delegation of the wcc visited the USSR in June 1962, and returned with a new and in some ways sobering understanding of the Soviet interest in the organization. According to its official report, the delegation concluded that "the thin thread which holds [the Russian Church] to the World Council at the moment is [the] predominant interest in peace. . . . It seems clear to us that the wcc, if it is to make relationship with the Orthodox Church of Russia continuously possible, must be more manifestly explicit on the question of peace."[84] The delegation also reported that the state authorities were present at every meeting, and that "no independent conversations with Church leaders were possible."

The entry of the Russian Orthodox Church into the wcc was followed by the first formal contacts between the wcc and the Soviet government. Shortly before the Geneva summit of 1955 the wcc had sent copies of its "Call to Prayer"—a request that all pray for the success of the meeting—to the four participating governments. The British and U.S. governments replied to the appeal; the Soviet (and French) did not. This standoffish posture was maintained for the next several years, even though the wcc had expressed criticism of certain U.S. policies.[85] But in 1961 the Soviet government took a much more positive attitude toward a wcc initiative. Concerned about the problem of atmospheric testing, in that year the wcc proposed that a consultation be held at the Ecumenical Institute in Geneva between Christians from various countries and government representatives, especially of the two major powers, at which testing and related issues could be discussed. The USSR accepted the invitation and offered to send Ambassador Tsarapkin.[86]

The Soviet rapprochement with the wcc should be seen in conjunction with other international activities of the Church, and in particular its role in the founding of the Christian Peace Conference (cpc). Although the Russian Church had been reaching out since 1954 to the Western religious establishment, it had by no means severed contact with clerical fellow-travelers in the West. It developed close ties, for example, with Canon Collins, the so-called Red Dean who had extensive dealings with both the Moscow Patriarchate and the Soviet Peace Committee.[87] The founding of the cpc was an attempt to make greater use of contact with people such as Collins at a time when the Soviet government was engaged in a massive campaign against the deployment of U.S. nuclear weapons in Europe.

In late 1957 the Ecumenical Council of Churches of Czechoslovakia began preparations for an international conference to discuss the Christian position on atomic weapons. Czechoslovakia was in some respects ideally suited to manage an international religious front on behalf of the USSR. In addition to having a large Protestant population, it was the country in Eastern Europe whose legal and administrative pattern of church-state relations most closely approximated that of the USSR.[88] Preliminary meetings involving delegates from Eastern Europe and West Germany took place in 1958, 1959, and 1960, and a well-prepared All Christian Peace Assembly was convened in Prague in 1961.[89] The Prague meeting, which drew 700 delegates from throughout the world, launched the Christian Peace Conference.

The cpc was to function as a permanent organization with headquarters in Prague as well as hold mass assemblies at four-year intervals. It also established "regional" (in fact national) committees that maintained contact with the central organization and each other. The largest regional committee outside Eastern Europe was the West German, which had about 400 members, most of whom were Protestant clergymen. Other active regional committees were in Britain and the Netherlands. In 1965 the regional committees began holding annual conferences, meeting first in Prague and the following year in Zagorsk.[90] The committees were involved in all the main Communist-sponsored campaigns of the 1960s: against the MLF, for a European security conference, and against U.S. involvement in Vietnam.

Although in preparation since 1957, the launching of the cpc probably was connected with the decision to join the wcc. It provided the USSR with a controlled Communist fallback and a sounding board for initiatives to be introduced in the wcc. It is noteworthy that the cpc held its first (1961) and third (1968) All Christian Peace assemblies just before general assemblies of the wcc, even though the wcc hierarchy warned it against doing so. The June 1962 wcc delegation to Moscow also reported that "the great emphasis in every conversation was on peace" and that "the most lively and critical discussion took place concerning the Prague Peace Conference."[91]

Much as it previously had urged the wcc to give direct support to the wpc, the Russian Church began calling for cooperation between what it portrayed as two parallel international church movements, the one representing the major churches of North America and Western Europe, the other an effectively controlled Soviet front. The wcc would not give an unqualified endorsement to the cpc, but it did agree to exchange delegations of observers during important meetings. The cpc's prestige was enhanced in 1966 when it was admitted to unesco as a nongovernmental observer.[92] By 1968 the bulletin of the cpc could boast that Prague had become, "along with Geneva and Rome, the third pole of world ecumenical life."[93]

However, the USSR was soon to suffer a severe, if temporary, setback in the cpc. Early in 1968 the Soviets and East Europeans began losing control of the front, in part to Third World delegations, some of which were subject to Chinese influence. At one meeting Japanese and Indian delegates attacked the npt as a "selfish treaty" drafted by the three most powerful "have nations" and imposed upon the "have nots."[94] Subsequently, the Communist-controlled churches had difficulty in fulfilling one of the cpc's main functions, passing resolutions and appeals supportive of Soviet foreign policy. The invasion of Czechoslovakia dealt a further blow to the organization. The International Secretariat of the cpc, headed by the Czech Joseph Hromadka, issued a sharp and immediate protest. Hromadka later resigned, and the national affiliates of the cpc in West Germany, Switzerland, Italy, France, and the Netherlands ceased to function. Metropolitan Nikodim was chosen as interim president, but the Russians and supporting delegations failed in a bid to move the headquarters from Prague to Budapest or East Berlin.[95]

In addition to participating in the cpc and the wcc, the Russian Church expanded its bilateral relations with Western churches. A noteworthy bilateral development was the first *Arnoldshainer Gespräche* between representatives of the ekd and the Russian Orthodox Church in October 1959. These "conversations" were mainly concerned with theological matters, and remained "more or less aloof from political ups and downs and interference of politically engaged fellow-Christians."[96] Between 1959 and 1987 eleven such conversations took place, alternately in the USSR and the Federal Republic.[97]

The Russian Orthodox Church also was involved in two other international religious assemblies: a meeting of all Orthodox churches and the Conference of European Churches (CEC). In late 1960 Alexei became the first Russian patriarch to visit Constantinople since 1589. His discussions there with Patriarch Athenagoras led to a pan-Orthodox conference on the Greek island of Rhodes in the fall of 1961, the first meeting of all the Eastern Orthodox churches since the Council of Nicea in A.D. 787. Archbishop Nikodim, the Russian representative at this meeting, called on the conference to "define its position" with respect to world peace.[98] In private sessions the Russian churchmen made clear that their participation in future conferences could not be assured if some political points were not included in the documents of the meeting.[99] The conference adopted three topics for ongoing discussion proposed by Nikodim, one dealing with racial discrimination, another with peace, and a third entitled "Orthodoxy and Christian Duty in Areas of Rapid Social Change." The Russian delegation also failed to get its way in an important organizational dispute and thus was unable to undermine the primacy traditionally accorded the Ecumenical patriarch of Constantinople.[100] In formulating its closing message affirming Orthodox unity, the conference rejected proposals by the Russian Church for an overt appeal to the great powers regarding peace and disarmament, and instead called for peace in general terms using traditional Biblical phraseology.

The CEC was primarily a Western venture that attracted cautious Eastern participation. (Unlike the WCC, which was worldwide in scope and aimed to establish grass roots contact with the laity in its constituent member churches, the CEC had a narrower focus. It was confined to Europe and aimed to bring together mainly clergy and officials of the member churches.) It held its first meeting in Nyborg, Denmark in 1959. The Soviet-bloc churches adopted a fairly low profile in the CEC until the fifth Nyborg assembly in the fall of 1967, at which the CEC endorsed the convening of a European security conference and announced the beginning of a special round of consultations on the theme of peace in Europe.

At the sixth Nyborg conference in 1971 the Eastern-bloc churches staged something of a coup by introducing a memorandum proposing that in all future assemblies peace be given overwhelming emphasis.[101] The memorandum declared that "up to now CEC has been insufficiently concerned with the problem of European security," which it characterized as "the problem which should surely be the most important and most central in its work in the service of peace."[102] At the conclusion of the meeting the conference adopted a message to the churches declaring that it was the duty of the churches to promote "all plans which give hope for better international relations in Europe," including the convening of a conference on European security.[103] A number of Western delegations opposed adoption of a final "message," but yielded to the combined efforts of the Eastern-bloc churches and sympathetic West Europeans. The 1971 assembly also established a permanent working group on peacemaking in Europe charged with holding periodic consultations and issuing recommendations. The CEC and the CPC also agreed to form a joint committee to study problems of European security.[104]

Another significant institutional breakthrough occurred in August 1972, when the Russian Church met in the Netherlands for the first time with Pax Christi, the Roman Catholic peace organization. Subsequent Orthodox-Pax Christi conferences took place at approximately two-year intervals: in Vienna in 1974, Leningrad in 1976, London in 1978, Zagorsk in 1980, Antwerp in 1983, Odessa in 1985, and Antwerp in 1987.[105] Relations with the Vatican remained rather distant, however. The two churches initiated theological conversations in 1967, which subsequently took place at approximately three-year intervals but with a significant break in the first part of the 1980s.[106] The focus of the dialogue was largely theological, and final communiqués contained only generalities on arms control and political issues, as well as overt acknowledgment of different points of view regarding "particular political and military proposals for the application of [general] principles."[107]

From the perspective of the Soviet political authorities, by the late 1960s and early 1970s the Russian Orthodox Church was well positioned to use its bilateral and multilateral contacts to support Soviet foreign policy objectives in Europe and elsewhere.[108] In 1968 local Soviet churches began making contributions, ranging to as much as 30 percent of their annual income, to the Soviet Peace Committee. Soviet clergymen, already severely taxed for the "unproductive" way in which they earned their living, were pressed to give a month of each year's salary to the committee.[109]

In the 1970s the WCC became the focal point of Russian Orthodox international activism, with nuclear disarmament the chief policy issue on its agenda. The WCC never embraced the Soviet peace program, but its 1972 "Statement on European Security and Cooperation," its 1973 "Memorandum on Disarmament," and its 1975 "Declaration on the World Armaments Situation" were close to the Soviet viewpoint on many issues and were welcomed in Moscow.[110] As a sympathetic Western observer concluded, "especially from 1975 onwards, the World Council of Churches has gained in the field of nuclear issues a moral authority that has gone beyond its own constituency of member churches. WCC statements on the nuclear issue have given strong impulses to the Christian peace movements, influencing their orientation and direction."[111]

At the Nairobi assembly in 1975 the WCC adopted the "Program to Combat Militarism and the Arms Race" that was in effect a mandate for various unilateral, bilateral, and multilateral initiatives by the organization and its constituent churches. In March 1977 the WCC held its first consultation with representatives of all its member churches from the USSR and Eastern Europe. These consultations, which dealt almost exclusively with the peace issue, were institutionalized and occurred at approximately three-year intervals.

Russian Orthodox membership in the WCC was also regarded as helpful in moderating international criticisms of Soviet policy. In 1956 the WCC unequivocally condemned the Soviet invasion of Hungary. Twelve years later the WCC initially refrained from issuing any statement on the Warsaw Pact's suppression of the Prague Spring and instead polled its members on their attitudes toward "recent events in Czechoslovakia." The Soviet and East European churches vigorously defended the invasion. (The WCC's reaction was thus more hesitant and less forceful than that of the CPC, a Communist-controlled front.) Under pressure from member churches the WCC deplored the action after a week's delay, which in turn elicited a strong protest from the Russian Orthodox Church.[112] WCC reaction to the Soviet invasion of Afghanistan was weaker still. The second round of WCC–East European church consultations took place in January 1980, a few weeks after the invasion, and issued a concluding document that did not even mention Afghanistan but expressed concern about the "accelerated arms race in Europe and the postponement of SALT II." It went on to recommend that "especially under the present circumstances, the churches should not acquiesce in the estrangement in political relations, but seek cooperation for world peace between persons [and] groups of different ideologies and nations."[113] A month later the executive committee of the WCC did express "serious concern" about "the military action of the USSR in Afghanistan," but prefaced this remark by stating that "no single event should be seen in isolation" and expressing concern about several other developments, including the NATO INF decision.[114] The WCC avoided any further mention of Afghanistan, but intensified its criticisms of U.S. policy and especially alleged U.S. plans for waging a limited nuclear war.[115]

Russian Orthodox participation in the WCC also helped to mute Western responses to religious persecution in the USSR. In 1975 the dissident Orthodox priest Gleb Iakunin and his colleague Lev Regelson sent an appeal to the Nairobi assembly of the WCC, asking it to look into Soviet religious persecution and to prescribe actions such as discussion and meditation in local churches and the organization of appropriate protests to support persecuted believers in the USSR. Russian Orthodox clergymen rebutted the charges and strongly suggested that the Church might have to consider withdrawal from the organization if the USSR was singled out in any WCC resolution.[116] In 1980 Iakunin was arrested for "anti-Soviet agitation and propaganda" and sentenced to five years in a labor camp. The WCC did not respond to appeals for intervention on Iakunin's behalf (individual Western churchmen such as the archbishop of Canterbury did send letters to President Brezhnev and the patriarch). A dissident church historian and a group called the Christian Committee for the Defense of Believers in the USSR also sent letters to the next assembly of the WCC in 1983, but no action was taken.[117]

Another international milestone was the 1981 Public Hearing on Nuclear Weapons and Disarmament that was organized by the WCC and took place in Amsterdam. After hearing evidence from various invitees, including many representing Soviet organizations, the hearing pronounced that "the time has come when the churches must unequivocally declare that the production and deployment as well as the use of nuclear weapons are a crime against humanity." This finding was subsequently endorsed by the WCC as a body at the 1983 Vancouver assembly.[118]

The growing salience of the peace issue also was seen in the CEC. At its eighth assembly in Switzerland in September 1974 the CEC adopted a report calling for the strengthening of "cooperation between European churches on peace questions" and recommended that the CEC "establish a working group for coordinating post-CSCE work and gathering together the findings and conclusions of peace research institutes for use in the churches."[119] Subsequently, "the main thrust of CEC activities" became, in the words of the organization's general secretary, "the monitoring and the encouraging of the Helsinki process."[120] At the 1979 ninth CEC assembly in Crete the conference adopted a Churches' Human Rights Program for the Implementation of the Helsinki Final Act which was in effect a mandate for a wide range of consultations and activities by member churches.

On the basis of this mandate the Russian Church sponsored the June 1984 conference on Peace and Human Rights: Theological Origins and Political Consequences of Confidence-Building Measures, which attracted church leaders from throughout Europe.[121] In "monitoring" the human rights provisions of the Final Act, the CEC leaned strongly toward Soviet and Eastern interpretations. The CEC "was able to publicly witness to its specific aim of promoting peace in Europe, by insisting on the ten principles and the three baskets of the Final Act seen as a whole, instead of singling out [as the West was accused of doing by the East] basket three on humanitarian co-operation and human rights to underline the opposition between West and East. This attitude was of great help to and encouragement to the church-affiliated peace movements."[122] At its ninth assembly in Scotland in 1986 the CEC proposed an assembly of all churches in countries participating in the CSCE, which led to the European Ecumenical Convocation on Peace and Justice in Basel in May 1989.[123]

The antinuclear controversies of the late 1970s and early 1980s also gave an impetus to numerous new bilateral contacts between the Russian Orthodox Church and Western counterparts. To give just one example, in April 1979 the Tutzing Evangelical Academy of the West German EKD and the Bavarian Society for the Promotion of Relations between the FRG and the Soviet Union sponsored its first International Colloquium on Questions of Disarmament. Participants on the Soviet side included Orthodox churchmen as well as state and party officials. Similar colloquia, to which U.S. as well as Soviet officials were invited, were held at three-year intervals and focused on various peace issues.[124]

In addition to implementing mandates from the WCC and the CEC, the Moscow Patriarchate became increasingly bold in convening its own conferences, which in turn mandated various ongoing activities. In 1977 the Patriarchate convened an international religious forum—a world conference of the Religious Workers for Lasting Peace, Disarmament, and Just Relations among Nations—at Zagorsk that was attended by 633 delegates from 107 countries representing Buddhists, Hindus, Jews, Sikhs, Shintoists, and Christians.[125] The Zagorsk meeting was in the tradition of the 1952 and 1969 forums, which were held on an ad hoc basis in response to a perceived foreign policy need.

In May 1982—the height of the anti-INF campaign—the Patriarchate organized another meeting—the World Conference of Religious Workers for Saving the Sacred Gift of Life from Nuclear Catastrophe—that decided to transform itself into a permanent institution by holding annual meetings. Subsequent assemblies attracted up to six hundred religious leaders each year. In addition, the Patriarchate organized smaller meetings of European church leaders, "in accordance with [the] mandate of the 1982 inter-religious conference to facilitate the implementation of its ideas and decisions."[126]

In the increasingly favorable political climate of the late 1970s even the CPC, which was pronounced moribund by Western experts in the early 1970s, made a comeback. Following the events of 1968 the organization continued to function under tight political control. It continued to pronounce on European issues and especially the CSCE, but for a period of years its activities were mainly directed at the Third World. In 1975 Bishop Károly Tóth of the Reformed

Church in Hungary replaced Nikodim as president. Tóth had some success in cultivating an independent image for the CPC, but managed to back all Soviet foreign policy initiatives and to condemn the "naive pacifism" of the independent peace movements in Eastern Europe.[127] Regional committees that ceased to function in 1968 were revived, particularly in West Germany. Metropolitan Philaret attended the 1987 meeting of the West German committee, the theme of which was "Our 'Yes' to the Creation of God and Our 'No' to the Militarization of Earth and Space: A Nuclear-free World by the Year 2000."[128]

Russian Orthodox involvement in international activities continued to increase under Gorbachev. The 1988 celebrations marking 1,000 years of Christianity in Russia would have meant a higher profile for the Church under any Soviet leader, but Gorbachev had particular reasons to encourage Church activism.[129] His "new political thinking" was at least superficially compatible with church teachings. In his report to the Twenty-Seventh Party Congress he noted pointedly that "the Soviet public is prepared to continue developing links with non-communist tendencies and organizations, *including* religious ones, which come out against war."[130] In *Perestroika* Gorbachev noted "old Russia was united with Europe by Christianity." Iakovlev also hinted at the role of Christianity as a part of the historical underpinning of the "common European home."[131]

Russian Orthodox and foreign clergymen played a prominent part in the peace forum convened by Gorbachev in February 1987 under the slogan "For a Nuclear-Free World, For the Survival of Humanity."[132] The religious section of the forum attracted 215 religious leaders from 56 countries, including representatives of the World Council of Churches and the Conference of European Churches. Even though front involvement in the forum was kept to a minimum, the CPC leadership played a leading role in organizing the religious section of the forum. The religious leaders adopted the "Appeal for Joint Efforts" that was handed to Gorbachev at the closing plenary. It noted the "special role" of people of religion in increasing international contacts, intensifying education for peace, and eliminating "enemy images," and endorsed Gorbachev's plan for the elimination of nuclear weapons by the year 2000 and called on all nuclear weapons states to renounce doctrines of deterrence.[133]

Throughout 1988 the state authorities took a positive stance toward the millennium celebrations organized by the Church. The celebration attracted the archbishop of Canterbury, a delegation from the Roman Catholic Church led by two cardinals, and many other prominent Western church leaders. The EKD and the Russian Church jointly sponsored a mobile exhibition on religion in the USSR that traveled throughout West Germany, and high-level Russian Orthodox delegations attended symposia and services in Regensburg and Hannover.[134]

While Gorbachev no doubt hoped to use the Russian Orthodox Church to enhance the USSR's international image, he also was responsible for very real improvements in the conditions of the Church. On April 29, 1988, he met in the Kremlin with Patriarch Pimen and other members of the Holy Synod. Prominently featured on Soviet television, the meeting was the first between the leaders of the party and the Church since Stalin had received the three hierarchs in September 1943. Gorbachev acknowledged that the churches had been affected "by the tragic events of the period of the personality cult," and promised a return to Leninist principles in church-state relations. While the Russian Orthodox Church was the main beneficiary of Gorbachev's reforms, other Christian churches as well as Jews, Muslims, and other religions also welcomed the new tolerance.

In 1989 an increasing number of churches were reopened, Bibles became more available, and churches were allowed to engage in charity work.[135] Five religious leaders—one Muslim, the Armenian Catholicos, and three figures from the Russian Orthodox Church (including Patriarch Pimen)—were elected in March 1989 to the new Congress of People's Deputies. Previously, religious leaders were barred from holding any state office.[136] These improvements were given wide international publicity and approval when the Central Committee of the wcc met for the first time in Moscow in July 1989.[137]

The most tangible foreign policy result of Gorbachev's internal reforms was a rapprochement between the Soviet government and the Vatican and, to a lesser extent, closer ties between the Russian Orthodox and Roman Catholic churches. In 1987 the Vatican resumed the theological conversations with the Russian Orthodox Church that had been suspended after 1980. Cardinal Casaroli, the Vatican foreign minister, attended the millennium celebrations in Moscow, and was received by Gorbachev. The Vatican also began receiving a large number of high-ranking Orthodox visitors.[138]

In January 1989 Pope John Paul II received a delegation of the Soviet Committee for the Defense of Peace led by G. Borovik. According to Izvestiia, this was the first Vatican reception for representatives of a Soviet "mass organization." There was no communiqué or other tangible result of the meeting, but a Soviet participant announced that "contacts between the Vatican and Soviet mass organizations will continue."[139] Gorbachev met with Pope John Paul II during his trips to Italy in November 1989 and November 1990, and the USSR and the Holy See exchanged diplomatic missions in early 1990. The Vatican remained fairly cautious in its dealings with the Kremlin, however. Pope John Paul turned aside Gorbachev's invitations to visit the USSR, and the Vatican stopped short of reestablishing full diplomatic relations.

While the status of the Uniate Church remained a source of tension between the Vatican and the Soviet government, by 1988 it was increasingly clear that the main obstacle to re-recognition of the Uniate Church was not the Soviet government but the hierarchy of the Orthodox Church. The state reregistered the Church in late 1989, but there were bitter disputes between the Orthodox and Uniates over such matters as property that had been owned by the Uniates and transferred to the Orthodox Church in 1946.[140] These matters were taken up in a separate dialogue between the Vatican and the Russian Church.[141] The Vatican was less satisfied with the policy of the Soviet state toward predominantly Catholic Lithuania, which declared its independence from the USSR in early 1990 and was subjected to political and economic pressures by the authorities in Moscow.

Despite its differences with the Vatican, the Russian Church remained a strong supporter of closer political and ecclesiastical ties with the rest of Europe. Archbishop Kirill of Smolensk and Kaliningrad, the newly appointed chairman of the Department of External Church Relations of the Moscow Patriarchate (the unofficial "foreign minister" of the Church) declared that "without unity among Christians I cannot imagine, for example, the building of a common European home."[142] A concrete new element in the Russian Church's relations with churches in the West was its ability to accept material aid for the restoration of church buildings and other activities. In late 1989, for example, it accepted, with the approval of the state authorities, offers from the Protestant churches of East and West Germany for help in restoring the Kaliningrad cathedral.[143]

Peace Groups

The "dawning perception of the Peace Movement as a novel and, hopefully, decisive factor in world politics"[144] became apparent in Soviet policy only after World War II, and was described by Marshall Shulman in his *Stalin's Foreign Policy Reappraised*. Even after this "dawning," however, the Soviet leadership remained wary of contact with groups not under the control of the international Communist movement. The peace movement was envisioned as an enterprise to be directed by a core of loyal Communists, assisted by fellow-travelers who were useful in attracting a mass following. Only gradually did the Soviet authorities come to value cooperation with groups that were interested in peace but that had no open or disguised link with the international Communist movement.

Unlike the popular front, which was based on an appeal to the Socialist parties and trade unions, the peace movement was to be drawn primarily from the intellectuals. In August 1948 the Polish Communist Party organized the World Conference of Intellectuals for Peace, which attracted a number of prominent non-Communist intellectuals. The conference was followed by the Cultural and Scientific Conference for World Peace in New York in March 1949, and the World Peace Congress in Paris the following month. The Paris meeting resulted in the founding of the most important of the Communist peace fronts, the World Peace Council (WPC).[145] A year later the WPC launched the Stockholm peace appeal, which reportedly gathered 500 million signatures in support of its "ban the atomic bomb" proposition.

In the mid-1950s the USSR began drawing distinctions between "mass" peace activities and those directed at Western elites. In August 1955 four Soviet scientists participated in a London conference sponsored by the Association of Parliamentarians for World Government, "the first time since the war that any Russian Communists had attended a conference in the West."[146] It was at this meeting that Bertrand Russell unveiled the famous Russell-Einstein manifesto. Russell was concerned that the document "should not in any way offend those of Communist ideology,"[147] and worked to obtain the signature of Joliot-Curie, head of the World Federation of Scientific Workers (WFSW). But he would not allow Communist fronts to capture the movement and even refused offers from the WFSW for formal association.

After what appears to have been some initial hesitation, the USSR decided to endorse the budding movement of scientists for peace. A meeting scheduled for January 1957 was postponed because of the Hungarian and Suez crises, but in July scientists met in Pugwash, Nova Scotia, to found the movement of that name. Three Soviet scientists were part of the founding group. The meeting resulted in a public statement on disarmament that, although devoid of ideological formulations, was endorsed by the Soviet Academy of Sciences. It also concluded with an agreement to institutionalize further scientific meetings. The Russell-Einstein manifesto had envisioned a single meeting of scientists, but a continuing committee was set up to organize follow-on events.

Pugwash conferences subsequently were held at least once each year, always with Soviet participants present.[148] The meetings generally were dominated by British, U.S., and Soviet participants and often focused on U.S.-Soviet or global issues. But European issues were first discussed as a distinct topic at the ninth Pugwash Conference in 1962, and a permanent study group on European issues was established. Beginning in 1967 smaller symposia on European issues were held under Pugwash auspices. Pugwash later formulated unofficial proposals for nuclear-free zones and undertook various other Europe-specific initiatives. The group's 1982 annual conference took place in Warsaw, and "was the first important international East-West meeting held in Poland after the introduction of martial law."[149] Under the theme "The Current Danger of Nuclear War: the Relevance of the Russell-Einstein Manifesto Today," the conference adopted the Declaration of the Pugwash Movement which was signed by 111 Nobel laureates in the natural sciences.

The Soviet decision to cooperate with the movement of scientists long remained somewhat of an exception to a general pattern. For the most part Soviet officials were reluctant to sanction activities they did not control. In his account of the 1962 International Conference on Disarmament and Reduction of World Tensions, Canon Collins, the chief organizer of the event, recalled that the Soviet Peace Committee was hesitant to become involved in an independent, if even very left-leaning, enterprise. Collins had been campaigning for a "cultural and political peace conference along the lines of the Pugwash Conferences for scientists, a conference in which Communists and fellow travellers would not be the dominating element."[150] The peace committee officials to whom he talked "were enthusiastic, but insisted on the presence of Western Communists and communist sympathizers." This drove away already hesitant candidates for sponsorship on the Western side such as the British CND.

In response to an "impassioned appeal for some such meeting" by the Soviet Peace Committee, in early 1961 Collins redoubled his efforts and an arrangement was worked out under which invitations to the conference would be allocated on the basis of "not less than six Westerners to every five Communists," with "anyone thought by Western members to be a fellow traveller" to count as a Communist. This arrangement failed to convince even the CND, and the conference attracted far less attention and respectability than it would have had the Soviets been more willing to be flexible on the question of participation. The Soviet authorities apparently were satisfied with the arrangement, however, and sent the writer Ilya Ehrenburg and another delegate to the London meeting.

Soviet analysts saw a regular ebb and flow in the activities of the West European peace movement, with periods of high activity in the mid-1950s, late 1960s, and between 1977–83, followed by periods of relative quiescence. According to one writer, "there was an obvious decline in antiwar activity in Western Europe in the late 1950s and early 1960s," after which "the peace organizations did not have any perceptible influence again until the middle 1960s."[151] The revival of activity in the latter period was largely attributable to the Vietnam War, which according to Soviet writers drew the new left into a joint struggle with "leftist democratic peace organizations."

At the International Conference of Communist and Workers' Parties in Moscow in 1969 the participating parties concluded that "the existing situation calls for unity of action of the Communists and all anti-imperialist forces so that maximum use can be made of all the new possibilities for launching a broader offensive against imperialism, against the forces of reaction and war."[152] Using Vietnam as a unifying element, the Soviet- and Communist-controlled elements in the "antimilitarist coalitions" advanced demands specific to Europe, such as the call for an early convening of the European security conference. In November 1969 representatives from twenty-six European countries met in Vienna to support the conference. The Soviet Committee for European Security was founded in 1971, and analogous national committees were formed under the direction of the local Communist parties throughout Western Europe. This phase of activism culminated with the 1973 World Congress of Peace Forces.

Soviet writers concede that in the mid-1970s the peace movement declined in most West European countries. But they argued that this decline differed from that of the late 1950s and early 1960s in that it grew out of victory rather than defeat: "Détente was developing, and the population in many West European countries did not see any immediate reasons for mass demonstrations."[153] The movement revived in the late 1970s in response to the "reactionary counterattack on détente."

The turning point was the "neutron bomb" episode of 1977–78. In August 1977 the WPC sponsored an International Ban the Neutron Bomb Week, which was followed in February 1978 by an Amsterdam international forum against the neutron bomb. The tiny Dutch Communist Party played a major role in mobilizing resistance to the weapon in the Netherlands, leading to spillover effects in West Germany and ultimately to President Carter's decision not to go ahead with development of the weapon.

These events seemed to confirm the orthodox Marxist-Leninist view that "unity of action" under Communist hegemony could be effective in shaping Western policy, which in turn may help to explain Soviet behavior during the INF controversy. The bureau of the WPC held a special session in Helsinki in December 1979 to plan a strategy, and in May 1980 the presidium of the WPC met in Budapest and issued an appeal for "joint action to prevent another world war." In late September the WPC sponsored the Sofia World Parliament of the Peoples for Peace, which culminated in the adoption of the People's Charter for Peace.[154] A delegation of the German Peace Union (DFU)—a front controlled by the German Communist Party (DKP)—went to Moscow as guests of the Soviet Peace Committee for what was apparently a strategy session. In November 1980 the DKP, DFU, and allied organizations launched the Krefeld Appeal, which gathered 800,000 signatures in opposition to the NATO deployments.[155]

Soviet writers characterized the peace movement as "generally democratic in character," but acknowledged the diversity of its social makeup, the contradictory stands taken by its participants, ideological dissimilarities, and even "irreconcilable views."[156] These qualities called for careful management by Communists thrust into a "vanguard" role, and the CPSU often was critical of the performance of the West European parties for their excessively dogmatic approach to the non-Communist peace movement. According to a mid-1983 *Kommunist* editorial, "certain comrades were unable to grasp the nature of the antiwar movements . . . , were not always able to overcome their prejudices against pacifist and ecological organizations with their inconsistent and contradictory arguments, and did not perceive the members of these movements as their objective allies in the struggle for peace."[157] The same editorial praised the work of the U.S., French, West German, Greek, Austrian, Swedish, and Swiss Communist parties in the antiwar movement, but pointedly made no mention of parties in four of the five deployment countries: Italy, Britain, Belgium, and the Netherlands. In the end the failure of the anti-INF campaign probably damaged the prestige of the International Department and strengthened the position of those who argued that peace activities and propaganda were not a substitute for intergovernmental negotiations.[158]

In addition to ebb and flow of the West European peace movement noted by Soviet analysts, there were secular changes in the relationship between it and the CPSU, as the latter slowly became more open to cooperation with non-Communist peace groups in the West. The Soviet authorities always promoted, with the limited means available, horizontal linkages between West European Communists and the local peace movements, but they moved more slowly in opening direct channels to non-Communist groups and individuals interested in working for peace. The Soviet Peace Committee began hosting peace-oriented Western groups in the late 1950s, and in October 1961 the Soviet Peace Committee hosted a delegation of Western peace marchers, most of whom were pacifists critical of Soviet as well as Western nuclear testing. But the effect of these meetings often was to reinforce concerns about the uncontrollability of non-Communist peace activists. Professors at Moscow State University had difficulty channeling the discussion between Soviet and Western interlocutors in purely anti-Western directions.[159]

Nonetheless, this kind of interaction grew steadily, especially in the 1970s and early 1980s. In 1984 it was estimated that two such delegations per week were arriving in Moscow, where they were briefed on Soviet international peace initiatives and such domestic activities as demonstrations, signature campaigns, and peace lessons in the schools.[160] Responding to overtures from primarily U.S. groups, Soviet organizations became involved in such enterprises as Grandmothers for Peace, the International Peace Lantern Project, Young Storytellers for Peace, and the Larry's Ice Cream "Building of Peace—One Scoop at a Time" ice cream exchange.[161]

Less of this kind of activity took place between the USSR and Western Europe, but a few such enterprises began developing in the early 1980s. A turning point was the Norwegian women's march that took place in the summer of 1982. This venture was proposed to the Soviet Peace Committee in November 1981 (through the Soviet representative at the Helsinki offices of the WPC) and approved in February 1982. After preparatory discussions with the Soviets about 250 women and 20 men from Norway, Sweden, Denmark, and Finland set out from Stockholm, accompanied by Grigorii Lokshin, secretary of the Soviet Peace Committee. Once inside the USSR they were joined by Soviet marchers and welcomed by people "weeping in the streets at the sight of the peace banners."[162] Apart from a contingent of Finnish Communists, most of the Nordic marchers were "liberal professional women" with no Communist affiliations. Building upon the pattern established in 1982, in 1984 ten Mothers for Peace from Britain made a nine-day visit to the USSR. Subsequently, a mixed group of British, Danish, and Soviet mothers went to the United States to spread their message.[163]

From the Soviet perspective there were both advantages and drawbacks to institutionalizing ties with non-Communist peace groups. By dealing with non-Communists, Soviet organizations vastly increased the range of groups and individuals in the West they were able to influence and lent greater credibility to whatever joint appeals and proclamations were concluded. But Soviet officials remained extremely sensitive to the slightest criticism of Soviet foreign and defense policy. In dealing with the West European Communist parties the International Department insisted upon a rigid double standard according to which Western military measures were condemned as war preparations while those of the USSR and its allies were justified as the main bulwark of world peace. Efforts to impose the same standard on the peace movement alienated many potential allies and even disturbed some non-Soviet functionaries in the WPC.[164] Even under Gorbachev the USSR continued to reject the "so-called theory of the 'equal responsibility' of the United States and the USSR for international tensions and the arms race."[165]

Apart from their tendency to criticize Soviet as well as NATO and U.S. policies, the other danger posed by non-Communist peace groups was their affinity for Soviet and East European dissidents, and especially for the independent peace groups that sprang up in the early 1980s. These groups quickly became a focal point of interest for sections of the non-Communist peace movement in the West, which saw them as a natural counterpart whose very existence answered charges that the Western peace movement was a one-sided phenomenon targeted at U.S. but not Soviet weapons.[166]

The most prominent such organization in the Soviet Union was the Group for the Establishment of Trust Between the USSR and the U.S.A., whose formation was announced at a Moscow press conference in early June 1982.[167] The group issued its "Appeal to Governments and Citizens of the USSR and the U.S.A.," that endorsed certain arms control measures and called on the Soviet and U.S. governments and the peoples of both countries to form a four-sided committee to seek ways to establish mutual trust. The Soviet authorities quickly moved to suppress the movement and to block contact between it and visiting Western peace delegations. Members of the group were placed under house arrest (Sergei Batovrin, the group's spokesman, was forcibly interned in a psychiatric hospital), while the official Soviet peace movement launched a counteroffensive against those in the West who had taken up the cause of these groups. In late 1982 Zhukov sent a series of sharply worded telegrams to Western peace groups in which he claimed that "not a single person supporting peace and disarmament has ever been detained."[168] In subsequent telegrams Zhukov acknowledged that members of the group had been arrested but attributed this to criminal behavior.

Nonetheless, the group on balance fared better than virtually any dissident organization in the USSR, in part because of the government's reluctance to alienate the Western peace movement. In September 1982 twenty members of the U.S. freeze movement appealed for Batovrin's release in a letter to Brezhnev.[169] Two days after the letter was reported in the Western press Batovrin was released as an outpatient, pending the findings of a medical commission that was to rule on his sanity. According to Peter Reddaway, by 1983 the Group for the Establishment of Trust was virtually the only Soviet dissident group still functioning openly in Soviet society, albeit in the face of intensive KGB harassment.[170]

Harassment of dissidents at home undercut implementation of what appears to have been a decision in principle to expand the links between the official Soviet peace movement and non-Communist peace groups in the West. Official Soviet and East European representatives took part in an all-European gathering of non-Communist disarmament groups for the first time in July 1984 in Perugia, Italy.[171]

The Soviet debut was marred, however, by sharp disputes over a variety of issues. Participants jeered as Evgenii Silin, the deputy chairman of the Committee for European Security and Cooperation, and Lokshin, secretary of the Soviet Peace Committee, denounced as hooligans members of the Group for the Establishment of Trust, defended the Soviet Union's INF countermeasures, and explained why there could be no differences in the USSR between official and public opinion. The Soviet representatives also threatened to withdraw in protest against a demonstration by Italians on behalf of Charter 77 and Solidarity.

The general decline of the mass peace movement after the initial INF deployments in late 1983 led to a shift in emphasis in Soviet peace activities, as the peace establishment began devoting more attention to smaller, elite groups such as physicians, scientists, and other specialists.[172] One of the important new forms of elite interaction to emerge was the International Physicians for the Prevention of Nuclear War (IPPNW), which won the 1985 Nobel Peace Prize.[173] Like other public organizations in the USSR, the Soviet section of the IPPNW was controlled by the party, but it was granted certain special privileges that enhanced its credibility. For example, in 1982 Soviet and U.S. members of the IPPNW appeared on Soviet television for a live roundtable discussion of nuclear issues.

Another new group was the Soviet Scientists Committee for Peace, against the Nuclear War Threat that was set up in 1983 to conduct studies on such issues as the destabilizing effects of INF deployments and SDI. Initially intended to be a propaganda instrument directed at Western scientists, the committee later evolved into a source of genuine expertise for the civilian leadership, which was dissatisfied with its total reliance on the general staff for information about military issues.[174]

Efforts to cultivate the scientific community and the intellectual elite increased dramatically under Gorbachev, whose "new political thinking" consciously echoed the wording of the Russell-Einstein manifesto, and who obviously enjoyed meeting personally with writers and intellectuals. The high point of these efforts was the holding in February 1987 of the Moscow forum, For a Nuclear-Free World, For the Survival of Humanity, which was billed as a gathering of the world's intellectual elite and had virtually no connection to the "masses." Apart from the section composed of Western religious leaders, Communist and front participation in the forum was kept to a minimum, and in contrast to the usual Soviet practice there was no attempt to gather signatures on a concluding appeal or communiqué.

Another breakthrough of the Gorbachev period was the founding of the International Foundation for the Survival and Development of

Humanity, of which Andrei Sakharov was a leading member. The foundation was established in January 1988 with offices in Washington, Moscow, and Stockholm. Although its positions (especially criticism of SDI) coincided with those of the Soviet government on some points, the foundation itself was independent and transnational, and as such reflected regime acceptance of an unprecedented element of pluralism in international contacts.

While Gorbachev's reforms led to a revitalization of the Soviet peace dialogue with Western elites, they spelled disaster for what was left of the mass-oriented Communist peace movement that was launched in the late 1940s and that as recently as the early 1980s had managed to adapt somewhat to changing conditions in Europe. By the end of 1989 the future of the WPC was very much in doubt as the East European countries withdrew their financial support, as the USSR shifted its own priorities, and as domestic liberalization made it increasingly difficult to organize peace delegations that would parrot the official line (which in any case was constantly changing in radical directions) on every issue. Officials from the Soviet Committee for the Defense of Peace acknowledged attempts to "enlist the informals in their work," but enjoyed little success in this regard.[175]

9 CSCE and the "All-European Process"

The CSCE, 1973–75

Background

In the Western literature the origins of the CSCE usually are traced to the February 1954 foreign ministers conference, at which Molotov introduced his proposal for a general European treaty on collective security in Europe.[1] Molotov did not actually call for a single all-European meeting such as Brezhnev later achieved with the Helsinki conference, but rather an institutionalized system of "regular or, when required, special conferences at which each state shall be represented by a member of its government or by some specially designated representative."[2] In addition to these conferences, the draft provided for two standing bodies, a "consultative political committee" and a "military consultative organ." As permanent members of the UN Security Council, the United States and China would be permitted to send observers to the organs set up in accordance with the treaty. The USSR never was able to generate much support in the West for this proposal, even after it was altered to provide for U.S. participation, and the campaign for a conference was quietly shelved.[3]

Eastern interest in an all-European conference revived in the mid-1960s, shortly after Khrushchev's ouster. In a December 1964 speech before the UN General Assembly, Polish foreign minister Rapacki proposed that a conference be convened to implement the Polish plan for a freeze on nuclear armaments in central Europe.[4] In January 1965 the PCC endorsed a "conference of European states to discuss measures for ensuring collective security in Europe."[5] At the Twenty-Third Party Congress in early 1966 several speakers including Brezhnev referred to the need for an "appropriate international conference" to discuss security.[6]

The Warsaw Pact launched a full-scale campaign on behalf of the conference at the July 1966 Bucharest meeting of the PCC. The Bucharest declaration called for a "general European conference" that would deal with the peaceful settlement of disputes and the development of economic, scientific, and cultural relations, and would result in a "general European declaration."[7] The Pact also called for the simultaneous dissolution of NATO and the Warsaw Pact or, as a first step, of the military organizations of the two alliances. The provisions of the declaration were substantially reiterated in the "Statement on European Security" adopted by the 1967 Karlovy Vary meeting of European Communist parties.[8]

The most remarkable aspect of the Soviet campaign for a European conference was the way it advanced in the face of Western skepticism. This advance cannot be attributed, at least in its early stages, to the inherent attractiveness of the Soviet proposals, which were more militant and transparently anti-U.S. than that of 1955. Nor did public pressure, which came too late to influence government decisions and was in any case confined to marginally effective front organizations, play a decisive role.[9] Two other factors probably did help to assure the success of the Soviet campaign: the active bilateral diplomacy conducted by the USSR in the late 1960s, much of it by Kosygin, and the West's own growing interest in a package deal in which the USSR would secure the conference in exchange for progress on conventional arms reductions and Berlin.

After a temporary halt caused by the 1968 crisis in Czechoslovakia, in March 1969 the East resumed its campaign for a conference. The Budapest meeting of the PCC issued the "Appeal to All European Countries" for a "general European conference to consider questions of European security and peaceful cooperation."[10] The following month the North Atlantic Council expressed its desire "to explore with the Soviet Union and the other countries of Eastern Europe which concrete issues best lend themselves to fruitful negotiation and early resolution."[11] It added that "any negotiations must be well prepared in advance, and that all governments whose participation would be necessary to achieve a political settlement should take part." This formulation sidestepped the question of East German recognition, but clearly implied the inclusion of the United States (with its four-power rights) and Canada (which had troops stationed in West Germany and would take part in any force reduction talks). In June 1970 the PCC declared that "the question of the makeup of the conference participants has been clarified," and endorsed the participation of the GDR and the FRG, "on an equal footing with each other and on the basis of equal rights with the other European states," as well as of the United States and Canada.[12]

Having secured, as was seen in chapter four, certain bilateral commitments to the discussion and possible holding of a conference, the USSR began pressing for multilateral preparatory consultations. At Oreanda in September 1971 Brandt agreed to promote what in effect would be a series of multiple bilateral consultations. Two months later Pompidou went a step further by endorsing multilateral contacts "as soon as possible." But the real breakthrough occurred in May 1972 when Nixon and Brezhnev agreed that multilateral consultations could begin after the final signature of a Berlin agreement and that the conference itself should be convened "without undue delay." Meeting shortly after the May summit, the North Atlantic Council endorsed the Nixon-Brezhnev formulation, and in July the Finnish government issued invitations to the multilateral consultations to all "interested states," including the United States, Canada, and the two Germanies. In the ensuing months, thirty-four participating countries accepted the Finnish invitation, and the exploratory phase of the conference got under way in November 1972.[13]

The Pact first formally proposed a conference agenda in Prague in October 1969. It contained two items: "European security and renunciation of the use of force or the threat of its use in the mutual relations among States in Europe," and "expansion of trade, economic, scientific and technical relations on the principle of equal rights aimed at the development of political co-operation among European States." In their May 1970 response the NATO ministers proposed that the agenda include "the development of international relations with a view to contributing to the freer movement of people, ideas and information."[14] The East was critical of the NATO call for talks on freer movement, but eventually came to accept that some discussion of what later were called Basket III issues was inevitable. In June 1970 the Pact added a third item to its proposed agenda: "The establishment at the all-European conference of an organ for questions of security and co-operation in Europe." Thus by the time the Helsinki preparatory consultations convened, there was an informal understanding among the participants about four items to be discussed: (1) security; (2) economic, technological, and environmental cooperation; (3) cultural and humanitarian cooperation; and (4) the possible establishment of a permanent body to promote European cooperation.

The preparatory consultations were "in many ways the key to the entire subsequent negotiation, since they set the agenda and the procedures that guided the Conference throughout its existence."[15] The Soviet objective was to move as rapidly as possible from the consultations to the convening of a formal conference at the highest possible level. Soviet delegates called for a quick preparatory meeting that would be concerned chiefly with organizational matters and that would leave the elaboration of a detailed agenda to the foreign ministers at the first stage of the conference.[16] Accordingly, the Eastern delegations refrained from introducing substantive proposals, and engaged in all kinds of complex maneuvers (including opposing a Christmas break) to speed the talks.

Led by the members of the European Community, the Western participants took a different approach. They proposed that the consultations draw up a series of agreed mandates that would be given to the committees of the second stage of the CSCE to serve as instructions for the drafting of the final document. Thus in early 1973 Italy, Belgium, and Denmark submitted, by prearrangement with their EC partners, detailed proposals for instructions to the drafting committees in each of the three CSCE "baskets" (the term itself came into use during the consultations): security; economic cooperation and environmental protection; and human contacts and cultural and information exchange. The East strongly objected to this approach, which it claimed was tantamount to transforming the consultations into a preliminary conference. Thus one of the earliest disputes in the talks was over the term "mandate" itself, which the Soviet delegates at first purported not to understand, and later rejected as "totally unacceptable."[17]

By refusing to agree to a formal conference until instructions to the committees had been drafted, the West was able to exert considerable leverage over the USSR, which was eager for the conference to begin. Thus in early 1973 the Soviet Union reluctantly adopted the Western approach by putting forward four sets of tasks (*zadanie*) for the drafting committees, three of which corresponded to the Western proposals, and a fourth which was concerned with the creation of a permanent consultative body.

In the next six months the delegates thrashed out a ninety-six-paragraph document entitled "Final Recommendations of the Helsinki Consultations" that presaged in condensed form the Final Act. The recommendations gave the committees a mandate to work on such controversial topics as "the freer and wider dissemination of information of all kinds" and "the question of prior notification of major military movements." They also established the format of the conference. On the basis of a French proposal that was intended to partially satisfy the Soviet demand for a high-level opening, it was agreed that the conference would take place in three stages: the first at the ministerial level in Helsinki, the second at the working level in Geneva, and the third in Helsinki at a level that would be decided in the course of the conference. As was seen in chapter four, the Western delegations were able to use Brezhnev's desire for a summit-level conclusion to exert leverage in the drafting of the Final Act. The Final Recommendations also included a set of rules of procedure for the conference. These rules, which became known as the Blue Book (after the color of the paper on which they were printed), stipulated that decisions would be taken by consensus, that the chairmanship would rotate by country (this was disadvantageous to the Warsaw Pact, which had only seven members) and that the host country would provide a temporary executive secretariat.

The Final Act

In accordance with the agreement worked out in the preliminary consultations, the foreign ministers of the thirty-five met in Helsinki in July 1973. Technically their main order of business was to formally adopt the Final Recommendations concerning rules of procedure, agenda, and instructions and to set the date for the second stage of the conference. These tasks were accomplished in the communiqué issued at the conclusion of the meeting, which stipulated that the second stage of the conference would begin in Geneva in September, "in order to pursue the study of the questions on the agenda and in order to prepare drafts of declarations, recommendations, resolutions or any other final documents on the basis of the proposals submitted during the first stage as well as those to be submitted."[18] In addition to these formalities, many countries introduced draft proposals. The USSR introduced a draft "General Declaration," East Germany and Hungary an economics proposal, Bulgaria and Poland a human contacts proposal, and Czechoslovakia a plan for an advisory committee responsible for conference follow-up.[19]

In these proposals and the accompanying speeches the Eastern foreign ministers tried to win back ground they had been forced to yield in the preliminary consultations. Gromyko "blithely ignored the laborious work at [Helsinki] and went back to formulations which his negotiators had tried in vain to include in the Final Recommendations."[20] Otto Winzer of East Germany misquoted the recommendations by referring to the (nonexistent) "stipulation in the Final Recommendations that . . . cooperation must be conducive to the strengthening of peace, understanding among peoples and the spiritual enrichment of the human being."[21] The East also tried to downplay the overall significance of the drafting instructions by refusing to annex them to the conference communiqué. Although the communiqué stated that the ministers had adopted the Final Recommendations, they were not made an integral part of the communiqué and not published in the USSR.

Nevertheless, in drafting the Final Act the Eastern delegations were forced to work in general conformity with the mandate contained in the Final Recommendations. The proposals they submitted differed from the specific wordings contained in the recommendations on many points, but conformed to the agenda and general provisions hammered out in Helsinki. The East even began to invoke the conference mandates to counter delaying tactics on the Western side, opposing, for example, Western proposals for the adoption of "work programs" or "agendas" for the work of each subcommittee which the East argued would mean a renegotiation of the mandates concluded in the preparatory phase.[22] At other points in the confer-

ence Eastern participants complained about the "multitude of detailed draft documents, often exceeding the mandate set out in the
Final Recommendations," and about the West's "unbalanced" approach to the conference. (Of twenty-six proposals tabled by Western
countries, fifteen related to Basket III and only two to Basket I.)[23]

Like many international documents, the Final Act was not negotiated from scratch but was drawn, by mutual agreement of the
conference participants, from existing sources. At the preparatory
consultations East and West differed over the particular sources to be
used. Speaking on behalf of the East, Poland proposed that in drafting
the final document the committees should draw upon four sources:
the UN Charter, the 1970 UN Declaration on Principles of International Law Concerning Friendly Relations and Co-operation among
States, the 1970 UN Declaration on the Strengthening of International Security, and all "appropriate formulations of the agreements
made between states in view of a lessening of international tensions
and to ensure security in Europe."[24] The Western participants maintained as acceptable only the first two items on this list, the Charter
and the Declaration on Friendly Relations.[25]

The reasons for the differing positions on the question of sources
were fairly obvious. One of the USSR's main objectives was to obtain
multilateral endorsement for its bilateral settlement with the Federal Republic of Germany. Therefore, it wanted to transfer passages
from the Eastern treaties of 1970–73 to the Final Act. Western governments, in contrast, were strongly opposed to any drafting instructions that would have facilitated the multilateralization of existing
bilateral agreements, and were understandably suspicious of Soviet
efforts to introduce an array of UN resolutions into the drafting process. The West came out somewhat ahead on this issue, although it
did not win a complete victory. The Final Recommendations referred
to "the purposes and principles of the United Nations," listed the ten
key principles later to become the Helsinki "decalogue," and stated
that in drafting, "the Committee/Sub-committee shall take into account in particular" the friendly relations declaration "in accordance
with the Charter of the United Nations."[26]

Other documents that influenced the wording of particular provisions included the International Covenant on Civil and Political
Rights and its companion document, the Covenant on Economic, Social and Cultural Rights, both of which contained "escape clauses"
that could be interpreted as sanctioning the suspension of human
rights by governments under certain conditions. The Eastern countries traditionally had been unenthusiastic about all international
agreements dealing with human rights, and did not accede to the covenants when they were adopted by the General Assembly and opened
for signature in 1966. As it became clear, however, that human rights

would become a topic in the European security conference, the USSR and its allies realized the potential utility of these documents, which all but one bloc country signed and ratified in 1972–74.[27] The East also managed to secure the inclusion in the Final Recommendations of a passage stipulating that the drafting committee "shall bear in mind the results of the Intergovernmental Conference on Cultural Policies in Europe, Helsinki, June 1972 including the broader concept of culture outlined by that Conference." This conference had been convened under UNESCO auspices, and had devoted considerable attention to the role of governments in promoting the "democratization of culture."[28] As an Italian participant later wrote, the reference to UNESCO and the conference had "a substantially negative influence on the entire mandate on cultural matters."[29]

The form of the final document also was a matter of dispute, as the negotiators recognized that the placing of provisions and the interrelationship of the different baskets to each other would have an effect on content. The centerpiece of the Soviet negotiating effort was the draft "General Declaration" introduced by Gromyko. The USSR wanted to lend greater political and legal stature to this document than to those provisions spelling out concrete obligations, thereby making fulfillment of the latter conditional upon compliance with the former. This dispute was resolved by an ambiguous compromise. The Declaration on Principles Guiding Relations between Participating States (as the "General Declaration" came to be called) did come to occupy a special place in the Final Act, and Eastern legal scholars subsequently developed the theory that the act incorporated "decisions of a differentiated legal character."[30] In this interpretation, the norms contained in the Declaration on Principles "are absolutely binding in international law," whereas the other provisions were more provisional and hortatory.[31] From the Western perspective, the somewhat special status of the Declaration on Principles was counterbalanced by the fact that the Final Act was, as the West had insisted, a single document of which both the security and human rights provisions formed integral parts.

A related issue of form concerned the so-called "mini-preamble" to Basket III, the drafting of which the Soviets at first insisted would have to precede the drafting of all substantive points on information and human contacts. The suspected Soviet intent was to introduce caveats—such as making fulfillment of Basket III provisions subject to national "laws and customs"—that would negate the force of any commitments. In the face of adamant Soviet resistance, the West agreed to a separate preamble, but managed to water down its provisions in a way that in the Western view did not give the East an excuse for not carrying out the obligations that followed.

Even as they tried to use formal devices and references to earlier documents to shade the meaning of the Final Act, the participants left nothing to chance when it came to individual words and phrases. These became the real battleground of the negotiations. Of the hundreds of disputes on wording, the most noteworthy concerned the inviolability of frontiers and human rights. Gromyko's draft "General Declaration" stipulated that the signatories would "regard the existing frontiers in Europe as inviolable now and in the future, will make no territorial claims upon each other and acknowledge that peace in the area can be preserved only if no-one encroaches upon the present frontiers." This language was much too sweeping and categorical, not only for the West Germans, who wanted to hold open the door to reunification by peaceful means, but for countries such as Spain and Ireland with unresolved territorial disputes.[32] After a prolonged deadlock a compromise was reached in which the signatories affirmed the inviolability of frontiers and pledged to "refrain now and in the future from assaulting these frontiers." Elsewhere in the Final Act it was stated that "frontiers can be changed, in accordance with international law, by peaceful means and by agreement." The 1970 treaty between the USSR and West Germany made no provision for the change of frontiers, peacefully or otherwise. The Soviet Union thus in effect was forced to give back some of what it had gained from Brandt five years earlier.

Human rights was another area in which particular words were the object of prolonged debate. Britain and the USSR were involved in a dispute over the translation of the word "belief" (*conviction/Bezeugung/credo/credo*) into Russian, which was never really resolved in the negotiation of the actual text, but dealt with through a series of unilateral statements in the conference journal.[33] In the preliminary consultations the USSR had won an important victory by having language from Article 18 of the International Covenant on Civil and Political Rights, with its qualifying provisions, adopted as the title of point seven in the CSCE decalogue.[34] Although the word *ubezhdenie* appeared in this title (and five times in Article 18), the USSR insisted upon substituting *vera* (which did not appear in Article 18) for it in the Final Act.[35] No amount of Western pressure could restore the original term, and Britain and eight supporting delegations finally made a declaration in the journal that it was willing to accept the Soviet language on the understanding that it meant *vera*, a position to which the USSR gave a qualified assent in the parallel statement in the journal.[36]

Perhaps more important than the "real" meaning of the Final Act as determined by its sources, form, and wording were the interpretations placed upon it by political leaders, scholars, journalists, and others. Politically, what people in the East and West *thought* the Final Act meant became more important than what was painstakingly worked out by the negotiators. In promoting its interpretation of the Final Act, the USSR drew distinction between what it saw as the static and dynamic elements in the document. Although the Western negotiators managed to secure language that sanctioned the possibility of peaceful change in Europe and even to "win back" points that the West Germans had conceded in their bilateral *Ostpolitik*, the USSR later acted as if CSCE represented the final closing of all territorial and political issues in Europe and that any discussion of change was illegal under the Final Act. Western commentators critical of the Final Act lent credence to this position by uncritically repeating Soviet claims about ratification of the postwar territorial and political status quo. In addition, Soviet officials claimed that the Final Act barred attempts by the West to challenge the social status quo in the East through actions the Communist authorities regarded as subversive. In his speech to the concluding session of the conference, Brezhnev remarked that the "information media can serve the goals of peace and confidence, or they can spread the poison of discord," and expressed the hope that the results of the conference would serve as a "correct guideline" in determining cooperation in this area.[37]

While claiming that the Final Act ruled out most forms of change in the East, Soviet officials argued that the Final Act constituted a mandate for change in East-West relations and especially for the transition to a new phase of "military détente." In his opening speech to the conference Gromyko had spoken of "setting long-range guidelines for peaceful development in Europe," which he called the "main political import of the all-European conference's decisions."[38] In his closing speech two years later, Brezhnev proclaimed that "the document we are to sign, while summarizing the results of the past, addresses itself in content to the future. . . . [It] is a broad but clearcut platform of unilateral, bilateral and multilateral action by the states for years and perhaps decades to come."[39] The 1976 Berlin Conference of European Communist Parties (which the USSR had postponed to ensure that it took place after the completion of the CSCE) issued a final document, "For Peace, Security, Cooperation and Social Progress in Europe," that called for "strict observance" of the Final Act and reiterated many of the positions taken by the Eastern delegations at the CSCE.[40]

Conference Follow-up

While the Soviet leaders portrayed the Final Act as a mandate for change in Europe, by 1975 they were not enthusiastic about creating permanent institutions responsible for monitoring or implementing its provisions. This represented a change in Soviet policy, which at one point strongly favored a "permanent organ" for security in Europe. As far back as 1954 Molotov had proposed a pan-European system of institutionalized consultation. In an interview with the *New York Times* more than three years later Khrushchev suggested that "the question of establishing European security should lead to the liquidation of military blocs and perhaps the creation of some kind of body where members could exchange views and prevent new tensions. It might be a special body or if enough confidence could be established, the discussions might be carried out in the United Nations."[41]

Soviet interest in a permanent European body resurfaced in June 1970, when the Pact's Budapest appeal added a third item to the two-point agenda it had put forward in Prague nine months earlier. It called for the "establishment at the all-European conference of an organ for questions of security and cooperation in Europe." The appearance of this item on the agenda may have been motivated by tactical considerations. In December 1969 the government of British prime minister Wilson had put forward a proposal for a "standing commission" on East-West relations that would handle the preparatory work for a security conference and that might also serve as a permanent follow-up institution to a conference.[42] Some Western experts thought that such a commission could be modeled on the Western European Union and hoped, among other things, that it could be used to "train Eastern experts in arms control skills."[43] The idea was disliked by most of the other Western powers, but in deference to Wilson was placed on the agenda of the May 1970 meeting of the NATO foreign ministers, who cautiously concluded that "the establishment of a permanent body could be envisaged as one means, among others, of embarking on multilateral negotiations in due course."[44] At this same meeting the NATO ministers called for "exploratory talks" on force reductions in Europe. The Pact's June 1970 proposal thus was probably a response of sorts to the Western call for conventional force reduction talks. According to the Budapest Memorandum, "the question concerning the reduction of foreign armed forces . . . could be discussed in the organ which it is proposed to establish at the all-European conference."[45] The January 1972 Prague summit again endorsed the idea of a standing organ, but appeared to back off from assigning it an arms control role, and instead mentioned its potential use in promoting economic and cultural cooperation.[46]

The Helsinki consultations got under way in November 1972 with the Soviet Union introducing a three-part agenda, much along the lines of the 1970 declaration. Item three called for discussion of a consultative organ, similar to the one that Molotov and Bulganin had proposed in the mid-1950s. The chief Soviet negotiator stressed that a permanent organ would not limit the sovereignty of the participating states, was not intended to drive the United States out of Europe, and was compatible "with the system of relationships between some of the European states"—a formulation that the Western delegates took to mean the EC.[47] But Western delegations were not swayed by the arguments in favor of the permanent organ, and were reluctant even to mention it in the final recommendations. Instead they argued that follow-up to the conference should be discussed only after the results of the CSCE were known. The Soviets eventually agreed to a compromise French suggestion that the Final Recommendations mandate the consideration of a "follow-up to the conference" that would "give effect to the decisions of the Conference and to further the process of improving security and developing co-operation in Europe." The modalities of the follow-up were not otherwise defined, but at Eastern insistence "proposals of an organizational nature" were explicitly sanctioned in the recommendations.

In his opening speech to the July 1973 Helsinki Conference, Foreign Minister Gromyko stated that "the expansion of cooperation in the interests of peace would be served by the development of political consultations and exchange of information between States in Europe."[48] He went on to argue that consultations among states "seeking a better understanding of their respective positions with a view to bringing them closer together broaden possibilities for actions to consolidate peace." At the same session Czechoslovakia submitted a draft proposal for the creation of an advisory committee on security and cooperation in Europe. In addition to arranging future all-European conferences, the committee would "undertake periodic exchanges of views and information on questions of general interest relating to the strengthening of security and the development of cooperation in Europe."[49] It would also, "as the need arises and as may be agreed in each particular case . . . convene meetings of experts or set up working groups to prepare practical measures relating to the strengthening of security and the development of cooperation between States in Europe." The committee would be composed of "representatives of all the interested States of Europe, the United States and Canada."[50]

The USSR at first championed the Czechoslovak proposal, but gradually lost interest in it in the face of Western opposition and out of concern that a permanent organ would become a standing tribunal for the condemnation of Soviet human rights violations. The communiqué issued after the Warsaw Pact summit of April 1974 endorsed the creation of a "permanent security council for Europe aimed at building new relations between all states," but this was the last time a permanent CSCE organ was mentioned in a Pact document.

The following month the USSR accepted the basic outlines of a follow-up proposal put forward by Denmark on behalf of the EC nine. It called for the convening, in 1977, of a meeting of high officials from the participating states for two purposes: (1) to evaluate the way in which the decisions of the conference had been implemented; and (2) to present, in the light of this evaluation, proposals for further CSCE-related activities.[51] The Danish proposal became the basis for the follow-up section in the Final Act, in which the signatories "resolve to continue the multilateral process initiated by the Conference." The first step in this process was to be a meeting in Belgrade, which in turn would "define the appropriate modalities for the holding of other meetings which could include further similar meetings and the possibility of a new Conference." It was further stipulated that the Belgrade and all subsequent meetings would use the same rules of procedure and working methods that had applied in the CSCE.

In addition to the Belgrade meeting, the Final Act mandated the convening of two expert meetings: one of specialists "to pursue the examination and elaboration of a generally acceptable method for the peaceful settlement of disputes," and a scientific forum comprised of leading personalities from the participating states. The scientific forum was a West German initiative that provoked little controversy but that was important in establishing the precedent for other such meetings after Belgrade. The other meeting grew out of a dispute between Switzerland and the USSR regarding a Swiss proposal to include within the Final Act a convention on a European system for the peaceful settlement of disputes.[52] The Eastern delegations refused to consider any dispute resolution mechanism other than consultations, but in a compromise intended to mollify the Swiss they agreed to a provision in the Final Act mandating the convening of a meeting of experts to discuss methods for the peaceful resolution of disputes and specifically the Swiss proposal.

While these meetings were authorized in the Final Act, the section on follow-up made clear that the *first* post-Helsinki meeting was to be one scheduled to take place in Belgrade in 1977, and that the Belgrade meeting was to define the "modalities" of all subsequent CSCE meetings. This stipulation took on some importance in December 1975, when Brezhnev made an early attempt to hijack the CSCE process by proposing, in a speech to the Polish Communist Party Congress, the convening of all-European conferences in the fields of environmental protection, transportation, and energy.[53] Soviet representatives subsequently introduced the Brezhnev proposals in the ECE, where they cited the passage in the Final Act endorsing "meetings of experts of the participating States" as the basis of their approach. Western representatives countered that the Soviet proposals fell under the category of "other meetings" and thus could be discussed and mandated only at the Belgrade follow-up conference.[54]

The West thus managed to establish the principle, which had been expressed in somewhat muddled form in the Final Act, that meetings of plenipotentiaries would have a "coordinating" relationship to all expert meetings.[55]

_____

The Process

From Belgrade to Madrid

The Review Conference. The preparatory phase of the Belgrade meeting took place over a two and one-half-month period in the summer of 1977, and resulted in a detailed set of decisions that were to guide the follow-up conference. This document (which became known as the Yellow Book, after the paper supplied by the Yugoslav foreign ministry), included an agenda, timetable, and instructions for the establishment of five subsidiary working bodies. It specified which agenda items were to be discussed in open plenary sessions and which were to be discussed in closed meetings of the working bodies, and set mid-February 1978 as the time by which a final document should be completed. An annex to the Belgrade decisions contained an even more detailed work program that outlined a schedule of meetings for the plenary and working bodies.

The most controversial feature of this document was what became known as the "optical division"—the physical space between that part of the agenda providing for a "thorough exchange of views" on the implementation of the Final Act and that part concerned with "the deepening of mutual relations, the improvement of security and the development of cooperation in Europe, and the development of the process of détente in Europe."[56] This division allowed the Western delegates to claim that the review of implementation and the submission of new proposals were separate agenda items, and that a debate on compliance was the first order of business. The Eastern side wanted to avoid any review and to proceed immediately to the discussion of new proposals, particularly those related to military détente.

When the Western delegates began to conduct their review and to accuse the USSR and its allies of human rights violations, the Soviets initially responded by arguing that such a discussion was counter to point seven of the Final Act's Declaration on Principles Guiding Relations between Participating States, which forbids interference in internal affairs. This was a clear case of the East's invoking the declaration to qualify all other understandings in the Final Act, much as had been feared by the drafters in Geneva. In the end, however, the Soviets were goaded into defending themselves against the charges and into counterattacking, for example, by criticizing the United

States for everything from the trials of Sacco and Vanzetti to domestic unemployment. The Soviet response actually was welcomed by the Western delegations, who took it as a tacit admission that domestic conditions were a legitimate topic for discussion in the CSCE.

Under the second item on the agenda, the delegations submitted nearly 100 proposals. Two basic kinds of proposals were submitted. The first was for the adoption, in the concluding document of the Belgrade meeting itself, of language on issues related to the three CSCE baskets. Examples included proposals by Hungary affirming the right to work, by Bulgaria and the GDR calling on all participating states to accede to the International Covenants on Human Rights, and an Eastern Basket II proposal calling for the universal application of MFN among CSCE signatories and the elimination of all barriers to trade. The second kind of proposal called for the mandating, in the concluding document, of further activities and meetings linked to the CSCE process. Examples included the Soviet proposal for the convening of all-European, high-level meetings on the environment, energy, and transportation.

The fate of these proposals was virtually sealed from the outset by differences between East and West over the content of a concluding document. The USSR submitted a three-page draft that contained only its security and economic proposals, and made clear that it would not accept a document with any reference to human rights—much less one that endorsed any of the actual proposals put forward by NATO or neutral countries. For its part, the West would not accept a substantive document which dealt with Baskets I and II but that was silent on III.

The participants finally agreed on a short concluding document that did little more than call for a second review meeting, to take place in Madrid in 1980 following a preparatory conference that would determine the "appropriate modalities" for the meeting. The latter were to be framed on the basis of the Final Act and three other documents: the decisions adopted before the Belgrade meeting, the 1973 Final Recommendations, and the Belgrade Concluding Document.[57] The final document also established the date and duration of the two expert meetings mentioned in the Final Act and, in deference to Malta, mandated a third such meeting to consider Mediterranean affairs that was to take place in Valletta.

Expert Meetings.   In accordance with the mandate in the Final Act, the Swiss took the lead at the Montreux meeting, reintroducing the draft convention that had been rejected by the USSR and its allies. For disputes involving the interpretation of existing agreements, they proposed that all states submit to a mandatory court of arbitration. In disputes of a more political nature they proposed that states be required to submit the dispute to an independent investigation, mediation, and settlement commission. The decisions of this commission would not necessarily be binding, but participation in its work would be mandatory. The Swiss further proposed that both bodies be composed of independent individuals rather than state representatives, who would hold office for a fixed and lengthy term.[58]

The Warsaw Pact countries rejected the Swiss proposal and introduced their own draft proposal for a system of institutionalized consultation.[59] The Eastern proposal thus was both defensive in that it aimed to counter the unacceptable Swiss proposal, and offensive in that it pointed to a possible long-term Soviet interest in using consultations as a means of pressure over other states. The Montreux meeting ended without producing any agreement on matters of substance, but it did result in a formal report to the Madrid conference in which the participants recommended the convening of a second such meeting to continue discussion of the issue.[60]

The Hamburg scientific forum convened in February 1980, very much under the shadow of the Soviet invasion of Afghanistan and the resulting deterioration of East-West relations. The forum was brief—only two weeks—but helped to establish a strong precedent for future expert meetings on cooperation of various kinds. Western scientists condemned the treatment of their counterparts in the USSR (notably Sakharov), while the East took a studiously nonpolitical view of the forum, calling for "businesslike" discussion of scientific exchange, free from political interference.[61] The meeting adopted a final report for the Madrid review conference that outlined specific proposals for scientific cooperation.[62]

The Montreux, Hamburg, and Valletta meetings established the standard by which future meetings of experts within the CSCE process were judged. All three meetings technically fulfilled their mandates from the Belgrade conference by resulting in a concluding document that was reported back, as an agreed statement by the participants, to the next review conference. The Valletta meeting and, despite the controversies that surrounded it, the Hamburg forum both adopted long and relatively noncontroversial documents containing lists of recommended areas for cooperation.[63] The concluding document of the Montreux conference fulfilled the Belgrade mandate only in the purely formal sense, in that it adopted a document that said little more than that the experts had met and recommended meeting again in the future.

From Madrid to Vienna

The Review Conference.   The Madrid meeting was a crucial make-or-break point in the development of the CSCE process. After the outcome in Belgrade, failure to agree on a third follow-up meeting probably would have meant a breakdown in the CSCE process, while agreement to hold such a meeting, when it finally was reached, was widely seen as an irrevocable step toward institutionalization.[64]

At the preparatory meeting that was to adopt the agenda and rules of procedure, the Western delegations were surprised when the Eastern countries objected to a proposal by the Spanish hosts that the Yellow Book that had been used at Belgrade be applied to Madrid. Instead, the East proposed a long list of amendments, the most important of which was the elimination of the optical division. This would allow for the immediate discussion of new proposals and rule out an extended session exclusively devoted to implementation. In addition, the East wanted a stipulation that the review of implementation would not extend beyond six weeks. The East further surprised the other delegations by refusing to agree that in accordance with the precedent established at Belgrade the Madrid meeting would mandate a second review conference. The message was that Soviet agreement to another meeting was conditional upon what happened at Madrid, and that a heavy focus on human rights without sufficient attention to military détente would mean the effective end of the CSCE process.

These and other procedural disputes delayed the conclusion of the preparatory consultations, resulting in a somewhat comical beginning to the conference. At midnight on November 11 the Spanish foreign minister entered the deadlocked procedural deliberations to announce that he had a mandate to open the formal review conference, which he proceeded to do. This action deprived the East of further opportunities to delay the convening of the conference while it extracted concessions on procedural matters. This outcome was possible only because the conference was held in Spain, at that time not a member of NATO but very much associated with the EC countries and the United States. Whether a Finnish or other neutral foreign minister would have acted thus in defiance of Soviet wishes is uncertain.

The participants eventually agreed, three days after the formal conference was convened, on an agenda and rules of procedure. This agreement, which became known as the Purple Book, was based on a compromise worked out by the NNA.[65] The Soviet effort to radically revise the Belgrade procedures had failed, largely as a result of the decisive action of the Spanish government, but the East did manage to obtain some of what it demanded. The optical division was eliminated, although this in fact had no practical effect on the conference. The East decided not to introduce new proposals during what the West regarded as the implementation phase, lest their public relations effect be diluted. The East also secured an explicit six-week limit on the review phase of the conference. Western delegations later ignored this provision, however, claiming that it was based on a tacit understanding that the East would not commit egregious new violations of the Final Act in the course of the conference and that the Eastern side failed to observe this understanding, especially after the December 1981 imposition of martial law in Poland.[66]

In the most significant procedural change, the Purple Book differed from the Belgrade rules in that it did not set a definite date for closure and adoption of a final document. It stipulated that "every effort should be made to agree on the concluding document not later than 5 March 1981," but that the meeting itself would determine the date of closure. Given the consensus rule that governed CSCE meetings, this meant that one side or even a single country could literally compel the other participants to continue the meeting against their wishes. Finally, the Eastern delegations managed to prevent the inclusion of another follow-up meeting on the agenda, and would agree only to a discussion of the modalities for "other meetings." The chairman issued an interpretive statement claiming that "other meetings" was a category that included "the next meeting similar to the present one," but the Soviets would not agree in advance to a more precise commitment. While the West promised unconditionally to attend a third follow-up meeting, the East again signaled that it would withhold commitment to a continuation of the follow-up process until consensus was reached on a post-Madrid European disarmament conference.[67]

The mere fact that the Soviets were prepared to threaten a breakdown of the CSCE process to reshape the rules of procedure suggested the shift in negotiating leverage between East and West that had taken place in the CSCE since the early 1970s. In the Helsinki consultations and the early stages of the CSCE the USSR was the *demandeur*, while the West could exert leverage and extract concessions by raising the prospect of an inconclusive or delayed outcome. But by 1980 Western governments had developed their own vested interest in the process and could no longer exert that kind of leverage. Earlier toughness on the human rights issue only aggravated the problem, as the United States was widely criticized for its confrontational pose at Belgrade and thus was especially wary of causing a breakdown in Madrid. The general deterioration in East-West relations also neutralized potential Western leverage, as pressure groups and public opinion in Western Europe strongly supported ongoing talks with the East.

The review session was characterized by bitter charges and countercharges concerning the Soviet invasion of Afghanistan, the NATO dual track decision, and domestic conditions in East and West. In these arguments the USSR and its allies developed the thesis, first adumbrated at Belgrade, that their obligations to fulfill the provisions of Basket III were not absolute but conditional upon "the level of détente." The Soviets in effect were saying that if the East was not living up to the human rights provisions in the Final Act it was because the West had launched a counterattack on détente. Questions of implementation and compliance

thus could not be given priority if only for the simple reason that the only possible soil and invariable condition for the development of cooperation in humanitarian areas is the steady expansion of détente. . . . It is the level of détente that determines how rapidly the provisions of the Final Act dealing with the broadening of ties in the fields of culture, education and communication are implemented. The higher this level, the more favourable opportunities are created for interstate cooperation in the humanitarian field. Conversely, a worsening of the international situation leads to the scaling down of such cooperation.[68]

After six weeks the conference moved to the proposal stage. Eighty-seven proposals were submitted for inclusion in the final document, of which thirty-six were by Warsaw Pact countries, alone or in combination. (Eleven proposals were by Romania, which pursued an independent policy in the CSCE.) Of the twenty-five non-Romanian WTO proposals, three concerned basic principles, one related to Basket I (military détente), nine to Basket II, and twelve to Basket III. The USSR individually sponsored only one proposal, a call for the adoption of language in which states would pledge greater cooperation with regard to the content of school textbooks and would make particular efforts to include in them facts of "universal and pan-European significance," such as the defeat of fascism in World War II.[69]

As at Belgrade, the Madrid proposals were of two types: those consisting of language to be incorporated in a concluding document that would supplement the Final Act, and those calling for follow-up meetings and forums. The centerpiece of the Eastern effort was the Polish proposal for a conference on military détente, the counterpart to the French proposal along similar lines that was backed by the NATO countries.[70] The East put forward one other meeting proposal: a revamped call by Poland and the USSR for the convening of a high-level meeting on energy.[71] Most of the other proposals for follow-up meetings came from NATO countries. They included a French proposal for a cultural forum of leading artists and cultural figures, a proposal by Canada, Spain, and the United States for a meeting of experts on human rights, and a proposal by Canada, Denmark, Greece, the United Kingdom, and the United States for a meeting of experts to discuss emigration and family reunification.[72] Although Western delegations put forward most of the proposals for meetings of experts, they did so with reservations. Some governments were concerned that expert meetings would detract from the review conferences and channel discussion of compliance with the Final Act into a welter of discussions regarding technicalities. Instead of being held accountable for failing to observe the provisions of the Final Act, the USSR would be able to create the appearance of compliance by participating in meetings that would discuss differing interpretations of what compliance *meant*.

The Madrid meeting was a close-run thing. The imposition of martial law in Poland occurred just as it was ready to move to the drafting stage. The USSR and its allies argued that developments in Poland were an internal matter and insisted that the conference proceed in a businesslike way with the next task on the agenda—the drafting of the final document and a mandate for a new arms control forum. But in light of the events in Poland the Western delegations refused to schedule further meetings of the drafting group. However, they were in a "strange situation" thanks to the "inexorable consensus rule," which enabled the USSR and its allies to block an adjournment.[73] Unable to resolve an impasse over whether the meeting should adjourn or consider an East German work plan for the drafting group, the delegations sat through what became known as the "night of long silences" before the chairman finally called a "coffee break." The break lasted fifty-four and one-half hours and was used by various delegations to negotiate a compromise solution. The Soviets agreed that once three meetings of the drafting group were held, the conference could adjourn.

When it reconvened in November 1982 the climate of East-West relations was still bad, but passions over Poland had cooled. Both sides showed interest in a successful outcome, albeit for different reasons. The USSR wanted to secure a mandate for an all-European conference in the security field while giving up as little as possible in the area of human rights. The West also wanted the security conference, in part to defuse pressures from the peace movement. It also sought to ensure the continuity of the CSCE process. By July 1983 all parties had agreed to the essence of a Spanish draft, and in September the ministers gathered in Madrid to sign a concluding document.[74]

The West largely failed in its efforts to strengthen the Basket III provisions of the Final Act. It was unable to secure even partial endorsement of its main textual proposals in this area, which included prohibition of interference with foreign radio broadcasts, pledges that journalists would not be expelled for articles published in their newspapers, and guarantees of free access by citizens to reading rooms and cultural centers, of the right to strike, and of freedom of expression for dissidents and Helsinki monitors. The more extreme Eastern proposals—such as a Hungarian proposal for a guaranteed right to work and a joint GDR/USSR proposal on the responsibility of the mass media and journalists to promote disarmament, détente, and mutual cooperation between states—also disappeared without a trace.

But the West was able to secure agreement to several nonsecurity expert meetings. Notwithstanding earlier reservations about such meetings, the Western countries, and especially the United States and Canada, became increasingly committed to such meetings as a way of maintaining a balance between the security and nonsecurity aspects of the CSCE process. "The clearer it became that within the Concluding Document there was to be nothing in the human dimension sufficient to counterbalance the [CDE], the more the two North American participants . . . insisted on the two expert meetings they had proposed . . . in order to redress the balance."[75] The Madrid concluding document mandated five expert meetings: the Athens conference on the peaceful settlement of disputes, a Venice seminar on the Mediterranean, the Ottawa meeting on human rights, the Budapest Cultural Forum, and the Bern meeting on human contacts.[76] In addition, of course, the Madrid Concluding Document mandated the convening of and established the terms of reference for the Stockholm CDE. No country was fully satisfied with the outcome at Madrid, but all agreed that it was a distinct advance over what had been achieved at Belgrade, where the only result was preservation of the CSCE process itself.

The Expert Meetings.   The first post-Madrid expert meeting was the Athens conference on peaceful settlement of disputes. It met for six weeks in March–April 1984, attracted little public attention, and was even less productive than the Montreux meeting of six years earlier.[77] The Soviet and East European delegations basically adhered to the stance they had adopted at Montreux, and called for a system of obligatory consultation. They proposed that two states in a dispute could agree among themselves, on the basis of the required consultations, to bring in a third country mediator, but that setting up such machinery in advance was impermissible. Many of the smaller countries, notably Switzerland and Austria, were suspicious of the Soviet proposal for obligatory consultation, which they feared could open the way for small states to be bullied by the USSR.[78] The Athens meeting did succeed in adopting a formal report—shorter than the Montreux document but with an even longer title. It noted that "some progress was made" and called for further discussions "in an appropriate framework within the CSCE process," but did not recommend another meeting of experts.[79]

The Venice seminar on Mediterranean cooperation was brief (ten days as opposed to the six weeks provided for most expert meetings), and was mandated chiefly to satisfy Malta's perennial demand that consideration of Mediterranean issues be institutionalized with the CSCE framework.[80]

The Ottawa meeting, which the United States and other Western delegations had proposed partly in exchange for their assent to the disarmament conference, convened in May 1985. The mere fact that it was held reinforced two long-standing Western themes: the centrality of human rights and the full involvement of North America in the CSCE process. The Soviet and East European delegations took the position that in accordance with the Madrid mandate and the Final Act each state was permitted only to report on the human rights situation at home. The Soviet representative offered a glowing report of Soviet democracy and social and economic achievements, while seeking to rule out of order Western criticisms of Soviet and East European human rights performance. This approach failed, however, and as at Belgrade the Soviets and East Europeans were goaded into launching a strong attack on alleged Western violations of social, economic, and cultural human rights, such as the right to work, the right to health care, and the right to education.[81] Soviet delegates also elaborated the line they began to develop in Belgrade and Madrid which held that progress in "humanitarian cooperation" was dependent on the "level of détente" and introduced the concept of the "human right of the third generation" (first generation human rights being the classic political and civil rights traditionally championed by the West; second generation human rights being the social, economic and cultural rights stressed by the East), which they called the "right to life in peace."

East and West both introduced draft final documents. The Western draft included a number of concrete recommendations, including the admission of trial observers, the banning of the misuse of psychiatry, and further meetings on human rights in the CSCE context.[82] The Warsaw Pact draft included the concept of the "right to life in peace" and did not call for any concrete actions on implementation.[83] In an effort to bridge the gap and produce a document that would minimally fulfill the Madrid mandate, the NNA introduced a draft that basically repeated and reaffirmed language already in the Final Act and contained only a single recommendation: that the participating countries in the follow-up meeting in Vienna should "take into consideration" the calling of an additional meeting of experts on the respect for human rights.[84] The NATO countries indicated they would accept the NNA draft, but the Soviets refused. The East had the last word by introducing another draft that was based on the NNA proposal, but that excised the reference to possible future meetings. This was unacceptable to the West and the NNAs. Ottawa was thus the first CSCE meeting that failed to fulfill even the minimum requirements of its mandate.[85]

The Budapest Cultural Forum was the first CSCE meeting of any kind to be held in a Warsaw Pact country, and attracted considerable international interest. There were 116 proposals officially introduced, of which the USSR individually sponsored seven and cosponsored fifteen others. Of the fifteen cosponsored resolutions, fourteen were with one or more Warsaw Pact allies, and one, "Cooperation in the preservation of cultural heritage when under threat," was with Greece.[86] Many of the Soviet proposals were crudely political, although less so than those of its allies. Of the twenty-two proposals with which the USSR was associated, five dealt with peace, five were for symposia on various themes, five were calls for the "democratization" of culture or attacks on Western cultural "pollution," and five dealt with the dissemination of culture.

The West (the NATO countries plus Ireland) and the East (the Warsaw Pact countries minus Romania) submitted draft reports for adoption by the forum and submission to the Vienna review conference.[87] The Western draft endorsed cultural exchanges and cooperation as a "stabilizing factor" in interstate relations and called for practical measures that reflected the traditional Western emphasis on opening up Eastern societies through the removal of censorship and elimination of restrictions on communication. The Western draft also explicitly referred to "the North American heritage" and its relationship to Europe. The Eastern draft was more political, and contained long preambular language on "the continuing international tension as a result of the unrestrained arms race and the increasing danger of nuclear war," and the need for all persons active in the field of culture to strengthen "the humane ideas of peace, antimilitarism, social progress, mutual understanding and friendship among nations." It endorsed various bilateral and multilateral exchanges, but with the familiar caveats regarding nonintervention in internal affairs and respect for different "cultural systems."

Working from these drafts the Hungarians produced a bland compromise that would have been adopted, had it not been vetoed by Romania, which apparently did so to spite the Hungarian hosts and to protest Western criticisms of the architectural destruction of Bucharest. The compromise draft was harmless enough from the Western perspective. It contained no references to peace or other political themes, and for the most part avoided references to cultural systems and the kind of qualifying language favored by the East. It made no mention of individual rights or of breaking down barriers, but it had high praise for the meeting itself: the representatives "agreed that the Cultural Forum in Budapest was a valuable contribution both to the development of mutual understanding and to the promotion of international cultural cooperation and exchanges."[88]

The Bern meeting on human contacts took place in April–May

1986 and resulted in a major propaganda triumph for the USSR, as the United States was responsible for blocking the adoption of a document that the other thirty-four participants were prepared to accept. The Soviet sense of triumph was all the greater for its having occurred in Basket III, an area in which the USSR generally had been on the defensive. Although at Madrid the Soviet Union had been skeptical about the Bern meeting and had given only conditional assent to attend, under the influence of the Gorbachev reforms it adopted a positive stance, offering to discuss concrete improvements in visa issuing procedures and other matters. The positive Eastern approach brought to the fore tensions between the United States and Western Europe that had been evident as far back as the Belgrade conference, but that had been subsumed by the USSR's refusal to consider *any* substantive result in the area of human rights. Whereas the United States tended to regard CSCE meetings as forums in which to spotlight Eastern failures to observe the Final Act, the West Europeans saw these meetings as opportunities to reach concrete agreements in specific areas of interest, such as visa issuance procedures or conditions for journalists.[89] The West Europeans thus were willing to accept an NNA compromise draft that had been approved by the USSR and its allies that provided for concrete progress in a few areas but that in the view of U.S. policymakers watered down the general provisions contained in the Final Act.[90] Soviet propaganda subsequently made much of the thirty-four to one vote against the United States, even though on the *substance* of the issue under discussion, namely human contacts, there were few real differences among the Western delegations.

The Vienna Conference

The Vienna review conference was the first major CSCE event to take place entirely during the Gorbachev period. As such it reflected the new leadership's growing commitment to the "all-European process" and its view that the CSCE agreements could serve as "the blueprints for the construction of a common European home."[91]

The conference was dominated by the negotiations (discussed in chapter six) to produce mandates for two new arms control forums: a further stage of the CDE and a new forum to replace the MBFR talks on force reductions.[92] The Eastern delegations came to Vienna with a single draft mandate that was intended to revise the CDE's terms of reference by instructing it to discuss both force reductions and a further set of CSBMs, preferably covering independent air and naval as well as ground force activities. As was seen, the Western delegations forced a change in the Eastern approach and the eventual division of the arms control process between two forums, one to include the thirty-five CSCE participants and the other limited to the twenty-three members of NATO and the Warsaw Pact.

In his opening speech to the conference Shevardnadze stressed the importance of the East's arms control initiatives and launched a forceful and, from the point of view of the Western foreign ministers, counterproductive attack on the United States, which he blamed for the failure of the recently concluded Reykjavik summit.[93] Shevardnadze also sprang a major surprise when he proposed the holding of a CSCE conference on humanitarian cooperation in Moscow. The background to this proposal almost certainly was the perceived Soviet triumph in Bern, to which Shevardnadze alluded in his speech. The other major Eastern proposals included an offer by Czechoslovakia for the holding of an economic forum in Prague, a Bulgarian offer to sponsor an ecological forum in Sofia, an East German proposal for the facilitation of political dialogue and arms reductions, and a Polish proposal for a symposium on cultural heritage to take place in Cracow.[94]

The first round of the Vienna conference took place slightly before the dramatic improvements in Soviet human rights performance that began with Gorbachev's telephone call to the exiled Andrei Sakharov in December 1986. Thus in the seven-week review phase the Western delegations strongly criticized the USSR and some East European countries for violations of the Final Act. Most Western delegations were skeptical of the proposal for a Moscow human rights conference, although none would condemn it outright. The Soviet response was characteristically defiant, and included a Soviet and Bulgarian walkout when U.S. ambassador Warren Zimmermann set aside a moment of silence for Anatolii Marchenko, a dissident who died in a Soviet prison during the fifth week of the conference. Unlike at Belgrade and Madrid, where the thrust of Soviet Basket III responses was to protest Western interference in internal affairs, at Vienna the Soviet and Czechoslovak delegations downplayed the interference argument and counterattacked the West's human rights record. This reflected the more pugnacious Gorbachev approach to human rights, which had been seen already in his personal meetings with Western leaders.

The Western countries waited until the second phase of the conference (January 27–April 10, 1987) to introduce their proposals, which included a West German proposal for an economic forum, a British proposal for an information forum, and textual proposals by different Western states or groups of states.[95] By the end of the second phase there were 120 proposals on the table, of which 32 were for follow-up conferences and other CSCE-related activities, and the remainder for language to be included in a concluding document.

The Soviet delegates were highly critical of the West's failure to introduce new proposals on arms control and military détente, and stressed that progress in Baskets II and III would not be made until the USSR's Basket I priorities were addressed. In a plenary speech General Tatarnikov compared the "piles of proposals" in Basket III with the West's reticence in the security area.[96] For their part, many Western delegations were concerned that the Eastern stress on military issues and the virtual certainty that the CDE mandate would be renewed in some form posed a danger that the CSCE would be transformed into a one-dimensional, all-European security forum.

As was seen in chapter six, in July 1987 the West finally put forward its draft mandate for a post-Vienna arms control process. While the East was critical of its substantive provisions, the tabling of a proposal cleared the way to progress in drafting a final document. In an indication of their eagerness to conclude the meeting, in late September the Soviets surprised most of the other delegations by agreeing to accept as a "point of departure" a compromise Austro-Swiss Basket III draft which incorporated many of the West's textual proposals. The East spent the entire fourth round trying to neutralize its provisions by proposing over 200 amendments, but the USSR had nonetheless accepted in principle the core element in the Western approach, a Dutch proposal for a human rights monitoring mechanism that in effect would institutionalize what Soviet officials had long rejected as interference in internal affairs.[97]

Throughout 1988 the drafting of a concluding document continued, with three sets of issues to be resolved: (1) mandates for the arms control forums; (2) mandates for other meetings; and (3) textual proposals, the most controversial of which were in Basket III. Progress toward new security forums and progress on the textual proposals were linked, as the West tried to exploit Soviet eagerness for the former to secure concessions in the latter. This leverage was rather limited, however, given the West's own stake in the security side of the CSCE process and its desire to get conventional arms control talks under way.

There was an additional complicating linkage between the arms control issue and the mandating of non-security follow-up meetings. The Western delegations were wary of a "trivialization" of the CSCE process through the endless proliferation of meetings, but at the same time were in the paradoxical position, as at Madrid, of needing these meetings to maintain balance in the CSCE process in the face of Soviet attempts to stress the security component. The United States, which had fiscal as well as policy reasons for opposing the proliferation of meetings, at one point suggested that Vienna mandate no more than six—the number established at Madrid. The Soviets, on the other hand, generally favored a large number of meetings (a reversal of their Belgrade and Madrid positions), not only because of their generally more activist stance, but because, as some Western delegates suspected, they saw advantages in being able to bargain over the question of meetings, as particular Western governments and individual politicians became identified with proposals which the USSR had the power to block.

The Moscow human rights meeting remained especially controversial in the West, and the United States, Britain, and Canada withheld approval until almost the very end of the conference.[98] In order to neutralize the symbolism of a human rights meeting being held exclusively in Moscow (as well as to maintain Western leverage over the USSR), Western delegations proposed to make the Moscow meeting a part of a larger series of meetings that would comprise a CSCE Conference of the Human Dimension. The Moscow meeting, scheduled to take place in September 1991, technically would be the last phase of a three-part Conference of the Human Dimension of the CSCE. The first meeting was to take place in Paris in June 1989, and the second in Copenhagen in June of the following year.

The result of all this bargaining was a remarkable seventy-nine-page document that was signed at the foreign minister level in January 1989.[99] It included strengthened language on human contacts, including faster visa-processing procedures and other concrete improvements. In the information field it incorporated language that appeared to rule out the jamming of radio broadcasts. The document also provided for monitoring Eastern compliance with the human rights provisions of the Final Act and other CSCE documents. As noted, the USSR and its allies initially were opposed to such an approach but eventually agreed, in the concluding document of the review conference, to a series of monitoring measures, including the holding of "bilateral meetings with other participating States that so request, in order to examine questions relating to the human dimension of CSCE." The dates and places of such meetings are to be arranged "by mutual agreement through diplomatic channels," but participating states were guaranteed the right to report on responses to their requests for meetings to CSCE follow-up meetings and to meetings of the Conference of the Human Dimension.[100]

From the thirty-two proposals for follow-up meetings that were tabled, ten meetings were mandated (eleven if the CFE talks are counted as within the CSCE process): a continuation of the CSBM talks, the three human rights meetings, an April 1989 information forum to take place in London, an October 1989 meeting on the environment in Sofia, a March 1990 meeting on economic cooperation in Bonn, a September 1990 meeting on the Mediterranean in Mallorca, a January 1991 meeting on the peaceful settlement of disputes in Valletta, and a September 1991 meeting on cultural heritage in

Cracow. The next review conference was scheduled to begin in Helsinki in March 1992.

In addition to increasing the number of expert meetings, the Vienna conference introduced sweeping new procedures for their conduct. The practice of holding preparatory meetings before each expert meeting was abandoned. Instead, the agenda, work programs, number of working groups, and rules of procedure were spelled out in the Vienna document itself. This change (which in part accounted for the length of the document) marked a further institutionalization of the CSCE process and minimized the likelihood of the kinds of prolonged procedural disputes that had preceded the adoption of the Blue, Yellow, and Purple books.

CSCE after Vienna

Soviet enthusiasm for the "all European process" entered a new stage in 1989. In a *Pravda* interview that was devoted exclusively to the Vienna meeting and published the day after the signing of the concluding document, Gorbachev declared that the Helsinki process had been raised to a new high and that a step had been taken toward realization of the "common European home."[101] In his concluding speech to the conference Shevardnadze called the agreement a "landmark on the way to a fundamentally new Europe."[102] In the West enthusiasm for the results of Vienna meeting ran almost as high.

The approval expressed in both the USSR and the West reflected the balanced results of the CSCE process since 1975 and perhaps differing expectations of where this process ultimately was headed. With the start of the CFE talks and a new stage of the CDE the USSR had come close to realizing an aspiration it had had since 1954: the creation of a permanent all-European forum for political and security dialogue. In exchange, it had had to accept the United States and Canada as full participants in the CSCE and to accommodate persistent Western pressures for an opening of Soviet and East European societies: to permit the monitoring of human rights conditions, to increase access to information, and to provide military data and agree to on-site inspections.

In the first half of 1989 the emphasis in Soviet CSCE policy was on the domestic reform process and the need to harmonize Soviet internal laws and procedures with broader European norms. At the London information forum in April–May 1989 Soviet delegates linked glasnost and the new freedom of expression at home with Soviet foreign policy, and called for the creation of a common European informational space. Western delegations praised the new openness in the

USSR, but remained somewhat wary of state involvement in the sensitive sphere of information.[103]

At the Paris meeting of the Conference of the Human Dimension in May–June, France and the USSR put forward a joint proposal for the creation of a common European legal space through the rapprochement and harmonization, on a long-term basis, of legal systems and norms throughout the continent. This was the first joint human rights proposal cosponsored by NATO and Warsaw Pact countries. As at the information forum, the Soviet delegation in Paris stressed the link between the USSR's foreign policy and the changes under way at home, notably the convening of the new Congress of People's Deputies, several members of which participated in the CSCE meeting.[104]

While the Western participants generally praised the reforms in the USSR, Poland, and Hungary, they continued to criticize Romania, Bulgaria, Czechoslovakia, and East Germany. The United States put forward a proposal for free and secret elections in all CSCE states that at the time was seen as too radical and that "once again revealed the gap between the [West Europeans'] results-oriented human rights policy and the [U.S.] declaratory approach."[105] Because of Romanian intransigence the Paris meeting did not produce a final document, but its work was expected to contribute to the Copenhagen meeting scheduled for the following year.[106]

In the second half of 1989 Soviet and Western interest in CSCE shifted from domestic reform to international security. As the Warsaw Pact crumbled and as Western leaders and the general public questioned the future rationale for NATO, CSCE was increasingly put forward as the basis for a future European security order that would either supersede or absorb the military alliances. The desire for the CSCE process to play a greater role in security affairs was reflected in Soviet and Western proposals for the creation of permanent CSCE institutions that would anchor the United States and the USSR in the future European order. In his December 1989 Brussels speech Shevardnadze called for regular summit and ministerial meetings under CSCE auspices, and for the establishment of a CSCE secretariat and other permanent bodies such as a European risk reduction center.[107] These ideas were refined and elaborated by Soviet officials in early 1990,[108] and in essence endorsed by NATO in July 1990.[109] Most of them were formally adopted at the November 1990 Paris summit. In addition, of course, the CSCE process was the locus of the highly successful Vienna CSBM and CFE talks, which produced the arms control treaty and the East-West non-aggression agreement that were signed in Paris and that were to form the basis for a new European order following the reunification of Germany within NATO and the withdrawal of the USSR from Eastern Europe.

On the concluding day of the three-day November 1990 Paris summit, the thirty-four CSCE participants signed a sweeping declaration, known as the Charter of Paris, that committed the signatories to "democracy based on human rights and fundamental freedoms, prosperity through economic liberty and social justice, and equal security for all countries." In contrast to the Final Act of 1975, the Paris agreement stressed the fundamental rights of the individual, and contained little of the qualifying language sought by the East in previous CSCE documents. The Paris meeting also resulted in the establishment of several small but permanent CSCE institutions: a CSCE secretariat to be located in Prague, a center for the prevention of conflict in Vienna, and a Warsaw office for monitoring free elections. The Paris document also endorsed the establishment of a CSCE parliamentary assembly and the regular foreign ministerial and summit meetings proposed the previous year by Gorbachev and Shevardnadze. The ministers were to meet annually as a Council, beginning in Berlin in 1991, and the heads of government biannually, beginning in Helsinki in 1992.

10 Conclusion

The "Era of Stagnation"

The background to the sweeping post-1985 changes in Soviet policy was the "era of stagnation," which began under Brezhnev and continued (with a brief and partial break under Andropov) until Chernenko's death in early 1985. The Brezhnev period originally was seen, both in the USSR and to some extent the West, as one of foreign policy success for what then was called the "world socialist system." Khrushchev had made a promising start in "normalizing" relations with the West, but had failed to secure Western recognition of East Germany or to change the status quo in Berlin.

In contrast, through patient diplomacy and the steady buildup of military power Kosygin and Brezhnev had managed, without precipitating the crises that were the hallmark of the Khrushchev era, to conclude the 1970 treaty with West Germany and (in the Soviet view) its multilateral endorsement in the 1975 CSCE Final Act. In addition, the USSR gained recognition from the United States, in the 1972 SALT I treaty, of strategic nuclear parity, thereby underscoring the futility of any Western reversion to a "positions of strength" policy.

In the second half of the 1970s Soviet policy in Europe did not achieve new breakthroughs, and largely consisted of rhetorical and diplomatic calls for the implementation of understandings said to have been reached "in principle" earlier in the decade. The USSR and its allies called for joint East-West efforts to make détente "irreversible" and to supplement political with military détente. Western complaints about the Soviet nuclear and conventional buildup were brushed aside, while expressions of support for dissidence in the East (partly fueled by the human rights provisions of the Final Act) were protested as inadmissible or even "illegal" under the terms of the Final Act and other agreements.

The communiqués and basic principle agreements concluded with West European countries in this period were replete with references to the need to continue, expand, and deepen the process of détente—to in effect implement the détente mandate embodied in the Final Act. Unilateral Soviet statements were even more effusive, and expounded on the "irreversibility" theme while elevating the advance of Soviet power and prestige through détente to the status of a law of science.[1]

Much of this language was boilerplate, drafted by working-level diplomats and propagandists, but it nonetheless reflected Brezhnev's view of détente as an "almost mechanical process" of regular meetings, grandiose agreements, and incessant talk about peace—all of which it was claimed were both the result of and a further contribution to the USSR's growing might.[2] Soviet ideologists even squared the policy of détente with a "principled" commitment to world revolution by the doctrine (later repudiated by Foreign Minister Shevardnadze) that peaceful coexistence was a means of conducting the class struggle.[3] Brezhnev refused to rule out Soviet support for "progressive" forces in the West, and rebuffed a proposal by French president Giscard d'Estaing that France and the USSR should sign an agreement pledging mutual *ideological* coexistence.[4]

Brezhnev's mechanical conception of détente was based on a set of optimistic assumptions that were partly rooted in reality, and partly the result of the leadership's own ideological blinders and growing remoteness from the objective circumstances of domestic and international life.[5] After the 1968 invasion of Czechoslovakia and a series of reforms in CMEA and the Warsaw Pact the Soviet leaders appeared reasonably confident that Eastern Europe would remain relatively stable and that in the USSR itself the few signs of dissidence could be contained. They were aware of Western arguments to the effect that détente would have corrosive effects on the Eastern social system, but were inclined to discount these arguments as post facto rationalizations for a policy that the West had been compelled to adopt. From the Soviet perspective, Western refusal to accept the legitimacy of the Eastern order, perceived West German revanchism, and U.S. pretensions to military and political superiority *also* had been destabilizing. To permanently eliminate these challenges was worth the risk associated with the expanded contacts and human rights pledges that the West demanded in exchange.

Soviet leaders also operated on the basis of certain assumptions about the relative economic and technological performance of the two systems. Already in the 1960s they realized the groundlessness of Khrushchev's more extravagant claims about Soviet economic performance and the prospects for "burying" the West through economic competition. This led to the Kosygin reforms of 1965. The failure of these reforms resulted in intensified efforts to import technology and capital from the West, which also proved somewhat disappointing.

Despite these failures, Soviet writers (using what now are known to have been highly erroneous statistics) claimed that the USSR was closing the gap in national income with the United States, and portrayed the East as the most dynamic region of the world economy. They also noted that the West was beset by economic problems, and that while it was ahead in the purely technical dimensions of the race to develop new industrial and information technologies, the East had long run advantages in applying these technologies. They claimed that in the West technological change would only exacerbate contradictions that did not exist in the East. There was in any case a pronounced tendency under Brezhnev to downplay the purely economic aspects of the competition and to reassert the importance of politics and the subjective factor.[6] Whether consciously or not, in the 1970s the USSR channeled competition onto the military plane, not so much through overt uses or threats to use force, but through arms control and the endless talk of peace, both of which directed world attention to precisely those areas of competition where the Soviet Union was strongest.

Three developments of the late 1970s and early 1980s called into question these assumptions and set the stage—after having little initial effect—for the changes under Gorbachev. First, NATO's 1979 dual-track decision undercut claims that political détente was being supplemented by military détente and that trends in the correlation of forces were moving in favor of the East. While the political leadership focused on INF and nuclear issues, farseeing military officers, notably Marshal Ogarkov, began to worry about potential trends in the conventional balance and about whether the USSR had the technology base to compete with the West.[7]

Second, the crisis in Poland that erupted in August 1980 brought the question of stability in the East to the fore. The Soviet leadership initially responded to the crisis in Poland by blaming "Western subversion" and the errors of the Polish Communist Party, but in February 1982 (after Jaruzelski had cracked down, making the issue less explosive) a sanctioned debate began in the Soviet press about the existence and nature of contradictions within socialism. This debate brought into the open many of the themes that were discussed with greater frankness after the adoption of glasnost.

Third, and closely related to the first two points, the USSR entered a period of severe economic slowdown and social decline. After decades in which it claimed to be closing the economic gap with the United States, in the late 1970s the gap again began to widen. There was also an increasingly obvious Soviet lag in science and technology, and Soviet claims about the social achievements of socialism had an increasingly hollow ring, given the alarming rise in alcoholism and an unprecedented drop in Soviet life-expectancy statistics.

The growing awareness of domestic difficulties and a more hostile international environment at first did not result in major changes in foreign policy. Brezhnev in his last years and Andropov throughout his brief period in power were almost totally preoccupied with the war in Afghanistan, the crisis in Poland, and above all the anti-INF campaign, to which they subordinated virtually every Soviet foreign policy priority.

This campaign was in some respects the supreme test of the Brezhnevian approach to détente in Europe. Early in the controversy Brezhnev used his personal contacts with Western leaders to argue that the INF decision was incompatible with the understandings upon which détente was based. When these arguments failed the USSR took the anti-INF campaign to Western parliaments, political parties, and ultimately the streets. INF was the subject of foreign ministry consultations, summit-level letters, and regular embassy contacts. It dominated Soviet behavior in arms control forums, and was injected into religious, cultural, and economic exchanges. In sum, the campaign made use of all the bilateral and multilateral institutions that had been built up in recent decades.

When it became clear to Andropov and his associates that the campaign nonetheless would fail and that the deployments would begin as scheduled, they faced a choice between two policy alternatives. They had the option of following through on the most dire of their own warnings and tearing down the entire structure of détente. In fact, they did take a few steps in this direction: they walked out of the INF talks, postponed the reconvening of MBFR, and for all practical purposes suspended high-level meetings with West Germany. But if they ever contemplated such a course they stopped well short of returning to the militant self-isolation of the late Stalin period.

The other policy option was to minimize losses: to undertake a set of face-saving military countermeasures, to single out West German leaders for punishment while preserving most other ties with the FRG, and position themselves to refight the INF and other issues another day. The USSR began tending toward this option as early as January 1983, almost a year before the denouement of the INF struggle. The Prague Political Declaration issued in that month (and the first major post-Brezhnev foreign policy document) contained in outline form many of the security proposals that Gorbachev later was to adopt. Chernenko continued the trend toward the second option by getting the U.S.-Soviet arms control talks back on track and by at least going through the motions at the Stockholm CDE.

Nonetheless, this was a period of drift in foreign policy. While the aging leadership resisted the emotional temptation to tear down the structure of Soviet-West European relations because of INF, it was unable to restore momentum or coherence in Soviet détente policy. The old slogans—making détente irreversible, supplementing military with political détente, and building upon the triumph of Helsinki—had failed to produce the right outcome in the INF struggle, and were increasingly irrelevant to the Europe of the 1980s. This was the situation that confronted Gorbachev as he assumed power in 1985.

Soviet Policy, 1985–89

Like all Soviet leaders in recent decades, Gorbachev had good economic and political reasons for wanting to pursue a policy of relaxation of tensions with Western Europe. But a mere "return to détente" was not without its drawbacks, especially for a new leader who had not fully consolidated his position at home. By 1985 it was the Western leaders—Kohl, Thatcher, Reagan, and others—who were pressing for a return to business as usual in East-West relations. Having "won" the INF battle, they were anxious to demonstrate that relations would improve, that the economic and cultural ties valued by Western publics were continuing, and that the alarmist scenarios put out by the peace movement were not to be taken seriously. Gorbachev thus faced a choice between continuing to sulk in relative isolation and returning to a détente relationship on terms laid down by the West.

This dilemma was not just a question of personal and national prestige. It went to the heart of Brezhnev's "mechanical" conception of détente and of the role of processes and institutions in promoting Soviet interests. Brezhnev had assumed that regular meetings with foreign leaders, arms control negotiations, and the other forms of contact that he assiduously cultivated would constrain Western governments and lead almost automatically to Soviet foreign policy gains. By 1985 Gorbachev knew that there was another side to the story. While his basic instincts were to follow Brezhnev's course and continue building up the network of Soviet-West European cooperation, he also understood that the West could use détente as a cover for pursuing policies inimical to Soviet interests, notably the deployment of new arms and the challenging of Soviet influence in Eastern Europe.

Gorbachev thus assumed power with a predisposition to question the value of routine meetings and negotiations. This manifested itself in an initial reluctance to engage in summitry for its own sake and in criticisms of what he saw as the bureaucratized arms control process. Already in the spring of 1985 he characterized the Geneva nuclear and space talks as "fruitless" and hinted at breaking them off.[8] In talks with Spanish prime minister González he made the cryptic but in some ways revealing remark that "there is too much cynicism among foreign ministers."[9] These sentiments eventually contributed to his decision to sabotage the MBFR talks and to go to Reykjavik where he hoped to "wrench arms control out of the hands of the bureaucrats."[10]

Gorbachev also sensed the need for a new détente mandate that would impart momentum to the ossified policies and network of institutions he inherited. Already in the spring of 1985 he began to speak of going "beyond détente." In an important speech marking the fortieth anniversary of the victory over Germany he stated that "we believe that the process of détente should be revived. This does not mean, however, a simple return to what was achieved in the 1970s. It is necessary to strive for something much greater. From our point of view, détente is not an end goal of politics. It is needed, but only as a transitional stage from a world cluttered with arms to a reliable and comprehensive system of international security."[11] In his report to the Twenty-Seventh Party Congress the following year he stated that it "is important, while preserving the capital that has been built up, to move forward from the initial phase of détente to a more stable, mature détente; then to the creation of reliable security on the basis of the Helsinki process and radical cuts in nuclear and conventional arms."[12]

While Gorbachev was groping his way toward a new conception of détente, his policies on specific issues remained for the most part rather traditional. He reiterated a very conservative line regarding change in Eastern Europe. The new edition of the CPSU program, the draft of which was circulated in the fall of 1985, espoused the standard view that détente with the West was conditional upon the maintenance of stability, as defined by the USSR, in the East.[13] Gorbachev personally identified with this view on many occasions, most notably at the June 1986 congress of the Polish Communist Party, where he praised General Jaruzelski for the imposition of martial law and reiterated that "the achievements in the socialist lands are irreversible."[14]

Gorbachev's slowness in instituting change in foreign policy was partly due to the presence of party conservatives in the Politburo, such as Gromyko. But he himself was still under the influence of what he later would come to dismiss as "old thinking." Many of his statements indicate that he was seriously concerned about what he saw as a perception in the West that the USSR was weak and could be forced to make concessions on issues such as SDI. In September 1985, for example, he told a U.S. audience that his upcoming summit meeting with President Reagan was "designed for negotiations, for negotiations on the basis of equality and not for signing an act of someone's capitulation. This is all the more true since we have not lost a war to the U.S., or even a battle, and we owe it absolutely nothing."[15] Shevardnadze struck a similarly defensive note in his speech to the UN in the same month: "Our country will not permit military superiority over itself. . . . Profoundly mistaken are those who may expect that the Soviet economy will fail to withstand the strain of a qualitatively new stage in the arms race which is currently being forced upon us."[16] This fear of being perceived as weaker than the United States was not conducive to making major arms control concessions.

Nor did Gorbachev seem to feel strong domestic pressures for a radical change in foreign policy. Contrary to what was often suggested in the West, he did not assume power convinced that the USSR would be required to retrench internationally because of its economic difficulties. He did argue that there was a two-sided relationship between domestic and international affairs, but tended to stress that domestic strength was needed to achieve foreign policy successes rather than that foreign policy achievements could play a role in remedying domestic deficiencies. As late as May 1986, for example, he argued that recent Soviet economic difficulties had had an effect on the USSR's "foreign-policy position," as the West sought to exploit these difficulties to replace the détente of the 1970s with a cold war. But he went on to state that "now, when one can note a change for the better in our domestic affairs, there also has been a certain improvement in the international situation." These arguments, which were forcefully repeated in *Perestroika*, in fact were variations on the Brezhnevian theme that détente was the product of Soviet strength and had to be imposed on the West, whereas tension and cold war were the result of Soviet weaknesses.[17]

In sum, it was unclear whether Gorbachev was prepared to strike out in new foreign policy directions. Just as he initially underestimated the difficulties facing the Soviet economy and assumed that more discipline, new personnel, higher investment, and imaginative mobilizing slogans soon would produce "acceleration," he seemed to believe that a more vigorous approach to foreign policy would lead to improved results.[18] He replaced Gromyko with Shevardnadze, appointed new ambassadors to key countries, improved the style of Soviet pronouncements on international issues, and appropriated for his own use a number of the attractive slogans which had been used in the anti-INF campaign under Brezhnev and Andropov.[19] Rather than making substantive concessions in negotiations he took unilateral steps, such as the INF deployment and nuclear test moratoria, intended to put the West on the defensive.

By mid-1986, however, Gorbachev was displaying signs of impatience with the results of Soviet foreign policy. In an unprecedented gesture for a general secretary, on May 23 he came to the foreign ministry to address a closed meeting of MFA officials and ambassadors, many of whom had returned to Moscow to attend. According to a brief TASS report, the conference was devoted to the subject of "implementing the decisions of the CPSU congress in the field of foreign policy."[20] Details were not made public, but it was rumored that its convening reflected dissatisfaction on Gorbachev's part with the performance of Soviet diplomacy, and in particular a concern that foreign audiences were not responding favorably enough to his recent initiatives, notably his January 15 plan for the complete elimination of nuclear weapons by the year 2000.[21] These reports were confirmed more than a year later, when a summary of the speech was published in an MFA journal.[22]

Parts of the speech were fairly militant. It argued that the West would "not balk at any means of disrupting our peace offensive" and called for a "truly dynamic, effective, combative diplomacy" to counter Western resistance. At the same time, however, Gorbachev demanded new flexibility in Soviet diplomacy and if necessary the making of concessions to produce results in negotiations. He praised the Soviet movement away from "dogmatic positions with respect to the EEC," called for efforts to anticipate the negotiating positions of other countries, and argued that "we must not allow persistence in defending a particular position to develop into senseless stubbornness, so that the Soviet representatives will be called 'Mister Nyet'." In effect Gorbachev was giving the Soviet foreign policy bureaucracy a difficult and in some ways self-contradictory assignment: it was not to abandon or compromise his vision of a nuclear-free world and a comprehensive system of security, but it was to make progress toward implementation of that vision, if need be through compromise and concessions.

Concern about the effectiveness of Soviet foreign policy was reinforced by a new pessimism about the Soviet domestic situation, which belatedly seems to have taken hold in the second half of 1986. Most observers date the radicalization of Gorbachev's domestic policy from the January 1987 plenum of the CPSU Central Committee, but this plenum had been postponed three times, suggesting that a behind-the-scenes battle over the need for radical change was under way for much of 1986. The Chernobyl disaster, which occurred on April 26, 1986, no doubt brought home many of the deficiencies of the Soviet system. It was followed by the June plenum, at which Gorbachev complained about the slow pace of perestroika.[23]

During the first half of 1987 Gorbachev's view of the domestic situation grew increasingly gloomy. At the January plenum he charged the party with stagnation and systemic failures and called for secret balloting and a choice of candidates in elections. In his May 1987 interview with *L'Unità* he spoke of "pre-crisis" phenomena. This set the stage for his report to the June plenum, in which he took a somber view of the USSR's economic prospects, claiming that the improvements achieved were "neither radical nor cardinal. The braking mechanism still has not been smashed nor replaced by the mechanism of acceleration."[24]

Henceforth, economic weakness was to become an increasingly salient theme in official discussions of Soviet foreign policy. This was made clear by Shevardnadze in a speech to the MFA some two weeks after the June plenum. He stressed that foreign policy was an extension of domestic policy and argued that the goal of diplomacy was to form an external environment favorable for internal development. "The main thing is that the country not incur additional expenses in connection with the need to maintain defensive capability and protect its lawful foreign policy interests. This means that we must seek ways to limit and reduce military rivalry, eliminate confrontational features in relations with other states, and suppress crisis situations. We must do this, of course, without sacrificing our principles, class interests, and our ideals."

A final factor that contributed to change in Soviet foreign policy was a reevaluation of the external and especially the U.S. threat. Until as recently as the spring and summer of 1986 Gorbachev took a very gloomy view of U.S. intentions. In his speech in Togliatti on April 8, for example, he referred to a series of recent U.S. actions, and asked rhetorically: "Do they in Washington think that they are dealing with faint hearts? Do they believe that today it is possible to behave like compulsive gamblers? Is this how they in the United States understand the spirit of Geneva? Do they think that we do not see how the just started Soviet-U.S. dialogue is being used to cover the implementation of military aims?"[25] The Chernobyl disaster only heightened Gorbachev's sensitivity to perceived U.S. hostility. Despite a rather concerted effort on the part of the U.S. administration not to gloat in the face of Soviet adversity, in his first public statement on the disaster Gorbachev charged that "the ruling circles of the U.S.A. and their most zealous allies—I would like to mention specially the FRG among them—regarded the mishap only as another possibility to put up additional obstacles [to cooperation] and to justify the arms race."[26]

These suspicions began to give way to a more nuanced view in the late summer and early fall of 1986. Gorbachev's annual vacation in the Crimea appears to have been a time of profound rethinking on his part. Although domestic problems no doubt were his main concern, he also gave considerable attention to foreign policy matters. Apart from his Vladivostok speech dealing primarily with Asian issues, the main foreign policy development of the summer of 1986 was an exchange of letters with President Reagan dealing primarily with arms control.

Preoccupied with saving SDI from mounting political pressure, on July 25 Reagan outlined a radical new proposal which envisioned the complete elimination by both sides of their land and sea-based ballistic missiles. As part of this deal, the USSR would be required to accept the U.S. claim that the ABM treaty permitted testing of space-based defensive systems. The United States would agree not to deploy a defensive system for seven and one-half years, after which it would have carte blanche to do so.[27] The Reagan offer initially caused perplexity on the Soviet side, but it no doubt contributed to a process of rethinking and helped set the stage for Gorbachev's own sweeping proposals at the Reykjavik summit.

Reykjavik had two long-term influences on Soviet policy. First, it crystallized the change in Soviet attitudes regarding the U.S. threat. It is likely that such a change would have occurred in any case. U.S. defense spending peaked in fiscal year 1985, and declined steadily thereafter. In the first half of 1986 the United States suffered a series of space disasters that placed the visionary SDI program in an ironic light. In November Reagan's party lost control of the Senate, and later in the same month Reagan himself was damaged by the surfacing of the Iran-Contra affair. But the Reykjavik meeting, which occurred amid these deepening U.S. problems (and was only made possible after Reagan had "blinked" on the Daniloff-Zakharov swap) brought home the reality of Reagan's weakness to Gorbachev in a uniquely personal way. In addition, Reykjavik provided a boost to the utopian strain in Gorbachev's own thinking and rhetoric, perhaps even rescuing them from creeping irrelevance. By agreeing, as the Soviets and many in the West insisted he had, to the complete elimination of nuclear weapons, Reagan had in effect endorsed the main thrust of Gorbachev's January 15 plan and his antideterrence rhetoric.[28]

These events set the stage for the major developments of 1987: the negotiation of the double zero INF treaty and the adoption of "reasonable sufficiency" and "defensive defense" in the conventional field. The INF treaty in particular was a major turning point. Because it eliminated a whole class of weapons, it was relatively easy to square with Gorbachev's utopian rhetoric. Nonetheless, it was widely and justifiably seen in the West as a major backdown from Brezhnev-era positions—a real as opposed to rhetorical shift in policy. This change in Western perceptions in turn led the Soviet leadership to conclude that the international atmosphere was improving and the threat of war receding, thus facilitating a series of other substantive changes in policy, beginning with the Geneva agreements on Afghanistan and culminating in the unilateral Soviet troop reductions announced in December 1988.

The adoption of the doctrine of "reasonable sufficiency" was rooted in economic requirements, but also reflected a rethinking of the relationship between the role of conventional and nuclear forces and of the potential contribution that political factors could make to diminishing and perhaps eventually eliminating the nuclear threat to the USSR. Although NATO long thought it prudent to plan against a bolt-from-the-blue Warsaw Pact invasion of Western Europe, many Western analysts believed that the USSR was not actually planning such an attack, but was positioning itself to neutralize NATO's deterrent capability in the event of hostilities. As Michael McGwire concluded in 1987, in a war "there is little doubt that the Soviets would seek to destroy all nuclear weapons and means of delivery in the theater, including most types of fixed-wing aircraft."[29] Prodded by influential theorists in the military, Gorbachev probably came to realize the drawbacks of this very demanding military doctrine. It was uncertain of success, expensive, depended heavily on both the contributions of East European armies and of East European territory, and, to the extent that it was difficult to distinguish from an overtly aggressive posture, provoked Western countermeasures that in turn raised the cost and lowered the prospects of successful implementation. Gorbachev's decision to conclude the zero option INF treaty in part reflected a decision to break out of this impasse by making the rapid denuclearization of Europe a foreign policy priority. This in turn permitted the restructuring and reduction of Soviet conventional forces, as well as downgraded the importance for Soviet military planning of both the East European armies and East European territory.

At the same time that the USSR increased the priority attached to eliminating the U.S. nuclear presence from Western Europe, Gorbachev and his advisers seemed less fearful than their predecessors of Western Europe as a potential center of military power. The revised IMEMO "Theses on the European Community" issued in mid-1989 concluded that "the idea of turning the Community into a West European superpower has also had to be abandoned. The national monopolistic complexes have proved to be very much alive and the common action of the member states has moved on to quite a different plane. . . . [T]he affirmation in a number of recent Community documents of the intention to create a European union bears a different meaning than that which was attached to the term 'political union' in the fifties and sixties."[30]

In his October 1989 report to the Supreme Soviet Shevardnadze cited the leadership's "confidence in the country's external security" as one of the factors that accounted for the difference between the "thaws" of earlier periods and the current phase of Soviet foreign policy. "In the fifties and sixties there were different realities and different ideas about the external threat. There was no sense of firm national security, and the threat of war was seen as an immediate and even inevitable reality. This could not fail to restrict the very scale of possible reform. It was necessary to acquire confidence and to eschew, if you will, our weakness complex so as to assess the situation objectively in a balanced way."[31] This growing sense of security (which was not necessarily shared in the military or by old-line Communists) in part explained the growing level of tolerance toward change in Eastern Europe, which before the events of 1989 was seen most clearly in the August 1988 decision not to block Jaruzelski's proposal to legalize Solidarity and begin the roundtable talks as a way out of Poland's lingering internal crisis.

Soviet Policy, 1989–90

The year 1989 began on a hopeful note for Soviet policy in Europe. Gorbachev and Shevardnadze praised the results of the Vienna CSCE review conference, which in their view reflected the happy convergence of change within the USSR and accelerating progress toward the creation of a new all-European order. As Gorbachev told reporters on the eve of the signing of the concluding document, the Soviet Union was rearranging its rooms within the emerging common European house.[32]

This seeming convergence of positive internal and foreign policy change continued throughout the spring and early summer. Internally, the Soviet scene was dominated by the partly free elections to the new Congress of People's Deputies and the establishment later in the spring of a new parliamentary system. These reforms created a favorable backdrop for Gorbachev's visits to Western Europe, as did the sweeping conventional arms control concessions that the USSR showed that it was prepared to make when the CFE talks got under way in March.

The main cloud on the horizon from the Soviet point of view, apart from the domestic economy, was Eastern Europe. Soviet officials stressed repeatedly that the Brezhnev doctrine was dead and that the East European countries were free to shape their internal destinies. At the same time, however, they appeared to set limits to how far change could go. In his Strasbourg speech in which he outlined his vision of a common European home, Gorbachev warned that it was a mistake to believe that "the overcoming of the division of Europe is the overcoming of socialism. This is a course for confrontation."[33]

Nor were there signs of a fundamental rethinking of the German question. Gorbachev had long expressed rather primitive views on this issue, frequently retelling his story of a 1975 encounter with a West German gas station owner in which he explained how Churchill and the United States had divided Europe.[34] There was some movement away from the dogmatic Brezhnevian view that the German question was irrevocably closed, but this had no operational effect on policy. To West Germans who pressed him on how a divided Germany was consistent with a common European house, Gorbachev replied that history would decide the ultimate fate of the German nation. The message to the Germans was that they should join with the USSR in a long-term effort to change the situation in Europe, and that this might change the status of Germany in some yet to be determined way. This line was consistent with that of the 1950s, when the Soviet Union had insisted on priority for the creation of a new all-European security system, which then would "facilitate" reunification.[35]

Moreover, there seemed to be a convergence of Soviet and West German views on this matter, which boded well for the future of Soviet policy. At the June 1989 Bonn summit the USSR endorsed the West German concept of a European peace order, while the West Germans endorsed the common European house.[36] Gorbachev refrained from saying "never" in regard to German reunification, while West Germans such as Foreign Minister Genscher assured the Soviets that reunification was a very distant prospect that would occur only in the context of a changed European system. Meanwhile, Gorbachev and Shevardnadze pressed such familiar themes as the need for further reductions in and the eventual elimination of nuclear weapons from the continent, and reiterated that their long-term objective was the dissolution of the blocs and the elimination of all foreign military bases.

The first blow to the Soviet position in Eastern Europe was the stunning defeat of the Polish Communists in the June elections. This was followed by talks regarding the formation of a coalition government, and the election of Mazowiecki as prime minister in August. Shevardnadze admitted that the USSR was unhappy with this turn of events, but expressed confidence that the Polish Communists would recover their positions. Elsewhere in Eastern Europe the Soviet leadership appeared to assume that the most desirable outcome would be the emergence of reform socialist systems, perhaps with the participation of non-Communist parties and popular movements. An Eastern Europe configured along these lines would cease to be a brake on the USSR's own reform process as well as win further goodwill in Western Europe, and thus contribute to the building of the common European home.

In October Gorbachev gave even the hardline East Germans a nudge in this direction by pointedly warning that history would leave behind those who failed to adapt. East Germany was beset by a simmering refugee crisis, as vacationing citizens occupied West

German embassies throughout Eastern Europe and demanded the right to emigrate. But few in either the East or the West saw this crisis as an immediate threat to the very survival of the East German state. The crisis continued to build, however. Demonstrations in East Germany grew larger, and pressures for open borders increased. Honecker was replaced by Egon Krenz in an effort to placate the population. On November 9 the East German authorities opened the border in an effort to defuse popular pressures. Emigration rose to 2,000 per day, threatening the economic viability of the East German state.

Reunification was at first little talked about by the East German protesters, but gradually became the dominant theme in the East German debate, as people sought immediate improvements in their economic situation and made clear that they did not want to be a part of yet another socialist experiment. On November 28 Chancellor Kohl seized the German issue by putting forward a ten-point plan for eventual confederation between the two states.

The USSR reacted nervously to these events. It discouraged the East Germans from using force, and apparently the government never considered using the 380,000 Soviet soldiers in East Germany to crush the demonstrations. But the Soviet Union quickly mobilized its diplomatic efforts to prevent the reopening of what was called as late as early December the "so-called German question."[37] These efforts included Gorbachev's call for a Helsinki II summit, talks with French president Mitterrand and foreign minister Dumas, and moves to revive the almost moribund four-power institutions. In addition, the USSR backed off somewhat from its dissolution of the blocs rhetoric and suggested that both blocs could be transformed and made components of a new all-European system. Shevardnadze underscored the shift by his December visit to NATO headquarters.[38]

But pressures for reunification continued to grow, and by late January 1990 Gorbachev was prepared to assure Chancellor Kohl that the USSR was not in principle opposed to reunification. Reverting to a theme heard earlier in the postwar period, Soviet officials stressed that the Soviet Union had been the original champion of German unity but had been thwarted by the West. Gorbachev also repeated his familiar theme that history would determine the fate of Germany, but rather plaintively acknowledged that "history has started working in an unexpectedly rapid way."[39] Whereas previously he had argued that progress toward creating a European home might lead to change in Germany, he now stressed that unexpected change in Germany required the acceleration of desired changes in Europe as a whole: "It follows that the process of the unification of Germany is organically linked with the all-European process and its pivotal line, the formation of a structure of European security that is new in principle and that will replace that which is based upon blocs." "Synchronization" thus became the major theme in Soviet policy toward Europe, as the USSR argued that it was necessary to slow the rush toward reunification while a new all-European order was built.

In practice this meant that Germany had to become neutral, as the USSR initially demanded. Later Shevardnadze proposed that Germany could become a member of both blocs. These ideas were rejected in West Germany, and the Soviet Union was forced to lower its sights and to call for the reform of NATO and the concurrent building up of all-European structures as preconditions for its assent to German unity within NATO.

At the Ottawa Open Skies conference in February 1990 the USSR agreed to take part in the "two plus four talks" regarding the external aspects of reunification.[40] Originally it pressed for a "four plus two" forum that would underscore the primacy of victors' rights over German self-determination, but was overruled. When the talks got under way in May the USSR took a maximal stance based on the Potsdam agreement. It demanded a peace treaty or other ratifiable document that at last would bring World War II to an end, and put forward a long list of political, military, and economic demands.[41] It was widely expected, however, that in time the Soviet leadership, beset by growing internal economic and nationality problems and failing to generate any support for its stance in Eastern or Western Europe, would cut the best possible deal.

As in the Austrian negotiations of 1955, the USSR sought to make a bilateral understanding with West Germany the essence of the settlement, even as it fulfilled the legalities of a four-power negotiation. Genscher and Shevardnadze met repeatedly over a period of months, and settled such issues as future troop strength of the Bundeswehr, German economic obligations to the USSR, the withdrawal of Soviet troops from the eastern part of Germany, and the future of bilateral relations between the two countries.[42] Convinced that further delay would only alienate the Germans, and given face-saving assurance by NATO in its London declaration, on July 14–16, 1990, Gorbachev met at his vacation retreat with Chancellor Kohl and settled the final arrangements. Germany would be united within NATO as early as the end of 1990, thus opening a new era in European history.

The foreign ministers of the six two plus four participating states met in Paris on July 17 and were joined by the foreign minister of Poland. They tentatively agreed that instead of a formal peace treaty the six would sign a document regulating all questions concerning unification and the reestablishment of full German sovereignty. This document would then be submitted for approval to the CSCE summit scheduled for November. Meanwhile, East and West Germany began establishing full economic and monetary union, and on August 23, 1990, the People's Chamber of the GDR set October 3 as the date for accession to the Federal Republic of Germany.

On September 12, 1990, the two plus four talks concluded in Moscow. In response to Soviet pressures, the West Germans abandoned their earlier preference for an international document rather than a full-fledged treaty, and agreed to sign the Treaty on the Final Settlement with Respect to Germany. On October 1 the World War II victors formally suspended their four-power rights and responsibilities over Germany and Berlin, leaving the two Germanies fully sovereign. On October 3, 1990, the German Democratic Republic ceased to exist.

The USSR and the Future of Europe

Having failed to dictate the terms of German unity, the Soviet Union faced an uncertain future as a European power. As part of the July settlement Gorbachev and Kohl agreed to conclude a treaty between the USSR and a united Germany that would regulate their political, economic, and cultural ties. This treaty was concluded in late September and formally signed by President Gorbachev and Chancellor Kohl in Bonn on November 9. It obliged the new Germany to strive for close cooperation with the USSR in virtually all fields, and contained a controversial nonaggression clause that some in the West regarded as in conflict with Germany's obligations under the NATO treaty. In addition, Germany became the strongest advocate, within the European Community and the seven-nation group of industrialized countries, of massive economic aid to the USSR. On September 28 representatives of the two governments initialed the Treaty on the Development of Comprehensive Cooperation in the Economic, Industrial, Scientific, and Technological Areas. It reaffirmed many of the provisions in existing bilateral economic agreements, as well as obliged the FRG to undertake measures to minimize the economic losses to the USSR arising from the GDR's withdrawal from CMEA.[43]

While the Soviet Union failed in its bid to weaken the links between Germany and the United States, many Soviet officials expressed confidence that the U.S. military presence in Germany was untenable, and that with the Soviet threat all but gone NATO would wither away as well. Foreign Minister Shevardnadze was criticized by Soviet conservatives for having "lost Germany," but in his own testimony to the Supreme Soviet International Affairs Committee regarding the Treaty on the Final Settlement with Respect to Germany he stressed the list of assurances the USSR had gained regarding the future German and NATO threats. He predicted that "in the future NATO and the Warsaw Treaty Organization will become component parts of all-European security structures and later will probably be dissolved in them."[44] Other Soviet officials were more blunt. For example, Nikolai Portugalov, a prominent Soviet expert on Germany, wrote in *Spiegel* in early October that "it is logical to assume that the U.S. military and, above all, nuclear presence in West Germany will not long survive the withdrawal of our troops from the East."[45]

The USSR supplemented and counterbalanced its new relationship with Germany by a search for closer relations with the other major countries of Western Europe, as well as the EC, which was seen in Moscow as a major potential source of economic aid. Soviet-EC relations entered a new stage in July 1990 with the visit to the USSR of Jacques Delors, the first ever by the head of the EC Commission. In October of the same year Gorbachev went to Madrid where he signed a Spanish-Soviet Joint Political Declaration, and to Paris where he and Shevardnadze signed, along with President Mitterrand, Prime Minister Rocard, and Foreign Minister Dumas, a Franco-Soviet treaty on accord and cooperation. The treaty did not contain the controversial non-aggression clause included in the treaty with Bonn, but it included an extensive list of commitments, including political consultations and regular talks between general staffs. Gorbachev formally signed the USSR-FRG treaty in Bonn in early November, and stopped in Rome on his way to the Paris summit later in the month to sign a similar treaty with Italy. All of these agreements hailed the overcoming of the division of Europe, and pledged the signatories to friendship and cooperation in the political, economic, cultural, and to some extent even military spheres.

But if the USSR could be somewhat reassured about the external dimensions of the threat from Europe and the new Germany, it was unclear whether it was internally configured to play its part in the new emerging European order. Soviet leverage in the German question was undercut by the separatist movements in the union republics and by the ever deepening economic crisis. These problems were certain to linger on into the post-postwar era and to threaten the USSR—or, in the event of its breakup, its constituent parts—with self-exclusion from a prosperous and stable Europe.[46]

As for the vast network of Soviet-West European institutions whose development since 1953 this book has documented, their future will depend on the evolution of the USSR and specifically on whether or not communism survives in some form as a comprehensive way of organizing society. If communism is utterly doomed, this network is likely to disappear as well. Joint economic commissions will become irrelevant, as Soviet firms deal directly with their Western counterparts, without the elaborate bureaucratic machinery that

was created to facilitate economic cooperation between two fundamentally different systems. The same will happen to cultural commissions, as Russia or what survives of the Soviet confederation is
fully integrated into a world cultural and scientific community dominated by private or quasi-governmental foundations, institutions,
museums, and universities. Parliamentarians and political parties
will participate in international parliamentary bodies and in their
respective political internationals, but their overwhelming concerns
will be domestic, as they seek to satisfy their constituents and assure
their own reelection. Summits will continue, as they do in Western
Europe, North America, and elsewhere, but Russian leaders will
have a greater stake in domestic affairs, and will not be able to portray every meeting with a foreign leader as a vital step toward peace.
Arms control will cease to be relevant as military antagonism fades.
The elaborate verification and confidence-building measures negotiated at Vienna will remain on the books, but they are likely to fall
into disuse, as parliaments and a free press verify from within the
activities of the residual military forces. Even the CSCE process,
which is widely seen as a key to the future of European stability, is
likely to fade in importance, as the United Nations assumes more of
the role envisioned for it in 1945.

Trends in this direction were evident already in the late 1980s, as
communism loosened its grip on most aspects of Soviet life and civil
society revived. Firms dealt directly with each other, albeit with difficulty. The state monopoly on cultural exchange broke down. Parliamentarians did direct their attention to domestic affairs and away
from the promotion of peace. Arms control was overshadowed by
political developments, and Western governments privately concluded that they could accept less stringent measures of verification
in light of the opening of Soviet society that was under way.

If, on the other hand, communism survives in the USSR or in Soviet Russia, one can expect a continuing process of further institu-
tion-building as the Soviet Union cooperates more intensively with
the West, but as institutions are still required to manage interaction
between systems that, even if no longer antagonistic, remain very
different. While in 1989 and 1990 the informals, the entrepreneurs,
and others outside the old Communist system either concentrated
exclusively on challenges at home or forged links on a decentralized
basis with foreign counterparts, Gorbachev, Shevardnadze, and the
official foreign policy institutes poured out proposals for new councils, commissions, crisis-management *troiky*, risk reduction centers,
open skies, open seas, liaison missions, hotlines, military exchanges,
seminars, central European air-control regimes, multinational peace-
keeping forces, multinational arms control verification forces, international satellite monitoring regimes, ecological risk reduction

centers, international disaster relief centers, multinational disaster response teams, confidence-building measures, secretariats, complex verification schemes, a European institute of human rights, and many other ideas. For the most part these proposals met with positive responses from Western governments eager to help Gorbachev and searching for ways to avoid instability in a period of extraordinary change. It is unclear, however, how much of this structure would be necessary if the USSR was to become a truly democratic, free-market country, as those terms are understood in the West.

For scholars, the task of sorting out the détente experience and its relevance for the changes of 1989–90 is just beginning. For now the discussion is politicized. The left has been quick to argue that recent events show that the Soviet military threat was always exaggerated and that the West might have been more forthcoming in arms control talks and less fearful of technology leakage. But the left clearly was wrong in arguing over the years that military competition with the USSR was futile since the Soviet people would bear any sacrifice to maintain their security, or that trying to deny the Soviet Union vital technologies was pointless, since doing so would only encourage redoubled efforts toward self-sufficiency. External pressure on the Soviet system did contribute to change and a rethinking of the very concept of security. Indeed, it could be argued that greater pressure—and less détente—might have cracked the system earlier.

For its part, the right has been quick to criticize the left for its embarrassing intimacy with the now discredited Communist regimes and parties and for its tacit collaboration in the Communist strategy of politicizing all forms of cooperation on behalf of peace. But much of this criticism is unjustified, if only because the right itself has little to be proud of in this area. Historically, conservative governments and parties played as much if not more of a role than their Socialist and Social Democratic rivals in building up the broad network of cooperation with Communist governments and nongovernmental organizations, often with little regard for actual or potential sources of anti-Communist opposition. More fundamentally, it is too early to know precisely what effect contacts and agreements with the regimes had on deeper processes within society. If détente flattered the vanity of corrupt Communists, it may also have helped to provide breathing space for civil society under communism or opened windows on the outside world that otherwise would have remained closed.

Whether or not these questions can ever be fully sorted out is unclear. But work on doing so can now begin, as the cold war and in a sense détente as well have ended, and have given way to a new and possibly less ambiguous era in relations between Russia and the West.

Appendix

Summits, 1955–90[1]

NATO Europe

Belgium

Oct. 1956	Moscow	Khrushchev-van Acker
June 1975	Moscow	Podgornyi-King Baudouin (H)

Denmark

March 1956	Moscow	Khrushchev-Hansen
Feb. 1964	Moscow	Khrushchev-Krag
June 1964	Copenhagen	Khrushchev-Krag
Dec. 1971	Copenhagen	Kosygin-Krag
Oct. 1973	Moscow	Brezhnev-Jorgensen
May 1975	Moscow	Podgornyi-Queen Margarethe II (H)
Oct. 1986	Moscow	Gorbachev-Schluter

France

July 1955****	Geneva	Khrushchev-Faure
May 1956	Moscow	Khrushchev-Mollet
April 1960	Paris	Khrushchev-de Gaulle
May 1960****	Paris	Khrushchev-de Gaulle
June 1966	Moscow	Kosygin-de Gaulle
Dec. 1966	Paris	Kosygin-de Gaulle
June 1967*	Paris	Kosygin-de Gaulle
July 1967*	Paris	Kosygin-de Gaulle
Oct. 1970	Moscow	Brezhnev-Pompidou
Oct. 1971	Paris	Brezhnev-Pompidou
Jan. 1973	Minsk (USSR)	Brezhnev-Pompidou
June 1973	Paris	Brezhnev-Pompidou
March 1974	Pitsunda (USSR)	Brezhnev-Pompidou
May 1974*	Paris	Podgornyi-Giscard
Dec. 1974	Paris	Brezhnev-Giscard
March 1975	Moscow	Kosygin-Chirac (PM)
Oct. 1975	Moscow	Brezhnev-Giscard
June 1977	Paris	Brezhnev-Giscard
Sep. 1977	Moscow	Kosygin-Barre (PM)
April 1979	Moscow	Brezhnev-Giscard

May 1980	Warsaw	Brezhnev-Giscard
Nov. 1982*	Moscow	Andropov-Mauroy (PM)
Feb. 1984*	Moscow	Chernenko-Mauroy (PM)
June 1984	Moscow	Chernenko-Mitterrand
March 1985*	Moscow	Gorbachev-Mitterrand
Oct. 1985	Paris	Gorbachev-Mitterrand
July 1986	Moscow	Gorbachev-Mitterrand
May 1987	Moscow	Ryzhkov-Chirac (PM)
Nov. 1988	Moscow	Gorbachev-Mitterrand
July 1989	Paris	Gorbachev-Mitterrand
Dec. 1989	Kiev	Gorbachev-Mitterrand
May 1990	Moscow	Gorbachev-Mitterrand
Oct. 1990	Paris	Gorbachev-Mitterrand

Federal Republic of Germany

Sep. 1955	Moscow	Khrushchev-Adenauer
Aug. 1970	Moscow	Kosygin-Brandt
Sep. 1971	Oreanda (USSR)	Brezhnev-Brandt
May 1973	Bonn	Brezhnev-Brandt
Oct. 1974	Moscow	Brezhnev-Schmidt
Nov. 1975	Moscow	Podgornyi-Scheel (H)
May 1978	Bonn	Brezhnev-Schmidt
June 1979*	Moscow	Kosygin-Schmidt
June 1980	Moscow	Brezhnev-Schmidt
Nov. 1981	Bonn	Brezhnev-Schmidt
Nov. 1982*	Moscow	Andropov-Carstens (H)
July 1983	Moscow	Andropov-Kohl
Feb. 1984*	Moscow	Chernenko-Kohl
March 1985*	Moscow	Gorbachev-Kohl
July 1987	Moscow	Gorbachev-Weizsäcker (H)
Oct. 1988	Moscow	Gorbachev-Kohl
June 1989	Bonn	Gorbachev-Kohl
Feb. 1990	Moscow	Gorbachev-Kohl
July 1990	Stavropol (USSR)	Gorbachev-Kohl
Nov. 1990	Bonn	Gorbachev-Kohl

Greece

Oct. 1979	Moscow	Kosygin-Karamanlis
Nov. 1982*	Moscow	Andropov-Papandreou
Feb. 1983	Athens	Tikhonov-Papandreou
Feb. 1984*	Moscow	Chernenko-Papandreou
Feb. 1985	Moscow	·Tikhonov-Papandreou

Iceland

Sep. 1977	Moscow	Kosygin-Hallgrimsson
Oct. 1986*	Reykjavik	Gorbachev-Hermannsson
March 1987	Moscow	Gorbachev-Hermannsson

Italy

Feb. 1960	Moscow	Khrushchev-Gronchi (H)
Aug. 1961	Moscow	Khrushchev-Fanfani
March 1964	Rome	Kosygin-Moro
Jan. 1967	Rome	Podgornyi-Saragat (H)
Oct. 1972	Moscow	Kosygin-Andreotti
Nov. 1975	Moscow	Podgornyi-Leone (H)
June 1979*	Moscow	Kosygin-Andreotti
Feb. 1984*	Moscow	Chernenko-Pertini (H)
March 1985*	Moscow	Gorbachev-Pertini (H)
May 1985	Moscow	Gorbachev-Craxi
Oct. 1988	Moscow	Gorbachev-De Mita
Nov. 1989	Rome	Gorbachev-Andreotti
July 1990	Moscow	Gorbachev-Andreotti
Nov. 1990	Rome	Gorbachev-Andreotti

Luxembourg

June 1972	Moscow	Podgornyi-Grand Duke Jean (H)
Oct. 1990	Moscow	Gorbachev-Santer

Netherlands

Nov. 1986	Moscow	Gorbachev-Lubbers

Norway

Nov. 1955	Moscow	Khrushchev-Gerhardsen
July 1964	Oslo	Khrushchev-Gerhardsen
June 1965	Moscow	Kosygin-Gerhardsen
Dec. 1971	Oslo	Kosygin-Bratteli
March 1974	Moscow	Kosygin-Bratteli
March 1985*	Moscow	Gorbachev-Willoch
Dec. 1986	Moscow	Gorbachev-Brundtland (as chairman of the International Commission for Environment and Development)
Jan. 1988	Oslo	Ryzhkov-Brundtland

Portugal

Oct. 1975	USSR	Podgornyi-Costa Gomes
Feb. 1984*	Moscow	Tikhonov-Soares
Nov. 1987	Moscow	Gorbachev-Soares

Spain

May 1984	Moscow	King Juan Carlos (H)
March 1985*	Moscow	Gorbachev-González

May 1986	Moscow	Gorbachev-González
Oct. 1990	Madrid	Gorbachev-González

Turkey

Aug. 1965	Moscow	Kosygin-Urguplu
Dec. 1966	Ankara	Kosygin-Demirel
Sep. 1967	Moscow	Kosygin-Demirel
April 1972	Ankara	Podgornyi-Sunay (H)
Dec. 1975	Ankara	Kosygin-Demirel
June 1978	Moscow	Kosygin-Ecevit
Nov. 1982*	Moscow	Tikhonov-Ulusu (H)
Feb. 1984	Moscow	Ozal-Tikhonov
Dec. 1984	Ankara	Tikhonov-Ozal
July 1986	Moscow	Ryzhkov-Ozal

United Kingdom

July 1955****	Geneva	Khrushchev-Eden
April 1956	London	Khrushchev-Eden
March 1959	Moscow	Khrushchev-Macmillan
May 1960****	Paris	Khrushchev-Macmillan
Feb. 1966	Moscow	Kosygin-Wilson
July 1966	Moscow	Kosygin-Wilson
Feb. 1967	London	Kosygin-Wilson
Jan. 1968	Moscow	Kosygin-Wilson
Feb. 1975	Moscow	Brezhnev-Wilson
June 1979*	Moscow	Kosygin-Thatcher
Feb. 1984*	Moscow	Chernenko-Thatcher
March 1985*	Moscow	Gorbachev-Thatcher
March 1987	Moscow	Gorbachev-Thatcher
Dec. 1987*	U.K.	Gorbachev-Thatcher
April 1989	London	Gorbachev-Thatcher
Sep. 1989*	Moscow	Gorbachev-Thatcher
June 1990	Moscow-Kiev	Gorbachev-Thatcher

Other Europe

Austria

April 1955	Moscow	Molotov-Raab
July 1958	Moscow	Khrushchev-Raab
Oct. 1959	Moscow	Voroshilov-Scharf (H)
June 1960	Vienna	Khrushchev-Raab
Nov. 1966	Vienna	Podgornyi-Klaus
March 1967	Moscow	Kosygin-Klaus
May 1968	Moscow	Podgornyi-Jonas (H)
July 1973	Vienna	Kosygin-Kreisky
May 1974	Moscow	Kosygin-Kreisky
Feb. 1978	Moscow	Brezhnev-Kreisky

June 1979*	Vienna	Brezhnev-Kirchschläger (H)
April 1981	Vienna	Tikhonov-Kreisky
May 1982	Moscow	Brezhnev-Kirchschläger (H)
Nov. 1984	Moscow	Tikhonov-Sinowatz
March 1985	Moscow	Gorbachev-Kirchschläger
April 1986	Moscow	Gorbachev-Sinowatz
July 1987	Vienna	Ryzhkov-Vranitzky
Oct. 1988	Moscow	Gorbachev-Vranitzky

Cyprus

June 1971	Moscow	Podgornyi-Makarios
Oct. 1982	Moscow	Brezhnev-Kiprianou

Finland

Sep. 1955	Moscow	Bulganin-Paasikivi
Aug. 1956	Helsinki	Voroshilov-Kekkonen
Jan. 1957	Moscow	Bulganin-Fagerholm (PM)
June 1957	Helsinki	Khrushchev-Kekkonen
Jan. 1959	Leningrad	Khrushchev-Kekkonen
Sep. 1960	Helsinki	Khrushchev-Kekkonen
Nov. 1960	Moscow	Khrushchev-Kekkonen
Sep. 1961	Helsinki	Brezhnev-Kekkonen
June 1966	Helsinki	Kosygin-Kekkonen
Oct. 1968	Gulf of Finland	Kosygin-Kekkonen
Oct. 1968*	Moscow	Kosygin-Koivisto
May 1969	Leningrad	Kosygin-Kekkonen
Oct. 1969	Leningrad	Kosygin-Kekkonen
July 1970	Moscow	Kosygin-Kekkonen
Oct. 1970	Helsinki	Podgornyi-Kekkonen
Feb. 1971	Moscow	Kosygin-Kekkonen
April 1971	Moscow	Kosygin-Karjalainen (PM)
Feb. 1972	Moscow	Kosygin-Kekkonen
Aug. 1972	Sukhumi (USSR)	Kosygin-Kekkonen
April 1973	Helsinki	Podgornyi-Kekkonen
Sep. 1973	Leningrad	Kosygin-Kekkonen
Feb. 1974	Moscow	Kosygin-Kekkonen
Oct. 1974	Moscow	Kosygin-Sorsa (PM)
Oct. 1974	Helsinki	Podgornyi-Kekkonen
March 1975	Moscow	Kosygin-Kekkonnen
Sep. 1975	Svetogorsk (USSR)	Kosygin-Kekkonnen
June 1976	USSR	Kosygin-Kekkonen
March 1977	Helsinki	Kosygin-Kekkonen
May 1977	Moscow	Brezhnev-Kekkonnen
Nov. 1977	Moscow	Kosygin-Kekkonnen
Nov. 1977	Moscow	Kosygin-Sorsa (PM)
Dec. 1977	Helsinki	Kosygin-Kekkonen
April 1978	Moscow	Kosygin-Sorsa (PM)

Sep. 1978	Karelian ASSR	Kosygin-Kekkonen
Nov. 1980	Moscow	Brezhnev-Kekkonen
March 1982	Moscow	Brezhnev-Koivisto
Dec. 1982	Moscow	Andropov-Koivisto
Oct. 1982	Moscow	Ponomarev-Sorsa (as head of party delegation)
Dec. 1982	Karelian ASSR	Tikhonov-Koivisto
Dec. 1982	Helsinki	Tikhonov-Koivisto
June 1983	Moscow	Andropov-Koivisto
April 1984	Moscow	Chernenko-Koivisto
Sep. 1984	Moscow	Tikhonov-Sorsa (PM)
March 1985*	Moscow	Gorbachev-Koivisto
June 1985	Karelian ASSR	Tikhonov-Koivisto
Sep. 1985	Moscow	Gorbachev-Koivisto
March 1986	Stockholm	Ryzhkov-Sorsa (PM)
Dec. 1986	Tallin, Estonia	Ryzhkov-Sorsa (PM)
Jan. 1987	Helsinki	Ryzhkov-Sorsa (PM)
Oct. 1987	Moscow	Gorbachev-Koivisto
Sep. 1988	Moscow	Ryzhkov-Holkeri (PM)
Oct. 1989	Helsinki	Gorbachev-Koivisto

Malta

| Dec. 1984 | Moscow | Tikhonov-Mintoff |
| Dec. 1989* | Valletta | Gorbachev-Fenech-Adami |

Sweden

March 1956	Moscow	Khrushchev-Erlander
June 1964	Stockholm	Khrushchev-Erlander
June 1965	Moscow	Kosygin-Erlander
July 1968	Stockholm	Kosygin-Erlander
June 1970	Moscow	Kosygin-Palme
April 1973	Stockholm	Kosygin-Palme
April 1976	Moscow	Kosygin-Palme
Dec. 1977*	Helsinki	Kosygin-Faldin
June 1978	Moscow	Brezhnev-King Carl Gustav (H)
March 1986*	Stockholm	Ryzhkov-Carlsson
April 1986	Moscow	Gorbachev-Carlsson
Jan. 1988	Stockholm	Ryzhkov-Carlsson

Switzerland

| Nov. 1985* | Geneva | Gorbachev-Fürgler (H) |

The Vatican

Jan. 1967	Vatican City	Podgornyi-Paul VI (H)
Nov. 1989	Vatican City	Gorbachev-John Paul II
Nov. 1990	Vatican City	Gorbachev-John Paul II

Other

United States

July 1955****	Geneva	Khrushchev-Eisenhower
Sep. 1959	Washington	Khrushchev-Eisenhower
May 1960****	Paris	Khrushchev-Eisenhower
June 1961	Vienna	Khrushchev-Kennedy
June 1967	Glassboro	Kosygin-Johnson
May 1972	Moscow	Brezhnev-Nixon
June 1973	Washington	Brezhnev-Nixon
June 1974	Moscow	Brezhnev-Nixon
July 1974*	Paris	Podgornyi-Nixon
Nov. 1974	Vladivostok	Brezhnev-Ford
June 1979	Vienna	Brezhnev-Carter
Nov. 1985	Geneva	Gorbachev-Reagan
Oct. 1986	Reykjavik	Gorbachev-Reagan
Dec. 1987	Washington	Gorbachev-Reagan
June 1988	Moscow	Gorbachev-Reagan
Dec. 1988	New York	Gorbachev Reagan
Dec. 1989	Malta	Gorbachev-Bush
June 1990	Washington	Gorbachev-Bush
Sept. 1990	Helsinki	Gorbachev-Bush

Canada

May 1971	Moscow	Kosygin-Trudeau
Oct. 1971	Ottawa	Kosygin-Trudeau
Nov. 1982*	Moscow	Andropov-Trudeau
Feb. 1984*	Moscow	Chernenko-Trudeau
March 1985*	Moscow	Gorbachev-Mulroney
Nov. 1989	Moscow	Gorbachev-Mulroney
June 1990	Ottawa	Gorbachev-Mulroney

Notes

Chapter 1: Introduction

1. Sir Roger Makins, "The World since the War, the Third Phase," *Foreign Affairs* 33, no. 1 (1954); Ia. Viktorov, "Vazhnye shagi na puti smiagcheniia mezhunarodnoi napriazhennosti," *Kommunist* 14 (1955); and Adam Ulam, *Expansion and Coexistence*, pp. 539–72.

2. See, for example, the criticism of SPD leader Willy Brandt in Martin Kriele, "Jetzt muss man auseinanderhalten, was nicht zusammengehört," *Frankfurter Allgemeine Zeitung*, January 13, 1990.

3. The most comprehensive book on the subject is Thomas W. Wolfe, *Soviet Power and Europe*. The only other relevant English language books have been specialized monographs or edited collections of essays. See, for example, Ray S. Cline, James Arnold, and Roger E. Kanet, eds., *Western Europe in Soviet Global Strategy*; Edwina Moreton and Gerald Segal, *Soviet Strategy Toward Western Europe*; Herbert J. Ellison, *Soviet Policy Toward Western Europe*; George Ginsburgs and Alvin Z. Rubinstein, *Soviet Foreign Policy Toward Western Europe*; and Richard Pipes, *Soviet Strategy in Europe*. For a useful monograph in German, see Christoph Royen, *Die sowjetische Koexistenzpolitik gegenüber Westeuropa*. See also the general comments on the literature in the review article by Randy Hagerty in *Soviet Studies* 37, no. 2 (1985): 280–81.

4. The titles of recent studies suggest their focus. Jerry Hough, "Soviet Perspectives on European Security," *International Journal* 40, no. 1 (1985): 20–41; Michael Sodaro, "Soviet Studies of the Western Alliance," in Ellison, *Soviet Policy Toward Western Europe*, pp. 234–65; Geoffrey Pridham, "The Soviet View of the Current Disagreements between the United States and Western Europe," *International Affairs* (London) 59, no. 1 (1983); William Garner, *Soviet Threat Perceptions of NATO's Eurostrategic Missiles*; Robbin Laird, "Soviet Perspectives on French Security Policy," *Survival* 27, no. 2 (1985); Robert Cutler, "Soviet Debates over the Conduct of Foreign Policy toward Western Europe: Four Case Studies, 1971–75," unpublished Ph.D. dissertation, University of Michigan, 1982; Coit Dennis Blacker, "The Soviet Perception of European Security," in Derek Leebaert, ed., *European Security: Prospects for the 1980s*, pp. 137–61; and Neil Malcolm, *Soviet Policy Perspectives on Western Europe*. Robbin F. Laird and Susan L. Clark, *The USSR and the Western Alliance*, is also mainly a perceptions study.

5. For a comprehensive discussion see J. F. Brown, *Eastern Europe and Communist Rule*.

Chapter 2: From Stalin to Khrushchev

1. For an overview of the literature, see John Lewis Gaddis, "The Emerging Post-Revisionist Synthesis on the Origins of the Cold War," *Diplomatic History* 7, no. 3 (1983): 171–90.

2. Vojtech Mastny, *Russia's Road to the Cold War*, pp. 40, 132.

3. See Iu. N. Rakhmaninov, *Problema evropeiskoi bezopasnosti*, pp. 145–50.

4. Charles de Gaulle, *The Complete War Memoirs: Salvation*, p. 738.

5. Charles Gati, *Hungary and the Soviet Bloc*, pp. 14–23; see also Geir Lundestad, *The American Non-Policy toward Eastern Europe, 1943–1947*, pp. 435–50.

6. Radio address of August 9, 1945, *Public Papers of the Presidents of the United States: Harry S. Truman, 1945*, p. 205.

7. James F. Byrnes, *Speaking Frankly*, pp. 69–71. For the Paris Peace Conference, see F. S. Marston, *The Peace Conference of 1919: Organization and Procedure*, and Harold Nicolson, *Peacemaking 1919*.

8. The record on this question is somewhat confused. See Winston S. Churchill, *The Second World War: Triumph and Tragedy*, p. 649; the exchange at the first plenary meeting, July 17, 1945, U.S. Department of State, *Foreign Relations of the United States* [hereinafter, *FRUS*]: *Conference of Berlin (Potsdam), 1945*, p. 57 (Thompson minutes), and p. 62 (Cohen notes); the more detailed Soviet record in Andrei A. Gromyko, ed., *Sovetskii soiuz na mezhdunarodnykh konferentsiakh perioda velikoi otechestvennoi voiny 1941–1945 gg.*, 6:50–53; and Sir Llewellyn Woodward, *British Foreign Policy in the Second World War*, 5:403. Details in these accounts vary, but none suggests strong opposition to the CFM on Stalin's part.

9. See Ruth B. Russell (assisted by Jeanette E. Muther), *A History of the United Nations Charter: The Role of the United States 1940–1945*; and Valentin M. Berezhkov, *Stranitsi diplomaticheskoi istorii*, pp. 335–440.

10. See Thomas M. Campbell and George Herring, eds., *The Diaries of Edward R. Stettinius, Jr.*, p. 244; and Churchill, *The Second World War: Triumph and Tragedy*, p. 356, for Stalin's complaints about the League of Nations.

11. Complete records in *FRUS, 1945*, 2:99–559.

12. Byrnes, *Speaking Frankly*, p. 109; and Alan Bullock, *The Life and Times of Ernest Bevin: Foreign Secretary, 1945–1951*, p. 199.

13. For the communiqué see *FRUS (Potsdam)*, pp. 815–17.

14. *Public Papers: Harry S. Truman, 1945*, p. 213.

15. U.S. Department of State, *Documents on Disarmament, 1945–1959*, 1:1–3.

16. See Vojtech Mastny, "Europe in U.S.-USSR Relations: A Topical Legacy," *Problems of Communism* 37, no. 1 (1988): 20. For a Soviet account see N. V. Novikov, *Vospominaniia diplomata*, pp. 342–52.

17. *FRUS, 1946*, 2:643–44; Molotov's position was foreshadowed at Yalta by Stalin. See *FRUS: The Conferences at Malta and Yalta*, p. 589.

The 21 countries at the conference were Australia, Belgium, Brazil, Bye-lorussia, Canada, China, Czechoslovakia, Ethiopia, France, Greece, India, Netherlands, New Zealand, Norway, Poland, Ukraine, Union of South Africa, United Kingdom, United States, USSR, and Yugoslavia. The presence of the 5 former German allies brought the total number of participants to 26.

18. See Byrnes, *Speaking Frankly*, p. 111; and Joseph I. Lieberman, *The Scorpion and the Tarantula: The Struggle to Control Atomic Weapons, 1945–1949*, pp. 204–24. See *Documents on Disarmament, 1945–1959*, 1:4, for the UN resolution.

19. *Documents on Disarmament, 1945–1959*, 1:6.

20. See Frederick Osborn, "Negotiating on Atomic Energy, 1946–47," in Raymond Dennett, ed., *Negotiating with the Russians*, pp. 209–36.

21. See Andrei A. Gromyko, *Memories*, p. 118.

22. *Documents on Disarmament, 1945–1959*, 1:60–61.

23. *New York Times*, March 23, 1946; and *Izvestiia*, October 31, 1946.

24. For the importance of February 1946 in U.S. deliberations, see John Lewis Gaddis, *The United States and the Origins of the Cold War, 1941–1947*, p. 284.

25. For the text of Byrnes's speech, see U.S. Department of State, *Documents on Germany, 1944–1985* (Washington, D.C.: GPO, 1986), pp. 91–99; for the text of the draft treaty of disarmament and demilitarization (first submitted to the CFM on April 29, 1946), ibid., pp. 79–82; and for German pressures, see Konrad Adenauer, *Memoirs: 1945–1953*, pp. 17–88.

26. Charles Bohlen, *Witness to History*, p. 263.

27. Bullock, *Devin*, p. 491.

28. For Stalin and the Marshall Plan, see Dmitrii Volkogonov, *Triumf i tragediia*, 2 (part 2): 91–92. See also Joseph M. Jones, *The Fifteen Weeks*. For the internal effects of the plan and the debate on its role in promoting economic recovery, see Lawrence S. Kaplan, "The Cold War and European Revisionism," *Diplomatic History* 11, no. 2 (1987): 143–56. For a leading revisionist work, see Alan S. Milward, *The Reconstruction of Western Europe, 1945–51*. For the position of Finland see Max Jakobson, "Paasikivi," *International Affairs* 1 (1990).

29. Vojtech Mastny, "Stalin and the Militarization of the Cold War," *International Security* 9, no. 3 (1984/85): 111; and Isaac Deutscher, *Stalin: A Political Biography*, 2d ed., pp. 580–87.

30. See Volkogonov, *Triumf i tragediia* 2 (part 2): 95–100; Gati, *Hungary and the Soviet Bloc*, pp. 108–23; and Milovan Djilas, *Rise and Fall*, pp. 133–42. For the domestic aspects of "Zhdanovism," see Werner G. Hahn, *Postwar Soviet Politics: The Fall of Zhdanov and the Defeat of Moderation, 1946–1953*.

31. "Report by Secretary Marshall, December 19, 1947," *A Decade of American Foreign Policy, 1941–49*, p. 106.

32. See Karel Kaplan, *Dans les archives du comité Central: 30 ans de secrets du bloc soviétique*, pp. 30–39; and Pavel Tigrid, "The Prague

Coup of 1948: The Elegant Takeover," in Thomas T. Hammond, ed., *The Anatomy of Communist Takeovers*, pp. 399–432; and James H. Billington, "Finland," in C. E. Black and T. P. Thornton, eds., *Communism and Revolution: The Strategic Uses of Political Violence*, pp. 117–44.

33. For various interpretations of the crisis, see Hannes Adomeit, *Soviet Risk-Taking and Crisis Behavior*, pp. 67–182.

34. *FRUS, 1948*, 2:909.

35. For the East-West exchanges of notes in this period, see *Documents on Germany*, pp. 150–221. See also Bullock, *Bevin*, pp. 578–79; and the exchanges in *FRUS, 1948*, 2:936–38, for internal Western deliberations.

36. Alexei Roshchin, "The UN in the Cold War Years," *International Affairs* 1 (1990): 217; and Viktor Israelian, "Zametki k istorii 'kholodnoi voinyi'," *SShA: Ekonomika, politika, ideologiia* [hereinafter, *SShA*] 9 (1989).

37. David Wightman, *Economic Co-operation in Europe: A Study of the United Nations Economic Commission for Europe*, pp. 7–8, 264; Gunnar Myrdal, "Twenty Years of the United Nations Economic Commission for Europe," *International Organization* 22, no. 3 (1968): 618; and UN, ECE, *Three Decades of the United Nations Economic Commission for Europe* (E/ECE/962).

38. See the various reports and resolutions in *Documents on Disarmament, 1945–1959*, 1:172, 178–79; and Bernhard G. Bechhoefer, *Postwar Negotiations for Arms Control*, pp. 123–42.

39. For activities in other organizations, see Herbert W. Briggs, *The International Law Commission*, pp. 78–80; Maureen Gallagher, "The World Health Organization: Promotion of U.S. and Soviet Foreign Policy Goals," *Journal of the American Medical Association* 186, no. 1 (1963): 30; and Leonard B. Schapiro, "The Soviet Union and International Organizations," *The Year Book of World Affairs, 1949*, pp. 214, 219.

40. See Mastny, "Europe in U.S.-USSR Relations," p. 28.

41. Royal Institute of International Affairs [hereinafter, RIIA], *Survey of International Affairs, 1951*, pp. 130–44.

42. See Andrei A. Gromyko, *Pamiatnoe*, 1:206–7.

43. For the text see *Documents on Disarmament, 1945–1959*, 1:252.

44. Wightman, *Economic Co-operation in Europe*, p. 264.

45. RIIA, *Survey of International Affairs, 1951*, p. 151.

46. Robert Loring Allen, "United Nations Technical Assistance: Soviet and East European Participation," *International Organization* 11 (1957); and Alexander Dallin, *The Soviet Union at the United Nations*, pp. 31–36.

47. RIIA, *Documents on International Affairs* [hereinafter, *Documents*], *1952*, pp. 85–88, for the note and enclosed treaty draft; see also *FRUS, 1952–1954*, 7 (part 1): 169–70.

48. Hans-Peter Schwarz, "Die Aera Adenauer," in Karl Dietrich Bracher, et al., *Geschichte der Bundesrepublik Deutschland*, 2:149–66; *FRUS, 1952–1954*, 7 (part 1): 169–327; and Marshall D. Shulman, *Stalin's Foreign Policy Reappraised*, p. 194.

49. See Adenauer, *Memoirs, 1945–1953*, pp. 310–28; and Schwarz, "Die Ära Adenauer," pp. 104–26.

50. Shulman, *Stalin's Foreign Policy Reappraised*, pp. 259, 264.

51. Ibid., p. 5.

52. See Audrey Kurth Cronin, *Great Power Politics and the Struggle over Austria*, pp. 50–52, 108–11.

53. Shulman, *Stalin's Foreign Policy Reappraised*, pp. 186–87.

54. See the concluding communiqué in RIIA, *Documents, 1952*, pp. 249–51.

55. Shulman did not explicitly mention the 1952 religious forum, but it clearly was analogous to the economic conference held in the same year.

56. "Sovetsko-norvezhkoe kommiunike," *Pravda*, November 16, 1955.

57. "Future Tasks of the Alliance," *Department of State Bulletin*, January 8, 1968, p. 51.

58. Andreas Meyer-Landrut, "Prospects for Allied Policy towards the East: The German View," *NATO Review* 35, no. 2 (1987).

59. *Razriadka* was still not a preferred term. *Smiagcheniia napriazhennosti* and *oslablenie napriazhennosti* also were used.

Chapter 3: Geneva and the Four-Power Process

1. Winston S. Churchill, *His Complete Speeches 1897–1963*, Robert Rhodes James, ed., 8:8484.

2. Ibid., 8:7944.

3. Minutes, Truman-Churchill meeting, January 18, 1952, *FRUS, 1952–1954*, 6 (part 1): 849.

4. Dean Acheson, *Present at the Creation. My Years at the State Department*, p. 268.

5. Dulles raised the six-power, two-China idea with Molotov at Vienna in May 1955, largely for bargaining purposes. *FRUS, 1955–1957*, 5:181. The other proposals are discussed in the text.

6. *FRUS, 1952–1954*, 6 (part 2): 964.

7. On Eden's opposition to a summit, see Robert Rhodes James, *Anthony Eden: A Biography*, pp. 365, 371, 400–403; and John Colville, *Fringes of Power: 10 Downing Street, Diaries 1939–1955*, pp. 705–6.

8. For the exchange of letters see *FRUS, 1952–1954*, 6 (part 2): 965.

9. For U.S. government deliberations immediately after Stalin's death, see W. W. Rostow, *Europe after Stalin: Eisenhower's Three Decisions of March 11, 1953*. See also the Policy Planning Staff paper recommending that the West "resist revival of CFM [and] . . . avoid referring issues to Deputies except for Austrian treaty." Leon W. Fuller of the Policy Planning Staff to PPS director Robert Bowie, January 5, 1954, *FRUS, 1952–1954*, 7 (part 1): 734.

10. James Reston, "Eisenhower and Churchill to Confer with French in Bermuda next Month," *New York Times*, May 22, 1953.

11. *Pravda*, May 24, 1953.

12. See Bohlen's telegram from Moscow, May 25, 1953, *FRUS, 1952–*

1954, 6 (part 1): 986. The Bermuda meeting was later postponed because of a political crisis in France.

13. Strobe Talbott, ed., *Khrushchev Remembers*, p. 393.

14. After Beria's fall in July 1953 it was rumored that he had favored far-reaching concessions to the West on Germany. See Ulam, *Expansion and Coexistence*, pp. 542–43; and Gromyko, *Memories*, p. 316.

15. *FRUS, 1952–1954*, 7 (part 1): 602.

16. Ibid., 7:604.

17. Harold Macmillan, *Tides of Fortune, 1945–1955*, p. 527. In all, 13 notes were exchanged.

18. See Bohlen's telegram from Moscow of November 27, 1953, *FRUS, 1952–1954*, 7 (part 1): 679.

19. The CFM which the Palais Rose Conference was attempting to arrange would have been held in Washington.

20. *FRUS, 1952–1954*, 7 (part 1): 682.

21. See Wilhelm G. Grewe, *Rückblenden 1976–1951*, p. 185; and Anthony Eden, *Full Circle*, p. 75.

22. U.S. Department of State, *Foreign Ministers Meeting: Berlin Discussions, January 25–February 18, 1954*, pp. 13–24.

23. Ibid., p. 34.

24. The Austrians took part in the sessions of the conference concerned with the state treaty. See Eden, *Full Circle*, pp. 82–83, for Molotov's "callous brutality" toward the Austrian delegation.

25. U.S. Department of State, *Berlin Discussions*, pp. 231–32.

26. *FRUS, 1952–1954*, 7 (part 1): 1205–6.

27. RIIA, *Documents, 1954*, pp. 39–43.

28. Ibid., pp. 46–51.

29. Ibid., pp. 58–61, for the Soviet note.

30. On the background to this telegram, see the correspondence between Churchill and Eisenhower of March–May 1954, *FRUS, 1952–1954*, 6 (part 2): 964–79; and Macmillan, *Tides of Fortune*, pp. 514–59.

31. The Soviet government later leaked this correspondence to rebut charges that it had delayed the convening of a conference. *New Times* 12 (1955): 2–4.

32. U.S. Department of State, *American Foreign Policy, 1950–1955*, 1:481.

33. Ibid., 1:488.

34. Ibid., 1:487.

35. For background see Cronin, *Great Power Politics and the Struggle over Austria*; Kurt Steiner, "Negotiations for an Austrian State Treaty," in Alexander George, et al., *U.S.-Soviet Security Cooperation: Achievements, Failures, Lessons*, pp. 75–76; and Vojtech Mastny, "Kremlin Politics and the Austrian Settlement," *Problems of Communism* 31, no. 4 (1982): 37–51.

36. *New Times* 7 (1955): 23.

37. Telegram from the State Department (hereinafter listed as State) to the high commissioner for Austria, February 15, 1955, *FRUS, 1955–1957*, 5:1.

38. See ibid., 5:2, for example, for the remarks by Soviet minister Kudryatsev, reported from Vienna on February 23.

39. For Austrian and three-power concerns about the drawbacks of a bilateral approach, see the telegrams from High Commissioner Thompson of March 23, 25, 1955, in ibid., 5:19–20.

40. See the Austrian aide-mémoire of March 14, RIIA, *Documents, 1955*, p. 220.

41. Bohlen to State, March 5, 1955, *FRUS, 1955–1957*, 5:8–9. See also Bohlen, *Witness to History*, p. 374. Bruno Kreisky expressed a similar view on March 21. See the telegram of March 5 from Thompson, *FRUS, 1955–1957*, 5:11.

42. For Bohlen's differences with Thompson, see his telegram from Moscow, March 31, 1955, ibid., 5:26.

43. Memorandum of conversation, Dulles and Austrian Ambassador Karl Gruber, Washington, D.C., March 25, 1955, ibid., 5:17. For Eden's views, see the remarks by the first secretary of the British embassy in Washington, D.C., ibid., 5:19 n. 3.

44. Convinced that Germany was the real object of Soviet interest, Dulles was skeptical they would attend an ambassadorial conference. See RIIA, *Documents, 1955*, p. 221, for the tripartite declaration by Britain, France, and the United States.

45. Mastny, "Kremlin Politics," pp. 46–48.

46. For the bilateral documents, see *New Times* 17 (1955), Special Supplement; and *New Times* 22 (1955), Special Supplement.

47. Note of April 19, 1955, RIIA, *Documents, 1955*, pp. 224–25.

48. U.S. delegation to State, May 3, 1955, *FRUS, 1955–1957*, 5:69.

49. Ibid., 5:89, for Dulles's remarks at the North Atlantic Council staff meeting, Paris, May 8, 1955.

50. Soviet Ambassador Ilichev yielded on May 12. See the delegation telegram of that day in ibid., 5:108; and Macmillan, *Tides of Fortune*, p. 596.

51. For the complete text of the treaty, see *Department of State Bulletin*, July 6, 1955, pp. 916–32.

52. Telegram from the U.S. high commissioner to State, May 14, 1955, *FRUS, 1955–1957*, 5:113.

53. For British thinking, see Macmillan, *Tides of Fortune*, pp. 594–95.

54. In his speech at the signing ceremony the following day, Molotov engaged in what Dulles called a bit of "characteristic trickery" by implying that the Western proposals had accepted the Soviet draft. See Dulles's report to the NSC of May 19, *FRUS, 1955–1957*, 5:116.

55. For the British-Austrian exchange (November 14 and December 6, 1955), see RIIA, *Documents, 1955*, p. 239.

56. Eden, *Full Circle*, pp. 320–21.

57. See State telegrams from Paris in *FRUS, 1955–1957*, 5:123, 126–28.

58. Churchill resigned on April 5.

59. Memorandum of conversation with Herbert Blankenhorn, March 9, 1955, *FRUS, 1955–1957*, 5:134.

60. James Reston, "President Backs Talks in Advance of Big 4 Parley," *New York Times*, March 24, 1955.

61. These views were relayed to Dulles in a telegram from Under Secretary Hoover, May 15, 1955, *FRUS, 1955–1957*, 5:180.

62. Tripartite note of May 10, United States, Department of State, *The Geneva Conference of Heads of Government, July 18–23, 1955*, pp. 1–2. This plan has been attributed to Macmillan. For his thinking at the time see his *Tides of Fortune*, p. 588.

63. *Pravda*, May 27, 1955.

64. As expressed by Blankenhorn, telegram from the delegation at the London working group to State, April 28, 1955, *FRUS, 1955–1957*, 5:154.

65. Eden, *Full Circle*, pp. 327–28. See also Eden's comments at the tripartite luncheon with Eisenhower and Faure, *FRUS, 1955–1957*, 5:345.

66. "Note de la Direction d'Europe," July 4, 1955, in France, Ministère des Affaires Etrangères, *Documents Diplomatiques Français, 1955* (hereinafter, *DDF, 1955*), 2:10–11. The French were urged by the Soviets to play a mediating role, but were determined not to do so. See Ambassador Joxe's report of a conversation in Moscow with Saburov, March 2, 1955, ibid., 2:3–5.

67. See the TASS declaration of June 14, 1955, cited in Andrei Gromyko and B. N. Ponomarev, *Soviet Foreign Policy*, 2:189. Khrushchev recognized that reunification was "the number one goal" of the Western powers, and that it "really meant the expulsion of Socialist forces from the German Democratic Republic." Talbott, *Khrushchev Remembers*, p. 400.

68. Bohlen, *Witness to History*, p. 379; and the memorandum of conversation, *FRUS, 1955–1957*, 5:243–47.

69. See also the TASS dispatch of July 12, and Joxe's telegram to Pinay from Moscow reporting on a conversation with the Soviet leadership, for Soviet thinking on the eve of the conference. *DDF, 1955*, 2:78–79.

70. For the text of the Soviet note see RIIA, *Documents, 1955*, pp. 245–48. The USSR had invited Adenauer to visit the Soviet Union in January 1955, but he had rejected the offer.

71. For Adenauer's views see the memorandum of conversation, Adenauer and Dulles, New York, June 17, 1955, *FRUS, 1955–1957*, 5:235; and the more forceful presentation by Blankenhorn to the Paris working group, telegram from the U.S. delegation to State, July 9, 1955, ibid., 5:310. For the further exchange of notes with the USSR see RIIA, *Documents, 1955*, p. 249.

72. Report of the Paris working group, July 15, 1955, *FRUS, 1955–1957*, 5:331.

73. Memorandum of discussion, NSC meeting of July 7, 1955, ibid., 5:276.

74. U.S. Department of State, *The Geneva Conference*, p. 39.

75. Delegation record, second plenary session, July 18, 1955, *FRUS, 1955–1957*, 5:370.

76. Telegram from U.S. delegation to State, July 20 [19], 1955, ibid., 5:383–84.

77. See also Eden, *Full Circle*, p. 330.

78. See, for example, Dulles's cable to Hoover, July 20, 1955, *FRUS, 1955–1957*, 5:403; and *New York Times*, July 20, 1955.

79. See the July 19 telegram from the delegation to State summarizing the third plenary session of July 19, 1955, *FRUS, 1955–1957*, 5:388–397.

80. Remarks at third plenary session, July 19, as reported in delegation telegram to State, July 19, 1955, ibid., 5:396.

81. Dulles telegram to the acting secretary, July 20, 1955, ibid., 5:403–4.

82. Ibid., 5:403; see also 5:397–98 for Dulles's memorandum to Eisenhower, urging him to take up the subject with Zhukov at their lunch scheduled for the following day.

83. Based on a brief Eden-Dulles conversation of the following day, reported by Dulles in ibid., 5:420.

84. These conclusions were drawn from conversations at the dinner which the British hosted for the Soviet leaders on July 19. Eisenhower and Dulles were briefed on the dinner at a breakfast meeting with Eden and Macmillan on July 20; see the memorandum of conversation in ibid., 5:398–403.

85. Ibid.

86. For the record of the meeting, see the telegram from the delegation to State, July 20, 1955, ibid., 5:405–7.

87. Memorandum of conversation with Dulles, July 20, 1955, ibid., 5:419.

88. For the text of the treaty see ibid., 5:516–19; for the record of the session, 5:421–24.

89. U.S. delegation to State, July 21, 1955, ibid., 5:436.

90. Ibid., 5:437.

91. U.S. delegation to State, July 22, 1955, ibid., 5:469.

92. Eden, *Full Circle*, p. 338. See also Eden's remarks at the first restricted session, July 23, 1955, where he made essentially the same point to the conference, *FRUS, 1955–1957*, 5:497.

93. In addition to the Germany-European security problem, there were four other unresolved issues on the table as the restricted session began: the question of consultation with the GDR and FRG; and three disarmament issues. The disarmament aspects of the conference are discussed in chapter 6.

94. See the memorandum of conversation prepared by Bohlen, July 23, 1955, *FRUS, 1955–1957*, 5:488–92. In his account of his meetings with Eisenhower, Zhukov noted only that the president expressed support for "the policies of U.S. imperialistic circles." G. K. Zhukov, *Vospominaniia i razmyshlenia*, p. 723.

95. Eden, *Full Circle*, p. 339. U.S. delegation record of the seventh (restricted) plenary session, July 23, 1955, *FRUS, 1955–1957*, 5:503–12.

96. Eden, *Full Circle*, p. 339.

97. U.S. Department of State, *The Geneva Conference*, pp. 67–68.

98. U.S. delegation record of the seventh (restricted) plenary session, July 23, 1955, *FRUS, 1955–1957,* 5:499.

99. Talbott, *Khrushchev Remembers,* p. 400. See also Gromyko and Ponomarev, *Soviet Foreign Policy,* p. 191: "the directives combined two different theses: the Western thesis for the reunification of Germany by means of 'free elections,' and the Soviet thesis that the German question should be settled in accordance with the national interests of the German people and the interests of European security"; and Gromyko's essentially negative evaluation of Geneva, in *Pamiatnoe,* 1:367.

100. Dwight D. Eisenhower, *Mandate for Change 1953–1956,* p. 524.

101. Ibid., p. 526. See also Bohlen, *Witness to History,* p. 384.

102. Message of Adenauer to Eisenhower, July 25, 1955, in State telegram, Geneva to the Secretary, No. 193, Dwight D. Eisenhower Library, Abilene, Kansas.

103. NSC meeting minutes, July 28, 1955, *FRUS, 1955–1957,* 5:531.

104. RIIA, *Documents, 1955,* p. 200.

105. *Pravda,* August 5, 1955.

106. RIIA, *Documents, 1955,* p. 201.

107. Ibid., p. 203.

108. Lester B. Pearson, *Memoirs,* 2:191–211.

109. For growing Western pessimism, see Macmillan, *Tides of Fortune,* pp. 642–43; the "Note du Directeur General Roland de Margerie," August 1, 1955, *DDF, 1955,* 2:165–69; and Grewe, *Rückblenden,* p. 229.

110. See the editorial note in *FRUS, 1955–1957,* 5:588, for this group.

111. See the deliberations of the Bonn group and statements by the Western ministers, especially Dulles's remarks to the British and French ambassadors, August 1, 1955, *FRUS, 1955–1957,* 5:542, in which he urged further use of the "continued reiteration technique" which had worked in the case of Austria.

112. The Soviet government published these instructions in an official history. See Gromyko and Ponomarev, *Soviet Foreign Policy,* 2:192.

113. U.S. Department of State, *The Geneva Meeting of Foreign Ministers, October 27–November 6, 1955,* pp. 18–23.

114. See Macmillan (conference chairman at the time of this incident), *Tides of Fortune,* p. 645, for details. Ivone Kirkpatrick, the British permanent under secretary who accompanied Macmillan, later wrote that "from the start Molotov made it clear that the Soviet government had no intention of fulfilling the understandings given by the two leaders in the summer." *The Inner Circle: Memoirs,* p. 262.

115. U.S. Department of State, *Geneva Meeting of Foreign Ministers,* pp. 38–45.

116. Ibid., p. 46.

117. Macmillan, *Tides of Fortune,* p. 646.

118. U.S. Department of State, *Geneva Meeting of Foreign Ministers,* pp. 75–76.

119. Macmillan, *Tides of Fortune,* pp. 644–45.

120. U.S. Department of State, *Geneva Meeting of Foreign Ministers,*

pp. 75–76. For the text of the Soviet proposal, see the U.S. delegation telegram of November 1, 1955, *FRUS, 1955–1957*, 5:659.

121. U.S. Department of State, *Geneva Meeting of Foreign Ministers*, pp. 105–22. Adenauer had made precisely this argument to Dulles in a letter of August 9, but Dulles disagreed in his reply. For Adenauer's letter see Konrad Adenauer, *Erinnerungen 1953–1955*, pp. 478–80; for the reply, see *FRUS, 1955–1957*, 5:549.

122. Memorandum of conversation, October 29, 1955, *FRUS, 1955–1957*, 5:649.

123. There were strong signs of British "softness" on the German issue even before the conference began. See the (still partially classified) letter from the U.S. representative on the Paris working group, Coburn Kidd, to Jacques Reinstein of October 17, 1955, ibid., 5:614–15.

124. Halvard Lange's observation was less significant in its own right than for having been recalled by Macmillan, *Tides of Fortune*, pp. 642–43. The French remained more wary than the British of possible Soviet-West German or German-German bilateral dealings, and especially of the position of the German Social Democrats. See, for example, the reports of de Margerie (chargé d'affaires in Bonn) to Pinay of November 10, 11, 1955, in *DDF, 1955*, 2:792–95.

125. Memorandum from Bohlen to Dulles, November 7, 1955, *FRUS, 1955–1957*, 5:701.

126. Macmillan, *Tides of Fortune*, p. 647.

127. Memorandum of conversation, November 15, 1955, *FRUS, 1955–1957*, 5:794.

128. U.S. Department of State, *Background of Heads of Government Conference, 1960: Principal Documents, 1955–1959*, p. 46.

129. See the internal memorandum of the French foreign ministry of November 21, 1955, especially the section, "La 'relance européenne,'" in *DDF, 1955*, 2:837–39.

130. Charles R. Planck, *The Changing Status of German Reunification in Western Diplomacy, 1955–1966*, p. 17.

131. As the same observer noted, Geneva "complicated infinitely the efforts of Presidents Kennedy and de Gaulle to explore new paths in East-West relations after 1960." Ibid.

132. U.S. Department of State, *American Foreign Policy: Current Documents, 1958*, p. 701.

133. Veljko Micunovic, *Moscow Diary*, pp. 327–28. According to this account, the Politburo issued a directive that nothing more about Soviet superiority in rocketry be published, and that peaceful coexistence again was to be emphasized. Bulganin's letter writing campaign was timed to coincide with the new propaganda line.

134. At Geneva the Soviet leaders had expressed to Eisenhower a desire to come to the United States. Stephen E. Ambrose, *Eisenhower: The President*, p. 266, citing a post-Geneva briefing of Congressional leaders. See also *FRUS, 1955–1957*, 5:487.

135. Micunovic, *Moscow Diary*, pp. 335, 338.

136. *Documents on Disarmament, 1945–1959*, 2:929.

137. Bulganin to Eisenhower, January 8, 1958, *American Foreign Policy, 1958*, p. 705.

138. Ibid., p. 703.

139. Dulles news conference, January 10, 1958, ibid., p. 713.

140. Eisenhower to Bulganin, January 12, 1958, ibid., p. 721.

141. Harold Macmillan, *Riding the Storm, 1956–1959*, p. 468; and *Correspondence with the Soviet Union on Summit Talks*, Cmnd. 381 and Cmnd. 423.

142. Bulganin to Eisenhower, February 1, 1958, *American Foreign Policy, 1958*, p. 742.

143. Soviet aide-mémoire of February 28, 1958, ibid., p. 751.

144. Declaration by the Western ambassadors, March 31, 1958, ibid., p. 778.

145. Ibid., p. 781.

146. Statement of the three ambassadors to the Soviet government, April 16, 1958, ibid., p. 787.

147. Statement of the three ambassadors to the Soviet government, May 3, 1958, ibid., p. 793; and aide-mémoire of May 28, 1958, p. 802.

148. Ibid., p. 803.

149. For confirmation that Khrushchev approved the execution of Nagy, see Evgenii Ambartsumov, "Zhertvoprinoshenie Imre Nadia," *Moskovskie novosti* 27 (1989). See Hans Kroll, *Lebenserinnerungen eines Botschafters*, pp. 378–83, for the organized Soviet attack on the West German embassy.

150. Kroll, *Lebenserinnerungen*, p. 384.

151. Note of November 27, 1958, *American Foreign Policy, 1958*, pp. 591–96.

152. See Kroll, *Lebenserinnerungen*, pp. 389–400 for this episode.

153. *Background, 1960*, p. 319.

154. Note of February 16, 1959, *Background, 1960*, p. 329.

155. See Macmillan's account of the trip in his *Riding the Storm, 1956–1959*, pp. 557–655.

156. *Background, 1960*, p. 330.

157. Foreign Minister Brentano voiced serious reservations about the plan in the Washington quadripartite talks. U.S. Department of State, outgoing telegram, April 1, 1959, Dwight D. Eisenhower Library.

158. *Department of State Bulletin*, August 24, 1959, p. 269; and *Documents on Disarmament, 1945–1959*, 2:1441.

159. *Background, 1960*, p. 461.

160. Andre Fontaine, *History of the Cold War: From the Korean War to the Present*, p. 326.

161. Shevchenko recalled a conversation with Khrushchev in 1960 in which he stated: "We threw a little scare into the NATO countries last year with the spirit of Camp David. . . . We must work further at turning the United States against Europe and Europe against the United States. That was the technique that Vladimir Ilyich taught us. I have not forgotten this lesson." Arkady Shevchenko, *Breaking With Moscow*, p. 103. See also Khrushchev's account in Strobe Talbott, ed., *Khrushchev Remembers: The Last Testament*, pp. 368–416.

162. Harold Macmillan, *Pointing the Way 1959–1961*, p. 209. For Khrushchev's opening statement, see *New Times* 21 (1960): 34–36.

163. See, for example, Michael R. Beschloss, *Mayday: Eisenhower, Khrushchev and the U-2 Affair*, pp. 374–80.

164. Charles de Gaulle, *Memoirs of Hope: Renewal and Endeavor*, p. 248. Khrushchev himself deepened the mystery when he claimed, at a diplomatic reception in 1962, that he had been opposed to going to Paris but had been forced to by others. "Reluctant at 1960 Summit," *New York Times*, June 8, 1962. In his memoirs he implausibly asserted that the Soviet delegation left for Paris with the "necessary documents" prepared for discussions on the German problem and especially disarmament, but that on the plane Khrushchev decided to redraft his opening statement to make it a protest against the U-2. See Talbott, *Khrushchev Remembers: The Last Testament*, pp. 449–61; and Michel Tatu, *Power in the Kremlin*, pp. 49–68, for a discussion of Soviet internal politics.

165. This was the view of Vernon Walters, who attended the meetings as an interpreter. See his *Silent Missions*, p. 348.

166. "Peace Plea on Vietnam in Moscow," *The Times*, December 2, 1965.

167. Text in Boris Meissner, ed., *Moskau-Bonn: Die Beziehungen zwischen der Sowjetunion und der Bundesrepublik Deutschland 1953–1975*, 2:1270–71. For general background see William E. Griffith, *The Ostpolitik of the Federal Republic of Germany*. For the legal status of Germany after the Moscow Treaty, see Monica H. Forbes, *Feindstaatenklauseln, Viermaechteverantwortung und Deutsche Frage*.

168. Text in Meissner, *Moskau-Bonn*, 2:1271–72.

169. See Adomeit, *Soviet Risk-Taking and Crisis Behavior*, pp. 200–201, for this phase of the crisis.

170. Arthur Schlesinger, Jr., *A Thousand Days: John F. Kennedy in the White House*, p. 348. See also Frank Costigliola, "The Pursuit of Atlantic Community: Nuclear Arms, Dollars, and Berlin," in Thomas G. Paterson, ed., *Kennedy's Quest for Victory: American Foreign Policy, 1961–1963*, pp. 24–56.

171. The text appeared in *Pravda*, June 10, 1961.

172. Pierre Salinger, *With Kennedy*, p. 191.

173. See Curtis Cate, *The Ides of August: The Berlin Wall Crisis, 1961*.

174. Adomeit, *Soviet Risk-Taking*, p. 213; and Theodore Sorenson, *Kennedy*, pp. 598–99.

175. See Salinger, *With Kennedy*, pp. 190–99.

176. Dean Rusk, *As I Saw It*, p. 221.

177. Schlesinger, *A Thousand Days*, p. 398.

178. See Sorenson, *Kennedy*, p. 599.

179. Rusk, *As I Saw It*, p. 221.

180. Talbott, *Khrushchev Remembers: The Last Testament*, pp. 501–9.

181. *SSSR-GDR: 30 let otnoshenii 1949–1979: Dokumenty i materialy*, pp. 96–104.

182. The Brezhnev-Kosygin leadership appears to have resisted East German calls to heat up the Berlin situation as a way of putting pressure on West Germany. See the account by Gomulka's interpreter of an April 1967 conversation among Gomulka, Brezhnev, and Honecker, in which the latter vainly appealed for an "offensive" approach. Erwin Weit, *Ostblock Intern*, pp. 166–67.

183. See Griffith, *The Ostpolitik of the Federal Republic of Germany*, pp. 196–200, for background.

184. *Pravda*, July 11, 1969.

185. For a definitive account of the talks, see Werner Link, "Aussen- und Deutschland Politik in der Aera Brandt, 1969–74," Bracher et al., *Geschichte der Bundesrepublik*, 5:198–206.

186. For the agreement, annexes, and accompanying protocol, see Charles I. Bevans, *Treaties and Other International Agreements of the United States of America, 1776–1949*, 24 (part 1) (1973): 283–392.

187. See A. James McAdams, *East Germany and Détente: Building Authority after the Wall*, pp. 110–15.

188. Link, "Aussen- und Deutschland Politik," p. 203.

189. There were differences between the West German government and the three Western powers on the Berlin issue. The Basic Law and the Berlin Constitution of 1950 both stipulated that West Berlin was a *Land* of the Federal Republic. However, the Western governments expressed reservations on these provisions, which they claimed were irreconcilable with their four-power rights. The West German government contended that the application (but not the validity) of the Basic Law had been suspended in Berlin. See Ernst R. Zivier, *The Legal Status of the Land Berlin: A Survey after the Quadripartite Agreement*, pp. 74–77. This dispute became moot in 1990, when the four powers relinquished all of their rights in Berlin.

190. See Link, "Aussen- und Deutschland Politik," pp. 202–4, which draws heavily on French official papers.

191. See Bahr's extravagant assessment in Rudolf Steinke and Michael Vale, eds., *Germany Debates Defense: The NATO Alliance at the Crossroads*; and Henry A. Kissinger, *White House Years*, pp. 830–32. For a balanced assessment see Jonathan Dean, "Berlin in a Divided Germany: An Evolving International Regime," in George et al., *U.S.-Soviet Security Cooperation*, pp. 98–104.

192. See Meissner, *Moskau-Bonn*, 2:1571, for the UN; and John J. Maresca, *To Helsinki*, pp. 81–85, for CSCE.

193. Serge Schmemann, "Shevardnadze Seeks Curbs on Forces in New Germany," *New York Times*, June 23, 1990.

Chapter 4: Diplomacy

1. According to Khrushchev, "the Geneva meeting was an important breakthrough for us on the diplomatic front. We had established ourselves as able to hold our own in the international arena." Talbott, *Khrushchev Remembers*, p. 400.

2. Mastny, "Kremlin Politics and the Austrian Settlement," p. 47.

3. Orjan Berner, *Soviet Policies toward the Nordic Countries*, p. 75; and Max Jakobson, *Finland: Myth and Reality*, pp. 102–5.

4. Adenauer, *Erinnerungen*, p. 492. See also Bohlen, *Witness to History*, p. 376; and Talbott, *Khrushchev Remembers: The Last Testament*, pp. 357–60. For an overview of German policy, see Peter Siebenmorgen, *Gezeitenwechsel: Aufbruch zur Entspannungspolitik*.

5. Briefing for Dulles by Ambassador Krekeler, August 28, 1955, *FRUS, 1955–1957*, 5:555.

6. Adenauer to Livingston Merchant, August 31, 1955, *FRUS, 1955–1957*, 5:567.

7. Ibid., 5:568.

8. Adenauer, *Erinnerungen*, p. 513; the same conversation is summarized in *FRUS, 1955–1957*, 5:576.

9. Adenauer, *Erinnerungen*, pp. 514–15. (Italics in the original.)

10. The Soviet leaders later partially reneged on Bulganin's informal offer by refusing to agree in writing to the return of the prisoners. Bulganin agreed only to give his word that the prisoners would be released following the establishment of relations, as they ultimately were. The West Germans were left bitter "about [the] Soviets using 9,000 human beings as [a] method of forcing diplomatic relations." See Carlo Schmid, *Erinnerungen*, pp. 566–82; and the telegrams from U.S. Ambassador Conant, September 15, 16, 1955, *FRUS, 1955–1957*, 5:585, 587.

11. U.S. embassy telegram, September 14, 1955, *FRUS, 1955–1957*, 5:582.

12. See the accounts of the harsh exchange between Bohlen and Adenauer in Adenauer, *Erinnerungen*, p. 492; and Bohlen, *Witness to History*, p. 376.

13. See de Margerie's briefing to the North Atlantic Council, November 23, 1955, telegram from the U.S. representative to State, *FRUS, 1955–1957*, 5:807.

14. See the various accounts cited in the next chapter, but especially George Brown, *In My Way*, p. 75.

15. See Christian Pineau, *Nikita Sergueevitch Khrouchtchev*, p. 142, and the discussion in chapter 7 of this book. In a corollary to this argument, Soviet spokesmen told the West Germans that only they were strong enough to count for anything in Europe and thus able to stand up to the Americans. See Kroll's account of a 1958 conversation with Khrushchev in his *Lebenserinnerungen*, p. 363.

16. Pearson, *Memoirs*, 2:208.

17. See Adenauer's letter to Dulles, September 23, 1955, *FRUS, 1955–1957*, 5:592.

18. "Sovetsko-norvezhkoe kommiunike," *Pravda*, November 16, 1955.

19. Curt Gasteyger, "Gegenseitige Staatsbesuche als Teil des neuen Kurses in der sowjetischen Aussenpolitik," *Europa Archiv* 11 (1956): 8908–9.

20. "Pledge to Soviet Evaded by Danes," *New York Times*, March 7, 1956; for the text see "Sovetsko-datskoe kommiunike," *Pravda*, March 7, 1956.

21. Hansen briefing to the North Atlantic Council, May 4, telegram from the U.S. delegation to State, May 5, 1956, in *FRUS, 1955–1957*, 4:355.

22. See Berner, *Soviet Policies toward the Nordic Countries*, p. 83.

23. See Tage Erlander's account in *1955–1960*, pp. 298–311; and "Sovetskoe-shvedskoe kommiunike," *Pravda*, April 4, 1956.

24. For the draft text see *Documents, 1956*, pp. 579–80.

25. *Pravda*, February 15, 1956.

26. Arnaldo Cortesi, "Italian Red Asks Pact with Soviet," *New York Times*, March 15, 1956. See also "Zaiavlenie Pravitel'stva SSSR Pravitel'stvu Italii o zakliuchenii Dogovora o Druzhbe i Nenapadenii mezhdu SSSR i Ital'ianskoi Respublikoi," *Pravda*, May 28, 1958, reprinted in USSR, Ministerstvo Inostrannykh Del (hereinafter listed as MID), *SSSR-Italiia: Stranitsy istorii, 1917–1984, Dokumenty i materialy*, pp. 95–98.

27. There were some exceptions. In 1958 British prime minister Macmillan offered to explore the prospects for a U.K.-USSR nonaggression treaty. But nothing came of this offer, which was overtaken by the Berlin crisis. Macmillan, *Riding the Storm*, p. 463.

28. Eden, *Full Circle*, p. 340; *FRUS, 1955–1957*, 5:399; and Macmillan, *Tides of Fortune*, p. 623.

29. "Soviet Asks a Visit by Faure and Pinay," *New York Times*, August 3, 1955.

30. Eden, *Full Circle*, pp. 397–98.

31. *Documents, 1956*, pp. 646–53.

32. "Zaiavlenie o peregovorakh Predsedatelia Soveta Ministrov SSSR N. A. Bulganina i Chlena Prezidiuma Verkhovnogo Soveta SSSR N. S. Khrushcheva c Prem'er-Ministrom Soedinennogo Korolevstva Serom Antoni Idenom," *Pravda*, April 27, 1956.

33. Eden, *Full Circle*, p. 397. After a long discussion in the cabinet it was decided that because of his recent anti-British remarks Khrushchev could have only tea with the queen rather than lunch. "Lunch with the Queen Was Banned by Eden," *The Times*, January 2, 1986.

34. See Kirkpatrick, *The Inner Circle*, p. 262.

35. "Faure Sees Coty on Offer," *New York Times*, August 4, 1955.

36. *U.S. News and World Report*, April 6, 1956.

37. See the account by Christian Pineau, Mollet's foreign minister, in his *Khrouchtchev*, pp. 136–48.

38. "Zaiavlenie o peregovorakh," *Pravda*, May 20, 1956.

39. Macmillan, *Riding the Storm*, p. 288.

40. Micunovic, *Moscow Diary*, p. 241.

41. Khrushchev later confirmed that the Soviet Union cancelled these visits solely because "we were more eager to visit the United States." See Talbott, *Khrushchev Remembers: The Last Testament*, p. 370.

42. Macmillan, *Riding the Storm*, p. 585.

43. Dwight D. Eisenhower, *Waging Peace, 1956–1961*, pp. 405–6.

44. Murphy misunderstood his instructions and forgot to attach conditions—by which time Khrushchev had already agreed to come and could not be disinvited. Murphy acknowledged that Eisenhower "agreed

very reluctantly" to issue the invitation. Robert Murphy, *Diplomat among Warriors*, p. 438.

45. For the Nixon administration, see Henry Kissinger, *Years of Upheaval*, p. 288. On the hopes of the Reagan administration, see Bill Keller, "Politics and Security Concerns Dash Hopes for Extended Trip by Gorbachev," *New York Times*, October 31, 1987.

46. De Gaulle, *Memoirs of Hope*, pp. 213–39. For Khrushchev's surprise at de Gaulle's invitation, see Talbott, *Khrushchev Remembers: The Last Testament*, p. 417.

47. For the visits to Scandinavia see Talbott, *Khrushchev Remembers: The Last Testament*, pp. 515–27.

48. Speculation in the West has long centered on the role that internal opposition to the trip might have played in Khrushchev's ouster. A few days after the trip was announced in Bonn a West German engineer working at the FRG's Moscow embassy was attacked with mustard gas while attending a church service. When the authorities in Bonn protested the attack, they were told that the engineer was a spy. After another West German protest, the Soviet government sent a conciliatory reply, but a few hours later Khrushchev was removed from office. For this incident see Tatu, *Power in the Kremlin*, pp. 388–91.

49. For general background see Marshall D. Shulman, "Recent Soviet Foreign Policy: Some Patterns in Retrospect," *Journal of International Affairs* 22, no. 1 (1968): 26–47.

50. "Soviet Delegation Arrives for Visit to Turkish Cities," *New York Times*, January 5, 1965.

51. "Gromyko to Visit Turkey," *New York Times*, April 2, 1965.

52. "Kosygin Says Soviet Wants Turkish Nonaggression Pact," *New York Times*, June 26, 1965.

53. "Gromyko Discusses Cyprus with Turk," *New York Times*, May 19, 1965.

54. For the joint communiqué see USSR, MID, *SSSR-Italiia*, pp. 124–29.

55. De Gaulle, *Memoirs of Hope*, p. 232.

56. Quoted in Alfred Grosser, *Franco-Soviet Relations Today*, p. 43.

57. Accounts of these trips appear in Peter Scholl-Latour, *Im Sog des Generals: Von Abidjan nach Moskau*, pp. 318–56; and in Grosser, *Franco-Soviet Relations Today*, pp. 41–46.

58. Gromyko, *Pamiatnoe*, 1:423.

59. Excerpts from Kosygin's speech appeared in *The Times*, February 10, 1967. The Wilson government agreed to start negotiations on a treaty of friendship and peaceful cooperation, but declined to negotiate nonaggression language, which it saw as incompatible with Britain's obligations to NATO. The negotiations lagged and ultimately were terminated after the Soviet invasion of Czechoslovakia. Terence Prittie, "Solid, Sober End to Kosygin Visit—But No Big Breakthrough," *Guardian*, February 14, 1967. The text of the joint communiqué appeared in *Pravda* of the same date.

60. See Wolfe, *Soviet Power and Europe*, p. 292. U.S. officials were

aware of but did not encourage Wilson's efforts. See Lyndon B. Johnson, *The Vantage Point*, pp. 253–54.

61. "Vietnam Challenge to Mr. Wilson Today," *The Times*, July 18, 1966.

62. "Sovetsko-frantsuzskoe kommiunike," *Izvestiia*, May 1, 1965.

63. On the other hand, Kosygin was not successful in inducing de Gaulle to record, in a bilateral communiqué, acceptance of the Oder-Neisse line as Poland's western border, even though he had taken this position privately in his talks with Stalin in 1944 and publicly in remarks to a press conference in March 1959. See Grosser, *Franco-Soviet Relations Today*, p. 71.

64. USSR, *Vneshniaia politika Sovetskogo Soiuza: Sbornik dokumentov, 1966* (hereinafter, *VpSS: Sbornik dokumentov*), p. 62.

65. Ibid., p. 300.

66. *The Times*, February 14, 1967.

67. Text in *The Times*, January 25, 1968.

68. *VpSS: Sbornik dokumentov, 1967*, pp. 29–30.

69. *VpSS: Sbornik dokumentov, 1968*, p. 199.

70. *XXV s"ezd Kommunisticheskoi Partii Sovetskogo Soiuza, 24 fevralia–5 marta 1976 g.: Stenograficheskii otchët* (hereinafter *Stenograficheskii otchët, 1976*), 1:40.

71. For the interaction of domestic and international factors leading to this turn of events, see Archie Brown, "In the Corridors of the Kremlin," *Times Literary Supplement*, April 1, 1983.

72. Bernard Gwertzman, "Pompidou Is Warmly Welcomed in the Soviet Union," *New York Times*, October 7, 1970.

73. This did not mean that relations between the three men were good or, as was to be seen later in the decade, that Brezhnev would prolong this arrangement for foreign policy purposes. See Brown, "In the Corridors of the Kremlin"; and Harry Gelman, *The Brezhnev Politburo and the Decline of Détente*, pp. 78–79.

74. Willy Brandt, *People and Politics: The Years 1960–1975*, p. 323.

75. Ibid., p. 328.

76. Ibid., p. 345.

77. Pierre Hassner, "Moscow and the Western Alliance," *Problems of Communism* 30, no. 3 (1981): 52.

78. *Pravda*, October 31, 1971.

79. "Kommiunike o vstreche mezhdu General'nym Sekretarem TsK KPSS L. I. Brezhnevym i Federal'nym kantslerom FRG Brandtom," *Pravda*, September 19, 1971.

80. Hedrick Smith, "Brandt Supports a Europe Parley," *New York Times*, September 19, 1971.

81. *Department of State Bulletin*, June 26, 1972, p. 901.

82. Maresca, *To Helsinki*, p. 10.

83. Ibid., p. 47.

84. Ibid., p. 56.

85. Ibid., p. 137; and William G. Hyland, *Mortal Rivals*, pp. 114–20.

86. Kissinger, *Years of Upheaval*, p. 293.

87. "M. Tindemans seduit par M. Gromyko," *Le Soir*, June 26, 1975.

88. Michel Tatu, "Moscou multiplie les efforts pour assurer le success de la visite de M. Brejnev à Paris," *Le Monde*, October 24–25, 1975; see also Edward A. Kolodziej, *French International Policy Under De Gaulle and Pompidou: The Politics of Grandeur*, p. 157.

89. "La sécurité européene au centre des conversations belgosoviétiques," *Le Soir*, June 26, 1975.

90. Leonid Brezhnev, *Leninskom kursom*, 5:338.

91. Iu. Kashlev, *Europe Five Years After Helsinki: The Soviet Viewpoint*, p. 35. See *Ot Khel'sinki do Belgrada: Sovetskii soiuz i osushchestvlenie Zakliuchitel'nogo akta obshcheevropeiskogo soveshchaniia, dokumenty i materiali*, pp. 129–61, for the texts of 14 such agreements concluded with West European countries in the first two years after the conference.

92. *Pravda*, May 20, 1980.

93. Neville Waites, "France under Mitterrand: External Relations," *The World Today* 6 (1982): 229.

94. German Federal Institute for East European and International Studies, *The Soviet Union 1984/85*, p. 241.

95. The term had been used by Brezhnev on his trip to Bonn in 1981 and by Gorbachev in his December 1984 speech to the House of Commons.

96. See the remarks attributed to Lev Zaikov in *Corriere della Sera*, April 9, 1986; the announcement of a Gorbachev visit to Italy in early 1987, *Avanti*, September 30, 1986; and a Greek government announcement that Gorbachev would make an official visit to Greece in the spring of 1987. Athens Domestic Service, January 13, 1987, Foreign Broadcast Information Service, *Daily Report: West Europe* (hereinafter, FBIS-WEU), same date.

97. For the text see *Pravda*, November 28, 1986.

98. "Zhit' i deistvovat' po mandatu Zhenevy," *Izvestiia*, December 24, 1985.

99. Robert J. McCartney, "Allies Rebuff Soviet Arms Forum Proposal," *Washington Post*, July 14, 1988.

100. For the agreements see *Izvestiia*, April 2, 1987. For the disagreements on deterrence, see the dinner speeches of the two leaders, *Pravda*, April 1, 1987; and Martin Walker and James Nauhgtie, "Thatcher Sparring for Points," *Guardian*, March 31, 1987.

101. Moscow Television, March 31, 1987, Foreign Broadcast Information Service, *Daily Report: Soviet Union* (hereinafter, FBIS-SU), April 3, 1987.

102. See the unusual op-ed article by retiring West German ambassador to the Soviet Union Joerg Kastl, "Einen Schritt zurück, um zwei Schritte voran tun zu können," *Frankfurter Allgemeine Zeitung*, April 25, 1987.

103. *The Economist*, October 29, 1988.

104. *Visit of Mikhail Gorbachev to Great Britain, April 5–7, 1989: Documents and Materials*.

105. "Sovmestnoe zaiavlenie," *Pravda*, June 14, 1989.

106. Fred Oldenburg, "Vier Tage im Juni 1989—Gorbatschow in Bonn," *Osteuropa* 39, nos. 11–12 (1989): 981–94.

107. James M. Markham, "Gorbachev Says French and Soviets Are Similar," *New York Times*, July 5, 1989.

108. *Pravda*, July 7, 1989.

109. Vitalii Zhurkin, "Obshchii dom dliaa Evropy: Razmyshleniia o tom, kak ego stroit'," *Pravda*, May 17, 1989.

110. "Sovetsko-finliandskaia deklaratsiia," *Pravda*, October 27, 1987. Also noteworthy was the USSR-Canada declaration signed a month later, on the occasion of Prime Minister Brian Mulroney's visit to Moscow. "Sovetsko-kanadskaia politicheskaia deklaratsiia," *Pravda*, November 22, 1989.

111. John Wyles, "Companies Flock to Sign Deals with Soviet Union," *Financial Times*, December 1, 1989.

112. For controversies concerning the choices of Teheran, Yalta, and Potsdam, see Churchill, *The Second World War: Closing the Ring*, p. 282; Sherwood, *Roosevelt and Hopkins*, pp. 844–45; the correspondence in *FRUS: The Conferences at Malta and Yalta*, pp. 3–23; and Churchill, *The Second World War: Triumph and Tragedy*, pp. 215, 571, 578. For the early postwar period, see the Eisenhower-Churchill correspondence in *FRUS: 1952–1954*, 6 (part 1): 978–80; and Macmillan, *Tides of Fortune*, p. 535.

113. The Western powers originally proposed Lausanne. The Soviets countered with Vienna, and Geneva was the compromise choice. See the exchange of notes in U.S. Department of State, *The Geneva Conference*, pp. 6–11.

114. RIIA, *Documents, 1955*, pp. 198–200.

115. In the joint statement issued the two countries "resolutely rejected attacks on the sovereign right of the GDR to safeguard the security and inviolability of her borders." "Sovmestnoe soobshenie," *Pravda*, June 10, 1989. This clearly was a reply to those who were calling for Gorbachev to announce the tearing down of the Berlin wall on his upcoming trip.

116. Macmillan, *Tides of Fortune*, p. 600.

117. Harold Wilson, *Final Term: The Labour Government 1974–1976*, p. 155.

118. Anatoliev distinguished between three kinds of nontreaty documents that could result from summits and other meetings. A communiqué was a "general and standard kind of document" whose purpose was "to inform the press and the public at large of the results of the talks and the atmosphere in which they passed." A joint statement was "more binding on the sides" and "presumes that something substantial has come out of the negotiations." A declaration was "a still more weighty and binding document," which "proclaims identical views and joint intentions." K. Anatoliev, *Modern Diplomacy: Principles, Documents, People*, p. 235.

119. On political treaties see Jan F. Triska and Robert M. Slusser, *The Theory, Law, and Policy of Soviet Treaties*, pp. 227–83.

120. Anatoliev, *Modern Diplomacy*, p. 243 (italics added).

121. Wilson, *Final Term*, p. 158.

122. Robert A. D. Ford, "The Soviet Union: The Next Decade," *Foreign Affairs* 62, no. 5 (1984): 1141.

123. German Federal Institute, *The Soviet Union 1978–79*, p. 206. Some West European diplomats privately expressed nervousness about the term "good neighborly" that began to appear in agreements with the Nordic countries in 1956 and that some feared could imply acknowledgment that geographical proximity to the Soviet Union entailed special political obligations going beyond those applying to all states in accordance with the UN Charter and international law. But Canada, Turkey, Greece, Finland, and Sweden concluded "good neighborly" agreements or provisions with the Soviet Union before 1989. See also the Treaty on Good-Neighborliness, Partnership, and Cooperation Between the Soviet Union and the FRG, concluded in September 1990. Text in *Izvestiia*, September 22, 1990.

124. The last Soviet-Swedish joint communiqué was issued at the conclusion of Palme's April 1976 visit to Moscow. For the text see *Pravda*, April 10, 1976.

125. Lars Christiansson, "Tone Down Gorbachev's Promises," *Svenska Dagbladet*, May 4, 1986, in FBIS-WEU, June 2, 1986.

126. Jacques Amalric, "A Dialogue without Major Concessions," *Le Monde*, October 6–7, 1985, in *FBIS-WEU*, October 11, 1985. The text of the press conference appears in Mikhail S. Gorbachev, *A Time for Peace.*

127. "Moscow: Draw Up a Communiqué with Lubbers," *NRC Handelsblad*, November 11, 1986, in *FBIS-WEU*, November 20, 1986.

128. See the interview with Petrovskii, *Süddeutsche Zeitung*, June 23, 1989.

129. *Pravda*, July 9, 1989.

130. TASS, September 27, 1989.

131. *Pravda*, December 1, 1989.

132. *Pravda*, December 20, 1989.

133. John M. Goshko, "U.S., Allies Divided on European Summit," *Washington Post*, January 29, 1990.

134. Georgii A. Arbatov, "Such Different Meetings: ... Soviet-American Relations and the Four Summit Meetings," in Abel Agenbegyan, ed., *Perestroika Annual* (London: Futura, 1988), p. 225; see also Mikhail Gorbachev, *Perestroika: New Thinking for Our Country and the World*, p. 239.

135. *Pravda*, October 17, 1988, quoted in George G. Weickhardt, "New Soviet Style in Arms Control Negotiations," *Report on the USSR* 29 (1989): 8.

136. "Zavershenie peregovorov," *Pravda*, January 20, 1988.

137. "Sovetsko-frantsuzskii dialog," *Pravda*, October 11, 1988.

138. *Izvestiia*, May 30, 1990.

139. See the final declaration, *New York Times*, July 7, 1990.

140. For background see John Van Oudenaren, *Political Consultation Agreements in Soviet-West European Relations.*

141. USSR, *Vneshniaia politika Sovetskogo Soiuza: 1948 god*, pp. 183–85.

142. U.S. Department of State, *Foreign Ministers Meeting: Berlin Discussions*, pp. 233–34.

143. U.S. Department of State, *The Geneva Conference*, pp. 48–51.

144. Ibid., p. 54. Cf. the 1949 NATO Treaty, which obligated the parties to "consult together" under certain circumstances. Bevans, *Treaties and Other International Agreements* 4:828–31.

145. *New Times* 21 (1955): 201–5.

146. Scholl-Latour, *Im Sog des Generals*, p. 348.

147. "Sovetsko-frantsuzskaia deklaratsiia," *Pravda*, July 1, 1966.

148. "Sovetsko-frantsuzskii protokol," *Pravda*, October 14, 1970. For an account of the extreme care taken on the Soviet side in the negotiation of the agreement, see Nicolas Polianski, *M.I.D.: 12 ans dans les services diplomatiques du Kremlin*, p. 65.

149. *XXIV s"ezd Kommunisticheskoi Partii Sovetskogo Soiuza, 30 marta–9 aprelia 1971 g.: Stenograficheskii otchët* (hereinafter, *Stenograficheskii otchët, 1971*), 1:48.

150. Robert A. D. Ford, *Our Man in Moscow*, p. 118.

151. "Sovetsko-kanadskii protokol o konsul'tatsiiakh," *Pravda*, May 20, 1971.

152. "Sovetsko-ital'ianskii protokol o konsul'tatsiiakh," *Pravda*, October 27, 1972.

153. "Sovetsko-angliskii protokol o konsul'tatsiiakh," in *Dokumenty i materialy sovetsko-angliskii peregovorov v Moskve*, pp. 45–48; English text in Cmnd. 5924.

154. "Sovetsko-datskii protokol o konsul'tatsiiakh," *Pravda*, October 8, 1976.

155. For reasons that are not clear, the text of the Greece-USSR protocol did not appear in *Pravda* or *Izvestiia*, or in *VpSS: Sbornik dokumentov* for 1985.

156. "Sovmestnoe zaiavlenie," *Pravda*, October 31, 1974.

157. "Sovmestnaia deklaratsiia," *Pravda*, May 7, 1978.

158. "Sovmestnaia sovetsko-bel'giiskaia deklaratsiia," *Pravda*, June 26, 1975.

159. According to reports in the Norwegian press, the USSR has been pressing hard for the conclusion of a "special 'consultation agreement'" with the Oslo government. "Soviet Arrogance" (editorial), *Aftenposten*, August 15, 1987, in *FBIS-WEU*, August 21, 1987.

160. G. L. Rozanov, *SSSR-FRG: Perestroika otnoshenii*, pp. 19–21.

161. CG [Claus Gennrich], "Genschers Gespraeche mit Schewardnadse," *Frankfurter Allgemeine Zeitung*, January 20, 1988. For the text see "Protokol o konsul'tatsiiakh," *Vestnik Minerstva Inostrannykh Del SSSR* (hereinafter, *Vestnik MID*), no. 3 (1988).

162. B. M. Klimenko (ed.), *Slovar' mezhdunarodnogo prava*, pp. 138–39. Western authorities are much less definite about the legal status of consultation agreements. Cf. Lassa Oppenheim, *International Law: A Treatise*, H. Lauterpacht, ed., 2:8.

163. See Kardelj's account of the midnight episode in Vladimir Dedijer, *Tito*, pp. 323–24; the Soviet denunciation is reported in Vladimir Dedijer, *The Battle Stalin Lost: Memoirs of Yugoslavia, 1948–1953*,

p. 33. See also Milovan Djilas, *Conversations with Stalin*, pp. 182–83, for Stalin's role in the crisis. Further details emerged from a 1971 television appearance by Kardelj, reproduced in Vladimir Dedijer, ed., *Dokumenti 1948*, pp. 185–87. Neither government has published text of the agreement.

164. "Soobshchenie o besedakh Predsedatel'ia Soveta Ministrov SSSR N. S. Khrushcheva s Prezidentom Finliandskoi Respubliki I. K. Kekkonenom," *Pravda*, November 26, 1961.

165. For background see D. G. Kirby, *Finland in the Twentieth Century*, pp. 181–87; and Billington, "Finland," in Black and Thornton, *Communism and Revolution: The Strategic Uses of Political Violence*, pp. 137–39, who noted that Kekkonen did echo the Soviet claim that Norwegian policy had helped to bring on the crisis.

166. "K predlozheniiu o dogovore," *Pravda*, May 8, 1984.

167. See Shevardnadze's interview, *Pravda*, June 3, 1989.

168. Before the talks the foreign office issued a statement emphasizing that Britain's nuclear deterrent would not be on the agenda. London Press Association, April 18, 1986, in *FBIS-WEU*, April 18, 1986.

169. See "Vazhnoe sobytie mirovoi politiki (K itogam sovetsko-frantsuzskoi vstrechi na vysshem urovne)," *Mirovaia Ekonomika i Mezhdunarodnaia Otnoshenia* (hereinafter, *MEiMO*) 6 (1979): 8–9, for the 1970s.

170. Interview with N. N. Uspenskii, chief of the USSR MFA Second European Department, in *Sovetskaia Rossiia*, March 25, 1989, in *FBIS-SU*, March 29, 1989.

171. "Sovmestnoe zaiavlenie," *Pravda*, June 14, 1989.

172. "Sovmestnaia sovetsko-ital'ianskaia deklaratsiia," *Pravda*, December 1, 1989.

173. "Sovetsko-kanadskaia politicheskaia deklaratsiia," *Pravda*, November 22, 1989.

174. Klimenko, *Slovar' mezhdunarodnogo prava*, p. 175. The first Franco-Soviet group appears to have been set up in November 1988. See the report of the legal affairs working group session in *Vestnik MID* 23 (1989): 50. The West Germans followed shortly thereafter.

176. Iuri Gremitskikh MFA press briefing, December 1, 1989, reported by TASS, same day.

177. Recognition and the maintenance of diplomatic relations are not identical, but "the existence of diplomatic relations necessarily implies mutual recognition." Clive Parry, et al., *Encyclopaedic Dictionary of International Law*, p. 93. For Soviet thinking on the importance of recognition, see G. I. Tunkin, *Theory of International Law*, p. 70.

178. See George F. Kennan, *Russia and the West Under Lenin and Stalin*, p. 228, for the debate in Britain.

179. For a complete listing with all temporary breaks, see "Diplomaticheskie otnosheniia SSSR," *Vestnik MID* 14 (1988): 46–55.

180. Beschloss, *Mayday*, p. 172.

181. Grosser, *Franco-Soviet Relations Today*, pp. 34–35.

182. "Soviet Envoy Punched in Netherlands Tussle over Defector's Wife," *New York Times*, October 10, 1961; and Seymour Topping,

"Dutch and Russians Expel Ambassadors," *New York Times*, October 14, 1961.

183. See Gustav Hilger and Alfred G. Meyer, *Incompatible Allies: A Memoir-History of German Soviet Relations, 1918–1941*, p. 19; von Rauch, *A History of Soviet Russia*, p. 192; and Kennan, *Russia and the West Under Lenin and Stalin*, p. 226, for the most noteworthy disputes with Britain and Germany.

184. On the importance of the espionage function, see Sir William Hayter, *Russia and the World*, pp. 18–23.

185. For comprehensive documentation see "Expulsions of Soviet Representatives from Foreign Countries, 1970–81" (February 1982); "Expulsions of Soviet Officials Worldwide, 1982" (January 1983); and subsequent annual updates in the U.S. Department of State, *Foreign Affairs Note* series.

186. "Expulsion of 47 Soviet Officials Creates Serious Tension between Paris and Moscow," *Le Monde*, April 6, 1983, in *FBIS-WEU*, April 7, 1983.

187. *The Economist*, September 21, 1985.

188. For international agreements on the proper conduct of diplomats, see Marjorie M. Whiteman, *Digest of International Law*, 7:142–48, 223–52.

189. John Vinocur, "KGB Officers Try to Infiltrate Antiwar Groups," *New York Times*, July 26, 1983; and Bruce Porter, "The Soviet Peace Offensive: An Analysis of Tactics," *RFE-RL Research*, May 3, 1982.

190. German Federal Institute, *The Soviet Union, 1983/84*, p. 243.

191. See Shevardnadze's speech at the July 1988 MFA conference, *International Affairs* 10 (1988); and the section reports from the conference in *International Affairs* 11 (1988); and the articles by Leonid Ilichev and Iuli Kvitsinskii, *International Affairs* 5 (1989).

192. The Soviet ambassador to Finland gave the first such conference in April 1986. Biweekly press conferences at the Soviet embassy in Lisbon were instituted in late 1986. See also Nikolai Lunkov, "The Embassy in the Eternal City," *International Affairs* 12 (1989): 52.

193. Deutsche Presse Agentur (DPA), April 10, 1987, in *FBIS-SU*, April 13, 1987.

194. "Soviet Advertising Campaign in Denmark," *Berlingske Tidende*, February 26, 1986, in *FBIS-WEU*, March 4, 1986.

195. For these performances see accounts by men who served in Moscow at the time: Micunovic, *Moscow Diary*; Hayter, *Russia and the World*; Kroll, *Lebenserinnerungen*; and Bohlen, *Witness to History*.

196. *Pravda*, December 28, 1985.

197. *Pravda*, February 8, 1989.

198. See Götz von Groll, "The Helsinki Consultations," *Aussenpolitik* 24, no. 2 (1973): 123–29.

199. Frank J. Prial, "Talks on Cutting Forces in Europe Are Broken Off," *New York Times*, December 16, 1983.

200. See, for example, the notification provisions of the 1986 Conference on Disarmament in Europe (CDE) agreement, which stipulates that the participating states will "give notification in writing through

diplomatic channels," 42 days in advance of certain military maneuvers. "Document of the Stockholm Conference," CSCE/SC.9, para. 29.

201. Anatoliev, *Modern Diplomacy*, pp. 35, 58.

202. A. N. Kovalev, *Azbuka diplomatii*, p. 29. Technically a note is "a formal communication from the head of a mission to a government that may be written either in the first or the third person." Nicolson, *Diplomacy*, p. 133. See also Lord Gore-Booth, ed., *Satow's Guide to Diplomatic Practice*, pp. 41–54; and Anatoliev, *Modern Diplomacy*, pp. 86–87.

203. Disarmament was a principal subject in 26 of the exchanges, a summit in 20, and "territorial questions" in only 7. See Elmer Plischke, "Eisenhower's 'Correspondence Diplomacy' with the Kremlin: Case Study in Diplomatics," *Journal of Politics* 30, no. 1 (1968): 137–59; and Jacob D. Beam, *Multiple Exposure*, p. 273.

204. Macmillan, *Riding the Storm*, p. 467.

205. *The Economist*, March 4, 1978; and *New York Times*, January 24, 1978. According to reports in the West German press, the letter to Schmidt was written "in a rude manner." See Hannes Adomeit, *The Soviet Union and Western Europe: Perceptions, Policies, Problems*, p. 99.

206. *Washington Star*, February 10, 1979; excerpts from the Brezhnev letter to Italian prime minister Andreotti appeared in *La Stampa*, January 17, 1979. See also Jimmy Carter, *Keeping Faith: Memoirs of a President*, pp. 200, 234.

207. For the text see *Bild*, November 2, 1985.

208. See, for example, Gorbachev's letters to Maurice Marois, head of the International Institute of Life, TASS, March 12, 1986; to Finnish eighth graders, *Hufvudstadsbladet*, February 7, 1986, in *FBIS-SU*, February 12, 1986; and to a West German tenth-form pupil, in TASS, April 23, 1986.

209. "Andropow wirbt, droht und verschickt Briefe an die Europäer," *Frankfurter Allgemeine Zeitung*, August 31, 1983; and Serge Schmemann, "Andropov Bids Lawmakers in Bonn Curb U.S. Missiles," *New York Times*, September 21, 1983.

210. According to a standard Soviet source that appeared in 1972, the note verbale is the most common method used by the Soviet foreign ministry to deliver a protest. Anatoliev, *Modern Diplomacy*, p. 126.

211. Ibid., p. 125.

212. USSR, *Vneshniaia politika Sovetskogo Soiuza, 1949 god*, p. 165.

213. *Pravda*, November 24, 1954. In May 1955 the Supreme Soviet denounced the treaties with Britain and France. *Pravda*, May 8, 1955.

214. Grosser, *Franco-German Relations Today*, p. 36.

215. W.A., "Moskau: Ein gefaehrlicher Schritt," *Frankfurter Allgemeine Zeitung*, July 13, 1984.

216. Theo Sommer, "Bonn's New Ostpolitik," *Journal of International Affairs* 22, no. 1 (1968): 61–62.

217. "Memorandum to the Government of the Federal Republic of Germany," TASS, July 12, 1984.

218. [ckn], "Bonn spricht von 'nicht akzeptabler Einmischung' Moskaus," *Frankfurter Allgemeine Zeitung*, July 13, 1984.

219. German Federal Institute, *The Soviet Union 1980–81*, p. 221.

220. "Frantsiia narushaet chetyrekhstoronnee soglashenie po Zapadnomu Berlinu," *Vestnik MID* 23 (1988): 31–32.

221. German Federal Institute, *The Soviet Union, 1975–76*, p. 244.

222. "Zaiavlenie Minerstva Inostrannykh Del SSSR pravitel'stvam SShA, Velikobritanii i Frantsii," *Pravda*, June 12, 1984.

223. The text of this note was broadcast on Moscow radio shortly after it was delivered. For the text see *FBIS-SU*, September 9, 1981.

224. John Miller, "Russia Sends Cruise Protest to Thatcher," *Daily Telegraph*, November 29, 1983.

225. Christopher Walker, "Moscow Calls in British Envoy over Missiles," *The Times*, July 8, 1987; full text of the protest released by TASS on the day of the meeting, July 7, 1987.

226. Johan Jorgen Holst, "Norway's Search for a Nordpolitik," *Foreign Affairs* 60, no. 1 (1981): 81.

227. Kazimierz Grzybowski, *Soviet Public International Law*, p. 203.

228. Agence France-Presse (AFP), February 6, 1987.

229. Robert K. German, "Norway and the Bear: Soviet Coercive Diplomacy and Norwegian Security Policy," *International Security* 7, no. 2 (1982): 55–82.

230. Olof Santesson, "The Soviet Response" (editorial), *Dagens Nyheter*, May 7, 1983, in *FBIS-WEU*, May 12, 1983.

231. The Soviet embassy in Stockholm made public the text of Pankin's remarks, which were delivered orally to Palme. *Dagens Nyheter*, May 10, 1983, in *FBIS-WEU*, May 19, 1983.

232. "Our Aircraft Did not Violate Swedish Airspace," *Dagens Nyheter*, October 21, 1984.

233. "Soviet Ambassador Protests Book," *Süddeutsche Zeitung*, October 29, 1984.

234. *Le Monde*, March 31–April 1, 1985.

235. *Le Monde*, February 4–5, 1985.

236. David Marsh, "Anger over French Film Star's 'War Spectacular'," *Financial Times*, April 20, 1985.

237. TASS, January 27, 1981.

238. Mitterrand recalled that he was very much taken aback by this action: "An amazing situation! A Russian ambassador in Paris, talking to the first secretary of the French Socialist Party about Portugal's right to decide her own fate!" François Mitterrand, *The Wheat and the Chaff*, p. 154.

Chapter 5: Parliaments, Political Parties, and Trade Unions

1. See James Douglas, *Parliaments Across Frontiers: A Short History of the Inter-Parliamentary Union*, pp. 51–52.

2. See the 1919 Bolshevik program in Jan F. Triska, ed., *Soviet Communism: Programs and Rules*, p. 137; and V. L. Shvetsov, "Mezhparlamentskii soiuz," in G. I. Morozov, ed., *Obshchestvennost' i problemy voiny i mira*, p. 350.

3. Vernon V. Aspaturian, "Soviet Politics," in Roy Macridis, ed.,

Modern Political Systems: Europe, p. 432; and V. Grigoryev, *The Soviet Parliament (A Reference Book),* p. 12.

4. "Invitation to Moscow Accepted," *The Times,* August 12, 1954.

5. See *Inter-Parliamentary Bulletin* 5 (1954): 135–36; 6 (1954): 146; 1 (1955): 1.

6. For the text see *New Times* 7 (1955).

7. Z. A. Lebedeva, *Parlamentskaia gruppa sovetskogo soiuza,* pp. 13–14, for background.

8. *Inter-Parliamentary Bulletin* 1 (1955): 28.

9. Clifton Daniel, "Khrushchev Irks French Visitors," *New York Times,* September 23, 1955.

10. "M. Pineau Questioned," *The Times,* November 3, 1956.

11. Lebedeva, *Parlamentskaia gruppa,* pp. 53–58.

12. See Philip M. Williams, ed., *The Diary of Hugh Gaitskell,* pp. 496–516.

13. "Obrashenie Verkhovnogo Soveta SSSR Kongressu Soedinenennykh Shtatov Ameriki Parlamentu Velikobritanii," *Pravda,* May 11, 1957.

14. L. Rozanov, *SSSR-FRG: Perestroika otnoshenii,* p. 29.

15. See Grigoryev, *The Soviet Parliament;* and *Verkhovnii sovet SSSR.*

16. "Visit by Soviet Parliamentarians," *The Times,* March 15, 1973.

17. Nicholas Comfort, "Whitelaw to See Gorbachev in Moscow," *Daily Telegraph,* May 20, 1986.

18. There were additional private or unofficial meetings in this period which partially undercut official boycotts on exchange. In December 1968, for example, five left-wing British Labour M.P.s hosted a Soviet delegation at a private meeting in the House of Commons. "MPs Speak Out to Soviet Group," *The Times,* December 23, 1968.

19. Gorbachev was named chairman of the Foreign Affairs Commission of the Council of the Union in April 1984.

20. *Izvestiia,* October 25, 1986.

21. TASS, January 22, 1980; and Reuter, January 23, 1980.

22. Claude Estier, chairman of the Foreign Affairs Commission of the National Assembly, quoted on Moscow International Service, October 26, 1984, in *FBIS-WEU,* October 29, 1984.

23. L. Tolkunov, "Ravnopravnye peregovory, a ne voennoe protivoborstvo," *Kommunist* 7 (1984): 104.

24. *Izvestiia,* May 28, 1985.

25. Ibid., March 12, 1987.

26. Douglas, *Parliaments Across Frontiers,* pp. 55–69, 75–77.

27. United States, Congress, House of Representatives, Committee on Foreign Affairs, *Inter-Parliamentary Union Conference: Report of the United States Delegation to the Spring Meeting of the Inter-Parliamentary Union, Held at Oslo, Norway, April 7–12, 1980;* and idem, *Inter-Parliamentary Union Conference: Report of the United States Delegation to the 70th Conference of the Inter-Parliamentary Union, Seoul, Korea, Oct. 2–13, 1983.*

28. For the early period see Peter H. Juviler, "Inter-Parliamentary

Contacts in Soviet Foreign Policy," *American Slavic and East European Review* (February 1961).

29. See *Inter-Parliamentary Bulletin* 3–4 (1973): 176; and 1 (1974): 31–34.

30. See Jukka Huopaniemi, *Parliaments and European Rapprochement: The Conference of the Inter-Parliamentary Union on European Co-operation and Security (Helsinki, January 1973).*

31. For an account by a Soviet participant, see L. Tolkunov, "MPs for Peace and Cooperation in Europe," *International Affairs* 5 (1973): 59–64.

32. "Final Act of the Inter-Parliamentary Conference on European Cooperation and Security," *Inter-Parliamentary Bulletin* 1 (1973): 15–23.

33. See Luigi Ferraris, *Testimonianze di un Negoziato*, pp. 118, 122, for a brief analysis, by members of the Italian CSCE delegation, of the 1st and 2d parliamentary conferences.

34. Huopaniemi, *Parliaments and European Rapprochement*, p. 99; and "Further Inter-Parliamentary Activities in the Field of Cooperation and Security in Europe," *Inter-Parliamentary Bulletin* 2 (1983): 97–98.

35. "Final Act of the 2nd Inter-Parliamentary Conference on European Cooperation and Security," *Inter-Parliamentary Bulletin* 1 (1975): 22–33.

36. "Concluding Resolutions of the 3rd Inter-Parliamentary Conference on European Cooperation and Security," *Inter-Parliamentary Bulletin* 2 (1978): 93–105.

37. "Concluding Resolutions of the 4th Inter-Parliamentary Conference on European Cooperation and Security," *Inter-Parliamentary Bulletin* 2 (1980): 71–82.

38. "Final Resolutions of the 5th Inter-Parliamentary Conference on European Cooperation and Security," *Inter-Parliamentary Bulletin* 2 (1983).

39. "Concluding Resolutions of the 6th Inter-Parliamentary Conference on European Cooperation and Security," *Inter-Parliamentary Bulletin* 3 (1986).

40. Communist delegates from Western Europe did not go to the 1983 meeting in Seoul, "apparently under instructions from Moscow." See Committee on Foreign Affairs, *Inter-Parliamentary Union Conference: Report of the United States Delegation to the 70th Conference,* p. 2.

41. Huopaniemi, *Parliaments and European Rapprochement*, p. 100.

42. In the course of the discussion, Tolkunov had the temerity to suggest that since the Bundestag had already been dissolved, Hans-Jürgen Wischnewski, the leader of the West Germans, had no powers to speak on behalf of his national group. Ibid., p. 14.

43. "Priem delegatsii," *Pravda*, December 20, 1985.

44. *Izvestiia*, March 23, 1987.

45. "L'UEO accepte l'invitation de Moscou," *Le Monde*, February 19, 1987.

46. *Izvestiia*, July 15, 1989.

47. "Gaststatus für vier osteuropäische Staaten im Europarat," *Frankfurter Allgemeine Zeitung*, June 10, 1989; and "Pozitivnyi shag," *Pravda*, June 10, 1989.

48. Boris Pyadyshev, "Will We Be Prepared," *International Affairs* 9 (1989): 157–58.

49. *Vestnik MID* 15 (1989).

50. Text in *Pravda*, July 7, 1989. An agreement on the opening of consulates in Strasbourg and Kiev was concluded during Foreign Minister Dumas's November 1989 visit to Moscow. *Pravda*, November 15, 1989.

51. TASS, September 23, 1989.

52. *Pravda*, July 5, 1989; and *Vestnik MID* 15 (1989): 33–34.

53. "Vstrecha M. S. Gorbacheva s R. Ziusmuti i L. Fabiusom," *Pravda*, November 18, 1989; and Helmut Herles, "Ein deutschfranzösisches Gespann in Moskau," *Frankfurter Allgemeine Zeitung*, November 20, 1989.

54. *Izvestiia*, November 13, 1983.

55. East Berlin ADN (Allgemeiner Deutscher Nachrichtendienst) report of September 14, 1988, in *FBIS-EEU*, September 16, 1988.

56. For the text of the appeal, see *Izvestiia*, July 10, 1987. For Gorbachev's message to the meeting, see the Polish Press Agency (PAP) dispatch of November 26, 1988, in *FBIS-SU*, December 8, 1988.

57. See Vladimir Baranovskii, "Parlamentarizm: Evropeiskii rakurs," *Moskovskie novosti* 27 (1989): 3.

58. For background see Boris Meissner, "Gorbatschows Umbau des Sowjetsystems," *Osteuropa* 39, nos. 11–12 (1989); and 40, no. 1 (1990). See also the transcripts of the relevant Congress and Supreme Soviet sessions in *Izvestiia*.

59. Interview with A. S. Dzasokhov, chairman of the International Affairs Committee, *Izvestiia*, April 26, 1990.

60. See the letter from a group of Labour M.P.s calling for a joint session of the Supreme Soviet and the European Parliament, *Guardian*, November 18, 1989.

61. *Pravda*, June 15, 1989.

62. In March 1990 he gave up this position when he became president of the USSR. His replacement was Anatolii Lukianov, a close associate.

63. See the interview with S. M. Rogov, deputy chairman of the group, in *Krasnaia zvezda*, May 16, 1989, in *FBIS-SU*, May 22, 1989.

64. Aleksei Kazannik, "People's Deputies: Words before the Congress," *Sovetskaia kultura*, December 12, 1989, in *FBIS-SU*, December 20, 1989.

65. J. W. Bruegel, "Contact between Socialist and Communist Internationals: 1919–79," *Socialist Affairs* 5 (1978): 139–41.

66. See Hilger and Meyer, *Incompatible Allies*, p. 70.

67. See Arvo Tuominen, *The Bells of the Kremlin: An Experience in Communism*, pp. 235–45.

68. For an account of Attlee's 1936 visit to Moscow and his contacts with Litvinov, see Kenneth Harris, *Attlee*, pp. 125–26.

69. Bill Jones, *The Russia Complex: The British Labour Party and the Soviet Union*, p. 36; and Julius Braunthal, "The Rebirth of Social Democracy," *Foreign Affairs* 27, no. 4 (July 1949): 587–88.

70. Julius Braunthal, *History of the International*, 3:5.

71. For the second front issue see John Campbell, *Aneurin Bevan and the Mirage of British Socialism*, pp. 116–17. Eden reported that Stalin was "pretty outspoken in criticism of the Labour party as at present led" in his Moscow meetings with Eden in October 1944. Anthony Eden, *The Reckoning*, p. 560.

72. Joseph Frankel, *British Foreign Policy 1945–1973*, p. 192.

73. For a Soviet history of this period, see V. A. Ryzhikov, *Britanskii leiborizm segodnia: Teoria i praktika politika poslevoennykh pravitel'stv Velikobritanii*, pp. 40–53.

74. Richard Löwenthal, "Democratic Socialism as an International Force," *Social Research* 47, no. 1 (1980): 84.

75. Braunthal, *History of the International*, p. 191.

76. See Denis Healey, ed., *The Curtain Falls: The Story of the Socialists in Eastern Europe*, p. 6.

77. *Pravda*, October 6, 1952.

78. See Harold Wilson, *Memoirs: The Making of a Prime Minister*, pp. 143–44; and Janet Morgan, ed., *The Backbench Diaries of Richard Crossman*, pp. 249–50.

79. "Labour Delegates' Stay in Moscow," *The Times*, August 7, 1954; and Cecil Parrott (at the time chargé d'affaires in the British embassy), *The Serpent and the Nightingale*, p. 62.

80. For an account of the trip and extracts from Bevan's unpublished diary see Michael Foot, *Aneurin Bevan: A Biography, 1945–1960*, pp. 443–46.

81. Parrott, who interpreted for Bevan in a private conversation with Malenkov, recalled that this visit was arranged at Bevan's initiative. Parrott, *The Serpent and the Nightingale*, pp. 64–65. See also Morgan, *The Backbench Diaries of Richard Crossman*, p. 343.

82. Haakon Lie (secretary of the Norwegian Labour Party), speech to the Council Conference, *Socialist International Information* 11 (1956): 176.

83. "Norway Bars Red 'Contact'," *New York Times*, December 21, 1955. Khrushchev's letter to Gerhardsen accepting the exchange of journalists appeared in *Pravda*, December 20, 1955.

84. *Pravda*, February 16, 1956.

85. Welles Hangen, "Soviets Pressing Drive to Foster Popular Fronts," *New York Times*, April 1, 1956. For the Ponomarev article see *Pravda*, March 31, 1956.

86. Wolfgang Leonhard, *The Kremlin Since Stalin*, p. 201.

87. "Statement on the Relations between the Socialist International and Other Political Forces," *Socialist International Information* 10 (1956): 158.

88. Ibid., 11 (1956): 181.

89. R. Löwenthal, "Post-Stalin Russia and Coexistence," *Socialist International Information* 34 (1956): 597.

90. Morgan, *The Backbench Diaries of Richard Crossman*, p. 477.

91. Williams, *The Diary of Hugh Gaitskell*, pp. 484–91.

92. Ibid., p. 503.

93. Ibid., pp. 506–16; and Morgan, *The Backbench Diaries of Richard Crossman*, pp. 624, 486–94. See also Herbert Morrison, *An Autobiography*, pp. 301–5; and Brown, *In My Way*, pp. 71–75.

94. Reports later circulated that Gaitskell, who died in 1963 of a rare tropical disease, was poisoned by the KGB. See Chapman Pincher, *Their Trade Is Treachery*, pp. 64–66; Peter Wright, *Spycatcher*, pp. 362–64; and "Was Gaitskell Poisoned?" *The Economist*, July 18, 1987. These reports appear to have been taken seriously by British and U.S. intelligence, but had no apparent effect on Labour Party relations with the Soviet Union and the CPSU.

95. See J. M. Domenach, "Again the Popular Front," *Foreign Affairs* 34, no. 4 (1956).

96. Morgan, *The Backbench Diaries of Richard Crossman*, p. 752.

97. Micunovic, *Moscow Diary*, pp. 55–56.

98. Foot, *Aneurin Bevan*, 2:563–65.

99. For the text of the letter see *New York Times*, October 16, 1957. Letters were sent to the Norwegian Labor Party, the French Socialist Party, the SPD, and socialist parties in Italy, Denmark, Belgium, and the Netherlands.

100. Philip M. Williams, *Hugh Gaitskell: A Political Biography*, p. 460; see also Macmillan, *Riding the Storm*, pp. 284–85; and *Izvestiia*, October 17, 1957.

101. "Norwegian Party's Action," *The Times*, October 16, 1957.

102. For the Hungarian government statement see *Pravda*, June 17, 1958.

103. See Williams, *Hugh Gaitskell*, p. 519.

104. "Foreign Secretary Sees Mr. Suslov," *The Times*, March 18, 1959.

105. For an account see Foot, *Aneurin Bevan*, 2:617–20.

106. "New Berlin Proposal by Mr. Khrushchev," *The Times*, March 10, 1959.

107. Sydney Gruson, "Khrushchev Sees No German Unity," *New York Times*, March 19, 1959. For an account of the visit see Harmut Söll, *Fritz Erler, Eine politische Biographie*, 2:379–86.

108. See Söll's account based on SPD archives, in Soell, *Fritz Erler*, p. 659 n. 229. Kreisky confirmed that he and Austrian ambassador Hans Thalberg played a mediating role, but claimed that Khrushchev issued the invitation and that acceptance of it was blocked by U.S. chief of mission Bernard Gufler. Bruno Kreisky, *Zwischen den Zeiten: Erinnerungen aus fünf Jahrzehnten*, pp. 450–51.

109. Triska, *Soviet Communism: Programs and Rules*, pp. 52, 62.

110. Pineau, *Khrouchtchev*, p. 232.

111. François Fejtö, *The French Communist Party and the Crisis of International Communism*, p. 158.

112. Brandt, *People and Politics*, p. 109.

113. Weit, *Ostblock intern*, pp. 166–67.

114. M. A. Suslov, *Marksizm-Leninizm i sovremennaia epokha: Iz-brannye rechi i staty*, 3:185.

115. Hans Georg Lehmann, *Öffnung nach Osten: Die Ostreisen Helmut Schmidts und die Entstehung der Ost- und Entspannungspolitik*, pp. 71–76.

116. "Resolutions Adopted by Eleventh Congress," *Socialist International Information* 14 (1969): 147–48.

117. The PS was founded in 1971 by the merger of the SFIO, several political clubs, and Mitterrand's organization of non-Communist resistance veterans.

118. "Special Bureau Meeting in Amsterdam," *Socialist Affairs* 5 (1972): 94.

119. The bureau also proposed that the category of consultative member be discontinued. This proposal, which would have ended the individual memberships of the nine (counting the three Baltic states) East European Social Democratic parties-in-exile, elicited favorable comment in the East, but ultimately was dropped under pressure from "right wing" parties. "Important Decisions for Future Structure," *Socialist Affairs* 12 (1972): 222. For a typical Eastern commentary see Dimitr Dimitrov, "Notes on the Theory and Policy of the Socialist International," *World Marxist Review* 18, no. 9 (1975): 87–88.

120. *Tasks at the Present Stage of the Struggle Against Imperialism and United Action of the Communist and Workers' Parties and All Anti-Imperialist Forces, Conference of Communist and Workers' Parties*.

121. *Stenograficheski otchët, 1971*, 1:45.

122. Brezhnev, *Leninskim kursom*, 3:352. This speech is best known for containing Brezhnev's invitation to the West to "taste the wine" of conventional arms control talks.

123. Iu. Zhilin, "Sotsintern pered litsom mezhdunarodnykh problem," *Pravda*, August 18, 1971. See also Bruno Pittermann, "A Reply to Zhilin's *Pravda* Article," *Socialist Affairs* 2 (1972).

124. "Sovmestnoe kommiunike Kommunisticheskoi Partii Sovetskogo Soiuza i Bel'giiskoi Sotsialisticheskoi Partii," *Pravda*, November 9, 1972.

125. "Soviet Delegation in Belgium," *Socialist Affairs* 4 (1973): 74; and "Belgian Socialists in USSR," *Socialist Affairs* 4 (1974): 76.

126. Ray Hayward, "Labour Party Journey to Moscow," *Socialist Affairs* 4 (1973): 74. A Soviet account appears in V. A. Ryzhikov, *SSSR-Velikobritaniia: Razvitie otnoshenii 60–70-e gody*, pp. 44–45.

127. "Best Forgotten," *The Economist*, November 6, 1976; and Hugh Noyes, "Hostile Reception for Russians," *The Times*, October 29, 1976.

128. The official communiqué was published in *Socialist Affairs* 3 (1975): 49–51.

129. See Mitterrand, *The Wheat and the Chaff*, p. 153.

130. "Razvitie kontaktov," *Pravda*, December 12, 1977.

131. "Sovmestnoe kommiunike delegatsii KPSS i Ispanskoi Sotsialisticheskoi Rabochei Partii," *Pravda*, December 16, 1977.

132. See N. G. Sibilev, *Sotsialisticheskii Internatsional: istoriia, ideologiia, politika.*

133. B. Ponomarev, "Za sotrudnichestvo v bor'be protiv gonki vooruzhenii za razoruzhenie," *Kommunist* 7 (1978): 49–50.

134. Alexander Weber, "In Face of Complex Problems," *New Times* 49 (1978): 13.

135. "Moscow Encounter," *Socialist Affairs* 6 (1979): 172.

136. *Pravda*, October 18, 1985.

137. *Stenograficheskii otchët, 1976,* 1:56.

138. *Stenograficheskii otchët, 1981,* 1:36.

139. "Leadership Election Decision Is Deferred," *The Times,* September 27, 1980.

140. Jonathan Steele, "Labour Leaders Seek Nuclear Peace Treaty with Andropov," *Guardian*, May 6, 1983.

141. This campaign was orchestrated by a committee which included representatives of the foreign ministry, International Department of the Central Committee, KGB, and the military. See Paul H. Nitze, "Living with the Soviets," *Foreign Affairs* 62, no. 2 (1983/84): 362.

142. *Pravda*, November 27, 1984.

143. Celestine Bohlen, "Chernenko Delineates Arms Talks," *Washington Post*, November 27, 1984.

144. Heinz Timmermann, "Moskau und die Linke in Westeuropa: Aspekte und Perspektiven des Verhältnisses zu den Eurokommunisten und zu den demokratischen Sozialisten (II)," *Osteuropa* 30, no. 6 (1980): 498.

145. Excerpts from Ponomarev's speech appeared in *Die Neue Gesellschaft* 6 (1978): 482–83. See the article by Zamiatin, "Auf dem Weg zu einem dauerhaften Frieden," *Die neue Gesellschaft* 10 (1979): 873–75) and Doris Kamaikov, "Sowjetische Erfahrungen bei der Rekonversion," *Die Neue Gesellschaft* 2 (1979): 108–11.

146. *Pravda*, June 30, 1981.

147. CG [Claus Gennrich], "Andropow wendet sich an SPD-Abgeordnete Bonn," *Frankfurter Allgemeine Zeitung*, September 21, 1983.

148. Bernhard Küppers, "Tschernenko warnt im Gespraech mit Vogel vor einer nuklearen Katastrophe," *Süddeutsche Zeitung*, March 13, 1984.

149. Ibid., May 29, 1985.

150. Claus Gennrich, "Die SPD sucht das Gespräch mit dem Osten über die Sicherheitspolitik," *Frankfurter Allgemeine Zeitung*, August 30, 1984.

151. *Süddeutsche Zeitung*, June 20, 1985.

152. For the text see *Neues Deutschland*, August 28, 1987.

153. [ban], "Abrüstungsinitiative der SPD und der polnischen Kommunisten," *Frankfurter Allgemeine Zeitung*, June 28, 1989.

154. *Pravda*, September 18, 1988.

155. "PZPR-SPD Joint Declaration on European Security and Cooperation Through Means of Building Mutual Trust," *Trybuna Ludu*, November 26, 1985, in *FBIS-EEU*, December 3, 1985.

156. "Apropos of a Document of the French Socialist Party," *New*

Times 1 (1980); and Iuri Sedov, "In the Cold War Spirit," *New Times* 5 (1979): 14.

157. *Pravda*, August 29, 1980.

158. "Vstrecha parlamentariev," *Pravda*, October 7, 1982.

159. See the unilateral communiqué issued by the Soviet side at the conclusion of the Brandt visit, "Vstrecha M. S. Gorbacheva c Villi Brandtom," *Izvestiia*, May 28, 1985.

160. *Pravda*, March 7, 1986; draft in *Pravda*, October 26, 1985.

161. For the list of delegations see *Pravda*, February 22, 23, 24, 25, 1986.

162. *Argumenty i fakty*, no. 30 (1989). For the text see *Socialist Affairs* 1–2 (1989): 28–35.

163. *Pravda*, July 20, 1989.

164. See the account by the Danish party defense and security policy spokesman Lasse Budtz, "East-West Dialogue," *Aktuelt*, November 12, 1986, in *FBIS-SU*, December 1, 1986.

165. See the discussion between CPSU and Socialist International officials, "Communists and Social Democrats: A Time to Gather Stones Together," *World Marxist Review* 32, no. 8 (1989): 57–58.

166. [hls], "Vogel bestätigt Veränderungen der Deutschlandpolitik der SPD," *Frankfurter Allgemeine Zeitung*, September 20, 1989; and [hls], "Die SPD will künftig mit den Sozialdemokraten in der DDR vorrangig Kontakt halten," *Frankfurter Allgemeine Zeitung*, October 25, 1989.

167. "Opfer der Eitelkeit," *Spiegel*, no. 39 (1989).

168. See the account of meetings between Iakovlev and Zagladin and the leaders of the two Communist parties and the Social Democratic Party to discuss the prospects for such a meeting, *Pravda*, October 27, 1989.

169. Martin Kettle, "Socialists Pave Way for All-Europe Federation," *Guardian*, February 9, 1990.

170. For the early work of the committee in promoting the European security conference, see Luigi Ferraris, *Testimonanze di un Negoziato*, pp. 114–16.

171. "Kommunike o peregovorakh delegatsii KPSS i Partii Tsentra Finliandii," *Pravda*, December 6, 1986. The Center Party's privileged status was similar to that accorded the Congress Party of India.

172. Reported in DPA, April 21, 1986; and *Pravda*, April 15, 20, 1986.

173. *Pravda*, January 10, 1989.

174. "Cooperation and Dialogue with Political Parties and Movements," *International Affairs* 11 (1988): 37.

175. *Die Presse*, May 12, 1989, in *FBIS-SU*, May 16, 1989.

176. See the report on a five-day visit to West Germany, PAP, October 18, 1986; and FDP Bundestag group chairman Mischnick's visit to East Germany, DPA, April 9, 1987.

177. Sofia BTA (Bulgarian Telegraph Agency), September 23, 1986, August 13, 1986.

178. Budapest MTI (Hungarian News Agency), April 28, 1987.

179. An indication of Soviet thinking was the appearance in the

MFA's monthly journal of an article by the leader of one of these parties. See Roman Malinowski, "The Role of the United Peasants' Party in the Polish Foreign Policy," *International Affairs* 10 (1988): 65–75. Malinowski was speaker of the Sejm (since November 1985) and played an important role in the September 1988 meeting of the chairmen of the parliaments of Warsaw Pact countries. See his speech of September 14, 1988, reported by PAP on the same day.

180. *Izvestiia*, July 4, 1987.

181. Reported in *Hufvudstadsbladet*, November 3, 1986, in *FBIS-WEU*, November 6, 1986.

182. Paavo Vayrynen, "The Finnish Centre Party, a Unique Party," *International Affairs* 11 (1989): 57.

183. In response to this development the USSR stepped up its direct ties to these parties. On August 11 the Polish news agency PAP reported that Soviet ambassador Vladimir Brovikov met separately with the leaders of the Democratic Party (DP) and the United Peasant Party (UPP) to discuss starting interparty cooperation with the CPSU.

184. Cortez Ewing, "The British Labor Party and Soviet Russia 1918–25," *American Federationist* 37, no. 1 (January 1930): 70–81.

185. TUC, *British Labour Delegation to Russia, 1920, Report.*

186. Stuart Chase et al., *Soviet Russia in the Second Decade. A Joint Survey by the Technical Staff of the First American Trade Union Delegation*, p. xi.

187. "Memorandum on the Activities of the Red International of Labor Unions during the First Decade of Its Existence," Enclosure no. 1 to Dispatch no. 7695 from the U.S. Legation at Riga, May 8, 1931 (typescript in the library of the U.S. Department of Labor).

188. Much of this discussion follows Daniel F. Calhoun, *The United Front, the TUC and the Russians, 1923–28.* See also Georgii Kanaev, *Soviet Trade Unions and the International Trade Union Movement: The Struggle for Unity*, pp. 14–15, for a Soviet view.

189. Calhoun, *The United Front*, p. 82.

190. Ibid., pp. 72–80; and the Riga dispatch, pp. 52–53.

191. *Russia: The Official Report of the British Trades Union Delegation to Russia and Caucasia, Nov. and Dec. 1924.*

192. Calhoun, *The United Front*, p. 67.

193. Stephen F. Cohen, *Bukharin and the Bolshevik Revolution*, pp. 230, 260.

194. Walter M. Citrine, *Men and Work: An Autobiography*, p. 93.

195. Walter M. Citrine, *I Search for Truth in Russia*, pp. 248, 300.

196. Walter M. Citrine, *Two Careers*, p. 236.

197. For the text of the resolution see TUC, *Report of Proceedings at the 73rd Annual Trades Union Congress* (1941), p. 243.

198. TUC, *Report of Proceedings at the 74th Annual Trades Union Congress* (1942), pp. 57–69.

199. Citrine, *Two Careers*, p. 98.

200. Jones, *The Russian Complex*, pp. 83–84, 70.

201. See, for example, N. V. Matkovskii, *Kratkii ocherk profsoiuznogo dvizheniia v anglii*, p. 71.

202. See J. H. Oldenbroek, "The Russians and the ILO," *Free Labour World* 49 (1954): 1–2; and Harold Karan Jacobson, "The USSR and ILO," *International Organization* 14, no. 3 (1960): 405–8.

203. Jacobson, "The USSR and ILO," p. 425; and *Pravda*, June 6, 1957, for the text of the message.

204. "Invitation from Russia," *The Times*, September 8, 1954.

205. "Trades Union Congress," *The Times*, September 9, 1954.

206. A. Adamczyk, "The WFTU's Unity Offer," *Free Labour World* 65 (1955): 24–27.

207. John P. Windmuller, "Realignment in the I.C.F.T.U.: The Impact of Détente," *British Journal of Industrial Relations* 14, no. 3 (1976): 247.

208. "Foreign Secretary Sees Mr. Suslov," *The Times*, March 18, 1959.

209. See the Drew Middleton dispatch in *New York Times*, June 11, 1957.

210. T. Barten'ev and Iu. Komissarov, *SSSR-Finlandiia*, p. 93.

211. "TUC Men in Russia 'Out of Curiosity'," *The Times*, September 13, 1966.

212. "European Unions Watching TUC Moscow Mission," *The Times*, September 14, 1966.

213. See Helmut Allardt, *Moskauer Tagebuch: Beobachtungen, Notizen, Erlebnisse*, pp. 223–24.

214. "Ostkontakte: Eine Diskussion in Moskau," *Die Quelle* 5 (1966): 194.

215. "Ein nützlicher Schritt," *Die Quelle* 12 (1966): 529.

216. "Ostkontakte: Möglichkeiten und Grenzen der Information," *Die Quelle* 2 (1967): 58–60.

217. An exchange with Poland's trade unions had been scheduled for early 1968, but was cancelled when the Poles demanded as a precondition that the DGB recognize the Oder-Neisse line. The DGB's difficulties with the Polish trade unions were somewhat surprising, in that they stood in such dramatic contrast to the pioneering role played by the PUWP in developing party-to-party contacts with the SPD.

218. "Ludwig Rosenbergs Moskauer Gespräche," *Die Quelle* 7/8 (1968): 290–91.

219. "DGB zu Ostkontakte," *Die Quelle* 9 (1968): 342; and "Ohne Vorbedingungen," *Die Quelle* 4 (1970): 162.

220. TUC, *Report of 100th Annual Trades Union Congress* (1968), p. 608.

221. Eric Wigham, "Unions Cold Shoulder Russia over Czechoslovak Crisis," *The Times*, August 30, 1968.

222. "Bundeskongress des DGB: Antrage und Entschliessungen," *Die Quelle* 5 (1969): 196.

223. Allardt, the ambassador at the time, gave an account of this dinner in *Moskauer Tagebuch*, pp. 217–28.

224. "DGB-Bündesvorstand über Ostkontakte," *Die Quelle* 1 (1970): 10.

225. See the interview with Vetter in *Die Quelle* 6 (1970): 251–54.

226. Text in ibid., 6:254.

227. "DGB-Delegation zu Gast in Bulgarien," and "Ein 'historischer Dialog' in Warschau," *Die Quelle* 5 (1970): 204–6, 206–7; and "Gewerkschaftskontakte sind Beiträge zur Entspannung," *Die Quelle* 11 (1972): 505.

228. "Kongress der sowjetischen Gewerkschaften," *Die Quelle* 4 (1972).

229. Brezhnev, *Leninskim Kursom*, 3:490.

230. "Breschnew-Besuch fand einen starken Widerhall," *Die Quelle* 6 (1973): 246.

231. Paul Routledge, "Closer Links with Britain is Feather in Soviet Unions' Cap," *The Times*, July 23, 1973; and TUC, *Report of the 105th Annual Trades Union Congress* (1973), p. 212.

232. "K prebyvaniiu v SSSR delegatsii general'nogo soveta Britanskogo kongressa tred-iunionov," *Trud*, July 21, 1973.

233. For the controversy see reports in *The Times*, March 3, 5, 11, 15, 27, and April 1, 11, 1975.

234. "Kommiunike ob itogakh peregovorov mezhdu delegatsiiami VTSSPS i BKT," *Trud*, April 2, 1975.

235. Paul Routledge, "Mr. Shelepin Says Campaign against Him Is Work of a Small Group Opposed to Détente," *The Times*, April 2, 1975.

236. "Two Days in the Life of Alexander Shelepin," *The Economist*, April 5, 1975, p. 27.

237. See B. C. Roberts and Bruno Liebhaberg, "The European Trade Union Confederation: Influence of Regionalism, Détente, and Multinationals," *British Journal of Industrial Relations* 14, no. 3 (1976): 265.

238. V. Rogov, "V dukhe druzhby i sotrudnichestva," *Trud*, April 2, 1975

239. German Federal Institute, *The Soviet Union 1973*, pp. 146–47.

240. Roy Godson, *The Kremlin and Labor: A Study in National Security Policy*, p. 47; and "Reds under the Blanket," *The Economist*, March 8, 1975, p. 76.

241. The AFL-CIO reaffiliated with the ICFTU on January 1, 1982.

242. P. T. Pimenov, "Rabochii klass i profsoiuzy v bor'be za mir," in Morozov, ed., *Obshchestvennost' i problemy voiny i mira*, p. 188.

243. TUC, *Report of the General Council, 1978*, p. 260.

244. "ILO Says It Cannot Aid Dissident Soviet Workers," *New York Times*, April 15, 1978.

245. "ILO Assails Soviet Labor Tactic," *New York Times*, March 6, 1981.

246. "ILO Says Soviet Violates Pact Barring Forced Labor," *New York Times*, May 13, 1980.

247. TUC, *Report of the General Council, 1980*, pp. 219–20.

248. "DGB-Erklärung zu Frieden und Entspannung," *Die Quelle* 2 (1980): 72.

249. "Eugen Loderer: Entspannungspolitik trotz Afghanistan," *Die Quelle* 3 (1980): 131.

250. Donald Macintyre, "TUC Leaders Call Off Visit to Poland," *The*

Times, September 6, 1980; and "Journalists' Union Drops Visit to Soviet Union," *The Times*, October 16, 1980.

251. Iain Guest, "Poland Inquiry Dropped," *Guardian*, November 15, 1982.

252. "Poland Is Criticized by an i.l.o. Inquiry for Solidarity Curb," *New York Times*, June 28, 1988; and "Poland Quitting i.l.o.," *New York Times*, November 17, 1984.

253. L. Toporkov, "мот: Postydnaia stranitsa," *Izvestiia*, December 8, 1984.

254. Stepan Shalaev, "Sovetskie profsoiuzy v bor'be za mir," *Kommunist* 5 (1984): 97.

255. See Bohdan Nahaylo, "Gorbachev's Visit to London and the Elusive Anglo-Soviet Thaw," *Radio Liberty Research*, November 26, 1984.

256. Leonid Kostin, as reported in TASS, July 17, 1983.

257. Reported in *FBIS-SU*, March 19, 1983.

258. Tim Jones, "TUC Split over Mission to Moscow," *The Times*, January 8, 1987.

259. Information from Rudolf G. Kolchanov, deputy chief editor of Trud, on "International Observers Roundtable," Moscow Domestic Service, March 1, 1987, in *FBIS-SU*, March 3, 1987.

260. *Trud*, March 1, 1987.

261. "M. Gorbatchev va recevoir une delegation de la Confederation internationale des syndicats libres," *Le Monde*, October 9, 1987.

262. *Free Labour World* 6 (1981): 9; 4 (1983): 10–12.

263. "Statement on Poland," *Free Labour World* 6 (1981): 1; and "Soviets Arrest Two Free Trade Unionists," *Free Labour World* 4 (1982): 21–22.

264. "ICFTU Delegation Meets Mikhail Gorbachev," *Free Labour World* 12 (1987): 1.

265. By raising human rights questions, the ICFTU seemed to be going against its own decision to constitute a fact-finding group dealing with security issues. The reasons for this anomaly are not clear.

266. *Pravda*, October 10, 1987.

267. See Vladimir Volin, "An Alternative Trade Union," *Moscow News*, no. 25 (1989), describing the founding of a new Association of Socialist Trade Unions, "Sotsprof," which was denied recognition by the Soviet authorities.

Chapter 6: Arms Control

1. *Documents on Disarmament, 1945–1959*, 1:258.
2. Ibid., 1:337–39.
3. Ibid., 1:340–41.
4. Ibid., 1:345–46.
5. Ibid., 1:391–93.
6. *Documents, 1955*, pp. 110–18.
7. Dulles to Department of State, July 23, 1955, *FRUS, 1955–1957*, 5:484–86.
8. U.S. Department of State, *The Geneva Conference*, p. 68.

9. Stassen and Dulles, memorandum of conversation, November 15, 1955, *FRUS, 1955–1957*, 5:782.

10. Morgan, *The Backbench Diaries of Richard Crossman*, p. 492.

11. *Documents, 1956*, pp. 562–70.

12. The Yugoslav ambassador met with Khrushchev on November 12, who remarked that the West was "weak and divided," that "the weakness of the British and French had been revealed to the whole world," and that even though the Soviet Union was not thinking of going to war, its "latest threats of war had been correct and necessary." In the same conversation Khrushchev remarked that he and his colleagues were thinking of "starting up a new campaign in favor of disarmament." Micunovic, *Moscow Diary*, pp. 156–57.

13. Eisenhower, *Waging Peace*, pp. 472–73; and Macmillan, *Riding the Storm*, pp. 300–307.

14. *Documents on Disarmament, 1945—1959*, 2:849–68.

15. *New York Times*, September 21, 1957.

16. *Documents on Disarmament, 1945–1959*, 2:904–6.

17. *Pravda*, November 6, 1957.

18. Ibid., December 27, 1957.

19. Bechhoefer, *Postwar Negotiations for Arms Control*, p. 456.

20. In their communiqué of September 1959, the ministers requested the secretary-general to convene the Disarmament Commission in order to inform it of the nature and purpose of the new committee. For the DC response see *Documents on Disarmament, 1945–1959*, 2:1443.

21. Khrushchev's proposal was amplified in a detailed Soviet government declaration of September 19.

22. The General Assembly had no formal responsibility for the new ten-power committee, but in November 1959 it unanimously adopted a resolution "expressing the hope that measures leading towards the goal of general and complete disarmament under effective international control will be worked out in detail and agreed upon in the shortest possible time." *Documents on Disarmament, 1945–1959*, 2:1545.

23. While this withdrawal has been attributed by some analysts to the U2 incident and the breakdown of the Paris summit, these events appear to have had little to do with each other, as is suggested by the fact that Khrushchev actually used the bloc walkout in an unsuccessful attempt to revive his personal correspondence with Eisenhower. For Khrushchev's letter see *Documents on Disarmament, 1960*, pp. 132–36. The United States refrained from replying at the head of government level, using instead a diplomatic note to rebut Khrushchev's charges. For the text see ibid., pp. 140–42.

24. Iu. Khvostov, "Disarmament Negotiations," *International Affairs* 2 (1961): 65–66.

25. Louis J. Halle, *The Cold War as History*, p. 389.

26. *Documents on Disarmament, 1961*, p. 80.

27. See John J. McCloy, "Balance Sheet on Disarmament," *Foreign Affairs* 40, no. 3 (1962); and Arthur H. Dean, *Test Ban and Disarmament: The Path of Negotiation*, pp. 30–33.

28. *Department of State Bulletin*, November 6, 1961, pp. 766–67.

29. Text in ibid., October 9, 1961, pp. 589–90.

30. *Documents on Disarmament, 1960*, p. 722.

31. This was noted by arms control officials in the Kennedy administration. See Glenn T. Seaborg, *Kennedy, Khrushchev and the Test Ban*, pp. 101–2.

32. The 18-nation Disarmament Committee continued its deliberations throughout the 1960s, with general and complete disarmament still its ostensible objective. France boycotted the sessions, so the committee in effect had only 17 members. See Thomas W. Wolfe, "The Soviet Union and Arms Control," Rand Corporation, P-3337, April 1966, for Soviet policy.

33. *Documents on Disarmament, 1945–1959*, 2:1188; see also de Gaulle, *Memoirs of Hope*, pp. 205–6.

34. For the text of the treaty see Arms Control and Disarmament Agency (hereinafter listed as ACDA), *Arms Control and Disarmament Agreements*, pp. 41–43.

35. Schlesinger, *A Thousand Days*, p. 914.

36. François de Rose, "Atlantic Relationships and Nuclear Problems," *Foreign Affairs* 41, no. 3 (1963): 480. See also William B. Bader, *The United States and the Spread of Nuclear Weapons*, p. 49.

37. *Documents on Disarmament, 1945–1959*, 2:870.

38. *Documents on Disarmament, 1964*, p. 8. For an account of this period see Glenn T. Seaborg, with Benjamin S. Loeb, *Stemming the Tide: Arms Control in the Johnson Years*.

39. *Documents on Disarmament, 1964*, pp. 15–16.

40. *Documents on Disarmament, 1965*, p. 347.

41. Ibid., p. 444.

42. Johnson, *The Vantage Point*, p. 477.

43. *Documents on Disarmament, 1964*, p. 339.

44. Gerhard Wettig, "Soviet Policy on the Nonproliferation of Nuclear Weapons, 1966–68," *Orbis* 12, no. 4 (1969): 1064.

45. For the text see ACDA, *Arms Control and Disarmament Agreements*, pp. 91–95.

46. See Shevardnadze's speech at the Geneva Conference on Disarmament, *Pravda*, August 7, 1987.

47. See William C. Potter, "Nuclear Proliferation: U.S.-Soviet Cooperation," *The Washington Quarterly* 8, no. 1 (1985): 151.

48. See H. J. Neuman, *Nuclear Forces in Europe: A Handbook for the Debate*, p. 35.

49. See Rusk, *As I Saw It*, pp. 239–41; Arthur Schlesinger, *Robert Kennedy and His Times*, pp. 519–25; James G. Blight, Joseph S. Nye, and David A. Welch, "The Cuban Missile Crisis Revisited," *Foreign Affairs* 66, no. 1 (1987): 178–79; Raymond L. Garthoff, *Reflections on the Cuban Missile Crisis*; and Gromyko, *Memories*, p. 179.

50. John Newhouse, *Cold Dawn: The Story of SALT*, p. 176.

51. Ibid., p. 127.

52. Ibid., p. 93.

53. The USSR received some indirect support for its position by

securing an advantage in missile launchers which American officials justified as an offset to the American advantage in forward-based systems.

54. Gerhard Wettig, "Dimensions of Soviet Arms Control Policy," *Comparative Strategy* 7, no. 1 (1988): 5.

55. Cyrus Vance, *Hard Choices*, (1983), p. 139; Carter, *Keeping Faith*, p. 255; and Raymond L. Garthoff, *Détente and Confrontation*, p. 735.

56. See Jonathan Dean, *Watershed in Europe*, pp. 117–18.

57. "The 1977 Alastair Buchan Memorial Lecture," *Survival* 20, no. 1 (1978).

58. Helmut Schmidt, *Menschen und Mächte*, pp. 89–90.

59. *Pravda*, October 7, 1979.

60. The situation was complicated by the decision of the United States not to ratify the SALT II treaty, which ruled out an early round of SALT III in which INF could be considered. This allowed the Soviets to score propaganda points by claiming that the United States had not fulfilled the conditions of the original two-track decision, but did not affect the fundamental differences between the sides on the issues, which may well have been exposed even sooner if negotiations had not been delayed.

61. Details of Schmidt's conversations were leaked and appeared in *Die Welt*, July 7, 1980.

62. "Ob itogakh peregovorov rukovoditelei SSSR i FRG," *Pravda*, July 5, 1980.

63. *Documents on Disarmament, 1980*, p. 436.

64. For the background to the resumption of the talks, see Alexander M. Haig, Jr., *Caveat: Realism, Reagan and Foreign Policy*, pp. 228–31.

65. The best sources for the period up to 1983 are Strobe Talbott, *Deadly Gambits*, and the three-part series by John Barry in *The Times*, May 31, June 1, 2, 1983; for the post-1983 period, Strobe Talbott, *The Master of the Game: Paul Nitze and the Nuclear Peace*; and Paul H. Nitze, *From Hiroshima to Glasnost: At the Center of Decision—A Memoir*. See also David T. Jones, "How to Negotiate with Gorbachev's Team," *Orbis* 33, no. 3 (1989).

66. Talbott, *Deadly Gambits*, p. 184.

67. John Barry, "New Men Take over in Moscow," *The Times*, June 2, 1983.

68. These accounts appeared in Talbott, *The Master of the Game*, pp. 174–81; *Deadly Gambits*, pp. 116–51; and more definitively in Nitze, *From Hiroshima to Glasnost*, pp. 376–85. For Kvitsinskii's version see "Soviet View of Geneva," *New York Times*, January 12, 1984.

69. For a typical Soviet commentary see Igor Malashenko, "Reasonable Sufficiency and Illusory Superiority," *New Times* 24 (1987). In contrast, a retired MFA official made the point that the 1987 treaty "is not at all the same thing as the 'zero option' President Reagan was talking about in 1981." G. M. Kornienko, "Pravda i domysly o raketakh SS-20," *SShA* 4 (1989): 52.

70. Stephen Dryden, "Belgium to Deploy Cruise Missiles," *Washington Post*, March 15, 1985. For Belgian policy see "Wilfried Martens, Loyal Wobbler," *The Economist*, January 19, 1985.

71. *Pravda*, April 7, 1985.

72. John Tagliabue, "Dutch Say Soviet Missile Freeze Will Not Affect Plan for Cruise," *New York Times*, April 8, 1985.

73. Sandro Viola, "Gorbachev Revives Andropov Proposal over Compromise," *La Repubblica*, May 31, 1985, in *FBIS-WEU*, June 4, 1985.

74. *Pravda*, October 4, 1985.

75. Speech to the North Atlantic Assembly, San Francisco, October 14, 1985, in *Department of State Bulletin*, December 1985, p. 24.

76. *Izvestiia*, January 16, 1986.

77. This was the essence of the U.S. counterproposal tabled in February 1986.

78. Talbott, *Master of the Game*, p. 304.

79. For accounts see Nitze, *From Hiroshima to Glasnost*; and Donald T. Regan, *For the Record*, p. 347.

80. M. S. Gorbachev, *Perestroika: New Thinking for Our Country and the World*, p. 238.

81. See, for example, André Fontaine, "Europe and East-West Relations," *Le Monde*, October 22, 1986, *FBIS-WEU*, October 27, 1986; the editorial "Zeroing in on Europe," *The Times*, October 24, 1986; and David S. Yost, "The Reykjavik Summit and European Security," *SAIS Review* 7, no. 2 (1987): 2–6.

82. See Gorbachev's interview with Indian journalists, reprinted in *Pravda*, November 24, 1986; see also Shevardnadze's harsh speech to the opening session of the Vienna CSCE review conference, *Pravda*, November 6, 1986.

83. *Pravda*, March 1, 1987.

84. Gorbachev, *Perestroika*, p. 246. See also his speech to the February 1987 Moscow forum, which presaged his position in the talks with Shultz. *Pravda*, February 17, 1987.

85. See, for example, Volker Rühe's interview in *Bild am Sonntag*, April 26, 1987.

86. Reprinted in *Pravda*, July 23, 1987.

87. At various points the Soviet side demanded that the United States agree in the treaty not to deploy INF in Alaska (which it had no intention of doing). The essence of this demand was political, and reflected the Soviet desire to secure equal treatment for U.S. and Soviet territory.

88. In 1990 it was revealed that East Germany, Bulgaria, and Czechoslovakia had obtained SS-23 missiles, possibly in violation (on the part of the USSR) of the INF treaty. See Douglas L. Clarke, "The East German SS-23 Missiles and the INF Treaty," *Report on Eastern Europe* 1, no. 12 (1990); and Bill Geertz, "Senate Seeks Report to Determine if Soviets Violated Arms Treaty," *Washington Times*, August 6, 1990.

89. See "Third Country Risk" (editorial), *The Times*, August 28,

1987, for the argument that Kohl "breached a principle" in yielding on the PIA matter.

90. See Thomas Risse-Kappen, "Zero Option: The Global Elimination of Ground-Launched Intermediate-Range Missiles," Peace Research Institute Frankfurt, Report No. 2, 1988, p. 24.

91. *International Affairs* 10 (1988): 19. See also his interview with *Argumenty i Fakty* 18 (1989).

92. James M. Markham, "Soviet Bloc Seeks Battlefield Nuclear-Arms Talks," *New York Times*, January 6, 1988.

93. Alan J. Vick and James A. Thomson, *The Military Significance of Restrictions on Strategic Nuclear Force Operations*, p. 1. See also F. Stephen Larrabee and Allen Lynch, *Confidence-Building Measures and U.S.-Soviet Relations*; and O. Bykov, *Confidence-Building Measures*, pp. 8–10.

94. The proposals are outlined in Soviet Committee for European Security and Cooperation, *How to Avert the Threat to Europe*, p. 74. See also *New York Times*, December 8, 1983. However, at the June 1979 Vienna summit President Carter proposed, in a handwritten note to Brezhnev, an agreement to "provide safe ocean haven areas for missile submarines to prevent destabilizing asw [antisubmarine warfare] developments." Carter, *Keeping Faith*, p. 253.

95. Michael Gordon, "U.S.-Soviet Talks Fail to Complete New Arms Accord," *Washington Post*, May 29, 1988.

96. Gerard Smith, *Doubletalk: The Story of the First Strategic Arms Limitation Talks*, pp. 190–91.

97. Kissinger, *White House Years*, p. 1208.

98. See *Strategic Survey, 1973* (London: IISS, 1974), p. 64.

99. For the text and the Gromyko speech, see *Documents on Disarmament, 1982*, pp. 349–52.

100. *Pravda*, December 23, 1982.

101. Ibid., January 7, 1983.

102. M. A. Milstein, "K voprosu o neprimenii pervym iadernogo oruzhiia," *SShA* 3 (1983).

103. See Henry Kissinger, "The Long Journey," *Washington Post*, December 17, 1985.

104. See *Department of State Bulletin*, January 1986, pp. 7–10; and *Sovetsko-amerikanskaia vstrecha na vyshem urovne*, pp. 13–17.

105. *Pravda*, January 13, 1958.

106. Ibid., January 12, 1958.

107. Osmo Apunen, "The Problem of the Guarantees of a Nordic Nuclear-Free Zone," *Ulkopolitiikka* (special issue, 1975), pp. 13–27.

108. For a listing of various Balkan proposals, see Athanassios G. Platias and R. J. Rydell, "International Security Regimes: The Case of a Balkan Nuclear-Free Zone," in David Carlton and Carlo Schaerf, eds., *The Arms Race in the 1980s*, p. 278.

109. William J. Jorden, "Soviet Suggests a Neutral Italy and Scandinavia," *New York Times*, January 12, 1958.

110. *Documents on Disarmament, 1945–1959*, 2:1423–26.

111. Outside Europe Khrushchev also called for a nuclear-free zone

in the Middle East and for the creation of a "zone of peace, above all an atom-free zone" in the Far East and Pacific. The Middle East proposal was made in January 1958; the Pacific proposal in Khrushchev's speech to the 21st CPSU Congress in early 1959.

112. *Izvestiia*, August 14, 1959.

113. See William E. Griffith, *Albania and the Sino-Soviet Rift*, p. 51.

114. *Izvestiia*, August 14, 1959.

115. For a general overview see Y. Tomilin, "Nuclear-Free Zones: How to Make Them Effective," *International Affairs* 8 (1975).

116. For Kekkonen's role see Osmo Apunen, "Three 'Waves' of the Kekkonen Plan and Nordic Security in the 1980s," *Bulletin of Peace Proposals* 11, no. 1 (1980): 16–32.

117. *Pravda*, May 20, 1963.

118. *Stenograficheskii otchët*, 1971, 1:53.

119. *Pravda*, July 17, 1974.

120. *Stenograficheskii otchët*, 1981, 1:45. In the second peace program (1976), Brezhnev made no specific mention of nuclear-free zones.

121. Iu. Komissarov, "Dva podkhoda k problemam bezopasnosti na Severe Evropy," *Mirovaia ekonomika i mezhdunarodnye otnoshenii* [hereinafter, *MEiMO*] 7 (1986): 17. For a thorough discussion of individual country positions on the zone, see Falk Bomsdorf, *Sicherheit im Norden Europas . . .*, pp. 235–67.

122. See Karl Bildt, "Sweden and the Soviet Submarine," *Survival* 25, no. 4 (1983): 165–69. The Treholt affair erupted into public view in January 1984 when Norwegian diplomat Arne Treholt was arrested for spying on behalf of the USSR. It was suggested by some in Norway that Treholt, who eventually was convicted, had served as an agent of influence and that he had worked on behalf of the Soviet Union to drum up support for the zone.

123. *Pravda*, June 27, 1981.

124. "Moscow Bars Key Area from Atom-Free Zone," *New York Times*, July 24, 1981.

125. John F. Burns, "Andropov Offers Atom-Free Baltic," *New York Times*, June 7, 1983. Inclusion of the Baltic in the zone was a complicated issue. Some Swedes were concerned that any arms control regime limited to the Baltic could advance what some suspected was a long-term Soviet design to transform the Baltic into a *mare clausum*, access to which by nonlittoral powers would be prohibited or circumscribed. For Swedish concerns about Soviet intentions, see the Lars Christiansen dispatch in *Svenska Dagbladet*, June 6, 1984.

126. See Palme's interviews in *Stern*, October 21, 1983, and *Le Monde*, October 17–18, 1982.

127. See the favorable assessment by N. N. Uspenskii (deputy in the 2d European Department of the MFA), "Godovshchina Murmanskikh initsiativ," *Vestnik MID* 19 (1988): 30–31.

128. See the report of a conversation with journalists with former Norwegian prime minister Kåre Willoch, in Erick Magnusson, "Pressure to Change Norwegian Foreign Policy," *Dagens Nyheter*, December 21, 1985, *FBIS-WEU*, January 8, 1986.

129. The Kola pledge was reported by Anker Jorgensen in the Western media, but was not confirmed by the Soviet side. See the AFP dispatch of October 6, *FBIS-SU*, October 7, 1988.

130. Sven Svensson, "Norway Says 'Yes' to Nordic Zone," *Dagens Nyheter*, May 16, 1986, *FBIS-WEU*, May 21, 1986.

131. "Press-konferentsiia v Khel'sinki," *Pravda*, November 14, 1986.

132. Mikhail S. Gorbachev, *The Speech in Murmansk*, pp. 28–29.

133. MFA press briefing, March 14, 1989.

134. Bill Keller, "Gorbachev Plan to Destroy His A-Armed Subs in Baltic," *New York Times*, October 27, 1989.

135. Independent Commission on Disarmament and Security Issues, *Common Security: A Blueprint for Survival.*

136. Ibid., p. 147.

137. Serge Schmemann, "Soviet Union Indicates Its Support for Nuclear-Free Zone in Europe," *New York Times*, January 28, 1983.

138. G. Vorontsov, "Bez'iadernye zony—put' k miru i razoruzheniiu," *MEiMO* 8 (1984): 55.

139. *Pravda*, October 23, 1986.

140. *Nuclear-Weapon-Free Corridor in Central Europe*, p. 11.

141. See Robert R. King, "The Athens Conference and the Balkans," *Radio Free Europe Research*, March 1, 1976, for Romanian motives.

142. Henry Kamm, "Greek Chief, Due in Soviet, Says U.S. Rift Is between Friends," *New York Times*, February 11, 1985.

143. WT.37. Under the CSCE document classification scheme, official documents from the 1973–75 conference are prefaced by "CSCE"; documents for subsequent CSCE meetings are prefaced by an initial designating the meeting, generally in the language of (or an official language chosen by) the host country. Thus "BM" denotes "Belgrade Meeting," "WT" stands for "Wiener Treffen," "OM" for "Ottawa Meeting," and so forth.

144. See also Shevardnadze's message to Yugoslav foreign minister Loncar, *Pravda*, February 25, 1988.

145. Ibid., January 7, 1983.

146. Ibid., March 27, 1986.

147. Paris AFP, June 25, 1986, *FBIS-WEU*, June 30, 1986.

148. "Otvet M. S. Gorbacheva na obrashchenie K. Livingstona," *Pravda*, January 3, 1986.

149. V. F. Davidov, *Beziadernye zony i mezhdunarodnaia bezopasnost'*, p. 184.

150. Philip E. Mosely, "The Meanings of Coexistence," *Foreign Affairs* 41, no. 1 (1962): 37.

151. Letter to Karamanlis in *Pravda*, January 12, 1958. Letters to Gerhardsen of Norway and Hansen of Denmark in *Pravda*, January 12, 13, respectively.

152. Frank K. Roberts, "Encounters with Khrushchev," in Martin McCauley, ed., *Khrushchev and Khrushchevism*, p. 222.

153. Walters, *Silent Missions*, p. 361. See also Khrushchev's August 11, 1961 speech at a Soviet-Romanian friendship meeting, at which he

spoke of blasting NATO weapons located in Italian orange and Greek olive groves. *Pravda*, August 12, 1961.

154. See Alec Douglas-Home's account of his first meeting with Gromyko at the UN in New York, at which the Soviet foreign minister "made an aggressive remark on the possibility of nuclear war." Alec Douglas-Home, *The Way the Wind Blows*.

155. In April 1984 Gromyko warned Italian foreign minister Andreotti that nuclear weapons could turn all of Italy "into a Pompeii." See also the vaguely threatening "How Britain Could Secure a Pledge of Nuclear Survival," letter to the *Guardian*, January 15, 1985, by Lev Semeiko of the U.S.A. and Canada Institute.

156. Lawrence D. Weiler, "No First Use: A History," *Bulletin of the Atomic Scientists* 39, no. 2 (1983): 30–31, for background.

157. *Documents on Disarmament, 1978*, p. 348.

158. See the draft convention of September 8 in ibid., pp. 558–60.

159. *Stenograficheskii otchët, 1981*, 1:44; and *Pravda*, April 4, 1981.

160. The Soviet ambassador to the Netherlands gave a speech in March 1984 in which he stated that the USSR would promise never to attack the Netherlands with nuclear arms if it decided not to accept the deployment of U.S. cruise missiles. Editorial, *De Volkskrant*, March 29, 1984, *FBIS-WEU*, April 5, 1984. A guarantee offer was made to Spain in February 1986, as disclosed by the Soviet press attaché in Madrid, and publicly rejected by Spanish foreign minister Fernández-Ordóñez. See the reports from Spanish radio, *FBIS-WEU*, March 3, 1986.

161. UN, *Disarmament Yearbook, 1982*, pp. 230–32.

162. For an assessment based on a reading of the Soviet press, see Robbin F. Laird, *France, the Soviet Union, and the Nuclear Weapons Issue*.

163. Williams, *Hugh Gaitskell*, p. 455.

164. Ibid., p. 520.

165. *Documents on Disarmament, 1960*, pp. 39–40.

166. Government statement on the resumption of nuclear weapons tests, August 30, 1961, *Documents on Disarmament, 1961*, p. 341.

167. Speech by Khrushchev on the Vienna meeting, June 15, 1961, in ibid., p. 179.

168. Pineau, *Khrouchtchev*, p. 237.

169. The agreement was embodied in a July 1976 exchange of letters between foreign ministers. Texts in France, Ministère des Affaires Etrangères, *Les Relations Franco-Soviétiques: Textes et Documents 1965–1976*, pp. 176–78.

170. *The Times*, February 14, 1967.

171. *Stenograficheskii otchët, 1971*, 1:53–54.

172. Garthoff, *Détente and Confrontation*, p. 351. The approach to Britain was in August 1973.

173. *Documents on Disarmament, 1978*, p. 348.

174. Carter, *Keeping Faith*, p. 257.

175. For the text of the aide-mémoire addressed to the five powers, see *Pravda*, June 22, 1983; see also A. N. Kaliadin and Iu. Nazarkin, *Disarmament Negotiating Machinery*, p. 63.

176. "Otvet M. S. Gorbacheva na obrashchenie K. Livingstona," *Pravda*, January 3, 1986.

177. The Soviet offer to Britain was in the form of a personal letter from Gorbachev to Prime Minister Thatcher. Rodney Cowton, "Moscow Arms Talks Offer Formalized," *The Times*, October 18, 1985.

178. *Izvestiia*, January 16, 1988.

179. See the comments by Arbatov in Martin Walker, "Moscow to Resist PM over Missiles," *Guardian*, March 26, 1987; and Aleksandr Lebedev, "Bomb for Europe? The British and French Nuclear Arsenals," *New Times* 3 (1987).

180. "L'affaire des euromissiles divise la majorité," *Le Monde*, March 6, 1987.

181. A. A. Kokoshin, "The New Soviet Military Doctrine and Unilateral Cuts of the USSR Armed Forces," statement before the Armed Services Committee, U.S. House of Representatives, March 10, 1989.

182. Published versions of the study suggest that in fact third country forces received very little consideration. See Committee of Soviet Scientists for Peace, Against the Nuclear Threat, *Strategic Stability Under the Conditions of Radical Nuclear Arms Reductions: Report on a Study (Abridged)*, Moscow, April 1987; A. A. Kokoshin, "Sokrashchenie iadernykh vooruzhenie i strategicheskaia stabil'nost," *SShA* 2 (1988); and A. Arbatov and G. Lednev, "Strategic Equilibrium and Stability," *Disarmament and Security Yearbook, 1987*.

183. Iuli Vorontsov, section report, "The Military-Political Aspects of Security," at the July 1988 MFA Scientific and Practical Conference, *International Affairs* 10 (1988): 41.

184. See Sergei Vybornov, Andrei Gusenkov, Vladimir Leontiev, "Nothing Is Simple in Europe," *International Affairs* 3 (1988): 34–41; Vladimir Stupishin, "Indeed, Nothing in Europe Is Simple," *International Affairs* 5 (1988): 69–73; and Vybornov and Leontiev, "The Future of the Old Weapon," *International Affairs* 9 (1988): 81–89. For a discussion of the "scientists" versus "diplomats" debate, see Stephen Shenfield, *Minimum Nuclear Deterrence: The Debate Among Soviet Civilian Analysts*, pp. 7–18.

185. Peter Stothard and Robin Oakley, "Thatcher Urged Not to Raise Trident at Gorbachev Talks," *The Times*, June 7, 1990.

186. DPA, July 31, 1985, *FBIS-WEU*, August 1, 1985.

187. See Smith, *Doubletalk*, p. 470; and Dean, *Watershed in Europe*, p. 117.

188. TASS, July 15, 1986.

189. For a view of the effectiveness of Soviet "spin controllers" by a member of the U.S. INF negotiating team in Geneva, see Jones, "How to Negotiate with Gorbachev's Team," p. 361.

190. RIIA, *Documents, 1955*, pp. 552–55.

191. *Documents on Disarmament, 1945–1959*, 1:456–67.

192. U.S. Department of State, *The Geneva Conference*, p. 38.

193. Ibid., pp. 55–56.

194. Eden, *Full Circle*, p. 77.

195. U.S. Department of State, *The Geneva Conference*, pp. 31–34.

196. Ibid., p. 59.

197. See Grewe, *Rückblenden 1976–1951*, p. 225; and Dulles's remarks to the British ambassador about the danger of the plan, and his suggestion that the experiment "might be done in relation to Norway or Turkey where there were real national boundaries to deal with rather than a divided country." Memorandum of conversation, August 31, 1955, *FRUS, 1955–1957*, 1:563.

198. U.S. Department of State, *Foreign Ministers Meeting*, p. 29.

199. Ibid., pp. 45–48.

200. Ibid., pp. 184–86.

201. Ibid., p. 194.

202. See his statement of October 31, 1955, in ibid., pp. 75–76; and the U.S. delegation report, *FRUS, 1955–1957*, 1:658–59.

203. *Documents on Disarmament, 1945–1959*, 1:603–7.

204. For the text and Bulganin's letter see RIIA, *Documents, 1957*, pp. 125–29, 2–11.

205. Macmillan letter of June 14, 1957, in ibid., p. 14.

206. *Documents on Disarmament, 1945–1959*, 2:948.

207. Ibid., p. 1218.

208. "New Point in Moscow Communiqué," *The Times*, March 4, 1959.

209. For a discussion of some of the Western proposals, see James E. Dougherty, "Zonal Arms Limitation in Europe," *Orbis* 7, no. 3 (1963): 481–82.

210. *Documents on Disarmament, 1959*, pp. 304–8.

211. *Pravda*, January 15, 1960. For background see Raymond L. Garthoff, "Estimating Soviet Military Force Levels: Some Light from the Past," *International Security* 14, no. 4 (1990).

212. *Documents on Disarmament, 1960*, pp. 79–80; and *Documents on Disarmament, 1962*, 1:103–27.

213. *Documents on Disarmament, 1961*, pp. 496–504.

214. For the text see USSR, *SSSR v borbe za bezopasnost'*, pp. 7–9.

215. See Wolfe, "The Soviet Union and Arms Control"; for the Soviet and Warsaw Pact conventional buildup, see Phillip A. Karber, "To Lose an Arms Race: The Competition in Conventional Forces Deployed in Central Europe, 1965–80," in Uwe Nerlich, ed., *Soviet Power and Western Negotiating Policies*, 1: 31–88.

216. NATO, *Texts of Final Communiqués, 1949–1970*, p. 189.

217. Ibid., p. 198.

218. Like the Harmel report, the Reykjavik declaration did not posit a tight linkage between progress on arms control and change in the European political order. However, it suggested that the former could facilitate the latter. The ministers "recognized that the unresolved issues which still divide the European Continent must be settled by peaceful means, and are convinced that the ultimate goal of a lasting peaceful order in Europe requires an atmosphere of trust and can only be reached by a step-by-step process." Ibid., p. 199.

219. Ibid., p. 223.

220. Quoted in Mojmir Povolny, "The Soviet Union and the European Security Conference," *Orbis* 18, no. 1 (1974): 215.

221. *Pravda*, June 27, 1970.

222. *Stenograficheskii otchët, 1971*, 1:54.

223. The speech was widely credited with defusing pressures in the United States for Congressionally mandated unilateral troop withdrawals from Europe, and thus was interpreted by many Western observers as proof that the Soviet leadership wanted the United States to remain militarily in Europe. See, for example, John G. Keliher, *The Negotiations on Mutual and Balanced Force Reductions*, p. 29; and the Aspen Strategy Group, *After the INF Agreement: Conventional Forces and Arms Control in European Security*, 1987, which noted that "many in the West believed that Soviet leaders feared that precipitate U.S. withdrawals would spur the West Germans into a massive buildup of forces that would destabilize Central Europe" (p. 12).

224. Brezhnev, *Leninskim kursom*, 3:352–53.

225. Ibid., p. 353.

226. Thomas W. Wolfe, "Soviet Attitudes toward MBFR and the USSR's Military Presence in Europe," Rand Corporation, P-4819, April 1972, p. 11.

227. *New York Times*, June 5, 1971.

228. TASS, June 5, 1971.

229. "Russians Are Said to Link Troop and Security Talks," *New York Times*, June 8, 1971.

230. Brandt, *People and Politics*, p. 352.

231. Povolny, "The Soviet Union and the European Security Conference," p. 221.

232. "Deklaratsiia o mire, bezopastnosti i sotrudnichestve v Evrope," *Pravda*, January 27, 1972.

233. For confirmation that there was a U.S.-Soviet understanding on a link between CSCE and MBFR by a former American official, see Garthoff, *Détente and Confrontation*, p. 404.

234. Ibid., p. 481.

235. *Washington Post*, January 12, 1973, quoted in Keliher, *The Negotiations on Mutual and Balanced Force Reductions*, p. 32.

236. According to Brandt, "more than half" of the time was taken up with CSCE. See Brandt, *People and Politics*, p. 263. Brezhnev also urged Pompidou to participate in MBFR but failed in this regard.

237. Ferraris, *Report on a Negotiation*, pp. 23–24.

238. This interpretation was confirmed by several statements in the Gorbachev period. During his 1989 trip to Bonn Gorbachev was asked point blank whether "it is preferable from the Soviet standpoint for U.S. troops to stay in Europe or leave," and in effect gave "leave" for an answer: "I would not like to go into details now, although you did ask me to do so. It is in the details that divergences have arisen. But in principle we have been right to raise the question of the reduction and the presence of foreign troops, and undoubtedly this process will proceed and should result logically in there being no foreign troops on others' territory." Press conference, *Pravda*, June 16, 1989. In early 1990

Shevardnadze admitted to an interviewer that until "quite recently our aim was to oust the Americans from Europe at any price." *Izvestiia*, February 20, 1990.

239. Pact delegates protested when the Austrian hosts inadvertently provided official placards which read MBFR. Garthoff, *Détente and Confrontation*, p. 480.

240. Robin Ranger, "MBFR: Political or Technical Arms Control," *The World Today* 30, no. 10 (1974): 412.

241. Brezhnev, *Leninskim kursom*, 4:327–28.

242. Clive Rose, "Mutual and Balanced Force Reductions," *NATO's Sixteen Nations* 29, no. 4 (1984/85): 34.

243. Dean, *Watershed in Europe*, pp. 108–9.

244. This point is stressed by Keliher, *The Negotiations on Mutual and Balanced Force Reductions*, p. 36. European negotiators suspected that Soviet stubbornness on this issue was in part attributable to the fact that Kissinger had already conceded the issue to Dobrynin in earlier talks. Garthoff confirmed these suspicions in *Détente and Confrontation*, p. 481.

245. *Department of State Bulletin*, July 23, 1973, pp. 130–34.

246. Keliher, *The Negotiations on Mutual and Balanced Force Reductions*, p. 42.

247. *Documents on Disarmament, 1973*, p. 364.

248. The East provided a detailed account of its proposal in K. Borisov, "Vienna: Two Positions," *New Times* 50 (1973): 4–5.

249. Brezhnev, *Leninskim kursom*, 4:327–28.

250. Borisov, "Vienna: Two Positions," p. 5.

251. Rose, "Mutual and Balanced Force Reductions," p. 35.

252. Option 3 eventually was withdrawn in late 1979, when NATO, as part of its dual-track INF decision, announced the unilateral withdrawal of many of the systems it had proposed to trade for reductions in Soviet tank forces.

253. U.K., Foreign and Commonwealth Office, "MBFR from the Soviet Viewpoint," *Foreign Policy Documents* 23 (1978): 7–8.

254. *Pravda*, January 19, 1977.

255. News conference statement by Dutch representative De Vos, July 19, 1978, *Documents on Disarmament, 1978*, p. 248.

256. Schmidt, *Menschen und Mächte*, pp. 91–94, for an account of the talks. The text of the statement is in *Pravda*, May 7, 1978.

257. De Vos news conference statement, July 19, 1978, *Documents on Disarmament, 1978*, p. 450.

258. Ibid.

259. Western intelligence services later concluded that the withdrawal was more than offset by a buildup in other units. Richard Burt, "Soviet Said to Add to Its Bloc Troops," *New York Times*, June 8, 1980.

260. Dean, *Watershed in Europe*, p. 167, for Schmidt's authorship.

261. G. Evgenev and I. Mel'nikov, "Vena: nuzhny konstruktivnye rezul'taty," *MEiMO* 7 (1982): 88.

262. Richard F. Staar, "The MBFR Process and Its Prospects," *Orbis* 27, no. 3 (1984): 1003–4.

263. For details of the proposal see Thomas C. Hammond, "MBFR—Further Western Attempts to Break the Impasse," *NATO Review* 32, no. 4 (1984): 14–15.

264. See the interview with Mikhailov in *Volkstimme*, July 2, 1983.

265. Hammond, "MBFR—Further Western Attempts," pp. 15–16.

266. Dusko Doder, "Soviets Offer New Cuts at Europe Troop Talks," *Washington Post*, February 15, 1985.

267. Michael Alexander, "MBFR—Verification Is the Key," *NATO Review* 34, no. 3 (1986): 8.

268. "West Is Cool to Soviet Plan on Cutting Forces in Europe," *New York Times*, February 16, 1985.

269. Dean, *Watershed in Europe*, p. 167.

270. Alexander, "MBFR—Verification Is the Key," p. 10.

271. "Vystuplenie Tovarishcha Gorbacheva M. S.," *Pravda*, April 19, 1986.

272. *Pravda*, June 12, 1986.

273. Patrick Blum, "East 'Ready to Break Troop Cut Impasse,'" *Financial Times*, October 24, 1986.

274. See Eisenhower, *Mandate for Change*, pp. 521–22; and the record of Eisenhower's informal conversation with Khrushchev (Bohlen's memorandum of conversation), *FRUS, 1955–1957*, 5:456–57.

275. See Walt W. Rostow, *Open Skies: Eisenhower's Proposal of July 21, 1955*, for background.

276. *Documents on Disarmament, 1945–1959*, 1:516–21.

277. Ibid., pp. 603–7.

278. For details, including maps, see Bechhoefer, *Postwar Negotiations for Arms Control*, pp. 377–86. The 800-kilometer proposal was broached in a government statement attached to Bulganin's letter to Eisenhower of November 17. See *Documents, 1956*, p. 611. It was formally tabled at the UN in March 1957.

279. At a news conference in Helsinki in June 1957 Khrushchev characterized the Arctic proposal as "quite comical," and objected to the fact that it included large swaths of Soviet and Canadian territory, but very little of the United States. Drew Middleton, "Khrushchev Asks Atom Test Check," *New York Times*, June 14, 1957.

280. Maresca, *To Helsinki*, pp. 168–69.

281. CSCE/I/3. Documents from the 1973–75 CSCE conference appear in Igor I. Kavass, et al., eds., *Human Rights, European Politics, and the Helsinki Accord: The Documentary Evolution of the Conference on Security and Co-operation in Europe 1973–1975*.

282. CSCE/II/C/1.

283. Maresca, *To Helsinki*, p. 171; and CSCE/II/C/12.

284. Ferraris, *Report on a Negotiation*, pp. 184–85.

285. Ljubivoje Acimovic, *Problems of Security and Cooperation in Europe*, pp. 218–19.

286. Wilson, *Final Term*, p. 156; and James Callaghan, *Time and Chance*, p. 366.

287. The USSR was not explicitly mentioned in the Final Act. The following formulation, which applied to the USSR and Turkey, was

used: notification would apply to maneuvers "on the territory, in Europe, of any participating State as well as, if applicable, in the adjoining sea area and air space," with the following exception: "In the case of a participating State whose territory extends beyond Europe, prior notification need be given only of maneuvers which take place in an area within 250 kilometers from its frontier facing or shared with any other European participating state."

288. "The Other Side of the Hill," *The Times*, September 23, 1986.

289. See the semi-annual reports of the Commission on Security and Cooperation in Europe, *Implementation of Helsinki Final Act*, and the Commission's *The Helsinki Process and East-West Relations: Progress in Perspective*, pp. 22–31.

290. See David S. Yost, *France's Deterrent Posture and Security in Europe*, part 2, "Strategic and Arms Control Implications," pp. 39–42.

291. See Benoit d'Aboville, "CBMs and the Future of European Security," in F. Stephen Larrabee and Dietrich Stobbe, eds., *Confidence-Building Measures in Europe*, p. 202.

292. *Pravda*, November 28, 1976.

293. CSCE/BM/5; see also Adam-Daniel Rotfeld, "CBMs between Helsinki and Madrid," in Larrabee and Stobbe, *Confidence-Building Measures in Europe*, p. 109; and Jean-Christophe Romer, "L'URSS et la Conference de Stockholm," *Defense Nationale* 8/9 (1984): 46–48, for a survey of Soviet comments on the origins of the conference.

294. Communiqué of the Committee of Foreign Ministers, *Pravda*, May 16, 1979.

295. Milstein, "K voprosu o neprimenii pervym iadernogo oruzhiia," p. 18.

296. *Pravda*, May 16, 1979.

297. *Stenograficheski otchët, 1981*, 1:46.

298. In his *Spiegel* interview of November 1981, Brezhnev said only that "insular territories adjacent to Europe and respective sea and ocean areas and air spaces over them must . . . be included."

299. This new term was adopted by the conference in March 1981 at the suggestion of Yugoslvia in order to signify that the measures contemplated would be more substantial than those mandated in the Final Act. David S. Yost, "Arms Control Prospects at Madrid," *The World Today* 38, no. 10 (1982): 392.

300. Nicole Gnesotto, "Conference on Disarmament in Europe Opens in Stockholm," *NATO Review* 31, no. 6 (1983): 4.

301. For an account and analysis of the negotiations by a former U.S. negotiator, see James Goodby, *The Stockholm Conference: Negotiating a Cooperative Security System for Europe*.

302. *Pravda*, January 19, 1984; and John Vinocur, "Gromyko Attacks the U.S. at European Security Talks," *New York Times*, same date.

303. *Pravda*, January 19, 1984.

304. Malta, Romania, and the neutral and nonaligned also put forward proposals. The NNA proposal eventually played a major role in the

conference, in that it helped to bridge the Warsaw Pact-NATO differences.

305. John Borawski, Stan Weeks, and Charlotte E. Thompson, "The Stockholm Agreement of September 1986," *Orbis* 30, no. 4 (1987): 650.

306. Quoted in John Vinocur, "Mystery of Stockholm: What's on the Agenda?" *New York Times*, January 18, 1984.

307. John Vinocur, " 'Non-Use of Force' Issue Is Examined at NATO," *New York Times*, March 23, 1984.

308. *Public Papers of the Presidents: Ronald Reagan, 1984* (Washington, D.C.: GPO, 1986), 1:808.

309. Goodby, *The Stockholm Conference*, p. 17.

310. See the proposals tabled on May 20, 1985: SC/WGB.3 by Bulgaria, Poland, and the USSR dealing with naval exercises; and SC/WGB.2 by the GDR, Hungary, and the USSR dealing with air force operations.

311. Borawski, et al., "The Stockholm Agreement of September 1986," p. 650.

312. *Izvestiia*, January 16, 1986.

313. "Document of the Stockholm Conference," CSCE/SC.9, in *CSCE: Public Documents and Statements*, pp. 388–415; and for a convenient summary of the agreement see Leif Mevik, "The CDE: A Solid Achievement," *NATO Review* 34, no. 5 (1986): 15–17.

314. The USSR refused to accept a last minute American proposal that aerial inspections be carried out by neutral aircraft, and insisted that aircraft of the country subject to the inspection be used.

315. Adam-Daniel Rotfeld, "CSBMs in Europe: A Future-Oriented Concept," UNIDIR/88/25 (UN Institute for Disarmament Research), January 1989, p. 15.

316. Joseph Schaerli, "Verification of Confidence- and Security-Building Measures," UNIDIR/88/26, January 1989, p. 9.

317. Günther Gillessen, "German Complaints about Soviet Inspection Practices Show Results," *Frankfurter Allgemeine Zeitung*, April 1, 1989, in *JPRS Report: Arms Control*, June 6, 1989.

318. Schaerli, "Verification of Confidence- and Security-Building Measures," p. 10.

319. Gillessen, "German Complaints."

320. Maresca, *To Helsinki*, p. 173; and the texts of the proposals, CSCE/II/C/6, and CSCE/II/C/16.

321. Macmillan, *Tides of Fortune*, p. 623.

322. *FRUS, 1955–1957*, 5:479–80.

323. "Navy on Way to Leningrad," *The Times*, October 10, 1955.

324. "Danish, Soviet Navies to Visit," *New York Times*, April 20, 1956; and "Danish Ships to Visit Soviet," *New York Times*, July 31, 1956.

325. Dana Adams Schmidt, "President Rules Twining Is to Go to Moscow Fete," *New York Times*, May 31, 1956.

326. "Russian Air Power," *The Times*, June 25, 1956.

327. Basil Gingell, "Soviet Snub over Naval Visit," *The Times*, June 7, 1967.

328. "Russian Officers in Britain," *The Times*, March 28, 1977.

329. Schmidt, *Menschen und Mächte*, p. 92.

330. In 1987 the Swedish government "decided to demonstrate the improved relations" by sending the commander of the Swedish air force on an official visit to the USSR. Stockholm International Service, June 9, 1987, in *FBIS-WEU*, June 10, 1987.

331. *Pravda*, January 7, 1983. Until 1983 Soviet budget limitation proposals did not spell out a role for the blocs and were made in the UN context. See Abraham S. Becker, *Military Expenditure Limitation for Arms Control: Problems and Prospects*, pp. 137–40; *Pravda*, November 24, 1978, for a PCC budget freeze and reduction proposal; and *Pravda*, May 16, 1980, for a PCC call for cuts in military budgets, "above all of the major powers."

332. *Pravda*, October 17, 1985. See also the statement adopted the next week by the PCC, "For the Elimination of the Nuclear Threat and a Change for the Better in European and World Affairs." *Pravda*, October 24, 1985.

333. Reported by East Berlin ADN, December 9, 1986, in *FBIS-SU*, December 10, 1986; and *Die Presse*, December 11, 1986, in *FBIS-WEU*, December 12, 1986.

334. Text in *FBIS-EEU*, June 1, 1987.

335. *Pravda*, April 11, 1987.

336. The first high-level U.S.-Soviet military contacts took place at the June 1979 Vienna summit. Contacts later were suspended, but were resumed in late 1987. "Top Soviet Military Official Makes History at the Pentagon," *Washington Post*, December 10, 1987; George C. Wilson, "Soviet Military Chief Calls Forces Defensive," *Washington Post*, March 17, 1988; and Michael R. Gordon, "Top Soviet Commander Plans 6-Day U.S. Tour," *New York Times*, July 6, 1988.

337. *Krasnaia zvezda*, April 2, 1989.

338. *Pravda*, July 6, 1989.

339. *Krasnaia zvezda*, August 2, 1989.

340. "Wellershoff für mehr militaerische Kontakte," *Die Welt*, May 6, 1989.

341. [fy], "Die Bundesmarine besucht Leningrad," *Frankfurter Allgemeine Zeitung*, October 11, 1989.

342. "Achromejev trifft Stoltenberg und Wellershoff," *Frankfurter Allgemeine Zeitung*, June 14, 1989.

343. Magarditsch Hatschikjan and Wolfgang Pfeiler, "Deutsch-sowjetische Beziehungen in einer Periode der Ost-West-Annäherung," *Deutschland Archiv* 22, no. 8 (1989): 884. The hotline established during the same visit was considered a political rather than a military link. The Dutch agreement was signed by Defense Minister Relus Ter Beek and Yazov during the former's visit to Moscow. See TASS, June 19, 1990. For Sweden, see the Anders Steinvall dispatch in *Dagens Nyheter*, September 27, 1990, in *FBIS-WEU*, October 25, 1990.

344. Halifax Statement on Conventional Arms Control, *NATO Review* 34, no. 3 (1986): 30.

345. *NATO Review* 34, no. 6 (1986): 27–28.

346. For a succinct statement of the French position, see the statement by French Vienna delegation head Pierre-Henri Renard, *Le Monde*, February 1–2, 1987.

347. WT.1.

348. Interview with Soviet delegation head Iuri Kashlev, *Diario 16*, May 9, 1987.

349. U.S. Department of State, *CSCE Vienna Follow-up Meeting: A Framework for Europe's Future*, no. 35, January 1989.

350. Dual-capable systems could be addressed in the negotiations, but were not singled out in a separate category.

351. For a summary of Eastern and Western thinking, see Robert D. Blackwill and F. Stephen Larrabee, *Conventional Arms Control and East-West Security*; see also Edward L. Warner, III, and David A. Ochmanek, *Next Moves: An Arms Control Agenda for the 1990s*, pp. 89–128.

352. *Pravda*, February 26, 1986.

353. See James A. Thomson and Nanette C. Gantz, *Conventional Arms Control Revisited: Objectives in the New Phase*.

354. See his address to the Moscow Forum for a Nuclear-Free World, for the Survival of Humanity, *Pravda*, February 17, 1987.

355. *Trybunu Ludu*, May 8–9, 1987.

356. "O voennoi doktrine gosudarstv-uchastnikov Varshavskogo Dogovora," *Pravda*, May 30, 1987.

357. *Pravda*, March 31, 1988.

358. See Eduard Shevardnadze, "Towards a Safe World," *International Affairs* 9 (1988): 12–13; and Dmitrii Yazov, "The Soviet Proposal for European Security," *Bulletin of the Atomic Scientists* 9 (1988): 9.

359. Paul Lewis, "Soviet Offers to Adjust Imbalance of Conventional Forces in Europe," *New York Times*, June 24, 1988.

360. *Pravda*, July 16, 1988.

361. See Paul K. Davis, et al., *Variables Affecting Central-Region Stability: The 'Operational Minimum' and Other Issues at Low Force Levels*.

362. *Pravda*, December 8, 1988. These cuts were planned as far back as the summer of 1988, shortly after ratification of the INF treaty. See Akhromeev's interview in *Krasnaia zvezda*, July 2, 1989.

363. *Pravda*, January 20, 1989.

364. A detailed report was issued. See *Pravda*, January 30, 1989.

365. *Pravda*, March 7, 1989.

366. William Tuohy, "Soviet Missile Cuts Could Upset NATO Modernization," *Los Angeles Times*, January 21, 1989.

367. *Pravda*, July 7, 1989.

368. According to one scenario widely discussed by institute researchers in the summer of 1989 (very much under the shadow of the rapid changes in Poland and Hungary), the USSR and the West might strike a deal in which the Soviet Union would not press for rapid denuclearization, while in return the West would not call for the rapid breakup of the Warsaw Pact, and thus help to shore up a residual Soviet influence in Eastern Europe.

369. Pavel Bayev, Vitali Zhurkin, Sergei Karaganov, Viktor Shein, *Tactical Nuclear Weapons in Europe: The Problem of Reduction and Elimination* (Moscow: Novosti, for the Institute of Europe and the Soviet Committee for European Security and Cooperation, 1990).

370. Michael R. Gordon, "Warsaw Pact Offers Details of Its European Arms Proposal," *New York Times*, May 31, 1989.

371. "Comprehensive Concept," *Department of State Bulletin*, August 1989, p. 27. (Italics in the original).

372. *Washington Post*, May 31, 1989.

373. See R. Jeffrey Smith, "U.S., Britain Set Compromise in Treaty Verification Dispute," *Washington Post*, September 12, 1989.

374. CSCE.WV.2. The SPD and the Polish Communist Party lent support to an expanded role for naval issues by concluding, in June 1989, a joint working paper on CSBMs and arms limitation measures for the Baltic. [ban], "Abrüstungsinitiative der SPD und der polnischen Kommunisten," *Frankfurter Allgemeine Zeitung*, June 28, 1989; text in Sozialdemokratische Partei Deutschlands, *Materialien: Frieden und Abrüstung in Europa*, pp. 14–15.

375. For the complete range of WTO proposals, see the "Statement on Confidence- and Security-Building Measures and Disarmament in Europe," by the WTO Committee of Foreign Ministers, October 28, 1988, *FBIS-EEU*, October 31, 1988.

376. Text distributed by ADN, July 7, 1988.

377. *Pravda*, July 12, 1988.

378. "K novym mashtabam i kachestvu obshcheevropeiskogo dialoga," *Izvestiia*, January 20, 1989; also his interview in *Le Figaro*, January 10, 1989; and Rotfeld, "CSBMs in Europe: A Future-Oriented Concept," p. 17.

379. Jan Reifenberg, "Nach dem Absturz der MiG 23 erwägt die Nato ein Krisenzentrum mit dem Ostblock," *Frankfurter Allgemeine Zeitung*, July 8, 1989.

380. Jan Reifenberg, "A First Attempt to Increase Awareness of Others' Motives," *Frankfurter Allgemeine Zeitung*, February 2, 1990, in *Joint Publications Research Service Report: Arms Control*, April 3, 1990.

381. Paul Lewis, "Soviet Position at 'Open Skies' Talks Leaves West Wondering about Rifts in Moscow," *New York Times*, February 25, 1990.

382. See Shevardnadze's interview in *Ogonëk* 11 (1990), and Michael R. Gordon, "Bush Draws Fire over Troop Cuts," *New York Times*, March 1, 1990.

383. David Hoffman, "Soviets Propose Retaining 4 Powers' Role in Germany," *Washington Post*, June 23, 1990.

384. *New York Times*, July 17, 1990.

385. Treaty on the Final Settlement with Respect to Germany, official text distributed by the German Information Center, New York, 1990.

386. "Superpowers Consider New U.S. Force Cuts," *Washington Post*, September 11, 1990.

387. Thomas L. Friedman, "U.S. and Soviets Reach Agreement on New Arms Pact," *New York Times*, October 4, 1990.

388. "Warsaw Pact Arms Quotas Threaten Treaty," *Financial Times*, October 12, 1990.

Chapter 7: Economics

1. Cmnd. 1207, in Foreign Office, *Hertslet's Commercial Treaties*, 30:977–83. For an account of the negotiations see Richard H. Ullman, *Anglo-Soviet Relations, 1917–1921*, 3:397–453.

2. It canceled all claims and counterclaims for compensation for damages caused by the war, set aside the problem of czarist debts, and provided for the mutual granting of most favored nation treatment. The German government also pledged to assist private German firms in dealing with the Soviet government. Article 3 contained the treaty's only explicitly political provisions, and provided for the resumption of full diplomatic and consular relations. For the text see League of Nations, *Treaty Series: Treaties and International Engagements Registered with the Secretariat of the League of Nations* [hereinafter, *LNTS*] 19, no. 498.

3. E. H. Carr, *The Bolshevik Revolution, 1917–1923*, 3:283.

4. Ibid., 3:355.

5. V. Kozyrev, "Trade and Economic Relations between the USSR and France," *Foreign Trade* 7 (1970): 12.

6. A. S. Kovolenko, *Torgovye dogovory i soglasheniia SSSR*, pp. 303–10 for the text.

7. United Kingdom, *Treaty Series* 34 (1948), Cmnd. 7439. For an account of the negotiations see Wilson, *Memoirs: The Making of a Prime Minister*, pp. 91–92.

8. For the 1934 agreement see *LNTS* 149, no. 3446:445–70.

9. For the significance of this agreement see Geir Lundestad, *America, Scandinavia, and the Cold War, 1945–1949*, p. 60.

10. For the text of the 1947 treaty see Kari Mottola, O. N. Bykov, and I. S. Korolev, eds., *Finnish-Soviet Economic Relations*, pp. 250–55.

11. Text in Kovolenko, *Torgovye dogovory*, pp. 310–14.

12. Angela Stent, *From Embargo to Ostpolitik*, pp. 34, 37, 52.

13. Unnamed officials quoted in Gunnar Adler-Karlsson, *Western Economic Warfare, 1947–1967*, p. 86.

14. See U.S. Department of State, *Geneva Meeting of Foreign Ministers*, pp. 239–40, 245–48, for the proposal texts; and *FRUS, 1955–1957*, 5:760–64, for the negotiations.

15. Lyman Burbank, "Scandinavian Integration and Western Defense," *Foreign Affairs* 1 (1956): 149.

16. Adenauer, *Erinnerungen*, p. 513. Saburov also held out the prospect of joint Soviet-West German efforts to industrialize China. See Schmid, *Erinnerungen*, p. 569.

17. Talbott, *Khrushchev Remembers: The Last Testament*, pp. 357–60.

18. Pineau, *Khrouchtchev*, p. 67.

19. Mastny, "Kremlin Politics and the Austrian Settlement," p. 46.
20. V. Medvedovsky, "USSR-Italy: Results and Prospects of Economic Cooperation," *Foreign Trade* 10 (1978): 26.
21. Meissner, *Moskau-Bonn*, 1:384–86. For background see Stent, *From Embargo to Ostpolitik*, pp. 64–67.
22. *Treaty Series* 34 (1960), Cmnd. 1076.
23. Britain claimed that the USSR had seized about £11 million worth of British assets in the Baltic states and other territories annexed after January 1939, while the Soviet Union claimed ownership of £7 million in gold formerly owned by the central banks of the Baltic states and lodged in London. "Negotiations on Russian Debt," *The Times*, August 19, 1964. After eight years of talks, it was agreed that Britain would pay the Soviet Union £500,000 in consumer goods, after which both sides would drop all claims. See the communiqué issued at the conclusion of the Kosygin-Wilson talks, *The Times*, February 14, 1967.
24. France, Ministère des Affaires Etrangères, *Les Relations Franco-Soviétiques*, pp. 62–63, 121–31.
25. Charles P. Kindleberger, *Foreign Trade and the National Economy*, p. 173.
26. Glenn Alden Smith, *Soviet Foreign Trade: Organization, Operations, and Policy, 1918–1971*, p. 166.
27. Arthur Jay Klinghoffer, *The Soviet Union and International Oil Politics*, p. 220. See also Marshall Goldman, "The Soviet Union," *Daedalus* (*The Oil Crisis: In Perspective*) 104, no. 4 (1975): 129–30.
28. Klinghoffer, *The Soviet Union and International Oil Politics*, pp. 220–21. For Italy as a whole, the dependence on Soviet oil was almost 23 percent.
29. Smith, *Soviet Foreign Trade*, p. 166.
30. For a full treatment of the embargo see Stent, *From Embargo to Ostpolitik*, pp. 93–115.
31. Gerard Curzon, *Multilateral Commercial Diplomacy: The General Agreement on Tariffs and Trade and Its Impact on National and Commercial Policies and Techniques*, p. 65.
32. For background see Jacob J. Kaplan and Günther Schleiminger, *The European Payments Union: Financial Diplomacy in the 1950s.*
33. K. Ovchinnikov, "Europe: Long-Term Agreements in East-West Trade and Economic Relations," *Foreign Trade* 6 (1974): 23.
34. The Finnish-Soviet system of payments was established in 1951. Payment was made through ruble accounts kept in Finland by the Bank of Finland and in the USSR by the Bank of Foreign Trade. By exporting to the Soviet Union, Finland earned rubles that were deposited in the latter account, and that could be spent only to purchase goods from the USSR. See Kari Holopainen, "The System of Payment between Finland and the Soviet Union," in Mottola et al., *Finnish-Soviet Economic Relations*, pp. 173–80. Consistent with the Soviet desire to convert all trade to a hard currency basis, in June 1990 Soviet officials told the Finns that they wanted to end the clearing account as early as January 1, 1991. Because of the hard currency shortage in the USSR there was speculation that the changeover would occur by 1992

at the earliest. "Clearing Account with USSR Will Continue Next Year," *Helsingin Sanomat*, August 30, 1990, in *FBIS-WEU*, September 21, 1990. However, it did not occur as scheduled in 1991.

35. Stent, *Embargo to Ostpolitik*, pp. 64–65.

36. V. Mikhailov, "Franco-Soviet Trade and Economic Relations," *Foreign Trade* 11 (1968): 12.

37. De Gaulle, *Memoirs of Hope*, p. 232.

38. Philip Hanson, *Trade and Technology in Soviet-Western Relations*, pp. 92–94.

39. Hilger, *Incompatible Allies*, pp. 137, 237.

40. It broke down again in May 1927 when the Russian members pulled out following the abrogation of the 1924 trade agreement, but resumed activity in 1934 with the restoration of trade ties. David Young, "Sixty Years of Experience Pays Off," *The Times*, October 21, 1976; and M. Tomashevskii, "Russko-britanskoi torgovoi-palate—50 let," *Vneshnaia torgolovaia* 4 (1966): 33.

41. *Treaty Series* 34 (1948), Cmnd. 7439.

42. *Treaty Series* 34 (1960), Cmnd. 1076.

43. Simone Alopaeus, "La Coopération de la Finlande avec l'Europe," in Johan Galtung, ed., *Co-operation in Europe*, pp. 220–21.

44. "K nauchno-tekhnicheskomu sotrudnichestvu mezhdu SSSR i Finlandiei," *Pravda*, August 17, 1955.

45. L. A. Ingul'skaia, "Rol' kul'turnogo obmena v razvitii dobrososedskikh otnoshenii mezhdu Finlandiei i SSSR," in USSR Academy of Sciences, *Sovetskaia kultura: istoriia i sovremennost'*, p. 240.

46. "Kommiunike o pervoi sessii sovetsko finliandskoi kommissii po nauchno-tekhnicheskomu sotrudnichestvu," *Pravda*, March 3, 1956.

47. "Sovetsko-norvezhkoe kommiunike," *Pravda*, November 16, 1955.

48. Susanne S. Lotarski, "Institutional Development and the Joint Commissions in East-West Commercial Relations," in U.S., Congress, Joint Economic Committee, *East European Economies Post-Helsinki: A Compendium of Papers Submitted to the Joint Economic Committee*, p. 1021.

49. These included the agreement by which France supplied the USSR with the technology for its PAL color television system (1965), an agreement on the exploration of space (1966), and a later agreement on cooperation in the field of atomic energy (1967). For the texts see France, Ministère des Affaires Etrangères, *Les Relations Franco-Soviétiques*, pp. 7–8, 20–22, 48–50.

50. Ibid., pp. 18–20; and Grosser, *Franco-Soviet Relations Today*, p. 48.

51. See Article 4 of "Soglashenie ob ekonomicheskom i nauchno-tekhnicheskom sotrudnichestve mezhdu Pravitel'stvom SSSR i Pravitel'stvom Italii," in USSR, MID, *SSSR-Italiia*, pp. 119–21.

52. Brandt discussed this subject in 1970 with Kosygin, who professed indifference to form, and did not insist on the creation of a *grande commission*. Brandt, *People and Politics*, p. 330.

53. For the text of the agreement see Meissner, *Moskau-Bonn*, 2:1559–61.

54. *Treaty Series* 59 (1968), Cmnd. 3710. For the origin of the working groups see Ian Taylor, "Britain and Eastern Europe," in Galtung, *Co-operation in Europe*, pp. 132–133, 137.

55. Ryzhikov, *SSSR-Velikobritaniia*, p. 39.

56. Kari Mottola, "The Finnish-Soviet Long-Term Programme—A Chart for Cooperation," in *Yearbook of Finnish Foreign Policy, 1977*, p. 48.

57. *Sotsialisticheskaia industriia*, July 17, 1985.

58. Joint communiqué in Meissner, *Moskau-Bonn*, 2:1481.

59. Y. Bolod and V. Nikitin, "New Steps in Cooperation between the USSR and the Federal Republic of Germany," *Foreign Trade* 3 (1973): 9. See the *Frankfurter Allgemeine Zeitung* report in Meissner, *Moskau-Bonn*, 2:1563.

60. *Izvestiia*, September 14, 1986.

61. I. A. Litvak and Carl H. McMillan, "Intergovernmental Cooperation Agreements as a Framework for East-West Trade and Technology Transfer," in Carl H. McMillan, ed., *Changing Perspectives in East-West Commerce*, p. 162.

62. For a critical assessment see A. Schüller, "Warum Gemischte Wirtschaftskommissionen?" *Neue Zürcher Zeitung*, April 2, 1977; and for a defense see J. Jahnke, "Gemischte Wirtschaftskommissionen," *Neue Zürcher Zeitung*, March 2, 1977.

63. The USSR All Union Chamber of Commerce was renamed the All Union Chamber of Commerce and Industry in 1972. For its charter see *Foreign Trade* 11 (1974): 57–60. The chamber also had an espionage function. In 1987 the U.S. State Department charged that the chamber was headed by a KGB general and was heavily engaged in commercial espionage. Clyde H. Farnsworth, "K.G.B. Runs Commerce Unit, U.S. Says," *New York Times*, October 28, 1987.

64. *Sotsialisticheskaia industriia*, July 17, 1985.

65. Ibid., January 16, 1986.

66. I. Shapovalov, "The 9th General Assembly of the Franco-Soviet Chamber of Commerce," *Foreign Trade* 10 (1975): 51–53.

67. The British-Soviet Chamber of Commerce opened an office in March 1987. *Izvestiia*, April 1, 1987.

68. A Turkish-Soviet Business Council and a counterpart Soviet-Turkish Committee for Business Cooperation were established in June 1988. TASS, June 10, 1988. A Soviet agreement with Malta's Federation of Industries was concluded in June 1987. TASS, June 2, 1987. Greece and the USSR formed a bilateral chamber in 1990. *Athens News*, May 27, 1990.

69. "Joint Trade Planning Offer by Russians," *The Times*, February 4, 1967.

70. For the text of the Finnish agreement see Mottola et al., *Finnish-Soviet Economic Relations*, pp. 261–62.

71. Lotarski, "Institutional Development and the Joint Commissions in East-West Commercial Relations," p. 1021.

72. V. Petrov, "Development of Trade and Economic Relations between the USSR and Britain," *Foreign Trade* 3 (1971): 7.

73. John Pinder defined industrial cooperation as "transfers of finance, skills and technology: everything that lies between direct investment at one end of the spectrum and the exchange of goods at the other." See John Pinder, "How Active Will the Community Be in East-West Economic Relations," in Ieuan John, ed., *EEC Policy towards Eastern Europe*, p. 78. See also ECE, *Register of Intergovernmental Agreements on Industrial Co-operation* (Report by the Executive Secretary), TRADE/252, November 10, 1971, and TRADE/252 Add. 1–13, October 4, 1971–April 22, 1972; ECE, *Activities of the Intergovernmental Joint Commissions in the Field of Industrial Cooperation* (Note by the Secretariat), COOP.IND./2, April 5, 1971; and ECE, *Analytical Report on Industrial Co-operation among ECE Countries*, E/ECE/844/Rev.1, November 1973.

74. For the agreement with Finland see *Foreign Trade* 7 (1971): 17–18; with France, *Foreign Trade* 2 (1972): 61–62; and with Italy, USSR, MID, *SSSR-Italiia*, pp. 196–98.

75. Text in *Foreign Trade* 11 (1974): 53–54.

76. Texts in ibid., 4 (1975): 3–9.

77. Brandt, *People and Politics*, pp. 360–61.

78. Schmidt, *Menschen und Mächte*, p. 53.

79. C. Sasse, "Kooperationsabkommen und EG-Handelspolitik: Parallelität oder Konflikt?" *Europa Archiv* 20 (1974): 699. See also Max Baumer and Hanns-Dieter Jacobsen, "CMEA and the World Economy: Institutional Concepts," in U.S., Congress, Joint Economic Committee, *East-European Economies Post-Helsinki*, p. 1006.

80. For the French program see *Foreign Trade* 11 (1974): 53–54, especially Article 4. For the West German program see *Foreign Trade* 12 (1974): 54–55. Except for a reference to the title of the 1958 agreement, the 1973 USSR-FRG agreement did not use the word "trade."

81. John Vinocur, "Brezhnev and Schmidt Sign Pact," *New York Times*, May 7, 1978.

82. Brezhnev, *Leninskim kursom*, 6:55.

83. Litvak and McMillan, "Intergovernmental Cooperation Agreements as a Framework for East-West Trade and Technology Transfer," p. 163.

84. Gorbachev, *Perestroika*, p. 204.

85. For a view of Gorbachev's early thinking on international economic issues and his apparent readiness to learn, see Friedrich Wilhelm Christians, "The Roads to Russia," *International Affairs* 5 (1990): 132–35.

86. *Ekonomichkeskaia gazeta*, No. 4, 1987.

87. John Tedstrom, "Western Joint Ventures in the Soviet Union: Problems and Prospects," *RFE/RL Research*, September 28, 1988, pp. 3–4.

88. [hal], "Gemeinschaftsunternehmen mit der Sowjetunion bleiben ein Wagnis," *Frankfurter Allgemeine Zeitung*, September 23, 1989.

89. The first such agreements were signed in early 1989 with Fin-

land and Belgium. An agreement with West Germany was signed in June 1989 during Gorbachev's visit to Bonn.

90. *Financial Times*, July 16, 19, 1986; and Martin Linton and Martin Walker, "Russians Pay up for Late Parrot," *Guardian*, May 24, 1990.

91. David Remnick, "Soviets Struggle to Pay Debts," *Washington Post*, June 27, 1990.

92. Ivan Silaev (Soviet deputy prime minister and chairman of the Soviet side of the USSR-FRG commission), *Handelsblatt*, December 30, 1988.

93. *Pravda*, July 6, 1989.

94. See the report of the commission session in Moscow led by economics minister Hausmann, "Bonn will Moskau stärker helfen," *Frankfurter Allgemeine Zeitung*, May 21, 1990. For the USSR-FRG treaty see *Izvestiia*, September 22, 1990.

95. For the interwar period see Christopher A. P. Binns, "From USE [United States of Europe] to EEC: The Soviet Analysis of European Integration," *Soviet Studies* 30, no. 2 (1978); Jerzy Lukazewski, "Western Integration and the People's Democracies," *Foreign Affairs* 46, no. 2 (1968): 385; and Vsevolod Kniazhinsky, *West European Integration: Its Policies and International Relations*, p. 40.

96. Burbank, "Scandinavian Integration and Western Defense," p. 149.

97. M. Burinsky, "The ECE and Problems of All-European Economic Cooperation," *Foreign Trade* 4 (1972): 24.

98. *Pravda*, March 17, 1957.

99. "O sozdanii 'obshchego rynka' i Evratomy (Tezisy)," *MEiMO* 1 (1957). See also Christopher A. P. Binns, "The Development of the Soviet Policy Response to the EEC," *Co-existence* 14, no. 2 (1977); and Adomeit, *The Soviet Union and Western Europe*, pp. 18–52.

100. "Ob imperialisticheskoi 'integratsii' v zapadnoi Evrope ('Obshchii Rynok')(Tezisy)," *MEiMO* 9 (1962).

101. N. S. Khrushchev, "Nasushchnye voprosy razvitiia mirovoi sotsialisticheskoi sistemy," *Kommunist* 12 (1962).

102. Seymour Topping, "Khrushchev Bids Italy Quit Bloc," *New York Times*, June 8, 1962.

103. Khrushchev, "Nasushchnye voprosy razvitiia mirovoi sotsialisticheskoi sistemy," p. 10.

104. Poland, Romania, Hungary, and Bulgaria all concluded sectoral agreements that entailed de facto recognition of the EC's authority over member-state trade policy.

105. Brezhnev, *Leninskim kursom*, 3:490.

106. Ilkka Tapiola, "Co-operation between Finland and the CMEA, 1973–77," *Yearbook of Finnish Foreign Policy*, 1977.

107. For the U.K. see the Shore-Patolichev exchange of letters (December 11, 1975) affirming the principles of the Temporary Commercial Agreement of 1934, *Foreign Trade* 5 (1976): 53; for the FRG see the Hermes-Manzhulo exchange of letters of October 30, 1974, *Foreign Trade* 1 (1975): 57; for Denmark, see the Norgard-Patolichev exchange of letters of August 28, 1975, *Foreign Trade* 3 (1976): 59; and for Italy,

see the Rumor-Gromyko exchange of letters (November 20, 1975) affirming the principles of the 1948 Treaty on Trade and Navigation, *Foreign Trade* 11 (1976): 53. Upon becoming an EC member in 1986, Spain denounced its 1972 bilateral commercial treaty with the USSR. Madrid EFE, December 13, 1986, in *FBIS-WEU*, December 15, 1986.

108. Michael Leigh, *European Integration and the Common Fisheries Policy*, p. 145.

109. Maresca, *To Helsinki*, p. 19.

110. *East-West* 151 (1976): 1. The text was never officially made public, but was leaked by the Soviets. See also John Pinder, "Economic Integration and East-West Trade," *Journal of Common Market Studies* 16, no. 1 (1977).

111. "An EEC Flea in Russia's Ear," *The Economist*, January 13, 1979.

112. See Kniazhinsky, *West European Integration*, pp. 347–48; and L. Minayev, "American Hegemonism and Interimperialist Contradictions," *International Affairs* 8 (1983): 54–55, for assessments reflecting the official view.

113. *Pravda*, June 16, 1984.

114. See the interview with Cervetti in *L'Unità*, May 22, 1985, *FBIS-WEU*, May 29, 1985.

115. "Rech' M. S. Gorbacheva," *Izvestiia*, May 31, 1985.

116. In his landmark speech to the MFA in May 1986, Gorbachev praised what he saw as movement away from "dogmatic positions with respect to the EC." *Vestnik MID* 1 (1987). See also Shevardnadze's July 1988 remarks discussed below.

117. David Buchan and Patrick Cockburn, "Moscow Hints at Trade Agreement with Brussels," *Financial Times*, June 28, 1985.

118. AFP, May 2, 1986.

119. John Wyles, "Hungary and EEC to Negotiate Trade Pact," *Financial Times*, January 25, 1984.

120. *Rude Pravo*, May 24, 1986.

121. *Izvestiia*, July 26, 1986; and TASS, October 27, 1986.

122. The GDR already enjoyed access to the EC market under a protocol to the Treaty of Rome. West Germany had certain obligations to regulate the reexport of GDR goods to other members of the Community, so access was not complete. See Fritz Homann, "Innerdeutscher Handel und EG-Binnenmarkt," *Deutschland Archiv* 3 (1989): 305–6.

123. "Kremlin Knocks at EC Door," *Frankfurter Rundschau*, November 25, 1986, *FBIS-WEU*, November 25, 1986; and Quentin Peel, "EEC, Soviet Union Hold First Round of Talks," *Financial Times*, January 17, 1987. For a Soviet account of the talks see the interview with Iurii Buzykin, the chief Soviet delegate, "USSR-European Commission: Dialogue Starts," *New Times* 5 (1987): 6–7.

124. AFP, June 14, 1985.

125. John Palmer, "Russia, EEC Set for Peace Move," *Guardian*, February 24, 1986.

126. Oleg Bogomolov, "Europe: Prospects for Economic Cooperation," *New Times* 8 (1986): 20.

127. *International Affairs* 10 (1988): 10.

128. *MEiMO* 4 (1989). See also the authoritative *The European Community: Theses of the Institute of the World Economy and International Relations of the Academy of the USSR.*

129. "EEC-Comecon to Discuss Formal Relations," *Financial Times,* March 18, 1987.

130. Peter Hort, "Détente between the EC and East Bloc," *Frankfurter Allgemeine Zeitung,* March 28, 1987, *FBIS-WEU,* March 30, 1987.

131. "Joint Declaration on the Establishment of Official Relations between the European Economic Community and the Council for Mutual Economic Assistance," *European Community News,* June 24, 1988.

132. "SEV-EES: Vzaimnyi interes," *Pravda,* June 24, 1988.

133. "Proshli konsul'tatsii," *Pravda,* November 18, 1988; *Vestnik MID* 22 (1988): 18. West German foreign minister Genscher and Commissioner Willy de Clerq signed for the EC; and Rudolf Rohlicek, deputy prime minister of Czechoslovakia, and Viacheslav Sychev of the CMEA for the latter organization.

134. P. Hanson and Vlad Sobell, "The Changing Relations between the EC and the CMEA," *Radio Free Europe Research,* May 3, 1989.

135. Under the terms of the economic agreement, the EC was to eliminate, in three stages by the end of 1995, all quota restrictions on Hungarian exports to the Community. In return, Hungary was to improve access to its market by EC firms. As part of its package of reciprocity measures, Hungary agreed not to give preferential treatment to barter trade. AFP, July 1, 1988. After Hungary broke with communism in 1989–90, the EC advanced its timetable for removing quotas and began to negotiate a "second generation" agreement with Hungary. EC relations with Poland, Czechoslovakia, Bulgaria, and Romania followed this basic pattern.

136. Paul Webster, "Paris and Moscow Agree on a Summit," *Guardian,* November 16, 1989.

137. The text of the Soviet aide-mémoire appeared in *Die Presse,* August 11, 1989.

138. Paul L. Montgomery, "Trade Pact for Soviets and Europe," *New York Times,* November 28, 1989.

139. *Pravda,* October 23, 1989; and Peter Guilford, "Moscow Trade Chief Attacks EC Attitude to Comecon," *The Times,* October 12, 1989.

Chapter 8: Culture, Churches, and the Peace Movement

1. Iu. Denisov, "Sixty Years of Relations between the USSR and North European Countries," *International Affairs* 7 (1984): 45.

2. The FSU was initially headquartered in Berlin but moved to Amsterdam after the Nazi takeover. Louis Nemzer, "The Soviet Friendship Societies," *Public Opinion Quarterly* 13, no. 2 (1949): 266, 269.

3. L. Larry Leonard, *International Organization*, p. 47; and Dallin, *The Soviet Union at the United Nations*, pp. 61–69.

4. See Ernest J. Simmons, "Negotiating on Cultural Exchange, 1947," in Dennett, *Negotiating with the Russians*, pp. 239–70.

5. There were a few signs of change in Soviet policy in this period. One was the decision to participate in the 1952 Helsinki Olympics, a decision that may have been taken as far back as December 1948 when the Central Committee issued a decree revitalizing the Soviet physical culture movement. John N. Washburn, "Sport as a Soviet Tool," *Foreign Affairs* 34, no. 3 (1956): 493.

6. Frederick C. Barghoorn, *The Soviet Cultural Offensive*, p. 16.

7. L. A. Ingul'skaia, "Rol' kul'turnogo obmena v razvitii dobrososedskikh otnoshenii mezhdu Finlandiei i SSSR," USSR Academy of Sciences, *Sovetskaia kultura: istoriia i sovremennost'*, pp. 241–42.

8. Bechhoefer, *Postwar Negotiations for Arms Control*, p. 231.

9. For these proposals, see U.S. Department of State, *The Geneva Meeting of Foreign Ministers*, pp. 239–40, pp. 245–48; and "Proekt zaiavleniia chetyrekh derzhav po voprosy razvitiia kontaktov mezhdu vostokam i zapadom," *Pravda*, November 16, 1955.

10. See the report of the U.S. delegation, November 2, 1955, *FRUS, 1955–1957*, 5:661–63.

11. See the U.S. delegation reports, ibid., 692-694; and C. D. Jackson's report to Dulles, November 12, 1955, ibid., pp. 760–64.

12. U.S. Department of State, *The Geneva Meeting*, p. 261.

13. "Sovetsko-norvezhkoe kommiunike," *Pravda*, November 16, 1955.

14. "Sovetsko-shvedskoe kommiunike," *Pravda*, April 4, 1956.

15. "Sovmestnoe zaiavlenie o dal'neishem razvitii sviazei mezhdu SSSR i Soedinennym Korolevstvom," *Pravda*, April 27, 1956.

16. "Sovmestnoe zaiavlenie o kul'turnyh sviaziakh mezhdu SSSR i Frantsiei," *Pravda*, May 20, 1956.

17. Barghoorn, *The Soviet Cultural Offensive*, pp. 251–52.

18. Drew Middleton, "Russians Promise Restraint in Sale of Mideast Arms," *New York Times*, April 27, 1956.

19. "Cultural Links with Russia," *The Times*, May 12, 1955.

20. See "Professional Visits to Russia," *The Times*, June 23, 1955, for the joint embassy-committee statement.

21. See Morgan, *The Backbench Diaries of Richard Crossman*, p. 711, for an account of a discussion of reciprocity in 1958 between Crossman and A. A. Surkov, secretary of the Soviet Writers Union, first head of the Soviet section of the USSR-Great Britain Society, and the leading guest of the Communist-controlled Anglo-Soviet Friendship Society during its celebrations of the 40th anniversary of the October Revolution.

22. Z. M. Kruglova, "Soiuz Sovetskikh Obshchestv Druzhby i Kul'turnoi Sviazi S Zarubezhnymi Stranami," in Morozov, ed., *Obshchestvennost' i problemy voiny i mira*, p. 288.

23. Persistent tensions between the MFA and the Union of Soviet Societies were alluded to by Valentina Tereshkova (head of the union)

in her speech to the July 1988 Scientific and Practical Conference at the MFA. See *International Affairs* 11 (1988): 59.

24. CIA, Directorate of Intelligence, *Directory of Soviet Officials: National Organizations*, November 1984, pp. 267–71.

25. Meissner, *Moskau-Bonn*, 2:1574–75, citing Soviet press accounts.

26. For an inside view of the workings of the Soviet-Swiss society, see Polianski, *M.I.D.: 12 ans dans les services diplomatiques du Kremlin*, p. 183ff.

27. "Okonchanie Sovetsko-frantsuzskikh peregovorov po voprosam kul'turnykh i nauchnykh sviazei," *Izvestiia*, October 10, 1957.

28. *Pravda*, May 31, 1959. See also Barghoorn, *The Soviet Cultural Offensive*, pp. 264–65.

29. For the text of the communiqué and annex, see *The Times*, March 4, 1959; see also Macmillan, *Riding the Storm*, p. 576.

30. "More Anglo-Soviet Exchanges," *The Times*, March 30, 1959.

31. "Great Britain-U.S.S.R. Association," *The Times*, June 29, 1959.

32. *Treaty Series* 82 (1959), Cmnd. 917, p. 9.

33. See Cmnds. 7645, 8300, 8981, 9663.

34. "Kul'turnoe Soglashenie Mezhdu SSSR i Italiei," USSR, MID, *SSSR-Italiia*, pp. 106–10, especially Articles 11 and 12.

35. In the summer of 1969 Soviet air traffic controllers diverted to Leningrad (allegedly because of fog) a plane carrying the Berlin Philharmonic to Moscow, in order to abort a welcoming reception for the orchestra planned by the German ambassador. The reception was to have occurred at the Prague Restaurant. When the ambassador tried to reschedule, he was informed that the restaurant was fully booked. See Allardt, *Moskauer Tagebuch*, pp. 187–88.

36. Federal Institute, *The Soviet Union, 1973*, p. 140. See also Schmidt, *Menschen und Mächte*, pp. 54–59.

37. *Pravda*, May 21, 1973.

38. "Agreement on Relations in the Scientific, Technological, Educational and Cultural Fields for 1967–69," *Treaty Series* 39 (1968), Cmnd. 3279.

39. Ryzhikov, *SSSR-Velikobritaniia*, p. 40.

40. See the Brezhnev-Wilson Joint Statement, February 17, 1975, Cmnd. 5924, reprinted in Wilson, *Final Term*, pp. 280–85.

41. Taylor, "Britain and Eastern Europe," pp. 132–34.

42. P. Demichev, "Otvetstvennye zadachi sotsial'isticheskoi kul'tury," *Kommunist* 17 (1983): 32. See also P. Demichev, "Aktual'nye problemy mezhdunarodnykh kul'turnykh obmenov na sovremennom etape," *Kommunist* 10 (1984): 16–28.

43. *Izvestiia*, April 28, 1986.

44. Vladimir Mikhailovich Zaitsev, *United Towns*, pp. 6–8.

45. Ibid., p. 11.

46. Ryzhikov, *SSSR-Velikobritaniia*, pp. 32–33. According to this source, there were 15 such pairings in the mid-1970s. Volgograd (formerly Stalingrad) is the USSR's premier "victim city," and also is paired with Hiroshima.

47. The Gaullist mayor of Brest terminated the partnership, charging it had become a vehicle for KGB espionage directed at a nearby French naval base. Peter Ruge, "Ost-Spionage per Partnerschaft," *Die Welt*, March 23, 1987. Some observers were struck by the number of important French ports twinned with Soviet cities.

48. "Für die Städtepartnerschaft mit Kiew muss München noch viel lernen," *Frankfurter Allgemeine Zeitung*, October 7, 1985.

49. E. Grigorev, *Pravda*, August 12, 1985, gave this figure.

50. N. V. Pavlov, *Vneshniaia politika FRG: kontseptsii i realii 80-kh godov.*

51. *Pravda*, June 14, 1989.

52. "V interesakh mira i sotrudnichestva," *Pravda*, November 12, 1985.

53. In October 1988 Khabarovsk and Alaska signed a "sister state" agreement. Reported in *Radio Liberty Research Bulletin*, November 4, 1988. In the same month Quebec and the RSFSR signed a cooperation agreement, the first between a Soviet republic and a Canadian province. TASS, October 29, 1988.

54. "Besedy v Bonne," *Pravda*, October 8, 1982, for Solomentsev visit to NRW.

55. DPA, May 21, 1986.

56. *Pravda*, September 24, 1984.

57. "Von Mainz nach Moskau," *Frankfurter Allgemeine Zeitung*, September 20, 1989.

58. Burbank, "Scandinavian Integration and Western Defense," p. 149.

59. Zaitsev, *United Towns*, p. 52.

60. For the text see *Izvestiia*, April 2, 1987.

61. Robert J. McCartney, "Soviets Reject U.S. Proposal on New Air Links to Berlin," *Washington Post*, October 5, 1988.

62. *Vestnik MID* 23 (1988): 24.

63. *Pravda*, June 12, July 6, 1989.

64. Yuri Khilchevsky, "Cultural Diplomacy," *International Affairs* 5 (1990): 58; and Joseph Haniman, "Provinzen: Ein Treffen von Europas Kulturministern," *Frankfurter Allgemeine Zeitung*, November 6, 1989.

65. According to Iu. Khilchevskii, USSR deputy minister of culture, "art today is one of the few domestic 'commodities' that can compete in the foreign marketplace." *Pravda*, May 2, 1989.

66. See the description of the decline of the France-USSR Society by Bertrand de Lesquen in *Valeurs Actuelles*, April 23–29, 1990.

67. [Me], "Ukrainische Volksbewegung ergreift das Wort," *Frankfurter Allgemeine Zeitung*, October 7, 1989.

68. Natalya Kraminova, "What We Understood in Finland," *Moscow News* 45 (1989).

69. In the early 1920s Zinoviev toyed with the idea of using the Living Church (a pro-Communist grouping which broke away from the Russian Orthodox Church) to develop an international movement, but the idea was not seriously pursued. Mikhail Heller and Aleksandr Nek-

rich, *Utopia in Power: The History of the Soviet Union from 1917 to the Present*, p. 138.

70. See Jane Ellis, *The Russian Orthodox Church: A Contemporary History*; J. A. Hebly, *The Russians and the World Council of Churches*, p. 12; and Wassilij Alexeev, *The Foreign Policy of the Moscow Patriarchate, 1939–1953*, p. 220.

71. William C. Fletcher, *Religion and Soviet Foreign Policy 1945–1970*, p. 5.

72. Ibid., p. 223.

73. M. M. Wojnar, "Ukrainian (Ruthenian) Rite," in *New Catholic Encyclopedia*, 14:374; and J. Chrysostomus Blaschkewitz, "USSR," *New Catholic Encyclopedia*, 14:410–11. New information about these events appeared in Georgii Rozhonov, "Eto my, gospodi!" *Ogonëk* 38 (1989): 6–8. The Uniate church apparently was asked to persuade the two Ukrainian resistance movements to lay down their arms. The church refused, causing Stalin to order its liquidation.

74. G. A. Maloney, "Orthodox Churches," *New Catholic Encyclopedia*, 10:798.

75. Darril Hudson, *The World Council of Churches in International Affairs*, pp. 223–24.

76. *Conference in Defence of Peace of All Churches and Religious Associations in the USSR* (Moscow: Moscow Patriarchate, 1952).

77. "Russian Confers with Eden," *The Times*, March 20, 1956. Welles Hangen, "U.S., Soviet Clerics Argue over Peace," *New York Times*, March 14, 1956.

78. Hebly, *The Russians and the World Council of Churches*, p. 81. This work by a Dutch historian draws extensively on wcc archives.

79. *Ecumenical Review* 11, no. 1 (1958): 79–80.

80. Hebly, *The Russians and the World Council of Churches*, p. 96.

81. Fletcher, *Religion and Soviet Foreign Policy*, p. 96.

82. For an appraisal of Russian motivations by the main adviser to the wcc on Soviet affairs, see John Lawrence, "East and West—The Opportunity," *Ecumenical Review* 14, no. 3 (1962). The Russians in the wcc later complained about this article, and no similarly frank appraisal appeared in subsequent wcc publications. See Hebly, *The Russians and the World Council of Churches*, p. 78.

83. Ibid., p. 94.

84. From the wcc archives, in ibid., pp. 78–79.

85. Hudson, *The World Council of Churches in International Affairs*, p. 230.

86. Ibid., pp. 240–42.

87. See L. John Collins, *Faith under Fire*, pp. 284–91.

88. See Otto Luchterhandt, "Die Religionsfreiheit im Verständnis der sozialistischen Staaten," in Eugen Voss, ed., *Die Religionsfreiheit in Osteuropa*, p. 52.

89. For background on the cpc see Fletcher, *Religion and Soviet Foreign Policy*, pp. 39–58.

90. Maurice Cavalié, "The Meeting of Representatives of cpc Regional Committees," *Christian Peace Conference* 20–21 (1966): 20–22.

91. Hebly, *The Russians and the World Council of Churches*, pp. 78–79.

92. *Christian Peace Conference* 20–21 (1966): 46.

93. Maurice Cavalié, "After the Third Assembly," *Christian Peace Conference* 27 (1968): 17. An interesting sidelight on the CPC is the role it probably played in introducing the term "Manichean" into the discussion of East-West issues. This term, which literally refers to a Christian heresy founded in the third century by a Persian named Manes, was used in CPC statements of the 1960s and later was appropriated by academic Sovietologists.

94. Yutaka Shishido, "Why Was the Disarmament Problem Dropped?" *Christian Peace Conference* 27 (1968): 19.

95. Marc Reuver, *Christians as Peacemakers: Peace Movements in Europe and the USA*, pp. 76–80.

96. J. A. Hebly, *Eastbound Ecumenism: A Collection of Essays on the World Council of Churches*, p. 28.

97. See the communiqué of "Arnoldshain-XI," *Journal of the Moscow Patriarchate* 12 (1987): 57–59.

98. Hebly, *The Russians and the World Council of Churches*, p. 92.

99. Dana Adams Schmidt, "Russians Puzzle Orthodox Parley," *New York Times*, October 1, 1961.

100. "Russian Proposals Win in Church Talk," *New York Times*, September 30, 1961. By long tradition Moscow ranks fifth in the patriarchal order of precedence, after Constantinople, Alexandria, Antioch, and Jerusalem. But the Russian church is by far the largest of the Orthodox churches, and were it not for political factors would have had a much stronger claim to precedence.

101. Hebly, *Eastbound Ecumenism*, pp. 34–35.

102. Council of European Churches, *This Happened at Nyborg VI: The Report of the Sixth Assembly of the Conference of European Churches*, pp. 241–46.

103. Ibid., p. 118.

104. Conference of European Churches, *Peace in Europe—The Churches' Role: Report of a Consultation Held at Engelberg, Switzerland, 28th May–1st June 1973*, pp. 6–7.

105. "Theological Peacemaking Conversations in Belgium," *Journal of the Moscow Patriarchate* 2 (1988): 45.

106. Meetings took place in Leningrad (1967), Bari (1970), Zagorsk (1973), Trent (1975), Odessa (1980), and Venice (1987).

107. "Theological Conversations between Representatives of the Roman Catholic and Russian Orthodox Churches: Communiqué," *Journal of the Moscow Patriarchate* 3 (1988).

108. See N. A. Koval'skii, "Religioznye sily i dvizhenii za mir," in Morozov, ed., *Obshchestvennost' i problemy voiny i mira*, pp. 250–63.

109. Ellis, *The Russian Orthodox Church*, pp. 47–50, 94.

110. World Council of Churches, *Peace and Disarmament: Documents of the World Council of Churches*, pp. 63–65, 66–70, 81–84.

111. Reuver, *Christians as Peacemakers*, p. 60.

112. Fletcher, *Religion and Soviet Foreign Policy*, pp. 136–38.

113. *Ecumenical Review* 32, no. 2 (1980): 198–99.

114. Ibid., pp. 189–90.

115. "Threats to Peace," *Ecumenical Review* 32, no. 4 (1980): 433–35.

116. See Ellis, *The Russian Orthodox Church*, pp. 355–61.

117. Kenneth Briggs, "2 Letters to Church Parley Assail Soviet," *New York Times*, August 9, 1983.

118. Reuver, *Christians as Peacemakers*, pp. 60–61.

119. Conference of European Churches, *Crossroads for the European Churches: The Report of the Seventh Assembly of the Conference of European Churches*, p. 127.

120. Jean Fischer, in the foreword to Reuver, *Christians as Peacemakers*, p. viii.

121. TASS, June 25, 1984.

122. Reuver, *Christians as Peacemakers*, pp. 64–65.

123. For this meeting see KAO, "Warnung vor 'lebensbedrohenden Strukturen' in der Gesellschaft," *Frankfurter Allgemeine Zeitung*, May 22, 1989.

124. Evangelical Academy Tutzing, *Dialog—Voraussetzung für Abrüstung und Friedenssicherung: III. Internationales Kolloquium*, p. 5.

125. Ellis, *The Russian Orthodox Church*, p. 274.

126. Metropolitan Philaret, quoted in TASS, January 3, 1984.

127. See the glowing assessment of the CPC in Reuver, *Christians as Peacemakers*, pp. 80–82.

128. "Conference of the CPC Regional Committee in the FRG," *Journal of the Moscow Patriarchate* 7 (1987).

129. Preparations for the celebration began in December 1980 with the formation of a special anniversary commission. Oxana Antic, "Celebrations in the Soviet Union and Abroad of the Millenium of the Christianization of Rus'," *RFE-RL Research*, June 1, 1988, p. 2.

130. *Politicheskii doklad*, p. 94 (italics added).

131. Gorbachev, *Perestroika*, p. 191. For Iakovlev see his speech in Rome, *Pravda*, March 21, 1989.

132. *CPC Information*, March 10, 1987; and Wallace Spaulding, "Communist Fronts in 1987," *Problems of Communism* 37, no. 1 (1980): 85; and K. Khachaturov, "Moskovskii forum i ego znachenie," *Mezhdunarodnaia zhizn'* 4 (1987): 100.

133. For the text see *Journal of the Moscow Patriarchate* 4 (1987): 31–32.

134. Antic, "Celebrations in the Soviet Union and Abroad of the Millenium of the Christianization of Rus'," pp. 3–5.

135. Two Soviet journals—*Literaturnaia Rossiia* and *Slovo*—began publishing excerpts from the Bible in 1989. See Jonathan Steele, "Die-Hards Fear Gorbachev's Divine Mission," *Guardian*, November 8, 1989.

136. Dawn Mann and Julia Wishnevsky, "The Composition of the Congress of People's Deputies," *Radio Liberty Research*, April 20, 1989. None of the five was elected to the smaller Supreme Soviet, but under the rotation principle they could expect to serve in the future.

137. [oll], "Abschluss der Moskauer Tagung des Ökumenischen Rates der Kirchen," *Frankfurter Allgemeine Zeitung*, July 28, 1989. Nonetheless, at least some in the Soviet leadership continued to show sensitivity to very close scrutiny of its policies, as was seen in October 1989, when the Soviet government refused a visa to Michael Bordeaux, a British researcher long involved in exposing Soviet religious persecution. *Guardian*, October 7, 1989.

138. Robert Suro, "Vatican Reaches Out to Russian Orthodox Church," *New York Times*, December 14, 1988.

139. M. Il'inskii, "Berech' planetu, vesti dialog," *Izvestiia*, January 17, 1989.

140. Bill Keller, "Ukrainian Catholic Church Wins Legal Status after a 43-Year Ban," *New York Times*, December 2, 1989.

141. John Wyles, "Russian Church Makes Appeal to Rome," *Financial Times*, January 12, 1990.

142. Quoted in Oxana Antic, "New 'Foreign Minister' of Russian Orthodox Church," *Report on the USSR* 2, no. 1 (1990): 9.

143. Ibid.

144. Shulman, *Stalin's Foreign Policy Reappraised*, p. 80.

145. See G. M. Lokshin, "Vsemirnyi Sovet Mira," and B. N. Polevoi, "Sovetskii Fond Mira," in Morozov, ed., *Obshchestvennost' i problemy voiny i mira*, pp. 267–81, 282–87.

146. Bertrand Russell, *The Autobiography of Bertrand Russell, 1944–1969*, p. 101.

147. Ibid., p. 97.

148. Josef Rotblat, *Pugwash: The First Ten Years*, pp. 13–17, 80–86; see also "The Pugwash Movement—Yesterday, Today, Tomorrow," *New Times* (special supplement), 1988; and V. G. Trukhanovskii, "Paguoshkoe dvizhenie," in Morozov, ed., *Obshchestvennost' i problemy voiny i mira*, pp. 383–95.

149. Marian Dobrosielski, "Europe: A Secure Continent," *New Times* (special supplement), 1988, p. 17.

150. Collins, *Faith under Fire*, p. 339.

151. L. G. Istiagin, "Antivoennoe dvizhenie v stranakh Zapadnoi Evropy: Osnovnye cherty i etapy razvitiia," in Iu. A. Zamoshkin, et al., eds., *Antivoennoe dvizhenie v Severnoi Amerike i Zapadnoi Evrope: tendentsii, problemi, perspektivi*, pp. 139–41.

152. For background on the conference see J. A. Emerson Vermaat, "Moscow Fronts and the European Peace Movement," *Problems of Communism* 31, no. 6 (1982): 46–47.

153. Istiagin, "Antivoennoe dvizhenie v stranakh Zapadnoi Evropy," p. 146.

154. TASS, September 27, 1980.

155. Alexander R. Alexiev, *The Soviet Campaign Against INF: Strategy, Tactics, Means*.

156. P. Fedoseev, "Sovremennoe antivoennoe dvizhenie i perspektivy ego razvitiia," *MEiMO* 2 (1985): 9.

157. *Kommunist* 12 (1983): 26, quoted in Elizabeth Teague, "Kom-

munist Editorial on Western Peace Movement," *RFE-RL Research*, September 2, 1983.

158. See Gorbachev's remarks to the 27th Party Congress, *Politicheskii doklad*, p. 84.

159. Seymour Topping, "Gag on Marchers Defied in Moscow," *New York Times*, October 6, 1961.

160. Martin Walker, "A Glimpse of the Peace Machine," *Guardian*, November 14, 1984.

161. *Surviving Together* 4 (1984): 16; 9 (1986): 69; 9 (1986): 42; and 12 (1987): 48.

162. The march was reportedly blocked by Fedorov, but rescued by Iuri Zhukov when he became head of the committee in February 1982. Jean Stead, "How They Went to Seek Peace in Russia," *Guardian*, August 13, 1982.

163. Doreen Taylor, "Why Pushing Peace Is Better than Pushing Buttons," *Guardian*, November 28, 1984.

164. See Grigorii Lokshin, "Pacifism Yesterday and Today," *International Affairs* 2 (1990): 96.

165. Iu. Krasin, "Strategiia mira—imperativ epokhi," *MEiMO* 1 (1986): 4.

166. See the article by E. P. Thompson in *Guardian*, February 21, 1983.

167. For background see Catherine A. Fitzpatrick, "Moscow's Independent Peace Movement," New York, Helsinki Watch Committee, November 1982 (unpublished typescript).

168. Iu. Zhukov, "Politika, za kotoroi budushchee," *Pravda*, November 30, 1982.

169. Judith Miller, "U.S. Group Assails Soviet Repression," *New York Times*, September 5, 1982.

170. Peter Reddaway, "Dissent in the Soviet Union," *Problems of Communism* 32, no. 6 (1983): 13.

171. It was reported that at least one East European country had wanted to send a delegation to a similar gathering in 1983, but was blocked by the USSR, and that the East Germans had lobbied within the bloc to prevent participation. Henry Kamm, "Soviet Group Is Jeered at Disarmament Parley," *New York Times*, July 20, 1984.

172. See E. Velikhov, "Nauka i aktual'nye problemy bor'by protiv ugrozy iadernoi voiny," *Mezhdunarodnaia zhizn'* 7 (1983): 21–32.

173. See William Drozdiak, "Nobel Peace Prize Winner Draws Fire," *Washington Post*, December 9, 1985, for the strong reaction in West Germany; Colman McCarthy, "The Nobel Prize for Scolding," *Washington Post*, October 23, 1985; and Walter Reich, "Inequality in the Nobel Peace-Prize Organization," *New York Times*, October 21, 1985.

174. Stephen M. Meyer (citing interviews with Soviet academics and officials), "The Sources and Prospects of Gorbachev's New Political Thinking on Security," *International Security* 13, no. 2 (1988): 130–31.

175. See the interview in *Komsomolskaia pravda*, May 29, 1990, *FBIS-SU*, June 7, 1990.

Chapter 9: CSCE and the All-European Process

1. See A. Ross Johnson, *The Warsaw Pact's Campaign for "European Security"*; Robert Spencer, "Canada and the Origins of the CSCE, 1965–73," in Robert Spencer, ed., *Canada and the Conference on Security and Cooperation in Europe*; and Mojmir Povolny, "The Soviet Union and the European Security Conference," *Orbis* 18, no. 1 (1974).

2. U.S. Department of State, *Foreign Ministers Meeting: Berlin Discussions*, p. 232.

3. See the exchange of notes in *Department of State Bulletin*, December 13, 1954, pp. 901–7.

4. Kathleen Teltsch, "Conference on European Security Urged by Poland in UN," *New York Times*, December 15, 1964.

5. *VpSS: Sbornik dokumentov, 1964–1965*, p. 113.

6. *23rd Congress of the Communist Party of the Soviet Union*, p. 56.

7. *VpSS: Sbornik dokumentov, 1966*, p. 175.

8. *VpSS: Sbornik dokumentov, 1967*, pp. 100–107.

9. In July 1965 the Communist controlled WPC staged a "peace congress" in Helsinki which endorsed the idea of a conference, and in June 1966 the WPC issued a "Memorandum on European Security" which also endorsed the project. A year later the Karlovy Vary statement called for a "popular" conference of European "nations," as well as endorsed a Yugoslav suggestion for a European parliamentary conference. This conference did not convene until 1973, well after the Western governments had all agreed in principle to participate in the CSCE.

10. *VpSS: Sbornik dokumentov, 1969*, p. 59.

11. NATO, *Texts of Final Communiqués, 1949–1970*, p. 207.

12. The form of the statement was itself significant. The PCC issued a memorandum, which the government of Hungary conveyed to all interested states, including the United States and Canada. For the text see USSR, MID, *SSSR v borbe za bezopasnost'*, pp. 37–39.

13. The selection of Finland as host country solved the mechanics of ensuring East and West German participation. Unlike the Austrians, Swiss, and Swedes, the Finns had never established full relations with either country. Finland thus was the only non-Communist country in Europe to accord the two Germanies strict equality of (non)status. Using their diplomatic list, the Finns seated the thirty-two ambassadors present and then placed the representatives (technically from the resident trade delegations) of the two German states to the right of the chairman.

14. NATO, *Texts of Final Communiqués, 1949–1970*, p. 222.

15. Maresca, *To Helsinki*, p. 7.

16. See von Groll, "The Helsinki Consultations," *Aussenpolitik* 24, no. 2 (1973): 123. See also the retrospective of L. I. Mendelevich, "Dipoli," *Vestnik MID* 9 (1987): 45–47; and his "Diplomaticheskie zametki o Khel'sinkskikh mnogostoronnikh konsul'tatsiakh, 1972–73 go-

dov po podgotovke obshcheevropeiskogo soveshchaniia," *Diplomatiche-skii vestnik, 1982.*

17. Ferraris, *Report on a Negotiation,* p. 14.

18. The communiqué, with the recommendations appended, appeared in *Department of State Bulletin,* July 30, 1973, pp. 181–88.

19. CSCE/I/3; CSCE/I/7; CSCE/I/8; and CSCE/I/5. The order in which these proposals were introduced was determined by the order in which the foreign ministers spoke.

20. Richard Davy, "Helsinki: Two Concepts of Détente," *The World Today* 29, no. 8 (1973): 318.

21. Ibid., 8:319. Winzer's speech is CSCE/I/PV.3.

22. Maresca, *To Helsinki,* p. 50.

23. Adam-Daniel Rotfeld, ed., *From Helsinki to Madrid: CSCE Documents,* p. 22; and A. L. Narochnitskii, *SSSR i bratskie sotsialisticheskie strany Evropy v 70-e gody,* p. 154.

24. Ferraris, *Report on a Negotiation,* p. 20.

25. For the origins of this document see Robert Rosenstock, "The Declaration of Principles of International Law Concerning Friendly Relations: A Survey," *American Journal of International Law* 65, no. 5 (1971); and Edward McWhinney, "'Peaceful Coexistence' and Soviet-Western International Law," *American Journal of International Law* 56, no. 4 (1962): 951–70.

26. The chief U.S. legal adviser at CSCE characterized the UN Declaration as the "principal progenitor" of the Final Act. Harold S. Russell, "The Helsinki Declaration: Brobdingnag or Lilliput?" *American Journal of International Law* 70, no. 2 (1976): 263.

27. Poland signed in 1976. For the texts see UN, *Human Rights: A Compilation of International Instruments,* pp. 3–8, 8–16. Russian texts in UN, *Prava Cheloveka: Mezhdunarodnyi bill' o pravakh cheloveka.* For the dates of accession, see UN, *United Nations Yearbook,* 1973–1977 editions.

28. See "Helsinki Conference Boosts European Cultural Policies," *UNESCO Chronicle* 18, nos. 8–9 (1972): 309–14.

29. Ferraris, *Report on a Negotiation,* p. 62.

30. Rotfeld, *From Helsinki to Madrid,* p. 30.

31. It was not until May 1974 that the East yielded to Western insistence that the signatures on the document be placed at the end of all the sections. Previously, the USSR wanted the signatures to follow the decalogue. See Thomas L. Krantz, "Moscow and the Negotiation of the Helsinki Accords, 1972–75," unpublished Ph.D. dissertation, Oxford University, 1981, p. 145.

32. Western countries also objected to the fact that the Soviet draft seemed to rule out peaceful change of borders by negotiated agreement, which was recognized as a fundamental attribute of sovereignty.

33. CSCE conference journal no. 46, July 20, 1975, in Kavass et al., *Human Rights, European Politics, and the Helsinki Accord.*

34. See Russell, "The Helsinki Declaration," p. 268.

35. *Prava Cheloveka,* p. 37.

36. Translation was a consistent problem at the CSCE, in part be-

cause the documents under discussion were so highly nuanced. One senior EC diplomat claimed that there were more than 100 variations between the Russian and English versions of the Final Act. See Krantz, "Moscow and the Negotiation of the Helsinki Accords," pp. 168–69. Western delegations at expert and follow-up conferences also expressed concern that the Russian translators hired by host governments were all Soviet citizens who at times appeared to receive instructions from the Soviet delegation.

37. Brezhnev, *Leninskim kursom,* 5:337.

38. CSCE/I/PV.2.

39. Brezhnev, *Leninskim kursom,* 5:336, 339. See also the party-government statement issued a week later to endorse the results of the conference. *Pravda,* August 7, 1975.

40. See James P. McGregor, "The 1976 European Communist Parties Conference," *Studies in Comparative Communism* 11, no. 4 (1978).

41. Interview with Turner Catledge, May 11, 1957.

42. For general background see Michael Palmer, *The Prospects for a European Security Conference,* pp. 14–16, 46–47, and especially chapter 7, pp. 56–63. See also Palmer, "A European Security Conference: Preparation and Procedure," *The World Today* 28, no. 1 (1972): 36–46; and V. Falin, "Auf dem Wege zur gesamteuropäischen Konferenz," *Europa Archiv* 21 (1972).

43. Palmer, *The Prospects for a European Security Conference,* p. 52.

44. Drew Middleton, "NATO Asks Talks with Soviet Bloc on Cut in Troops," *New York Times,* May 28, 1970. For U.S. opposition see Kissinger, *White House Years,* p. 534.

45. *Pravda,* June 27, 1970.

46. "Deklaratsiia o mire, bezopastnosti i sotrudnichestve v Evrope," *Pravda,* January 27, 1972. Western positions on the question of institutionalization wavered for a period before coming down firmly against any kind of permanent body. Brandt, *People and Politics,* p. 263.

47. Ferraris, *Report on a Negotiation,* p. 19.

48. CSCE/I/PV.2; text also in *Pravda,* July 4, 1973.

49. CSCE/I/5.

50. According to an Italian participant, the Soviets pressed for the establishment of a pan-European organ, "reviving a recurrent element in Soviet thinking, according to which political consultation (bilateral and in this case multilateral) constituted the cornerstone of peaceful coexistence and détente." Ferraris, *Testimonianze di un Negoziato,* p. 488.

51. The Danish proposal represented a compromise among the views held by different EC governments. The French, after Pompidou's waverings of the early 1970s, had become the most adamant opponents of any permanent machinery: the Danes and, after the return to power of the Labour Party in 1974, the British, the most enthusiastic supporters.

52. CSCE/II/B/1.

53. Brezhnev, *Leninskim kursom*, 5:418.

54. See Ilka Bailey-Wiebecke and Paul J. Bailey, "ECE and the Belgrade Follow-up Conference," *Aussenpolitik* (Eng. ed.) 28, no. 3 (1977): 262.

55. Maresca, *To Helsinki*, p. 203.

56. Sizoo and Jurrjens, *CSCE Decision-making*, p. 137. See also Dante B. Fascell, "Did Human Rights Survive Belgrade?" *Foreign Policy* 31 (1978): 110.

57. For the text see U.S. Department of State, Bureau of Public Affairs, *The Conference on Security and Cooperation in Europe*, pp. 148–49.

58. For the details of the proposal see the RFE dispatch by Ian MacDonald in Mastny, ed., *Helsinki, Human Rights, and European Security*, pp. 187–88.

59. For the English text of this treaty see Rotfeld, *From Helsinki to Madrid*, pp. 334–37.

60. "Report of the Meeting of Experts Representing the Participating States of the Conference on Security and Cooperation in Europe, Foreseen by the Final Act of the CSCE in Order to Pursue the Examination and Elaboration of a Generally Acceptable Method for Peaceful Settlement of Disputes Aimed at Complementing Existing Methods," December 9, 1978, U.S. Department of State, *The Conference on Security and Cooperation in Europe: Public Statements and Documents*, pp. 158–60.

61. See the RFE dispatch by Morton Vonduyke, in Mastny, ed., *Helsinki, Human Rights, and European Security*, pp. 215–16.

62. "Report of the 'Scientific Forum' of the Conference on Security and Cooperation in Europe," March 3, 1980, in *CSCE: Public Statements and Documents*, pp. 183–204.

63. For the Valletta document see "Final Report of the CSCE Meeting of Experts on Mediterranean Cooperation," March 26, 1979, in *CSCE: Public Statements and Documents*, pp. 167–74.

64. See Jorg Kastl, "The CSCE Review Meeting in Madrid," *NATO Review* 31, no. 5 (1983): 19; and Sizoo and Jurrjens, *CSCE Decision-making*, p. 277.

65. For the text see Sizoo and Jurrjens, *CSCE Decision-making*, pp. 290–95.

66. Ibid., p. 138.

67. Nancy M. Stetson, *The Madrid Meeting of the Conference on Security and Cooperation in Europe: A Report to the Committee on Foreign Relations*, pp. 10–12.

68. Sh. Sanakoyev, "At the Madrid Meeting," *International Affairs* 2 (1981): 47.

69. RM/H.20.

70. The Polish proposal was RM.6; the French RM.7.

71. RM.5.

72. RM.8; RM.16; RM/H.21.

73. Sizoo and Jurrjens, *CSCE Decision-making*, pp. 203–8.

74. *CSCE: Public Documents and Statements*, pp. 230–42.

75. Sizoo and Jurrjens, *CSCE Decision-making,* p. 260.

76. The USSR acquiesced in the human contacts meeting as a concession needed to secure Western participation in the disarmament conference, but refused to allow the meeting to be mentioned in the Madrid concluding document. Instead, it acquiesced in a unilateral statement by the chairman noting a consensus that a meeting would be held. In this way the Soviet Union satisfied the Western delegations, and in particular the West Germans, with their strong interest in family reunifications and other issues concerning human contacts, but did not establish a precedent for the mandating of subsequent meetings.

77. Rudolf Dolzer, "Moskau will allenfalls Konsultationen," *Frankfurter Allgemeine Zeitung,* September 18, 1984.

78. See the report by RFE correspondent Roland Eggleston, in Mastny, ed., *Helsinki, Human Rights, and European Security,* pp. 188–89.

79. "Report of the Meeting of Experts Representing the Participating States of the Conference on Security and Cooperation in Europe, Foreseen by the Final Act of the CSCE and the Concluding Document of the Madrid Meeting, in Order to Pursue the Examination of a Generally Acceptable Method for Peaceful Settlement of Disputes Aimed at Complementing Existing Methods," April 30, 1984, in *CSCE: Public Statements and Documents,* pp. 269–70.

80. "Report of the CSCE Venice Seminar on Economic, Scientific and Cultural Cooperation in the Mediterranean within the Framework of the Results of the Valletta Meeting of Experts," October 26, 1984, in ibid., pp. 275–80.

81. See Ekkehard Eickhoff, "Das KSZE-Experttreffen über Menschenrechte in Ottawa—eine Bewertung," *Europa Archiv* 19 (1985): 573–80 (English translation in Mastny, ed., *Helsinki, Human Rights, and European Security,* pp. 304–11.)

82. OME.47.

83. Ibid., 48.

84. Ibid., 49.

85. Ernst Levy, "Menschenrechts-Konferenze ohne Ergebnis beendet," *Frankfurter Allgemeine Zeitung,* June 19, 1985.

86. CSCE/CFB.115, November 21, 1985. See the complete table in *CSCE: Cultural Forum: Budapest: 1985* (London: Foreign and Commonwealth Office, Foreign Policy Document No. 146, April 1986).

87. CSCE/CFB.116, and CSCE/CFB.117.

88. CSCE/CFB.118. See also Jackson Diehl, "East-West Cultural Forum Ends Amid Angry Rhetoric," *Washington Post,* November 26, 1986.

89. Fascell, "Did Human Rights Survive Belgrade?" p. 113.

90. For the text see *Mezhdunarodnaia zhizn'* 9 (1986): 157–60; for the precise nature of U.S. objections, see the Congressional testimony of Michael Novak, head of the U.S. delegation, June 18, 1986, in *Department of State Bulletin,* September 1986, pp. 69–71. For the preferred Western draft see *Department of State Bulletin,* September 1986, pp. 71–72.

91. Gorbachev, *Perestroika*, p. 197. See also the new edition of the CPSU program, *Pravda*, March 7, 1986 (emphasis in the original).

92. This account of the Vienna meeting is based in part on U.S. Commission on Security and Cooperation in Europe, *Phase I of the Vienna Review Meeting of the Conference on Security and Cooperation in Europe*; and subsequent reports by the commission on Phase II (1987), and Phases III and IV (1988).

93. *Pravda*, November 6, 1986.

94. WT.1; WT.2; WT.3; WT.4; WT.5. According to the rules of procedure adopted at the preliminary consultations, new proposals could be introduced at any time, but not formally considered by the conference until the final week of its first phase. The East informally outlined its proposals in the opening speeches by the ministers, but did not formally table drafts until the second week of December.

95. WT.58; WT.45.

96. U.S. Commission on Security and Cooperation in Europe, *Phase II of the Vienna Review Meeting of the Conference on Security and Cooperation in Europe*, p. 10.

97. See Kashlev's evaluation at the end of the round, "Vena: na rubezhe otvetsvennykh reshenii," *Vestnik MID* 2 (1988): 29.

98. Don Oberdorfer and Lou Cannon, "'91 Moscow Conference Endorsed," *Washington Post*, January 4, 1989.

99. U.S. Department of State, *CSCE Vienna Follow-up Meeting: A Framework for Europe's Future.*

100. Ibid., p. 37.

101. "Otvety M. S. Gorbacheva na voprosy redaktsii gazety 'Pravda'," *Pravda*, January 17, 1989.

102. Shevardnadze, "K novym mashtabam i kachestvu obshcheev-ropeiskogo dialoga," *Izvestiia*, January 20, 1989. The MFA also announced the formation of an intradepartmental Commission for the Coordination of Questions Relating to the All-European Process. Kashlev was named chairman. "Sozdana komissiia," *Vestnik MID* 5 (1989).

103. Yuriy Deryabin, "Milestones of the 'Year of Europe'," *International Affairs* 2 (1990): 62–63.

104. Ibid., 2:62.

105. Michael Staack, "Fortschritte in der Menschenrechtspolitik: Perspektiven nach der KSZE-Konferenz in Paris," *Europa Archiv* 17 (1989): 534–35.

106. [EL], "KSZE-Treffen endet ohne Schluss-dokument," *Frankfurter Allgemeine Zeitung*, June 24, 1989. The other CSCE meeting in 1989 was the October–November Conference on Environmental Protection in Sofia, which was marked by large antigovernment rallies. The meeting failed to produce a final document, as Romania objected to a provision, endorsed by the USSR, affirming the right of individuals and nongovernmental organizations to be involved in environmental decisionmaking. "Thousands in Bulgaria Rally to Urge Shift to Democracy," *New York Times*, November 4, 1989. Michael Simmons, "Romania Veto Scuppers Environment Conference," *Guardian*, November 4, 1989.

107. *Pravda*, December 20, 1989.

108. See Shevardnadze's articles in *Izvestiia*, May 30, 1990, and *NATO's Sixteen Nations* 35, no. 3 (1990).

109. NATO declaration, *New York Times*, July 6, 1990.

Chapter 10: Conclusion

1. Brezhnevian optimism reached a high point in the 25th Party Congress of early 1976. See the comparative analysis of congress reports in Franklyn Griffiths, "Ideological Development and Foreign Policy," in Seweryn Bialer, ed., *The Domestic Context of Soviet Foreign Policy*, pp. 19–48. For a Soviet analysis questioning the prevailing assessments of the 1970s, see Sergei Karaganov, "The Common European Home: The Military Angle," *International Affairs* 8 (1988).

2. Ferraris, *Testimonanze di un Negoziato*, p. 302.

3. See his speech to the July MFA conference, *International Affairs* 10 (1988); and to the UN General Assembly, *Pravda*, September 28, 1988. Brezhnev told the 25th Party Congress that "détente does not in the slightest abolish, and it cannot abolish or alter, the laws of class struggle." *Stenograficheskii otchët*, 1976, 1:51–58.

4. See his interview in *Le Monde*, "La lutte idéologique ne doit pas conduire à une confrontation politique et militaire," June 16, 1977.

5. Shevardnadze criticized the MFA and other foreign policy institutions for failing to "deliver the warning signals about our lagging behind in the scientific-technical revolution," to predict structural changes in the world economy, and to "caution against lopsided infatuation with trade in energy products." In Shevardnadze's overall assessment, the Soviet Union "in the last 15 years [had] been steadily losing its position as one of the leading industrially developed countries." *Vestnik MID* 2 (1987).

6. See V. V. Zagladin, *The World Communist Movement: Outline of Strategy and Tactics*, p. 13.

7. See Ogarkov's *Vsegda v gotovnosti k zashchite Otchestva*; Jeremy Azrael, *The Soviet Civilian Leadership and the High Command, 1976–1986*; and Abraham S. Becker, *Ogarkov's Complaint and Gorbachev's Dilemma: The Soviet Defense Budget and Party-Military Conflict*.

8. Seth Mydans, "Gorbachev Calls Talks in Geneva Fruitless So Far," *New York Times*, May 28, 1985.

9. The transcript of the Gorbachev-González talks was leaked and appeared in *Cambio 16*, December 15, 1986.

10. Talbott, *Master of the Game*, p. 315.

11. *Pravda*, May 9, 1985.

12. *Politicheskii doklad*, p. 95.

13. *Pravda*, March 7, 1986.

14. *Pravda*, July 2, 1986.

15. *Time*, September 9, 1985.

16. Shevardnadze, UNGA speech, *Pravda*, September 25, 1985.

17. See Gorbachev, *Perestroika*, pp. 193–94.

18. "Acceleration" (*uskorenie*) was the dominant theme of the early Gorbachev period; it was supplanted by "restructuring" (perestroika) as Gorbachev's views were radicalized.

19. The phrase "new thinking" was used by Anatoly Gromyko and Vladimir Lomeiko in their 1984 book, *Novoe myshlenie v iadernyi vek.*

20. TASS, May 23, 1986, in *FBIS-SU*, May 27, 1986.

21. "Diplomats Hear Critical Speech by Gorbachev," *Los Angeles Times*, May 25, 1986; and Serge Schmemann, "Gorbachev Gives Critique of Soviet Foreign Policy," *New York Times*, May 24, 1986. See also Charles Glickham, "New Directions for Soviet Foreign Policy," RFE/RL, *Radio Liberty Research*, September 6, 1986.

22. *Vestnik MID* 1 (1987).

23. *Pravda*, June 26, 1987.

24. *Vestnik MID* 2 (1987).

25. *Pravda*, April 9, 1986. The actions cited by Gorbachev were the U.S. demand that the USSR cut its UN staff in New York by 40 percent; the challenge by two U.S. naval vessels of Soviet claims in the Black Sea; the bombing of Libya; and a nuclear test in Nevada.

26. May 14 address on Soviet television; text in *Pravda*, May 15, 1986. UPI, quoting a source in Kiev, reported that the death toll in the disaster may have passed 2,000. This report was cited by ACDA director Kenneth Adelman. *New York Times*, April 30, 1986.

27. For the Reagan letter see John Walcott, "New Reagan Gambit on Arms Control Is a Tall Order for Russians to Accept," *Wall Street Journal*, August 25, 1986.

28. See Shevardnadze's speech to the Vienna CSCE review conference, claiming that Reagan had agreed to the elimination of all nuclear weapons "in an even shorter time than was originally proposed in our 15 January statement." *Pravda*, November 6, 1986.

29. Michael McGwire, *Military Objectives in Soviet Foreign Policy*, p. 83.

30. See also Henry Kissinger, "Living with the Inevitable," *Newsweek*, December 4, 1989, quoting an "eminent Russian scientist," who reportedly told Kissinger that "the thrust of Soviet policy should be to remove U.S. nuclear weapons from Eurasia."

31. *Pravda*, October 24, 1989.

32. Ibid., January 16, 1989.

33. Ibid., July 7, 1989.

34. See Gorbachev, *Perestroika*, pp. 200–201; his interview with *Spiegel* in October 1988, reprinted in *Pravda*, October 24, 1988; and Friedrich Wilhelm Christians, "The Roads to Russia," *International Affairs* 5 (1990): 134. See also his inscription in the museum guest book at the conclusion of his visit to Potsdam in April 1986. "Prebyvanie delegatsii KPSS," *Pravda*, April 21, 1986. For scholarly discussions of this subject, see F. Stephen Larrabee, "Soviet Policy toward Germany: New Thinking and Old Realities," *The Washington Quarterly* 12, no. 3 (1989); Wolfgang Seiffert, "Die Reformpolitik Gorbatschows und die deutsche Frage," *Osteuropa* 39, no. 4 (1989): 317–31; and Jens Hacker,

"Lange wurde in Moskau die Existenz einer Deutschen Frage geleugnet," *Frankfurter Allgemeine Zeitung*, May 28, 1990.

35. See Gorbachev, *Perestroika*, p. 200; his remarks at the joint news conference with French president Mitterrand, Paris, July 5, 1989, in *Pravda*, July 7, 1989; and Aleksandr Bovin's unofficial commentary: "When this process [German reunification] will take place and in what form and whether it will take place at all no one can say at the moment. But one thing is clear: Only the gradual formation of an integral European space, a space of economic and political cooperation, a space of free interplay of ideas and interaction between people can create conditions for a new stage of European history. And Moscow cannot be bypassed on this path. . . ." *Izvestiia*, July 12, 1989 (ellipsis in original).

36. See the joint statement, *Pravda*, June 14, 1989.

37. *Izvestiia*, November 19, 1989.

38. See Shevardnadze's speech to the Political Commission of the European Parliament, *Pravda*, December 20, 1989. For the French role see Walter Schuetze, "Frankreich angesichts der deutschen Einheit," *Europa Archiv* 4 (1990): 133–38.

39. Interview, *Frankfurter Allgemeine Zeitung*, March 8, 1990.

40. Paul Lewis, "West and Soviets Agree With a Germanys on Rapid Schedule for Unification Talks," *New York Times*, February 14, 1990.

41. Serge Schmemann, "Soviets Unyielding on a New Germany in Western Orbit," *New York Times*, May 6, 1990.

42. Serge Schmemann, "Bonn and Moscow Ministers Consult on Germany," *New York Times*, June 12, 1990.

43. For the USSR-FRG talks, see "Das grosse historische Werk," *Spiegel* 38 (1990). See also Hannes Adomeit, "Gorbachev and German Unification: Revision of Thinking, Realignment of Power," *Problems of Communism* 39, no. 4 (1990): 1–23; and Alan Riding, "Gorbachev, in France, Says His Envoy Found Signs of Shift by Iraq," *New York Times*, October 30, 1990.

44. For Shevardnadze's testimony, see TASS, September 20, 1990.

45. Nikolai Portugalov, *Spiegel*, October 8, 1990, in *FBIS-SU*, October 10, 1990.

46. For an expression of Soviet concern about this prospect, see Sergei Karaganov, "Common European Home and Confederation," *Moscow News* 3 (1990).

Appendix

1. Main participants. Does not include the July 30–August 1, 1975 CSCE-summit in Helsinki or the November 1990 Paris all-European summit.

* denotes funerals and brief stopovers.

(H) indicates head of state who is not constitutionally responsible for the conduct of foreign affairs.

**** denotes four-power meeting.

(PM) denotes prime ministerial meeting in presidential systems (France and Finland) in which the prime minister is not chiefly responsible for foreign policy.

Bibliography

Western Sources

Documents

Bevans, Charles I. *Treaties and Other International Agreements of the United States of America, 1776–1949.* Washington, D.C.: U.S. Government Printing Office [hereinafter, GPO], 1969.

Churchill, Winston S. *His Complete Speeches 1897–1963.* Robert Rhodes James, ed. New York: Chelsea House, 1974.

Conference of European Churches. *Crossroads for the European Churches: The Report of the Seventh Assembly of the Conference of European Churches.* Geneva: Conference of European Churches, 1974.

———. *Peace in Europe—The Churches' Role: Report of a Consultation Held at Engelberg, Switzerland, 28th May–1st June 1973.* Geneva: CEC, 1973.

———. *This Happened at Nyborg VI: The Report of the Sixth Assembly of the Conference of European Churches.* Geneva: CEC, 1971.

Dedijer, Vladimir, ed. *Dokumenti 1948.* Belgrade: Izdavacka Radna Organizacija "Rad," 1979.

Degras, Jane, ed. *Soviet Documents on Foreign Policy,* 3 vols. London: Oxford University Press, 1953.

Evangelical Academy Tutzing. *Dialog—Voraussetzung für Abrüstung und Friedenssicherung: III. Internationales Kolloquium.* Tutzing: Evangelical Academy Tutzing, 1986.

France. Ministère des Affaires Etrangères. *Documents Diplomatiques Français, 1955,* 2 vols. Paris: Imprimerie Nationale, 1987–88.

———. *Les Relations Franco-Soviétiques: Textes et Documents 1965–1976.* Paris: La Documentation Française, 1976.

Germany, Federal Republic of. Auswärtiges Amt. *KSZE-Dokumentation: Phraseologie der KSZE-Schlussakte.* Bonn: Auswärtiges Amt, 1975.

Kavass, Igor I., Jacqueline Paquin Granier, and Mary Frances Dominick, eds. *Human Rights, European Politics, and the Helsinki Accord: The Documentary Evolution of the Conference on Security and Co-operation in Europe 1973–1975.* Buffalo: William S. Hein, 1981.

League of Nations. *Treaty Series: Treaties and International Engagements Registered with the Secretariat of the League of Nations.* Geneva: League of Nations, various years.

Meissner, Boris, ed. *Moskau-Bonn: Die Beziehungen zwischen der*

Sowjetunion und der Bundesrepublik Deutschland 1953–1975, 2 vols. Cologne: Wissenschaft und Politik, 1975.

North Atlantic Treaty Organization. *Texts of Final Communiqués, 1949–1970*. Brussels: NATO, 1971.

Royal Institute of International Affairs. *Documents on International Affairs*. London: Oxford University Press, various years.

Schapiro, Leonard. *Soviet Treaty Series 1917–1928*. Washington, D.C.: Georgetown University Press, 1950.

Sozialdemokratische Partei Deutschlands. *Materialien: Frieden und Abrüstung in Europa*. Bonn: SPD, 1989.

Trades Union Congress (TUC). *Report of Proceedings*. London: TUC, various years.

———. *Report of the General Council*. London: TUC, various years.

United Kingdom. *Foreign and Commonwealth Office. CSCE: Cultural Forum: Budapest: 1985*. Foreign Policy Document No. 146, London: FCO, April 1986.

———. Parliament. *Parliamentary Papers, Treaty Series* (Command Papers), various years.

United Nations. "Comprehensive Study of the Group of Governmental Experts on Confidence-Building Measures." UN doc. A/36/474, October 6, 1981.

———. *Human Rights: A Compilation of International Instruments*. New York, UN, 1978.

———. *Prava Cheloveka: Mezhdunarodnyi bill' o pravakh cheloveka*. New York: UN, 1988.

———. *United Nations Yearbook*. New York: UN, 1973–77.

United Nations. Economic Commission for Europe. *Three Decades of the United Nations Economic Commission for Europe* (E/ECE/962). New York: UN, 1978.

———. *ECE, 1947–1987* (E/ECE/1132). New York: UN, 1987.

United States. Arms Control and Disarmament Agency. *Arms Control and Disarmament Agreements: Texts and Histories of Negotiations*. Washington, D.C.: GPO, 1982.

———. *Documents on Disarmament*. Washington, D.C.: GPO, various years.

United States. Commission on Security and Cooperation in Europe. *The Belgrade Follow-up Meeting to the Conference on Security and Cooperation in Europe: A Report and Appraisal*. Washington, D.C.: GPO, 1978.

———. *The Helsinki Process and East-West Relations: Progress in Perspective*. Washington, D.C.: GPO, 1985.

———. *Implementation of Helsinki Final Act*. Washington, D.C.: GPO, various years.

———. *Phase I of the Vienna Review Meeting of the Conference on Security and Cooperation in Europe*. Washington, D.C.: GPO, 1987.

———. *Phase II of the Vienna Review Meeting of the Conference on Security and Cooperation in Europe*. Washington, D.C.: GPO, 1987.

———. *Phase III and IV of the Vienna Review Meeting of the Confer-*

ence on Security and Cooperation in Europe. Washington, D.C.: GPO, 1988.

United States. Congress. House Committee on Foreign Affairs. *Interparliamentary Union Conference: Report of the United States Delegation to the 70th Conference of the Interparliamentary Union, Seoul, Korea, Oct. 2–13, 1983.* Washington, D.C.: GPO, 1984.

————. *Interparliamentary Union Conference: Report of the United States Delegation to the Spring Meeting of the Interparliamentary Union, Held at Oslo, Norway, April 7–12, 1980.* Washington, D.C.: GPO, 1980.

United States. Congress. Joint Economic Committee. *East European Economies Post-Helsinki: A Compendium of Papers Submitted to the Joint Economic Committee.* Washington, D.C.: GPO, 1977.

United States. Congress. Senate Committee on Foreign Relations. *A Decade of American Foreign Policy, Basic Documents 1941–49.* Washington, D.C.: GPO, 1950.

United States. Congress. Senate Committee on Foreign Relations, Subcommittee on Disarmament. *Disarmament and Security: A Collection of Documents 1919–55.* Washington, D.C.: GPO, 1956.

United States. Department of State. *American Foreign Policy: Current Documents.* Washington, D.C.: GPO, various years.

————. *Background of Heads of Government Conference, 1960: Principal Documents, 1955–1959.* Washington, D.C.: GPO, 1960.

————. *CSCE Vienna Follow-up Meeting: A Framework for Europe's Future.* Washington, D.C.: Department of State, 1989.

United States. Department of State, Bureau of Public Affairs, Office of the Historian. *The Conference on Security and Cooperation in Europe: Public Statements and Documents, 1954–1986.* Washington, D.C.: Department of State, 1986.

————. *Documents on Disarmament, 1945–1949,* 2 vols. Washington, D.C.: GPO, 1960.

————. *Documents on Germany, 1944–1985.* Washington, D.C.: GPO, 1986.

————. *Foreign Ministers Meeting: Berlin Discussions, January 25–February 18, 1954.* Publication 5399. Washington, D.C.: GPO, 1954.

————. *Foreign Relations of the United States, Diplomatic Papers: The Conferences at Malta and Yalta, 1945.* Washington, D.C.: GPO, 1955.

————. *Foreign Relations of the United States: Conference of Berlin (Potsdam), 1945.* 2 vols. Washington, D.C.: GPO, 1960.

————. *Foreign Relations of the United States, 1945,* vol. 2 (*General Political and Economic Matters*). Washington, D.C.: GPO, 1967.

————. *Foreign Relations of the United States, 1946,* vol. 3 (*Paris Peace Conference: Proceedings*), and vol. 4 (*Paris Peace Conference: Documents*). Washington, D.C.: GPO, 1970.

————. *Foreign Relations of the United States, 1948,* vol. 2 (*Germany and Austria*). Washington, D.C.: GPO, 1973.

————. *Foreign Relations of the United States, 1949,* vol. 3 (*Council of Foreign Ministers, Germany and Austria*). Washington, D.C.: GPO, 1974.

———. *Foreign Relations of the United States: 1952–1954*, vol. 7 (*Germany and Austria*). Parts 1 and 2. Washington, D.C.: GPO, 1986.

———. *Foreign Relations of the United States, 1952–1954*, vol. 6 (*Western Europe and Canada*). Parts 1 and 2. Washington, D.C.: GPO, 1986.

———. *Foreign Relations of the United States, 1955–1957*, vol. 4 (*Western European Security and Integration*). Washington, D.C.: GPO, 1986.

———. *Foreign Relations of the United States: 1955–1957*, vol. 5 (*Austrian State Treaty; Summit and Foreign Ministers Meetings, 1955*). Washington, D.C.: GPO, 1988.

———. *The Geneva Conference of Heads of Government, July 18–23, 1955*. Washington, D.C.: GPO, 1955.

———. *The Geneva Meeting of Foreign Ministers, October 27–November 6, 1955*. Washington, D.C.: GPO, 1955.

United States. National Archives. Office of the Federal Register. *Public Papers of the Presidents: Harry S. Truman.* 8 vols. Washington, D.C.: GPO, 1961–66.

———. *Public Papers of the Presidents: Ronald Reagan.* 14 vols. Washington, D.C.: GPO, 1982–90.

World Council of Churches. *Peace and Disarmament: Documents of the World Council of Churches.* Geneva: WCC, 1982.

Memoirs, Diaries, and Biographies

Acheson, Dean. *Present at the Creation: My Years at the State Department.* New York: W. W. Norton, 1969.

Adenauer, Konrad. *Erinnerungen 1953–1955*, vol. 2. Stuttgart: Deutsche Verlags-Anstalt, 1966.

———. *Memoirs, 1945–1953* (translated by Beate Ruhm von Oppen). Chicago: Regnery, 1965.

Allardt, Helmut. *Moskauer Tagebuch: Beobachtungen, Notizen, Erlebnisse.* Düsseldorf: Econ, 1973.

Ambrose, Stephen E. *Eisenhower: The President.* New York: Simon and Schuster, 1984.

Beam, Jacob D. *Multiple Exposure.* New York: W. W. Norton, 1978.

Bohlen, Charles. *Witness to History.* New York: W. W. Norton, 1973.

Brandt, Willy. *People and Politics: The Years 1960–1975.* Boston: Little, Brown, 1976.

Brown, George. *In My Way.* New York: St. Martin's, 1970.

Bullock, Alan. *The Life and Times of Ernest Bevin: Foreign Secretary, 1945–1951.* New York: W. W. Norton, 1983.

Byrnes, James F. *Speaking Frankly.* New York: Harper, 1947.

Callaghan, James. *Time and Chance.* London: Collins, 1987.

Campbell, John. *Aneurin Bevan and the Mirage of British Socialism.* New York: W. W. Norton, 1987.

Campbell, Thomas M., and George Herring, eds. *The Diaries of Edward R. Stettinius, Jr.* New York: New Viewpoints, 1975.

Carter, Jimmy. *Keeping Faith: Memoirs of a President.* New York: Bantam, 1982.

Churchill, Winston S. *The Second World War,* 6 vols. Boston: Houghton Mifflin, 1948–53.

Citrine, Walter M. *I Search for Truth in Russia.* London: Routledge, 1936.

――――. *Men and Work: An Autobiography.* London: Hutchinson, 1964.

――――. *Two Careers.* London: Hutchinson, 1967.

Collins, L. John. *Faith under Fire.* London: Leslie Frewin, 1966.

Colville, John. *Fringes of Power: 10 Downing Street, Diaries 1939–1955.* New York: W. W. Norton, 1987.

Dean, Arthur H. *Test Ban and Disarmament: The Path of Negotiation.* New York: Harper and Row, 1966.

Dedijer, Vladimir. *The Battle Stalin Lost: Memoirs of Yugoslavia, 1948–1953.* New York: Viking, 1970.

――――. *Tito.* New York: Simon and Schuster, 1953.

De Gaulle, Charles. *The Complete War Memoirs: The Call to Honour, Unity, Salvation.* New York: Simon and Schuster, 1964.

――――. *Memoirs of Hope: Renewal and Endeavor.* New York: Simon and Schuster, 1971.

Deutscher, Isaac. *Stalin: A Political Biography.* 2d ed. New York: Oxford University Press, 1967.

Djilas, Milovan. *Conversations with Stalin.* New York: Harcourt Brace, 1962.

――――. *Rise and Fall.* San Diego: Harcourt Brace Jovanovich, 1983.

Douglas-Home, Alec. *The Way the Wind Blows.* New York: Quadrangle, 1976.

Eden, Anthony. *Full Circle.* Boston: Houghton Mifflin, 1960.

――――. *The Reckoning.* Boston. Houghton Mifflin, 1965.

Eisenhower, Dwight D. *Mandate for Change, 1953–1956.* Garden City, N.Y.: Doubleday, 1963.

――――. *Waging Peace, 1956–1961.* Garden City, N.Y.: Doubleday, 1965.

Erlander, Tage. *1955–60.* Stockholm: Tidens, 1976.

Foot, Michael. *Aneurin Bevan: A Biography, 1945–1960.* New York: Atheneum, 1974.

Ford, Gerald R. *A Time to Heal.* New York: Harper and Row, 1979.

Ford, Robert A. D. *Our Man In Moscow.* Toronto: University of Toronto Press, 1989.

Grewe, Wilhelm G. *Rückblenden 1976–1951.* Berlin: Propyläen, 1979.

Haig, Alexander M., Jr. *Caveat: Realism, Reagan and Foreign Policy.* New York: Macmillan, 1984.

Harris, Kenneth. *Attlee.* New York: W. W. Norton, 1982.

Hayter, Sir William. *Russia and the World.* New York: Taplinger, 1970.

Hilger, Gustav, and Alfred G. Meyer. *Incompatible Allies: A Memoir-History of German-Soviet Relations, 1918–1941.* New York: Macmillan, 1953.

Hyland, William G. *Mortal Rivals.* New York: Random House, 1987.

James, Robert Rhodes. *Anthony Eden: A Biography.* New York: McGraw-Hill, 1987.

Johnson, Lyndon B. *The Vantage Point*. New York: Holt, Rinehart and Winston, 1971.

Kennan, George F. *Memoirs: 1925–1950*. Boston: Little, Brown, 1967.

Kirkpatrick, Ivone. *The Inner Circle: Memoirs*. London: Macmillan, 1959.

Kissinger, Henry A. *White House Years*. Boston: Little, Brown, 1979.

———. *Years of Upheaval*. Boston: Little, Brown, 1982.

Kreisky, Bruno. *Zwischen den Zeiten: Erinnerungen aus fünf Jahrzehnten*. Berlin: Siedler, 1986.

Kroll, Hans. *Lebenserinnerungen eines Botschafters*. Berlin: Kiepenheuer and Witsch, 1967.

McCauley, Martin, ed. *Khrushchev and Khrushchevism*. Bloomington: Indiana University Press, 1988.

McGhee, George. *At the Creation of a New Germany: From Adenauer to Brandt—An Ambassador's Account*. New Haven, Conn.: Yale University Press, 1989.

Macmillan, Harold. *At the End of the Day, 1961–1963*. New York: Harper and Row, 1973.

———. *Pointing the Way, 1959–1961*. New York: Harper and Row, 1972.

———. *Riding the Storm, 1956–1959*. New York: Harper and Row, 1971.

———. *Tides of Fortune, 1945–1955*. New York: Harper and Row, 1969.

Mitterrand, François. *The Wheat and the Chaff*. New York: Seaver, 1982.

Micunovic, Veljko. *Moscow Diary*. Garden City, N.J.: Doubleday, 1980.

Morgan, Janet, ed. *The Backbench Diaries of Richard Crossman*. New York: Holmes and Meier, 1981.

Morrison, Herbert. *An Autobiography*. London: Odhams, 1960.

Murphy, Robert. *Diplomat among Warriors*. Garden City, N.Y.: Doubleday, 1964.

Nitze, Paul H. *From Hiroshima to Glasnost: At the Center of Decision—A Memoir*. New York: Grove Weidenfeld, 1989.

Parrott, Cecil. *The Serpent and the Nightingale*. London: Faber and Faber, 1977.

Pearson, Lester B. *Memoirs*, 3 vols. Toronto: University of Toronto Press, 1972–1975.

Pineau, Christian. *Nikita Sergueevitch Khrouchtchev*. Paris: Perrin, 1965.

Polianski, Nicolas. *M.I.D.: 12 ans dans les services diplomatiques du Kremlin*. Paris: Belford, 1984.

Regan, Donald T. *For the Record*. San Diego: Harcourt Brace Jovanovich, 1988.

Rusk, Dean. *As I Saw It*. New York: W. W. Norton, 1990.

Russell, Bertrand. *The Autobiography of Bertrand Russell, 1944–1969*. New York: Simon and Schuster, 1969.

Salinger, Pierre. *With Kennedy*. Garden City, N.J.: Doubleday, 1966.

Schlesinger, Arthur, Jr. *Robert Kennedy and His Times*. Boston: Houghton Mifflin, 1978.

———. *A Thousand Days: John F. Kennedy in the White House*. Boston: Houghton Mifflin, 1965.

Schmid, Carlo. *Erinnerungen.* Bern: Scherz, 1979.

Schmidt, Helmut. *Menschen und Mächte.* Berlin: Siedler, 1987.

Seaborg, Glenn T., with Benjamin S. Loeb. *Stemming the Tide: Arms Control in the Johnson Years.* Lexington, Mass.: Lexington Books, 1988.

Sherwood, Robert E. *Roosevelt and Hopkins: An Intimate History.* New York: Harper and Row, 1948.

Shevchenko, Arkady. *Breaking with Moscow.* New York: Knopf, 1985.

Smith, Gerard. *Doubletalk: The Story of the First Strategic Arms Limitation Talks.* New York: Doubleday, 1980.

Söll, Hartmut. *Fritz Erler, Eine politische Biographie,* 2 vols. Bonn: J. H. W. Dietz, 1976.

Sorenson, Theodore. *Kennedy.* New York: Harper and Row, 1965.

Tuominen, Arvo. *The Bells of the Kremlin: An Experience in Communism.* Lily Leino, trans. Hanover: University Press of New England, 1983.

Vance, Cyrus. *Hard Choices.* New York: Simon and Schuster, 1983.

Walters, Vernon. *Silent Missions.* Garden City, N.Y.: Doubleday, 1978.

Weit, Erwin. *Ostblock intern.* Hamburg: Hoffmann and Campe, 1970.

Williams, Philip M. *Hugh Gaitskell: A Political Biography.* London: Jonathan Cape, 1979.

Williams, Philip M., ed. *The Diary of Hugh Gaitskell.* London: Jonathan Cape, 1983.

Wilson, Harold. *Final Term: The Labour Government 1974–1976.* London: Weidenfeld and Nicolson, 1979.

———. *Memoirs: The Making of a Prime Minister.* London: Weidenfeld and Nicolson and Michael Joseph, 1986.

Books

Acimovic, Ljubivoje. *Problems of Security and Cooperation in Europe.* Alphen aan den Rijn: Sijthoff and Nordhoff, 1981.

Adler-Karlsson, Gunnar. *Western Economic Warfare, 1947–1967.* Stockholm: Almqvist and Wiksell, 1968.

Adomeit, Hannes. *Soviet Risk-Taking and Crisis Behavior.* London: Allen and Unwin, 1982.

———. *The Soviet Union and Western Europe: Perceptions, Policies, Problems.* Kingston, Ontario: Centre for International Relations, Queen's University, 1979.

Alexeev, Wassilij. *The Foreign Policy of the Moscow Patriarchate, 1939–1953.* New York: Research Program on the USSR, 1955.

Alexiev, Alexander R. *The Soviet Campaign Against INF: Strategy, Tactics, Means.* Santa Monica, Calif.: Rand Corporation, N-2280-AF, February 1985.

Aspaturian, Vernon. *Process and Power in Soviet Foreign Policy.* Boston: Little, Brown, 1971.

Azrael, Jeremy. *The Soviet Civilian Leadership and the High Command, 1976–1986.* Santa Monica, Calif.: Rand Corporation, R-3521-AF, June 1987.

Bader, William B. *The United States and the Spread of Nuclear Weapons.* New York: Pegasus, 1968.

Bialer, Seweryn, ed. *The Domestic Context of Soviet Foreign Policy.* Boulder, Colo.: Westview, 1981.

Barghoorn, Frederick C. *The Soviet Cultural Offensive.* Princeton, N.J.: Princeton University Press, 1960.

Bark, Dennis L. *Agreement in Berlin: A Study of the 1970–72 Quadripartite Negotiations.* AEI-Hoover Policy Study 10, August 1974.

Bechhoefer, Bernhard G. *Postwar Negotiations for Arms Control.* Washington, D.C.: Brookings Institution, 1961.

Becker, Abraham S. *Military Expenditure Limitation for Arms Control: Problems and Prospects.* Cambridge, Mass.: Ballinger, 1977.

————. *Ogarkov's Complaint and Gorbachev's Dilemma: The Soviet Defense Budget and Party-Military Conflict.* Santa Monica, Calif.: Rand Corporation, R-3541-AF, December 1987.

Berner, Orjan. *Soviet Policies toward the Nordic Countries.* Lanham, Md.: University Press of America, 1986.

Beschloss, Michael R. *Mayday: Eisenhower, Khrushchev and the U-2 Affair.* New York: Harper and Row, 1986.

Black, C. E., and T. P. Thornton. *Communism and Revolution: The Strategic Uses of Political Violence.* Princeton, N.J.: Princeton University Press, 1964.

Blackwill, Robert D., and F. Stephen Larrabee. *Conventional Arms Control and East-West Security.* Durham, N.C.: Duke University Press, 1989.

Bomsdorf, Falk. *Sicherheit im Norden Europas: Die Sicherheitspolitik der fünf nordischen Staaten und die Nordeuropapolitik der Sowjetunion.* Baden-Baden: Nomos, 1989.

Borawski, John. *From the Atlantic to the Urals: Negotiating Arms Control at the Stockholm Conference.* Washington, D.C.: Pergamon-Brassey's, 1988.

Bracher, Karl Dietrich, et al. *Geschichte der Bundesrepublik Deutschland,* 6 vols. Stuttgart: Deutsche Verlags-Anstalt, 1981–87.

Braunthal, Julius. *History of the International,* 3 vols. Boulder, Colo.: Westview, 1980.

Briggs, Herbert W. *The International Law Commission.* Ithaca, N.Y.: Cornell University Press, 1965.

Brown, J. F. *Eastern Europe and Communist Rule.* Durham, N.C.: Duke University Press, 1988.

Calhoun, Daniel F. *The United Front, the TUC and the Russians, 1923–28.* Cambridge: Cambridge University Press, 1976.

Carlton, David, and Carlo Schaerf, eds. *The Arms Race in the 1980s.* New York: St. Martin's, 1982.

Carr, E. H. *The Bolshevik Revolution, 1917–1923.* London: Pelican, 1966.

Cate, Curtis. *The Ides of August: The Berlin Wall Crisis, 1961.* New York: M. Evans, 1978.

Catudal, Honore M., Jr. *The Diplomacy of the Quadripartite Agreement* on Berlin: A New Era in East-West Politics. Berlin: Berlin Verlag, 1978.

Chase, Stuart, et al. Soviet Russia in the Second Decade. A Joint Survey by the Technical Staff of the First American Trade Union Delegation. New York: John Day, 1928.

Cline, Ray S., James Arnold, and Roger E. Kanet, eds. Western Europe in Soviet Global Strategy. Boulder, Colo.: Westview, 1987.

Cohen, Stephen F. Bukharin and the Bolshevik Revolution. New York: Vintage, 1971.

Couve de Murville, Maurice. Une politique étrangère. Paris: Plon, 1971.

Cronin, Audrey Kurth. Great Power Politics and the Struggle over Austria. Ithaca, N.Y.: Cornell University Press, 1986.

Curzon, Gerard. Multilateral Commercial Diplomacy: The General Agreement on Tariffs and Trade and Its Impact on National and Commercial Policies and Techniques. New York: Praeger, 1966.

Dallin, Alexander. The Soviet Union at the United Nations. New York: Praeger, 1962.

Davis, Paul K., Robert D. Howe, Richard L. Kugler, and William G. Wild. Variables Affecting Central-Region Stability: The "Operational Minimum" and Other Issues at Low Force Levels. Santa Monica, Calif.: Rand Corporation, N-2976-USDP, September 1989.

Dean, Jonathan. Watershed in Europe. Lexington, Mass.: D. C. Heath, 1987.

Dennett, Raymond, ed. Negotiating with the Russians. Boston: World Peace Foundation, 1951.

Douglas, James. Parliaments Across Frontiers: A Short History of the Inter-Parliamentary Union. London: HMSO, 1975.

Ellis, Jane. The Russian Orthodox Church: A Contemporary History. Bloomington: Indiana University Press, 1986.

Ellison, Herbert J. Soviet Policy Toward Western Europe. Seattle: University of Washington Press, 1983.

Fejtö, François. The French Communist Party and the Crisis of International Communism. Cambridge, Mass.: MIT Press, 1967.

Ferraris, Luigi. Report on a Negotiation. Alphen aan den Rijn: Sijthoff and Nordhoff, 1979.

———. Testimonianze di un Negoziato. Padua: CEDAM, 1977.

Fletcher, William C. Religion and Soviet Foreign Policy 1945–1970. London: Oxford University Press, 1973.

Fontaine, Andre. History of the Cold War: From the Korean War to the Present. New York: Vintage, 1969.

Forbes, Monica H. Feindstaatenklauseln, Viermaechteverantwortung und Deutsche Frage. Baden-Baden: Nomos, 1983.

Frankel, Joseph. British Foreign Policy 1945–1973. London: Oxford University Press, 1975.

Fritsch-Bournazel, Renata. L'Union Soviétique et les Allemagnes. Paris: Presses de la Fondation nationale des sciences politiques, 1979.

Gaddis, John Lewis. The United States and the Origins of the Cold War, 1941–1947. New York: Columbia University Press, 1972.

Galtung, Johan, ed. *Co-operation in Europe.* Assen, the Netherlands: Van Gorcum, 1970.

Garner, William. *Soviet Threat Perceptions of NATO's Eurostrategic Missiles.* Paris: Atlantic Institute, 1983.

Garthoff, Raymond L. *Détente and Confrontation.* Washington, D.C.: Brookings Institution, 1985.

———. *Reflections on the Cuban Missile Crisis,* revised edition. Washington, D.C.: Brookings Institution, 1989.

Gati, Charles. *Hungary and the Soviet Bloc.* Durham, N.C.: Duke University Press, 1986.

Gelman, Harry. *The Brezhnev Politburo and the Decline of Détente.* Ithaca, N.Y.: Cornell University Press, 1984.

———. *Gorbachev's Policies Toward Western Europe: A Balance Sheet.* Santa Monica, Calif.: Rand Corporation, R-3588-AF, October 1987.

George, Alexander, Philip J. Farley, and Alexander Dallin, eds. *U.S.-Soviet Security Cooperation: Achievements, Failures, Lessons.* New York: Oxford University Press, 1988.

German Federal Institute for East European and International Studies. *The Soviet Union 1984/85.*

Ginsburgs, George, and Alvin Z. Rubinstein. *Soviet Foreign Policy Toward Western Europe.* New York: Praeger, 1978.

Godson, Roy. *The Kremlin and Labor: A Study in National Security Policy.* New York: Crane Russak, 1977.

Goodby, James. *The Stockholm Conference: Negotiating a Cooperative Security System for Europe.* Foreign Service Institute, Center for the Study of Foreign Affairs, Occasional Paper No. 6, 1987.

Gordon, Lincoln, ed. *Eroding Empire: Western Relations with Eastern Europe.* Washington, D.C.: Brookings Institution, 1987.

Gore-Booth, Lord, ed. *Satow's Guide to Diplomatic Practice.* 5th ed. London: Longman, 1979.

Griffith, William E. *Albania and the Sino-Soviet Rift.* Cambridge, Mass.: MIT Press, 1963.

———. *The Ostpolitik of the Federal Republic of Germany.* Cambridge, Mass.: MIT, 1978.

Grosser, Alfred. *Franco-Soviet Relations Today.* Santa Monica, Calif.: Rand Corporation, RM-5382-PR, 1967.

Grzybowski, Kazimierz. *Soviet Public International Law.* Leyden: A. W. Sijthoff, 1970.

Hahn, Werner G. *Postwar Soviet Politics: The Fall of Zhdanov and the Defeat of Moderation, 1946–1953.* Ithaca, N.Y.: Cornell University Press, 1982.

Halle, Louis J. *The Cold War as History.* New York: Harper and Row, 1967.

Hammond, Thomas T., ed. *The Anatomy of Communist Takeovers.* New Haven, Conn.: Yale University Press, 1975.

Hanson, Philip. *Trade and Technology in Soviet-Western Relations.* New York: Columbia University Press, 1981.

Healey, Denis, ed. *The Curtain Falls: The Story of the Socialists in Eastern Europe.* London: Lincolns-Prager, 1951.

Hebly, J. A. *Eastbound Ecumenism: A Collection of Essays on the World Council of Churches.* Lanham, Md.: University Press of America, 1986.

———. *The Russians and the World Council of Churches.* Belfast: Christian Journals, 1978.

Henry, I. D., and M. C. Wood. *The Legal Status of Berlin.* Cambridge: Grotius, 1987.

Hudson, Darril. *The World Council of Churches in International Affairs.* London: Faith Press for the Royal Institute of International Affairs, 1977.

Huopaniemi, Jukka. *Parliaments and European Rapprochement: The Conference of the Inter-Parliamentary Union on European Co-operation and Security. (Helsinki, January 1973).* Leiden: A. W. Sijthoff, 1973.

Hyland, William G. *Soviet-American Relations: A New Cold War?* Santa Monica, Calif.: Rand Corporation, R-2763-FF/RC, May 1981.

Independent Commission on Disarmament and Security Issues. *Common Security: A Blueprint for Survival.* New York: Simon and Schuster, 1982.

Jakobson, Max. *Finland: Myth and Reality.* Helsinki: Otava, 1987.

———. *Finnish Neutrality: A Study of Finnish Foreign Policy Since the Second World War.* New York: Praeger, 1969.

Jensen, Lloyd. *The Postwar Disarmament Negotiations: A Study in American-Soviet Bargaining Behavior.* Ann Arbor: University of Michigan, Center for Conflict Resolution, November 1962.

John, Ieuan, ed. *EEC Policy towards Eastern Europe.* Westmead, England: Saxon House, 1975.

Johnson, A. Ross. *The Warsaw Pact's Campaign for "European Security".* Santa Monica, Calif.: Rand Corporation, R-565-PR, November 1970.

Jones, Bill. *The Russia Complex: The British Labour Party and the Soviet Union.* Manchester: Manchester University Press, 1977.

Jones, Joseph M. *The Fifteen Weeks.* New York: Viking, 1955.

Jonsson, Christer. *Soviet Bargaining Behavior: The Nuclear Test Ban Case.* New York: Columbia University Press, 1979.

Kampelman, Max M. *Three Years at the East-West Divide.* New York: Freedom House, 1983.

Kaplan, Jacob J., and Günther Schleiminger. *The European Payments Union: Financial Diplomacy in the 1950s.* New York: Oxford-Clarendon, 1989.

Kaplan, Karel. *Dans les archives du comité central. Trente ans de secrets du bloc soviétique.* Paris: Albin Michel, 1978.

Keliher, John G. *The Negotiations on Mutual and Balanced Force Reductions.* New York: Pergamon, n.d.

Kennan, George F. *Russia and the West Under Lenin and Stalin.* New York: Mentor, 1960.

Kindleberger, Charles P. *Foreign Trade and the National Economy.* New Haven, Conn.: Yale University Press, 1962.

Kirby, D. G. *Finland in the Twentieth Century.* Minneapolis: University of Minnesota Press, 1979.

Klinghoffer, Arthur Jay. *The Soviet Union and International Oil Politics.* New York: Columbia University Press, 1977.

Kolodziej, Edward A. *French International Policy Under De Gaulle and Pompidou: The Politics of Grandeur.* Ithaca, N.Y.: Cornell University Press, 1974.

Korbel, Josef. *Détente in Europe: Real or Imaginary?* Princeton, N.J.: Princeton University Press, 1972.

Laird, Robbin F. *France, the Soviet Union, and the Nuclear Weapons Issue.* Boulder, Colo.: Westview, 1985.

Laird, Robbin F., and Susan L. Clark. *The USSR and the Western Alliance.* Boston, London: Unwin, Hyman, 1989.

Larrabee, F. Stephen, and Allen Lynch. *Confidence-Building Measures and U.S.-Soviet Relations.* New York: Institute for East-West Security Studies, 1986.

Larrabee, F. Stephen, and Dietrich Stobbe, eds. *Confidence-Building Measures in Europe.* New York: Institute for East-West Security Studies, 1983.

Leebaert, Derek, ed. *European Security: Prospects for the 1980s.* Lexington, Mass.: Lexington Books, 1978.

Lehmann, Hans Georg. *Öffnung nach Osten: Die Ostreisen Helmut Schmidts und die Entstehung der Ost- und Entspannungspolitik.* Bonn: Neue Gesellschaft, 1984.

Leigh, Michael. *European Integration and the Common Fisheries Policy.* London: Croom Helm, 1983.

Leonard, L. Larry. *International Organization.* New York: McGraw-Hill, 1951.

Leonhard, Wolfgang. *The Kremlin Since Stalin.* New York: Praeger, 1963.

Lieberman, Joseph I. *The Scorpion and the Tarantula: The Struggle to Control Atomic Weapons, 1945–1949.* Boston: Houghton Mifflin, 1970.

London, Kurt, ed. *The Soviet Impact on World Politics.* New York: Hawthorn Books, 1974.

Lundestad, Geir. *America, Scandinavia, and the Cold War, 1945–1949.* New York: Columbia University Press, 1980.

———. *The American Non-Policy toward Eastern Europe, 1943–1947.* New York: Humanities, 1975.

McAdams, A. James. *East Germany and Détente: Building Authority after the Wall.* New York: Cambridge University Press, 1985.

McGwire, Michael. *Military Objectives in Soviet Foreign Policy.* Washington, D.C.: Brookings Institution, 1987.

McMillan, Carl H., ed. *Changing Perspectives in East-West Commerce.* Lexington, Mass.: Lexington Books, 1974.

Macridis, Roy, ed. *Modern Political Systems: Europe.* Englewood Cliffs, N.J.: Prentice-Hall, 1987.

Malcolm, Neil. *Soviet Policy Perspectives on Western Europe.* London: Routledge (for the Royal Institute of International Affairs), 1989.

Maresca, John J. *To Helsinki.* Durham, N.C.: Duke University Press, 1983.

Marston, F. S. *The Peace Conference of 1919: Organization and Procedure.* London: Oxford University Press, 1944.

Mastny, Vojtech. *Russia's Road to the Cold War.* New York: Columbia University Press, 1979.

Mastny, Vojtech, ed. *Helsinki, Human Rights, and European Security: Analysis and Documentation.* Durham, N.C.: Duke University Press, 1986.

"Memorandum on the Activities of the Red International of Labor Unions during the First Decade of Its Existence," Enclosure No. 1 to Despatch No. 7695 from the TEE Legation at Riga, May 8, 1931 (typescript in the library of the U.S. Department of Labor).

Meyer, Stephen M. *Soviet Theatre Nuclear Forces.* Adelphi Papers 187 and 188, London: International Institute for Strategic Studies, 1983–84.

Milward, Alan S. *The Reconstruction of Western Europe, 1945–51.* Berkeley: University of California Press, 1984.

Moreton, Edwina, and Gerald Segal. *Soviet Strategy Toward Western Europe.* London: Allen and Unwin, 1984.

Heller, Mikhail, and Aleksandr Nekrich. *Utopia in Power: The History of the Soviet Union from 1917 to the Present.* New York: Summit, 1986.

Nerlich, Uwe, ed. *Soviet Power and Western Negotiating Policies,* 2 vols. Cambridge: Ballinger, 1983.

New Catholic Encyclopedia. 17 vols. New York: McGraw-Hill, 1967–89.

Neuman, H J *Nuclear Forces in Europe: A Handbook for the Debate.* London: International Institute for Strategic Studies, 1982.

Newhouse, John. *Cold Dawn: The Story of SALT.* New York: Holt, Rinehart and Winston, 1973.

Nicolson, Harold. *Peacemaking 1919.* New York: Harcourt Brace, 1939.

Oppenheim, Lassa. *International Law: A Treatise,* H. Lauterpacht, ed. 2 vols. New York: David McKay, 1961.

Palmer, Michael. *The Prospects for a European Security Conference.* London: Chatham House, 1971.

Parry, Clive, et al. *Encyclopaedic Dictionary of International Law.* New York: Oceana, 1986.

Parsons, Talcott. *Essays in Sociological Theory.* rev. ed. Glencoe, Ill.: Free Press, 1954.

Paterson, Thomas G., ed. *Kennedy's Quest for Victory: American Foreign Policy, 1961–1963.* New York: Oxford University Press, 1989.

Pincher, Chapman. *Their Trade Is Treachery.* London: Sidgwick and Jackson, 1981.

Pipes, Richard. *Soviet Strategy in Europe.* New York: Crane Russak, 1976.

Planck, Charles R. *The Changing Status of German Reunification in Western Diplomacy, 1955–1966.* Baltimore: Washington Center of

Foreign Policy Research, SAIS, Johns Hopkins University, Studies in International Affairs, no. 4, 1967.

Rauch, Georg von. *A History of Soviet Russia*. New York: Praeger, 1957.

Reuver, Marc. *Christians as Peacemakers: Peace Movements in Europe and the USA*. Geneva: World Council of Churches, 1988.

Rostow, W. W. *Europe after Stalin: Eisenhower's Three Decisions of March 11, 1953*. Austin: University of Texas Press, 1982.

————. *Open Skies: Eisenhower's Proposal of July 21, 1955*. Austin: University of Texas Press, 1982.

Rotblat, Josef. *Pugwash: The First Ten Years*. New York: Humanities, 1967.

Royal Society of International Affairs. *Survey of International Affairs*. London: Oxford University Press, various years.

Royen, Christoph. *Die sowjetische Koexistenzpolitik gegenüber Westeuropa*. Baden-Baden: Nomos, 1978.

Russell, Ruth B. (assisted by Jeanette E. Muther). *A History of the United Nations Charter: The Role of the United States 1940–1945*. Washington, D.C.: Brookings Institution, 1958.

Satow, Sir Ernest. *A Guide to Diplomatic Practice*. 2d ed. London: Longmans, Green, 1922.

Scholl-Latour, Peter. *Im Sog des Generals: Von Abidjan nach Moskau*. Stuttgart: Deutsche Verlagsanstalt, 1966.

Seaborg, Glenn T. *Kennedy, Khrushchev and the Test Ban*. Berkeley: University of California Press, 1981.

Shenfield, Stephen. *Minimum Nuclear Deterrence: The Debate Among Soviet Civilian Analysts*. Center for Policy Development, Brown University, November 1989.

Shulman, Marshall D. *Beyond the Cold War*. New Haven, Conn.: Yale University Press, 1966.

————. *Stalin's Foreign Policy Reappraised*. New York: Atheneum, 1965.

Siebenmorgen, Peter. *Gezeitenwechsel: Aufbruch zur Entspannungspolitik*. Bonn: Bouvier, 1990.

Sizoo, Jan, and Rudolf Th. Jurrjens. *CSCE Decision-making: The Madrid Experience*. The Hague: Martinus Nijhoff, 1984.

Smith, Glen Alden. *Soviet Foreign Trade: Organization, Operations, and Policy, 1918–1971*. New York: Praeger, 1973.

Spencer, Robert, ed. *Canada and the Conference on Security and Cooperation in Europe*. Toronto: University of Toronto, Center for International Studies, 1984.

Stehle, Hansjakob. *Eastern Politics of the Vatican 1917–1979*. Athens: Ohio University Press, 1981.

Steinke, Rudolf, and Michael Vale. *Germany Debates Defense: The NATO Alliance at the Crossroads*, Armonk, N.Y.: M. E. Sharpe, 1983.

Stent, Angela. *From Embargo to Ostpolitik*. Cambridge: Cambridge University Press, 1981.

Stetson, Nancy M. *The Madrid Meeting of the Conference on Security and Cooperation in Europe: A Report to the Committee on Foreign Relations*. U.S. Senate, 97th Congress, 2d Session, July 1982.

Strategic Survey, 1973. London: International Institute for Strategic Studies, 1974.

Talbott, Strobe. *Deadly Gambits.* New York, Knopf, 1984.

———. *The Master of the Game: Paul Nitze and the Nuclear Peace.* New York: Knopf, 1988.

Tatu, Michel. *Power in the Kremlin.* New York: Viking, 1969.

Thomson, James A., and Nanette C. Gantz. *Conventional Arms Control Revisited: Objectives in the New Phase.* Santa Monica, Calif.: Rand Corporation, N-2697-AF, December 1987.

Trade Unions Congress. *British Labour Delegation to Russia, 1920, Report.* London: TUC and the Labour Party, 1920.

TUC. *Russia: The Official Report of the British Trades Union Delegation to Russia and Caucasia, Nov. and Dec. 1924.* London: TUC, 1925.

Triska, Jan F., ed. *Soviet Communism: Programs and Rules.* San Francisco: Chandler, 1962.

Triska, Jan F., and Robert M. Slusser. *The Theory, Law, and Policy of Soviet Treaties.* Stanford, Calif.: Stanford University Press, 1962.

Ulam, Adam. *Expansion and Coexistence.* New York: Holt, Rinehart and Winston, 1974.

Ullman, Richard H. *Anglo-Soviet Relations,* 3 vols. Princeton, N.J.: Princeton University Press, 1968–72.

Van Oudenaren, John. *Political Consultation Agreements in Soviet-West European Relations.* Santa Monica, Calif.: Rand Corporation, N-3090-RC, 1990.

Vick, Alan J., and James A. Thomson. *The Military Significance of Restrictions on Strategic Nuclear Force Operations.* Santa Monica, Calif.: Rand Corporation, N-2113-FF, April 1984.

Voss, Eugen, ed. *Die Religionsfreiheit in Osteuropa.* Zollikon: G2W-Verlag, 1984.

Warner, Edward L., III, and David A. Ochmanek. *Next Moves: An Arms Control Agenda for the 1990s.* New York: Council on Foreign Relations, 1989.

Whiteman, Marjorie M. *Digest of International Law,* 13 vols. Washington, D.C.: GPO, 1970.

Wolfe, Thomas W. *Soviet Power and Europe.* Baltimore: Johns Hopkins University Press, 1970.

Woodward, Sir Llewellyn. *British Foreign Policy in the Second World War,* vol. 5. London: HMSO, 1976.

Wightman, David. *Economic Co-operation in Europe: A Study of the United Nations Economic Commission for Europe.* New York: Praeger, 1956.

Wright, Peter. *Spycatcher.* New York: Viking, 1987.

Yearbook of Finnish Foreign Policy, 1977. Helsinki: Finnish Institute of International Affairs, 1977.

The Year Book of World Affairs, 1949. London: Stevens and Sons, 1949.

Yost, David S. *France's Deterrent Posture and Security in Europe. Adelphi Papers,* nos. 194–95. London: International Institute for Strategic Studies, 1985.

Zimmerman, William. *Soviet Perspectives on International Relations 1956–1967*. Princeton, N.J.: Princeton University Press, 1969.
Zivier, Ernst R. *The Legal Status of the Land Berlin: A Survey after the Quadripartite Agreement*. Berlin: Berlin Verlag, 1977.

Unpublished Dissertations

Cole, Paul M. "Neutralité du Jour: The Conduct of Swedish Security Policy Since 1945," unpublished Ph.D. dissertation, Johns Hopkins University, Nitze School of Advanced International Studies, 1990.
Cutler, Robert. "Soviet Debates over the Conduct of Foreign Policy toward Western Europe: Four Case Studies, 1971–75," unpublished Ph.D. dissertation, University of Michigan, 1982.
Griffiths, Franklyn. "Images, Politics, and Learning in Soviet Behaviour toward the United States," unpublished Ph.D. dissertation, Columbia University, 1972.
Krantz, Thomas. "Moscow and the Negotiation of the Helsinki Accords, 1972–75," unpublished Ph.D. dissertation, Oxford University, 1981.

Soviet and East European Sources

Documents

Brezhnev, Leonid. *Leninskim kursom*, 9 vols. Moscow: Politizdat, 1972.
Gorbachev, Mikhail S. *The Speech in Murmansk*. Moscow: Novosti, 1987.
Gromyko, Andrei, ed. *Sovetskii soiuz na mezhdunarodnykh konferentsiakh perioda velikoi otechestvennoi voiny 1941–1945 gg.*, vol. 6. Moscow: Politizdat, 1980.
Nikolskii, A. V., ed. *Sovetsko-amerikanskaia vstrecha na vyshem urovne*. Moscow: Politizdat, 1985.
Ot Khel'sinki do Belgrada: Sovetskii soiuz i osushchestvlenie Zakliuchitel'nogo akta obshcheevropeiskogo soveshchaniia, dokumenty i materiali. Moscow: Politizdat, 1977.
Nuclear-Weapon-Free Corridor in Central Europe. East Berlin: Verlag Zeit im Bild, 1986.
Politicheskii doklad Tsentral'nogo Komiteta KPSS XXVII s"ezdu Kommunisticheskoi partii Sovetskogo Soiuza. Moscow: Politizdat, 1986.
Rotfeld, Adam-Daniel, ed. *From Helsinki to Madrid: CSCE Documents*. Warsaw: Polish Institute of International Affairs, 1985.
Suslov, M. A. *Marksizm-Leninizm i sovremennaia epokha: Izbrannye rechi i staty*. Moscow: Politizdat, 1982.
Tasks at the Present Stage of the Struggle Against Imperialism and United Action of the Communist and Workers' Parties and All Anti-Imperialist Forces, Conference of Communist and Workers' Parties. Moscow: Novosti, 1969.
23rd Congress of the Communist Party of the Soviet Union. Moscow: Novosti, 1966.
USSR. Ministerstvo Inostrannykh Del. *Diplomaticheskii vestnik, 1982*. Moscow: Mezhdunarodnye Otnosheniia, 1983.

———. *Dokumenty i materialy sovetsko-angliskii peregovorov v Moskve.* Moscow: Politizdat, 1975.

———. *Dokumenty vneshnei politiki SSSR.* Moscow, various years.

———. *SSSR-GDR: 30 let otnoshenii 1949–1979: Dokumenty i materialy.* Moscow: Politizdat, 1981.

———. *SSSR-Italiia: Stranitsy istorii, 1917–1984, Dokumenty i materialy.* Moscow: Politizdat, 1985.

———. *SSSR v borbe za bezopasnost' i sotrudnichestvo v Evrope, 1964–1987: Sbornik dokumentov.* Moscow: Mezhdunarodnye Otnosheniia, 1988.

———. *Vneshniaia politika Sovetskogo Soiuza, 1948 god.* Moscow: Politizdat, 1950.

———. *Vneshniaia politika Sovetskogo Soiuza: Sbornik dokumentov,* various years. Moscow: Mezhdunarodnye Otnosheniia, 1981–1985.

Visit of Mikhail Gorbachev to Great Britain, April 5–7, 1989: Documents and Materials. Moscow: Novosti, 1989.

XXIV s"ezd Kommunisticheskoi Partii Sovetskogo Soiuza, 30 marta–9 aprelia 1971 g.: Stenograficheski otchët, 2 vols. Moscow: Politizdat, 1971.

XXV s"ezd Kommunisticheskoi Partii Sovetskogo Soiuza, 24 fevralia–5 marta 1976 g.: Stenograficheski otchët. Moscow: Politizdat, 1976.

XXVI s"ezd Kommunisticheskoi Partii Sovetskogo Soiuza, 23 fevralia–3 marta 1981 g.: Stenograficheskii otchët. 2 vols. Moscow: Politizdat, 1981.

Books

Agenbegyan, Abel, ed. *Perestroika Annual.* London: Futura, 1988.

Anatoliev, K. *Modern Diplomacy: Principles, Documents, People.* Moscow: Novosti, 1972.

Arbatov, Alexei, ed. *Razoruzhenie i bezopasnost': 1987 ezhegodnik.* Moscow: Novosti, 1988.

Barten'ev T., and Iu. Komissarov. *SSSR-Finlandiia.* Moscow: Politizdat, 1978.

Bayev, Pavel, Vitali Zhurkin, Sergei Karaganov, Victor Shein. *Tactical Nuclear Weapons in Europe: The Problem of Reduction and Elimination.* Moscow: Novosti, for the Institute of Europe and the Soviet Committee for European Security and Cooperation, 1990.

Berezhkov, Valentin M. *Stranitsi diplomaticheskoi istorii.* Moscow: Mezhdunarodnye Otnosheniia, 1987.

Bykov, O. *Confidence-Building Measures.* International Peace and Disarmament Series of the Scientific Research Council on Peace and Disarmament, Moscow: Nauka, 1983.

Conference in Defence of Peace of All Churches and Religious Associations in the USSR. Moscow: Moscow Patriarchate, 1952.

Davidov, Iu. *SShA i obshcheevropeiskii protsess.* Moscow: Nauka, 1989.

Davidov, V. F. *Beziadernye zony i mezhdunarodnaia bezopasnost'.* Moscow: Mezhdunarodnye Otnosheniia, 1988.

Dictionary of International Law. Moscow: Progress, 1986.

Disarmament and Security Yearbook, 1987. Moscow: IMEMO, 1988.

Gorbachev, Mikhail S. *Perestroika: New Thinking for Our Country and the World.* New York: Harper and Row, 1986.

———. *A Time for Peace.* New York: Richardson and Steirman, 1985.

Grigoryev, V. *The Soviet Parliament (A Reference Book).* Moscow: Progress, 1967.

Gromyko, Anatoly, and Vladimir Lomeiko. *Novoe myshlenie v iadernyi vek.* Moscow: Mezhdunarodnye Otnosheniia, 1984.

Gromyko, Andrei A. *Memories,* translated by Harold Shukman, London: Hutchinson, 1989.

———. *Pamiatnoe,* 2 vols. Moscow: Politizdat, 1988.

Gromyko, Andrei A., and B. N. Ponomarev, eds. *Soviet Foreign Policy,* 2 vols. Moscow: Progress, 1981.

Institute of the World Economy. *The European Community: Theses of the Institute of the World Economy and International Relations of the Academy of the USSR.* Moscow: IMEMO, 1989.

Kaliadin, A. N., and Iu. Nazarkin. *Disarmament Negotiating Machinery.* Moscow: Nauka (Scientific Research Council on Peace and Disarmament), 1984.

Kanaev, Georgii. *Soviet Trade Unions and the International Trade Union Movement: The Struggle for Unity.* Moscow: Novosti, 1970.

Kashlev, Iu. *Europe Five Years After Helsinki: The Soviet Viewpoint.* Moscow: Novosti, 1980.

Klimenko, B. M., ed. *Slovar' mezhdunarodnogo prava.* Moscow: Mezhdunarodnye Otnosheniia, 1986.

Kniazhinsky, Vsevolod. *West European Integration: Its Policies and International Relations.* Moscow: Progress, 1984.

Kovalev, A. N. *Azbuka diplomatii.* Moscow: Mezhdunarodnye Otnosheniia, 1984.

Kovolenko, A. S. *Torgovye dogovory i soglasheniia SSSR.* Moscow: Vneshtorgizdat, 1953.

Kuznetsov, Vladen. *A Nuclear Age Peace Code Is Needed.* Moscow: Novosti, 1984.

Lebedev, N. I. *Istoriia mezhdunarodnykh otnoshenii i vneshnei politiki SSSR, 1968–1978.* Moscow: Mezhdunarodnye Otnosheniia, 1979.

Lebedeva, Z. A. *Parlamentskaia gruppa sovetskogo soiuza.* Moscow: Mezhdunarodnye Otnosheniia, 1958.

Matkovskii, N. V. *Kratkii ocherk profsoiuznogo dvizheniia v anglii.* Moscow: Izdatel'stvo VTSSPS, 1954.

Morozov, G. I., ed. *Obshchestvennost' i problemy voiny i mira.* Moscow: Mezhdunarodnye Otnosheniia, 1978.

The Moscow Patriarchate 1917–1977. Moscow: Moscow Patriarchate, 1978.

Mottola, Kari, O. N. Bykov, and I. S. Korolev, eds. *Finnish-Soviet Economic Relations.* London: Macmillan (in association with the Finnish Institute of International Affairs), 1983.

Narochnitskii, A. L. *SSSR i bratskie sotsialisticheskie strany Evropy v 70-e gody.* Moscow: Nauka, 1988.

Novikov, N. V. *Vospominaniia diplomata: zapiski 1938–1947.* Moscow: Politizdat, 1989.

Ogarkov, N. V. *Vsegda v gotovnosti k zashchite Otchestva.* Moscow: Voenizdat, 1982.

Pavlov, N. V. *Vneshniaia politika FRG: kontseptsii i realii 80-kh godov.* Moscow: Mezhdunarodnye Otnosheniia, 1989.

Rakhmaninov, Iu. N. *Problema evropeiskoi bezopasnosti.* Moscow: Mysl', 1979.

Rozanov, G. L. *SSSR-FRG: Perestroika otnoshenii.* Moscow: Znanie, 1977.

Ryzhikov, V. A. *Britanskii leiborizm segodnia: Teoria i praktika politika poslevoennykh pravital'stv Velikobritanii.* Moscow: Mysl', 1984.

———. *SSSR-Velikobritaniia: Razvitie otnoshenii 60–70-e gody.* Moscow: Mezhdunarodnye Otnosheniia, 1977.

Sibilev, N. G. *Sotsialisticheskii Internatsional: Istoriia, ideologiia, politika.* Moscow: Mezhdunarodnye Otnosheniia, 1980.

Sobakin, V. K. *Ravnaia bezopasnost': printsip ravenstva i odinakovoi bezopastnosti v sovremennykh mezhdunarodnykh otnosheniakh.* Moscow: Mezhdunarodnye Otnosheniia, 1984.

Soviet Committee for European Security and Cooperation. *How to Avert the Threat to Europe.* Moscow: Progress, 1983.

The Soviet Parliament. Moscow: Progress, 1967.

Talbott, Strobe, ed. *Khrushchev Remembers.* Boston: Little, Brown, 1970.

———. *Khrushchev Remembers: The Last Testament.* Boston: Little, Brown, 1974.

Tunkin, G. I. *Theory of International Law.* trans., William E. Butler. Cambridge, Mass.: Harvard University Press, 1974.

USSR Academy of Sciences, *Sovetskaia kultura: istoriia i sovremennost'.* Moscow: Nauka, 1983.

Verkhovnii sovet SSSR. Moscow: Izdatel'stvo "Izvestiia sovetov trudiashchikhcia SSSR," 1975.

Volkogonov, Dmitrii. *Triumf i tragediia: politicheskii portret I. V. Stalina,* 2 vols. Moscow: Novosti, 1989.

Zagladin, V. V., ed. *Mirovoe kommunisticheskoe dvizhenie.* Moscow: Politizdat, 1984.

———. *The World Communist Movement: Outline of Strategy and Tactics.* Moscow: Progress, 1973.

Zaitsev, Vladimir Mikhailovich. *United Towns.* Moscow: Novosti, 1972.

Zamoshkin, Iu. A., et al., eds. *Antivoennoe dvizhenie v Severnoi Amerike i Zapadnoi Evrope: tendentsii, problemi, perspektivi.* Moscow: Mezhdunarodnye Otnosheniia, 1986.

Zhukov, G. K. *Vospominaniia i razmyshlenia.* Moscow: Novosti, 1969.

Zuev, F. G. *Sotsialisticheskoe sodruzhestvo i razriadka v Evrope.* Moscow: Nauka, 1984.

Index

Abrasimov, Petr, 136
Acheson, Dean, 25
Adenauer, Konrad, 22, 28, 36–37, 42, 48–49, 71, 77, 111; Moscow visit, 37–38, 65–67, 258–59, 389n
Adzhubei, Aleksei, 72
Afghanistan, war in, 83, 112, 119, 121, 159, 234, 238, 240, 266, 278, 291, 305, 333, 335, 351, 357
Air France, 111
Akhromeev, Sergei, 128, 240
Alaska, 226–27, 416n, 441n
Albania, 190, 229
Algeria, 69, 70, 105
Allied Control Council, 12
Allied High Commission, 31
All-Union Central Council of Trade Unions (AUCCTU), 149–53, 155, 158–59; abolition of, 162–63; desire for pan-European forum, 156–57, 161
All-Union Society for Cultural Relations with Foreign Countries, 283
American Federation of Labor and Congress of Industrial Organizations (AFL-CIO), 157, 411n
Amnesty International, 158
Anatoliev, K., 110
Andreotti, Guilio, 103
Andropov, Iuri, 83, 84, 109, 110, 112, 181, 185, 192–93, 212, 348, 351
Anglo-French Trades Union Council, 150–51
Anglo-Russian Trade Union Unity Committee, 150–51, 152, 156
Anglo-Soviet Friendship Society, 287, 439n
Anti-Ballistic Missile Systems, Treaty on the Limitation of, 92, 112, 357
Arctic Circle, 226–27
Arctic "zone of peace," 193–94
Arbatov, Georgii, 95, 128, 194

Arms control and disarmament, 10–11, 133, 140; bilateralization of talks, 169; complete and general disarmament, proposals for, 169, 207; East-West parity in negotiations, 52–53, 55, 168–69; institutional setting, 164–70; partial measures, Soviet proposals for, 206, 208; Soviet proposal (May 10, 1955), 165, 170, 203–4; Soviet proposal (March 1956), 206, 226. See also Confidence building measures; Conventional arms control; Nuclear arms control; Open Skies
Arnoldshainer Gespräche, 302–3
Association for Relations between Soviet and Foreign Cities, 292
Association of Southeast Asian Nations (ASEAN), 185
Atatürk, Kemal, 116
Atoms for Peace, 226
Attlee, Clement, 9, 129, 131
Austria, 6–8, 87, 99, 117, 119, 282, 371; Communist coup attempts, 19. See also Austrian State Treaty
Austrian State Treaty, 3, 13, 24, 29–35, 64, 90, 259, 362

Backfire bomber, 177
Baden-Württemberg, 293
Bahr, Egon, 60, 78, 203
Baker, James, 249–50, 252
Balkans, 100, 161, 190–92, 195
Baltic republics, 126, 406n. See also Lithuania
Baltic Sea, 192–94, 418n, 430n
Bandera, Stefan, 153
Barghoorn, Frederick C., 284
Baruch plan, 10
Batovrin, Sergei, 316
Baudouin, king of Belgium, 81
Belgium, 70, 81, 104, 117, 119, 248–49, 322, 367

About the Author

John Van Oudenaren is Associate Corporate Research Manager in the International Policy department of the RAND Corporation, Santa Monica, California, and a member of the faculty of the RAND Graduate School and the RAND-UCLA Center for Soviet Studies.

He was educated at Princeton University and the Massachusetts Institute of Technology, and has been a Research Associate at the International Institute for Strategic Studies, London, and a Research Scholar at the Kennan Institute for Advanced Russian Studies, Woodrow Wilson International Center for Scholars, Washington, D.C. In 1985–1987 he was a member of the Policy Planning Staff of the U.S. Department of State.